EMPIRE OF THE CZAR

Portrait of Custine
Watercolor by the Comtesse de Menou, Rome, 1846.

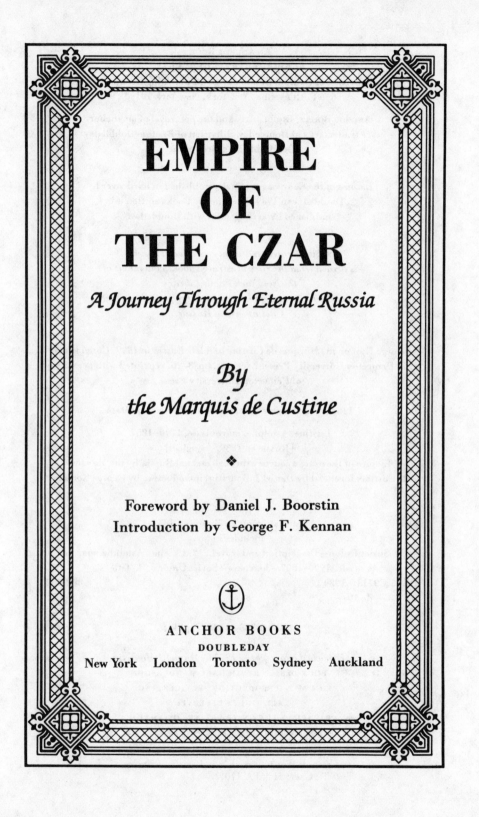

EMPIRE
OF
THE CZAR

A Journey Through Eternal Russia

By
the Marquis de Custine

❖

Foreword by Daniel J. Boorstin
Introduction by George F. Kennan

ANCHOR BOOKS
DOUBLEDAY
New York London Toronto Sydney Auckland

AN ANCHOR BOOK
PUBLISHED BY DOUBLEDAY
a division of Bantam Doubleday Dell Publishing Group, Inc.
666 Fifth Avenue, New York, New York 10103

ANCHOR BOOKS, DOUBLEDAY, and the portrayal of an anchor
are trademarks of Doubleday, a division of Bantam Doubleday
Dell Publishing Group, Inc.

Empire of the Czar was originally published in hardcover by
Doubleday in 1989. The Anchor Books edition is
published by arrangement with Doubleday.

*All illustrative material reproduced herein
is drawn from the rare illustrated books collections of
the New York Public Library
and is broadly contemporaneous to the period in which
Custine visited Russia.*

George F. Kennan, *Marquis de Custine and His Russia in 1839*. Copyright ©
1971 Princeton University Press. Excerpts, pp. 3–26, reprinted with permission
of Princeton University Press.

Library of Congress Cataloging-in-Publication Data

Custine, Astolphe, marquis de, 1790–1857.
    [Russie en 1839.   English]
Empire of the czar: a journey through eternal Russia/by the Marquis
de Custine; foreword by Daniel J. Boorstin; introduction by George Kennan.

        p.   cm.
    Translation of: La Russie en 1839.
        Includes index.
    1. Soviet Union—Description and travel.   2. Custine, Astolphe, marquis
        de, 1790–1857—Journeys—Soviet Union.   I. Title
DK25.C9713   1989   88-23620
947'.07—dc 19   CIP

ISBN 0-385-41126-X (pbk.)

Foreword copyright © 1989 by Daniel J. Boorstin
BOOK DESIGN BY MICHAEL MENDELSOHN
OF M 'N O PRODUCTION SERVICES, INC.
ALL RIGHTS RESERVED
PRINTED IN THE UNITED STATES OF AMERICA
FIRST ANCHOR BOOKS EDITION: APRIL 1990

To All Intrepid Travelers

ACKNOWLEDGMENTS

Our thanks first of all must go to the anonymous translator who, so promptly after its first publication in French, put the book into this elegant and lively English. We have retained his spelling and punctuation as a way of reminding us of our debt to his work 150 years ago. Ruth F. Boorstin, editorial associate at Doubleday, has collaborated at every stage. Jacqueline Onassis has given generously of her time and advice and her knowledge of French culture in editing the manuscript and selecting the illustrations. We are grateful to Judy Sandman, who has helped with this project from the beginning.

We are especially indebted to Dr. Edward Kasinec, Chief of the Slavic and Baltic Division of the New York Public Library, assisted by Robert H. Davis, Jr., for his enthusiastic assistance and his scholarly expertise helping us to select the illustrations and providing accurate captions.

EDITOR'S NOTE

The text reproduced here is that of the Longman edition of 1843, an English translation of the three-volume French original. This translation, elegant and eloquent, is still a literary landmark and did much to bring fame to Custine in the English-speaking world. It is abridged by about 15 percent to make it available in this single substantial volume. The sections omitted are those devoted to subjects other than Russia, theological discourses, lengthy myths, extensive quotations, or retellings from other authors. Selections from Custine's book have been published before in English. This edition is the most copious reproduction to appear in this century. The Introduction by George F. Kennan has been adapted by him from his *Marquis de Custine and His Russia in 1839.* (Princeton University Press, 1971). In the present edition all omissions are indicated. The text follows the spelling and punctuation of the anonymous translator.

Daniel J. Boorstin

FOREWORD
BY
DANIEL J. BOORSTIN

This lively travel classic, we hope, will help Western readers discover what Russia really was and help us ask whether that Russia is still there. It has often been called the best book ever written by a foreigner about Russia. Custine's prophetic insights can help us grasp the problems faced by Gorbachev or anyone else who tries to bring change to the Empire of the Czar.

Besides being a vivid account of horse-drawn travels in an exotic land, this is an uncanny and tantalizing book. "It is true I have not fully seen," wrote Custine, "but I have fully divined." What gives any man the clairvoyant power to see the broad deep currents of a nation's life? This question becomes more interesting as we read Custine. Although he was in Russia for less than three months in 1839, he showed that power. He somehow sensed features of Russian life and institutions that reached back for millennia before his time and would extend forward for more than a century. Following the daily adventures of this witty, penetrating, but passionate and prejudiced observer, we are constantly amazed that his breadth of insight could so far exceed the scope of his observations. And we are tantalized by the thought that though some of his facts may be inaccurate or exaggerated or maliciously distorted, still many of his conclusions survive at this distance of time.

To be fair to Custine, we must first of all travel along with him, sharing the adventures and misadventures into which his aggressive curiosity and hypersensitivity led him. Few of us would have chosen him for a traveling companion. He did not have the good fortune of Tocqueville, who, about the same time, was making the brief trip to the United States that produced his classic *Democracy in America* and who had the companionship of an amiable and intimate friend and collaborator, Gustave de Beaumont. Tocqueville's observations would have the benefit of being tested by the sobering criticisms of this alter ego. But Custine was a loner. As George F. Kennan explains in the Introduction that follows, Custine's sensitivities had been sharpened by a life of personal tragedy, and his hypersensitivity had been cultivated by incidents that had made him the most notorious homosexual in Paris and caused his ostracism from the polite literary society where he belonged. What we have from Custine, then, are his extremely personal, untempered, and frequently intemperate opinions, based on the experiences that he describes here in unforgettable detail.

Custine had the insights of an outsider. Even without drawing any subtle conclusions from these episodes, we can enjoy the variety, the color, and the semi-Asiatic strangeness of Russia a century and a half ago, which he depicts with eloquence. We join the fêtes and royal weddings in St. Petersburg, we share his delight in the river-broken vistas of the city, we listen in on his conversations with the "truly Russian" Czar Nicholas I and the affable Czarina, and share his ambivalent admiration of the Autocrat of all the Russias. We jog and jiggle along in the rickety carriages on rough roads with the daily threat of being stuck up to our axles in mud. We overnight in flea-bitten inns. We share the warmth and festivity of country-fair music and dance, and admire the rounded beauty of the peasant women. We sense the urban provincialism of Yaroslaf and Nijni Novgorod, and become familiar with the Volga boatmen. We are dazzled by the oriental splendor of the Kremlin, day and night.

None of this calls for an elaborate ideological gloss. But we are soon struck, and sometimes dumbfounded, by the prophetic accuracy of some of his observations—beginning with the bureaucratic hassle at the border on the way in. We share Custine's irritation at the sullen police-spy who has been assigned to him as a servant and whom he cannot shake off. His portrait of the grim prison at Schlusselburg, of meaningless interrogations, of incarceration for indefinable crimes, of the pains of exile to Siberia, seems all too familiar. He described poignantly the miseries visited on the children of convicts, the omnipresence of secrecy and suspicion. His anecdotes make us wonder how much of the eternal Russia is still there. He gives us a discomfiting feeling of *déjà vu.*

As a venture into the world of political speculation, Custine's journey to Russia was a counterpart of Tocqueville's nine-month voyage to America. Tocqueville, the young liberal aristocrat witnessing the decline of aristocracy and the rise of equality at home in France, went with Beaumont to learn what he could from America. The first part of his *Democracy in America* depicted the great opportunities (and new risks) of an egalitarian society in a New World. The Marquis de Custine was haunted by the memory of his father and grandfather, whose guillotining by the French Revolutionaries he painfully recounts. He went to Russia to document the advantages of autocracy and confirm his prejudices against popular government. But it was there that he discovered the evils of autocracy, and he returned to France a strong advocate of constitutions.

His conclusions are sometimes surprising, but always interesting to an American democrat. For example, he was a firm believer in the social advantages of a true aristocracy—a class of people who were equipped, qualified, and trained to preserve liberties against a despot. He saw such a class in England. But in Russia, surprisingly, he found no aristocracy. For there all classes, including the "noblemen," were equally slaves of the autocrat Czar. Russian courtiers did not deserve to be dignified as aristocrats, for they were nothing but fawning sycophants. He was appalled at this "moral degradation of the higher classes." The Empire of the Czar, according to him, was already a truly "classless" society. Below the autocrat himself there were no grades of independence or dignity, but a whole nation of fear-struck slaves.

Today, some will say, while men of good will are trying to bring us together with the Russians, is no time to remind us of the deep currents of Russian history that separate them from us —the Mongolian invasions, the recurrent fears of attacks from the West, the unbroken traditions of autocracy and secrecy, and

the absence of any tradition of constitutions, of a legally autho-
rized opposition, of private rights of expression, or free worship
and free emigration. No two nations are more urgently in need of
understanding each other.

What this book can do is to encourage realistic hopes and
discourage utopian expectations.

Custine can help us correct the Modern Myopia. Custine's spirited and readable narrative can remind us that beneath the veil
of the U.S.S.R. there still remains a Russia—a legacy of the Empire of the Czar. Is the Empire that marched westward across
half of Europe and eastward across all of Asia still there? The
endless outpouring of print and movie and TV images about
"U.S.S.R. Today" should not blind us to the fact that, no more
than anyone else can the Russian people escape their history. To
understand the "Soviets," we must more than ever try to know
the history of their institutions, their ways of life, and their rul-
ers. For those were the makings of the Empire of the Czar.

*History can bring charity to our judgment of the Russians, and
patience to our expectations of their treatment of their citizens.*
Perhaps, then, we will not blame them so blatantly for refusing to
grant what their history and institutions make difficult or impossible for them (e.g., free emigration, free press, free speech, freedom of religion, an opposition party). The Russians can no more
forget the millennia of Mongolian occupation, the traditions of
expansion across Europe and Asia, the sacredness of Czarist autocracy, the identity of State and Religion, the traditions of secrecy and police tyranny, of knouting and Siberian exile, than
Americans can forget the millennia of Magna Carta tradition, of
parliaments, Bills of Rights, constitutions, habeas corpus, com-
mon-law judges, free land, copious immigration, and a moving
frontier. We will have greater sympathy for and patience for Russian efforts, however slow or small, to inch away from the historic
institutions that Custine describes in his *Empire of the Czar*.

New England Puritans of our colonial age could never be *disil-
lusioned*, simply because they were never illusioned. Their concept of Original Sin made them surprised and grateful that corrupt Man could accomplish anything. Similarly, a sense of
history can rescue us, too, from extravagant optimism and pain-

ful disappointments about Russian gropings to escape the ways of life described in this book.

Custine, depicting the grandeur and color as well as the backwardness of the Russian Empire in the nineteenth century, can remind us that some tendencies that we attribute to "Communism" today may simply be Russian: expansionism, autocracy, bureaucracy, centralism, secrecy, contempt for personal rights and public opinion, and so on. In all these ways, Custine can help us to a deeper, more charitable understanding of our willy-nilly partner in preserving the peace of the world—and the world.

This book is a brilliant example of an ancient genre, as old as Herodotus, which brings together the arts of literature and the techniques of social science to enrich our understanding of our fellow human beings. From the very beginning of Western culture, travelers and traveler-historians have put flesh and blood on the fearful abstractions of politics. After reading Custine's account of his conversations with Nicholas I, we have a more intimate view of the autocrat's problems—his strengths and weaknesses. We can plainly see that the Czar, too, was only another man. While Custine may make us more wary of Russians as political animals, he also makes us more sympathetic to them as human beings. I know of no other book that more vividly and suspensefully uses travel narrative to sketch institutions. The bizarre personality of the author, his uncompromising prejudices and passions, and the uncertain authenticity of particular facts simply add interest. Every reader is challenged by one of the more acute and eloquent travelers of the last century.

The American reader may also find Custine his guide to rediscovering America. The astonishing symmetry—Hegel would have called it "antithesis"—between the history of Russia and the history of the United States has often been noticed. It was in the mind of Tocqueville himself as he concluded the book that made him famous. The first volume of his *Democracy in America* (1835), written about the same time that Custine was journeying in Russia, ends with these prophetic words:

. . . The Russians and the Americans . . . have suddenly placed themselves in the front rank among the nations, and the world learned their existence and their greatness at almost the same time.

All other nations seem to have nearly reached their natural limits, and they have only to maintain their power; but these are still in the act of growing. All the others have stopped, or continue to advance with extreme difficulty; these alone are proceeding with ease and celerity along a path to which no limit can be perceived. The American struggles against the obstacles that nature imposes to him; the adversaries of the Russians are men. The former combats the wilderness and savage life; the latter, civilization with all its arms. The conquests of the American are therefore gained by the plowshare; whose of the Russian by the sword. The Anglo-American relies upon personal interest to accomplish his ends and gives free scope to the unguided strength and common sense of the people; the Russian centers all authority of society in a single arm. The principal instrument of the former is freedom; of the latter, servitude. Their starting-point is different and their courses are not the same; yet each of them seems marked out by the will of Heaven to sway the destinies of half the globe. (Trans. Henry Reeve, 1838)

Tocqueville was not far wrong.

Where are there better examples of the contrasting possibilities of history and civilization on this planet? A cosmic Plutarch writing the *Parallel Lives of Great Nations* could not find a more rewarding subject. Perhaps it could be called *Mark Twain or Dostoyevsky?*

Custine's vivid overstatements of the features of Russian history throw the large contours of American history into bold relief. At his entrance through the port of Kronstadt, "ice-locked during six months of the year" and with the "simple formalities" of the customs police in St. Petersburg, the miasma of fear and suspicion of all foreigners arises and is never dispelled. To the question " 'What is your object in Russia?' " Custine responds, " 'To see the country.' " To which the officer objects, " 'That is not here a motive for travelling!' (What humility in this objection!)" Custine repeatedly reminds us that the Russian fear of foreigners and obsession with government secrecy is no whim of bureaucrats but the understandable reaction to centuries of rule by Mongolian invaders, repeated later invasions and threats of invasion, and landlocked isolation. Lacking year-round seaborne access to the Western world, menaced by continent-spanning land borders, what more natural than that the Russian of 1839 should view foreigners with suspicion? Who but an invader or his agent would come "to see the country"?

All this had enduring consequences for Russia's diplomatic relations, as Custine observed!

Let but the liberty of the press be accorded to Russia for twenty-four hours, and we should learn things that would make us recoil with horror. Silence is indispensible to oppression. Under an absolute government every indiscretion of speech is equivalent to a crime of high treason.

If there are found among Russians, better diplomatists than among nations the most advanced in civilisation, it is because our journals inform them of every thing which is done or projected among ourselves, and because, instead of prudently disguising our weaknesses, we display them, with passion, every morning; whilst, on the contrary, the Byzantine policy of the Russians, working in the dark, carefully conceals from us everything that is thought, done, or feared among them. We march exposed on all sides, they advance under cover. The ignorance in which they leave us blinds our view; our sincerity enlightens theirs; we suffer from all the evils of idle talking, they have the advantages of secrecy; and herein lies all their skill and ability.

The reader must be constantly cautioned, and reminded that the land he is travelling is the Russia of 1839, a century and a half ago. Obviously we cannot understand any nation, including our own, without knowing its past. And especially in the case of Russia we need every kind of help that can be found toward a fuller knowledge of that past. For in recent decades the Russians —even after becoming Soviets—have not given themselves or us much reliable help. When Custine reports the words of the Russian nobleman Prince K., he describes this problem:

"Russian despotism not only pays little respect to ideas and sentiments, it will also deny facts; it will struggle against evidence, and triumph in the struggle!!! for evidence, when it is inconvenient to power, has no more voice among us than has justice. . . . The people, and even the great men, are resigned spectators of this war against truth; the lies of the despot, however palpable, are always flattering to the slave . . . in Russia . . . despotism is more powerful than nature; the emperor is not only the representative of God, he is himself the creative power: a power greater than that of Deity, for it only extends its action to the future, whereas the emperor alters and amends the past: the law has no retroactive effect, the caprice of a despot has."

Which makes the republication of Custine's travels and the reports of other outsiders all the more welcome.

On its first appearance in French and English this book sold widely. Custine claimed the sale of some two hundred thousand within three years, which was enormous in those days. This could hardly have been the result of the reviews. Such French reviews as appeared were predominantly unfavorable, some of them savage. Custine wittily attributed the large sale of the first printing to the fact that the leading Paris editors had ignored the book. In England also the major reviews were unfavorable. The poet-politician Richard Monckton Milnes, not entirely unfairly, called Custine "a theorist and generalizer of the wildest character." "He is sincere, although his sincerity may not be of the purest stamp—he is earnest, though his earnestness may be affected by self-conceit—he is fair, in so far as fairness consists in giving us the separate impressions, as they successively passed across his mind." When *Empire of the Czar* first appeared in English, it was ignored in the United States. Of course the book was banned in Russia, where even discussion of it was forbidden.

It is not surprising that the book aroused passions when it first appeared, as it will perhaps now once again. For it is a delectable mixture, in George F. Kennan's phrase, of "things sufficiently inaccurate to be annoying (mostly matters of detailed fact) and ones that were sufficiently true to hurt." If the book was never a *succès d'estime,* it has the distinction nevertheless of being a *suc-*

cès d'histoire. The reader today will be grateful to the unhappy Marquis for having made his journey and for having left this unvarnished record. Which gives us all a much-needed incentive and opportunity, with the aid of his acute eye and acerbic pen, to speculate on the relation between Russia's past and its present.

Despite its shortcomings and distortions, and Russian efforts to pretend that the book never existed, the book lives on—an antique mirror in which to see one of the most mysterious nations of our time. Custine himself finally saw his book as just that—a mirror for himself and for us. He concluded:

> If ever your sons should be discontented with France, try my receipt; tell them to go to Russia. It is a useful journey for every foreigner: whoever has well examined that country will be content to live anywhere else. It is always well to know that a society exists where no happiness is possible, because by a law of his nature, man cannot be happy unless he is free.
>
> Such a recollection renders the traveller less fastidious; and, returning to his own hearth, he can say of his country what a man of mind once said of himself: "When I estimate myself, I am modest; but when I compare myself, I am proud."

❖

INTRODUCTION
BY
GEORGE F. KENNAN

THE MAN

ASTOLPHE DE CUSTINE was a man of good family, even by the more fastidious standards of his own day. On his father's side, the family was a wealthy Lotharingian one, in which the marquisal title had been passed down (rather casually, to be sure) since the early eighteenth century. Astolphe's grandfather had purchased the well-known porcelain factory at Niderwiller in the Haute-Lorraine (now part of the Department of the Moselle); and it was in the chateau at that place that the boy grew up. His mother was a Sabran—the child, that is, of one of the great noble families of France.[1]

Custine's own childhood was agitated and tragic in the extreme. He was born in 1790, on the eve of the most harrowing period of the French Revolution. He might be described, as we shall see presently, as himself an emotional casualty of the Terror. His relatively young paternal grandfather, a man then only in his late forties, had sympathized with the Revolution in its early stages and had become a general in the revolutionary armies. His name will be remembered as that of the commander of the armies on the Rhine. This service to the Revolution did not, however, save him from the Terror. In 1792, he was recalled, imprisoned, and finally guillotined. His young son, Astolphe's father, then only in his twenties, rose gallantly to his own father's defense and was guillotined in his turn. Astolphe's mother, who had stood loyally by her young husband, visiting him in prison down to the last night, was herself taken and thrown into the death house after his execution. She escaped only narrowly, almost miraculously, the fate of her father-in-law and her husband.

All this happened when the boy, Astolphe, was only two or

three years old. The house, meanwhile, was raided and sealed by the revolutionary police. The family fortune was confiscated. A faithful maidservant, a young peasant girl from Lorraine, took the child and cared for it in the one unsealed room of the house, which was the kitchen.

The mother was eventually released, came home, and set about with great resolution and ultimate success to restore the family fortunes. She was without question a remarkable person— a woman of great beauty, charm, and strength of character. Widely known under her first name of Delphine, she enjoyed a reputation and a general respect in French society greater than anything ever accorded in their time to her son. Madame de Staël took her name, precisely with a view to immortalizing it, as the title of one of her own novels. Delphine was for many years the intimate friend—the mistress, one must suppose—of the writer and statesman Chateaubriand. The little boy was in fact brought up in part under the shadow of this impressive figure, whom he claims to have regarded as a sort of foster-father. But Chateaubriand's was not, unfortunately, the only male figure, and not even the only distinguished one, that fluttered around the candle of Delphine's great beauty, and it could not replace, emotionally, that of the missing father.

The boy thus remained throughout his youth the object of all the affection, attention, and protective patronage that a beautiful, high-powered, and solitary mother was capable of lavishing upon a beloved only son.* One cannot blame her; he was in a sense all she had. But it is clear that this unbalanced relationship, coming on top of the trauma of violent separation from both parents in early childhood, was too much for the boy's normal emotional development. He grew up handsome, brilliant, sensitive, delicate in health, in many ways talented, but with a latent, at first subconscious and repressed but ultimately overpowering, homosexual orientation.

For long—out of respect, I suppose, for his mother—Custine contrived to lead an outwardly normal life. At the time of the

---

* Custine had had an older brother, Gaston, born in 1788. After being inoculated against smallpox, Gaston died in July 1792.

Restoration, his mother wangled for him a military commission in one of the guard regiments. For a few weeks he trailed miserably around after his unit, buttoned into an uncomfortable uniform, a great sword clanking incongruously at his side; but he obviously failed to enjoy it, and was soon relieved of this duty. An effort was also made to use him as an aide to Talleyrand at the Congress of Vienna. But it was not long in becoming apparent that he was little better fitted for diplomacy than for life at court. His primary interest was literary. He became an enthused romantic, after the fashion of the day. The great figures of German literary romanticism formed the focus of his admiration. Some of them— including Heine, Varnhagen von Ense, and Varnhagen's remarkable wife, Rahel—became his warm personal friends.

In the early 1820s Custine acquiesced, amiably enough, in a marriage arranged for him by his mother. He became very fond, actually, of his young wife—even had a child by her. But when, in 1823, she—to his genuine and deep sorrow—suddenly died, something gave way within him. The effort to lead a conventional life failed. Other impulses, too long repressed, broke through with great and dangerous violence.

On the night of October 28, 1824, catastrophe ensued. Custine's unconscious and misused person was found that night, lying in the mud on the road from Versailles to St. Denis, stripped to the waist, beaten, robbed, the fingers broken, the ring ripped off. The deed had been done by a group of common soldiers with one of whom, allegedly, Custine had attempted to have a rendezvous.

Whether this was or was not the truth makes little difference. All of Paris believed that it was. The scandal was immense and spectacular. The whole affair came at once into the newspapers. Custine's reputation and his position in society were damaged beyond repair. From this time on to the end of his life he would figure, in the cruel gossip of the day, primarily as France's most distinguished and notorious homosexual.

The plight to which this personal catastrophe consigned him has been perhaps best described by Pierre de Lacretelle, in the introduction to the small volume of Custiniana which he published in 1956: "Imperturbable, le Marquis de Custine glissera désormais parmi les chuchotements, les sourires furtives, les regards moqueurs, méprisé par les uns, pris en pitié par les autres, problème pour tous."* The social rejection was cruel and drastic. One might note, as an example, the reaction of the Marquise de Montcalm, who responded to the news of the incident by sending word to Custine suggesting that he expiate his disgrace by a glorious death.

The episode of October 28, 1824, was only one of a series of disasters that overwhelmed Custine in just those years. He himself, in a letter to the Marquise de Montcalm, written (January 8, 1824) some months before his disgrace, described only the initial stage of this tragic series of events.[2] On January 7, 1823, according to this account, only a few months, that is, after the birth of Custine's small son, an old abbé, who had been a tutor to Custine's uncle and a virtual member of the family, died after pronouncing (Custine says he had lost his mind) a curse upon the entire family. Exactly six months later the young wife died, in terrible agony. At the lapse of just a year the same occurred with another member of the household—an old family friend. The child's nurse, meanwhile, had become insane. Successively, there perished everyone, except Custine himself and his mother, who had been connected with the wedding.

But Custine, writing that letter, did not yet know the full measure of the tragedy. Before that year of 1824 was out, there would come his own disgrace. Then, in the first days of 1826, his little son would die, and six months later his shattered and broken-hearted mother as well.†

Thrown back now upon himself, literally engulfed in humiliation, bereavement, and loneliness, Custine appears to have performed at this point an act of inner renunciation, and to have accommodated himself with relative dignity and reasonable suc-

---

* *Marquis de Custine, Souvenirs et portraits. Textes choisis et présentés par Pierre de Lacretelle.* Monaco: Editions du Rocher, 1956. The passage is difficult to translate. It might be rendered: "Henceforth the Marquis de Custine would make his way through life imperturbably, amid whisperings, furtive smiles, and mocking glances, held in contempt by some, pitied by others, a problem for everyone."

† Delphine's epitaph was written, in effect, by the Marquise de Montcalm: "Je ne croyais pas . . . qu'on peut mourir de chagrin, et la pauvre Madame de Custine est la preuve du contraire."[3]

cess to his unhappy condition. He became calm and resigned where he had once been nervous and agitated. He learned to accept his exclusion from the aristocratic society of Paris. He sought fulfillment, for the rest of his life, in travel, in literature, and in religion. He had always been devout. His piety now received an even deeper foundation. He found in the serene paternalism of the Roman Church, in which he had been reared, not only the absolution and tolerance for his emotional abnormality which society had denied him, but a substitute for the guillotined father, and a replacement for the element of majesty and hierarchy which he so deeply missed in the public life of the France of his day.

This solace notwithstanding, Custine's life remained tragic and uncompleted. His emotional frailty hung everlastingly, like a stone, around his neck, weighing down his hopes, interfering with his personal relations, limiting at crucial points his creative literary power. This quality of his fate was well described by Madame Ancelot, in her *Les Salons de Paris.* * "Over everything that M. de Custine did," she wrote (pp. 239–240),

> there hovered some baneful influence which diminished all his good fortunes. He united in himself, it is true, the greatest advantages of nature and society: he was tall and handsome, very witty, well-bred, extremely well educated, quite rich, and every inch the *grand seigneur* by ancestry, manners and feelings; but all these blessings did not prevent him from having a restless and tormented soul, which left him no peace. He was unable to find repose: he seemed driven by some inexplicable derangement of equilibrium which tore him away from everything that gave happiness to other men.

It must be noted that in the adjustment to his personal misfortunes and in the creation of a new life for himself Custine was decisively aided by the devoted attention and companionship of an English friend, Edward St. Barbe—Édouard de Sainte-Barbe,

---

* Mme. Marguerite-Louise Virginie Chardon Ancelot (1792–1875) was the wife of the French man of letters and member of the Académie Française, Jacques-Arsène-François-Polycarpe Ancelot. They collaborated in the writing of *Reine, Cardinal et Page,* and other works. Mme. Ancelot wrote works for the theatre, novels (including *Emerance, Renée de Varville),* as well as *Les Salons de Paris.*

as he called himself in France. Sainte-Barbe, the son of a prominent family of Hampshire gentry with estates near Lymington on
the south coast of England (the family traced its origins, and its
French name, to a companion-in-arms of William the Conqueror), joined Custine, as a constant associate, shortly *before*
(one notes this timing with a new tinge of pity for the parties to
Custine's marital tragedy), the death of the young marquise. He
then remained with Custine as a devoted companion and helper
(Custine, in his private correspondence, often referred to him
facetiously and affectionately as *"l'esclave")* until Custine's death
in 1857, running the household and bearing a large part of the
burden of management of Custine's personal affairs. The *ménage
à deux* which these two gentlemen conducted for over thirty
years, transformed occasionally into a *ménage à trois* when—as
happened more than once—Custine expended his hospitality and
patronage for a time on some other male figure as well, was naturally the cause of much malicious merriment in Paris society. But
contemporary witnesses who knew Sainte-Barbe are unanimous
in the judgment that he was a man of great delicacy and distinction of character: loyal, self-effacing, and dignified, and that he
carried his own part in this unusual arrangement with exemplary
tact and discretion. He dedicated his life to Custine; and the
latter's appreciation for this devotion is evident from an an-
guished reference to him, in a letter written by Custine to another friend when Sainte-Barbe was seriously ill in 1856, as *"un
homme sans lequel je ne puis vivre."* It is clear that what was
involved here was a profound, abiding, and in many ways touching relationship, going far deeper than could be explained by just
those physical impulses to which a cynical Paris loved to ascribe
it, and one which probably alone enabled Custine to endure his
disgrace and to go forward with his life and his work as a literary
person.

For the remainder of his life, Custine was seen primarily in
literary circles. The literary salons of Paris, in contrast to the
purely social ones, remained open to him—partly, no doubt, because his own hospitality was extended in the grandest and most

lavish manner to prominent people of the literary world.* He was
well acquainted with many of the great literary figures of the day:
with Victor Hugo, George Sand, Balzac, Stendhal, Baudelaire,
Lamartine, Sophie Gay. He was permitted to read aloud his own
works in the salon of Madame Récamier, and Balzac paid him the
compliment of doing the same *chez Custine*. Chopin played, on
occasion, at his soirées.

None of these friendships, it seems, were close or lasting ones
—except perhaps that with Sophie Gay. For this, Custine's lurid
private life, and the different orientation of his deeper human
attachments, constituted a barrier. It is also true that many who
were outwardly on good terms with him and accepted his hospitality were unable to resist the general tendency to sneer at him
behind his back. But it is not too much to say that Custine was a
well-known, if somewhat dubious, figure in the literary society of
the Paris of his day.

To be recognized as a "real" writer—to be accepted as a major
literary personality: this was Custine's greatest desire.† In the
attempt to realize this ambition, he tried almost every form of
literature. Poems, novels, drama: all these flowed at one time or
another from his hopeful and aspiring pen. None was a disgrace-
ful failure; none, on the other hand, was a serious success. In
1833, he contrived to have a play produced; but this was at great
cost to himself (he literally bought the theatre for the purpose),
and it was unceremoniously yanked from the repertoire after
three performances. He was often accused, at least in the gossip
of the day, of trying to bribe the critics and to buy favorable
publicity; but if there was anything in these charges, the effort
was singularly unsuccessful: the critics were seldom kind to him.
Until the appearance of *La Russie en 1839* he had no great repu-

---

* Custine's great town house (6, Rue de la Rochefoucauld), once (before Custine)
the residence of the sculptor Pigalle, survived, but only as part of the headquarters
of the *Compagnie des Ateliers et Forges de la Loire*. The grand salon, with its ornate
Empire ceiling and its lovely parquet-inlaid floors, where once Chopin played and
Chateaubriand read aloud from his works, later served as the company's boardroom.

† The Marquis de Luppé, in his biography, quotes Custine as saying, in a letter to
Sophie Gay, after the success of *La Russie en 1839*: "I have had only one ambition
in my life: to find a place among the good writers of my time and to be considered by
them as one of themselves." *Astolphe de Custine*, p. 236.

tation. His friend Heine was able, with some justification, to damn him with the cutting description of *"un demi-homme de lettres."* It was *La Russie en 1839* that finally established him and gave him his reputation as a serious literary figure; and even here the success flowed from the reception of the book by the public, not from any particular appreciation for it on the part of the French critics, who, as we shall see, were divided and largely unenthusiastic.

In spirit and style, Custine was in the deepest sense a romantic. Everything he wrote was burdened with the characteristic affectations of this literary school. For him, as for all the other romanticists (but perhaps for better reason than was commonly the case), it was the image of the noble, misunderstood individual, the unappreciated hero, that commanded the imagination and inspired the posture. He, like the others, ensconced himself figuratively on his own lonely pinnacle of pride and estrangement, hugging to his breast sensibilities which, you were permitted to feel, were too exquisite to stand full exposure to the gaze of an unfeeling world, prepared to let you glimpse or sense these sensibilities occasionally through the veils of reticence with which a noble nature required that they be obscured, but never prepared to inflict upon them the brutality either of disciplined analysis or of frank expostulation. This, if I am not mistaken, was, in part at least, what it meant to be a literary romanticist of the 1820s. Custine never wholly shook off this spirit. Its imprint rested on all that he wrote. It shines through at many points even in *La Russie en 1839.*

But the romantic spirit, as the history of literary taste has shown, was not in itself enough to make a great writer. It was often a handicap rather than an aid to creative immortality. It constituted a crust of intellectual and emotional convention which had to be broken through, as it was in the case of such men as Byron, Pushkin, Lermontov, and Walter Scott, by some deeper and stronger source of creative vitality, if greatness was to be achieved.

As a poet, a novelist, and a dramatist, Custine simply lacked this extra power. There was, however, one field where he was eventually able to develop it, and this was the travel account.

Custine adored travel. He spent a good part of his life in the pursuit of it. He found it, he says, *une douce manière de passer la vie* for one who was out of accord with the ideas of his time (he might have added: "and was rejected by the society into which he had been born"). He "read" countries, he claimed, as other people read books. Travel was, as he saw it, a means of changing not only scenes but centuries as well. What one had from it was *"l'histoire analysée dans ces résultats."*[*4] It was in the travel account that his qualities, such as they were, came into their own.

I am not familiar with the first of his efforts along this line. They were sketches of travel in Switzerland, Italy, England, and Scotland—travel that had been performed when he was very young, but the account of which was not edited for publication until many years later.[5] I have heard this work criticized with extreme severity—as the most atrocious romantic nonsense, written much under the influence of the Ossian legend. A later work on Spain, published only a year before Custine embarked on his journey to Russia, was obviously a much more serious effort.[6] I have the impression that this last work was unjustly ignored by contemporaries and committed to oblivion by later generations; but of this, of course, only someone familiar with Spain and its history could be a proper judge.

With the account of the journey to Russia, in any case, such abilities as Custine possessed as a literary person came to their final fruition. Forty-nine years old when he performed the journey, and fifty-two when he began his account of it, he was now at the height of his powers. The stinging challenge of confrontation with Russian realities—a challenge that has evoked the best from more than one western observer over the course of the centuries —brought out all that he had it in him to give in the way of vigor of reaction. It drew on all his qualities, but above all on his moral discrimination, his sense of the fitness of things, and his feeling for the essentials of a decent and hopeful civilization. In the

* Quotations from the text of *La Russie en 1839*, such as this one, are taken from the second Amyot edition, of 1844, and are cited simply as *La Russie*, followed by the volume and page numbers. The translations are not of uniform origin. Some are my own. Some are taken *in toto* from the Longman English edition. Some are mixtures of the two.

confrontation with the Russia of Nicholas I, Custine's abilities as a writer, wasted for lack of real artistic talent when it came to other forms of literature, were finally permitted to find their ultimate realization.

La Russie en 1839 represented very nearly the culmination of Custine's literary career. He wrote one more novel, of mediocre success, did a bit more traveling—mostly to Italy, survived most of his friends, sold his Paris house, and finally, after sensing clearly the approach of death, died suddenly at his suburban home in St. Gratien, in September 1857, his passing almost unnoticed in a France which had long forgotten him. He was survived for only little more than a year by his faithful companion and heir, Sainte-Barbe. His papers appear to have been completely lost in a confused series of vicissitudes that included destruction of a part of them (no doubt on his own instructions) by Sainte-Barbe, bouts of litigation over the estates of both men, and much indifference, neglect, and even rumors of misuse for purposes of blackmail, on the part of later heirs and others. With the disappearance of these papers there were denied to the historian, we must suppose, the last important clues to the various mysteries surrounding the memorable journey which Custine had made to Russia nearly two decades before his death and for which, alone, his name continues to be known to later generations.

Astolphe de Custine cannot be classed a great man. The artificiality and narrowness of horizon that marked his upbringing; the inner timidity which he was often able to conceal but never really to overcome; the scars of his painful emotional experience; the romantic distortion in his view of reality: these posed tragic strictures on the degree to which he was able to develop what might, in other circumstances, have been talents approaching the level of greatness.

But Custine was, by anyone's standards, a man of unusual qualities. The overpowering influence of his mother, and the streak of effeminacy in his nature that resulted from it, had endowed him with intuitive powers beyond those common to members of his sex. With these were coupled a keen intellect, the best sort of classical education that the private tutoring of that age was able to give, the broadening effects of many years of travel, and a real passion for language and literature. Personal adversity, finally, had made of him a philosopher of sorts—had endowed him with a great sensitivity to moral values, a fine nose for cant and hypocrisy of every sort, and in certain respects an elevation of outlook that carried him well above some of the prejudices and conventions of his time. It was these qualities that he brought to the performance of his journey and to the drafting of his account of it.

THE MOTIVES OF THE JOURNEY

WHAT moved Custine to undertake the journey to Russia, and to undertake it at the time he did, is not wholly clear. But there are three points that deserve notice in this connection.

It was, first of all, only the previous year—1838—that had seen the publication of his four-volume work on Spain. He had been guilty of the most egregious delay in the writing and publication of that work. The journey on which the book was based had been performed in the year 1831. By the time the book appeared, the regime in Spain had changed and much of the subject matter had become out of date. It was this inordinate lapse of time between completion of the journey and publication of the account of it that obliged Custine to change the title of the work and to emphasize its historical quality by calling it *L'Espagne sous Ferdinand VII*. Despite this staleness in the subject matter, the book was relatively well received by the critics— better than any of his previous works. This circumstance alone would have been sufficient to encourage him in the conclusion that the travel account—not the novel or the poem or the drama —was his true *forte*.

Beyond these connotations of the Spanish journey for Custine's concept of his true literary genre, there were also connotations relating to subject matter. No one was ever more profoundly a Western-European than Custine. Everything about his tastes, his interests, his political philosophy, and his faith had the deepest sort of roots in the history and culture of his native France, and, beyond that, in the traditions of the Roman Church and the Roman Empire. But Spain, as he himself at once recognized, was only partly a European country. His visit to it represented in a sense his first contact with the non-European world. He was keenly conscious of this fact, and highly sensitive to those subtle differences in thought and feeling and reaction that set Spain off from the Europe he knew. His success in spotting and describing these differences in *L'Espagne sous Ferdinand VII* inspired in him the thought of testing these same abilities by a visit to another semi-European country—Russia. He himself confessed this in so many words, in the text of his book on Spain. He was curious, he wrote, to compare Russia and Spain; both, he thought, constituting as they did only the extremities of the European continent, were more closely related to the Orient than any of the other nations of Europe.[7]

All of this would alone have been sufficient to permit us to ascribe the motivation for Custine's Russian journey in large measure to his experience with the book on Spain. But this effect, whatever it might otherwise have been, must have been immensely and spectacularly multiplied when he received, in August 1838, a letter from Balzac praising the book on Spain—a letter which would have turned the head of a man far less ambitious, and more successful, than Custine. One can imagine with what intense delight—greater, probably, than anything else experienced in his entire professional career as a writer—he must have read such phrases as these:

. . . il y a peu de livres modernes qui puissent être comparés à ces lettres.

Je ne dis cela qu'entre nous, car le livre sur l'Espagne est une oeuvre qui ne serait écrite par aucun des littérateurs de métier.

Vous êtes le voyageur par excellence. Ce que vous faites me confond, car il me semble que je serais incapable d'écrire de semblables pages.

Words such as these, coming from the pen of the famous author of *Le Père Goriot* and *Le Lys dans la vallée,* must have come like nectar to the palate of Custine, who had no higher ambition in life than to receive just this sort of recognition; and they would alone have sufficed to assure the formation in his mind of an intention to perform further such journeys. But Balzac did not let it go at that. "Si vous faites," he added,

> la même chose sur chaque pays, vous aurez fait une collection unique en son genre, et qui aura le plus grand prix, croyez-moi. En ceci, je m'y connais. Je ferai tout ce qui sera en mon pouvoir pour vous engager à peindre ainsi l'Allemagne, l'Italie intérieure, *le Nord,* la Prusse. Ce sera un grand livre et une grande gloire.*8

I have taken the liberty of italicizing, in this passage, the words "le Nord," for this was, of course, the term used in France at that time to refer to Russia. We see from this that Custine had from Balzac not only the most warm encouragement to make the writing of travel accounts his true *métier* but also the specific suggestion that Russia be included among the countries to which he should address his talent. It seems inconceivable that, in setting about as he did less than half a year later to prepare a journey to Russia, Custine should not have been acting at least partially under the influence of these words.

The acquaintance between Balzac and Custine had begun in the early thirties, when Balzac wrote appreciatively to Custine about one of the latter's early literary works—a favor which Custine returned, with interest, on the occasion of the one and only performance of Balzac's *Vautrin.* The two men met in Vienna, in 1835; and it was on that occasion that Custine made the acquaintance of Balzac's future wife, Madame Hanska. The pleasant relationship endured until the appearance of *La Russie en 1839.* Balzac, though often warned by others of Custine's lurid reputation, resolutely declined on grounds of principle to allow their relationship to be influenced by gossip about matters which he regarded as Custine's private affair. After Custine's visit to Russia, however, a concern on Balzac's part for Madame Hanska's

---

* I have given these passages in the original French because only this can convey the effect they must have produced on Custine. A translation will be found in the reference notes at the end of this Introduction.

financial and political interests in Russia caused him to distance himself from Custine—even to the point of forbidding Madame Hanska to write to Custine. When Balzac himself went to St. Petersburg, very shortly after the appearance of Custine's book, he toyed with the idea of writing something in the nature of a corrective to it. The coolness of his reception in Russia, however (on the Emperor's part, a result, no doubt, of the reaction to Custine's visit), together with the lessons of his own observations on the Russian scene, caused him to drop this idea entirely. When Balzac passed through Berlin, on his way back to Western Europe after his sojourn in Russia, the French ambassador in that city reported to the French Government that the way Balzac talked about Russia sounded no different than the book by Custine. Madame Hanska, too, in whose experience with official Petersburg there was no lack of bitterness, appears to have had a high opinion of Custine's work.

The second of the factors that might be mentioned in connection with the motivation for Custine's journey to Russia is also one that cannot be proven. It has its existence, admittedly, only in the imagination of this writer. It is the example set for Custine, as an object of both admiration and emulation, by the appearance of the first volume of Tocqueville's *De la Démocratie en Amérique.*

This volume had appeared in 1835. Its immense success was one of the commanding phenomena of the French literary-political scene just in the years 1836 and 1837 when, presumably, Custine was drafting his work on Spain. That Custine read it, and that it made a deep impression on him, is evident not only from the fact that he enlivened the title page of *L'Espagne sous Ferdinand VII* with a quotation from it,* but also from the highly respectful mention of it, and discussion of some of Tocqueville's views, in Letter XXXI of that same book. He must have wished, as he completed his own book, that he could emulate it. But

---

* The quotation was: "Mon but n'a pas été de préconiser telle forme de gouvernement en général; car je suis du nombre de ceux qui croient qu'il n'y a presque jamais de bonté absolue dans les lois."

Spain, as a subject, was not a suitable counterpart of Tocqueville's America. Russia, on the other hand, was.

The third factor affecting Custine's decision to go to Russia may have been, as some have professed to think, a major one, or it may have been, as I myself prefer to believe, of minor importance; but its existence, as a motive, is at least better documented than are the other two.

Among the Polish political exiles who took refuge in France after the Polish uprising of 1830–31, there was one—a very young man, dashing and handsome—whom Custine, beginning in 1835 and for a period of about five years thereafter, took under his wing, befriended, supported financially, and housed whenever he had no other place to go. The young man in question was Ignace de Gurowski, brother of the well-known Pan-Slavist Adam Gurowski who, at a much later date, was to go to the United States, to become a translator in the State Department, and to annoy and alarm Lincoln with a series of violent letters about policy questions during the Civil War.

In the period 1838–39, Gurowski was desirous of obtaining permission to return to the Russian Empire and to live there, as his brother Adam was then doing. Custine, it is clear, was anxious to help him in the realization of this aspiration (in the hopes, some think, of being rid of him at long last); and he made, in connection with his own journey, several efforts in this direction, including introducing Gurowski to the Russian Crown Prince while passing through Germany on the way to Russia; then taking the matter up personally in Russia with the Empress; and finally, after return from Russia, presenting Gurowski to the Empress on one of the latter's periodic visits to a German spa.

Custine's connection with Gurowski, nevertheless, has a more than negligible importance for the understanding of his book, because it had its place in the extensive pattern of Polish influences by which Custine, both before and after his journey, was affected. Young Gurowski was, of course, only one—and a very obscure one—of the many, and in part distinguished, Polish figures who had fled their native country and taken up residence in Paris at the time of the uprising of 1830–31. These people were of course anti-Russian to a man; and they did not hesitate to recommend themselves to the French as experts on Russia and authorities on the iniquities of Russian power. Nor was their expertise on this subject to be underrated. As my friend Sir Isaiah Berlin once observed to me in this connection: "Victims make acute observers."

REFERENCE NOTES

[1] Custine's mother is mentioned in many sources, but particular note should be made of the volume by B. J. A. Bardoux: *Madame de Custine, d'après des documents inédits,* Paris, 1888. For her relations with Chateaubriand, see particularly E. Chedieu de Robethon, *Chateaubriand et Madame de Custine,* Paris, Librairie Plon, 1893.

[2] Emmanuel de Lévis-Mirepoix, *Correspondance de la Marquise de Montcalm,* Paris, Éditions de Grand Siècle, 1949, p. 70.

[3] *Loc. cit.*

[4] *Là Russie,* I, 162.

[5] The work in question was entitled *Mémoires et voyages; lettres écrites à diverses époques, pendant des courses en Suisse, en Calabre, en Angleterre et en Écosse.* It was published in Paris, by A. Vézard, in 1830, in four volumes.

[6] The account of the travels in Spain was published in Paris, in 1838, by the publisher Ladvocat, in four volumes, under the title *L'Espagne sous Ferdinand VII.*

[7] *L'Espagne sous Ferdinand VII,* vol. 2, p. 212 of the Brussels edition of 1838, end of Letter xxviii.

[8] These passages are taken from vol. III, pp. 424–426, of the collection of Balzac's correspondence (H. de Balzac, *Correspondance*) recently put out (this volume in 1964) by Éditions Garnier Frères, in Paris. In translation, the passages would read as follows:
The first:

. . . there are few modern books that could be compared with these letters. I say this only between ourselves, but the book on Spain is a work that could not have been written by any of [our] professional *littérateurs.*
You are the traveller *par excellence.* What you write covers me with confusion, for it seems to me that I would be incapable of writing such pages.

And the second:

If you do the same thing for each country, you will have produced a unique collection of this sort, and one which, believe me, will have great value. This is a matter in which I know what I am talking about. I shall do everything in my power to get you committed to the description of Germany, the interior of Italy, Russia, and Prussia, in this manner. It will be a great book—and a great glory.

EMPIRE OF THE CZAR

CONTENTS

CHAPTER IV   Page 43

Conversation at Lübeck on Peculiarities in the Russian
Character.

CHAPTER V   Page 47

Prince K——— ❖ Definitions of Nobility ❖ The English
Nobility ❖ Freedom of Speech ❖ Canning ❖ Napoleon ❖
Confidential Conversation ❖ Glance at Russian History ❖
Institutions and Spirit of Chivalry unknown in Russia ❖ The
Nature of an Autocracy ❖ Politics and Religion are identical in
Russia ❖ Future Influence of Russia ❖ Fate of Paris ❖
Good Manners of the Higher Orders in Russia ❖ Society in
France before the Revolution ❖ His mauvais Ton ❖ Agreeable
Society on the Steam-Boat ❖ Russian NationalDances ❖ Two
Americans ❖ Steam-Boat Accident ❖ Isle of Dago.

CHAPTER VI   Page 61

Tragedy of Baron de Sternberg ❖ Type of Lord Byron's Heroes
❖ Parallel between Sir W. Scott and Byron ❖ Historical
Romance ❖ Marriage of Peter the Great ❖ Romodanowski ❖
Influence of the Greek Church in Russia ❖ Tyranny supported
by Falsehood ❖ Corpse in the Church of Revel ❖ The
Emperor Alexander deceived ❖ Russian Sensitiveness as to the
Opinions of Foreigners ❖ A Spy.

CHAPTER VII   Page 75

The Russian Marine ❖ Remark of Lord Durham's ❖ Great
Efforts for small Results ❖ The Amusements of Despotism ❖
Kronstadt ❖ Russian Custom-House ❖ Gloomy Aspect of
Nature ❖ Recollections of Rome ❖ English Poetical Name for
Ships of War ❖ Object of Peter the Great ❖ The Finns ❖
Batteries of Kronstadt ❖ Abject Character of the Lower
Classes of Russian Employés ❖ Inquisitions of the Police, and
the Custom-House ❖ Sudden Change in the Manners of
Fellow-Travellers ❖ Fickleness of Northern People.

CHAPTER VIII   Page 87

Approach to Petersburg by the Neva ❖ Incongruity between
the Climate and Aspect of the Country and the Style of

Architecture ❖ Absurd Imitation of the Monuments of Greece ❖ The Custom-House and Police ❖ Inquisitorial Examination ❖ Difficulties of Landing ❖ Appearance of the Streets ❖ Statue of Peter the Great ❖ The Winter Palace ❖ Rebuilt in one Year ❖ The Means employed ❖ Russian Despotism ❖ Citation from Herberstein ❖ Karamsin ❖ The Character of the People accords with that of the Government.

CHAPTER IX   Page 99

The Drowska ❖ Costume of the Lower Orders ❖ Wooden Pavements ❖ Petersburg in the Morning ❖ Resemblance of the City to a Barrack ❖ Contrast between Russia and Spain ❖ Difference between Tyranny and Despotism ❖ The Tchinn ❖ Peculiar Character of the Russian Government ❖ The Arts in Russia ❖ A Russian Hotel ❖ The Evils to be encountered there ❖ The Michael Palaces ❖ Death of Paul I ❖ The Spy baffled ❖ The Neva, its Quays and Bridges ❖ Cabin of Peter I ❖ The Citadel, its Tombs and Dungeons ❖ Church of St. Alexander Newski ❖ Russian Veterans ❖ Austerity of the Czar ❖ Russian Faith in the Future, and its Realisation ❖ Munich and Petersburg compared ❖ Interior of the Fortress ❖ The Imperial Tombs ❖ Subterranean Prison ❖ Russian Prisoners ❖ Moral Degradation of the Higher Classes ❖ Catholic Church ❖ Precarious Toleration ❖ Tomb of the last King of Poland, and of Moreau.

CHAPTER X   Page 115

Visit to the Islands ❖ Character of the Scenery ❖ Artificial Beauties ❖ Comparison between Russian and English Taste ❖ Aim and Characteristics of Russian Civilisation ❖ Happiness impossible in Russia ❖ Fashionable Life in St. Petersburg ❖ Equality under Despotism ❖ Characteristic Traits of Russian Society ❖ Absolute Power ❖ Pavilion of the Empress ❖ Vermin in the Houses and Palaces of St. Petersburg ❖ Costume of the Lower Orders ❖ Beauty of the Men when of pure Slavonian Race ❖ The Women ❖ Condition of the Russian Peasantry ❖ The Sale of Serfs ❖ Commerce can alone alter the present State of Things ❖ Care taken to conceal the Truth from Foreigners ❖ Religious Usurpation of Peter the Great ❖ His Character and Monstrous Cruelties ❖ Culpability of the Aristocracy ❖ The Author suspected ❖ State of Medical Art in Russia ❖ Universal Mystery ❖ Permission to be present at the Marriage of the Grand Duchess.

Description of the Emperor ❖ Continuation of his
Conversation ❖ His Political Opinions ❖ Sincerity of his
Language ❖ Fête at the Duchess of Oldenburg's ❖ Bal
Champêtre ❖ Flowers in Russia ❖ The Friend of the Empress
❖ Several Conversations with the Emperor ❖ His noble
Sentiments ❖ Confidence with which he inspires those who
approach him ❖ Aristocracy the only Bulwark of Liberty ❖
Parallel between Autocracies and Democracies ❖ The Arts in
Petersburg ❖ All true Talent is national.

The Population of Petersburg ❖ Solitude of the Streets ❖ The
Architecture ❖ Place du Carrousel in Paris ❖ Square of the
Grand Duke at Florence ❖ The Perspective Newski ❖
Pavements ❖ Effects of the Thaw ❖ Interior of the Houses—
The Beds ❖ Visit to Prince —— ❖ Bowers in the Drawing-
Rooms ❖ Beauty of the Slavonian Men ❖ Russian Coachmen
and Postillions ❖ The Feldjäger ❖ The Poetical Aspect of the
Land ❖ Contrast between Men and Things ❖ Architecture of
the Churches ❖ A General View of Petersburg ❖ Picturesque
and beautiful notwithstanding its Architecture ❖ Nature
beautiful even near the Pole ❖ Antipathy between the
Teutonic and Russian Races ❖ Its Effects in Poland ❖
Resemblance between the Russians and Spaniards ❖ Heat of
the Summer ❖ Fuel in Petersburg ❖ Address of the Russian
People ❖ The Designs of Providence ❖ Future Scarcity of Fuel
in Russia ❖ Want of Inventive Mechanical Genius among the
People ❖ The Romans of the North ❖ Relation between
People and their Governments ❖ The Plasterers ❖ Ugliness
and Dirtiness of the Women of the Lower Classes ❖ Their
Disproportion in point of Number, and its Result ❖ Asiatic
Manners ❖ Russian Politeness.

Fête of Peterhoff ❖ The People in the Palace of their Master
❖ Immense Power of the Emperor ❖ The Empress Catherine's
Motives for instituting Schools ❖ Views of the present
Emperor ❖ Russian Hospitality ❖ Foreigners' Descriptions of
Russia ❖ The Author's Motives in writing his Travels ❖ No
Middle Class in Russia ❖ The Children of the Priests ❖
Capital Punishments ❖ Abject Misery of the People ❖ Rules
for Foreigners who would seek Popularity in Russia ❖ Probity
of the Peasants ❖ Pick-pockets in the Palace ❖ The Journal
des Débats ❖ The Site of Peterhoff ❖ The Park Illuminations
❖ A Citizen Bivouac ❖ The English Palace ❖ Silence of the
Crowd ❖ The Ball ❖ Good Order of the Peasants ❖ Accident

in the Gulf ❖ Evil Omens ❖ The Empress's Mode of Life
❖ Description of the Illuminations ❖ Review of the
Corps of Cadets ❖ A Cadet in favour ❖ The Circassian Guard.

CHAPTER XVI Page 255

Cottage of Peterhoff ❖ A Surprise ❖ The Empress ❖ Her
Dress, Manners, and Conversation ❖ The Hereditary Grand
Duke ❖ An embarrassing Question ❖ Interior of the Cottage
❖ The Grand Duke acts as Cicerone ❖ Timidity in Society ❖
The Prince and the young Lady ❖ Cabinet of the Emperor ❖
Castle of Oranienbaum ❖ Fortress of Peter III ❖ Account of
his Assassination ❖ The Summer Houses of the Empress
Catherine ❖ The Camp of Krasnacselo.

CHAPTER XVII Page 267

Responsibility of the Emperor ❖ Effects of the Storm at
Peterhoff ❖ Death of Two Englishmen ❖ The Mystery in
which all Occurrences are enveloped ❖ A Steam-Boat saved by
an Englishman ❖ The Russian Police ❖ Disappearance of a
Femme de Chambre ❖ Politeness and Brutality united ❖
Cruelty of a Feldjäger ❖ Quarrel among Work-people, and the
revolting Cruelty of the Police ❖ The Emperor a Reformer ❖
The Column of Alexander ❖ Reform in the Language of the
Court ❖ The Church of Saint Isaac ❖ Its Immensity ❖ Spirit
of the Greek Religion ❖ Its Degradation ❖ Conversation with
a Frenchman ❖ A travelling Prison ❖ Insurrection caused by a
Speech of the Emperor's ❖ Bloody Scenes on the Wolga ❖
History of the Poet Pouskine ❖ His Duel and Death ❖ Fate of
his ambitious Successor ❖ The Poetry of Pouskine ❖ Effects of
the Adoption of Foreign Languages in Russia.

CHAPTER XVIII Page 291

Disturbances in Russia ❖ Parallel between French and Russian
Crimes and Cruelties ❖ Characteristics of Revolt in Russia ❖
Order in Disorder ❖ Danger of inculcating liberal Ideas among
ignorant Populations ❖ Reasons for Russian Superiority in
Diplomacy.

CHAPTER XIX Page 297

Petersburg in the Absence of the Emperor ❖ Character of the
Courtiers ❖ The Tchinn ❖ Its Nature and Origin ❖
Destruction of the Aristocracy ❖ Character of Peter the Great
❖ The Tchinn divided into fourteen Classes ❖ An immense

Contents

Power in the Hands of the Emperor ❖ Opposite Opinions on the future Influence of Russia ❖ Russian Hospitality ❖ Polite Formalities ❖ Resemblance to the Chinese ❖ Difference between the Russians and the French ❖ Russian Honesty ❖ Opinion of Napoleon ❖ The only sincere Man in the Empire ❖ Spoiled Savages ❖ Errors of Peter the Great ❖ The Hermitage ❖ Picture Gallery ❖ Private Social Code of the Empress Catherine.

CHAPTER XX   Page 319

The Minister of War ❖ An Evasion ❖ The Fortress of Schlusselburg ❖ Formalities ❖ Troublesome Politeness ❖ Hallucinations ❖ Kotzebue in Siberia ❖ The Feldjäger ❖ Manufactories of Petersburg ❖ Houses of Russian Peasants ❖ A Russian Inn ❖ Dirtiness of the People ❖ The Country Women ❖ Bad Roads ❖ The Engineer and his Wife ❖ The Sluices of Schlusselburg ❖ Union of the Caspian and Baltic ❖ The Source of the Neva ❖ Inundations of Petersburg ❖ The Interior of the Fortress of Schlusselburg ❖ The Tomb of Ivan ❖ Anger of the Commandant ❖ State Prisoners ❖ A Dinner with the Middle Classes in Russia ❖ Natural Causticity of the People ❖ Polite Conversation ❖ Madame de Genlis ❖ French Modern Literature prohibited ❖ A National Dish ❖ Difference in the Manners of the Higher and Middle Classes ❖ Return to Petersburg.

CHAPTER XXI   Page 343

Literary Candour ❖ The Bridge of Neva at Night ❖ Petersburg compared to Venice ❖ The Gospel dangerous ❖ Religion in Russia ❖ Janus ❖ New Poland ❖ The Future ❖ A Delay ❖ History of the Prince and Princess Troubetzkoi ❖ Devotion of the Princess ❖ Fourteen Years in the Uralian Mines ❖ Mercy of the Emperor ❖ The Children of a Convict ❖ Colonisation in Siberia ❖ A Mother's Anguish ❖ Second Petition to the Emperor, and his Answer ❖ A final Opinion on the Character of the Emperor ❖ The Family of the Exiles ❖ Change in the Author's Plans ❖ Means taken for deceiving the Police.

CHAPTER XXII   Page 359

Road from Petersburg to Moscow ❖ Speed of travelling ❖ A Livonian ❖ Punishment of a Postillion ❖ English Carriages on Russian Roads ❖ The Country People ❖ Aspect

of the Country ❖ The Post-house ❖ Mountains of Valdai ❖
Costume of the Peasantry ❖ Russian Ladies en Déshabillé ❖
Small Russian Towns ❖ Torjeck Russian Leather ❖ Chicken
Fricassee ❖ A double Road.

CHAPTER XXIII   Page 373

Boy Coachmen ❖ The Road ❖ Gracefulness of the
People ❖ Dress of the Women ❖ The See-saw ❖ Beauty of the
Female Peasants ❖ Russian Cottages ❖ Customs of the Serfs
❖ Devout Thieves ❖ Want of Principle in the Higher Classes
❖ Female Politicians ❖ Domestic Happiness of the Serfs ❖
Casuistical Reflections ❖ Connection of the Church and State
❖ Fundamental Difference between Sects and a Mother
Church ❖ History of a Foal ❖ The Author injured by the
Moral Atmosphere ❖ National Moral Responsibility ❖
Spain and Russia compared ❖ Dews of the North.

CHAPTER XXIV   Page 393

First View of Moscow ❖ Symbolic Architecture of Greek
Churches ❖ Castle of Petrowski ❖ Entrance to Moscow ❖
Aspect of the Kremlin ❖ Church of Saint Basil ❖ The French
at Moscow ❖ Anecdote relative to the French in Russia ❖
Battle of Moskowa ❖ The Kremlin a City ❖ Origin of the
word Czar ❖ An English Hotel in Russia ❖ The City by
Moonlight ❖ Population of Moscow ❖ The Object of
Conscience ❖ Gardens under the Walls of the Kremlin ❖
Description of the Fortress ❖ Ivan III ❖ Napoleon and the
Kremlin ❖ Modern Grandiloquence.

CHAPTER XXV   Page 409

The Kremlin by Daylight ❖ Character of its Architecture ❖
Symbolic Imagery ❖ Relation between the Character of
Buildings and Builders ❖ Ivan IV ❖ Patience criminal ❖
Introduction to the History of Ivan IV. *

CHAPTER XXVII   Page 417

English Club ❖ Reunion of Nations ❖ Peculiar Character of
Architecture in Moscow ❖ Observation of Madame de Staël ❖
Advantage of obscure Travellers ❖ Kitaigorod ❖ Madonna of
Vivielski ❖ Church of Vassili Blagennoï ❖ The Holy Gate ❖
Church of the Assumption ❖ Foreign Artists ❖ Tower

* Chapter XXVI has been omitted.

of John the Great ❖ Convent of the Ascension ❖ Interior of
the Treasury ❖ New Works at the Kremlin.

CHAPTER XXVIII   Page 433

Oriental Aspect of Moscow ❖ Horace Vernet ❖ Want of
superior Works of Art ❖ Russian Fickleness ❖ Silk
Manufactories ❖ Appearances of Liberty ❖ Railroads
❖ Russian Piety ❖ Church and State in England ❖ Devotees
and Statesmen ❖ Error of the Liberals in rejecting Catholicism
❖ French Policy ❖ Newspaper Government ❖ The Greco-
Russian Church ❖ Its Sects and their Origin ❖ Polygamy ❖
Merchants of Moscow ❖ A Russian Fair ❖ Rural Scenery in
Moscow ❖ Drunkenness among the Russians.

CHAPTER XXIX   Page 439

The Noblemen's Club ❖ Polite Education of the
Russians ❖ Habits of the Higher Classes ❖ A Russian Coffee-
house ❖ Religious Belief of the old Serfs ❖ Society in Moscow
❖ A Country House in a City ❖ Real Politeness ❖ Review
of Russian Character ❖ Murder in a Nunnery ❖
Conversation at a Table-d'hôte ❖ The Lovelace of the Kremlin
❖ A Burlesque Petition ❖ Modern Prudery ❖ Parting Scene
with Prince —— ❖ An elegant Coachman ❖ Morals of the
Citizens' Wives ❖ Libertinism the Fruit of Despotism ❖ Moral
Licence in lieu of Political Freedom ❖ Condition of the Serfs
and other Classes ❖ Nature of Russian Ambition ❖ Results of
the System of Peter the Great

CHAPTER XXX   Page 453

Roads in the Interior ❖ Farms and Country Mansions ❖
Monotony the great Characteristic of the Land ❖ Pastoral Life
of the Peasants ❖ Beauty of the Women and old Men ❖
Policy attributed to the Poles ❖ A Night at the Convent of
Troïtza ❖ Pestalozzi on Personal Cleanliness ❖ Interior of the
Convent ❖ Pilgrims ❖ Saint Sergius ❖ History of the Convent
❖ Its Tombs and Treasures ❖ Inconveniences of a Journey in
Russia ❖ Bad Quality of the Water ❖ Want of Probity
a National Characteristic.

CHAPTER XXXI   Page 469

Commercial Importance of Yaroslaf ❖ A Russian's Opinion of
Russian Architecture ❖ Description of Yaroslaf ❖ Monotonous
Aspect of the Country ❖ The Boatmen of the Volga ❖ Coup-

d'oeil on the Russian Character ❖ Primitive Drowskas ❖
Antique Costume ❖ Russian Baths ❖ Difference between
Russian and German Children ❖ Visit to the Governor ❖ An
agreeable Surprise ❖ Souvenirs of Versailles ❖ Influence
of French Literature ❖ Visit to the Convent of the
Transfiguration ❖ Russian Piety ❖ Byzantine Style in the Arts
❖ Great Points of Religious Discussion in Russia ❖ The
Zacuska ❖ The Sterled ❖ Russian Dinners ❖ Family Soirée ❖
Moral Superiority of the Female Sex in Russia ❖ Justification
of Providence ❖ A Lottery ❖ French Ton changed by Politics
❖ Want of a beneficent Aristocracy ❖ The real Governors
of Russia ❖ Bureaucracy ❖ Children of the Popes ❖
Propagandism of Napoleon still operates in Russia ❖ The Task
of the Emperor.

CHAPTER XXXII   Page 493

The Banks of the Volga ❖ Russian Coachmen in Mountain
Roads ❖ Kostroma ❖ Ferry on the Volga ❖ Accident in a
Forest ❖ Beauty of the Women ❖ Civilisation injurious ❖
Rousseau justified ❖ Etymology of the Word Sarmatian ❖
Elegance, Industry, and Humility of the Peasants ❖ Their
Music ❖ National Music dangerous to Despotism ❖ The Road
to Siberia ❖ A Picture of Russia ❖ Exiles on the Road.

CHAPTER XXXIII   Page 507

Site of Nijni-Novgorod ❖ Predilection of the Emperor for that
City ❖ The Kremlin of Nijni ❖ Concourse at the Fair ❖ The
Governor ❖ Bridge of the Oka ❖ Difficulty in obtaining a
Lodging ❖ The Plague of Persicas ❖ Pride of the Feldjäger
❖ The Fair-Ground ❖ Subterranean City ❖ Singular
Appearance of the River ❖ The City of Tea ❖ Of Rags ❖ Of
Wheelwrights' Work ❖ Of Iron ❖ Origin of the Fair ❖ Persian
Village ❖ Salt Fish from the Caspian ❖ Leather ❖ Furs ❖
Lazzaronis of the North ❖ Badly chosen Site ❖ Commercial
Credit of the Serfs ❖ Their Mode of calculating ❖ Bad Faith
of the Nobles ❖ Prices of Merchandise ❖ Turquoises of the
Bucharians ❖ Kirguis Horses ❖ The Fair after Sunset ❖ The
Effects of Music in Russia.

CHAPTER XXXIV   Page 529

Financial Phenomenon ❖ Financial Reform of the Emperor's
❖ Means taken by the Governor of Nijni to induce the
Merchants to obey ❖ Their nominal Compliance ❖ Enquiry
into their Motives ❖ Improvements at Nijni ❖ The Serf and

the Lord ❖ The Governor of Nijni's Explanations of despotic
Administration ❖ Forbearance of the Authorities ❖ A Ride
with the Governor—Value of the Commodities at the Fair of
Nijni ❖ Visits with the Governor ❖ The Bureaucracy
❖ The Author's Feldjäger ❖ Flag of Minine ❖ Bad Faith of
the Government ❖ Modern Vandalism ❖ Peter the Great ❖
The Governor's Camp ❖ Song of the Soldiers ❖
Church of the Strogonoffs ❖ Russian Vaudeville.

Contents

AUTHOR'S PREFACE

. . . Wherever I have set foot on earth, from Morocco to the frontiers of Siberia, I have seen smouldering the fires of religious war—not any longer, let us hope, to be the war of the armed hand, the least decisive of any, but the war of ideas. God alone knows the secret of events; but every man who observes and reflects can foresee some of the questions that will be resolved by the future: those questions are all religious. Upon the attitude which France may take in the world as a Catholic power, will depend her political influence. In the proportion that revolutionary spirits leave her, catholic hearts will draw around her. In this respect, the force of things so governs men, that a king supremely tolerant, and a minister who is a Protestant, have become throughout the world the most zealous defenders of Catholicism, simply because they are Frenchmen. . . .

The circumstance which renders Russia the most singular State now to be seen in the world is that extreme barbarism, favoured by the enslavement of the church, and extreme civilisation, imported by an eclectic government from foreign lands, are there to be seen united. To understand how tranquillity, or at least immobility, can spring from the shock of elements so opposed, it will be necessary to follow the traveller into the heart of this singular country.

The mode which I employ of describing places and defining characters, appears to me, if not the most favourable to the author, at least the most likely to inspire confidence in the reader, whom I oblige to follow me, and whom I render the judge himself of the development of those ideas that may be suggested to me.

I arrived in a new country without any other prejudices, than those which no man can guard against: those which a conscientious study of its history impart. I examined objects, I observed facts and individuals, while candidly permitting daily experience to modify my opinions. Very few exclusive political notions incommoded me in this spontaneous labour, in which religion alone was my unchanging rule; and even that rule may be rejected by the reader without the recital of facts and the moral consequences that flow from them being discarded, or confounded with the reprobation that I shall meet with from those whose creeds do not agree with mine.

I may be accused of having prejudices, but I shall never be reproached with intentionally disguising the truth.

The descriptions of what I saw were made upon the spot, the recitals of what I heard each day were committed to paper on the same evening. Thus, my conversations with the Emperor, given word for word in the ensuing chapters, cannot fail to possess a species of interest: that of exactitude. They will also serve, I hope, to render this prince, so differently viewed among us and throughout Europe, better known.

The chapters that follow were not all destined for the public. Several of the early ones were written as purely confidential letters. Fatigued with writing, but not with travelling, I resolved, this time, to observe without any methodical plan, and to keep my descriptions for my friends. The reasons that decided me to publish the whole will be seen in the course of the work.

The principal one was the feeling that my views were daily modified by the examination to which I subjected a state of society absolutely new to me. It struck me that in speaking the truth of Russia, I should be doing something bold and novel: hitherto, fear and interest have dictated exaggerated eulogies; hatred has also published calumnies: I am not afraid of making wreck either on the one rock or the other.

I went to Russia to seek for arguments against representative government, I return a partisan of constitutions. A mixed government is not the most favourable to action; but in their old age, nations have less need of acting: this government is the one which most aids production, and which procures to man the greatest amount of prosperity; it is, above all, the one which imparts the highest activity to mind within the sphere of practical ideas: in short, it renders the citizen independent, not by the elevation of sentiments, but by the operation of laws; assuredly these are great compensations for great disadvantages.

As I gradually became acquainted with the tremendous and singular government, regulated, or I might say founded, by Peter I., I became aware of the importance of the mission which chance had entrusted to me.

The extreme curiosity with which my work inspired the Russians, who were evidently rendered unquiet by the reserve of my language, first led me to think, that I had more power than I previously attributed to myself; I therefore became attentive and prudent, for I was not long in discovering the danger to which my sincerity might expose me. Not daring to send my letters by post, I preserved them all, and kept them concealed with extreme care; so that on my return to France, my journey was written, and in my own hands. Nevertheless, I have hesitated to publish it for three years: this is the time which I have needed to reconcile, in the secret of my conscience, what I believed to be the conflicting claims of gratitude and of truth! The latter at last prevails, because it appears to me to be truth of a nature that will interest my country. I cannot forget that, above all else, I write for France, and I hold it my duty to reveal to her useful and important facts.

I consider myself competent and authorised to judge, even severely if my conscience urges me, a country where I have friends, to analyse, without descending into offensive personalities, the character of public men, to quote the words of political persons, to commence with those of the highest personage in the state, to recount their actions, and to carry out to the last stage of inquiry the reflections which these examinations may suggest; provided, however, that in capriciously pursuing the course of my ideas, I do not give them to others except for just the worth that they have in my own eyes: this, it appears to me, is all that constitutes the probity of an author.

But in thus yielding to duty, I have respected, at least I hope so, all the rules of social propriety; for I maintain that there is a proper manner of expressing severe truths: this manner consists in speaking only upon conviction, whilst repelling the suggestions of vanity.

Besides, having seen much to admire in Russia, I have been able to mingle many praises in my descriptions.

The Russians will not be satisfied; when was self-love ever known to be? And yet no one has ever been struck more than I, by the greatness and political importance of their nation. The high destinies of these people, these last comers upon the old theatre of the world, engaged my mind during the whole time of my stay among them. The Russians, viewed as a body, appeared to me as being great, even in their most shocking vices; viewed as individuals, I considered them amiable. In the character of the common people I found much to interest: these flattering truths ought, I think, to compensate for others less agreeable. But, hitherto, the Russians have been treated as spoiled children by the greater number of travellers.

If the discordances that one cannot help remarking in their social state, if the spirit of their government, essentially opposed to my ideas and habits, have drawn from me reproaches, and even cries of indignation, my praises, equally voluntary, must have the greater weight.

But these Orientals, habituated as they are to breathe and dispense the most direct incense of flattery, will be sensible to nothing but blame. All disapprobation appears to them as treachery; they call every severe truth a falsehood; they will not perceive the delicate admiration that may sometimes lurk under my apparent criticisms—the regret and, on some occasions, the sympathy that accompany my most severe remarks.

If they have not converted me to their religions (they have several, and among these, political religion is not the least intolerant), if, on the contrary, they have modified my monarchical ideas in a way that is opposed to despotism and favourable to representative government, they will be offended simply because I am not of their opinion. I regret that such is the case, but I prefer regret to remorse. . . .

ARRIVAL OF THE HEREDITARY GRAND DUKE OF RUSSIA AT EMS ❖
CHARACTER OF RUSSIAN COURTIERS ❖ THE PERSON OF THE GRAND DUKE ❖
HIS FATHER AND UNCLE AT THE SAME AGE ❖ HIS EQUIPAGES AND SUITE
❖ SUPERIORITY OF THE ENGLISH IN ALL EXTERNAL APPURTENANCES
❖ THE RHINE ❖ THE RIVER MORE BEAUTIFUL THAN
ITS BANKS ❖ FIRE-FLIES ON
THE RHINE
❖

CHAPTER I

❖

I date from yesterday the commencement of my Russian Travels.* The Hereditary Grand Duke has arrived at Ems, preceded by ten or twelve carriages, and attended by a numerous court.

What has chiefly struck me in my first view of Russian courtiers is the extraordinary submissiveness with which, as grandees, they perform their *devoirs*. They seem, in fact, to be only a higher order of slaves; but the moment the Prince has retired, a free, unrestrained, and decided manner is reassumed, which contrasts unpleasantly with that complete abnegation of self, affected only the moment before. In a word, there appears to reign throughout the suite of the heir of the imperial throne, a habit of servile docility from which the nobles are not more exempt than the valets. It is not merely the etiquette that regulates other courts, where official respect, the importance of the office rather than that of the person, the compulsory part, in short, that has to be played, produces ennui, and sometimes ridicule: it is something more; it is a spontaneous and involuntary humility, which yet does not altogether exclude arrogance: it seems to me as though I could hear them say, "since it cannot be otherwise, we are glad to have it so." This mixture of pride and humiliation displeases me, and by no means prepossesses me in favour of the country I am about to survey.

I found myself amid the crowd of curious spectators close to

* 5th June, 1839.

the Grand Duke, just as he descended from his carriage; and as he stood for some time before entering the gate of the *maison des bains*, talking with a Russian lady, the Countess ——, I was able to observe him at my leisure. His age, as his appearance indicates, is twenty: his height is commanding, but he appears to me, for so young a man, rather fat. His features would be handsome were it not that their fulness destroys their expression. His round face rather resembles that of a German than a Russ; it suggests an idea of what the Emperor Alexander's must have been at the same age, without however recalling, in any degree, the physiognomy of the Calmuc. A face of this cast will pass through many changes before assuming its definitive character. The habitual humour which it, at present, denotes, is gentleness and benevolence; but between the youthful smile of the eyes, and the constant contraction of the mouth, there is, nevertheless, a discordance which does not bespeak frankness, and which, perhaps, indicates some inward suffering. The sorrows of youth—of that age in which happiness is, as it were, the right of man—are secrets the better guarded, because they are mysteries inexplicable even to those who experience them. The expression of this young prince is amiable; his carriage is graceful, imposing, and altogether princely; and his manner modest, without being timid, which must alone gain him much good will. The embarrassment of great people is so embarrassing to others, that their case always wears the character of affability, to which in fact it amounts. When they believe themselves to be something more than common mortals, they become constrained, both by the direct influence of such an opinion, and by the hopeless effort of inducing others to share it. This absurd inquietude does not disturb the Grand Duke. His presence conveys the idea of a perfectly well-bred man, and if he ever reign, it will be by the charm inherent in graceful manners that he will cause himself to be obeyed: it will not be by terror, unless, at least, the *necessities* attached to the office of a Russian Emperor should, in changing his position, change his disposition also.

Since writing the above, I have again seen the Hereditary Grand Duke, and have examined him more nearly and leisurely. He had cast off his uniform, which appeared to fit him too closely, and gave to his person a bloated appearance. In my opinion he looks best in undress. His general bearing is certainly pleasing; his carriage is lofty, yet without military stiffness. The kind of grace by which he is distinguished, reminds one of that peculiar charm of manner which seems to belong to the Slavonic race. It is not the expression of the quick passions of southern climes, neither is it the imperturbable coolness of the people of the north: it is a combination of simplicity, of southern mobility, and of Scandinavian melancholy. The Slavonians are fair-complexioned Arabs*; the Grand Duke is more than half German, but in Mecklenburg and Holstein, as in some parts of Russia, there are Germans of Slavonian extraction.

The countenance of this prince, notwithstanding his youth, presents fewer attractions than his figure. His complexion has already lost its freshness†; one can observe that he is under the influence of some cause of grief; his eye-lids are cast down with a sadness that betrays the cares of a riper age. His well-formed mouth is not without an expression of sweetness; his Grecian profile reminds me of antique medals, or of the portraits of the Empress Catherine; but notwithstanding his expression of amiableness (an expression which almost always imparts that also of beauty), his youth, and, yet more, his German blood, it is impossible to avoid observing in the lines of his face a power of dissimulation which one trembles to see in so young a man. This trait is doubtless the impress of destiny. It convinces me that this prince will be called to the throne. The tones of his voice are sweet, which is not commonly the case in his family; they say it is a gift which he has inherited from his mother.

He shines among the young people of his suite without our discovering what it is that preserves the distance which may be easily observed to exist between them, unless it be the perfect gracefulness of his person. Gracefulness always indicates an amiable mental endowment: it depicts mind upon the features, embodies it in the carriage and the attitudes, and pleases at the very time that it commands. Russian travellers had spoken to me of

* "Des Arabes blonds."
† The Grand Duke had been ill some time before his arrival at Ems.

the beauty of the prince as quite a phenomenon. Without this exaggeration I should have been more struck with it; besides, I could not but recollect the romantic mien, the archangelic form, of his father and his uncle, the Grand Duke Michael, who, when, in 1815, they visited Paris, were called *"the northern lights,"* and I felt inclined to be severe, because I had been deceived: yet, notwithstanding this, the Grand Duke of Russia appears to me as one of the finest models of a prince that I have ever met with.

With the inelegance of his equipages, the disorder of the baggage, and the carelessness of the servants, I have been much struck. In contrasting this imperial *cortège* with the magnificent simplicity of English equipages, and the careful superintendence that English servants bestow upon everything, one is reminded that to have one's carriages and harness made in London would not be all that is requisite towards attaining that perfection in material, or external arrangements, the possession of which constitutes the superiority of the English in so matter-of-fact an age as our own.

Yesterday I went to see the sun setting on the Rhine. It was a magnificent spectacle. It is not, however, the banks of the river, with their monotonous ruins and parched vineyards, which occupy too much of the landscape to be agreeable to the eye, that I chiefly admire in this beautiful yet overlauded country. I have seen elsewhere banks more commanding, more varied, more lovely; finer forests, a more luxuriant vegetation, and more picturesque and striking points of view: it is the river itself, especially as viewed from the shore, that appears to me the most wonderful object in the scene. This immense body of water, gliding with an ever equal motion through the country which it beautifies and enlivens, reveals to me a power in creation that overwhelms my senses. In watching its movements I liken myself to a physician examining the pulse of a man in order to ascertain his strength. Rivers are the arteries of our globe, and before their manifestation of universal life I stand fixed in awe and admiration; I feel myself to be in the presence of my sovereign; I see eternity, I believe, and I almost grasp the infinite. There is in this a sublime mystery; in nature what I cannot comprehend I admire, and my ignorance takes refuge in adoration. Thus it is, that science to me is less necessary than to discontented minds.

We shall literally die of heat. It is many years since the air of the valley of Ems, always oppressive, has risen to the present temperature. Last night, in returning from the banks of the Rhine, I saw in the woods a swarm of fire-flies—my beloved Italian *luccioli.* I had never before observed them, except in hot climates.

I set out in two days for Berlin and St. Petersburg.

❖

CHAPTER II*

❖

 . . . The death which my father sought and met in Paris under the influence of a sense of duty, was attended with a circumstance, unknown to the public, that in my opinion invests it with a character of sublimity. The circumstance deserves to be recited at length; but as my other parent will occupy a conspicuous part in the recital, I will first relate another story which will give some idea of her character.

My travels are my memoirs. I do not therefore scruple to commence those to Russia with a history that more concerns myself personally, than the topics on which I shall have to dwell hereafter.

It was while with the army, and before his recall to Paris, that General Custine was apprised of the death of the king. His expressions of indignation on this occasion were not moderated even in presence of the commissioners of the convention. These overheard him say, "I serve my country against foreign invasion, but who would fight for those who now govern us?" These words, reported to Robespierre by Thionville, decided the fate of the General.

My mother at that time lived in a retired manner in a village in Normandy. The moment she learnt the return of General Custine to Paris, this noble-minded young woman conceived it to be her duty to quit her asylum, and her child, who was then quite an

* Written at Berlin.

infant, to repair to the assistance of her father-in-law, with whom her family had been for some years on bad terms, owing to a difference in political opinions.

It was a great trial to her to part with me, for she was a mother in the truest sense of the word; but misfortune always had the first claim upon her heart.

Could General Custine have been saved, it would have been by the devotion and courage of his daughter-in-law. Their first interview was most touching. No sooner did the veteran recognise my mother than he believed himself safe. In fact, her youth, her extreme beauty, her mingled heroism and timidity, so interested the journalists, the people, and even the judges of the revolutionary tribunal, that the men who were determined on the death of the General, felt it necessary first to silence the most eloquent of his advocates, his daughter-in-law.

The government, however, at that time, had not thrown off all appearance of law; yet the men who hesitated to throw my mother into prison did not scruple to attempt her assassination. The *Septembriseurs*, as these hired ruffians were called, were placed for several days about the precincts of the Palais de Justice; but though my mother was warned of her danger, nothing could deter her from daily attending the trial, and seating herself at the feet of her father-in-law, where her devoted mien softened even the hearts of his murderers.

Between each sitting of the court she employed her time in privately soliciting the members of the committees and of the revolutionary tribunal. A friend of my father's, in costume *à la carmagnole*, generally accompanied her, and waited for her in the anti-room.

In one of the last sittings of the tribunal her looks had drawn tears even from the women in the gallery, commonly called "the furies of the guillotine," and the *tricoteuses* of Robespierre. This so enraged Fouquier-Tinville, that he sent secret peremptory instructions to the assassins outside.

After the accused was re-conducted to prison, his daughter-in-law prepared to descend the steps of the palace, in order to regain, on foot and alone—for none dared openly to accompany her—the hackney coach, which waited for her in a distant street.

My mother, naturally timid in a crowd, stood trembling at the head of this long flight of steps, pressed on all sides by an enraged and blood-thirsty populace. Her eyes involuntarily sought the spot where Madame de Lamballe had been murdered some time before. She felt her presence of mind departing, as from the ferocious mob the cry, "It is the daughter of the traitor, it is La Custine," mingled with horrid imprecations, reached her ears. How was she to pass through this crowd of infernal, rather than human beings? Already some, with naked swords, had placed themselves before her; others, half clothed, had placed themselves before her; others, half clothed, had caused their women to draw back—a certain sign that murder was about to be enacted. My mother felt that the first symptom of weakness she might betray would be the signal for her death: she has often related to me that she bit her hands and tongue so as to bring blood, in her endeavour to preserve a calm countenance at this juncture. At length she observed a fish-woman among the foremost of the crowd. This woman, who was revolting in appearance, had an infant in her arms. Moved by the God of mothers, *the daughter of the traitor* approached this mother, (a mother is something more than a woman,) and said to her, "What a sweet babe you have in your arms!" "Take it," replied the parent, who understood her by one word and glance; "you can return it to me at the foot of the steps."

The electricity of maternal feeling had thrilled through these two hearts. It communicated itself also to the crowd. My mother took the child, pressed it to her bosom, and held it as an aegis in her arms.

Man, as the child of nature, resumed his superiority over man brutalised under the influence of social evils. The "civilised" barbarians were vanquished by two mothers. She, who was mine, descended, thus rescued, into the court of the Palais de Justice, unsaluted by even an abusive word. She returned the infant to her who had lent it: they parted without interchanging a syllable: the place was not favourable to thanks or explanations, and they never saw each other afterwards; but assuredly the souls of these mothers will meet in another world.

The young woman thus miraculously saved, could not save her

father. He died, and to crown the glory of his life, the veteran soldier had the courage to die a Christian. A letter to his son attests this humble sacrifice, the most difficult of all, in an age of practical crimes and philosophical virtues. In proceeding to the scaffold he embraced the crucifix. This religious courage ennobled his death, as much as his military courage ennobled his life; but it gave great offence to the Brutus's of Paris.

During the trial of General Custine, my father had published a sober but manly defence of the former's political and military conduct. This defence, which had been placarded on the walls of Paris, only served to bring upon the author the hatred of Robespierre. He was imprisoned soon after the death of his father. At this period the Reign of Terror was making rapid progress: to suffer arrest was to receive sentence; the process of trial had become a mere form.

My mother had obtained permission to see her husband daily. Ascertaining that his death was determined, she put in requisition every means that might enable him to escape. By aid of large bribes and larger promises, she won over even the daughter of the gaoler to second her design.

My father was not tall. He was slightly and elegantly made. It was arranged therefore that he should put on the clothes of his wife in the prison, that she should dress herself in those of the gaoler's daughter, and while the latter was to reach the street by another stair, the prisoner and his wife were to pass out together by the ordinary passage, which the two women had been, purposely, in the habit of doing very frequently.

Every thing was duly arranged, and a day fixed, for the execution of this plan. On that day my mother, full of hope that it was her last visit, repaired to the prison, though only on the previous evening the convention had published a decree against all who should aid or connive at the escape of a political prisoner.

This monstrous law was purposely placed before the eyes of the prisoners. My mother, on arriving at the appointed hour, found Louise, the young woman whose good will as well as interested services she had enlisted, in tears, on the prison stairs. Upon enquiring the cause, she learnt, to her inexpressible surprise, that it was owing to her husband having peremptorily refused to entertain any farther the projected plan of escape. My mother, fearing they had been betrayed, turned, without reply, to gain her husband's apartment. Louise followed her, and apprised her, in a low voice, that he had read the law. She immediately guessed the rest. She knew his inflexible character, and his high and delicate sense of honour: despair almost deprived her of all physical power. "Come with me," she said to Louise, "you will have more influence with him than I; for it is in order to avoid exposing your life that he is about to sacrifice his own."

They both entered together, and a scene commenced which may be better imagined than described. Never but on one single occasion did my mother summon sufficient fortitude to describe it to me. Suffice to say, that nothing could shake the stoical resolution of the young prisoner: the two women on their knees, the weeping wife, the agonized mother reminding him that his child would be an orphan, the stranger urging the utmost willingness to risk her life in his service,—all was unavailing. The sentiments of honour and of duty were stronger in the soul of this man than love of life, than love for a tender and exquisitely beautiful woman, than the impulses of paternal affection. The time accorded to my mother for her visit was passed in useless remonstrances. She had, at length, to be carried out of the chamber. Louise conducted her into the street, where our friend M. Guy de Chaumont Quitry awaited her with an anxiety that may be easily imagined.

"All is lost," said my mother; "he will not save himself."

"I was sure he would not," replied M. de Quitry.

This answer, worthy of the friend of such a man, appears to me almost as sublime as the conduct to which it referred.

And of all this the world has hitherto known nothing. Supernatural virtue passed unobserved in a time when the sons of France were as lavish of their heroism as they had been of their genius fifty years before.

My mother saw her husband but once more after this scene. By means of money she procured permission to bid him the last adieu, when condemned, and in the Conciergerie. . . .

My mother, Delphine de Sabran, was one of the most lovely

women of those times. The devotion she displayed to her father-
in-law, assures to her a glorious place in the annals of a revolution in which the heroism of the women has
often atoned for the ferocity
and fanaticism of the
men. . . .

❖

CONTINUATION OF THE LIFE OF MADAME DE CUSTINE ❖ HER ARREST ❖ PROVIDENTIAL CONCEALMENT OF HER PAPERS ❖ DEVOTION OF NANETTE ❖ SCENE AT THE TOMB OF MARAT ❖ MADAME DE BEAUHARNAIS IN PRISON ❖ ANECDOTES OF PRISON LIFE ❖ INTERROGATION OF MADAME DE CUSTINE ❖ INSPIRES ONE OF HER JUDGES WITH THE DESIRE OF SAVING HER ❖ THE MEANS WHICH HE USES DURING SIX MONTHS TO RETARD HER EXECUTION ❖ END OF THE REIGN OF TERROR ❖ CHARACTER OF ROBESPIERRE ❖ THE PRISONS AFTER HIS FALL ❖ PETITION OF NANETTE ❖ EXTRAORDINARY DELIVERANCE OF MADAME DE CUSTINE ❖ RETURNS TO HER HOUSE ❖ SICKNESS AND POVERTY ❖ DEATH IN 1826

❖

CHAPTER III

❖

As I have begun to relate the misfortunes of my family, I will finish the recital. Perhaps this episode of our revolution, as recounted by the son of two individuals who performed conspicuous parts in it, will not be found altogether without interest.

My mother having lost all that could attach her to her country, had now no duty to perform but that of saving her life, and watching over the welfare of her child.

Her situation was, in fact, much worse than that of the other French fugitives. Our name, tainted with Liberalism, was as odious to the aristocrats of that period as to the Jacobins. . . .

Soon after the catastrophe which rendered her a widow, she became aware of the necessity of leaving France. This, however, required a passport, which it was very difficult to obtain. By means of money she procured a false one, under the name of a dealer in lace about to visit Belgium. It was arranged that my nurse, a faithful servant of our family in Lorraine, and who had brought me to Paris, should proceed with me by way of Alsace to Pyrmont in Westphalia, where we were to meet my mother, and from thence journey together to Berlin, in which city she expected to join her own mother and her brother also. To no other servant but the nurse herself was this plan confided. All preliminary arrangements having been made, Nanette departed with me for the office of the Strasburg diligence, leaving my mother, who was to set out immediately after us on her journey to Flanders, at her lodging in the Rue de Bourbon. She was employing the last minutes that were to precede her departure, in her cabinet, assorting papers and burning such as might compromise others; for among these papers were letters from officers in the army, and from parties already suspected of being aristocrats, of a character that would have sufficed to bring to the guillotine, in four and twenty hours, herself and fifty other individuals.

Seated on a large sofa near to the fire-place, she was busy burning the most dangerous letters, and placing others, which, as having been written by her parents and dearest friends she felt unwilling to destroy, in a separate box, when suddenly she heard the door of the outer apartment open, and forewarned by one of those presentiments which had never failed to admonish her in moments of danger, she said within herself, "I am betrayed; they are coming to arrest me;" whereupon, without further deliberation, for it was too late to burn the heaps of dangerous documents by which she was surrounded, she gathered them hastily together and stuffed them, with the box also, under the sofa, the hangings of which fortunately reached to the floor.

This accomplished, she arose, and received, with an air of perfect composure, the persons who instantly after entered her cabinet. They were the members of the Committee of General Safety, with their attendants. These beings, whose external appearance was at once ridiculous and terrible, surrounded her with muskets and drawn swords.

"You are under arrest," said the president.

My mother made no answer.

"You are arrested, for intent to emigrate."

"It was my intention," she replied, on seeing her false passport already in the hands of the president; for it had been taken from her pocket by the agent of the municipality, whose first care was to search her person. . . .

Before departing they examined the drawers, cabinets, and each piece of furniture in the room, and searched every where except beneath the sofa. The papers remained where they had been placed. My mother was conveyed to the Carmelite convent, which had been converted into a prison, and on whose walls was still to be seen the blood of the victims of the 2d September, 1792.

Meanwhile the friend who waited for her at the barrier, convinced from her non-appearance that she had been arrested, hurried to the office of the diligence to prevent Nanette from proceeding with me to Strasburg. He arrived in time, and I was taken back to our residence. My mother was no longer there; the seals had already been affixed upon the doors of her apartments; all the servants had been dismissed; not, however, before they had found time to plunder the plate and linen. The house was robbed of all its valuables, and deserted, except by the civic guard, who kept the door. The kitchen was the only room left to us. Here my poor nurse made her bed close to my cradle, and tended me for eight months with the affection of a mother; and with a devotion that could not have been exceeded had I been a great nobleman.

After the money, which had been destined for our journey, was expended, she supported me by selling, one by one, the articles of her dress. If my mother perished, her intention was to carry me to her own country, and to bring me up among the little peasants of her family. . . .

The latter [my mother], in her prison, derived some consolation from the society of several distinguished female fellow prisoners, who evinced for her the sincerest sympathy. Among others were Mademoiselle Picot, and Mesdames de Lameth, d'Aiguillon, and de Beauharnais, afterwards the Empress Josephine. This last named lady was placed in the same room with my mother, and they mutually performed for each other the offices of a *femme de chambre*. . . .

The prisoners, both male and female, used to meet at certain hours in a kind of garden, where the men played at prisoners' bars. It was usually during these moments of recreation that the revolutionary tribunal sent to summon its victims. If the one singled out was in the midst of a game, he bade a simple adieu to his friends, *after which the party continued their play!!* This prison was a world in miniature, of which Robespierre was the god. What could so much resemble hell, as this caricature of providence?

After having been five months in prison, my mother saw M. de Beauharnais depart for the scaffold. In passing her, he presented her with an arabesque talisman set in a ring. She always kept it, and it is now worn by me.

Time was then no longer reckoned by weeks, but by periods of ten days; the tenth was termed *décadi,* and answered to our Sunday, as they neither worked nor guillotined on that day. Its arrival, therefore, assured to the prisoners an existence of twenty-four hours; this appeared an age in prospect, and the day was always viewed as a fête in the prison.

Such was the life of my mother after the death of her husband. It continued during the last six months of the reign of terror. Considering her connections, her celebrity, and the circumstances of her arrest, it was wonderful that she had escaped the scaffold so long. On three different occasions she was taken from prison to her own house, where her inquisitors examined before her, and questioned her upon every insignificant paper which they could find in the drawers and secretaries; searching every corner of the apartment, and omitting only to examine the sofa, which it was the will of God should be overlooked. It may be readily imagined that my mother's heart would irrepressibly beat every time they approached this spot. She has often told me that she did not dare, in one single instance, to look towards the fatal sofa, and yet that she equally feared her eyes might have the appearance of being too consciously averted. . . .

Two days after the 9th Thermidor, the greater number of the prisons of Paris were empty. Madame de Beauharnais, through her connection with Tallien, came out in triumph: Mesdames d'Aiguillon and de Lameth were also speedily liberated. My mother was almost the only one left in the Carmelite prison. She beheld her noble companions in misfortune give place to the terrorists, who, after the political revolution that had been effected, daily changed places with their victims. All the friends and relatives of my mother were dispersed; no one thought of her. Jérôme, proscribed, in turn, as a friend of Robespierre, was obliged to conceal himself and could not aid her.

For two months she remained thus abandoned, under a desolation of feeling, that, she has often told me, was more difficult to endure than the previous more immediate sense of peril. . . .

At length Nanette, having saved my life by her careful nursing, set seriously about rescuing that of her mistress. She went to the house of one Dyle, a manufacturer of china, in order to consult with about fifty workmen of our province, who were then employed by this rich individual, and who had formerly worked at a porcelain manufactory founded by my grandfather at Niderviller, at the foot of the Vosges, and subsequently confiscated with his other property.

It was to these men, among whom was Malriat her father, that Nanette applied, urging them to interest themselves in the fate of their former mistress.

They eagerly signed a petition, framed by Nanette, who both spoke and wrote the German-French of Lorraine. This document she herself carried to Legendre, formerly a butcher, and then president of the bureau to which petitions in favour of prisoners were addressed. The paper of Nanette was received and thrown aside, among a multitude of similar petitions.

One evening, three young persons, connected with Legendre, entered the bureau, rather heated with wine, and amused themselves with chasing each other over the tables, and with other similar freaks. In the midst of this sport, some of the surrounding papers were disturbed; one fell, and was picked up by a member of the party. "What have you there?" asked the others.

"No doubt a petition," replied Rossigneux, which was the name of the person addressed,

"Yes; but for what prisoner?"

They called for lights. In the interval of their appearing, the three hot-headed youths took an oath among themselves to obtain, that very evening from Legendre, the signature that would give liberty to the captive, whoever he might be, and to announce to him his freedom within the same hour.

"I swear it, though it should be the liberation of the Prince de Condé," said Rossigneux.

"No doubt," said the others, laughing; "he is no longer a prisoner."

They read the petition; it was that dictated by Nanette, and signed by the workmen of Niderviller.

"How fortunate," shouted the young men; "the lovely Custine, a second Roland! We will go and fetch her from prison in a body."

Legendre returned home at one o'clock in the morning, under the influence of wine like the others. The petition for my mother's liberty was presented by three giddy youths, signed by a drunken man, and at three o'clock in the morning, the former, empowered to open her prison gates, knocked at the door of her apartment.

She at that time slept alone; and would neither open her door, nor consent to leave the prison.

Her liberators explained to her as well as they could, the circumstances of their coming; but she resisted all their urgent entreaties; she feared to enter a hackney coach with strangers in the middle of the night; and all they could obtain from her was the permission to return at the hour of ten.

When she finally left the prison, they related to her, with many details, the circumstances to which the liberation was owing, more especially with the view of proving to her that she had nobody to thank for it; for at that time a species of traffic in liberty was carried on by certain intriguers, who would often extort largely from the liberated parties, for the most part already ruined by the revolution.

A lady of rank, and nearly related to my mother, was not ashamed to ask her for 30,000 francs, which she pretended had been expended in bribes to procure her release. My mother replied by simply relating the story of Rossigneux, and saw her relative no more.

What a scene had she to encounter on returning to her own residence! The house bare and desolate, the seals yet on the doors, and I in the kitchen, still deaf and imbecile, in consequence of the malady that had so nearly ended in my death. My mother had remained firm before the terror of the scaffold, but she sank under this misery. The day after her return she was attacked with jaundice, which lasted five months, and left an affection of the liver, from which she suffered throughout her life.

At the end of six months, the small part of the estate of her husband that had remained unsold, was restored to her. We were then both recovered. . . .

My poor mother passed in struggling with poverty the best years of that life which had been so miraculously preserved.

Of the enormously rich estate of my grandfather, nothing remained to us but the debts. The government took the property, but left the task of paying the creditors to those whom it had robbed of the means for so doing. . . .

Our involved and complicated affairs were her torment. We were ever kept suspended betwixt fear and hope, and struggling meanwhile with want. At one time riches would appear within our grasp; at another, some unforeseen reverse, some chicanery of the law, deprived us of every prospect. If I have any taste for the elegancies of life, I attribute it to the privations of my early youth. . . .

I had the happiness of having her life preserved to me until the 13th of July, 1826. She died of the same disease that proved fatal to Bonaparte. This malady, of which the germ had long existed, was accelerated by grief, caused by the death of my wife and only child.

It was in honour of my mother that Madame de Staël, who knew her well and loved her warmly, gave the name of Delphine to the heroine of her first romance.

At the age of fifty-six years she still retained a beauty that
struck even those who had not known her in
her youth, and were not, therefore,
seduced by the charms
of memory.

❖

Conversation at Lübeck on Peculiarities in the Russian Character.

❖

CHAPTER IV

❖

. . . This morning, at Lübeck, the landlord of the hotel, hearing that I was going to embark for Russia, entered my room with an air of compassion which made me laugh. This man is more clever and humorous than the sound of his voice, and his manner of pronouncing the French language, would at first lead one to suppose.

On hearing that I was travelling only for my pleasure, he began exhorting me, with the good-humoured simplicity of a German, to give up my project.

"You are acquainted with Russia?" said I to him.

"No, sir; but I am with Russians; there are many who pass through Lubeck, and I judge of the country by the physiognomy of its people."

"What do you find, then, in the expression of their countenance that should prevent my visiting them?"

"Sir, they have two faces. I do not speak of the valets, who have only one; but of the nobles. When they arrive in Europe they have a gay, easy, contented air, like horses set free, or birds let loose from their cages: men, women, the young and the old, are all as happy as schoolboys on a holiday. The same persons when they return have long faces and gloomy looks; their words are few and abrupt; their countenances full of care. I conclude from this, that a country which they quitted with so much joy, and to which they return with so much regret, is a bad country."

"Perhaps you are right," I replied; "but your remarks, at least, prove to me that Russians are not such dissemblers as they have been represented."

"They are so among themselves; but they do not mistrust us honest Germans," said the landlord, retiring, and smiling knowingly.

Here is a man who is afraid of being taken for a good-natured simpleton, thought I: he must travel himself in order to know how greatly the description, which travellers (often superficial and careless in their observations) give of different nations, tends to influence these nations' character. Each separate individual endeavours to protest against the opinion generally established with respect to the people of his country.

Do not the women of Paris aspire to be simple and unaffected? It may be here observed, that nothing can be more opposite than the Russian and the German character. . . .

❖

PRINCE K——— ❖ DEFINITIONS OF NOBILITY ❖ THE ENGLISH NOBILITY ❖
FREEDOM OF SPEECH ❖ CANNING ❖ NAPOLEON ❖ CONFIDENTIAL
CONVERSATION ❖ GLANCE AT RUSSIAN HISTORY ❖ INSTITUTIONS AND
SPIRIT OF CHIVALRY UNKNOWN IN RUSSIA ❖ THE NATURE OF AN
AUTOCRACY ❖ POLITICS AND RELIGION ARE IDENTICAL IN RUSSIA ❖
FUTURE INFLUENCE OF RUSSIA ❖ FATE OF PARIS ❖ GOOD MANNERS OF THE
HIGHER ORDERS IN RUSSIA ❖ SOCIETY IN FRANCE BEFORE THE
REVOLUTION ❖ HIS MAUVAIS TON ❖ AGREEABLE SOCIETY ON THE STEAM-
BOAT ❖ RUSSIAN NATIONAL DANCES ❖ TWO AMERICANS ❖
STEAM-BOAT ACCIDENT ❖
ISLE OF DAGO
❖

CHAPTER V

❖

. . . Among the passengers on board the steamer I observed an elderly man, whose immensely swollen legs could hardly support his corpulent frame. His head, well set between his large shoulders, had a noble cast: it was a portrait of Louis XVI.

I soon learnt that he was the Russian Prince K——, a descendant of the conquering Varegues, and therefore one of the most ancient of the Russian nobility.

As I observed him, supported by his secretary, and moving with difficulty towards a seat, I could not help saying to myself, here is a sorry travelling companion; but on hearing his name, which I well knew by reputation, I reproached myself for this incorrigible mania of judging by appearances.

As soon as seated, the old gentleman, the expression of whose face was shrewd, although noble and sincere, addressed me by name.

Apostrophised thus suddenly, I rose without replying. The prince continued in that truly aristocratic tone, the perfect simplicity of which excludes all idea of ceremony:—

"You, who have seen almost all Europe, will, I am sure, be of my opinion."

"On what subject, my prince?"

"On England. I was saying to Prince ——, here," indicating with his finger, and without further presentation, the individual with whom he was talking, "that there is no noblesse among the

❖ 47 ❖

English. They have titles and offices; but the idea which we attach to a real order of nobility, distinguished by characteristics which can neither be purchased nor conferred, is unknown to them. A monarch may create a prince; education, circumstances, genius, virtue, may make a hero; but none of these things are sufficient to constitute a nobleman." . . .

Struck with this easy manner of making acquaintance, I began to examine the countryman of the Prince K——, Prince D——, the celebrity of whose name had already attracted my attention. I beheld a man still young: his complexion wore a leaden hue; a quiet patient expression was visible in his eye; but his forehead was full, his figure tall, and throughout his person there was a regularity which accorded with the coldness of his manners, and the harmony produced by which was not unpleasing. . . .

The tone of society among the higher ranks in Russia is marked by an easy politeness, the secret of which is almost lost among ourselves.

Every one, not even excluding the French secretary of Prince K., appears modest, superior to the little cares and contrivances of vanity and self-love, and consequently, exempt from their mistakes and mortifications. If it is this that one gains from living under a despotism, *vive la Russie!** How can polished manners subsist in a country where nothing is respected, seeing that *bon ton* is only discernment in testifying respect. Let us begin again by showing respect to those who have a right to deference, and we shall again become naturally, and so to speak, involuntarily polite.

Notwithstanding the reserve which I threw into my answers to the Prince K——, the old diplomatist quickly discovered the tendency of my views.

"You do not belong either to your country or to your age," said he, "you are an enemy to the power of speech as a political engine."

"It is true," I replied; "any other way of ascertaining the

---

* The author here requests a liberal construction on the part of the reader, in order to reconcile his apparent contradictions. It is only from a frank statement of the various contradictory views that present themselves to the mind that definitive conclusions are eventually to be attained.

worth of men appears to me preferable to public speaking, in a country where self-love is so easily excited as in mine. I do not believe that there could be found in France many men who would not sacrifice their most cherished opinions to the desire of having it said that they had made a good speech."

"Nevertheless," pursued the liberal Russian prince, "everything is included in the gift of language; everything that is in man, and something even beyond, reveals itself by discourse: there is divinity in speech."

"I agree with you," I replied; "and it is for that very reason that I dread to see it prostituted."

"When a genius like that of Mr. Canning's," continued the prince, "enchained the attention of the first men of England and of the world, surely political speech was something great and glorious."

"What good has this brilliant genius produced? And what evil would he not have caused if he had had inflammable minds for auditors? Speech employed in private, as a means of persuasion, to change the direction of ideas, to influence the action of a man, or of a small number of men, appears to me useful, either as an auxiliary, or as a counterbalance to power; but I fear it in a large political assembly whose deliberations are conducted in public. It too often secures a triumph to limited views and fallacious popular notions, at the expense of lofty, far-sighted conceptions, and plans profoundly laid. To impose upon nations the domination of majorities is to subject them to mediocrity. If such is not your object, you do wrong to laud oratorical influence. The politics of large assemblies are almost always timid, sordid, and rapacious. You oppose to this the case of England: that country is not what it is supposed to be. It is true that in its houses of parliament questions are decided by the majority; but this majority represents the aristocracy of the land, which for a long time has not ceased, except at very brief intervals, to direct the affairs of the state. Besides, to what refuges of lies have not parliamentary forms compelled the leaders of this masked oligarchy to descend? Is it for this that you envy England?"

"Nevertheless, man must be led either by fear or by persuasion."

"True; but action is more persuasive than words. Does not the Prussian government prove this? Does not Buonaparte? Buonaparte at the commencement of his reign governed by persuasion as much as, or more than, by force, and yet his eloquence, though great, was never addressed except to individuals; to the mass he never spoke except by deeds: to discuss the laws in public is to rob them of that respect which is the secret of their power."

"You are a friend to despotism?"

"On the contrary, I dread the lawyers, and their echo the newspapers,* which are but speeches whose echo resounds for twenty-four hours. Such is the despotism which threatens us in the present day."

"Come among us, and you will learn to fear some other kinds."

"It will not be you, prince, who will succeed in imbuing me with a bad opinion of Russia."

"Do not judge of it, either by me, or by any other Russian who has travelled: our natural flexibility renders us cosmopolites the moment we leave our own land; and this disposition of mind is in itself a satire against our government!"

Here, notwithstanding his habit of speaking openly on all subjects, the prince began to distrust both himself, me, and every one else, and took refuge in some remarks not very conspicuous for their perspicuity. He afterwards, however, availed himself of a moment when we were alone to lay before me his opinion as to the character of the men and the institutions of his country. The following, as nearly as I can recollect, forms the sum of his observations.

"Russia, in the present age, is only four hundred years removed from the invasions of barbarian tribes, whilst fourteen centuries have elapsed since western Europe experienced the same crisis. A civilisation older by one thousand years of course places an immeasurable distance between the manners of nations.

"Many ages before the irruption of the Mongols, the Scandinavians placed over the Slavonians (then altogether savages) chieftains, who reigned at Great Novogorod and at Kiew, under the name of Varegues. These foreign heroes, supported by a

---

* These allusions, it must be remembered, refer more especially to France.—*Trans.*

small retinue of armed followers, became the first princes of the Russians; and their companions in arms are the stock whence proceeds the more ancient nobility. The Varegue princes, who were a species of demigods, governed this nation while still composed of wandering tribes. It was from the emperors and patriarchs of Constantinople that they at this period derived all their notions of luxury and the arts. Such, if I may be allowed the expression, was the first laid stratum of civilisation in Russia, afterwards trampled on and destroyed by the Tartar conquerors.

"A vast body of saints, who were the legislators of a newly converted Christian people, illume, with their names, this fabulous epoch of Russian history. Princes also, great by their savage virtues, ennoble the early period of the Slavonian annals. Their names shine out from the profound darkness of the age, like stars piercing the clouds of a stormy night. The very sound of these strange names excites the imagination and challenges curiosity. Rurick, Oleg, the Queen Olga, Saint Wladimir, Swiatopolk, and Monomaque, are personages whose characters no more resemble those of the heroes of the west than do their appellations.

"They have nothing of the chivalrous about them; they are like the monarchs of Scripture; the nation which they rendered great remained in the vicinity of Asia; ignorant of our romance, it preserved manners that were in a great measure patriarchal.

"The Russian nation was not formed in that brilliant school of good faith, by whose instructions chivalrous Europe had so well profited, that the word *honour* was for a long period synonymous with truth, and the *word of honour* had a sanctity which is still revered, even in France, where so many things have been forgotten.

"The noble influence of the Knights of the Cross stopped, with that of Catholicism, in Poland. The Russians are warriors, but they fight under the principle of obedience, and with the object of gain; the Polish chevaliers fought for the pure love of glory; and thus, though these people spring from the same stock, and have still many points of resemblance, the events of history have separated them so widely that it will require a greater number of ages of Russian policy to reunite them than it has required of religion and of social habitudes to part them asunder.

"Whilst Europe was slowly recovering from the efforts she had made during centuries to rescue the tomb of Christ from the unbelievers, Russia was paying tribute to the Mohammedans under Usbeck, and at the same time drawing her arts and sciences, her manners, religion, and politics, as also her principles of craft and fraud, and her aversion to the Latin cross, from the Greek empire. If we reflect on all these civil, religious, and political influences, we shall no longer wonder at the little confidence that can be placed in the word of a Russian (it is the Russian prince who speaks), nor that the Russian character in general should bear the impress of that false Byzantine stamp which influences social life even under the empire of the Czars—worthy successors of the lieutenants of Bati.

"The unmitigated despotism that reigns over us established itself at the very period that servitude ceased in the rest of Europe. From the time of the invasion of the Mongols, the Slavonians, until then one of the freest people in the world, became slaves, first to their conquerors, and afterwards to their own princes. Bondage was thenceforward established among them, not only as an existing state, but as a constituent principle of society. It has degraded the right of speech in Russia to such a point that it is no longer considered anything better than a snare: our government lives by lies, for truth is as terrible to the tyrant as to the slave. Thus, little as one speaks, in Russia, one always speaks too much, since in this country all discourse is the expression of religious or political hypocrisy."

"Prince," I replied, after having listened attentively to this long series of deductions, "I will not believe you. It is enlightened to rise above national prejudices, and polite to deal gently with the prejudices of foreigners; but I have no more confidence in your concessions than I have in others' claims and pretensions."

"In three months you will render me greater justice; meanwhile, and as we are yet alone,"—he said this after looking round on all sides,—"I will direct your attention to a leading point, I will present you with a key which will serve to explain every thing to you in the country you are about to visit.

"Think at each step you take among this Asiatic people that the chivalrous and Catholic influence has never obtained in their land; and not only have they never adopted it, they have withstood it also, with bitter animosity, during long wars with Lithuania, Poland, and the knights of the Teutonic order."

"You make me proud of my discernment. I wrote lately to one of my friends that I conceived religious intolerance to be the secret spring of Russian policy.

"You anticipated clearly what you are going to see; you can have no adequate idea of the intense intolerance of the Russians; those whose minds are cultivated, and whom business brings into intercourse with western Europe, take the utmost pains to conceal the predominant national sentiment, which is the triumph of the Greek *orthodoxy*—with them synonymous with the policy of Russia.

"Without keeping this in view nothing can be explained either in our manners or our politics. You must not believe, for example, that the persecutions in Poland were the effect of the personal resentment of the Emperor: they were the result of a profound and deliberate calculation. These acts of cruelty are meritorious in the eyes of true believers; it is the Holy Spirit who so enlightens the sovereign as to elevate him above all human feelings; and it is God who blesses him as the executor of his high designs. By this manner of viewing things, judges and executioners become so much the greater saints as they are greater barbarians. Your legitimist journals little know what they are doing when they seek for allies among schismatics. We shall see an European revolution before we shall see the Emperor of Russia acting in good faith with a Catholic power; the Protestants are at least open adversaries; besides, they will more readily reunite with the pope than the chief of the Russian autocracy: for the Protestants, having beheld all their creeds degenerate into systems, and their religious faith transformed into philosophic doubt, have nothing left but their sectarian pride to sacrifice to Rome; whereas the Emperor possesses a real and positive spiritual power, which he will never voluntarily relinquish. Rome, and all that can be connected with the Romish church, has no more dangerous enemy than the autocrat of Moscow—visible head of his own church; and I am astonished that Italian penetration has not discovered the danger that threatens you from that quarter. After this veracious picture,

❖ 53 ❖

judge of the illusion with which the Legitimists of Paris nurse their hopes."

This conversation will give an idea of all the others. Whenever the subject became unpleasant to Muscovite self-love, the prince K—— broke off, at least until he was fully sure that no one overheard us.

The subjects of our discourse have made me reflect, and my reflections make me fear. . . .

Our Russian ladies have admitted into their little circle a French merchant, who is among the passengers. He is a man rather past the middle age, full of great schemes connected with steam-boats and railroads, but still exhibiting all his former youthful pretensions; agreeable smiles, gracious mien, winning grimaces, plebeian gestures, narrow ideas, and studied language. He is, notwithstanding, a good fellow, speaking willingly, and even well, when he speaks on subjects with which he is conversant, amusing also, though self-sufficient, and sometimes rather prosy.

He is going to Russia to *electrify* certain minds in favour of some great industrial undertakings. He travels as agent for several French commercial houses who have associated, he says, to carry into effect these important objects; but his head, although full of grave commercial ideas, finds place, nevertheless, for all the songs and bon mots that have been popular in Paris for the last twenty years. Before turning merchant he had been a lancer, and he has preserved, in his air and attitudes, some amusing traces of his former profession. He never speaks to the Russians without alluding to French superiority in matters of every description; but his vanity is too palpable to become offensive, or to excite anything beyond a laugh.

When singing he casts tender glances upon the ladies; when declaiming the *Parisienne* and the *Marseillaise,* he folds his cloak around him with a theatrical air: his store of songs and sayings, although rather jovial in character, much amuses our fair strangers. In listening to him they seem to believe they are on a visit to Paris. The *mauvais ton* of this specimen of French manners by no means strikes them, because they do not comprehend its source or its scope; a language which they cannot understand cannot disgust them; besides, persons belonging to really good society are always the last to be annoyed or alarmed. The fear of being lowered in position does not oblige them to take offence at everything that is said.

The old Prince K—— and myself laugh between ourselves at the language to which they listen; they laugh on their part with the innocence of an ignorance unacquainted with the point where good taste ceases, and where French vulgarity begins.

Vulgarity commences so soon as the individual thinks of avoiding it: such a thought never occurs to persons perfectly sure of their own good breeding.

When the gaiety of the ex-lancer becomes rather too exuberant, the Russian ladies moderate it by singing, in their turn, some of those national airs of which the melancholy and originality greatly charm me.

The Princess L—— has sung to us some airs of the Russian gypsies which, to my great surprise, bring the Spanish boleros to my mind. The Gitanos of Andalusia are of the same race as the Russian gypsies. This population dispersed, one knows not by what agency, throughout all Europe, has preserved in every region, its manners, its traditions and its national songs.

The sea voyage, so much dreaded in prospect, has proved so agreeable, that I look forward to its termination with real regret. Besides, who does not feel some sense of desolation in arriving in a large city, where one has no business and no friends. My passion for travel cools when I consider that it consists entirely of departures and arrivals. But what pleasures and advantages does not man purchase by this pain! Were it only that he can by this means obtain information without laborious study, it would be well thus to *turn over,* as the leaves of a book, the different countries of the earth.

When I feel myself discouraged in the midst of my pilgrimages, I say to myself, "If I wish for the result, I must take the means," and under this thought I persevere. I do more,—scarcely am I again in my own abode, than I think of recommencing my travels. Perpetual travel would be a delightful way of passing life, especially for one who cannot conform to the ideas which govern the world in the age in which he lives. To change one's country is tantamount to changing one's century. It is a long by-gone age which I now hope to study in Russia.

Never do I recollect having met in travelling, with society so agreeable and amusing as in this passage. Our life here, is like life in the country in wet weather; we cannot get out, but each tasks himself to amuse the others, so that the effort of each turns to the benefit of the whole. This however must be ascribed to the perfect sociability of some of our passengers, and more especially to the amiable authority of Prince K———. Had it not been for the part he took at the commencement of our voyage, no one would have broken the ice, and we should have continued observing each other in silence during the whole passage. Instead of such a melancholy isolation, we talk and chatter night and day. The light, lasting during the whole twenty-four hours, has the effect of so deranging habits, that there are always some ready for conversation at any hour. It is now past three o'clock, and as I write, I hear my companions laughing and talking in the cabin; if I were to go down, they would ask me to recite some French verses, or to tell some story about Paris. They never tire of asking about Mademoiselle Rachel or Duprez, the two great dramatic stars of the day. They long to draw to their own country the celebrated talents which they cannot obtain permission to come and see among us.

When the French lancer, the mercantile militaire, joins in the conversation, it is generally to interrupt it. There is then sure to be laughter, singing, and Russian dances.

This gaiety, innocent as it is, has proved offensive to two Americans going to Petersburg on business. These inhabitants of the New World do not permit themselves even a smile at the foolish pleasures of the young European women. They do not perceive that liberty and carelessness are the safeguards of youthful hearts. Their puritanism rebels not only against licence, but against mirth; they are Jansenists of the Protestant school; to please them, life must be made one protracted funeral. Happily, the ladies we have on board do not trouble themselves to render any reason to these pedantic merchants. Their manners are more simple than most of the women of the north, who, when they come to Paris, believe themselves obliged to distort their whole nature in order to seduce us. Our fair fellow-passengers please without seeming to think of pleasing; their French accent also appears to me better than that of most of the Polish women whom I have met in Saxony and Bohemia. In speaking our language they do not pretend to correct it, but endeavour to speak as we speak, and very nearly succeed.

Yesterday a slight accident which happened to our engine served to exhibit some of the secret traits of character in those on board.

The recollection of the former accident that befell to our boat has served to render the passengers rather timid and distrustful, though the weather has remained throughout extremely fine.

Yesterday after dinner, we were seated reading, when suddenly the motion of the paddles stopped, and an unusual noise was heard to proceed from the engine. The sailors rushed forward; the captain followed, without saying a word in reply to the questions of the passengers. At length he gave the order to sound. "We are on a rock," said a female voice, the first that had dared to break our solemn silence. "The engine is going to burst," said another.

I was silent, though I began to think that my presentiments were going to be realised, and that it was not, after all, caprice which had inclined me to renounce this voyage.

The Princess L——, whose health is delicate, fell into a swoon, murmuring some broken words of grief that she should die so far from her husband. The Princess D—— pressed the arm of *hers*, and awaited the result with a calm, which one would not have expected from her slight frail form and gentle features.

The fat and amiable Prince K—— neither changed his countenance nor his place; he would have sunk in his arm-chair into the sea without disturbing himself. The French ex-lancer, half merchant, half comedian, put on a bold face, and began to hum a song. This bravado displeased me, and made me blush for France, where vanity searches out of all things to extract some opportunity for display; true moral dignity exaggerates nothing, not even indifference to danger; the Americans continued their reading; I observed every body.

At length the captain came to inform us that the nut of the

screw of one of the pistons was broken, and that all would be made right again in a quarter of an hour.

At this news the fears that each party had more or less concealed betrayed themselves by a general explosion of rejoicing. Each confessed his thoughts and fears, all laughed at each other, and those who were the most candid in their confessions were the least laughed at. The evening that had commenced so ominously concluded with a dance and song.

Before separating for the night, Prince K—— complimented me for my good manners in listening with apparent pleasure to his stories. One may recognise the well-bred man, he observed, by the manner he assumes in listening to another. I replied that the best way by which to seem to be listening, was to listen. This answer, repeated by the prince, was lauded beyond its merit. Nothing is lost, and every thought is done more than justice to by persons whose benevolence even is intellectual.

The great charm of ancient French society lay in the art of making the best of others. If this amiable art is scarcely known among us in the present day, it is because it requires greater refinement of mind to praise than to depreciate. He who knows how to estimate all things, disdains nothing, and refuses to join in ridicule; but where envy reigns depreciation mixes with all that is said. Jealousy in the guise of wit, and under the mask of good sense, (for pretended good sense is always marked by a love of ridicule,) is the evil sentiment which in these days conspires against the pleasures of social life. In its endeavour to appear good and amiable, true politeness really becomes so; its possession seems to me to embrace that of all other virtues.

I shall here recount two stories, which will show how little meritorious was the attention for which I had been complimented.

We were passing the isle of Dago on the coast of Esthonia. The appearance of this spot is melancholy; it is a cold solitude, where nature appears naked and sterile, rather than savage and imposing; it seems as though she meant to repel man by the dulness, rather than by the terrors of her aspect."

"A strange scene has been witnessed in that isle," remarked Prince K——.

"At what period?"

"Not long ago, it was under the Emperor Paul."

"Pray relate it to us."

The prince then recounted, in a very
interesting manner, the history
of the Baron de
Sternberg.

❖

TRAGEDY OF BARON DE STERNBERG ❖ TYPE OF LORD BYRON'S HEROES ❖
PARALLEL BETWEEN SIR W. SCOTT AND BYRON ❖ HISTORICAL ROMANCE ❖
MARRIAGE OF PETER THE GREAT ❖ ROMODANOWSKI ❖ INFLUENCE OF THE
GREEK CHURCH IN RUSSIA ❖ TYRANNY SUPPORTED BY FALSEHOOD ❖
CORPSE IN THE CHURCH OF REVEL ❖ THE EMPEROR
ALEXANDER DECEIVED ❖ RUSSIAN SENSITIVENESS TO THE
OPINIONS OF FOREIGNERS ❖
A SPY
❖

CHAPTER VI

❖

It must be remembered that it is the Prince K—— who speaks.

"Baron Ungern de Sternberg had travelled over the greater part of Europe. He was a man of intelligence and observation, and his travels had made him all that he was capable of being made, namely, a great character developed by study and experience.

"On his return to St. Petersburg, in the reign of the Emperor Paul, he fell into undeserved disgrace; and, under the bitter feeling which this produced, determined to quit the court. He shut himself up in the island of Dago, of which he was lord; and in the retirement of this wild domain swore a mortal hatred to all human kind, to revenge himself on the emperor, whom he viewed as the representative of the whole race.

"This individual, who was living when we were children, has served as a model for more than one of Lord Byron's heroes.

"In his seclusion he affected a sudden passion for study, and, in order to pursue freely his scientific labours, he added to his mansion a very high tower, the walls of which you can see with the spy-glass."

Here the prince paused, and we took a view of the tower of Dago. The prince resumed:

"This tower he called his library, and crowned its summit with a sort of glazed lantern like an observatory, or rather light-house. He often repeated to his servants that he could only labour at night, and then no where but in this solitary place. It was there that he retired, as he said, to meditate, and to seek peace.

"No guests were admitted into this retreat except an only son, still a child, and his tutor.

"Towards midnight, when the baron believed them to be both asleep, he used often to shut himself up in his laboratory: the glass tower of which was then lighted with a lamp so brilliant, that, at a distance, it might be taken for a signal. This light-house, though not one in reality, was calculated to deceive strange vessels, that were in danger of being lost on the island, if their captains, venturing too far, did not perfectly know each point of the coast in the perilous Gulf of Finland.

"This error was precisely that which the terrible baron hoped for. Raised upon a rock, in the midst of a stormy sea, the perfidious tower became the beacon of inexperienced pilots; and the unfortunate beings, who were misled by the false hope that glittered before them, met their death at the moment they believed they had found a shelter from the storm.

"You may judge that nautical regulations were at that time very imperfectly maintained in Russia.

"As soon as a vessel was on the point of being wrecked, the baron proceeded to the shore, and secretly embarked with numerous active and determined men, whom he kept for the purpose of aiding him in these nocturnal expeditions. He then gathered together the stranger mariners and, instead of affording them the expected succour, murdered them under cover of the dark; after which he pillaged their ship, although actuated throughout much less by a desire of gain than by a pure love of evil, and a disinterested pleasure in destruction.

"Doubting all things, and disbelieving the principle of justice, he considered moral and social disorder as being most analogous to the state of man here below, and civil and political virtues as chimeras that only oppose nature without subduing it.

"He pretended that, in putting an end to the life of his fellow creatures, he was subservient to the schemes of Providence, who was pleased, he said, to extract life out of death.

"One evening, towards the end of autumn, when the nights were very long, he had exterminated the crew of a Dutch merchantman, and the pirates whom he kept under the title of guards, among the servants belonging to his house, were for several hours occupied in landing the cargo of the wrecked vessel, without observing that, during the massacre, the captain had profited by the darkness, and had saved himself in a boat which had followed him with some of the sailors of his vessel.

"Day-break surprised the baron and his emissaries at their work of darkness, and announced to them also the approach of a small boat. They immediately shut the gates of the secret vaults, where the produce of their pillage was disposed; after which the drawbridge was let down before the stranger.

"The baron, with that elegant hospitality which is an indelible characteristic of Russian manners, hastened to receive the leader of the newcomers.

"Affecting the most perfect security, he repaired to a saloon near the apartment of his son who was yet sleeping, and there awaited him. The tutor of his child was also in bed dangerously ill. The door of his chamber, which opened into the saloon, remained unclosed. The stranger was introduced.

" 'Sir Baron,' said the man, with an air of bold assurance, 'you know me, though you may not recognise me, for you have seen me but once, and then in the dark. I am the captain of the vessel, a part of whose crew perished last night under your walls. It is with pain I announce to you that some of your people have been recognised in the fray that took place, and that you yourself were seen stabbing with your own hand one of my men.'

"The baron, without replying, arose and gently closed the door of the tutor's chamber. The stranger continued—'If I speak to you thus freely, it is not because I intend to ruin you, I only wish to prove to you that you are in my power. Restore to me my cargo and my ship; which, damaged as it is, will still convey me to St. Petersburgh, and I promise secrecy; which promise I am ready to confirm with my oath. If the desire of revenge had influenced me I should have landed on the opposite coast, and proclaimed you in the first village. The proposal I make, proves my willingness to save you in thus apprising you of the danger to which you are exposed by your crimes.'

"The baron all this time maintained a profound silence. The

expression of his countenance was grave but not sinister. He requested a little time to reflect upon the course he should take, and withdrew, saying that in a quarter of an hour he would give his answer.

"Some minutes before the expiration of the stipulated time, he suddenly burst into the saloon through a secret door, threw himself upon the too adventurous stranger, and stabbed him to the heart.

"Orders had been meantime given to destroy the last man of the boat's crew. Silence, for a moment disturbed by so many murders, again reigned in this den of robbers. The tutor of the child had, however, overheard all that had passed: he continued to listen, but could at length only hear the step of the baron, and the deep snore of the Corsairs as, wrapped in their sheep-skins, they slept on the stairs of the tower.

"The baron, uneasy and suspicious, entered the chamber of this man; and examined his features with scrupulous attention. Standing near the bed, with the still bloody poniard in his hand, he watched a long time for the least signs which could betray a feigned slumber. At length, convinced that he was in a deep sleep, he resolved to let him live.

"Perfection in crime is as rare as in anything else," said the Prince K——, interrupting his narration.

We made no answer, for we were impatient to know the end of the history. He continued:—

"The suspicions of the tutor had been roused for some time past. As soon as the first words of the Dutch captain had met his ear he rose up, and witnessed through the chinks of the door, which the baron had locked upon him, all the circumstances of the murder. The instant afterwards he acted with the presence of mind before related, which deceived the assassin, and saved his life. After the baron had retired he rose, dressed, and, in spite of the fever that was upon him, let himself down from the window by cords, detached a skiff which he found fastened at the foot of the rampart, and pushed out to sea, steering towards the mainland, which he reached without accident, and where he immediately proclaimed the crime that he had witnessed.

"The absence of the sick man was soon noticed in the castle of

Dago. The baron, blinded by the infatuation of crime, imagined at first that he had cast himself into the sea while under the delirium of fever. Entirely occupied in searching for his body, he thought not of flight, although the cord attached to the window and the disappearance of the skiff were irrefragable proofs of the real fact.

"Convinced, at length, by these evidences, he was beginning to prepare for escape, when he found his castle surrounded by troops which had been instantly despatched against him. For one moment he thought of defence, but his people all forsook him. He was taken and sentenced by the Emperor Paul to hard labour for life in Siberia.

"It was there he died, and such was the end of a man who once shone alike by the powers of his mind, and the elegance of his manners, in the most polished circles of Europe. Our mothers can yet recollect him as having been everything that was agreeable.

"I should not have related to you this romantic tale if the circumstances of its occurrence, which would have been so appropriate to the middle-ages, had not belonged as it were to our own times. In everything, Russia is four centuries behind the world."

When Prince K—— had ceased speaking, we all exclaimed that the Baron de Sternberg was the type of Byron's Manfreds and Laras.

"It is unquestionable," said Prince K——, who had no fear of paradox, "that it is because Byron has drawn his models from real existences, that they appear to us to possess so few of the attributes of the probable. In poetry reality is never natural.

"That is so true," I replied, "that the fictions of Walter Scott produce a more perfect illusion than the exact copyings of Byron."

"Possibly, but you must look to yet other causes for this difference; Scott describes, Byron creates: the latter cares little for the reality, even in recounting it; the former is imbued with its instinct, even when inventing."

"Do not you think, prince," I replied, "that this instinct of reality, which you ascribe to the great romance-writer, is connected with his often being common-place? What masses of superfluous detail, and vulgar dialogue!—and, after all, it is in describing the dress and the apartments of his personages that he is most exact."

"Stay! I shall defend my favourite, Walter Scott," cried Prince K——, "I cannot permit so amusing a writer to be insulted."

"That he is amusing is just the species of merit which I deny him," I responded. "A romance writer who needs a volume to prepare a scene is anything but amusing. Walter Scott was very fortunate in appearing at an epoch when people no longer knew what amusement meant."

"How he describes the human heart," said Prince D——: for everybody was against me.

"Yes, provided he does not make it speak, for expression fails him whenever he attempts the passionate and the sublime: he draws characters by their actions admirably, for he has more skill and more power of observation than eloquence; his mind is methodical and calculating; he has appeared in a congenial age, and has marvellously revived and embodied the most vulgar and consequently the most popular ideas and images."

"He has been the first to solve, in a satisfactory manner, the difficult problem of historical romance: you cannot refuse him this merit," added Prince K——.

"Would that it were insolvable," I replied. "With what multitudes of false notions have the crowd of illiterate readers been imbued by the mixing of history with romance. This union is always mischievous, and, to me, scarcely appears amusing. I would prefer reading, even for amusement, M. Augustin Thierry, or any other equally grave author, to all the fables about real personages that have ever been invented."

"If it is a matter of taste," said Prince K——, smiling, "we will dispute no longer about it;" and, taking my arm, he begged me to assist him to his state-room, where, offering me a seat, he continued, in a low voice, "as we are alone, and you like history, I will relate to you a story of a higher order than the one you have just heard: it is to you alone that I relate it, because before Russians one must not talk of history.

"You know that Peter the Great, after much hesitation, destroyed the patriarchate of Moscow, in order to unite on the same head the crown and the tiara. The political autocracy thus openly usurped that unlimited spiritual power which it had coveted for so long—monstrous union, unknown before among the nations of modern Europe. The chimera entertained by the popes during the middle-ages is now actually realised in a nation of sixty millions of people, many of them Asiatics, whom nothing surprises, and who are by no means sorry to find a grand Lama in their Czar.

"The Emperor Peter sought to unite himself in marriage with Catherine, the sutler.

"To accomplish this supreme object of his heart it was necessary to begin by finding a family name for the future empress. This was obtained I believe in Lithuania, where an obscure private gentleman was first converted into a great lord *by birth*, and afterwards discovered to be the brother of the empress elect.

"Russian despotism not only pays little respect to ideas and sentiments, it will also deny facts; it will struggle against evidence, and triumph in the struggle!!! for evidence, when it is inconvenient to power, has no more voice among us than has justice."

The bold language of the prince startled me. He had been educated at Rome, and, like all who possess any piety of feeling, and independence of mind, in Russia, he inclined to the Catholic religion. While various reflections, suggested by his discourse, were passing in my mind, he continued his philosophical observations.

"The people, and even the great men, are resigned spectators of this war against truth; the lies of the despot, however palpable, are always flattering to the slave. The Russians, who bear so much, would bear no tyranny if the tyrant did not carefully act as though he believed them the dupes of his policy. Human dignity immersed and sinking in the gulf of absolute government, seizes hold of the smallest branch within reach, that may serve to keep it afloat. Human nature will bear much scorn and wrong; but it will not bear to be told in direct terms that it is scorned and wronged. When outraged by deeds, it takes refuge in words. Falsehood is so abasing, that to degrade the tyrant into the hypocrite is a vengeance which consoles the victim. Miserable and last illusion of misfortune, which must yet be respected, lest the serf should become still more vile, and the despot still more outrageous.

"There existed an ancient custom for two of the greatest noblemen of the empire to walk by the side of the patriarch of Moscow in solemn public processions.

"On the occasion of his marriage, the Czarinian pontiff determined to choose for acolytes in the bridal procession, on one side a famous boyard,* and on the other the new brother-in-law that he had created; for in Russia, sovereign power can do more than create nobles, it can raise up relatives for those who are without any; with us, despotism is more powerful than nature; the emperor is not only the representative of God, he is himself the creative power: a power indeed greater than that of Deity, for it only extends its action to the future, whereas the emperor alters and amends the past: the law has no retroactive effect, the caprice of a despot has.

"The personage whom Peter wished to associate with the new brother of the empress was the highest noble in Moscow, and after the Czar, the greatest individual in the empire, his name was Prince Romodanowski. Peter notified him through his first minister that he was to attend the ceremony in order to walk by the emperor's side—an honour which he would share with the brother of the empress."

" 'Very well,' replied the prince; 'but on which side of the Czar am I expected to place myself?'

" 'My dear prince,' replied the courtier, 'how can you ask such a question? Of course the brother-in-law of his majesty will take the right.'

" 'I shall not attend, then,' responded the haughty boyard.

"This answer reported to the Czar provoked a second message.

" 'You shall attend!' was the mandate of the tyrant; 'you shall either attend, or I will hang you!'

" 'Say to the Czar,' replied the indomitable Muscovite, 'that I entreat him first to execute the same sentence on my only son:

---

* The title of a Russian noble.

this child is only fifteen years old; it is possible that, after having seen me perish, fear will make him consent to walk on the left hand of his sovereign; but I can depend on myself, both before and after the execution of my child, never to do that which can disgrace the blood of Romodanowski.' "

"The Czar, I say it in his praise, yielded; but to revenge himself on the independent spirit of the Muscovite aristocracy, he built St. Petersburg.

"Nicholas," added prince K——, "would not have acted thus; he would have sent the boyard and his son to the mines, and have declared by an ukase, *conceived in legal terms,* that neither the father nor the son could have children; perhaps he would have decreed that the father had never been married; such things still often take place in Russia, the best proof of which is that we are forbidden to recount them."

Be this as it may, the pride of the Muscovite noble gives a perfect idea of that singular combination of which the actual state of Russian society is the result. A monstrous compound of the petty refinements of Byzantium, and the ferocity of the desert horde, a struggle between the etiquette of the Lower Empire, and the savage virtues of Asia, have produced the mighty state which Europe now beholds, and the influence of which she will probably feel hereafter, without being able to understand its operation.

We have just seen an instance of arbitrary power outbraved and humiliated by the aristocracy.

This fact, and many others, justify me in maintaining that it is an aristocracy which constitutes the greatest check on the despotism of an individual,—on an autocracy; the soul of aristocracy is pride, the spirit of democracy is envy. We will now see how easily an autocrat may be deceived.

This morning we passed Revel. The sight of that place, which has not long been Russian territory, recalled to our memories the proud name of Charles XII., and the battle of Narva. In this battle was killed a Frenchman, the Prince de Croï, who fought under the king of Sweden. His body was carried to Revel, where he could not be buried, because during the campaign he had contracted debts in the province, and had left nothing to pay them. According to an ancient custom of the land, his body was placed in the church of Revel until his heirs should satisfy his creditors. This corpse is still in the same church where it was laid more than one hundred years ago. The amount of the original debt has become so greatly augmented by interest, and by the daily charge made for the keeping of the corpse, that there are few fortunes which would now suffice to acquit it.

In passing through Revel about twenty years since the Emperor Alexander visited the church, and was so shocked with the hideous spectacle presented by the corpse, that he commanded its immediate interment. On the morrow the Emperor departed, and the body of the Prince de Croï was duly carried to the cemetry. The day after it was brought back to the church, and placed in its former position. If there is not justice in Russia, there are, it would appear, customs more powerful even than the sovereign will.

What most amused me during this too short passage was to find myself constantly obliged, in obedience to my instinctive notions of equity, to justify Russia against Prince K——'s observations. This won me the good will of all the Russians who heard our conversation. The sincerity of the opinions which the amiable Prince pronounces on his country, at least proves to me that in Russia there are some who may speak their mind.

When I remarked this to him, he replied, that he was not a Russian!! Singular assertion! However, Russian or stranger, he says what he thinks. He has filled the most important political posts, spent two fortunes, worn out the favour of several sovereigns, and is now old, and infirm, but especially protected by a member of the imperial family, who loves wit too well to fear it. Besides, in order to escape Siberia, he pretends that he is writing memoirs, and that he has deposited the finished volumes in France. The Emperor dreads publicity as much as Russia dreads the Emperor.

I am much struck by the extreme susceptibility of the Russians as regards the judgment which strangers may form respecting them. The impression which their country may make on the minds of travellers occupies their thoughts incessantly. What would be said of the Germans, the English, and the French if they indulged themselves in such puerility? If the satires of Prince K—— are disagreeable to his countrymen, it is not so much because their own sentiments are wounded, as on account of the influence these satires may have upon me, who am become an important person in their eyes since they have heard that I write my travels.

"Do not allow yourself to be prejudiced against Russia by this unpatriotic Russian; do not write under the influence of his statements; it is from a wish to display his French wit at our expense that he thus speaks, but in reality he has no such opinion."

This is the kind of language that is addressed to me, privately, ten times a day. It appears to me as though the Russians would be content to become even yet worse and more barbarous than they are, provided they were thought better and more civilised. I do not admire minds which hold the truth thus cheaply; civilisation is not a fashion, nor an artificial device, it is a power which has its result,—a root which sends forth its stalk, produces its flowers, and bears its fruit.

"At least you will not call us the barbarians of the north, as your countrymen do." This is said to me every time I appear amused by some interesting recital, some national melody, or some noble or poetic sentiment ascribed to a Russian. I reply to these fears by some unimportant compliment, but I think in my own mind that I could better love the barbarians of the north than the apes who are ever imitating the south.

There are remedies for primitive barbarism, there are none for the mania of appearing what one is not.

A kind of Russian *savant*, a grammarian, a translator of various German works, and a professor of I know not which college, has made as many advances towards me as he could during this passage. He has been travelling through Europe, and returns to Russia full of zeal, he says, to propagate there all that is valuable in the modern opinions of western Europe. The freedom of his discourse appeared to me suspicious: it was not that luxury of independence observable in Prince K——; it was a studied liberalism, calculated to draw out the views of others.

If I am not mistaken, there may be always found some *savant* of this kind, on the ordinary lines of route to Russia, in the hotels of Lübeck, the steamboats, and even at Havre, which, thanks to the navigation of the German and Baltic seas, has become the Muscovite frontier.

This man extracted from me very little. He was specially desirous of learning whether I should write my travels, and obligingly offered me the lights of his experience. He left me at last thoroughly persuaded that I travelled only to divert myself, and without any intention of publishing the relation of a tour which would be performed very rapidly. This appeared to satisfy him; but his inquietude which was thus allayed, awoke my own. If I write this journey I must expect to give umbrage to a government more artful and better served with spies than any other in the world. This is an unpleasant idea. I must conceal my letters,

I must be guarded in my language; but I will affect

nothing: the most consummate deception

is that which assumes

no mask.

❖

THE RUSSIAN MARINE ❖ REMARK OF LORD DURHAM'S ❖ GREAT EFFORTS
FOR SMALL RESULTS ❖ THE AMUSEMENTS OF DESPOTISM ❖ KRONSTADT ❖
RUSSIAN CUSTOM-HOUSE ❖ GLOOMY ASPECT OF NATURE ❖ RECOLLECTIONS
OF ROME ❖ ENGLISH POETICAL NAME FOR SHIPS OF WAR ❖ OBJECT OF
PETER THE GREAT ❖ THE FINNS ❖ BATTERIES OF KRONSTADT ❖ ABJECT
CHARACTER OF THE LOWER CLASSES OF RUSSIAN EMPLOYÉS ❖ INQUISITIONS
OF THE POLICE, AND THE CUSTOM-HOUSE ❖ SUDDEN CHANGE IN THE
MANNERS OF FELLOW-TRAVELLERS ❖
FICKLENESS OF NORTHERN
PEOPLE
❖

CHAPTER VII

❖

As we approached Kronstadt,—a sub-marine fortress of which the Russians are justly proud,—the Gulf of Finland suddenly assumed an animated appearance. The imperial fleet was in motion and surrounded us on all sides. It remains in port, icelocked during more than six months of the year; but during the three months of summer the marine cadets are exercised in nautical manoeuvres, between St. Petersburg and the Baltic.

After passing the fleet we again sailed on an almost desert sea; now and then, only, enlivened by the distant apparition of some merchant vessel, or the yet more infrequent smoke of a *pyroscaph,* as steam-boats are learnedly called in the nautical language of some parts of Europe.

The Baltic sea, by the dull hues of its unfrequented waters, proclaims the vicinity of a continent depopulated under the rigours of the climate. The barren shores harmonise with the cold aspect of the sky and water, and chill the heart of the traveller.

No sooner does he arrive on this unattractive coast than he longs to leave it; he calls to mind, with a sigh, the remark of one of Catherine's favourites, who, when the Empress complained of the effects of the climate of Petersburg upon her health, observed, "It is not God who should be blamed, Madame, because men have persisted in building the capital of a great empire in a territory destined by nature to be the patrimony of wolves and bears."

❖ 75 ❖

My travelling companions have been explaining to me, with much self-satisfaction, the recent progress of the Russian marine. I admire this prodigy without magnifying it as they do. It is a creation, or rather a re-creation of the present emperor's. This prince amuses himself by endeavouring to realise the favourite object of Peter I., but however powerful a man may be, he is forced sooner or later to acknowledge that nature is more powerful still. So long as Russia shall keep within her natural limits, the Russian navy will continue the hobby of the emperors and nothing more!

During the season of naval exercises, I am informed that the younger pupils remain performing their evolutions in the neighbourhood of Kronstadt, while the more advanced extend their voyages of discovery as far as Riga, and sometimes even to Copenhagen.

As soon as I found that the sole object of all this display of naval power which passed before my eyes, was the instruction of pupils, a secret feeling of ennui extinguished my curiosity.

All this unnecessary preparation which is neither the result of commerce nor of war, appears to me a mere parade. Now, God knows, and the Russians know, whether there is any pleasure in a parade! The taste for reviews in Russia is carried beyond all bounds, and here, before even landing in this empire of military evolutions, I must be present at a review on the water. But I must not laugh at this. Puerility on a grand scale appears to me a monstrous thing, impossible except under a tyranny, of which it is, perhaps, the most terrible result! Everywhere, except under an absolute despotism, men, when they make great efforts, have in view great ends; it is only among a blindly abject people that the monarch may command immense sacrifices for the sake of trifling results.

The view of the naval power of Russia, gathered together for the amusement of the Czar, at the gate of his capital, has thus caused me only a painful impression. The vessels which will be inevitably lost in a few winters, without having rendered any service, suggest to my mind images—not of the power of a great country, but of the useless toils to which the poor unfortunate seamen are condemned. The ice is a more terrible enemy to this

navy than foreign war. Every autumn after the three months'
exercise, the pupil returns to his prison, the plaything to its box,
and the frost begins to wage its more serious war upon the imperial finances. Lord Durham once remarked to the Emperor himself, with a freedom of speech which wounded him in the most
sensitive part, that the Russian ships of war were but the play-
things of the Russian sovereign.

As regards myself, this childish Colossus by no means predis-
poses me to admire what I may expect to see in the interior of the
empire. To admire Russia in approaching it by water, it is necessary to forget the approach to England by the Thames. The first
is the image of death; the last, of life,

On dropping anchor before Kronstadt, we learned that one of
the noble vessels we had seen manoeuvering around us had just
been lost on a sand bank. This shipwreck was dangerous only to
the captain, who expected to be cashiered, and, perhaps, punished yet more severely. Prince K—— said to me privately, that
he would have done better to have perished with his vessel. Our
fellow-traveller the Princess L—— had a son attached to the
unlucky ship. She was placed in a situation of painful suspense,
until news of his safety was brought to her by the governor of
Kronstadt.

The Russians are incessantly repeating to me that it is requisite to spend at least two years in their country before passing a
judgment upon it; so difficult is it to understand.

But though patience and prudence may be necessary virtues in
those learned travellers who aspire to the glory of producing eru-
dite works, I, who have been hitherto writing only for my friend
and myself, have no intention of making my journal a work of
labour. I have some fear of the Russian custom-house, but they
assure me that my *écritoire* will be respected.

Nothing can be more melancholy than the aspect of nature in
the approach to St. Petersburg. As one advances up the Gulf, the
flat marshes of Ingria terminate in a little wavering line drawn
between the sky and the sea; this line is Russia. It presents the
appearance of a wet lowland, with here and there a few birch
trees thinly scattered. The landscape is void of objects, and
colours; has no bounds, and yet no sublimity. It has just light

enough to be visible; the grey mossy earth well accords with the pale sun which illumines it, not from overhead, but from near the horizon, or almost indeed from below,—so acute is the angle which the oblique rays form with the surface of this unfavoured soil. In Russia the finest days have a blueish dimness. If the nights are marked by a clearness which surprises, the days are clothed with an obscurity which saddens.

Kronstadt, with its forest of masts, its substructures, and its ramparts of granite, finely breaks the monotonous reverie of the pilgrim, who is, like me, seeking for imagery in this dreary land. I have never seen, in the approaches to any other great city, a landscape so melancholy as the banks of the Neva. The *campagna* of Rome is a desert, but what picturesque objects, what past associations, what light, what fire, what poetry, if I might be allowed the expression, I would say, what passion animates this religious land. To reach St. Petersburg, you must pass a desert of water framed in a desert of peat earth: sea, shore, and sky, are all blended into one mirror, but so dull, so tarnished, that it reflects nothing.

The thought of the noble vessels of the Russian navy, destined to perish without having ever been in action, pursues me like a dream.

The English, in their idiom, which is so poetical when it relates to maritime subjects, call a vessel of the royal navy, *a man of war.* Never will the Russians be thus able to denominate their ships of parade. These *men of court,* or wooden courtiers, are nothing more than the hospital of the imperial service. If the sight of so useless a marine inspired me with any fear, it was not the fear of war but of tyranny. It recalled to mind the inhumanities of Peter I., that type of all Russian monarchs, ancient and modern.

Some miserable boats, manned by fishermen as dirty as Esquimaux, a few vessels employed in towing timber for the construction of the *imperial navy,* and a few steam-boats, mostly of foreign build, were the only objects that enlivened the scene. Such is the approach to St. Petersburg: all that could have influenced against the choice of this site, so contrary to the views of nature or to the real wants of a great people, must have passed before the mind of Peter the Great without striking him. The sea, at any cost;—such was his sentiment. Whimsical idea in a Russian to found the capital of the empire of the Slavonians among the Finns, and in the vicinity of the Swedes! Peter the Great might say that his only object was to give a port to Russia; but if he had the genius which is ascribed to him, he ought to have foreseen the scope of his work; and in my opinion he did foresee it. Policy, and, I fear, the revenge of imperial self-love, wounded by the independence of the old Muscovites, have created the destinies of modern Russia.

Russia is like a vigorous person suffocating for want of external air. Peter I. promised it an outlet, but without perceiving that a sea necessarily closed during eight months in the year, is not like other seas. Names, however, are everything in Russia. The efforts of Peter, his subjects, and successors, extraordinary as they are, have only served to create a city which it is difficult to inhabit; with which the Neva disputes the soil whenever the wind blows from the Gulf, and from which the people think of flying altogether, at each step that this war of elements compels them to take towards the south. For a bivouac, quays of granite are superfluous.

The Finns, among whom the Russians fixed their new capital, are of Seythian origin, they are still almost Pagans—suitable inhabitants of the soil of Petersburg. It was only in 1836 that an ukase appeared, commanding their priests to add a family name to the saint's name given to the children in baptism.

This race is almost without physiognomy. The middle of the face is flattened to a degree that renders it deformed. The men, though ugly and dirty, are said to be strong, which, however, does not prevent their being poor. Although the natives, they are seldom seen in Petersburg except upon market days. They inhabit the swamps, and slightly elevated granite hills of the environs.

Kronstadt is a very flat island in the middle of the Gulf of Finland: this aquatic fortress is raised above the sea only just sufficiently to defend the navigation to St. Petersburg. Its foundations and many of its works are under water. Its guns are disposed, according to the Russians, with great skill, and by virtue of the shower of ball that an order of the emperor could here pour upon an enemy, the place passes for impregnable. I am not aware whether these guns command both the passages of the Gulf; the Russians who could have informed me, would not. My experience, although of recent date, has already taught me to distrust the rodomontades and exaggerations in which the subjects of the Czar, inspired by an excess of zeal in the service of their master, indulge. National pride appears to me to be tolerable only among a free people.

We arrived at Kronstadt about the dawning of one of those days without real beginning or end, which I am tired of describing though not of admiring.

After casting anchor before the silent fortress, we had to wait a long time for the arrival of a host of official personages, who boarded us one after the other; commissaries of police, directors and subdirectors of the customs, and finally the Comptroller himself. This important personage considered himself obliged to pay us a visit on account of the illustrious Russian passengers on board. He conversed for a long time with the returned princes and princesses. They talked in Russian, probably because the politics of the West were the subject of their discourse; but when the conversation fell on the troubles of landing and the necessity of leaving our carriages at Kronstadt, French was freely spoken.

The Travemünde packet draws too much water to ascend the Neva, the passengers, therefore, have to proceed by a smaller steamer, which is dirty and ill-constructed. We are allowed to carry with us our lighter baggage, after it has been examined by the officers. When this formality is concluded we leave for Petersburg, with the hope that our carriages left in the charge of these people, may arrive safely on the morrow.

The Russian princes were obliged, like myself, to submit to the laws of the custom-house, but on arriving at Petersburg I had the mortification of seeing them released in three minutes, whilst I had to struggle with every species of trickery for the space of three hours.

A multitude of little superfluous precautions engender here a population of deputies and sub-officials, each of whom acquits himself with an air of importance and a rigorous precision, which seemed to say, though everything is done with much silence, "Make way, I am one of the members of the grand machine of state."

Such members, acting under an influence which is not in themselves, in a manner resembling the wheel-work of a clock, are called men in Russia! The sight of these voluntary automata inspires me with a kind of fear: there is something supernatural in an individual reduced to the state of a mere machine. If, in lands where the mechanical arts flourish, wood and metal seem endowed with human powers, under despotisms, human beings seem to become as instruments of wood. We ask ourselves, what can become of their superfluity of thought? and we feel ill at ease at the thought of the influence that must have been exerted on intelligent creatures before they could have been reduced to mere *things.* In Russia I pity the human beings, as in England I feared the machines: in the latter country, the creations of man lack nothing but the gift of speech; here, the gift of speech is a thing unnecessary to the creatures of the state.

These machines, clogged with the inconvenience of a soul, are, however, marvellously polite; it is easy to see they have been trained to civility, as to the management of arms, from their cradle. But of what value are the forms of urbanity when their origin savours of compulsion? The free-will of man is the consecration that can alone impart a worth or a meaning to human actions; the power of choosing a master can alone give a value to fidelity; and since, in Russia, an inferior chooses nothing, all that he says and does is worthless and unmeaning.

The numerous questions I had to meet, and the precautionary forms that it was necessary to pass through, warned me that I was entering the Empire of Fear, and depressed my spirits.

I was obliged to appear before an Areopagus of deputies who had assembled to interrogate the passengers. The members of this formidable rather than imposing tribunal were seated before a large table; some of them were turning over the leaves of the register with an attention which had a sinister appearance, for their ostensible employ was not sufficient to account for so much gravity.

Some, with pen in hand, listened to the replies of the passengers, or rather the accused, for every stranger is treated as culpable on arriving at the Russian frontier. All the answers were carefully written down, and the passports minutely examined, and detained, under the promise that they would be returned at Petersburg.

These formalities being satisfied, we proceeded on board the new steam-boat. Hour after hour elapsed, and still there was no talk of starting. Every moment fresh boats proceeded from the city, and rowed towards us. Although we were moored close to the walls, the silence was profound. No voice issued from this tomb. The shadows that were gliding in their boats around were equally silent. They were clad in coarse capotes of grey wool, their faces lacked expression, their eyes possessed no fire, their complexion was of a green or yellow hue; I was told that they were sailors attached to the garrison, but they more resembled soldiers. Sometimes the boats passed round us in silence, sometimes six or a dozen ragged boatmen, half covered with sheepskins, the wool turned within, and the filthy skin appearing without, brought us some new police agent, or tardy custom-house officer. These arrivals and departures, though they did not accelerate our matters, at least gave me leisure to reflect on the species of filthiness peculiar to the people of the North. Those of the South pass their life in the open air half naked, or in the water; those of the North, for the most part shut up within doors, have a greasy dirtiness, which appears to me far more offensive than the neglect of a people destined to live beneath the open heaven, and born to bask in the sun.

The tedium to which these Russian formalities condemned us, gave me also an opportunity of remarking that the great lords of the country were little inclined to bear patiently the inconveniences of public regulations, when those regulations proved inconvenient to themselves.

"Russia is the land of useless formalities," they murmured among themselves—but in French, that they might not be overheard by the subaltern *employés.* I have retained the remark, with the justice of which my own experience has only too deeply impressed me. As far as I have been hitherto able to observe, a work that should be entitled *The Russians judged by Themselves,* would be severe. The love of their country is with them only a mode of flattering its master; as soon as they think that master can no longer hear, they speak of every thing with a frankness which is the more startling because those who listen to it become responsible.

The cause of all our delay was at length revealed. The chief of chiefs, the director of the directors of the custom-house again presented himself: it was this visit we had been awaiting so long, without knowing it. At first it appeared as if the only business of the great functionary was to play the part of the man of fashion among the Russian ladies. He reminded the Princess D—— of their rencontre in a house where the Princess had never been; he spoke to her of court balls she had never seen: but while continuing to dispense these courtly airs, our drawing-room officer of the customs would now and then gracefully confiscate a parasol, stop a portmanteau, or recommence, with an imperturbable *sang froid,* the researches already conscientiously made by his subordinates.

In Russian administration, minuteness does not exclude disorder. Much trouble is taken to attain unimportant ends, and those employed believe they can never do enough to show their zeal. The result of this emulation among clerks and commissioners is, that the having passed through one formality does not secure the stranger from another. It is like a pillage, in which, after the unfortunate wight has escaped from the first troop, he may yet fall into the hands of a second and a third.

The chief turnkey of the empire proceeded slowly to examine the vessel. At length this perfumed Cerberus, for he scented of musk at the distance of a league, released us from the ceremonies attending an *entrée* into Russia, and we were soon under weigh, to the great joy of the princes and princesses, who were going to rejoin their families. Their pleasure belied the observation of my host in Lübeck; as for me, I could not partake in it: on the contrary, I regretted quitting their delightful society to go and lose myself in a city whose vicinity was so uninviting. But the charm of that society was already broken; as we drew towards the end of our journey the ties which had united us became severed—fragile ties, formed only by the passing requirements of the voyage.

The women of the North know wonderfully well how to make us believe that they would have desired to meet with that which destiny has brought in their way. This is not falsehood, it is refined coquetry, a species of complaisance towards fate, and a supreme grace. Grace is always natural, though that does not prevent its being often used to hide a lie. The rude shocks and uncomfortably constraining influences of life disappear among graceful women and poetical men; they are the most deceptive beings in creation; distrust and doubt cannot stand before them; they create what they imagine; if they do not lie to others, they do to their own hearts; for illusion is their element, fiction their vocation, and pleasures in appearance their happiness. Beware of grace in woman, and poetry in man—weapons the more dangerous because the least dreaded!

Such were my thoughts on leaving the walls of Kronstadt: we were still all together, but we were no longer united. That circle, animated, but the previous evening, by a secret harmony which rarely exists in society, now lacked its vital principle. Few things had ever appeared to me more melancholy than this sudden change. I acknowledged it as the condition attached to the pleasures of the world. I had foreseen it, I had submitted a hundred times to the same experience; but never before did it enlighten me in so abrupt a manner. Besides, what annoyances are more painful than those of which we cannot complain? I saw each individual about to re-enter his own path; the free interchange of feeling which unites those travelling together to the same goal no longer existed among them; they were returning into real life, whilst I was left alone to wander from place to place. To be ever wandering is scarcely to live. I felt myself abandoned, and I compared the cheerlessness of my isolation to their domestic pleasures. Isolation may be voluntary, but is it on this account any the more sweet? At the moment, everything appeared to me preferable to my independence, and I regretted even the cares of domestic life. I could read in the eyes of the women the thoughts of husband, children, milliners, hairdressers, the ball, and the court; and I could equally read there, that, notwithstanding the protestations of yesterday, I was no longer an object of concern to them. The people of the North have changeable hearts; their affections, like the faint rays of their sun, are always dying. Remaining fixedly attached neither to persons nor to things—willingly quitting the land of their birth—born for invasions—these people appear as though merely destined to sweep down from the pole, at the times and epochs appointed by God, in order to temper and refresh the races of the South, scorched by the fires of heaven and of their passions.

On arriving at Petersburg, *my friends,* favoured by their rank, were speedily liberated from their floating prison, in which they left me bound by the irons of the police and the custom-house, without so much as bidding me adieu. Where would have been the use of adieus? I was as dead to them. What are travellers to mothers of families? Not one cordial word, not one look, not one thought was bestowed on me. It was the white curtain of the magic lantern, after the shadows have passed. I repeat that I had expected this *dénouement,* but I had not expected the pain which it caused me; so true it is that within ourselves exists the source of all our unforeseen emotions.

Only three days before landing, two of our fair and amiable travellers had made me promise to visit them in Petersburg, where the court is now assembled.

❖

CHAPTER VIII

❖

The streets of Petersburg present a strange appearance to the eyes of a Frenchman. I will endeavour to describe them; but I must first notice the approach to the city by the Neva. It is much celebrated, and the Russians are justly proud of it, though I did not find it equal to its reputation. When, at a considerable distance, the steeples begin to appear, the effect produced is more singular than imposing. The hazy outline of land, which may be perceived far off between the sky and the sea, becomes, as you advance, a little more unequal at some points than at others: these scarcely perceptible irregularities are found on nearer approach to be the gigantic architectural monuments of the new capital of Russia. We first begin to recognise the Greek steeples and the gilded cupolas of convents; then some modern public buildings—the front of the Exchange, and the white colonnades of the colleges, museums, barracks, and palaces which border the quays of granite, become discernible. On entering the city, you pass some sphinxes, also of granite. Their dimensions are colossal and their appearance imposing; nevertheless these copies of the antique have no merit as works of art. A city of palaces is always magnificent, but the imitation of classic monuments shocks the taste when the climate under which these models are so inappropriately placed is considered. Soon, however, the stranger is struck with the form and multitude of turrets and metallic spires which rise in every direction: this at least is national architecture. Petersburg is flanked with numbers of large convents, surmounted by steeples; pious edifices, which serve as a rampart to the profane city. The Russian churches have preserved their primitive appearance; but it is not the Russians who invented that clumsy and capricious Byzantine style, by which they are distinguished. The Greek religion of this people, their character, education, and history, alike justify their borrowing from the Lower Empire; they may be permitted to seek for models at Constantinople, but not at Athens. Viewed from the Neva, the parapets of the quays of Petersburg are striking and magnificent; but the first step after landing discovers them to be badly and unevenly paved with flints, which are as disagreeable to the eye as inconvenient to the feet and ruinous to the wheels. The prevailing taste here is the brilliant and the striking: spires, gilded and tapering like electric conductors; porticoes, the bases of which almost disappear under the water; squares, ornamented with columns which seem lost in the immense space that surrounds them; antique statues, the character and attire of which so ill accord with the aspect of the country, the tint of the sky, the costume and manners of the inhabitants, as to suggest the idea of being captive heroes in a hostile land; expatriated edifices, temples that might have fallen from the summit of the Grecian mountains into the marshes of Lapland:—such were the objects that most struck me at the first sight of St. Petersburg. The magnificent temples of the pagan Gods, which so admirably crown, with their horizontal lines and severely chaste contours, the promontories of the Ionian shores, and whose marbles, gilded by the sunshine amid the rocks of the Peloponnesus, here become mere heaps of plaster and mortar; the incomparable ornaments of Grecian sculpture, the wonderful minutiae of classic art, have all given place to an indescribably burlesque style of modern decoration, which substitution passes among the Finlanders as proof of a pure taste in the arts. Partially to imitate that which is perfect is to spoil it. We should either strictly copy the model, or invent altogether. But the re-production of the monuments of Athens, however faithfully executed, would be lost in a miry plain, continually in danger of being overflowed by water whose level is nearly that of the land. Here nature suggests to man the very opposite of that which he has imagined. Instead of imitations of pagan temples, it demands bold projecting forms and perpendicular lines, in order to pierce the mists of a polar sky, and to break the monotonous surface of the moist grey steppes which form, farther than the eye or the imagination can stretch, the territory of Petersburg. I begin to understand why the Russians urge us with so much earnestness to visit them during winter: six feet of snow conceals all this dreariness, but in summer we see the country. Explore the territory of Petersburg and the neighbouring provinces, and you will find, I am told, for hundreds of leagues, nothing but ponds and morasses, stunted firs and dark-leaved birch. To this sombre vegetation the white shroud of winter is assuredly preferable. Every where the same plains and bushes seem to compose the same landscape; at least, until the traveller approaches Finland and Sweden. There he finds a succession of little granite rocks covered with pines, which change the appearance of the soil, though without giving much variety to the landscape. It will be easily believed that the gloom of such a country is scarcely lessened by the lines of columns which men have raised on its even and naked surface. The proper bases of Greek peristyles are mountains: there is here no harmony between the inventions of man and the gifts of nature; in short, a taste for edifices without taste has presided over the building of St. Petersburg.

But, however shocked our perceptions of the beautiful may be by the foolish imitations which spoil its appearance, it is impossible to contemplate without a species of admiration, an immense city which has sprung from the sea at the bidding of one man, and which has to defend itself against a periodical inundation of ice, and a perpetual one of water.

The Kronstadt steam-boat dropped her anchor before the English quay opposite the Custom-house, and not far from the famous square where the statue of Peter the Great stands mounted on its rock.

I would gladly spare my reader the detail of the new persecutions, which, under the name of *simple* formalities, I had to undergo at the hand of the police, and its faithful ally the custom-house; but it is a duty to give a just idea of the difficulties which attend the stranger on the maritime frontier of Russia: the entrance by land is, I am told, more easy.

For three days in the year the sun of Petersburg is insupportable. I arrived on one of these days. Our persecutors commenced by impounding us (not the Russians, but myself and the other foreigners) on the deck of our vessel. We were there, for a long time, exposed without any shelter to the powerful heat of the morning sun. It was eight o'clock, and had been daylight ever since one hour after midnight. They spoke of thirty degrees of Réaumur,* which temperature, be it remembered, is much more inconvenient in the North, where the air is surcharged with vapour, than in hot climates.

At length I was summoned to appear before a new tribunal, assembled, like that of Kronstadt, in the cabin of our vessel. The same questions were addressed to me, with the same politeness, and my answers were recorded with the same formalities.

"What is your object in Russia?"

"To see the country."

"That is not here a motive for travelling."

(What humility in this objection!)

"I have no other."

"Whom do you expect to see in Petersburg?"

"Every one with whom I may have an opportunity of making acquaintance."

"How long do you think of remaining in Russia?"

"I do not know."

"But, about how long?"

"A few months."

"Have you a public diplomatic mission?"

"No."

"A secret one?"

"No."

"Any scientific object?"

"No."

"Are you employed by your government to examine the social and political state of this country?"

* Nearly 100° Fahrenheit.—*Trans.*

"No."

"By any commercial association?"

"No."

"You travel, then, from mere curiosity?"

"Yes."

"What was it that induced you, under this motive, to select Russia?"

"I do not know," &c. &c. &c.

"Have you letters of introduction to any people of this country?"

I had been forewarned of the inconvenience of replying too frankly to this question; I therefore spoke only of my banker.

At the termination of the session of this court of assize I encountered several of my *accomplices.* These strangers had been sadly perplexed, owing to some irregularities that had been discovered in their passports. The blood-hounds of the Russian police are quick-scented, and have a very different manner of treating different individuals. An Italian merchant, who was among our passengers, was searched unmercifully, not omitting even the clothes on his person, and his pocket-book. Had such a search been made upon me, I should have been pronounced a very suspicious character. My pockets were full of letters of introduction, and though the greater number had been given me by the Russian ambassador himself, and by others equally well known, they were sealed; a circumstance which made me afraid of leaving them in my writing-case. The police permitted me to pass without searching my person; but when my baggage came to be unpacked before the custom-house officers, these new enemies instituted a most minute examination of my effects, more especially my books. These were seized *en masse,* and without any attention to my protestations, but an extraordinary politeness of manner was all the while maintained. A pair of pistols and an old portable clock were also taken from me, without my being able to ascertain the reason of the confiscation. All that I could get was the promise that they would be returned.

I have now been more than twenty-four hours on shore without having been able to recover any thing, and to crown my embarrassment, my carriage has, by mistake, been forwarded from Kronstadt to the address of a Russian prince. It will require trouble, and explanations without end, to prove this error to the custom-house agents; for the prince of my carriage is from home.

Between nine and ten o'clock I found myself, personally, released from the fangs of the custom-house, and entered Petersburg under the kind care of a German traveller, whom I met *by chance* on the quay. If a spy, he was at least a useful one, speaking both French and Russian, and undertaking to procure me a drowsky; while, in the mean time, he himself aided my valet to transport in a cart to Coulon's hotel such part of my baggage as had been given up.

Coulon is a Frenchman, who is said to keep the best hotel in Petersburg, which is not saying much. In Russia, foreigners soon lose all trace of their national character, without, at the same time, ever assimilating with that of the natives.

The obliging stranger found even a guide for me who could speak German, and who mounted behind in the drowsky, in order to answer my questions. This man acquainted me with the names of the buildings we passed in proceeding to the hotel, which occupied some time, for the distances are great in Petersburg.

The too celebrated statue of Peter the Great, placed on its rock by the Empress Catherine, first attracted my attention. The equestrian figure is neither antique nor modern; it is a Roman of the time of Louis XV. To aid in supporting the horse, an enormous serpent has been placed at his feet; which is an ill-conceived idea, serving only to betray the impotence of the artist.

I stopped for one moment before the scaffolding of an edifice which, though not yet completed, is already famous in Europe, the church, namely, of St. Isaac. I also saw the façade of the new winter palace; another mighty result of human will applying human physical powers in a struggle with the laws of nature. The end has been attained, for in one year this palace has risen from its ashes; and it is the largest, I believe, which exists; equalling the Louvre and the Tuilleries put together.

In order to complete the work at the time appointed by the emperor, unheard-of efforts were necessary. The interior works were continued during the great frosts; 6000 workmen were continually employed; of these a considerable number died daily, but the victims were instantly replaced by other champions brought forward to perish, in their turn, in this inglorious breach. And the sole end of all these sacrifices was to gratify the caprice of one man!

Among people naturally, that is to say, anciently civilised, the life of men is only exposed when common interests, the urgency of which is universally admitted, demand it. But how many generations of monarchs has not the example of Peter the Great corrupted!

During frosts when the thermometer was at 25 to 30 degrees below 0 of Réaumur, 6000 obscure martyrs—martyrs without merit, for their obedience was involuntary—were shut up in halls heated to 30 degrees of Réaumur, in order that the walls might dry more quickly; in entering and leaving this abode of death, destined to become, by virtue of their sacrifice, the abode of vanity, magnificence, and pleasure. Thus these miserable beings would have to endure a difference of 50 to 60 degrees of temperature.

The works in the mines of the Uralian mountains are less inimical to life; and yet the workmen employed at Petersburg were not malefactors. I was told that those who had to paint the interior of the most highly heated halls were obliged to place on their heads a kind of bonnet of ice, in order to preserve the use of their senses under the burning temperature. Had there been a design to disgust the world with arts, elegance, luxury, and all the pomp of courts, could a more efficacious mode have been taken? And yet the sovereign was called father, by the men immolated before his eyes in prosecuting an object of pure imperial vanity. They were neither spies nor Russian cynics who gave me these details, the authenticity of which I guarantee.

The millions expended on Versailles supported as many families of French workmen as there were Slavonian serfs destroyed by these twelve months in the winter palace; but, by means of this sacrifice, the mandate of the emperor has realised a prodigy; and the palace, completed to the general satisfaction, is going to be inaugurated by marriage fêtes. A prince may be popular in Russia without attaching much value to human life. Nothing colossal is produced without effort; but when a man is in himself both the nation and the government, he ought to impose on himself a law, not to press the great springs of the machine he has the power of moving, except for some object worthy of the effort. To work miracles at the cost of the life of an army of slaves may be great; but it is too great, for both God and man will finally rise to wreak vengeance on these inhuman prodigies. Men have adored the light, the Russians worship the eclipse: when will their eyes be opened?

I do not say that their political system produces nothing good; I simply say that what it does produce is dearly bought.

It is not now for the first time that foreigners have been struck with astonishment at contemplating the attachment of this people to their slavery. The following passage, which is an extract from the correspondence of the Baron Herberstein, ambassador from the Emperor Maximilian, father of Charles V., to the Czar Vassili Ivanowich, I have found in Karamsin.

Did the Russians know all that an attentive reader may gather even from this flattering historian, in whom they glory, and whom foreigners consult with extreme distrust, on account of his partiality as a courtier, they would entreat the emperor to forbid the perusal of his, and of all other historical works, and thus be left in a darkness equally favourable to the repose of the despot and the felicity of his subjects, who believe themselves happy so long as others do not stigmatise them as victims.

Herberstein, in characterising the Russian despotism, writes as follows:—"He (the czar) speaks, and it is done; the life and fortunes of laity and clergy, nobles and burghers, all depend on his supreme will. He is unacquainted with contradiction, and all he does is deemed as equitable as though it were done by Deity; for the Russians are persuaded that their prince is the executor of the Divine decrees. Thus, *'God and the prince have willed,' 'God and the prince know,'* are common modes of speech among them. Nothing can equal their zeal for his service. One of his principal officers, a venerable gray-haired person, formerly ambassador in Spain, came to meet us on our entry into Moscow. He galloped his horse, and displayed all the activity of a young man, until the sweat fell from his brow; and when I expressed my surprise to him, '*Ah, Monsieur le Baron,*' he replied, '*we serve our sovereign in a manner altogether different from that in which you serve yours.*'

"I cannot say whether it is the character of the Russian nation which has formed such autocrats, or whether it is the autocrats themselves who have given this character to the nation."

This letter, written more than three centuries ago, describes the Russians precisely as I now see them. Like the ambassador of Maximilian, I still ask, is it the character of the Russian which has made the autocracy, or is it the autocracy which has made the Russian character? and I can no more solve the question than could the German diplomatist.

It appears to me, however, that the influence is reciprocal: the Russian government could never have been established elsewhere than in Russia; and the Russians would never have become what they are under a government differing from that which exists among them.

I will add another citation from the same author, Karamsin. He repeats the observations of the travellers who visited Muscovy in the sixteenth century. "Is it surprising, say these strangers, that the grand prince is rich? He neither gives money to his troops nor his ambassadors; he even takes from these last all the costly things they bring back from foreign lands.* It was thus that the Prince Yaroslowsky, on his return from Spain, was obliged to place in the treasury all the chains of gold, the collars, the costly stuffs, and the silver vessels, which the Emperor and the Arch-duke Ferdinand had given him. Nevertheless, these men do not complain; they say, 'The great prince takes away, the great prince will give again.' " It was thus the Russians spoke of the czar in the sixteenth century.

At the present day you will hear, both in Paris and in Petersburg, numbers of Russians dwelling with rapture on the prodigious effects of the word of the emperor: and, in magnifying these results, not one troubles himself with dwelling upon the means. "The word of the emperor can create," they say. Yes; it can animate stones, by destroying human beings. Notwithstanding

* Dickens, in his Travels through the United States, informs us that the same practice is at this day observed in America.

this little restrictive clause, every Russian is proud of being able to say to us, "You take three years to deliberate on the means of rebuilding a theatre, whilst our emperor raises again, in one year, the largest palace in the universe." And this puerile triumph does not appear to them too dearly bought by the death of a few thousand wretched artisans, sacrificed to that sovereign impatience, that imperial fantasy, which constitutes the national glory. Whilst I, though a Frenchman, see nothing but inhuman ostentation in this achievement, not a single protestation is raised from one end of this immense empire to the other, against the orgies of absolute power.

People and government are here in unison. That a man brought up in the idolatry of self, a man revered as omnipotent by sixty millions of men, or at least of beings that resemble men, should not undertake to put an end to such a state of things— this does not surprise me: the wonder is, that among the voices that relate these things to the glory of this individual, not one separates itself from the universal chorus, to protest in favour of humanity, against such autocratic miracles. It may be said of the Russians, great and small, that they are drunk with slavery.

❖

THE DROWSKA ❖ COSTUME OF THE LOWER ORDERS ❖ WOODEN PAVEMENTS
❖ PETERSBURG IN THE MORNING ❖ RESEMBLANCE OF THE CITY TO A
BARRACK ❖ CONTRAST BETWEEN RUSSIA AND SPAIN ❖ DIFFERENCE
BETWEEN TYRANNY AND DESPOTISM ❖ THE TCHINN ❖ PECULIAR
CHARACTER OF THE RUSSIAN GOVERNMENT ❖ THE ARTS IN RUSSIA ❖
A RUSSIAN HOTEL ❖ THE EVILS TO BE ENCOUNTERED THERE ❖ THE
MICHAEL PALACES ❖ DEATH OF PAUL I ❖ THE SPY BAFFLED ❖ THE NEVA,
ITS QUAYS AND BRIDGES ❖ CABIN OF PETER I ❖ THE CITADEL, ITS TOMBS
AND DUNGEONS ❖ CHURCH OF ST. ALEXANDER NEWSKI ❖ RUSSIAN
VETERANS ❖ AUSTERITY OF THE CZAR ❖ RUSSIAN FAITH IN THE FUTURE,
AND ITS REALISATION ❖ MUNICH AND PETERSBURG COMPARED ❖ INTERIOR
OF THE FORTRESS ❖ THE IMPERIAL TOMBS ❖ SUBTERRANEAN PRISON ❖
RUSSIAN PRISONERS ❖ MORAL DEGRADATION OF THE HIGHER CLASSES ❖
CATHOLIC CHURCH ❖ PRECARIOUS TOLERATION
❖ TOMB OF THE LAST KING OF POLAND,
AND OF MOREAU
❖

CHAPTER IX

❖

It was on the day before yesterday, between nine and ten o'clock, that I obtained the liberty of entering Petersburg.

The city, whose inhabitants are not early risers, gave me at that hour of day the idea of a vast solitude. Now and then I met a few drowskas. The drivers were dressed in the costume of the country. The singular appearance of these men, their horses and carriages, struck me more than anything else on my first view of the city.

The ordinary costume and general appearance of the lower classes of Petersburg, (not the porters, but) the workmen, coachmen, the small tradespeople, &c. &c., is as follows:—on the head is worn either a cap, formed somewhat in the shape of a melon; or a narrow-brimmed hat, low crowned, and wider at the top than the bottom. This headdress slightly resembles a woman's turban or a Norman cap. It becomes the younger men. Both young and old wear beards. Those of the beaux are silken and carefully combed; those of the old and the careless appear dirty and matted. Their eyes have a peculiar expression, strongly resembling the deceitful glance of Asiatics—so strongly, that in casually observing them, you might fancy yourself in Persia.

Their locks, worn long on each side, fall upon the cheeks and conceal the ears; but their hair is cut closely off from the nape of the neck upwards, which original mode of wearing it leaves the neck behind quite bare, for they have no cravat. The beard sometimes falls upon the breast, sometimes it is cut close round the chin. Much value is attached to this ornament, which accords with the *tout ensemble* of the costume better than with the stocks, the frock coats, and the waistcoats of our young modern fops.

The Russian people have a natural perception of the picturesque; their customs, furniture, utensils, costume and figure, would all furnish subject for the painter, and the corner of every street in Petersburg might suggest material for a picture graceful in its kind.

But to complete the description of the national costume:—in place of our frock and great-coats, is substituted the cafetan, a long and loose Persian robe made of grey, olive, or yet more commonly, of blue cloth. The folds of this robe, which has no collar, but is cut close to the neck, form an ample drapery, drawn together round the loins by a brightly coloured silken or woollen girdle. The boots are large, and take the form of the foot. On the legs the high leather falls down, or is doubled back over itself, in not ungraceful folds.

The singular form of the drowska is well known; imitations, more or less exact, are to be seen every where. It is the lowest and smallest carriage imaginable, being almost hid by the two or three persons that it carries. It consists of a stuffed seat, protected by four splash-boards of polished leather. This seat is supported on four extremely low wheels, by four little springs, and is placed lengthwise. The driver sits before, his feet almost touching the hocks of his horses, and close behind, astride the seat, his masters are jammed together, for two men sometimes mount the same drowska. I have not seen how the women manage. To these singular vehicles, small as they are, one, two, and sometimes three horses are attached. The shaft horse has his head fixed in a large and raised semi-circle of wood, which gives the idea of a moving triumphal arch. It is not a collar, for the neck of the horse is far below the wood; it is rather a hoop, through which the animal seems to be proudly passing. The different parts of the harness are well adapted to correspond with this not ungraceful hoop, a bell attached to which announces the approach of the drowska.

In observing this lowest of all equipages gliding swiftly between two lines of the lowest built of all houses, one can scarcely realise the idea of being in Europe. The second horse, fastened on the near side of the former, is yet less confined; his head is left free, and he is kept constantly on the gallop, when even his comrade in harness only trots.

Originally the drowska was nothing more than a rough plank, placed between four little wheels, on axles almost touching the earth. This primitive coach has been greatly improved, but it still preserves its original lightness and its strange appearance. In striding the seat one feels as if mounting some tamed animal; but if this species of horseback is not liked, the party seats himself sideways, holding by the coachman, who always drives at a gallop.

There is a new kind of drowska, in which the seat is not fixed lengthwise, and the body of which has the form of a tilbury. It is an approach to the carriages of other lands, and savours of the English modes; so much the worse, for among all people I love that which is national, and regret that it should ever become obsolete! These scarcely perceptible coaches are rudely jolted over the uneven stones of the streets of Petersburg, though in certain quarters the pavement is improved by two lines of wooden blocks laid down on each side of the way. Over such pavements, which are found in the larger streets, the horses proceed with great rapidity, especially in dry weather, for the rain renders them slippery. These mosaics of the north are expensive by reason of the continual repairs which they require, but they are preferable to the stones.

The movements of the men whom I met appeared stiff and constrained; every gesture expressed a will which was not their own. The morning is the time for commissions and errands, and not one individual appeared to be walking on his own account. I observed few good looking women, and heard no girlish voices; every thing was dull and regular as in a barrack. Military discipline reigns throughout Russia. The aspect of the country makes me regret Spain as much as though I had been born an Andalusian: it is not however the heat which I want, for that here is almost suffocating: it is light and light-heartedness. Love and liberty for the heart, brilliancy and variety of colour for the eye, are

here unknown: in a word, Russia is in all respects the very opposite of Spain. Fancy can almost descry the shadow of death hovering over this portion of the globe.

Now appears a cavalry officer passing at full gallop to *bear an
order* to some commanding officer; then a chasseur carrying *an
order* to some provincial governor, perhaps at the other extremity
of the empire, whither he proceeds in a kibitka, a little Russian
chariot, without springs or stuffed seat. This vehicle, driven by an
old bearded coachman, rapidly conveys the courier, whose rank
would prevent his using a more commodious equipage had he one
at his disposal. Next are seen foot soldiers returning from exercise
to their quarters, in order to *receive orders* from their captain.
This automaton population resembles one side of a chess-board,
where a single individual causes the movements of all the pieces,
but where the adversary is invisible. One neither moves nor re-
spires here except by an imperial order; consequently everything
is dull, formal, and spiritless. Silence presides over and paralyses
life. Officers, coachmen, Cossacks, serfs, courtiers, all servants
under the same master, blindly obey the orders which they do not
understand; it is certainly the perfection of discipline; but the
sight of such perfection does not gratify me; so much regularity
can only be obtained by the entire absence of independence.

Among this people bereft of time and of will, we see only
bodies without souls, and tremble to think that, for so vast a
multitude of arms and legs, there is only one head. Despotism is a
union of impatience and of indolence; with a little more forbearance on the part of the governing power, and of activity on the
part of the people, equal results might be obtained at a far
cheaper cost; but what then would become of tyranny?

If I am reproached for confounding despotism with tyranny, I
answer that I do so with design. They are such near relatives,
that they never fail to unite in secret to the misfortune of mankind. Under a despotism, tyranny may maintain itself the longer,
because it preserves the mask.

When Peter the Great established what is here called the
tchinn, that is to say, when he applied the military system to the
general administration of the empire, he changed his nation into

a regiment of mutes, of which he declared himself and his successors the hereditary colonels.

Let the reader imagine the ambition, the rivalry, and all the other passions of war in operation during a state of peace; let his mind conceive an absence of all that constitutes social and domestic happiness and, in place of these, let him picture to himself the universal agitation of an ever-restless though secret intrigue, —secret, because the mask is essential to success; finally, let him realise the idea of the almost complete apparent triumph of the will of one man over the will of God, and he will understand Russia.

As the morning advances, the city becomes more noisy, without however appearing more gay; one sees only carriages, little distinguished for elegance, carrying at the full speed of their two, four, or six horses, people always in haste, because their life is passed in thus *making their way.* Pleasure without any ulterior aim—pleasure for its own sake, is here a thing unknown.

Thus, almost all the great *artistes* who visit Russia to reap the fruit of the fame they have acquired elsewhere, never remain beyond a very brief period; if ever they prolong their stay, they wrong their talents. The air of this country is unfavourable to the finer arts. Productions that spring spontaneously elsewhere, will only here grow in the hot house. Russian art will never be a hardy plant.

At the Hotel de Coulon, I found a degenerated French innkeeper. His house is at present nearly full, on account of the marriage of the Grand Duchess Marie; and he appeared almost annoyed at being obliged to receive another guest, and consequently gave himself little trouble to accommodate me. After several parleys, I was at length established on the second floor, in suffocating apartments, consisting of an *entrée,* a *salon,* and a bed-chamber, the whole without curtains or window blinds, though there is a sun for twenty-two hours daily above the horizon, the oblique rays of which penetrate more fully into the houses than the sun of Africa, which falls direct upon the roofs. The air of this lodging resembles that of a limekiln choked with dust, and charged with exhalations of insects mingled with musk, forming altogether an atmosphere that is insupportable.

Scarcely was I installed in this abode than (the fatigue of the night having got the better of my curiosity, which usually impels me to sally forth and lose myself in a large unknown city) I lay down, wrapped in a cloak, on an immense leather sofa, and slept profoundly during—three minutes.

At the end of this time I woke in a fever, and on casting my eyes upon the cloak, what a sight awaited them!—A brown but living mass: things must be called by their proper name—I was covered, I was devoured with bugs. Russia is, in this respect, not a whit inferior to Spain: but in the south we can both console and secure ourselves in the open air; here we remain imprisoned with the enemy, and the war is consequently more sanguine. I began throwing off my clothes, and calling for help. What a prospect for the night! This thought made me cry out more lustily. A Russian waiter appeared. I made him understand that I wished to see his master. The master kept me waiting a long time, and when he at length did come, and was informed of the nature of my trouble, he began to laugh, and soon left the room, telling me that I should become accustomed to it, for that it was the same every where in Petersburg. He first advised me however never to seat myself on a Russian sofa, because the domestics, who always carry about with them legions of insects, sleep on these articles of furniture. To tranquillise me he further stated, that the vermin would not follow me if I kept at a proper distance from the furniture in which they had fixed their abode.

The inns of Petersburg resemble caravanserais, where the traveller is simply housed, but not waited upon, unless by his own servants. Mine, not understanding the Russian language, is not only useless to me but troublesome, for I have to take care of him as well as myself!

However, his Italian quickness soon discovered in one of the dark corridors of this walled desert, called L'Hôtel Coulon, a footman, out of place, who speaks German, and whom the keeper of the hotel recommended. I engaged him, and told him of my distress. He immediately procured me a light iron bedstead, the mattress for which, I had stuffed with the freshest straw that could be obtained, and caused the four feet to be placed in as many jars of water, in the middle of the chamber, the furniture of which I also had removed. Thus intrenched for the night, I dressed, and attended by the footman, whom I had desired to forbear directing me, I issued from this magnificent hotel—a palace without, and an ornamented stable within.

The hotel Coulon opens on a kind of *"square,"* which is tolerably lively for this city. On one side of the square stands the new Michael Palace, the stately abode of the Grand Duke Michael, brother of the emperor. It was built for the Emperor Alexander, who never inhabited it. The other sides of the square are inclosed by fine ranges of buildings with noble streets opening between. Scarcely had I passed the new Michael Palace than I found myself before the old. It is a vast, square, and gloomy fabric, differing in all respects from the elegant modern edifice of the same name.

If the men are silent in Russia, the stones speak with a lamentable voice. I am not surprised that the Russians neglect their ancient architectural monuments; these are witnesses of their history, which, for the most part, they are glad to forget. When I observed the black steps, the deep canals, the massive bridges, and the deserted porticos of this ill-omened palace, I asked its name; and the answer called to my mind the catastrophe which placed Alexander on the throne, while all the circumstances of the dark scene which terminated the reign of Paul I. presented themselves to my imagination.

Nor was this all: by a kind of savage irony there had been placed before the principal gate of the sinister edifice, before the death, and by the order of the Emperor Paul, the equestrian statue of his brother Peter III., another victim whose memory the emperor delighted to honour in order to dishonour that of his mother. What tragedies are played in cold blood in this land, where ambition and even hate are calm in appearance! With the people of the south, their passion reconciles me, in some measure, to their cruelty; but the calculating reserve, and the coldness of the men of the north, adds to crime the varnish of hypocrisy. Snow is a mask. Here man appears gentle because he is impassible; but murder without hate inspires me with more horror than vindictive assassination. The more nearly I can recognise an involuntary impulse in the commission of evil, the more I feel consoled. Unfortunately, it was the calculation of interest and prudence, and not the impulses of anger, which presided over the murder of Paul. Good Russians pretend that the conspirators had only intended to place him in prison. I have seen the secret door opening into the garden, which led to the apartment of the emperor by a private staircase, up which Pahlen caused the assassins to ascend. His communication with them on the evening before was to this effect:—"You will either have killed the emperor by five o'clock to-morrow morning, or you will be denounced by me to the emperor, at half past five, as conspirators." The result of this eloquent and laconic harangue need not be questioned.

At five o'clock on the following morning, Alexander was an emperor, and also an imputed parricide, although he had only consented (this is true, I believe) to the confinement of his father, in order to save his mother from prison and perhaps death, to protect himself from a similar fate, and to preserve his country from the rage and caprice of an insane autocrat.

At the present day, the Russians pass the old Michael Palace without daring to look at it. In the schools, and elsewhere, the death of the Emperor Paul is forbidden to be mentioned or even believed.

I am astonished that this palace of inconvenient recollections has not been pulled down. The traveller congratulates himself at the sight of a monument whose antique appearance is remarkable in a land where despotism renders every thing uniform and new; where the reigning notion effaces daily the traces of the past. Its square and solid form, its deep moats, tragic associations, and secret gates and staircases favourable to crime, impart to it an imposing air, which is a rare advantage in Petersburg. At each step I take I am amazed to observe the confusion that has been every where made in this city between two arts so very different as those of architecture and decoration. Peter the Great and his successors seem to have taken their capital for a theatre.

I was struck with the startled air of my guide, when I questioned him, in the most easy and natural manner that I could assume, on the events that had taken place in the old palace. The physiognomy of this man replied, "it is easy to see you are a newcomer." Surprise, fear, mistrust, affected innocence, pretended ignorance, the experience of an old soldier who would not easily be duped, took possession, by turns, of his countenance, and made it a book equally instructing and amusing to peruse. When your spy is at fault by reason of your apparent security, the expression of his face is truly grotesque, for he believes himself compromised by you so soon as he sees that you do not fear being compromised by him. The spy thinks only of his vocation; and if you escape his nets, he begins at once to imagine that he is going to fall into yours.

A promenade through the streets of Petersburg, under the charge of a *domestique de place,* is not without interest, and little resembles a progress through the capitals of other civilised lands. One thing is singularly connected with and dependent on another in a state governed with so close a logic as that which presides over the policy of Russia.

After leaving the old and tragical Michael Palace, I crossed a large square resembling the Champ de Mars at Paris, so spacious is it and so empty. On one side is a public garden, on the other a few houses; there is sand instead of pavement in the middle of the area, and dust in every part of. This immense square, the form of which is vague and undefined, extends to the Neva, near which termination is a bronze statue of Suwaroff.

The Neva, its bridges and quays, form the real glory of Petersburg. The scene here is so vast, that all the rest seems little in comparison. The Neva is like a vessel, so full that its brim disappears under the water, which is ready to flow over on every side. Venice and Amsterdam appear to me better protected against the sea than St. Petersburg.

The vicinity of a river, large as a lake, and which flows on a level with the land through a marshy plain, lost in the mists of the atmosphere and the vapours of the sea, was assuredly of all the sites in the world the least favourable for the foundation of a capital. The water will here, sooner or later, teach a lesson to human pride. The granite itself is no security against the work of winters in this humid ice-house, where the foundations of rock and the ramparts of the famous citadel, built by Peter the Great, have already twice given way. They have been repaired, and will be yet again, in order to preserve this *chef-d'oeuvre* of human pride and human will.

I wished at once to cross the bridge in order to examine it more nearly; but my servant first conducted me, in face of the fortress, to the house of Peter the Great, which is separated from it by a road and an open piece of ground.

It is a cabin, preserved, as is said, in the same state as that in which the emperor left it. In the citadel the emperors are now buried, and the prisoners of state detained—singular manner of honouring the dead! In thinking of all the tears shed there, *under* the tombs of the sovereigns of Russia, one is reminded of the funerals of some Asian kings. A tomb bedewed with blood would, in my eyes, be less impious: tears flow for a longer period, and are perhaps accompanied with deeper pangs.

During the time that the imperial artisan inhabited the cabin, his future capital was built beneath his eye. It should be admitted in his praise, that, at that period, he thought much less of the palace than of the city.

One of the chambers of this illustrious cottage, that, namely, which was the workshop of the princely carpenter, is now transformed into a chapel. It is entered with as much reverence as are the most sacred churches in the empire. The Russians are ever ready to make saints of their heroes. They delight in confounding the dreadful virtues of their masters with the benevolent power of their patrons, and endeavour to view the cruelties of history through the veil of faith.

Another Russian hero, in my opinion little deserving of admiration, has been sanctified by the Greek priests; I mean Alexander Newski—a model of prudence, but a martyr neither to piety nor to generosity. The national church has canonised this wise rather than heroic prince—this Ulysses among the saints. An enormous convent has been built around his reliques.

The tomb, enclosed within the church of Saint Alexander, is in itself an edifice. It consists of an altar of massive silver, surmounted with a species of pyramid of the same metal, which rises to the vault of a vast church. The convent, the church, and the cenotaph form one of the wonders of Russia. I contemplated them with more astonishment than admiration; for though the costliness of this pious work is immense, the rules of taste and of art have been little heeded in its construction.

In the cabin of the Czar, I was shown a boat of his own building, and several other objects religiously preserved, and placed under the guard of a veteran soldier. In Russia, churches, palaces, public places, and many private houses, are entrusted to the keeping of military pensioners. These unfortunate beings would be left without means of subsistence in their old age, unless they were, on leaving the barracks, converted into porters. In such posts they retain their long military capotes, which are made of coarse wool, and are generally much worn and dirty. At each visit that you make, men, thus clad, receive you at the gates of the public buildings and at the doors of the houses. They are spectres in uniform that serve to remind one of the discipline which here rules over every thing. Petersburg is a camp metamorphosed into a city. The veteran who kept guard in the imperial cottage, after having lighted several wax-tapers in the chapel, led me to the sleeping apartment of Peter the Great, emperor of all the Russias. A carpenter of our days would not lodge his apprentice in such a place.

This glorious austerity illustrates the epoch and the country as much as the man. In Russia, at that time, every thing was sacrificed to the future; every one was employed in building the palaces of their yet unborn masters; and the original founders of the magnificent edifices, not experiencing themselves the wants of luxury, were content to be the purveyors of the future civilisation, and took pride in preparing fitting abodes for the unknown potentates who were to follow them. There is certainly a greatness of mind evidenced in this care which a chieftain and his people take for the power, and even the vanity, of the generations that are yet to come. The reliance which the living have thus placed in the glory of their distant posterity has something about it which is noble and original. It is a disinterested and poetical sentiment, far loftier than the respect which men and nations are accustomed to entertain for their ancestors.

Elsewhere, great cities abound with monuments raised in memory of the past. St. Petersburg, in all its magnificence and immensity, is a trophy raised by the Russians to the greatness of the future. The hope which produces such efforts appears to me sublime. Never, since the construction of the Jewish temple, has the faith of a people in its own destinies raised up from the earth a greater wonder than St. Petersburg. And what renders more truly admirable this legacy, left by one man to his ambitious country, is, that it has been accepted by history.

The prophecy of Peter the Giant, sculptured upon blocks of granite reared in the sea, has been fulfilled before the eyes of the universe. This is the first instance in which pride has appeared to me really worthy of admiration.

The history of Russia does not, however, date, as the ignorant and superficial in Europe seem to suppose, from the reign of Peter I.; it is Moscow which explains St. Petersburg.

The deliverance of Muscovy, after long ages of invasion, and afterwards the siege and capture of Kasan by Ivan the Terrible, the determined struggles with Sweden, and many other brilliant as well as patient deeds of arms, justified the proud attitude of Peter the Great, and the humble confidence of his people. Faith in the unknown is always imposing. This man of iron had a right to put his trust in the future: characters like his produce those results which others only hope. I can see him, in all the simplicity of greatness, seated in the threshold of this cabin, planning and preparing against Europe, a city, a nation, and a history. The grandeur of Petersburg is not unmeaning. This mighty metropolis, ruling over its icy marshes, in order from thence to rule the world, is superb—more superb to the mind than to the eye! Yet it may not be forgotten, that one hundred thousand men, victims of obedience, were lost in converting the pestilential swamps into a capital.

Germany is at present witnessing the accomplishment of a masterpiece of critical art—one of its cities is being learnedly transformed into a city of ancient Greece or Italy. But New Munich wants an ancient population; Petersburg was wanted by the modern Russians.

On leaving the house of Peter the Great, I again passed before the bridge of the Neva (which leads to the Islands), and entered the celebrated fortress of Petersburg.

I have already remarked that this edifice, of which the name alone inspires fear, has twice had its ramparts and its granite foundations undermined, although it is not yet 140 years old. What a struggle! The stones here seem to suffer violence like the men.

I was not permitted to see the prisons: there are dungeons under the water, and there are others under the roofs, all of which are full of human beings. I was only allowed to inspect the church, which incloses the tombs of the reigning family. My eyes were on these tombs while I was yet searching for them, so difficult was it to imagine that a square stone, of about the length and breadth of a bed, newly covered with a green cloth embroidered with the imperial arms, could be the cemetery of the Empress Catherine I., of Peter I., Catherine II., and of so many other princes, down to the Emperor Alexander.

The Greek religion banishes sculpture from its churches, by which they lose in pomp and religious magnificence more than they gain in mystical character*; while at the same time it accommodates itself to gilt work, chasings, and to pictures which do not show a very pure taste. The Greeks are the children of the Iconoclasts.† In Russia they have ventured to mitigate the doctrine of their fathers; but they might have gone further than they have done.

In this funereal citadel, the dead appeared to me more free than the living. If it had been a philosophical idea which suggested the inclosing in the same tomb the prisoners of the emperor and the prisoners of death—the conspirators and the monarchs against whom they conspired—I should respect it; but I see in it nothing more than the cynicism of absolute power— the brutal security of a despotism which feels itself safe. Strong in its superhuman power, it rises above the little humane delicacies, the observance of which is advisable in common governments. A Russian emperor is so full of what is due to himself, that he cannot afford to have his justice lost sight of in that of God's. We royalist *revolutionaries* of Western Europe see only in a prisoner of state at Petersburg an innocent victim of despotism; the Rus-

* En mysticité.
† Destroyers of images.

sians view him as a reprobate. Every sound appeared to me a complaint; the stones groaned beneath my feet. Oh, how I pity the prisoners of this fortress! If the existence of the Russians confined under the earth, is to be judged of by inferences drawn from the existence of the Russians who live above, there is, indeed, cause to shudder! A thrill of horror passed through me as I thought that the most stedfast fidelity, the most scrupulous probity, could secure no man from the subterranean prisons of the citadel of Petersburg, and my heart dilated, and my respiration came more freely, as I repassed the moats which defend this gloomy abode, and separate it from the rest of the world.

Who would not pity this people? The Russians, I speak now of the higher classes, are living under the influences of an ignorance and of prejudices which they themselves no longer possess. The affectation of resignation appears to me the lowest depth of abjectness into which an enslaved nation can fall: revolt or despair would be doubtless more terrible, but less ignominious. Weakness so degraded that it dare not indulge itself even in complaint, that consolation of the lower animal creation fear calmed by its own excess—this is a moral phenomenon which cannot be witnessed without calling forth tears of horror.

After visiting the sepulchre of the Russian sovereigns, I proceeded to the Catholic church, the services of which are conducted by Dominican monks. I went there to demand a mass for an anniversary which none of my travels have hitherto prevented my commemorating in a Catholic church. The Dominican convent is situated in the Perspective Newski, the finest street in Petersburg. The church is not magnificent, but decent: the cloisters are solitary, the courts encumbered with rubbish of mason work. An air of gloom reigns throughout the community, which, notwithstanding the toleration it enjoys, appears to possess little wealth, and still less sense of security. In Russia toleration has no guarantee, either in public opinion, or in the constitution of the state: like every thing else it is a favour conceded by one man; and that man may withdraw to-morrow what he has granted to-day.

While waiting for the prior in the church, I saw beneath my feet a stone on which was inscribed a name that awoke in me some emotion—Poniatowski! the royal victim of folly. This too credulous lover of Catherine II. is buried here without any mark of distinction; but though despoiled of the majesty of the throne, there remains for him the majesty of misfortune. The troubles of this prince, his blind fatuity punished so cruelly, and the perfidious policy of his enemies, attract the attention of all Christians and of all travellers to his obscure tomb.

Near to the exiled king has been placed the mutilated body of Moreau. The Emperor Alexander caused it to be brought there from Dresden. The idea of placing together the remains of two men so greatly to be pitied, in order to unite in the same prayer the memory of their disappointed destiny, appears to me one of the greatest conceptions of this prince, who, be it remembered, was truly great when he entered a city from whence Napoleon was flying.

Towards four o'clock in the evening I began, for the first time, to recollect that I had not come to Russia merely to inspect curious monuments of art, and to enter into the reflections, more or less philosophical, which they might suggest; and I hastened to the French ambassador's.

There I found my oversight had been great. The marriage of the Grand Duchess Marie was to take place on the day after the morrow, and I had arrived too late to be presented previously. To miss this ceremony of the court, in a land where the court is every thing, would be to lose my journey.

❖

CHAPTER X

❖

I am just returned from visiting the Islands. They form an agreeable marsh; never was the vase better concealed by the flowers. A shallow, left dry during the summer, owing to the channels that intersect it serving as drains to the soil, planted with superb groves of birch, and covered with numerous charming villas—such is the tract called the Islands. The avenues of birch, which, together with pines, are the only trees indigenous to these icy plains, create an illusion that might lead the traveller to imagine himself in an English park. This vast garden overspread with *"villas"* and *"cottages,"** serves instead of the country to the inhabitants of Petersburg: it is the camp of the courtiers, thickly inhabited during a brief portion of the year, and totally deserted during the remainder.

The district of the Islands is reached by various excellent carriage roads, connected with bridges thrown over the different arms of the sea.

In wandering among its shady alleys, it is not difficult to imagine one's self in the country, but it is a monotonous and artificial country. No undulations of the ground, always the same kind of trees,—how is it possible to produce pictorial effect from such materials! Under this zone the plants of the hot-house, the fruits of the tropics, and even the gold and precious stones of the

* The allusion here is evidently made to a *London* rather than to an *"English"* park.—*Trans.*

mines, are less rare than our commonest forest trees. With wealth every thing may be procured here that can exist under glass, and this is much towards furnishing the scenery of a fairy tale, but it is not sufficient to make a park. One of the groves of chestnut or beech which beautify our hills would be a marvel in Petersburg. Italian houses surrounded by Laponian trees, and filled with the flowers of all countries, form a contrast which is singular rather than agreeable.

The Parisians, who never forget Paris, call the tract of the Islands the Russian Champs Elysées, but it is larger, more rural, and yet more adorned and more artificial, than our Parisian promenade. It is also farther distant from the fashionable quarters, and includes both town and country. At one moment you may suppose yourself looking upon real woods, fields, and villages; in the next, the view of houses in the shape of temples, of pilasters forming the framework of hot-houses, of colonnaded palaces, of theatres with antique peristyles, prove that you have not left the city.

The Russians are rightly proud of this garden raised at so much expence on the spongy soil of Petersburg. But if Nature is conquered, she remembers her defeat, and submits with bad grace. Happy the lands where heaven and earth unite and mutually vie in embellishing the abodes of man, and in rendering his life pleasant and easy!

I should insist less on the disadvantages of this unfavoured land, I should not regret so greatly, while travelling in the north, the sun of the south, if the Russians affected less to undervalue the gifts of which their country is deprived. Their perfect content extends even to the climate and the soil; naturally given to boasting, they have the folly to glory even in the physical as well as the social aspect which surrounds them. These pretensions prevent my bearing so resignedly as I ought to do, and as I had intended, with all the inconveniences of northern countries.

The delta formed between the city and one of the *embouchures* of the Neva, is now entirely covered by this species of park; it is nevertheless included within the precincts of Petersburg: the Russian cities embrace the country also. This tract would have become one of the most populous quarters of the new city, had the plan of the founder been more exactly followed. But, little by little, Petersburg receded from the river, southward, in the hope of escaping the inundations; and the marshy isles have been reserved exclusively for the summer residences of the most distinguished courtiers. These houses are half-concealed by water and snow for nine months of the year, during which time the wolves roam freely round the pavilion of the Empress: but during the remaining three months, nothing can exceed the profusion of flowers which the houses display. Nevertheless, under all this factitious elegance, the character of the people betrays itself; a passion for display is the ruling passion of the Russians: thus, in their drawing-rooms, the flowers are not placed in such manner as may render the interior of the apartment more agreeable, but so as to attract admiration from without: precisely the contrary of what we see in England, where, above all things, people shrink from *hanging out a sign in the streets.* The English are, of all the people on the earth, those who have best known how to substitute taste for style: their public buildings are *chefs-d'oeuvre* of the ridiculous; their private houses are models of elegance and good sense.

Among the Islands, all the houses and all the roads resemble each other. The shade of the birch trees is transparent, but under the sun of the North a very thick foliage is not required. Canals, lakes, meadows, groves, cottages, villas and alleys, follow each other in constant succession. This dreamy landscape pleases without interesting, without piquing the curiosity; but it gives the idea of repose, and repose is a precious thing at the Court of Russia, even though it be not valued there as it ought to be.

A distant pine forest rears at intervals its thin and spiry foliage above the roofs of some *villas,* built of planks and painted. These remembrances of solitude pierce through the ephemeral gaiety of the gardens, as though to witness to the rigour of winter, and the neighbourhood of Finland.

The aim of civilisation in the North is serious. There, society is the fruit, not of human pleasures, not of interests and passions easily satisfied, but of a will ever persisting and ever thwarted, which urges the people to incomprehensible efforts. There, if individuals unite together, it is to struggle with a rebellious nature, which unwillingly responds to the demands made upon her.

This dulness and stubbornness in the external world engender a gloom which accounts to me for the tragedies in the political world so frequent at this court. Here the drama is enacted in actual life, whilst the theatre is occupied with farce. Empty amusements are those alone permitted in Russia. Under such an order of things, real life is too serious an affair to admit a grave and thoughtful literature. Low comedy, the idyll, and the apologue well veiled, can alone flourish in presence of so terrible a reality. If in this inhospitable clime the precautions of despotism shall yet further increase the difficulties of existence, all happiness will be taken from man,—repose will become impossible. Peace, felicity—these words here are as vague as is that of Paradise. Idleness without ease, inertia without quiet—such are the inevitable results of the Boreal Autocracy.

The Russians enjoy but very little of the country which they have created at the gate of their city. The women pass the summer at the Islands, and the winter at Petersburg. They rise late, spend the day at their toilets, the evening in visits, and the night at play. To forget themselves, to lose themselves in a round of excitement, such is the apparent end of their existence.

The summer of the Islands commences in the middle of June and lasts till the end of August. During these two months there is not generally (though with the exception of the present year) more than a week of hot weather. The evenings are damp, the night atmosphere clear, but cloudy above, the days grey and misty. Life would here become insupportably dull and melancholy to the individual who should allow himself to reflect. In Russia, to converse is to conspire, to think is to revolt: thought is not merely a crime, it is a misfortune also.

Man thinks only with a view of ameliorating his lot and that of his fellows, but when he can do nothing and change nothing, thought does but prey upon and envenom the mind, for lack of other employment. This is the reason why, in the Russian world of fashion, people of all ages join in the dance.

As soon as the summer is over, a rain, fine as the points of needles, falls for weeks without any cessation. In two days the birch trees of the isles may be seen stript of their leaves, the houses of their flowers and their inhabitants, and the roads and bridges crowded with carriages, drowskas, and carts engaged in the removal of furniture, all the different kinds of which are heaped together with a slovenliness and disorder natural to the Slavonian race. It is thus that the rich man of the North, awaking from the too fleeting illusions of his summer, flies before the north-cast wind, leaving the bears and wolves to re-enter into possession of their legitimate domain. Silence resumes its ancient rights over these icy swamps, and for nine months, the frivolous society of the city of wood take refuge in the city of stone. From this change of season they experience little inconvenience; for in Petersburg the snows of the winter nights reflect almost as much light as is shed by the summer sun, and the Russian stoves give more heat than its obliquely falling rays.

That which yearly occurs in the islands will be the fate one day of the entire city. Should this capital, without roots in history, be forgotten for even a brief space by the sovereign, should a new policy direct his attention elsewhere, the granite hid under the water would crumble away, the inundated low lands would return to their natural state, and the guests of solitude would again take possession of their lair.

These ideas occupy the mind of every foreigner who traverses the streets of Petersburg; no one believes in the duration of the marvellous city. But little meditation (and what traveller worthy of his occupation does not meditate?) enables the mind to prefigure such a war, such a change in the course of policy, as would cause this creation of Peter I. to disappear like a soap bubble in the air.

In no other place have I been so impressed with the instability of human things. Often in Paris and in London have I said to myself, a time will come when this noisy abode will be more silent than Athens or Rome, Syracuse or Carthage; but to no man is it given to foresee the hour nor the immediate cause of the destruction; whereas, the disappearing of St. Petersburg may be foreseen, it may take place tomorrow, in the midst of the triumphant songs of its victorious people. The decline of other capitals follows the destruction of their inhabitants, but this will perish at the moment even when the Russians will see their power extending. I believe in the duration of Petersburg, just as I believe in that of a political system, or in the constancy of man. This is what cannot be said of any other city in the world.

What a tremendous power is that which can thus cause a metropolis to spring up in the wilderness, and which, with one word, can restore to solitude all that it has taken! Here real existence seems to belong only to the sovereign: the fate, the power, the will of an entire people are all centred in one single head. The Emperor is the personification of social power; beneath him reigns the equality that forms the dream of the modern Gallo-American democrats, the Fourriérists, &c. But the Russians acknowledge a cause of storm that is unknown to others, the wrath of this emperor. Republican or monarchical tyranny is preferable to autocratic equality. I fear nothing so much as a strict logic applied to politics. If France has been practically prosperous during the last ten years, it is, perhaps, because the apparent absurdity which presides over her affairs is a high practical wisdom; action, instead of speculation, now governs us.

In Russia the spirit of despotism always exerts itself with a mathematical rigour, and the result of such extreme proceeding is an extreme oppression. In beholding this effect of an inflexible policy we feel shocked, and ask ourselves, with a kind of terror, how comes it that there is so little humanity in the actions of man? But to tremble is not to disdain; we never despise that which excites our fear.

In contemplating Petersburg, and in reflecting on the dreadful existence of the inhabitants of this camp of granite, one might be led to doubt the compassion of Deity. There is presented here a mystery that is incomprehensible, and at the same time a greatness which is prodigious. Despotism thus organised becomes an inexhaustible subject for observation and meditation. This colossal empire, which rises before me all at once in the east of Europe —of that Europe, where society is suffering from the decay of all recognised authority—appears to me like a resurrection. I feel as though in the presence of some nation of the Old Testament, and I stop with fear mingled with curiosity before the feet of the ante-diluvian giant.

The first view of society in Russia shows that its arrangements, as contrived by the Russians themselves, are only adapted to their own social system: he must be a Russian who would live in Russia, even though outwardly every thing may appear to pass as in other places. The difference lies in the foundations of things.

It was a review of the fashionable world which I took this evening at the islands. The fashionable world, they say, is the same every where; nevertheless each society has a soul, and this soul will be instructed, like any other, by the fairy which is called civilisation, and which is nothing more than the customs of the age.

This evening all the city of Petersburg, that is to say, the court and its followers, were at the islands; not for the pure pleasure of promenading on a fine day, such a pleasure would appear insipid to the Russian courtiers, but to see the *packet-boat* of the Empress, a spectacle of which they never tire. Here every sovereign is a god, every princess is an Armida or a Cleopatra. The train of these changeable divinities never changes: it is composed of a people ever equally faithful; the reigning prince is always in the fashion with the Russian people.

Nevertheless these submissive men, let them say and do their best, are forced and constrained in their enthusiasm. A people without liberty has instincts, but not sentiments; and their instincts often manifest themselves in an officious and little delicate manner. The emperors of Russia must be overwhelmed with submission: sometimes the incense wearies the idol. In fact, this worship admits of terrible interludes. The Russian government is an absolute monarchy moderated by assassination; and when the prince is not under the influence of lassitude, he is under that of terror. He lives, therefore, between fear and disgust. If the pride of the despot must have slaves, the feelings of the man must yearn for equals; but a czar has no equals: etiquette and jealousy maintain invidious guard around his solitary heart. He is more to be pitied than even his people, especially if he possesses any amiable qualities.

I hear much boast made of the domestic happiness of the Emperor Nicholas, but I see in it the consolations of a superior mind, rather than the proof of real happiness. Consolation is not felicity; on the contrary, the remedy proves the evil; an emperor of Russia must have a heart like other men if he has one at all. So much for the over-lauded private virtues of the Emperor Nicholas.

This evening the Empress, having proceeded from Peterhoff by sea, landed at her pavilion on the islands, where she will remain until the marriage of her daughter, which is to be celebrated to-morrow, in the new winter palace. While she remains at the islands, the leafy shade which surrounds her pavilion serves as a shelter during the day for her regiment of chevalier guards, one of the finest in the army.

We arrived too late to see her leave her sacred vessel, but we found the crowd still under the excitement caused by the rapid transit of the imperial star. The only tumults possible in Russia are those caused by the struggles of flatterers. This evening the human effervescence resembled the agitation of the waves, that continue boiling in the track of some mighty vessel long after she has entered port.

At last, then, I have breathed the air of the court! though the deities who exhale it upon mortals are still unseen.

It is now one o'clock in the morning; the sun is about to rise, and I cannot yet sleep: I will, therefore, finish my night as I commenced it, by writing *without lights.*

Notwithstanding Russian pretensions to elegance, foreigners cannot find in all Petersburg one hotel that is endurable. The great lords bring with them, from the interior of the empire, a suite which is always numerous. Man is their property and their luxury. The moment the valets are left alone in the apartments of their masters, they squat themselves, in oriental fashion, on the seats and couches, which they fill with vermin. These creatures pass into the walls and floors, and in a few days the house becomes infested past all remedy; for the impossibility of airing the houses in winter perpetuates the evil from year to year.

The new imperial palace, built at such cost of life and money, is already full of these vermin. It might be said, that the wretched workmen who were killed in order to ornament with greater celerity the habitation of their master, have avenged their own death by inoculating with their vermin those homicidal walls. If the palace is infected by these nocturnal foes, how should I be able to sleep at Coulons? I have given up the idea; but the clearness of the night consoles me for every thing.

On returning from the islands about midnight, I again went out on foot, and occupied my mind with reviewing the scenes and conversations which had most interested me during the day; of these I will presently give the summary.

My solitary walk led me to the beautiful street called the Perspective Newski. I saw in the twilight, shining from afar, the little pillars of the tower of the Admiralty, surmounted with its lofty metallic spire. The spire of this Christian minaret is more taper than any Gothic steeple. It is gilded all over with the gold of the ducats sent as a present to the emperor Peter I. by the States of the Netherlands.

The revolting dirtiness of this inn-chamber, and the almost fabulous magnificence of that building, present a correct picture of Petersburg. Contrasts are not wanting in a city where Europe and Asia exhibit themselves to each other in mutual spectacle. The people are handsome. The men of pure Slavonian race, brought from the interior by the rich nobles, who either retain them in their service, or permit them for a certain period to carry on various trades in the city, are remarkable for their fair hair, their rosy complexions, and yet more for their perfect profiles, which equal those of Grecian statues. Their eyes have the oval Asiatic shape, with the colouring of the North; they are generally of a light blue, and unite a singular expression of gentleness, grace, and cunning. This expression, always restless, gives to the iris those changing hues, which vary from the green of the serpent, and the grey of the cat, to the black of the gazelle, though the ground colour still remains blue. The mouth, adorned with a gold and silky moustache, is beautifully formed, and the brilliant whiteness of the teeth lights up the whole countenance. The latter are sometimes sharp and pointed, when they resemble those of the tiger, but more commonly their shape is perfectly regular. The costume of these men is always original. It consists, either of the Greek tunic, with a lively-coloured girdle, the Persian robe, or the short Russian pelisse lined with sheepskin, the wool of which is turned outwards or inwards according to the season.

The women of the lower orders are less handsome; but few are met in the streets, and those few have little to attract: they appear degraded and stupified. It is a singular fact, that the men take pains with their dress, and the women neglect it: this is perhaps owing to the former being attached by service to the houses of the nobles. The women have a clumsy carriage; they wear heavy boots, which deform the foot: their figures are without elegance; and their complexions, unlike those of the men, lose all freshness and clearness even while they are yet young. Their little Russian coats, short, and open before, are trimmed with fur, which is almost always hanging in rags. This costume would be pretty if it was less shabby, and if the effect was not generally spoilt by deformity or revolting dirtiness of person. The national head-dress of the Russian women is handsome, but it has become rare; being now only worn, I am told, by nurses, and by the ladies of the court on days of ceremony. It is a species of paste-board tower, gilt, embroidered, and much widened at the top.

The accoutrements of the horses are picturesque, and the horses themselves show speed and blood; but the equipages that I saw this evening at the islands, not excepting those of the highest nobles, were not elegant, nor even clean. This accounts to me for the disorder and carelessness of the servants of the hereditary Grand Duke, and for the clumsiness and wretched varnish of that prince's carriages, which I noticed at Ems. Magnificence on a large scale, a gaudy luxury, gilded trappings, and an air of showy grandeur, are natural to the Russian nobles; but elegance, carefulness, and cleanliness are things unknown. I have listened this evening to several curious traits, illustrative of what we call the slavery of the Russian peasants.

It is difficult for us to form a just idea of the real position of this class of men, who live in the possession of no acknowledged rights, and who yet form the nation. Deprived of every thing by law, they are still not so much degraded morally as they are socially. They have good mental capacity, and sometimes even elevation of character; but, nevertheless, the principle which chiefly actuates their conduct through life is cunning. No one has a right to reproach them with this too natural consequence of their situation. Ever on their guard against their masters, who are constantly acting towards them with open and shameless bad faith, they compensate themselves by artifice for what they suffer through injustice. The relations between the peasantry and the owner of the soil, as well as their less immediate relations with the country, that is to say, with the Emperor, would alone be a subject worthy of a long sojourn in the interior of Russia.

In many parts of the empire the peasants believe themselves to belong to the earth, a condition of existence which appears to them natural, even when they have difficulty in understanding how man can be the property of man. In many other countries the peasants believe that the earth belongs to them. Such are the most happy, if they are not the most submissive, of slaves. Not unfrequently the peasants, when about to be sold, send a deputation to some far off master, of whose character for kindness reports have reached them, imploring him to buy them, their lands, their children, and their cattle; and if this lord, thus celebrated for his gentleness, (I do not say his justice, for the sentiment of justice is unknown in Russia,)—if this desirable lord has no money, they provide him with it, in order to be sure of belonging only to him. The benevolent lord, therefore, buys his new serfs with their own money; after which he exempts them from taxes for a certain number of years: thus indemnifying them for the price of their bodies, which they have paid to him in advance, by furnishing the sum that represents the value of the domain to which they belong, and of which they have, as it were, obliged him to become the proprietor.

The greatest misfortune which can happen to these vegetating men is to see their native fields sold. They are always sold with the glebe, and the only advantage they have hitherto derived from the modern ameliorations of the law, is, that they cannot now be sold without it. This provision is, however, notoriously evaded. Instead, for instance, of selling an entire estate, a few acres are often sold with one or two hundred men per acre. If the government becomes aware of such collusion it punishes the guilty parties, but it has seldom an opportunity of interfering; for between the crime and the supreme authority, that is, the Emperor, are a whole multitude of people interested in concealing and perpetuating abuses. The proprietors suffer as much as the serfs from this state of things, especially those whose affairs are deranged. Estates are difficult to sell; so difficult, that a man who owes debts and is willing to pay them, is finally obliged to have recourse to the Imperial Bank, where he borrows the sum which he requires, the Bank taking his property in mortgage. By this means the Emperor becomes treasurer and creditor of all the Russian nobility; and the latter, thus curbed by supreme power, are placed in a situation which makes the fulfilment of their duties towards the people impossible.

On a certain day a nobleman declares his intention of selling an estate. The news of this project throws the country into alarm. The peasants send to their lord a deputation of the elders of their village, who throw themselves at his feet, imploring with tears that they may not be sold. "It must be," replies the lord: "I cannot conscientiously augment the tax which my peasants pay, and nevertheless I am not rich enough to keep an estate which scarcely brings me in any thing."

"Is that all?" cry the deputies; "we then are wealthy enough to enable you to keep us." Whereupon, of their own free will, they raise their rent to double the amount which they have paid from time immemorial." Other peasants, with less gentleness, and greater craft of character, revolt against their masters, solely with the hope of becoming serfs of the crown. This is the highest ambition of the Russian peasant.

To emancipate suddenly such men would be to set the country on fire. The moment that the serfs, separated from the land to which they are attached, were to see it sold, let, or cultivated without them, they would rise in a mass, crying that they were despoiled of their goods.

It is but a short time ago that, in a remote village which was on fire, the peasants, who complained of the tyranny of their master, availed themselves of the disorder they had perhaps caused purposely, to seize his person, impale it, and roast it in the flames of the conflagration. For such acts the Emperor usually orders the transportation of the entire village to Siberia. This is called in Petersburg *peopling Asia.*

When I reflect upon these, and a thousand other cruelties, which, with greater or less secrecy, take place daily in the bosom of this immense empire, where the distances equally favour oppression and revolt, I am ready to conceive a hatred against the land, the government, and the entire population: an indefinable sense of uneasiness takes possession of me, and I think only of flying.

The fortune of a wealthy man is here computed by the heads of peasants. The man who is not free is coined; he is equivalent (on an average) to ten roubles a year to his proprietor, who is called free because he is the owner of serfs. There are districts where each peasant brings three and four times this sum to his master. In Russia the human money alters in value, as, with us, the land, which doubles in price when markets can be opened for its produce. Here I involuntarily pass my time in calculating how many families it has taken to pay for a bonnet, a shawl, or a rose tree: nothing appears to me as it does elsewhere; every thing seems tainted with blood. The number of human beings condemned to suffer, even unto death, in order to furnish the requisite quantity of stuff which forms the dress of some lovely woman at court, occupies my thoughts more than all her finery or her beauty. Absorbed in the labour of this melancholy computation, I feel myself growing unjust. The most charming face reminds me, in spite of my efforts to banish such ideas, of those caricatures of Bonaparte which were spread all over Europe in 1815. At a little distance the colossal statue of the Emperor appeared a simple likeness, but, on inspecting it more nearly, each feature was found to be composed of mutilated corpses.

In all countries the poor work for the rich, who pay them for their labour; but these poor are not folded for life in some enclosure like mere herds of cattle; and, though obliged to toil at the labour which daily provides their children with bread, they at least enjoy a semblance of liberty; now semblance, or appearance, is almost every thing to a being whose views are limited, but whose imagination is boundless. With us the hireling has the right of changing his employers, his residence, and even his profession, but the Russian serf is a chattel of his lord's; enlisted from birth to death in the service, his life represents to this proprietor a part and parcel of the sum necessary to supply the caprices and fantasies of fashion. Assuredly, in a state thus constituted, luxury is no longer innocent. All communities in which a middle class of society does not exist, ought to proscribe luxury as a scandal, for in well-organised lands, it is the profits which this class draws from the vanity of the superior classes which produce general opulence. If, as is anticipated, Russia should become a land of industrial arts, the relations between the serf and the owner of the soil will be modified, and a population of independent dealers and artisans will rise up between the nobles and the peasants, but at present the commerce of the land is scarcely born; the manufacturers, merchants, and tradesmen, are almost all Germans.

It is here only too easy to be deceived by the appearances of civilisation. If you look to the court and the people who are its votaries, you may suppose yourself among a nation far advanced in social culture and in political economy; but when you reflect on the relations which exist between the different classes of society, when you observe how small the number of these classes—finally, when you examine attentively the groundwork of manners and of things—you perceive the existence of a real barbarism, scarcely disguised under a magnificence which is revolting.

I do not reproach the Russians for being what they are, what I blame in them is, their pretending to be what we are. They are still uncultivated: this state would at least allow room for hope; but I see them incessantly occupied with the desire of mimicking other nations, and this they do after the true manner of monkeys, caricaturing what they copy. They thus appear to me spoilt for the savage state, and yet wanting in the requisites of civilisation; and the terrible words of Voltaire or of Diderot, now forgotten in France, recur to my mind—"The Russians have rotted before they have ripened."

At Petersburg every thing has an air of opulence, grandeur, and magnificence; but if we should by this show of things judge of the reality we should find ourselves strangely deceived. Generally, the first effect of civilisation is to render what may be called, *material* life easy; but here every thing is difficult:—a cunning apathy is the secret of existence.

If you wish to ascertain precisely what is to be seen in this great city, and if Schnitzler does not satisfy you, you will find no

other guide*: no bookseller has on sale a complete directory to
the curiosities of Petersburg: either the well informed men whom
you question have an interest in not answering you, or they have
something else to do. The Emperor, his health, his movements,
the project with which he is ostensibly occupied, such are the
only subjects worthy of the thoughts of a Russian who thinks at
all. The catechism of the court is the only necessary knowledge.
All take pleasure in rendering themselves agreeable to their master, by hiding some corner of truth from the eyes of travellers. No
one has any idea of gratifying the curious; on the contrary, they
love to deceive them by false data: it requires the talents of a
great critic to travel to advantage in Russia. Under despotism,
curiosity is synonymous with indiscretion. The empire is the emperor.

And yet this frightful extent of greatness was not sufficient for
the Czar Peter. That man, not content with being the reason of
his people, would also become their conscience. The sovereign
who did not shrink before such a responsibility, and who, notwithstanding his long apparent, or real hesitation, finally rendered himself culpable of so enormous an usurpation, has inflicted more evil on the world by this single outrage against the
prerogatives of the priests, and the religious liberty of man, than
he has conferred benefit on Russia by all his warlike and political
talents, and his genius for the arts of industry. This emperor, type
and model of the empire, and of the emperors in all ages, was a
singular union of the great and the minute. With a lust of power
grasping as that of the most cruel tyrants of any age or nation, he
united the ingenuity of the artisan in a degree that made him the
rival of the best mechanics of his times; a sovereign scrupulously
terrible, an eagle and an ant, a lion and a beaver:—this monarch,
dreadful during life, now imposes himself on posterity as a species
of saint, and tyrannises over the judgments, as he formerly tyrannised over the acts of men. To pass an impartial opinion upon
him is at the present time a sacrilege which is not without danger,
even for a stranger, in Russia. I brave this danger every moment
of the day, for of all yokes, the most insupportable to me is that

* Schnitzler is author of the best work on Russian statistics that has been written.

which imposes the necessity of admiring.* In Russia, power, all unlimited as it is, entertains an extreme dread of censure, or even of free speech. An oppressor is of all others the man who most fears the truth; he only escapes ridicule by the terror and mystery with which he environs himself. Hence it is that there must be no speaking of persons here: one must not allude to the *maladies* of which the Emperors Peter III. and Paul I. died, any more than to the clandestine amours that certain malevolent persons have ascribed to the reigning emperor. The amusements of this prince are viewed only as relaxations from the cares of greatness. This once known, and with whatever consequences they may be attended to certain families, one must profess ignorance of them under pain of being accused of the greatest of all crimes in the eyes of a people composed of slaves and diplomatists—the crime of indiscretion.

I am impatient to see the Empress. She is said to be a charming, though at the same time a frivolous and haughty personage. It needs both hauteur and levity to support an existence like that of hers. She neither interferes with nor informs herself respecting any public affairs: knowledge is worse than useless, where there is no power to act upon it. The Empress does as the other subjects of the Emperor: all who are born Russians, or would live in Russia, must make silence upon public affairs the motto of their life. Secret conversations would be very interesting, but who dares indulge in them? To reflect, and to discern would be to render one's self suspected.

M. de Repnin governed the empire and the Emperor: he has been out of favour for *two years,* and for *two years* Russia has not heard his name pronounced, though that name was previously in every body's mouth. In one day he fell from the pinnacle of power into the lowest depth of obscurity. No one dared to remember that he was living, nor even to believe that he ever had

---

* In the *History of Russia and of Peter the Great,* by M. le Général Comte de Ségur, we read as follows, (the Strelitz are the parties referred to):—"Peter himself interrogated these criminals by the torture, after which, in imitation of Ivan the Tyrant, he acted as their judge and their executioner. . . . Drunk with wine and blood, the glass in one hand, the axe in the other, in one single hour twenty successive libations marked the fall of twenty heads of the Strelitz, which the emperor struck off, piquing himself all the while on his horrible address."

lived. In Russia, on the day that a minister falls from favour, his friends become deaf and blind. A man is as it were buried the moment he appears to be disgraced. Russia does not know to-day if the minister who governed her yesterday exists. Under Louis the XV. the banishment of M. de Choiseul was a triumph; in Russia the retirement of M. de Repnin is a funeral.

To whom will the people one day appeal, from the mute servility of the great? What explosion of vengeance is not the conduct of this cringing aristocracy preparing against the autocratic power? What are the duties of the Russian noblesse? To adore the Emperor, and to render themselves accomplices in the abuse of sovereign power, that they themselves may continue to oppress the people. Is such the position that Providence has ordained them to occupy in the economy of this vast empire? They fill its posts of honour. What have they done to merit them? In the history of Russia, no one except the Emperor has performed his part. The nobles, the clergy, and all the other classes of society, have each failed in their own. An oppressed people have always deserved the ills under which they suffer. Tyranny is the work of the nation. Either the civilised world will, before another fifty years, pass anew under the yoke of barbarians, or Russia will undergo a revolution more terrible than that, the effects of which we are still feeling in Western Europe.

I can perceive that I am feared here, which I attribute to its being known that I write under the influence of my convictions. No stranger can set foot in this country without immediately feeling that he is weighed and judged. "This is a sincere man," they think, "therefore he must be dangerous." Under the government of the lawyers* a sincere man is only useless!

"An indefinite hatred of despotism reigns in France," they say, "but it is exaggerated and unenlightened, therefore we will brave it. The day, however, that a traveller, who convinces because he himself believes, shall tell the real abuses, which he cannot fail to discover among us, we shall be seen as we really are. France now barks at us without knowing us; when she does know us, she will bite."

* Alluding to France.—*Trans.*

The Russians, no doubt, do me too great honour by this inquietude; which, notwithstanding their profound dissimulation, they cannot conceal from me. I do not know whether I shall publish what I think of their country; but I do know that they only do themselves justice in fearing the truths that I could publish.

The Russians have every thing in name, and nothing in reality. They have civilisation, society, literature, the drama, the arts and sciences—but they have no physicians. In case of illness you must either prescribe for yourself, or call in a foreign practitioner. If you send for the nearest doctor you are a dead man, for medical art in Russia is in its infancy. With the exception of the physician of the Emperor, who, I am told, is, though a Russian, learned, the only doctors who would not assassinate you are the Germans attached to the service of the princes. But the princes live in a state of perpetual motion. It is often impossible to ascertain where they may be; or, when that is known, to send twenty, forty, or sixty versts (two French leagues are equal to seven versts) after them. There are, therefore, practically speaking, no physicians in Russia. Should even the physician be sought at the known residence of his prince, and not be found there, there is no further hope. "The doctor is not here." No other answer can be obtained. In Russia every thing serves to show that reserve is the favourite virtue of the land. An opportunity for appearing discreet cannot but offer to those who know how to seize it, and what Russian would not do himself credit at so little cost? The projects and the movements of the great, and of those attached to their persons by so confidential an employ as that of physician, ought not to be known, unless officially declared, to persons who are born courtiers, and with whom obedience is a passion. Here mystery supplies the place of merit.

The most able of these doctors of the princes are far inferior to the least known among the medical men of our hospitals. The skill of the most learned practitioners will rust at court: nothing can supply the place of the experience gained by the bedside of the sick. I could read the secret memoirs of a Russian court physician with great interest, but I would not follow his prescriptions. Such men would make better chroniclers than doctors. When, therefore, a stranger falls sick among this *soi-disant* civilised people, his best plan is to consider himself among savages, and to leave every thing to nature.

On returning to my hotel this evening I found a letter, which has very agreeably surprised me. Through the influence of our ambassador, I am to be admitted to-morrow to the imperial chapel, to see the marriage of the Grand Duchess.

To appear at court before having been presented, is contrary to all the laws of etiquette, and I was far from hoping for such a favour. The Emperor has, however, granted it. Count Woronzoff, Grand Master of the Ceremonies, without pre-informing me, for he did not wish to amuse me with a false hope, had despatched a courier to Peterhoff, which is ten leagues from Petersburg, to solicit his Majesty in my favour. This kind consideration has not been unavailing. The Emperor has given permission for me to be present at the marriage, in the chapel of the court, and I am to be presented, without ceremony, at the ball on the same evening.

❖

CHAPTER XI

❖

I am writing on the 14th of July, 1839, fifty years after the taking of the Bastille, which event occurred on the 14th of July, 1789. The coincidence of these dates is curious. The marriage of the son of Eugene de Beauharnais has taken place on the same day as that which marked the commencement of our revolutions, precisely fifty years ago.

I have just returned from the palace, after having witnessed, in the Imperial chapel, all the Greek ceremonies of the marriage of the Grand Duchess Marie with the Duke de Leuchtenberg.

I will endeavour to describe in detail, but in the first place I must speak of the Emperor.

The predominant expression of his countenance is that of a restless severity, which strikes a beholder at the first glance; and, in spite of the regularity of his features, conveys by no means a pleasant impression. Physiognomists pretend, with much reason, that the hardness of the heart injures the beauty of the countenance. Nevertheless, this expression in the Emperor Nicholas appears to be the result of experience rather than the work of nature. By what long and cruel sufferings must not a man have been tortured, when his countenance excites fear, notwithstanding the voluntary confidence that noble features inspire.

A man charged with the management and direction, in its most minute details, of some immense machine, incessantly fears the derangement of one or other of its various parts. He who obeys suffers only according to the precise measure of the evil inflicted: he who commands, suffers first as other men suffer, and afterwards that common measure of evil is multiplied a hundred fold for him by the workings of imagination and self-love. Responsibility is the punishment of absolute power.

If he be the *primum mobile* of all minds, he becomes the centre also of all griefs: the more he is dreaded the more he is to be pitied.

He to whom is accorded unlimited rule sees, even in the common occurrences of life, the spectre of revolt. Persuaded that his rights are sacred, he recognises no bounds to them but those of his own intelligence and will, and he is, therefore, subject to constant annoyance. An unlucky fly, buzzing in the Imperial palace during a ceremony, mortifies the Emperor: the independence of nature appears to him a bad example: every thing which he cannot subject to his arbitrary laws becomes in his eyes as a soldier, who in the heat of battle revolts against his officer. The Emperor of Russia is a military chief, and every day with him is a day of battle.

Nevertheless, at times, some gleams of softness temper the imperious looks of this monarch, and then the expression of affability reveals all the native beauty of his classic features. In the heart of the husband and the father, humanity triumphs for a moment over the policy of the prince. When the sovereign rests from his task of imposing the yoke upon his subjects, he appears happy. This combat between the primitive dignity of the man and the affected gravity of the sovereign appears to me worthy the attention of an observer: it occupied mine the greater part of the time I passed in the chapel.

The Emperor is above the usual height by half a head; his figure is noble, although a little stiff: he has practised from his youth the Russian custom of girding the body above the loins to such a degree as to push up the stomach into the chest, which produces an unnatural swelling or extension about the ribs, that is as injurious to the health as it is ungraceful in appearance.

This voluntary deformity destroys all freedom of movement, impairs the elegance of the shape, and imparts an air of constraint to the whole person. They say that when the Emperor loosens his dress, the viscera, suddenly giving way, are disturbed for a moment in their equilibrium, which produces an extraordinary prostration of strength. The bowels may be displaced—they cannot be got rid of.

The Emperor has a Grecian profile—the forehead high, but receding; the nose straight, and perfectly formed; the mouth very finely cut; the face, which in shape is rather a long oval, is noble; the whole air military, and rather German than Slavonic. His carriage and his attitudes are naturally imposing. He expects always to be gazed at, and never for a moment forgets that he is so. It may even be said that he likes this homage of the eyes.

He passes the greater part of his existence in the open air, at reviews, or in rapid journeys. During summer the shade of his military hat draws across his forehead an oblique line, which marks the action of the sun upon the skin. This line produces a singular effect, but it is not disagreeable, as the cause is at once perceived.

In examining attentively the fine person of this individual on whose will hangs the fate of so many others, I have remarked with involuntary pity that he cannot smile at the same time with the eyes and the mouth, a want of harmony which denotes perpetual constraint; and which makes one remember with regret that easy natural grace, so conspicuous in the less regular but more agreeable countenance of his brother, the Emperor Alexander. The latter, always pleasing, had yet, at times, an assumed manner. The Emperor Nicholas is more sincere; but he has an habitual expression of severity, which sometimes gives the idea of harshness and inflexibility. If, however, he is less fascinating, he is more firm than his late brother: but then it must be added, that he has also a proportionately greater need of firmness. Graceful courtesy insures authority, by removing the desire of resistance. This judicious economy in the exercise of power is a secret of which the Emperor Nicholas is ignorant; he is one who desires to be obeyed, where others desire to be loved.

The figure of the Empress is very elegant; and, though she is extremely thin, I find an indefinable grace about her whole person. Her mien, far from being haughty, as I had been informed, is expressive of an habitual resignation. On entering the chapel she was much affected, and I thought she was going to faint. A nervous convulsion agitated every feature of her face, and caused her head slightly to shake. Her soft blue, but rather sunken eyes, told of deep sufferings supported with angelic calmness. Her look, full of feeling, has the more power, from its seeming unconscious of possessing any. Faded before her time, and so weak, that it is said she cannot live long, her appearance gives the idea of a passing shadow, or of something that belongs no more to earth. She has never recovered from the anguish she had to undergo on the day of her assession to the throne, and conjugal duty has consumed the rest of her life.

She has given too many idols to Russia,—too many children to the Emperor. "Exhausting herself in Grand Dukes! What a destiny!" said a great Polish lady, who did not think herself obliged to speak reverently with her lips of what she hated in her heart.

Every one sees the state of the Empress, but no one mentions it. The Emperor loves her: when ill in bed he attends her himself, watches by her bed-side, and prepares and administers her food or medicine. No sooner is she better, than he destroys her health with the excitement of fêtes and journeys; but the moment that danger is again apprehended, he renounces all his projects. Of the precautions that might prevent evil he has a horror. Wife, children, servants, relations, favorites,—all in Russia must follow in the imperial vortex, and smile on till they die. All must force themselves to conform to the wish of the sovereign, which wish alone forms the destiny of all. The nearer any one is placed to the imperial sun, the more he is a slave to the glory attached to his situation. The Empress is dying under the weight of this slavery.

Every one here knows this, but no one speaks of it; for it is a general rule never to utter a word which can excite much interest: neither he who speaks, nor he who listens, must allow it to be seen that the subject of conversation merits continued attention, or awakens any warm feelings. All the resources of language are exhausted, in order to banish from discourse idea and sentiment, without, however, appearing to repress them, which would be *gauche.* The excessive constraint which results from this prodigious labour,—prodigious especially through the art with which it is concealed,—embitters the life of the Russians. Such a torment serves as an expiation for the men who voluntarily deprive themselves of the two greatest gifts of God—mind, and its organ, speech; in other words, thought and liberty.

The more I see of Russia, the more I approve the conduct of the Emperor in forbidding his subjects to travel, and in rendering access to his own country difficult to foreigners. The political system of Russia could not survive twenty years' free communication with the west of Europe. Listen not to the fictions of the Russians: they mistake pomp for elegance, luxury for politeness, a powerful police, and a dread of government, for the fundamental principles of society. According to their notions discipline is civilisation. Notwithstanding all their pretensions to good manners, their superficial education, their precocious corruption, and their facility of comprehending and appropriating the materialism of life, the Russians are not yet civilised. They are enrolled and drilled Tartars, and nothing more.

I wish it not to be inferred that they are therefore to be despised: the more their mental rudeness is concealed under the softer forms of social intercourse, the more formidable I consider them. As regards civilisation, they have been hitherto contented with exhibiting its appearance; but if ever they should find an opportunity of revenging their real inferiority upon us, we shall have to make a tremendous expiation for our advantages.

This morning, after dressing myself in haste, in order to repair to the imperial chapel, I entered my carriage, and followed that of the French ambassador, through the squares and streets that led to the palace, examining with curiosity all that presented itself in the way. The troops which I observed in the approaches to the palace were less magnificent than I had been led to expect, though the horses were certainly superb. The immense square which separates the dwelling of the sovereign from the rest of the city, was crossed in various directions by lines of carriages, servants in livery, and soldiers in a variety of uniforms. That of the cossacks is the most remarkable. Notwithstanding the concourse, the square, so vast is its extent, was not crowded.

In new states there is a void every where; but this is more

especially the case when the government is absolute: it is the absence of liberty which creates solitude, and spreads sadness.

The equipages of the courtiers looked well, without being really elegant. The carriages, badly painted, and still more badly varnished, are of a heavy make. They are drawn by four horses, whose traces are immoderately long. A coachman drives the wheel horses; a little postillion, clothed in the long Persian robe similar to that of the coachman, rides on a fore horse, seated upon, or rather in, a hollow saddle, raised before and behind, and stuffed like a pillow. This child, named, I believe, after the German the Vorreiter,* and in Russia the *Faleiter,* is always perched upon the right, or off-side leader; the contrary custom prevails in all other countries, where the postillion is mounted on the left, in order to have the right hand free to guide his other horse. The spirit and power of the Russian horses, which have all some blood, if all have not beauty, the dexterity of the coachmen, and the richness of their dress, greatly set off the carriages, and produce altgether an effect which, if not so elegant, is more striking and splendid than that of the equipages of the other courts of Europe.

I was occupied with a crowd of reflections which the novelty of the objects around me suggested, when my carriage stopped under a grand peristyle, where I descended among a crowd of gilded courtiers, who were attended by vassals as barbaric in appearance as in reality. The costume of the servants is almost as brilliant as that of their masters. The Russians have a great taste for splendour, and in court ceremonies this taste is more especially displayed.

In descending from the carriage rather hastily, lest I should be separated from the persons under whose guidance I had placed myself, my foot struck with some force against the curb stone, which had caught my spur. At the moment I paid little attention to the circumstance; but great was my distress when immediately afterwards I perceived that the spur had come off, and, what was still worse, that it had carried with it the heel of the boot also. Having to appear in this dilapidated state, for the first time,

* The fore rider.

before a man said to be as precise as he is great and powerful, seemed to me a real misfortune. The Russians are prone to ridicule; and the idea of affording them a subject for laughter at my first presentation was peculiarly unpleasant.

What was to be done? To return under the peristyle to search for the remnant of my boot was quite useless. To quit the French ambassador and return home would, in itself, be the way to create a *scene*. On the other hand, to show myself as I was, would ruin me in the estimation of the Emperor and his courtiers; and I have no philosophy against ridicule to which I voluntarily expose myself. The troubles that pleasure draws one into at a thousand leagues from home, appear to me insupportable. It was so easy not to go at all, that to go awkwardly were unpardonable. I might hope to conceal myself in the crowd; but, I repeat, there never is a crowd in Russia; and least of all upon a staircase like that of the new winter palace, which resembles some decoration in the opera of Gustavus. This palace is, I believe, the largest and most magnificent of all existing royal or imperial residences.

I felt my natural timidity increase with the confusion which this ludicrous accident produced, until, at length, fear itself supplied me with courage, and I began to limp as lightly as I could across the immense saloons and stately galleries, the length and strong light of which I inwardly cursed. The Russians are cool, quick-sighted quizzes, possessing, like all the ambitious, little delicacy of feeling. They are, besides, mistrustful of strangers, whose judgment they fear, because they believe we have but little good feeling towards them. This prejudice renders them censorious and secretly caustic, although outwardly they appear hospitable and polite.

I reached, at length, but not without difficulty, the further end of the imperial chapel. There all was forgotten, even myself and my foolish embarrassment; indeed, in this place the crowd was more dense, and no one could see what was wanting to my equipment. The novelty of the spectacle that awaited me restored my coolness and self-possession. I blushed for the vexation which my vanity as a disconcerted courtier had produced, and with the resumption of my part as simple traveller in the scene, recovered the composure of a philosophic observer.

One word more upon my costume. It had been the subject of grave consultation: some of the young people attached to the French legation had advised the habit of the national guard. I feared, however, that this uniform would displease the Emperor, and decided upon that of a staff officer, with the epaulettes of a lieutenant-colonel, which are those of my rank.

I had been warned that the dress would appear new, and that it would become, on the part of the princes of the imperial family, and of the emperor himself, the subject of numerous questions which might embarrass me. Hitherto, however, none have had time to occupy themselves with so small an affair.

The Greek marriage rites are long and imposing. Every thing is symbolical in the Eastern church. It seemed to me that the splendours of religion shed a lustre over the solemnities of the court.

The walls and the roof of the chapel, the habiliments of the priests and of their attendants, all glittered with gold and jewels. There are riches enough here to astonish the least poetical imagination. The spectacle vies with the most fanciful description in the Arabian Nights; it is like the poetry of Lalla Rookh, or the Marvellous Lamp,—that Oriental poetry in which sensation prevails over sentiment and thought.

The imperial chapel is not of large dimensions. It was filled with the representatives of all the sovereigns of Europe, and almost of Asia; by strangers like myself, admitted in the suite of the diplomatic corps: by the wives of the ambassadors, and by the great officers of the court. A balustrade separated us from the circular enclosure, within which the altar was raised. This altar is like a low square table. Places in the choir were reserved for the imperial family: at the moment of our arrival they were vacant.

I have seen few things that could compare with the magnificence and solemnity which attended the entrance of the Emperor into this chapel, blazing with gold and jewels. He appeared, advancing with the Empress, and followed by the court retinue. All eyes were immediately fixed upon him, and his family, among whom the betrothed pair shone conspicuously. A marriage of inclination celebrated in broidered habiliments, and in a place so pompous, was a novelty which crowned the interest of the scene.

This was repeated by every one around me; for my own part I cannot give credit to the marvel, nor can I avoid seeing a politic motive in all that is said and done here. The Emperor perhaps deceives himself, and believes that he is performing acts of paternal tenderness, while in the bottom of his heart he may be secretly influenced in his choice by the hope of personal advantage.

It is with ambition as with avarice; misers always calculate, not excepting even the moment when they believe they are yielding to disinterested sentiments.

Although the court was numerous, and the chapel small, there was no confusion. I stood in the midst of the *corps diplomatique*, near the balustrade which separated us from the sanctuary. We were not so crowded, as to be unable to distinguish the features and movements of each of the personages, whom duty or curiosity had there brought together. No disorder interrupted the respectful silence that was maintained throughout the assembly. A brilliant sun illuminated the interior of the chapel, where the temperature had, I understood, risen to thirty degrees.* We observed in the suite of the Emperor, habited in a long robe of gold tissue, and a pointed bonnet, likewise adorned with gold embroidery, a Tartar Khan, who is half tributary, and half independent of Russia. This petty sovereign had come to pray the Emperor of all the Russians to admit among *his pages* a son, twelve years old, whom he had brought to Petersburg, hoping thus to secure for the child a suitable destiny. The presence of this declining power, served as a contrast to that of the successful monarch, and reminded me of the triumphal pomps of Rome.

The first ladies of the Russian court, and the wives of the ambassadors of the other courts, among whom I recognised Mademoiselle Sontag, now Countess de Rossi, graced with their presence the circumference of the chapel. At the lower end, which terminated in a brilliant, painted rotunda, were ranged the whole of the imperial family. The gilded ceiling, reflecting the ardent rays of the sun, formed a species of crown around the heads of the sovereigns and their children. The attire and diamonds of the ladies shone with a magic splendour in the midst of

* Of Réaumur.—*Trans.*

❖ 143 ❖

all the treasures of Asia, which beamed upon the walls of the sanctuary, where royal magnificence seemed to challenge the majesty of the God whom it honoured without forgetting its own.

All this gorgeous display is wonderful, especially to us, if we recall the time, not distant, when the marriage of the daughter of a Czar would have been scarcely heard of in Europe, and when Peter I. declared, that he had a right to leave his crown to whomsoever he pleased. How great a progress for so short a period!

When we reflect on the diplomatic and other conquests of this power, which not long since was considered as of but little importance in the civilised world, we are led to ask ourselves if that which we see is not a dream. The Emperor himself appeared to me not much accustomed to what was passing before him; for he was continually leaving his prayers, and slipping from one side to the other, in order to remedy the omissions of etiquette among his children, or the clergy. This proves, that in Russia, even the court has not yet finished its education. His son-in-law was not placed quite conveniently, whereupon he made him shift his position by about two feet. The Grand Duchess, the priests themselves, and all the great functionaries of the court seemed to be governed by his minute but supreme directions. I felt that it would have been more dignified to leave things as they were, and I could have wished that when once in the chapel, God only had been thought of, and each man had been left to acquit himself of his functions, without his master so scrupulously rectifying each little fault of religious discipline, or of court ceremonial: but in this singular country the absence of liberty is seen everywhere: it is found even at the foot of the altar. Here the spirit of Peter the Great governs the minds of all.

During the mass at a Greek marriage, there is a moment when the betrothed drink together out of the same cup. Afterwards, accompanied by the officiating priest, they pass three times round the altar, hand in hand, to signify the conjugal union, and the fidelity which should attend their walk through life. All these acts are the more imposing, as they recall to mind the customs of the primitive church.

These ceremonies being ended, a crown was next held for a considerable time over the head of each of the newly-married

pair; the crown of the Grand Duchess, by her brother the hereditary Grand Duke, the position of which the Emperor himself
(once more leaving his prayer desk) took care to adjust, with a
mixture of good nature and of minute attention that would be
difficult to describe.

The crown of the Duke of Leuchtenberg was held by the
Count de Pahlen, Russian ambassador at Paris, and son of the
too celebrated and too zealous friend of Alexander. This recollection banished from the conversation, and perhaps from the
thoughts, of the Russians of these days, did not cease to occupy
my mind the whole time that the Count de Pahlen, with the
noble simplicity which is natural to him, was engaged in the performance of an act envied, doubtless, by all who aspired to court
favour. That act was an invocation of the protection of heaven,
upon the head of the husband of Paul the First's grandchild! The
strange coincidence most probably occurred to no one except
myself. It appears that tact and propriety are here necessary only
for those who possess no power. Had the recollection of the fact
which occupied my mind occurred to that of the Emperor, he
would have commissioned some other individual to hold the
crown over the head of his son-in-law. But in a country where
they neither read nor speak of public affairs, nothing has less to
do with the events of to-day, than the history of yesterday; power
consequently sometimes acts inadvertently, and commits over-
sights which prove that it sleeps in a security not always well
advised. Russian policy is not shackled in its march either by
opinions or actions; the favour of the sovereign is every thing. So
long as it lasts it supplies the want of merit, of virtue, and even of
innocence in the man on whom it is lavished; and, in the same
manner, when it is withdrawn, it deprives him of every thing.

Every one contemplated with a species of anxious interest the
immovableness of the arms which sustained the two crowns. The
scene lasted for a considerable time, and must have been very
fatiguing for the performers. The young bride is extremely graceful; her eyes are blue, and her fair complexion has all the delicate
freshness of early youth: openness and intelligence united form
the predominant expression of her face. This princess and her
sister, the Grand Duchess Olga, appear to me the two most beau-

tiful persons at the Russian court:—happy unison of the advantages of rank and the gifts of nature.

When the officiating bishop presented the married pair to their august parents, the latter embraced them with a warmth that was affecting. The moment afterwards the Empress threw herself into the arms of her husband—an effusion of tenderness which would have better suited a chamber than a chapel: but in Russia the sovereigns are at home every where, not excepting the house of God. The tender emotion, however, of the Empress appeared altogether involuntary, and therefore did not shock the feelings. Woe to those who could find any thing to ridicule in the emotions produced by true and natural feeling! Such exhibitions of sensibility are sympathetic. German kindheartedness is never lost; there must indeed be soul when feeling is allowed to betray itself even upon the throne.

Before the benediction, two doves were, according to custom, let loose in the chapel; they quickly settled on a gilded cornice which jutted out directly over the heads of the wedded pair; and there they never ceased billing and cooing during the whole mass. Pigeons are well off in Russia: they are revered as the sacred symbol of the Holy Ghost, and it is forbidden to kill them: fortunately the flavour of their flesh is not liked by the Russians.

The Duke de Leuchtenberg is a tall, well-made young man, but there is nothing *distingué* in his features. His eyes are handsome, but his mouth projects and is not well formed. His figure is good without being noble: a uniform becomes him, and supplies that want of grace that may be observed in his person. He looks more like a smart sub-lieutenant than a prince. Not one relation on his side had come to St. Petersburg to assist at the ceremony.

During the mass he appeared singularly impatient to be alone with his wife; and the eyes of the whole assembly were directed, by a kind of spontaneous sympathy, towards the two pigeons perched above the altar.

I possess neither the cynicism nor the talent for description of St. Simon, nor yet the ingenious humour of the writers of the good old times; I must therefore here dispense with some details that might prove rather amusing to the reader. In the age of Louis XIV. they exercised a liberty of language, which was fos-

tered by the certainty of there being no hearers, except those
who all lived and spoke in the same manner: there was then
plenty of society, but no public. In these times, there is a public,
but no society. With our fathers, every narrator in his own circle
could state facts without reference to consequences: in the present day, all classes being mixed, there is a lack of benevolence,
and therefore of security. Freedom of expression would appear
mauvais ton to people who have not all learnt their French from
the same vocabulary. A certain degree of plebeian sensitiveness
has insinuated itself into the language of the best society in
France; the greater the number whom we address, the greater the
necessity for assuming a grave and precise mode of speaking; a
nation demands more respect than an intimate society, however
refined that society may be. As regards decorum in language, a
crowd is more precise than a court. Freedom of speech becomes
inconvenient in proportion to the number of listeners. Such are
the reasons which deter me from relating that which, this morning in the Imperial Chapel, brought a smile on the face of more
than one grave personage, and, perhaps, more than one virtuous
lady. But I could not pass over quite silently an incident which
singularly contrasted with the majesty of the scene, and the necessity for gravity imposed upon the spectators.

At one part of the Greek marriage ceremony every one is
obliged to kneel. Before prostrating himself with the others, the
Emperor cast around the assembly a searching, and by no means
pleasing glance. It appeared as though he would assure himself
that no one remained standing—a superfluous precaution: for
though there were among the foreigners present both Catholics
and Protestants, it never, I am certain, entered into the thoughts
of one not to conform, externally, to all the ceremonies of the
Greek church.*

---

* The fear of the emperor, is in some measure explained by an account sent me
from Rome, in the month of January, 1843, by one of the most veracious individuals
whom I know.

"The last day in December I was at the Church del Gesu; it was decorated in a
magnificent manner, the organs were playing beautiful symphonies, and all the most
distinguished people in Rome were present. Two chairs were placed on the left of the
superb altar for the Grand Duchess Marie daughter of the Emperor of Russia, and
her husband the Duke of Leuchtenberg. They arrived attended by their suite and

The possibility of a doubt on such a point, justifies some of my previous observations, and authorises my repeating that a restless severity has become the habitual expression of the physiognomy of the Emperor.

In these times, when revolt pervades, as it were, the very air, perhaps autocracy itself begins to fear lest some insult should be offered to its power. This idea would clash disagreeably, and even terrifically, with the notions which it preserves of its rights. Absolute power is most to be feared when it is itself under the influence of fear. In noticing the nervous affection, the weakness, and the emaciated frame of the Empress, I called to mind what this interesting woman must have suffered during the revolt at the time of her accession to the throne. Heroism repays itself; it is by fortitude, but a fortitude that exhausts life.

I have already said that every body had fallen on their knees, and, last of all, the Emperor; the lovers were united; the imperial family and the crowd arose; the priests and choir chanted the *Te Deum*, and discharges of artillery, outside, announced the consecration of the marriage to the city. The effect of this exquisite music, mingled with the thunder of the cannon, the ringing of the bells, and the distant acclamations of the people, was inexpressibly grand. All musical instruments are banished from the Greek church, and the voices of human beings only there celebrate the praises of God. This rigour of the oriental ritual is favourable to the art of singing, preserving to it all its simplicity, and producing an effect in the chants which is absolutely celestial. I could fancy I heard the heart-beating of sixty millions of subjects—a living orchestra, following, without drowning, the triumphal hymn of

---

the Swiss guards, who formed their escort, and seated themselves on their chairs without previously kneeling on the cushions opposite, or paying any attention to the holy sacrament exposed before their eyes. The ladies of honour sat behind, which obliged the prince and princess to turn their heads in order to carry on the conversation, which they continued to do as though they were in a saloon. Two chamberlains remained standing, whereupon a sacristan, supposing they wanted seats and busying himself to provide them, excited much unsuitable laughter on the part of the prince and princess. The Pope remained during the whole ceremony, which was a rendering of thanks to God for the blessings of the past year, upon his knees. A cardinal gave the benediction, when the Prince of Leuchtenberg knelt also, but the Princess continued seated."

the priests. I was deeply moved: music can make us forget for one moment even despotism itself.

I can only compare these choruses without accompaniment, to the *Miserere* as sung during the Passion Week in the Sixtine chapel at Rome; but the chapel of the Pope is but the shadow of what it formerly was. It is one ruin more amid the ruins of Rome. About the middle of the last century, when the Italian school shone in its brightest lustre, the old Greek chants were re-arranged, without being spoilt, by composers who were brought to Petersburg from Rome. The works of these strangers are *chefs-d'oeuvre*, which is mainly owing to all their talent and science having been applied in subservience to the works of antiquity. Their classic compositions are executed with a power worthy of the conception. The soprano, or children's parts—for no woman sings in the imperial chapel—are perfectly correct; the basses have a strength, depth, and purity, that exceed any thing I recollect having heard elsewhere.

To an amateur of the art, the music of the imperial chapel is alone worth a journey to Petersburg. The sweet, the powerful, and all the finest shades of expression, are observed with a depth of feeling and a skill which cannot be too much admired. The Russians are musical; this cannot be doubted by those who have heard the music in their churches. I listened without daring to breathe, and I longed for my learned friend Meyerbeer to explain to me the beauties which I so deeply felt, but which I was unable to comprehend. He would have understood them by the inspiration they would have communicated, for his admiration of models is expressed by his rivalling them.

During the Te Deum, at the moment when the two choirs were responding to each other, the tabernacle opened, and the priests were seen, their heads adorned with sparkling tiaras of jewels, and their bodies clothed in robes of gold, over which their silver beards fell majestically; some of these beards reach as far as the waist. The assistants make as dazzling an appearance as the priests. This court is certainly magnificent, and the military costume shines also in all its splendour. I saw with delight the people bringing to God the homage of their riches and their pomp. The sacred music was listened to by a profane auditory with a silence and attention, which would alone give an effect to chants less sublime than these. God was there, and his presence sanctifies even the court: the world and sense were nothing more than accessory objects—the reigning thought was heaven.

The officiating archbishop did not disgrace the majesty of the scene. If not handsome, he is venerable; his small figure is like that of a weasel, but his head is white with age. He has a care-worn and sickly appearance; a priest, old and feeble, cannot be an ignoble object. At the close of the ceremony, the Emperor came and bent before him, respectfully kissing his hand.

The autocrat never fails to give an example of submission, when there is a hope that this example may be of profit to himself. I was interested in the poor archbishop, who appeared dying in the midst of his glory. The majestic figure of the Emperor, and his noble countenance, bending before the representative of religious power—the youthful couple—the imperial family—the spectators—in short, the whole assemblage that filled and animated the chapel, formed a subject for a picture. Before the ceremony, I thought the archbishop would have fainted. The court kept him waiting a long time, unmindful of the saying of Louis XVIII., that "Punctuality is the politeness of kings." Notwithstanding the cunning expression of his countenance, this old man inspired me with compassion. He was so feeble, and yet he sustained fatigue with so much patience, that I pitied, if I did not respect him; for whether his patience was the result of piety, or of ambition, it was cruelly tried.

As to the person of the young Duke of Leuchtenberg, it was in vain that I endeavoured to reconcile myself to it; it did not please me better at the close of the ceremony than at the beginning. This young man has a fine military bearing, and that is all. He reminded me of what I knew before, namely, that, in our days, princes are more common than gentlemen. I should have said that the Emperor's guard would have been a more suitable place for the young duke than the Emperor's family. His countenance manifested no emotion at any of the ceremonies which appeared so touching to me—an indifferent spectator. I was carried there by mere curiosity, and yet I felt very deeply affected, whilst the son-in-law of the emperor, the hero of the scene, seemed uninterested with regard to all that passed around him. He has a vacant countenance, and appeared more taken up with his person than with what he was doing. It can be seen that he reckons but little upon the good will of a court, where interested calculation prevails more completely than in any other, and where his unexpected fortune may procure him more enemies than friends. This young prince has, nevertheless, a slight resemblance to his father, whose countenance was intelligent and kind. Notwithstanding the tight Russian uniform, in which every one must feel fettered and confined, it appeared to me that his step was light, like that of a Frenchman. He little thought when passing before me, that there was one near him who carried on his breast a relic so precious to both, but more particularly so to the son of Eugene Beauharnais. I allude to the Arabic talisman, that M. de Beauharnais, the father of the viceroy of Italy, and the grandfather of the Duke of Leuchtenberg, gave to my mother as he passed the chamber which she inhabited in the Carmelite convent, on his way to the scaffold.

The religious ceremony in the Greek chapel was followed by a second nuptial benediction by a Catholic priest, which took place in one of the halls of the palace, consecrated to this pious use for the day only. After these two marriages, the bride and bridegroom and their family met at table. I, not having permission to witness either the Catholic marriage or the banquet, followed the greater number of the courtly crowd, and went out to breathe a less stifling air, congratulating myself on the little effect that my dilapidated boot had produced. Some persons, however, spoke to me of it laughingly, and that was all. Both in good and in evil, nothing that merely regards ourselves is as important as we fancy it.

On departing from the palace I found my carriage again without any trouble. There is never, I repeat, a large concourse in Russia. The space is always too vast for what is done there. This is the advantage of a country where there is no nation. In a community thus ordered, a crowd would be equivalent to a revolution.

The void which is every where observable, causes the public structures to appear too small for the places in which they stand;

they seem lost in space. The column of Alexander passes for being higher than that of the Place Vendôme, owing to the dimensions of its pedestal. The shaft consists of one single block of granite, the largest that has ever been shaped by the hand of man. This immense column, raised between the winter palace and the crescent, which forms the other extremity of the square, when viewed from the palace, appears to the eye as nothing more than a pole, and the houses around might be taken for palisades. In the square a hundred thousand men can perform their manoeuvres, without its appearing filled or thickly peopled. It is enclosed by the winter palace, the façades of which are rebuilt on the model of the old palace of the Empress Elizabeth. Here is at least a relief to the eyes, after the poor and frigid imitations of the monuments of Athens and Rome. The style is that of the Regency, or Louis XIV. degenerated, but the scale is very large. The opposite side of the square is terminated by a semicircle or crescent of buildings, in which are established the bureaus of various ministers of state. These edifices are mostly constructed in the ancient Grecian style. Singular taste! Temples erected to clerks! The buildings of the Admiralty are in the same square. Their small pillars and gilded turrets produce a picturesque effect. An avenue of trees ornaments the square opposite this spot, and renders it less monotonous. On the other side of the immense Russian Champ de Mars stands the church of Saint Isaac, with its colossal peristyle, and its brazen dome, still half concealed by the scaffolding of the architect. Further on is seen the palace of the senate, and other structures still in the form of pagan temples. Beyond, in an angle of this long square, at its extremity on the Neva, stands the statue of Peter the Great, which disappears in immensity like a pebble on the shore. These above-named edifices contain material enough to build an entire city, and yet they do not complete the sides of the great square of Petersburg: it is a plain, not of wheat, but of pillars. The Russians may do their best to imitate all that art has produced of beautiful in other times and other lands; they forget that nature is stronger than man. They never sufficiently consult her, and therefore she is constantly revenging herself by doing them mischief. Masterpieces have only been produced by men who have listened to, and felt the power of, nature. Nature is the conception of God; art is the relation between the conceptions of man and those of the power which has created, and which perpetuates the world. The artist repeats on earth what he has heard in heaven; he is but the translator of the works of the Deity; those who would create by their own models produce only monsters.

Among the ancients the architects reared their structures in steep and confined spots, where the picturesque character of the site added to the effect of the works of man. The Russians, who flatter themselves they are reproducing the wonders of antiquity, and who, in reality, are only caricaturing them, raise their *soi-disant* Grecian and Roman structures in immense fields, where they are almost lost to the eye. The architecture proper for such a land would not be the colonnade of the Parthenon, but the tower of Pekin. It is for man to build mountains, when nature has not undulated the surface of the earth; but the Russians have raised their porticoes and pediments without thinking of this, and without recollecting that on a flat and naked expanse it is difficult to distinguish edifices with so small an elevation. We still recognise the steppes of Asia in cities where they have pretended to revive the Roman Forum.* Muscovy is more nearly allied to Asia than to Europe. The genius of the East hovers over Russia. The semicircle of edifices opposite the imperial palace, if observed sideways, at a proper distance, has the effect of an incomplete ancient amphitheatre. If examined more nearly, we see only a series of decorations that have to be replastered every year, in order to repair the ravages of the winter. The ancients built with indestructible materials under a favourable sky; here, under a climate which destroys everything, they raise palaces of wood, houses of plank, and temples of plaster; and, consequently, the Russian workmen pass their lives in rebuilding, during the summer, what the winter has demolished. Nothing resists the effects of this climate; even the edifices that appear the most ancient have been reconstructed but yesterday; stone lasts here no better

---

* These observations apply only to the buildings constructed from the time of Peter I. The Russians of the middle ages, who built the Kremlin, better understood the architecture which belonged to their land and their genius.

than lime and mortar elsewhere. That enormous piece of granite, which forms the shaft of the column of Alexander, is already worn by the frost. In Petersburg it is necessary to use bronze in order to support granite; yet notwithstanding these warnings, they never tire of imitating the taste of southern lands. They people the solitudes of the pole with statues and historical bas-reliefs, without considering that in their country monuments are even more evanescent than memories. Petersburg is but the scaffolding of a structure—when the structure is finished, the scaffolding will be removed. This chef-d'oeuvre, not of architecture but of policy, is the New Byzantium, which, in the deep and secret aspirations of the Russian, is to be the future capital of Russia and the world.

Facing the palace, an immense arcade pierces the already noticed semicircular range of buildings, and leads into the *Morskoë* street. Above this enormous vault is placed a car with six horses in bronze, guided by, I know not what kind of allegorical or historical figure. I doubt whether there could be elsewhere seen anything in such bad taste as this colossal gate opening under a house, and flanked on either side by ordinary dwellings, whose vicinity has nevertheless not prevented its being, under Russian architects, converted into a triumphal arch. I question the merit of the workmanship of the car, statue, and horses; but were they ever so good, they are so ill placed that I should not admire them. In objects of art it is the harmony and keeping of the whole which invite to the examination of details; without merit in the conception, what avails a delicacy in the execution? But, indeed, both one and the other are equally wanting in the productions of Russian art. Hitherto this art has been confined to imitating, without choice or taste, the good or the evil of other lands. If the design be entertained of reviving ancient architecture, it can only be done by strictly copying, and by placing such copies in analogous sites. Every thing here is mean, although colossal; for in architecture it is not the dimensions of the walls which constitute excellence, but the purity of the style.

I cannot cease marvelling at the passion they have conceived here for light, aerial structures. In a climate where there is sometimes a difference of eighty degrees between the temperature of winter and of summer, what have the inhabitants to do with porticoes, arcades, colonnades, and peristyles? But the Russians are accustomed to view even nature as a slave. Obstinate imitators, they mistake their vanity for genius, and believe themselves destined to renew, on a scale yet larger than the original, all the wonders of the world. Such creations of the Russian sovereigns, as I have hitherto seen, have evinced, not the love of the arts, but the love only of self.

Among other boasts, I hear it said by many Russians, that their climate also is ameliorating! Will God, then, connive at the ambition of this grasping people? Will he give them up even the sky and the breeze of the south? Shall we see Athens in Lapland, Rome at Moscow, the riches of the Thames in the Gulf of Finland, and the history of nations reduced to a question of latitude and longitude?

While my carriage, after leaving the palace, was crossing rapidly the immense square I have been describing, a violent wind raised immense clouds of dust, and I could only see, as through a veil, the equipages that were passing in all directions. The dust of summer is one of the plagues of Petersburg; it is so troublesome that I even wish for the winter snow. I had scarcely reached my hotel when a tremendous storm burst forth. Darkness at mid-day, thunder without rain, a wind which blew down houses, and, at the same time, a suffocating temperature, were the greeting which Heaven gave during the nuptial banquet. The superstitious viewed these signs as ominous, but soon became re-assured, by observing that the storm did not last long, and that the air was purer after it than before. I recount what I see, without sympathising with it, for I have no interest here but that which actuates a curious and attentive stranger. There is between France and Russia a Chinese wall—the Slavonic language and character. In spite of the notions with which Peter the Great has inspired the Russians, Siberia commences on the Vistula.

Yesterday at seven o'clock I returned to the palace with several other foreigners, in order to be presented to the emperor and empress.

It is easy to perceive that the former cannot for a single instant forget what he is, nor the constant attention which he excites; he studies attitude incessantly,—from whence it results that he is never natural, not even when he is sincere. He has three expressions, not one of which is that of simple benevolence. The most habitual appears to be that of severity. Another, though rarer expression, suits perhaps better his fine face—it is that of solemnity; a third is that of politeness, in which are mixed some shades of gentleness and grace, that serve to temper the chill produced by the two former. But notwithstanding this grace, there is still something which injures the moral influence of the man; it is, that each expression is assumed or cast off at will, without the least trace of one remaining to modify the one next adopted. For such change we are not prepared, and it therefore appears like a mask, that can be put on or off at pleasure. Let not my meaning of the word mask be misunderstood,—I employ it according to its strict etymology. In Greek, *hypocrite* means an actor: the hypocrite was a man who masked himself to perform a play. I would only say, then, that the emperor is always engaged in acting his part.

Hypocrite or actor are ill-sounding words, especially in the mouth of one who professes to be impartial and respectful. But it appears to me that, to intelligent readers, and it is only such that I address, words are nothing in themselves; their importance depends upon the sense that is given to them. I do not say that the physiognomy of this prince lacks candour, but it lacks natural expression. Thus, the chief evil under which Russia suffers, the absence of liberty, is depicted even on the countenance of its sovereign: he has many masks, but no face. Seek for the man, and you still always find the emperor.

I believe this remark may be turned to his praise: he acts his part conscientiously. He would accuse himself of weakness were he to be for a single moment plain and simple, or were he to allow it to be seen that he lived, thought, and felt as do common mortals. Without seeming to partake of any of our affections, he is always governor, judge, general, admiral, prince,—never anything more,—never anything less. He will surely grow weary of all this effort as he advances in life; yet it will place him high in the opinion of his people, and perhaps of the world, for the multi-

Portrait of Delphine, Custine's Mother
Mezzotint by Jules-Armand Hanriot, after a portrait by Pietro Campana.

Czar Nicholas I
Strong ruler of the Russian Empire (1825–55) while the revolution swept through Europe.
Lithograph after a drawing by P. I. Smirnov.

View of the Neva River at St. Petersburg
Moonlit view, framed by the austere façades of government buildings lining its banks.
Drawn by L. R. von Klenze.
GENERAL RESEARCH DIVISION

The Winter Traveling Carriage
The traditional Russian *troika* harness, hauling a carriage.
Color engraving, drawn by Mornay.
GENERAL RESEARCH DIVISION

The Winter Palace and the Admiralty, Viewed Here from the Bourse Embankment
The Winter Palace (now home of the Hermitage Art Museum) served as the Czar's
residence in the northern capital. The Admiralty, distinguished by its steeple
surmounted by a "needle," housed the administrative offices of the Russian Navy.
Tinted lithograph, ca. 1856, by A. Durand.
GENERAL RESEARCH DIVISION

Kazan Square and the Cathedral of St. Petersburg
This impressive edifice was associated with the Imperial Family
(now the Museum of the History of Religion and Atheism).
Lithograph by Mornay.
GENERAL RESEARCH DIVISION

Perspective Newski, St. Petersburg
The capital's scenic main shopping throroughfare.
Tinted lithograph, ca. 1856, by A. Durand.

Smol'nyi Monastery, St. Petersburg
The 18th-century Women's Monastery of Resurrection, which after 1764
housed the Catherine II Training Society for Well-bred Girls, an early
institution of higher learning for women in the empire.

Drunken Smiths
Tinted lithograph, ca. 1852, by I. S. Shchedrovskii.

A Traveling Animal Trainer
From a typical mini-circus, making its rounds through the provinces.
Lithograph by I. Iakovlev.

Summer Residence of Their Imperial Majesties on the Gulf of Finland
The Peterhoff Palace was part of a compound
of parks and palaces belonging to the Imperial Family.
Tinted lithograph by V. F. Timm, 1859.

Fortress of Schlusselburg
A notorious St. Petersburg prison for political offenders.
Tinted lithograph by A. Durand.

Panoramic View of Nijni-Novgorod (now called Gorky)
Commercial crossroad between East and West, the site of the famous annual fair.
Lithograph by V. F. Timm.

tude admire the efforts which astonish them,—they pride themselves in seeing the pains that are taken to dazzle them.

Those who knew the Emperor Alexander, eulogise that prince on entirely different grounds. The qualities and the faults of the two brothers were altogether opposite; there was no resemblance, and likewise no sympathy between them. In this country, the memory of a defunct emperor is little honoured, and in the present instance inclination accords with the policy that would always have the preceding reign forgotten. Peter the Great is more nearly resembled by Nicholas than by Alexander, and he is more the fashion at the present day. If the ancestors of the emperors are flattered, their immediate predecessors are invariably calumniated.

The present emperor never lays aside the air of supreme majesty except in his family intercourse. It is there only that he recollects that the natural man has pleasures independent of the duties of state; at least, I hope that it is this disinterested sentiment which attaches him to his domestic circle. His private virtues no doubt aid him in his public capacity, by securing for him the esteem of the world; but I believe he would practise them independently of this calculation.

Among the Russians, sovereign power is respected as is a religion the obligations and authority of which stand independently of the personal merit of its priests: the virtues of the prince being superfluous, are so much the more sincere.

If I lived at Petersburg I should become a courtier, not from any love of place or power, nor from any puerile vanity, but from the desire of discovering some road that might reach the heart of a man who differs from all others. Insensibility is not in him a natural vice, it is the inevitable result of a position which he has not chosen, and which he cannot quit.

To abdicate a disputed power would be sometimes a revenge, to abdicate an absolute power would be an act of cowardice.

The singular destiny of an Emperor of Russia inspires me, first, with a lively emotion of curiosity, and afterwards with a feeling of pity. Who would not commiserate the state of this glorious exile? I cannot tell whether the Emperor Nicholas has received from God a heart susceptible of friendship, but I feel as though the desire of testifying a disinterested attachment to a man to whom society refuses equals, might take the place of ambition. The danger even, would give to such zeal the charm of enthusiasm. What! it will be said, attachment for a man who has nothing of humanity about him; whose severe physiognomy inspires a respect always mingled with fear, whose firm and fixed looks, in excluding familiarity, command obedience, and whose mouth, when it smiles, does not harmonise with the expression of the eyes; attachment for a man, in short, who never for a moment forgets to play his part as an absolute monarch!

And wherefore not? This want of harmony, this apparent harshness, is not a crime but a misfortune. I view in it a forced habit, not a natural character; and believing that, I can see into this man whom you calumniate as much by your fears and your precautions as your flatteries, I can feel all that it must cost him to perform his duty as a sovereign, and I would not abandon so pitiable a deity of earth to the implacable envy and the hypocritical submission of his slaves. To find again the neighbour in the prince, to love him as a brother, would be a religious vocation, and a work of charity that would gain the blessing of heaven.

The more we see of the court, more especially of the court of Russia, the greater compassion must we feel for him who has to preside over it. It is a theatre, on whose boards the actors pass their life in rehearsals. No one knows his part, and the day for the representation never arrives, because the manager is never satisfied with the proficiency of his *corps*. Actors and managers thus pass their life in preparing, correcting and perfecting their interminable drama of society, the title of which is "The civilisation of the North." If it be so fatiguing to the audience, what must it be to the performers!

The emperor is, by extraction, more a German than a Russ. The fineness of his features, the regularity of his profile, his military figure, his bearing, naturally a little stiff, all remind one of Germany rather than of Muscovy. His Teutonic temperament must have been long schooled and fettered ere he could have become, as he now is, a thorough Russian. Who knows?—he was perhaps born a plain good-natured man! If so, what must he not have endured before he could appear only as the chieftain of the

Slavonians? The obligation of achieving a continual victory over himself in order to reign over others, will explain much in the character of the Emperor Nicholas.

Far from inspiring me with dislike, these things attract me. I cannot help viewing with interest one feared by the rest of the world, and who is, in reality, only so much the more to be commiserated.

To escape as much as possible from the constraint which he imposes on himself, he is as restless as a lion in a cage, or a patient in a fever; he is constantly moving on foot or on horseback; reviewing, carrying on little wars, sailing, manoeuvring his fleet, giving and receiving fêtes. Leisure is that which is most dreaded at this court; whence I conclude that no where else is ennui so much felt. The emperor travels incessantly; he journeys over at least 1500 leagues every season, and he has no notion that others have not the strength to do as he does. The empress loves him, and dreads leaving him; she therefore follows him as well as she can, and is dying of the fatigues and excitement consequent upon this life.

So complete an absence of quiet and regularity must be injurious to the education of their children. The young princes do not live sufficiently isolated to avoid the evil influences which the frivolity of a court always in motion, the absence of all interesting and connective conversation, and the impossibility of meditation, must exert upon their character. When I think of the distribution of their time, I have little hope even of the talents which they exhibit, I fear just as I would for the enduring beauty of a flower whose roots were not in their natural soil. Every thing is founded on appearance in Russia; whence it is that everything inspires mistrust.

I was presented this evening, not by the French ambassador, but by the grand master of the court ceremonies. Such was the order of the emperor, of which I was previously informed by our ambassador. I cannot tell whether this is the usual proceeding, but it was the manner in which I was presented to their imperial majesties.

All the foreigners admitted to the honour of approaching their persons, were assembled together in one of the saloons which they would have to cross in proceeding to open the ball. We arrived at the appointed hour, and had to wait a long time for the appearance of the illustrious personages.

There were with me two or three French, a Pole, a Genevese, and several Germans. The opposite side of the saloon was occupied by a row of Russian ladies, assembled there to pay their court.

The Emperor received us with a refined and graceful politeness. At the first glance it was easy to recognise a man who, notwithstanding his power, is obliged and accustomed to humour the self-love of others.

In order to intimate to me that I might, without displeasing him, survey his empire, his majesty did me the honour of saying that it was at least necessary to see Moscow and Nijni before a just idea of the country could be formed. "Petersburg is Russian," he added, "but it is not Russia."

These few words were pronounced in a tone of voice that could not be forgotten, so strongly was it marked by authoritativeness and firmness. Every body had spoken to me of the imposing manners, the noble features, and the commanding figure of the emperor, but no one had prepared me for the power of his voice: it is that of a man born to command. In it there is neither effort nor study, it is a gift developed only by habitual use.

The Empress, on a near approach, has a most winning expression of countenance, and the sound of her voice is as sweetly penetrating as that of the emperor is naturally imperious.

She asked me if I came to Petersburg with the simple object of travelling. I replied in the affirmative. "I know that you are a curious observer," she continued.

"Yes Madame," I answered, "it is curiosity which brings me to Russia; and this time, at least, I do not regret having yielded to a passion for travel."

"You really think so?" she replied with a gracefulness of manner that was very charming.

"It appears to me that there are such wonderful objects in this country, that to believe them requires that we should see them with the eyes."

"I should wish you to see much and to view favourably."

"This wish of your majesty's is an encouragement."

"If you think well of us, you will say so, but it will be useless; you will not be believed: we are ill understood, and people will not understand us better."

These words in the mouth of the Empress struck me, on account of the pre-occupation of idea which they discovered. It seemed to me also that she meant to manifest a kind of benevolence towards me, which was expressed with a politeness and a simplicity that are rarely seen.

The Empress, the moment she speaks, inspires confidence as well as respect. Through the reserve which the language and usages of court render compulsory, it is easy to see that she has a heart. This misfortune imparts to her an indefinable charm. She is more than an empress, she is a woman.

She appeared to be suffering from extreme fatigue. The thinness of her person is quite shocking. The agitation of the life she leads is consuming her, and they say that the ennui of a life more calm would be equally injurious.

The fête which followed our presentation was one of the most magnificent that I have ever seen. The admiration and astonishment with which each saloon of this palace (rebuilt in a year), inspired the whole court, imparted a dramatic interest to the formal pomp of the usual ceremonies. Every hall and every painting was a subject of surprise to the Russians themselves, who now for the first time saw the marvellous abode which the word of their Deity had caused to spring from its ashes. What an effort of human will, thought I, as I contemplated each gallery, sculpture and painting. The style of the ornaments calls to mind the age in which the palace was originally founded, and what I saw appeared already ancient. They copy everything in Russia, not excepting even the effects of time. These wonders inspired the crowd with an admiration that was contagious, and my internal indignation at the means by which the miracle was created, began to diminish. If I could feel such an influence after only two days' abode here, what allowance should not be made for the men who are born, and who pass their life in the air of the Russian court!—that is in Russia; for it is the air of the court which is breathed from one end of the empire to the other. Even the serfs, through their relations with their lords, feel the influence of that sovereign will which alone animates the country: the courtier who is their master, is for them the image of the emperor, and the court is present to the Russians wherever there is a man to command, and men to obey.

Elsewhere the poor are either beggars, or unruly members of society; in Russia they are all courtiers. The courtier is found in every rank of society, and for this reason it is that I say, the court is everywhere. There is, between the sentiments of the Russian nobles and those of men of family in ancient Europe, the same difference that there is between the courtier and the aristocrat, or between emotions of vanity and of pride;—true pride, which is almost as rare as virtue—is virtue. Instead of abusing courtiers as Beaumarchais and so many others have done, these men, who, whatever may be said, are like other men, deserve pity. Poor unfortunate courtiers! they are not the monsters that our modern plays and romances, or our revolutionary journals describe; they are merely weak creatures, corrupted and corrupting, as much as, but not more than, others who are less exposed to temptation. Ennui is the curse of riches, still it is not a crime: vanity and interest are more strongly excited, and therefore more eagerly sought in a court than on any other stage of action: and these passions abridge life. But if the hearts they agitate are more tormented, they are not more perverse than those of other men. Human wisdom would accomplish much if it could succeed in showing to the multitude how much it ought to feel of pity instead of envy towards the possessors of a fancied good.

I saw them dancing in the very place where they had themselves nearly perished under blazing ruins, and where others had since actually died, in order that they might be amused on the day appointed by the emperor. This thought made me reflect in spite of myself, and shed (for me) a gloom over the entire fête. Elsewhere liberty gives birth to a feeling of gladness which is favourable to illusion; here despotism suggests meditations which make it impossible to deceive one's self.

The kind of dance that is most common at the grand fêtes of this country, does not disturb the course of ideas. The company promenade in a solemn step to the sound of music, each gentleman taking his partner by the hand. In the palace, hundreds of couples thus follow in procession, proceeding from one immense hall to another, winding through the galleries crossing the saloons, and traversing the whole building in such order or direction as the caprice of the individual who leads, may dictate. This is called dancing *la Polonaise.* It is amusing at first, but for those destined to dance it all their lives, balls must, I think, be a species of torture.

The *Polonaise* at Petersburg recalled to my memory the congress of Vienna, where I had danced it in 1814. No etiquette was observed in the European fêtes celebrated on that occasion, every one's place in the dance was regulated by hazard, though in the midst of all the monarchs of the earth. My fate had placed me between the Emperor Alexander and his consort, who was a princess of Baden. All at once, the line of the dancing couples was stopped without our perceiving the reason, as the music continued playing. The emperor, growing impatient, put his head over my shoulder, and, addressing himself to the empress, told her in a very rude tone, to move on. The empress turned, and perceiving behind me the emperor, with a lady as his partner for whom he had for some days past manifested a violent passion, she retorted, with an expression altogether indescribable, "Toujours poli!" The autocrat bit his lips as he caught my eye, and the line of dance again moved forward.

I was dazzled with the splendour of the great gallery; it is now entirely gilded, though before the fire it was only painted white. That disaster has served to minister to the taste which the emperor has for the magnificent.

All the ambassadors of Europe had been invited to admire the marvellous achievement of this government, a government which is so much the more bitterly criticised by the vulgar, as it is admired and envied by political men,—minds essentially practical, and who, approve the simplicity of the machine of despotism. One of the largest palaces in the world built in a year! what a subject of admiration for men accustomed to breathe the air of courts!

Great objects are never attained without great sacrifices.

Unity, force, and authority in the direction of public affairs, are purchased here by the loss of liberty, while in France, political liberty and commercial wealth have been purchased at the cost of the ancient spirit of chivalry, and of that delicacy of feeling formerly called our national honour. This honour is replaced by other virtues less patriotic, but more universal—by humanity, religion and charity. Every one admits that in France there is more religion now than there was at a time when the clergy was all-powerful. A wish to embrace the advantages which do not belong to each situation, is to lose those which do belong to it. It is this which is not admitted in France, where we expose ourselves to the danger of destroying everything by our very wish to preserve everything. Each nation is governed by its own law of necessity, to which it must submit, under penalty of national ruin.

We want to be commercial like the English, free like the Americans, at liberty to follow our caprices like the Poles in the times of their dicts, and conquerors like the Russians; all which is tantamount to being nothing. The good sense of a nation consists in perceiving and choosing the object that suits its genius, and is indicated by nature and history, and then, in shrinking from no sacrifices necessary to attain it.

France wants good sense in her ideas, and moderation in her desires. She is generous, she is even resigned*; but she does not know how to employ and direct her powers. She acts by impulse and at random. A country where, from the time of Fenelon, they have done nothing but talk of politics, is, in the present day, neither governed nor served. There are plenty of men who see and deplore the evil; but as for the remedy, every one seeks it in his passion, and therefore no one finds it, for the passions persuade those only who are under their influence.

Nevertheless, it is at Paris that one still leads the most pleasant life. We there amuse ourselves with every thing by finding fault; at Petersburg people weary of every thing in bestowing praise; pleasure, however, is not the end of existence, not even for individuals, and still less for nations.

What appeared to me more splendid even than the ball-room

* Elle est même résignée.

in the winter palace, was the gallery in which supper was served. It is not entirely finished, and the lights in temporary paper transparencies had a fantastic appearance which did not displease me. So unexpected an illumination in honour of the marriage-day, did not certainly correspond with the general decorations of the magical palace, but it produced a light clear as that of the sun, and this was enough for me. Thanks to the progress of commercial economy, we no longer see in France anything but tapers; there seem to be yet in Russia real wax candles. The supper-table was splendid; in this fête every thing was colossal, every thing was also innumerable in its kind, and I scarcely knew which most to admire, the superb effect of the whole, or the magnificence and the quantity of the objects considered separately. A thousand persons were seated together at the table.

Among these thousand, all more or less blazing with gold and diamonds, was the Khan of the Kirguises, whom I had seen at the chapel in the morning. I remarked also an old Queen of Georgia, who had been dethroned thirty years previously. This poor woman languished, unhonoured, at the court of her conqueror. Her face was tanned like that of a man's used to the fatigues of the camp, and her attire was ridiculous. We are too ready to laugh at misfortune when it appears under a form that does not please us. We should wish to see a Queen of Georgia rendered more beautiful by her distress; but we here see just the contrary, and, when the eyes are displeased, the heart soon becomes unjust. This is not generous, but I confess I could not help smiling to see a royal head crowned with a kind of shako, from whence hung a very singular veil. All the other ladies wore trains; but the queen of the East had on a short embroidered petticoat. There was much of the worn-out and wearied courtier in her expression, and her features were ugly. The national dress of the Russian ladies at court is antique and striking. They wear on the head a kind of tower, formed of rich stuff, and something resembling in shape the crown of a man's hat, lowered in height, and open at the top. This species of diadem is generally embroidered with jewels: it is very ancient, and gives an air of nobleness and originality to handsome persons, while it singularly enhances the ugliness of plain ones. Unfortunately, these last are very numerous at the

Russian court, from whence people seldom retire, except to die, so attached are the aged people to the posts they there occupy. In general, female beauty is rare at Petersburg; but among the higher classes the charm of graceful manners often supplies the place of elegant forms and regular features. There are, however, a few Georgian women who unite the two advantages. These females shine amid the women of the north, like stars in the profound darkness of a southern night. The shape of the court robes, with their long sleeves and trains, gives to the whole person an oriental aspect which, in a large assembly thus robed, has a very imposing effect.

An incident, singular enough in its character, has afforded me a specimen of the perfect politeness of the emperor.

During the ball, a master of the ceremonies had indicated to such of the foreigners as appeared for the first time at this court, the places that were reserved for them at the supper-table. "When you see the ball interrupted," he said to each of us, "follow the crowd into the gallery, where you will find a large table laid out; take the side to the right, and seat yourselves in the first places you find unoccupied."

There was but one table, laid with one thousand covers, for the *corps diplomatique*, the foreigners, and all the attendants at court; but at the entrance of the hall, on the right hand side, was a little round table laid for eight.

A Genevese, an intelligent and well-educated young man, had been presented the same evening in the uniform of a national guard, a dress which is in general anything but agreeable to the emperor; nevertheless, this young Swiss appeared perfectly at home. Whether it was owing to natural assurance, republican ease, or pure simplicity of heart, he seemed neither to think of the persons around him, nor of the effect that he might produce upon them. I envied his perfect self-confidence, which I was far from participating. Our manners, though very different, had the same success; the emperor treated us both equally well.

An experienced and intelligent person had recommended to me, in a tone half serious, half jocose, to maintain a respectful and rather timid air if I wished to please the monarch. This counsel was quite superfluous, for if I were to enter the hut of a collier, in order to make his acquaintance, I should experience some little degree of physical embarrassment, so naturally do I shrink from society. A man has never German blood without showing it; I possessed, therefore, naturally, the degree of timidity and reserve requisite to satisfy the jealous majesty of the Czar, who would be as great as he wishes to appear, if he were less prepossessed with the notion that those who approach him are likely to fail in respect. This inquietude of the emperor does not, however, always operate; of which, and of the natural dignity of that prince, the following is an instance.

The Genevese, far from partaking of my old-fashioned modesty, was perfectly at his ease. He is young, and has about him all the spirit of the age mingled with a simplicity of his own; and I could not but admire his air of assurance each time the emperor addressed him.

The affability of the monarch was soon put by the young Swiss to a decisive proof. On passing into the banquet hall, the republican, turning towards the right, according to the instruction he had received, came across the little round table, and intrepidly seated himself before it, though there was no other person there to keep him company. The moment after, the crowd of guests being placed, the emperor, followed by some officers who enjoyed his special confidence, advanced and took his seat at the same table at which was placed the worthy Swiss national guardsman. I should state that the empress was not at this table. The traveller remained in his chair with the imperturbable ease which I had already so much admired in him, and which, under the circumstances, was really admirable.

A seat was wanting, for the emperor had not expected this ninth guest; but, with a politeness the completeness of which was equivalent to the delicacy of a kind heart, he spoke in a low voice to a servant, directing him to bring a chair and another cover, which was done without any noise or trouble.

Being placed at the extremity of the great table, close to that of the emperor, this occurrence could not escape my observation, nor, consequently, that of him who was its object. But, this happily-constituted young man, far from troubling himself because he perceived he had been placed contrary to the intention of the sovereign, maintained, with the most perfect *sang froid,* a conversation with his two nearest neighbours, which lasted during the whole repast. I thought to myself, he has good sense; he does not wish to make a public display: but, no doubt, he only waits the moment when the emperor rises, to approach him, and to offer some word of explanation. Nothing of the kind! When supper was over the young Swiss, far from excusing himself, seemed to view the honour he had received as nothing more than was quite natural. On returning to his lodging he would doubtless inscribe, with the most perfect simplicity, in his journal—"Supped with the emperor." However, his majesty rather abridged the pleasure: rising, before the guests who sat at the great table, he passed round behind our chairs, all the while desiring that we should remain seated. The Hereditary Grand-duke accompanied his father; I observed this young prince stop behind the chair of a great English nobleman, the Marquis ——, and exchange some jest with the young Lord ——, son of the same marquis. The foreigners remained seated, like every body else, before the prince and the emperor, answered them with their backs turned, and continued eating.

This exhibition of English politeness shows that the Emperor of Russia has greater plainness of manners than have many of the owners of private houses.

I had scarcely expected to find at this ball a pleasure altogether foreign to the persons and objects around. I allude to the impressions which the great phenomena of nature have always produced in me. The temperature of the day had risen to 50 degrees, and notwithstanding the freshness of the evening, the atmosphere of the palace during the fête was suffocating. On rising from table I took refuge in the embrasure of an open window. There, completely abstracted from all that passed around, I was suddenly struck with admiration at beholding one of those effects of light which we see only in the north, during the magic brightness of a polar night. It was half-past twelve o'clock, and the nights having yet scarcely begun to lengthen, the dawn of day appeared already in the direction of Archangel. The wind had fallen: numerous belts of black and motionless clouds divided the firmament into zones, each of which was irradiated with a light so brilliant, that it appeared like a polished plate of silver; its lustre was reflected on the Neva, to whose vast and unrippled surface it gave the appearance of a lake of milk or of mother-of-pearl. The greater part of Petersburg, with its quays and its spires, was, under this light, revealed before my eyes; it was a perfect composition of Breughel's. The tints of the picture cannot be described by words. The domes of the church of Saint Nicholas stood in the relief of lapis lazuli against a sky of silver; the illuminated portico of the Exchange, whose lamps were partially quenched by the dawning day, still gleamed on the water of the river, and was reflected—a peristyle of gold: the rest of the city was of that blue which we see in the distances of the landscapes of the old painters. This fantastic picture, painted on a ground of ultramarine, and framed by a gilded window, contrasted, in a manner that was altogether supernatural, with the light and splendour of the interior of the palace. It might have been said that the city, the sky, the sea and the whole face of nature had joined in contributing to the magnificence of the fête given to his daughter by the sovereign of these immense regions.

I was absorbed in the contemplation of the scene, when a sweet and penetrating female voice suddenly aroused me with the question—"What are you doing here?"

"Madame, I am indulging in admiration. I can do nothing else to-day."

It was the empress. She stood alone with me in the embrasure of the window, which was like a pavilion opening on the Neva.

"As for me, I am suffocating," replied her majesty. "It is less poetical, I admit; but you are right in admiring this picture; it is magnificent!" Continuing to contemplate it, she added—"I am certain that you and I are the only persons here who have remarked this effect of light."

"Every thing that I see is new to me, Madame; and I can never cease to regret that I did not come to Russia in my youth."

"The heart and the imagination are always young."

I ventured no answer; for the empress, as well as myself, had no longer any other youth but that of which she spake—of which fact I did not wish to remind her: she would not have given me the time, nor, indeed, should I have had the boldness to tell her how many indemnifications may be found to console us for the flight of years. On retiring she said, with a grace which is her distinguishing attribute—"I shall recollect having suffered and admired with you:" and she afterwards added, "I do not leave yet; we shall meet again this evening."

I am very intimate with a Polish family, which is that of the woman whom the empress loves best—the Baroness ——. This lady was brought up in Prussia with the daughter of the king, has followed that princess to Russia, and has never quitted her. She has married in Petersburg, where she has no other office but that of friend to the empress. Such constancy is honourable to both. The baroness must have been speaking well of me to the emperor and empress, and my natural timidity—a flattery so much the more refined as it is involuntary—has completed my good fortune.

On leaving the supper saloon, to pass into the ball room, I again approached a window. It opened into the interior court of the palace. A spectacle was there presented to me very different, but quite as unexpected as the former. The grand court of the winter palace is square, like that of the Louvre. During the ball, this enclosure had been gradually filling with people. The light of the dawning day had become more distinct; and in looking on the multitude, mute with admiration, motionless, fascinated as it were by the splendours of its master's palace, and drinking in, with a sort of timid animal delight, the emanations of the royal festival, I experienced an impression of pleasure. At last, then, I had found a crowd in Russia: I saw nothing below me but men: and so close was the press that not an inch of earth could be discovered. Nevertheless, in despotic lands, the diversions of the people, when they approach those of the prince, always appear to me suspicious. The fear and flattery of the low, and the pride and hypocritical generosity of the great, are the only sentiments which I can believe to be genuine among men who live under the régime of the Russian autocracy.

In the midst of the fêtes of Petersburg I cannot forget the journey of the Empress Catherine into the Crimea, and the façades of villages, made of planks or painted canvass, and set up in the distance at every quarter league of the route, in order to make the triumphant sovereign believe that the desert had become peopled under her reign. A spirit similar to that which dictated these illusions still possesses the minds of the Russians; every one masks the evil, and obtrudes the good in the eyes of his imperial master. There is a permanent conspiracy of smiles, plotting against the truth, in favour of the mental satisfaction of him who is reputed to will and to act for the good of all. The emperor is the only man in the empire who lives; for eating and drinking is not living.

It must be owned, however, that the people remained there voluntarily; nothing appeared to compel them to come under the windows of the emperor: they were amusing themselves, therefore, but it was only with the pleasures of their masters; and, as Froissart says, *very sorrily*. The head-dress of the women, and the Russian, that is to say, the Persian, costume of the men, in their long robes and brightly-coloured girdles, the variety of colours and the immovableness of each individual, created the illusion of an immense Turkey carpet, spread entirely over the court by the magician who presides here over every miracle:—a parterre of heads,—such was the most striking ornament of the palace of the emperor during the night of his daughter's nuptials. This prince thought as I did, for he pointed out to the foreigners, with much complacency, the silent crowd, whose presence alone testified its participation in the happiness of its master. It was the vision of a people on their knees before the invisible gods. Their majesties are the divinities of this Elysium, where the inhabitants, trained to resignation, invent for themselves a felicity made up of privation and sacrifices.

I begin to perceive that I am here talking like the radicals in Paris. But, though a democrat in Russia, I am not the less in France an obstinate aristocrat: it is because a peasant in the environs of Paris is freer than a Russian lord, that I thus feel and write. We must travel before we can learn the extent to which the human heart is influenced by optical effects. This experience confirms the observation of Madame de Staël, who said, that in France "every body is either Jacobin or ultra-something."

I returned to my lodgings overwhelmed with the grandeur and magnificence of the emperor, and yet more astonished at seeing

the disinterested admiration of his people for the good things
which they do not possess, nor ever will, and which they do not
dare even to regret. If I did not daily see to how many ambitious
egotists liberty gives birth, I should have difficulty
in believing that despotism could make
so many disinterested
philosophers.

❖

NOTE ❖ EXCITEMENT OF A PETERSBURG LIFE ❖ THE EMPEROR TRULY A RUSSIAN ❖ AFFABILITY OF THE EMPRESS ❖ COMPARISON BETWEEN PARIS AND PETERSBURG ❖ DEFINITION OF POLITENESS ❖ FÊTE AT THE MICHAEL PALACE ❖ CONVERSATION WITH THE GRAND DUCHESS HELENA ❖ BEAUTIFUL ILLUMINATION ❖ A GROVE IN A BALL-ROOM ❖ JET D'EAU ❖ FUTURE PROSPECTS OF DEMOCRACY ❖ INTERESTING CONVERSATION WITH THE EMPEROR ❖ RUSSIA EXPLAINED ❖ IMPROVEMENTS IN THE KREMLIN ❖ AN ENGLISH NOBLEMAN AND HIS FAMILY ❖ ENGLISH POLITENESS ❖ ANECDOTE IN NOTE ❖ THE FRENCH AMBASSADOR ❖ THE GRAND CHAMBERLAIN ❖ SEVERE REPRIMAND OF THE EMPEROR'S ❖

CHAPTER XII

❖

NOTE

The following chapter was forwarded, in the shape of a letter, from Petersburg to Paris, by a person whom I could depend upon: and the friend to whom it was addressed has preserved it for me, as some of the details appeared to him curious. If its tone seem more eulogistic than that of those I have kept myself, it is because too great a sincerity might, under certain circumstances, have compromised the obliging party who had offered to take charge of my despatch. In this chapter, therefore, and only in this, I felt obliged to magnify the good, and to extenuate the evil. This is a confession: but the least disguise would be a fault in a work, the value of which depends upon the scrupulous fidelity of the writer.

I wish therefore that this chapter be read with rather more caution than the others; and especially that the notes which serve to correct it may not be passed over.

One ought to be a Russian, or even the Emperor himself, to bear the fatigue of a life at Petersburg. In the evening there are fêtes, such as are only seen in Russia; in the morning, court ceremonies and receptions, public solemnities, or reviews upon sea or land. A vessel of 120 guns has just been launched on the Neva before the whole court; but, though the largest vessel that the river has ever borne, it must not be supposed that there was any crowd at this naval spectacle. Space is that which the Russians least want, and through which they most suffer. The four or five hundred thousand men who inhabit Petersburg without peopling it, are lost in the vast enclosure of the immense city, the heart of which is composed of granite and brass, the body of plaster and of mortar, and the extremities of painted wood and rotten planks. These planks are raised in a solitary marsh like walls around the city, which resembles a colossal statue with feet of clay.* It is like none of the other capitals of the civilised world, even though in its construction all have been copied; but man in vain seeks for models in distant lands: the soil and the climate are his masters, they oblige him to create novelties, when he desires only to revive the antique.

I was present at the Congress of Vienna, but I do not recollect seeing any thing to be compared to the richness of the jewels and dresses, the gorgeous variety of the uniforms, or the grandeur and admirable ordering of the whole spectacle, in the fête given by the emperor, on the evening of the marriage of his daughter, in this same winter palace—burnt down only a year ago.

Peter the Great is not dead! His moral strength lives, and operates still. Nicholas is the only Russian sovereign which Russia has had since the reign of the founder of its metropolis.

Towards the end of the soirée given at court to celebrate the nuptials of the Grand Duchess Marie, the empress sent some officers to look for me, who, after searching for a quarter of an hour, could not find me. I was standing apart, according to my frequent practice, still absorbed in contemplating the beauty of the heavens, and admiring the night, against the same window where the empress had left me. Since supper I had quitted this place only for an instant, to follow in the train of their majesties; but not having been observed I returned into the gallery, where I could contemplate at leisure the romantic spectacle of the sun rising over a great city during a court ball. The officers at length discovered me in my hiding-place, and hastened to lead me to the

---

* The quays of the Neva are composed of granite, the cupola of Saint Isaac of copper, the Winter Palace and the column of Alexander of fine stone, marble and granite, and the statue of Peter I. of brass.

empress, who was waiting for me. She had the goodness to say before all the court, "M. de Custine, I have been inquiring for you for a long time—why did you avoid me?"

"Madame, I twice placed myself before Your Majesty, but you did not observe me."

"It was your own fault, for I have been seeking for you ever since I entered the ball-room. I wish you to see every thing here in detail, in order that you may carry from Russia an opinion which may rectify that of the foolish and the mischievously disposed."

"Madame, I am far from attributing to myself a power that could effect this; but if my impressions were communicable, France would imagine Russia to be Fairy-land."

"You must not judge by appearances, you must look deeply into things, for you possess every thing that can enable you to do this. Adieu! I only wished to say good evening—the heat fatigues me. Do not forget to inspect my new apartments; they have been remodelled according to a plan of the emperor's. I will give orders for you to be shown every thing." On withdrawing, she left me the object of general curiosity, and of the apparent good-will of the courtiers.

This court life is so new that it amuses me. It is like a journey in the olden times: I could imagine myself at Versailles a century ago. Politeness and magnificence are here natural. It will be seen by this how different Petersburg is from our Paris of the present day. At Paris there is luxury, riches and even elegance; but there is neither grandeur nor courtesy. Ever since the first revolution, we have dwelt in a conquered country, where the spoilers and the spoiled consort together as well as they are able. In order to be polite, it is necessary to have something to give. Politeness is the art of doing to others the honours of the advantages we possess, whether of our minds, our riches, our rank, our standing, or any other source of enjoyment. To be polite, is to know how to offer and to accept with grace; but when a person has nothing certain of his own, he cannot give any thing. In France at the present time nothing is exchanged through mutual good will: every thing is snatched by means of interest, ambition, or fear. Conversation, even, becomes insipid, when the secret calculations of interest cease to animate it. Mind itself is only valued, when it can be turned to personal account.

A fixed security of position in society is the basis of courtesy in all its relations, and the source also of those sallies of wit that enliven conversation.

Scarcely had we rested from the fatigues of the court ball, when we had to attend, in the Michael Palace, another fête, given yesterday by the Grand Duchess Helena, sister-in-law of the emperor, wife of the Grand Duke Michael, and daughter of Prince Paul of Wirtemberg, who lives at Paris. She is spoken of as one of the most distinguished personages in Europe, and her conversation is extremely interesting. I had the honour of being presented to her before the ball commenced, when she only addressed a word to me, but during the evening she gave me several opportunities of conversing with her.

The following is, as far as I recollect, the summary of what was said:—

"I hear that, in Paris and its neighbourhood, you move in a very agreeable circle of society."

"It is true, madame, the conversation of persons of mind is my greatest pleasure, but I was far from venturing to suppose that your Imperial Highness would have been acquainted with this circumstance."

"We know Paris, and we are aware that there are there some few who are conversant with things as they now are, and who at the same time do not forget the past. These are, I doubt not, your friends. We admire, through their writings, several of the persons whom you see habitually, especially Madame Gay, and her daughter, Madame de Girardin."

"These ladies are very intellectual: I have the good fortune to be their friend."

"You possess in them friends of a superior character."

Nothing is so rare as to think ourselves obliged to feel modesty for others; it was however a sentiment which I, in a slight degree, experienced at this moment. It will be said, that of all modesty this costs the least in its manifestation. However much it may be ridiculed, it is not the less true, that I felt I should have wanted delicacy, had I endeavoured to excite for my friends an admiration, by which my own vanity might have profited. At Paris I should have said all that I thought: at Petersburg I was afraid of seeming to magnify myself, under the pretence of doing justice to others. The Grand Duchess persisted, saying, "We take great pleasure in reading the works of Madame Gay. What do you think of them?"

"My opinion is, madame, that we may find in them a description of the society of former days written by one who understands it."

"Why does not Madame de Girardin continue to write?"

"Madame de Girardin is a poetess, madame, and in a writer of poetry silence is the indication of labour."

"I hope that this is the cause of her silence; for, with her observing mind and poetical talent, it would be a pity that she should confine herself to the production of mere ephemeral works."*

During this conversation, I made it a rule merely to listen and to reply; but I expected to hear the Grand Duchess pronounce other names which might flatter my patriotic pride, and put my friendly reserve to new trials.

These expectations were deceived. The Grand Duchess, who passes her life in a country where society is remarkable for its tact, undoubtedly knew better than myself what to speak of, and what to omit. Equally fearing the significance of my words, and of my silence, she did not utter another syllable on the subject of our cotemporary literature.

There are certain names, whose sound alone would disturb the tranquillity of mind and the uniformity of thought, despotically imposed upon all who will live at the Russian court.

I must now describe some of the magic fêtes at which I am present every evening. With us the balls are disfigured by the sombre attire of the men, whereas the varied and brilliant uniforms of the Russian officers give an extreme brilliancy to the saloons of Petersburg.

In Russia the magnificence of the women's apparel is found to accord with the gold of the military dress; and the male dancers

---

* The conversation is repeated word for word as it occurred.

have not the appearance of being the clerks of attorneys, or the shopmen of their partners' apothecaries.

The whole length of the garden front of the Michael Palace is ornamented by an Italian colonnade. Yesterday they availed themselves of a temperature of twenty-six degrees to illuminate the spaces betwixt each pillar of this exterior gallery with clusters of small lamps, arranged in a manner that had a very original effect. The lamps were formed of paper in the shape of tulips, lyres, vases, &c. Their appearance was both tasteful and novel.

At each fête given by the Grand Duchess Helena, it is said that she invents something altogether new. Such a reputation must be troublesome, for it is difficult to maintain. This princess, so beautiful and intellectual, and so celebrated throughout Europe for the grace of her manners, and the charms of her conversation, struck me as being less natural and easy than the other females of the imperial family. Celebrity as a woman of wit, and high intellectual attainment, must be a heavy burden in a royal court. She is an elegant and distinguished-looking person, but has the air of suffering from weariness and lassitude. Perhaps she would have been happier had she possessed good sense, with less wit and mental acquirements, and had continued a German princess confined to the monotonous life of a petty sovereignty.

Her obligation of doing the honours of French literature at the court of the Emperor Nicholas, makes me afraid of the Grand Duchess Helena.

The light that proceeded from the groups of lamps was reflected in a picturesque manner upon the pillars of the palace, and among the trees of the garden. The latter was full of people. In the fêtes at Petersburg the people serve as an ornament, just as a collection of rare plants adorns a hot-house. Delightful sounds were heard in the distance, where several orchestras were executing military symphonies, and responding to each other with a harmony that was admirable. The light reflected on the trees had a charming effect. Nothing is more fantastically beautiful than the golden verdure of foliage illuminated during a fine night.

The interior of the grand gallery in which they danced was arranged with a marvellous luxury. Fifteen hundred boxes of the rarest plants in flower formed a grove of fragrant verdure. At one of the extremities of the hall, amid thickets of exotic plants, a fountain threw up a column of fresh and sparkling water: its spray, illumined by the innumerable wax lights, shone like the dust of diamonds, and refreshed the air, always kept in agitation by the movement of the dance. It might have been supposed that these strange plants, including large palms and bananas, all of whose boxes were concealed under a carpet of mossy verdure, grew in their native earth, and that the groups of northern dancers had been transported by enchantment to the forests of the tropics. It was like a dream; there was not merely luxury in the scene, there was poetry. The brilliancy of the magic gallery was multiplied a hundred-fold by a greater profusion of enormous and richly gilded pier and other glasses than I had ever elsewhere seen. The windows ranged under the colonnade were left open on account of the excessive heat of the summer night. The hall was lofty, and extended the length of half the palace. The effect of all this magnificence may be better imagined than described. It seemed like the palace of the fairies: all ideas of limits disappeared, and nothing met the eye but space, light, gold, flowers, reflection, illusion, and the giddy movement of the crowd, which crowd itself seemed multiplied to infinity. Every actor in the scene was equal to ten, so greatly did the mirrors aid the effect. I have never seen any thing more beautiful than this crystal palace; but the ball was like other balls, and did not answer to the gorgeous decorations of the edifice. I was surprised that this nation of dancers did not devise something new to perform on the boards of a theatre so different from all others where people meet to dance and to fatigue themselves, under the pretext of enjoyment. I should like to have seen the quadrilles and the ballets of other theatres. It strikes me that in the middle ages, the gratifications of the imagination had a greater influence in the diversions of courts than they have at present. In the Michael Palace the only dances that I saw were the polonaises, the waltz, and the degenerated country dances called quadrilles in the Franco-Russian. Even the mazourkas danced at Petersburg are less lively and graceful than the real dances of Warsaw. Russian gravity cannot accommodate itself to the vivacity, the whim, and the *abandon* of the true Polish dances.

Under the perfumed groves of the ball-room the empress reposed herself at the conclusion of every polonaise. She found there a shelter from the heat of the illuminated garden, the air of which during this summer night was as stifling as that of the interior of the palace.

I found leisure during the fête to draw a comparison in my own mind between France and Russia, on a subject regarding which my observations were not in favour of the former. Democracy cannot but be uncongenial to the ordering of a grand assembly. The one which I beheld in the Michael Palace was embellished with all the care and all the tokens of homage of which a sovereign could be the object. A queen is always indispensable to the maintenance of elegant pleasures. But the principles of equality have so many other advantages, that we may well sacrifice to them the luxuries of pleasure. It is this which we do in France with a disinterestedness that is meritorious; my only fear is lest our great grandchildren may have different views, when the time shall have arrived to enjoy the perfections prepared for them by their too generous ancestors. Who knows if these undeceived generations shall not say, when speaking of us, "Seduced by a sophistical eloquence, they became vague, unmeaning fanatics, and have entailed on us absolute misery?"

To return from the contemplation of the future which America is promising to Europe:—before the banquet, the empress, seated under her canopy of exotic verdure, made me a sign to approach her; and scarcely had I obeyed, when the emperor also came to the magic fountain, whose shower of diamonds was giving us both light and a freshened atmosphere. He took me by the hand, and led me some steps from the chair of his consort, where he was pleased to converse with me for more than a quarter of an hour on subjects of interest; for this prince does not, like many other princes, speak to you merely that it may be seen he does so.

He first said a few words on the admirable arrangements of the fête; and I remarked, in reply, that in a life so active as his, I was astonished that he could find time for every thing, including even a participation in the pleasures of the crowd.

"Happily," he replied, "the machine of government is very simple in my country; for, with distances which render every thing difficult, if the form of government was complicated, the head of one man would not suffice for its requirements."

I was surprised and flattered by this tone of frankness. The emperor, who understands better than any one that which is felt, though not expressed, proceeded—replying to my thought—"If I speak to you in this manner, it is because I know that you can understand me: we are continuing the labours of Peter the Great."

"He is not dead, sire; his genius and his will still govern Russia."

When any one speaks in public with the emperor, a large circle of courtiers gathers at a respectful distance, from whence no one can overhear the sovereign's conversation, though all eyes continue fixed upon him.

It is not the prince who is likely to embarrass you when he does you the honour of conversing; it is his suite.

The emperor continued:—"It is not very easy to prosecute this work: submission may cause you to believe that there is uniformity among us, but I must undeceive you; there is no other country where is found such diversity of races, of manners, of religion, and of mind, as in Russia. The diversity lies at the bottom, the uniformity appears on the surface, and the unity is only apparent. You see near to us twenty officers, the two first only are Russians; the three next to them are conciliated Poles; several of the others are Germans; there are even the Khans of the Kirguises, who bring me their sons to educate among my cadets. There is one of them," he said, pointing with his finger to a little Chinese monkey, in a whimsical costume of velvet all bedizened with gold.

"Two hundred thousand children are brought up and instructed at my cost with this child."

"Sire, every thing is done on a large scale in this country—every thing is colossal."

"Too colossal for one man."

"What man has ever stood in nearer relation to his people?"

"You speak of Peter the Great?"

"No, sire."

"I hope that you will not be content with merely seeing Petersburg. What is your plan of route in visiting my country?"

"Sire, I wish to leave immediately after the fête of Peterhoff."

"To go——?"

"To Moscow and Ninji."

"Good: but you will be there too soon: you will leave Moscow before my arrival, and I should have been glad to see you there."

"This observation of your majesty's will cause me to change my plan."

"So much the better; we will show you the new works that we are making at the Kremlin. My object is to render the architecture of these old edifices better adapted to the uses now made of them. The palace was inconveniently small for me. You will be present also at a curious ceremony on the plain of Borodino: I am to place there the first stone of a monument which we are about to erect in commemoration of that battle."

I remained silent, and no doubt the expression of my face became serious. The emperor fixed his eyes on me, and then continued, in a tone of kindness and with a delicacy and even sensibility of manner which touched my heart,—"The inspection of the manoeuvres *at least* will interest you."

"Sire, every thing interests me in Russia."

I saw the old Marquis D——, who has only one leg, dance the polonaise with the empress. Lame as he is, he can get through this dance, which is nothing more than a solemn procession. He has arrived here with his sons: they travel like real great lords; a yacht brought them from London to Petersburg, where they have had forwarded English horses and carriages in great number. Their equipages are the most elegant, if they are not the most sumptuous, in Petersburg. These travellers are treated with marked attention. They are intimate with the imperial family. The emperor's love of field sports, and the recollection of his journey to London when Grand Duke, have established between him and the Marquis D—— that kind of familiarity which, it appears to me, must be more pleasant to the princes than to the private individuals who have become the objects of such favour. Where friendship is impossible, intimacy I should think can be only constraining. One would have said, to have sometimes seen the manners of the marquis's sons towards the members of the imperial family, that they thought on this subject as I did. If freedom of manners and speech should gain a footing at court, where will falsehood and politeness find a refuge?*

Young —— is at Petersburg: we meet every where, and with pleasure; he is a type of the Frenchman of the present day, but truly well bred. He appears to be enchanted with every thing. This satisfaction is so natural that it becomes contagious, and I doubt not the young man pleases as much as he is pleased. He travels to advantage, is well informed, and collects numerous facts, which he can number better than he can class; for at his age it is more easy to sum up than to arrange. But what a richly varied conversation is that of our ambassador! and how much will literature regret the time which he gives to politics, unless the latter be only a study by which the former will profit hereafter! Never was a man more perfectly adapted to his place, or one who played his part with greater ability, united with more apparent case and freedom from any assumption of importance. It is this combination which appears to me to constitute, in the present day, the condition of success for every Frenchman occupied with public affairs. No one, since the revolution of July, has ful-

* Some days after this was written, a little scene occurred at court which will give some idea of the manners of the most fashionable young people among the English in the present day: they have no right to reproach, nor yet any reason to envy, the least polite of our Parisian exquisites:—what a difference between this kind of blackguard elegance, and the politeness of the Buckinghams, the Lauzuns, and the Richelieus! The empress wished to give a private ball as a mark of attention to this family before their leaving Petersburg. She began by inviting the father, who dances so well with an artificial leg. "Madame," replied the old Marquis D——, "I have been loaded with kindnesses at Petersburg; but so many pleasures surpass my powers: I hope that your majesty will permit me to take my leave this evening, that I may get on board my yacht tomorrow morning, in order to return to England: otherwise I shall die of pleasure in Russia." "Well, then, I must give you up," replied the empress, satisfied with this polite and manly answer, worthy of the times in which the old lord must have first entered the world; then turning towards the sons of the marquis, whose stay in Petersburg was to be prolonged: "At least I may depend on you?" she said to the eldest. "Madame," replied this individual, "we are engaged to hunt the rein-deer to-day." The empress, who is said to be proud, was not discouraged, and, addressing herself to the younger brother, said, "You, at least, will remain with me?" The young man, at a loss for an excuse, and not knowing what to answer, in his vexation turned to his brother, murmuring, loudly enough to be overheard, "Am I then to be the victim?" This anecdote went the round of the whole court.

filled, so well as M. de Barante, the difficult charge of French ambassador at Petersburg.

In connection with the marriage fetês given in honour of the Grand Duchess Marie, a little incident occurred which will remind the reader of what often happened at the court of the Emperor Napoleon.

The grand chamberlain had died shortly before the marriage, and his office had been given to Count Golowkin, formerly Russian ambassador to China, to which country he could not obtain access. This nobleman, entering upon the functions of his office on the occasion of the marriage, had less experience than his predecessor. A young chamberlain, appointed by him, managed to incur the wrath of the emperor, and exposed his superior to a rather severe reprimand: it was at the ball of the Grand Duchess Helena.

The emperor was talking with the Austrian ambassador. The young chamberlain received from the Grand Duchess Marie an order to carry her invitation to this ambassador to dance with her. In his zeal the unfortunate *débutant* broke the circle of courtiers which I have before described as forming at a respectful distance around the emperor, and boldly approached his majesty's person, saying to the ambassador, "Monsieur le Comte, Madame la Duchesse de Leuchtenberg requests that you will dance with her the first polonaise."

The emperor, shocked with the ignorance of the new chamberlain, said to him, in an elevated tone of voice, "You have been appointed to a post, sir; learn, therefore, how to fulfil its duties: in the first place, my daughter is not the Duchess of Leuchtenberg—she is called the Grand Duchess Marie*; in the second place, you ought to know that no one interrupts me when I am conversing with any individual."†

The new chamberlain who received this harsh reprimand was, unfortunately, a poor Polish gentleman. The emperor, not content with what he had said, caused the grand chamberlain to be

---

* This title had been secured to her at her marriage.

† Did I not truly say that, at this court, life is passed in general rehearsals? An Emperor of Russia, from Peter the Great, downwards, never forgets that it is his office personally to instruct his people.

called, and recommended him to be, in future, more circumspect in his selection of deputies.

I left the ball of the Michael Palace at an early hour. I loitered on the staircase, and could have wished to remain there longer: it was a wood of orange trees in flower. Never have I seen any thing more magnificent or better directed than this fête: but there is nothing so fatiguing as admiration too greatly prolonged, especially if it does not relate to the phenomena of nature, or the works of the higher arts.

I lay down my pen in order to dine with a Russian officer, the young Count ———, who took me this morning to the cabinet of mineralogy, the finest I believe in Europe, for the Uralian mines are unequalled in the variety of their mineral wealth. Nothing can be seen here alone. A native of the country is always with you to do the honours of the public establishments and institutions, and there are not many days in the year favourable for seeing them. In summer they are repairing the edifices damaged by the frosts, in winter there is nothing but visiting: every one dances who does not freeze. It will be thought I am exaggerating when I say that Russia is scarcely better seen in Petersburg than in France. Strip the observation of its paradoxical form and it is strictly true. Most assuredly it is not sufficient to visit this country in order to know it. Without the aid of others, it is not possible to obtain an idea of any thing, and often this aid tyrannises over its object, and imbues him with ideas only that are fallacious.*

❖

* This is done designedly.

THE LADIES OF THE COURT ❖ THE FINNS ❖ THE OPERA ❖ THE EMPEROR THERE ❖ IMPOSING PERSON OF THIS PRINCE ❖ HIS ACCESSION TO THE THRONE ❖ COURAGE OF THE EMPRESS ❖ THE EMPEROR'S RECITAL OF THIS SCENE TO THE AUTHOR ❖ ANOTHER DESCRIPTION OF THE EMPEROR ❖ CONTINUATION OF HIS CONVERSATION ❖ HIS POLITICAL OPINIONS ❖ SINCERITY OF HIS LANGUAGE ❖ FÊTE AT THE DUCHESS OF OLDENBURG'S ❖ BAL CHAMPÊTRE ❖ FLOWERS IN RUSSIA ❖ THE FRIEND OF THE EMPRESS ❖ SEVERAL CONVERSATIONS WITH THE EMPEROR ❖ HIS NOBLE SENTIMENTS ❖ CONFIDENCE WITH WHICH HE INSPIRES THOSE WHO APPROACH HIM ❖ ARISTOCRACY THE ONLY BULWARK OF LIBERTY ❖ PARALLEL BETWEEN AUTOCRACIES AND DEMOCRACIES ❖ THE ARTS IN PETERSBURG ❖ ALL TRUE TALENT IS NATIONAL

❖

CHAPTER XIII

❖

Several of the ladies of this court, but their number is not great, have a reputation for beauty which is deserved; others have usurped this reputation by means of coquetries, contrivances, and affectations—all copied from the English; for the Russians in high life pass their time in searching for foreign models of fashion. They are deceived sometimes in their choice, when their mistake produces a singular kind of elegance—an elegance without taste. A Russian left to himself would spend his life in dreams of unsatisfied vanity: he would view himself as a barbarian. Nothing more injures the natural disposition, and consequently the mental powers, of a people, than this continual dwelling upon the social superiority of other nations. To feel humbled by the very sense of one's own assumption is an inconsistency in the actings of self-love which is not unfrequently to be seen in Russia, where the character of the *parvenu* may be studied under all its grades and phases.

As a general rule applicable to the different classes of the nation, beauty is less common among the women than the men; though among the latter also may be found great numbers whose faces are flat and void of all expression. The Finns have high cheek bones, small, dull, sunken eyes, and visages so flattened that it might be fancied they had all, at their birth, fallen on their noses. Their mouth is also deformed, and their whole appearance bears the impress of the slave. This portrait does not apply to the Slavonians.

I have met many people marked with the smallpox, a sight rarely now seen in other parts of Europe, and which betrays the negligence of the Russian administration on an important point.

In Petersburg the different races are so mingled, that it is impossible to form a correct idea of the real population of Russia. Germans, Swedes, Livonians, Finns (who are a species of Laplanders), Calmucs and other Tartar races, have so mixed their blood with that of the Slavonians, that the primitive beauty of the latter has, in the capital, gradually degenerated; which leads me often to think of the observation of the emperor, "Petersburg is Russian, but it is not Russia."

I have been witnessing at the opera what is called a *gala* representation. The building was magnificiently lighted: it is large, and well proportioned. Galleries and projecting boxes are unknown here: there is at Petersburg no citizen class for whom to provide seats. The architect, therefore, unfettered in his plan, can construct theatres of a simple and regular design, like those of Italy, where the women who are not of the highest ranks are seated in the pit.

By special favour I obtained a chair in the first row of the pit. On gala days these chairs are reserved for the greatest nobles, and the high court functionaries, and none are admitted to them except in the uniform or costume of their rank or office.

My right-hand neighbour, seeing from my dress that I was a stranger, addressed me in French with that hospitable politeness, which in Petersburg is a characteristic of the higher, and, to a certain extent, of all classes; for here every one is polite—the great, through the vanity of showing their good breeding, the little, through sentiments of fear.

After a few common-place observations, I asked my obliging neighbour the name of the piece that was to be performed. "It is a translation from the French," he answered: "The Devil on two Sticks." I puzzled my head to no purpose to make out what drama could have been translated under this title; at length it turned out that the *translation* was a pantomime founded on our ballet of the same name.

I did not much admire it, and directed my attention chiefly to the audience. At length, the court arrived. The imperial box is an elegant saloon, which occupies the back part of the theatre, and which is even yet more brilliantly illuminated.

The entrance of the emperor was imposing. As he advanced to the front of his box, accompanied by the empress, and followed by their family and the attendant courtiers, the public rose simultaneously. The emperor was dressed in a singularly splendid red uniform. That of the Cossacks looks well only on very young men: the one which the emperor wore better suited his age, and greatly set off the nobleness of his features and his stature. Before seating himself, he saluted the assembly with the peculiarly polite dignity by which he is characterised. The empress did the same, and, what appeared to me a want of respect towards the public, their suite followed their example. The whole theatre rendered to the sovereigns bow for bow, and, furthermore, overwhelmed them with plaudits and *hurras*. These demonstrations had an official character which greatly diminished their value. Wonderful that an emperor should be applauded by a pit-ful of courtiers! In Russia, real flattery would be the appearance of independence. The Russians have not found out this indirect mode of pleasing; and, in truth, its use might sometimes become perilous, notwithstanding the feeling of *ennui* which the servility of his subjects must often produce in the prince.

The compulsory manifestations of submission with which he is every where received is the reason why the present emperor has only twice in his life had the satisfaction of testing his personal power upon the assembled multitude—and this was during an insurrection. The only free man in Russia is the revolted soldier.

Viewed from the point where I sat, the emperor appeared truly worthy of commanding men, so noble was his face, and so majestic his figure. My mind involuntarily recurred to the period when he mounted the throne, and the contemplation of that bright page of history led my thoughts away from the scene that was enacting before me.

What I am now about to narrate was detailed to me by the emperor himself, only a few days ago. The reason that it was not stated in the last chapter is because the papers* containing such details could not be confided either to the Russian post or to any traveller.

The day on which Nicholas ascended the throne was that in which rebellion broke out among the guards. At the first intimation of the revolt of the troops, the emperor and empress proceeded alone to their chapel, and falling on their knees on the steps of the altar, bound each other by mutual oath before God, to die as sovereigns, if they should be unable to triumph over the insurrection.

The emperor might well view the evil as serious, for he had been informed that the archbishop had already vainly endeavoured to appease the soldiers. In Russia, when religious power loses its influence, disorder is indeed formidable.

After solemnly making the sign of the cross, the emperor proceeded to confront the rebels, and to overmaster them by his presence, and by the calm energy of his countenance. He stated this to me in terms more modest than those which I now use, and of which, unfortunately, I have not preserved the recollection, for at first I was rather taken by surprise, owing to the unexpected turn of the conversation. Of what passed after recovering from this surprise my memory is more tenacious.

"Sire, your majesty drew your strength from the right source."

"I did not know what I was about to do or say—I was inspired."

"To receive such inspirations, it is necessary to merit them."

"I did nothing extraordinary; I said to the soldiers, 'Return to your ranks!' and at the moment of passing the regiment in review, I cried, 'On your knees!' They all obeyed. What gave me power was, that the instant before I had resigned myself to meet death. I am grateful for having succeeded; but I am not proud of it, for it was by no merit of my own."

Such were the noble expressions which the emperor made use of in relating to me this contemporary tragedy.

From the above relation an idea may be formed of the interesting nature of the subjects on which he converses with the travel-

---

* Despatched in the form of a letter to Paris.—*Trans.*

lers whom he honours with his good-will. It will also explain the character of the influence he exercises over ourselves, as well as over his people and his family. He is the Louis XIV. of the Slavonians.

Eye-witnesses have informed me that his form seemed to dilate and grow more lofty and commanding at each step that he made in advancing towards the mutineers. Taciturn, melancholy, and absorbed in trifles as he had appeared during his youth, he became a hero the moment he was a monarch. The contrary is usually the case—and princes promise more than they perform.

This prince is, on the throne, as perfectly in his proper sphere as a great actor would be on the boards. His attitude before the rebel-guard was so imposing, that while he harangued the troops one of the conspirators, it is said, advanced four times towards him with the intention of killing him, and four times his courage failed, like that of the Cimbrian's before Marius.

An absurd falsehood was the instrument that the conspirators had employed to incite the army to this outbreak. They had spread a report that Nicholas had usurped the crown of his brother Constantine, who was, they said, on his way to Petersburg, to defend his rights by force of arms. The means through which they had induced the rebels to cry under the palace windows in favour of the Constitution, was by persuading them that this word *Constitution* was the name of the wife of Constantine. It was therefore an idea of duty which actuated the soldiers, who believed the emperor an usurper, and who could only be led into rebellion by a fraud. The fact is, that Constantine had refused the crown through weakness: he dreaded being poisoned. God knows, and there are perhaps some men who know also, if his abdication saved him from the peril which he thus expected to avoid.

It was then in support of legitimacy that the deceived soldiers revolted against their legitimate sovereign. People remarked that, during the whole time the emperor remained among the troops, he did not once put his horse in rapid motion, but though so calm, he was very pale. He was putting his power to the test, and the success of the proof assured him of the future obedience of his people.

Such a man cannot be judged by the standard applied to ordinary characters. His grave and authoritative voice—his magnetic and piercing look, which is often cold and fixed rather through the habit of suppressing his passions than of dissimulating his thoughts, for he is frank—his superb forehead—his features, which are those of an Apollo or a Jupiter—his immovable, imposing, and imperious expression—his figure, more noble than easy, more monumental than human, exercise upon all who approach his person a power which is irresistible. He becomes master of the wills of others, because it is seen that he is master of his own.

The following is what I have retained of the remainder of our conversation:—

"The insurrection thus appeased, your majesty must have entered the palace with feelings very different to those under which it was left; not only the throne, but the admiration of the world, and the sympathy of all lofty minds being, by this event, assured to your majesty."

"I did not thus view it: what I then did has been too much praised."

The emperor did not tell me that on his return he found his wife afflicted with a nervous trembling of the head, of which she has never been entirely cured. This convulsive motion is scarcely visible; indeed, on some days, when calm and in good health, the empress is entirely free from it: but whenever she is suffering, either mentally or physically, the evil returns and augments. This noble woman must have fearfully struggled with the inquietude occasioned by her husband's daring exposure of himself to the assassin's blow. On his return, she embraced him without speaking; but the emperor, after having soothed her, felt himself grow weak, and threw himself into the arms of one of his most faithful servants, exclaiming—"What a commencement of a reign!"

I publish these details, because it is well they should be known, in order to teach the obscure to envy less the fortune of the great.

Whatever apparent inequality legislation may have established in the different conditions of civilised men, the equity of Providence justifies itself by maintaining a secret equality, which nothing can alter or disturb. This is done by the agency of mental evils, which generally increase in the same ratio that physical evils diminish. There is less injustice in the world than the founders and legislators of nations have endeavoured to produce, or than the vulgar imagine they perceive: the laws of nature are more equitable than the laws of man.

These reflections passed rapidly through my mind as I conversed with the emperor, producing in me a sentiment which he would, I believe, have been rather surprised to learn that he had inspired—it was that of indescribable pity. I took care to conceal the emotion, and continued:

"I can truly say, sire, that one of the chief motives of my curiosity in visiting Russia was the desire of approaching a prince who exercises such power over men."

"The Russians are amiable; but he should render himself worthy who would govern such a people."

"Your majesty has better appreciated the wants and the position of this country than any of your predecessors."

"Despotism still exists in Russia: it is the essence of my government, but it accords with the genius of the nation."

"Sire, by stopping Russia on the road of imitation, you are restoring her to herself."

"I love my country, and I believe I understand it. I assure you, that when I feel heartily weary of all the miseries of the times, I endeavour to forget the rest of Europe by retiring towards the interior of Russia."

"In order to refresh yourself at your fountainhead?"

"Precisely so. No one is more from his heart a Russian than I am. I am going to say to you what I would not say to another, but I feel that you will comprehend me."

Here the emperor interrupted himself, and looked at me attentively. I continued to listen without replying, and he proceeded:
—

"I can understand republicanism: it is a plain and straightforward form of government, or, at least, it might be so; I can understand absolute monarchy, for I am myself the head of such an order of things; but I cannot understand a representative monarchy: it is the government of lies, fraud, and corruption; and I would rather fall back even upon China than ever adopt it."

"Sire, I have always regarded representative government as a compact inevitable in certain communities at certain epochs; but like all other compacts, it does not solve questions—it only adjourns difficulties."

The emperor seemed to say, Go on. I continued:

"It is a truce signed between democracy and monarchy, under the auspices of two very mean tyrants, fear and interest; and it is prolonged by that pride of intellect which takes pleasure in talking, and that popular vanity which satisfies itself on words. In short, it is the aristocracy of oratory, substituted for the aristocracy of birth: it is the government of the lawyers."

"Sir, you speak the truth," said the emperor, pressing my hand: "I have been a representative sovereign,* and the world knows what it has cost me not to have been willing to submit to the exigencies of *this infamous* government (I quote literally). To buy votes, to corrupt consciences, to seduce some in order to deceive others; all those means I disdained, as degrading those who obey as much as those who command, and I have dearly paid the penalty of my straightforwardness; but, God be praised, I have done for ever with this detestable political machine. I shall never more be a constitutional king. I have too much need of saying all that I think ever to consent to reign over any people by means of stratagem and intrigue."

The name of Poland, which presented itself incessantly to our thoughts, was not once uttered in this singular conversation.

The effect it produced on me was great. I felt myself subdued. The nobleness of sentiment which the emperor displayed, and the frankness of his language, seemed to me greatly to temper his omnipotence.

I confess I was dazzled! A man who could, notwithstanding my ideas of independence, make himself forgiven for being absolute monarch of sixty millions of fellow-beings, was, in my eyes, something beyond our common nature; but I distrusted my own admiration. I felt like the citizens among us, who, when surprised by the grace and address of the men of other days are tempted by their good taste to yield to the captivating lure, but their princi-

* In Poland.

ples resisting, they remain uncomfortably stiff, and endeavour to appear as insensible as possible. It is not in my nature to doubt a man's words at the moment they are addressed to me. A human being who speaks is to me the organ of Deity: it is only by dint of reflection and experience that I recognise the possibility of design and disguise. This may be called a foolish simplicity, which perhaps it is; but I solace myself for such mental weakness by the recollection that its source is a mental virtue: my own good faith makes me believe in the sincerity of others, even in that of an emperor of Russia.

The beauty of his face is also another instrument of persuasion, for this beauty is moral as well as physical. I attribute its effect to the truth of his sentiments, yet more than to the regularity of his features. It was at a ball at the Duchess of Oldenburg's that I had this interesting conversation with the emperor. The fête was singular, and deserves describing.

The Duchess of Oldenburg, who was a princess of Nassau, is nearly allied, through her husband, to the emperor. She wished to give a soirée on the occasion of the marriage of the Grand Duchess but being unable to excel the magnificence of the former fêtes, or to vie with the splendours of the court, she conceived the idea of a bal champêtre at her house in the Islands.

The Archduke of Austria, who arrived two days ago to be present at the festivities of Petersburg; the ambassadors of the whole world (singular actors in a pastoral); all Russia, and finally, all the high-born foreigners, gathered together to promenade with an air of innocent simplicity, in a garden where orchestras were concealed among the distant groves.

The emperor prescribes the character of each fête: the direction for this day was, the elegant simplicity of Horace.

The humour of all minds, including even the *corps diplomatique*, was throughout the evening modelled in conformity with this order. It was like reading an eclogue, not of Theocritus or Virgil, but of Fontenelle.

We danced in the open air until eleven in the evening, and then, the heavy dews having sufficiently inundated the heads and shoulders of the women, young and old, who assisted at this triumph over the climate, we re-entered the little palace which forms the usual summer-residence of the Duchess of Oldenburg.

In the centre of the villa* was a rotunda, quite dazzling with gold and wax lights, in which the dancers continued their amusement, while the others wandered over the rest of the house, to which this bright rotunda formed, as it were, a central sun.

There presided throughout the fête, which was smaller than the preceding ones, a species of splendid disorder that struck me more than the pomp of all the others. Without speaking of the comical constraint depicted on the countenances of certain parties who were obliged, for a time, to affect rural simplicity, it was a soirée altogether original, a species of Imperial Tivoli, where people felt themselves almost free, although in presence of an absolute master. The sovereign who enjoys himself seems no longer a despot, and this evening the emperor enjoyed himself.

The excessive heats of the present summer had fortunately favoured the design of the duchess. Her summer-house is situated in the most beautiful part of the Islands, and it was in the midst of a garden radiant with flowers (in pots), and upon an English grass-plot—another marvel here—that she had fixed her dancing saloon. This was a superb inlaid flooring, surrounded by elegant balustrades, richly embellished with flowers, and to which the sky served as ceiling. In Petersburg the luxury of rare flowers, reared in the hot-house, supplies the place of trees. Its inhabitants— men who have left Asia to imprison themselves among the snows of the north—recollect the oriental luxury of their earlier country, and do their best to supply the sterility of nature, which, left to herself, produces only pine and birch trees. Art raises here an infinite variety of shrubs and plants; for as every thing is artificial, it is just as easy to grow the exotic flowers of America as the violets and lilacs of France.

The empress, delicate as she is, danced, with her neck bare and her head uncovered, every polonaise at this magnificent ball in the garden of her cousin. In Russia every body pursues his career to the limits of his powers. The duty of an empress is to amuse herself to death.

* In Russian, "the datcha."

This German princess, the victim of a frivolity which must surely press as heavily as chains upon captives, enjoys in Russia a happiness rarely enjoyed in any land, or in any rank, and unexampled in the life of an empress—she has a friend. Of this lady, the Baroness de ——, I have already spoken. She and the empress, since the marriage of the latter, have scarcely ever been separated. The baroness, whose character is sincere, and whose heart is devoted, has not profited by her position. The man whom she has married is one of the officers in the army to whom the emperor is most indebted; for the Baron —— saved his life on the day of the revolt that attended the accession to the throne, by exposing his own with a devotedness unprompted by interest. Nothing could be sufficient reward for such an act of courage, it has, consequently, gone unrewarded.

As the garden became dark, a distant music answered to the orchestra of the ball, and harmoniously chased away the gloom of the night, a gloom too natural to these monotonous shades. The desert recommences on the Islands, where the pines and morasses of Finland adjoin the prettiest parks. An arm of the Neva flows slowly—for here all water appears stagnant—before the windows of the little princely house of the Duchess of Oldenburg. On this evening the water was covered with boats full of spectators, and the road also swarmed with pedestrians. A mixed crowd of citizens, who are as much slaves as the peasants, and of work-people, all courtiers of courtiers, pressed among the carriages of the grandees to gaze on the livery of the master of their masters. The whole spectacle was striking and original. In Russia, the names are the same as elsewhere, but the things are altogether different. I often escaped from the throng of the ball to walk beneath the trees of the park, and muse on the melancholy that insinuates itself into the festivals of such a land. But my meditations were short, for on this day the emperor seemed as though determined to keep possession of my mind. Was it because he had discovered in the bottom of my heart some prejudices little favourable towards him, though the result only of what I had heard before being presented; or did he find it amusing to converse for a few moments with one who differed from those that daily came in his way, or was it that Madame de ——had created an influence in his mind in my favour? I could not explain to my own satisfaction the cause of receiving so much honour.

The emperor is not only accustomed to command actions, he knows how to reign over hearts: perhaps he wished to conquer mine; perhaps the ices of my shyness served to stimulate his self-love. The desire of pleasing is natural to him: to compel admiration would still be to make himself obeyed. Perhaps he had a desire of trying his power on a stranger; perhaps, in short, it was the instinct of a man who had long lived deprived of the truth, and who believed he had for once met with a sincere character. I repeat, I was ignorant of his motives; but on that evening I could not stand before him, nor even place myself in a retired corner of the room where he might be, without his obliging me to approach and talk with him.

On seeing me enter the ball-room, he said, "What have you seen this morning?"

"Sire, I have been visiting the Cabinet of Natural History, and the famous Mammoth of Siberia."

"It is an object unequalled, in its kind, in the world."

"Yes, sire; there are many things in Russia that are not to be seen elsewhere."

"You flatter me."

"I respect your majesty too much to dare to flatter; but perhaps, sire, I do not fear you sufficiently; and I therefore ingenuously speak my thoughts, when even truth appears like compliment."

"This is a delicate compliment, monsieur: you strangers spoil us."

"Sire, your majesty was pleased to desire that I should be at my ease with you, and you have succeeded, as in every thing else that you undertake. Your majesty has cured me, for a time at least, of my natural timidity."

Obliged to avoid all allusion to the great political interests of the day, I wished to lead the conversation towards a subject which interested me quite as much; I added, therefore, "Each time that I am permitted to approach your majesty, I recognise the power which caused your enemies to fall at your feet on the day that your majesty ascended the throne."

"In your country there are prejudices entertained against us, which are more difficult to triumph over than the passions of a revolted army."

"Sire, you are seen from too great a distance: if your majesty were better known you would be better appreciated, and would find among us, as well as here, abundance of admirers. The commencement of your majesty's reign has already called forth just praises; it was also equally, or even yet more highly lauded at the time of the cholera; for in this second insurrection your majesty displayed the same authority, but tempered with the most generous devotion to the cause of humanity. Energy has never failed you, sire, in times of danger."

"The moments of which you recall the recollection have been, doubtless, the best in my life; nevertheless, they have appeared to me as the most frightful."

"I can well understand that, sire; to subdue nature in ourselves and in others requires an effort——"

"An effort which is terrible," interrupted the emperor, with an energy which startled me, "and one that is felt long after."

"Yes; but there is the consolation of having acted heroically."

"I have not acted heroically. I only performed my part: in such circumstances none can tell what he will say. We run into the danger, without previously inquiring how we are to get out of it."

"It was God who inspired you, sire; and if two so dissimilar things as poetry and government may be compared, I should say that you acted in the same way that poets sing, in listening to the voice from above."

"There was no poetry in that action."

I could perceive that my comparison had not appeared flattering, because it had not been understood in the sense of the Latin poet. At court they are in the habit of viewing poetry as merely an exhibition of wit; and it would have been necessary to have launched into a discussion to prove that it is the purest and most brilliant light that irradiates the soul. I therefore preferred remaining silent; but the emperor, being unwilling, doubtless, to leave me under the regret of having displeased him, detained me yet further, to the great astonishment of the court, and resumed the conversation with a kindness that was very gratifying. "What is your decided plan of route?" he asked.

"Sire, after the fête at Peterhoff, I propose leaving for Moscow, from whence I wish to proceed to Nijni, to see the fair, and to return to Moscow before the arrival of your majesty."

"So much the better: I shall be glad for you to examine, in detail, my works at the Kremlin. My residence there was too small, I am therefore building another more suitable; and I will explain to you myself all my plans for the embellishment of this part of Moscow, which we view as the cradle of the empire. But you have no time to lose, for you have immense distances to travel over—the distances! these are the curse of Russia."

"Do not, sire, regret them: they form the canvas of pictures that are to be filled up; elsewhere the earth is too confined for the inhabitants; but it will never fail your majesty."

"The time fails me."

"You have the future."

"They little know me who reproach my ambition: far from seeking to extend our territory, I am desirous of drawing closer around me the entire population of Russia. It is simply over misery and barbarism that I wish to achieve conquests: to ameliorate the condition of the Russians would be more gratifying than to aggrandise myself. If you knew what an amiable people the Russians are! how gentle, and how naturally polite! You will see them at Peterhoff; but it is here, on the first of January, that I would have especially desired to show them to you." Then, returning to his favourite theme, he continued: "But it is not easy to render one's self worthy of governing such a people."

"Your majesty has already done much for Russia."

"I fear sometimes that I have not done all that might have been effected."

This Christian speech came from the depths of the heart, and affected me even to tears: it made so much impression on me that I said to myself, The emperor has quicker perceptions than I; and if he had any motive for saying this he would have felt greater difficulty in saying it. He has, then, only betrayed a beautiful and noble sentiment, the scruple of a conscientious king. This cry of humanity uttered by a mind which every thing must contribute to render proud, touched my heart. We were in public, and I endeavoured to hide my feeling; the emperor, who answers to what is thought more than to what is said, (and in this sagacity lies the great charm of his conversation, as well as the potency of his influence,) perceiving the impression which he had produced, and which I attempted to disguise, approached me at the moment of parting, took my hand with an air of kindness, and pressing it, said, *"Au revoir."*

The emperor is the only man in the empire with whom one may talk without fear of informers; he is also the only one in whom I have as yet recognised natural sentiments and sincere language. If I lived in this country, and had a secret to conceal, I should begin by confiding it to him.

If he has, as I think, more pride than vanity, more dignity than arrogance, the general impression of the various portraits I have successively traced of him, and especially the effect his conversation produced on me, ought to be satisfactory to him: in fact, I did my best to resist the influence of his attractions. I am certainly any thing but revolutionary, still I am revolutionised: such is the consequence of being born in France, and of living there. But I have a yet better reason to give in explanation of my endeavour to resist the influence of the emperor over me. Aristocrat, both from character and conviction, I feel that the aristocracy alone can resist either the seductions or the abuses of absolute power. Without an aristocracy, there would be nothing but tyranny both in monarchies and in democracies. The sight of despotism is revolting to me in spite of myself: it offends all the ideas of liberty which spring alike from my natural feelings and my political creed. No aristocrat can submit without repugnance to see the levelling hand of despotism laid upon the people. This however happens in pure democracies as much as in absolute monarchical governments.

It appears to me, that if I were a sovereign I should like the society of those who would recognise in me the fellow-being as well as the prince, especially if, when viewed apart from my titles, and reduced to myself, I should still have a right to the title of a sincere, firm, and upright man.

Let the reader seriously ask himself, if that which I have recounted of the Emperor Nicholas, since my arrival in Russia places this prince lower in his opinion than before he had read these chapters.

Our frequent communications in public gained me numerous acquaintances, as well as renewal of acquaintances. Many persons whom I had met elsewhere cast themselves in my way, though only after they had observed that I was the object of this particular good-will on the part of the sovereign. These men were the most exalted persons at court; but it is the custom of people of the world, and especially of placemen, to be sparing of every thing except ambitious schemes. To preserve at court sentiments above the vulgar range, requires the endowment of a very lofty mind, and lofty minds are rare.

It cannot be too often repeated, that there are no great noblemen in Russia, because there are no independent characters, with the exception, at least, of those superior minds, which are too few in number to exercise any general influence on society. It is the pride inspired by high birth, which, far more than riches or rank acquired by industry, renders man independent.

This country, in many respects so different from France, still resembles it in one—it is without any social hierarchy. By reason of this gap in the body politic, universal equality reigns in Russia as in France, and therefore, in both countries, the minds of men are restless and unquiet: with us this is demonstrated by visible agitations and explosions, in Russia, political passions are concentrated. In France every one can arrive at his object, by setting out from the tribune, in Russia, by setting out at court. The lowest of men, if he can discover how to please his sovereign, may become to-morrow second only to the emperor. The favour of that god is the prize which produces as many prodigies of effort, and miraculous metamorphoses, as the desire of popularity among us. A profound flatterer in Petersburg is the same as a sublime orator in Paris. What a talent of observation must not that have been in the Russian courtiers, which enabled them to discover that a means of pleasing the emperor was to walk in winter without a great coat in the streets of Petersburg. This flattery of the climate has cost the life of more than one ambitious individual. Under a despotism which is without limits, minds are as much agitated and tormented as under a republic; but with this difference, the agitation of the subjects of an autocracy is more painful on account of the silence and concealment that ambition has to impose upon itself in order to succeed. With us, sacrifices, to be profitable, have to be public; here, on the contrary, they must be secret. The unlimited monarch dislikes no one so much as a subject *publicly* devoted. All zeal that exceeds a blind and servile obedience is felt by him as both troublesome and suspicious: exceptions open the door to pretensions, pretensions assume the shape of rights, and under a despot, a subject who fancies that he has rights is a rebel.

Marshal Paskiewitch can attest the truth of these remarks: they do not dare to ruin him, but they do all that is possible to make him a cipher. Before this journey, my ideas of despotism were suggested by my study of society in Austria and Prussia. I had forgotten that those states are despotic only in name, and that manners and customs there serve to correct institutions. In Germany, the people despotically governed appeared to me the happiest upon earth: a despotism thus mitigated by the mildness of its customs caused me to think that despotism was not after all so detestable a thing as our philosophers had pretended. I did not then know what absolute government was among a nation of slaves.

It is to Russia that we must go in order to see the results of this terrible combination of the mind and science of Europe with the genius of Asia—a combination which is so much the more formidable as it is likely to last: for ambition and fear, passions which elsewhere ruin men by causing them to speak too much, here engender silence. This forced silence produces a forced calm, an apparent order, more strong and more frightful than anarchy itself. I admit but few fundamental rules in politics, because in the art of government I believe more in the efficacy of circumstances than of principles, but my indifference does not go so far as to tolerate institutions which necessarily exclude all dignity of human character in their objects.

Perhaps an independent judiciary and a powerful aristocracy would instill a calm and an elevation into the Russian character, and render the land happy; but I do not believe the emperor dreams of such modes of ameliorating the condition of his people. However superior a man may be, he does not voluntarily renounce his own way of doing good to others.

But what right have we to reproach the Emperor of Russia with his love of authority? Is not the genius of revolution as tyrannical at Paris as the genius of despotism at Petersburg?

At the same time, we owe it to ourselves to make here a restriction that will show the difference between the social state of the two countries. In France, revolutionary tyranny is an evil belonging to a state of transition; in Russia, despotic tyranny is permanent.

It is fortunate for the reader that I have wandered from the subject with which I commenced my chapter, namely, the illuminated theatre, the gala representation, and the *translated* pantomime (a Russian expression) of a French ballet. Had I continued my description, he might have experienced a little of the *ennui* with which this dramatic solemnity inspired me; for the dancing at the Opera of Petersburg, without Madamoiselle Taglioni, is as cold and stiff as the dances of all European theatres when they are not executed by the first talents in the world; and the presence of the court encourages neither actors nor audience, for, before the sovereign, it is not permitted to applaud. The arts, disciplined as they are in Russia, produce interludes which do very well to amuse soldiers during the intervals of military command. They are magnificent, royal, imperial—but they are not really amusing. Here the *artistes* obtain wealth, but they do not draw inspiration: riches and elegance foster talents; but that which is yet more indispensable to them is the good taste and the freedom of public opinion.

The Russians have not yet reached the point of civilisation at which there is real enjoyment of the arts. At present their enthusiasm on these subjects is pure vanity; it is a pretence, like their passion for classic architecture. Let these people look within themselves, let them listen to their primitive genius, and, if they have received from Heaven a perception of the beauties of art, they will give up copying, in order to produce what God and nature expect from them. So far, all their magnificent works together will never be equivalent, in the eyes of those few real amateurs of the beautiful who vegetate at Petersburg, to a sojourn in Paris, or a journey in Italy.

The Opera-house is built on the plan of those of Milan and Naples; but these latter are more stately, and more harmonious in their proportions, than any thing
of the kind which I have yet
seen in Russia.

❖

CHAPTER XIV

❖

The population of Petersburg amounts to four hundred and fifty thousand souls, besides the garrison. So say patriotic Russians; but those who are well informed, and who consequently pass here for evil-disposed persons, assure me that it does not reach to four hundred thousand, in which number the garrison is included. Small houses of wood occupy the quarters beyond those immense spaces, called squares, that form the centre of the city.

The Russians, descended from a junction of various warlike and wandering tribes, have not yet quite forgotten the life of the bivouac. Petersburg is the head-quarters of an army, and not the capital of a nation. However magnificent this military city may be, it appears bare and naked in the eyes of one from the West of Europe.

"The distances are the curse of Russia," said the emperor; and it is a remark the justice of which may be verified even in the streets of Petersburg. Thus, it is not for the sake of display that people's carriages are drawn by four horses: here every visit is an excursion. The Russian horses, though full of mettle and sinew, have not so much bone as ours: the badness of the pavement soon tires them; two horses could not easily draw for any considerable time an ordinary carriage in the streets of Petersburg. To drive four is therefore an object of the first necessity to those who wish to live in the fashionable world. Among the Russians, however, all have not the right to attach four horses to their carriage. This permission is only accorded to persons of a certain rank.

After leaving the centre of the city the stranger loses himself in vaguely-defined lines of road, bordered by barracks which seem as though destined for the temporary accommodation of labourers employed in some great work; they are the magazines of forage, clothes, and of other supplies for the military. The grass grows in these *soi-disant* and always deserted streets.

So many peristyles have been added to houses, so many porticoes adorn the barracks that here represent palaces, so great a passion for borrowed decorations has presided over the construction of this temporary capital, that I count fewer men than columns in the squares of Petersburg, always silent and melancholy, by reason of their size alone, and their unchangeable regularity. The line and rule figure well the manner in which absolute sovereigns view things, and straight angles may be said to be the blocks over which despotic architecture stumbles. Living architecture, if the expression may be permitted, will not rise at command. It springs, so to speak, from itself, and is an involuntary creation of the genius and wants of a people. To make a great nation is infallibly to create an architecture. I should not be astonished if some one succeeded in proving that there are as many original styles of architecture as mother tongues. The mania for rules of symmetry is not, however, peculiar to the Russians: with us, it is a legacy of the Empire. Had it not been for this bad taste of the Parisian architects, we should, long since, have been presented with some sensible plan for ornamenting and finishing our monstrous Place du Carrousel, but the necessity for parallels stops every thing.

When architects of genius successively contributed their efforts to making the square of the Grand Duke at Florence one of the most beautiful objects in the world, they were not tyrannised over by a passion for straight lines and arbitrary proportions: they conceived the idea of the beautiful in all its liberty, without reference to mathematical diagrams. It has been a want of the instinctive perceptions of art, and the free creations of fancy working upon popular data, which has caused a mathematical eye to preside over the creation of Petersburg. One can never for a moment forget, in surveying this abode of monuments without genius, that it is a city built by a man, and not by a people. The conceptions appear limited, though their dimensions are enormous.

The principal street in Petersburg is the Perspective Newski, one of the three lines which meet at the palace of the Admiralty. These three lines divide into five regular parts the southern side of the city, which, like Versailles, takes the form of a fan. It is more modern than the port, built near to the islands by Peter the Great.

The Perspective Newski deserves to be described in detail. It is a beautiful street, a league in length, and as broad as our Boulevards. In several places trees have been planted, as unfortunate in their position as those of Paris. It serves as a promenade and rendezvous for all the idlers of the city. Of these, however, there are but few, for here people seldom move for the sake of moving; each step that is taken has an object independent of pleasure. To carry an order—to pay their court—to obey their master, whoever he may be—such are the influences which put in motion the greater part of the population of Petersburg and of the empire.

Large uneven flint-stones form the execrable pavement of this boulevard called the Perspective: but here, as in some other principal streets, there are deeply imbedded in the midst of the stones, blocks of fir-wood in the shape of cubes, and sometimes of octagons, over which the carriages glide swiftly. Each of these pavements consists of two lines, two or three feet broad, and separated by a stripe of the ordinary flint pavement on which the shaft horse runs. Two of these roads, that is to say, four lines of wood, run the length of the Perspective Newski, one on the left, the other on the right of the street, without touching the houses, from which they are separated by raised flags for the foot passengers. This beautiful and vast perspective extends—gradually becoming less populous, less beautiful, and more melancholy—to the undetermined limits of the habitable city, in other words, to the confines of the Asiatic barbarism by which Petersburg is always besieged; for the desert may be found at the extremity of its most superb streets.

A little below the bridge of Aniskoff is the street named Jelognaia, which leads to a desert called the square of Alexander. I doubt whether the Emperor Nicholas has ever seen this street. The superb city created by Peter the Great, and beautified by Catherine II., and other sovereigns, is lost at last in an unsightly mass of stalls and workshops, confused heaps of edifices without name, large squares without design, and in which the natural slovenliness and the inborn filthiness of the people of the land, have for one hundred years permitted every species of dirt and rubbish to accumulate. Such filth, heaped up year after year in the Russian cities, serves as a protestation against the pretension of the German princes, who flatter themselves that they have thoroughly polished the Slavonian nations. The primitive character of these people, however disguised it may have been by the yoke imposed upon it, at least shows itself in some of the corners of the cities; and if they have cities it is not because they wanted them, but because their military masters compel them to emulate the West of Europe. These unfortunate animals, placed in the cage of European civilisation, are victims of the mania, or rather of the ambition of the Czars, conquerors of the future world, and who well know that before subjugating us, they must imitate us.

Nothing, I am told, can give any idea of the state of the Petersburg streets during the melting of the snow. Within the fortnight which follows the breaking up of the ice on the Neva, all the bridges are carried away, and the communications between different quarters of the city are, during several days, interrupted, and often entirely broken off. The streets then become the beds of furious torrents; few political crises could cause so much damage as this annual revolt of nature against an incomplete and impracticable civilisation. Since the thaw at Petersburg has been described to me I complain no longer of the pavements, detestable though they be; for I remember they have to be renewed every year.

After mid-day, the Perspective Newski, the grand square of the palace, the quays and the bridges are enlivened by a considerable number of carriages of various kinds and curious forms: this rather relieves the habitual dulness of the most monotonous capital in Europe. The interior of the houses is equally gloomy, for notwithstanding the magnificence of certain apartments destined to receive company, and furnished in the English style, there may be seen in the back ground various signs of a want of cleanliness and order which at once reminds the observer of Asia.

The articles of furniture least used in a Russian house are beds. The women servants sleep in recesses similar to those in the old fashioned porters' lodges in France; whilst the men roll themselves up on the stairs, in the vestibule, and even, it is said, in the saloons upon the cushions, which they place on the floor for the night.

This morning I paid a visit to Prince ———. He is a great nobleman, but decayed in estate, infirm and dropsical. He suffers so greatly that he cannot get up, and yet he has no bed on which to lie,—I mean to say, nothing which would be called a bed in lands where civilisation is of older date. He lives in the house of his sister, who is absent. Alone in this naked palace, he passes the night on a wooden board covered with a carpet and some pillows. In all the Russian houses that I have entered, I have observed that the screen is as necessary to the bed of the Slavonians as musk is to their persons:—intense dirtiness does not always exclude external elegance. Sometimes however they have a bed for show, an object of luxury, which is maintained through respect for European fashions, but of which no use is ever made. The residences of several Russians of taste are distinguished by a peculiar ornament—a little artificial garden in the corner of the drawing-room. Three long stands of flowers are ranged round a window so as to form a little verdant saloon or kind of chiosc, which reminds one of those in gardens. The stands are surmounted by an ornamented balustrade, which rises to about the height of a man, and is overgrown with ivy or other climbing plants that twist around the trellis work, and produce a cool agreeable effect in the midst of a vast apartment blazing with gilt work, and crowded with furniture. In this little verdant boudoir are placed a table and a few chairs: the lady of the house is generally seated there, and there is room for two or three others, for whom it forms a retreat, which, if not very secret, is secluded enough to please the imagination.

The effect of this household thicket is not more pleasing than the idea is sensible in a land where secrecy should preside over all private conversation. The usage is, I believe, imported from Asia.

I should not be surprised to see the artificial gardens of the Russian saloons introduced some day into the houses of Paris. They would not disfigure the abode of the most fashionable female politician in France. I should rejoice to see the innovation, were it only to cope with the Anglo-manes who have inflicted an injury on good taste and the real genius of the French, which I shall never pardon. The Slavonians, when they are handsome, are lightly and elegantly formed, though their appearance still conveys the idea of strength. Their eyes are all oval in shape, and have the deceitful, furtive glance of the Asiatics. Whether dark or blue, they are invariably clear and lively, constantly in motion, and when they laugh their expression is very graceful.

This people, grave by necessity rather than by nature, scarcely dare to laugh except with their eyes; but, words being thus repressed, these eyes, animated by silence, supply the place of eloquence, so strongly is passion depicted in their expression. That expression is almost always intelligent, and sometimes gentle, though more often anxious even to a degree of wildness that conveys the idea of some animal of the deer kind caught in the toils.

The Slavonians, born to guide a chariot, show good blood, like the horses which they drive. Their strange appearance and the activity of their steeds render it amusing to traverse the streets of Petersburg. Thanks to its inhabitants, and, in despite of its architects, this city resembles no other in Europe.

The Russian coachmen sit upright on their seats: they always drive with great speed, but with safety. The precision and quickness of their eye is admirable. Whether with two or four horses, they have always two reins to each horse, which they hold with the arms much extended. No impediment stops them in their course; men and horses, both half wild, scour the city at full speed: but nature has rendered them quick and adroit, consequently, notwithstanding the reckless daring of these coachmen, accidents are of rare occurrence in the streets of Petersburg. They have often no whip, or when they have one, it is so short that they can make no use of it. Neither do they have recourse to the voice: the reins and the bit are their only instruments. One may traverse Petersburg for hours without hearing a single shout. If the pedestrians do not get out of the way sufficiently quickly, the falleiter, or postillion, utters a little yelp, like the sharp cry of a marmot roused in his nest, on hearing which every one gives way, and the carriage rushes past without having once slackened its speed.

The carriages are in general void of all taste, badly furnished, and badly kept. If brought from England they do not long resist the wear and tear of the pavement of Petersburg. The harness is strong, and at the same time light and elegant: it is made of excellent leather; in short, notwithstanding the want of taste, and the negligence of the servants, the *tout ensemble* of these equipages is original, and, to a certain degree, picturesque.

They only harness four horses abreast for long journeys. In Petersburg they are placed two and two; the traces by which they are attached are long beyond all proportion. The child who guides them is, like the coachman, dressed in the Persian robe called the *armiac*. However well it may suit the man who is seated, it is not convenient on horseback; notwithstanding which the Russian postillion is bold and dextrous.

I do not know how to describe the gravity, the haughty silence, the address, and the imperturbable temerity of these little Slavonian monkeys. Their pertness and dexterity are my delight every time that I go in the city, and they have, which is less often seen here than elsewhere, the appearance of being happy. It is the nature of man to experience satisfaction when what he does is done well. The Russian coachmen and postillions being the most skilful in the world, are perhaps content with their lot, however hard it may be in some respects.

It must also be observed that those in the service of the nobles pique themselves on their personal appearance, and take pains with it; but those who ply on hire, excite, as do also their unfortunate horses, my sincere pity. They remain in the street from morning till evening, at the door of the person who lets them out, or on the stands assigned by the police. The horses eat always in harness, and the men always on their seat. I pity the former more than the latter, for the Russians have a taste for servitude.

The coachmen live, however, in this manner only during the summer. In the winter, sheds are built in the midst of the most frequented squares, and near the theatres, and the palaces where fêtes are most frequently given. Around this shelter, large fires are lighted, where the servants warm themselves; nevertheless, in the month of January, scarcely a night passes on which there is a ball, without a man or two dying of cold in the streets.

A lady, more sincere than others to whom I addressed questions on this subject, replied, "It is possible, but I have never heard it talked about." A denial which involved a strange avowal. It is necessary to visit this city in order to learn the extent to which the rich man will carry his contempt for the life of the poor, and the slight value which life in general has in the eyes of men condemned to live under absolutism.

In Russia existence is painful to every body. The Emperor is scarcely less inured to fatigue than the lowest of his serfs. I have been shown his bed, the hardness of which would astonish our common labourers. Here every one is obliged to repeat to himself the stern truth, that the object of life is not to be found on earth, and that the means of attaining it is not pleasure. The inexorable image of duty and of submission appears at each instant, and makes it impossible to forget the hard condition of human existence—labour and sorrow!

If for a moment, in the midst of a public promenade, the appearance of a few idlers should inspire the illusive idea that there may be in Russia, as elsewhere, men who amuse themselves for the sake of amusement, men who make pleasure a business, I am soon undeceived by the sight of some feldjäger, passing rapidly in his telega. The feldjäger is the representative of power— he is the word of the sovereign: a living telegraph, he proceeds to bear an order to another similar automaton, who awaits him, perhaps, a thousand leagues off, and who is as ignorant as himself of the thoughts that put them both in motion. The telega, in which the man of iron travels, is of all travelling vehicles the most uncomfortable. It consists of a little cart with two leather seats, without springs or back. No other kind of carriage could stand the roads of this savage empire. The first seat is that of the coachman, who is changed at each stage; the second is reserved for the courier, who travels till he dies; and among men devoted to such a life this happens early.

Those whom I see rapidly traversing in every direction the fine streets of this city, seem to represent the solitudes in which they are about to plunge. I follow them in imagination, and at the end of their course appears to me Siberia, Kamtschatka, the Salt Desert, the Wall of China, Lapland, the Frozen Ocean, Nova Zembla, Persia, or the Caucasus. These historical or, almost, fabulous names, produce on my imagination the effect of a dim and vapoury distance in a vast landscape, and engender a species of reverie which oppresses my spirits. Nevertheless, the apparition of such blind, deaf, and dumb couriers is a poetical aliment, constantly presented to the mind of the stranger. This man, born to live and die in his telega, imparts of himself a melancholy interest to the humblest scene of life. Nothing prosaic can subsist in the mind when in the presence of so much suffering and so much grandeur. It must be owned that if despotism renders unhappy the people that it oppresses, it is conducive to the amusement of travellers, whom it fills with an astonishment ever new. Where there is liberty, every thing is published and speedily forgotten, for every thing is seen at a glance: but, under an absolute government, every thing is concealed, and therefore every thing is conjectured: the greater the mystery, the greater the curiosity, which is enhanced even by the necessary absence of apparent interest.

Russia has no past history, say the lovers of antiquity. True, but the immense field she occupies, and the prospect of the future, might serve as a pasture for the most ardent imaginations. The philosopher in Russia is to be pitied, the poet there may and ought to be gratified.

The only poets really unhappy, are those condemned to languish under a system of publicity. When all the world may say what they please, the poet must hold his peace. Poetry is a mystery which serves to express more than words; it cannot subsist among a people who have lost the modesty of thought. Vision, allegory, apologue, are the truth of poetry; and in a country where publicity pervades every thing this truth is destroyed by reality, which is always coarse and repulsive to the eye of fancy.

Nature must have implanted a sentiment profoundly poetical in the souls of this satirical and melancholy people, or they could never have found the means of giving an original and picturesque aspect to cities built by men entirely destitute of imagination: and this in the most flat, dull, naked and monotonous region in the earth. Nevertheless, if I could describe Petersburg as I see it, I should draw a picture in every line; so strikingly has the genius of the Slavonian race reacted against the sterile mania of its government. This anti-national government advances only by military evolutions: it reminds one of Prussia under its first king.

I have been describing a city without character, rather pompous than imposing, more vast than beautiful, and full of edifices without style, taste, or historic interest. But to make the picture complete, that is, faithful, I should have inserted the figures of men naturally graceful, and who, with their oriental genius, have adapted themselves to a city built by a people which exist no where, for Petersburg has been constructed by wealthy men, whose minds were formed by comparing, without deep study, the different countries of Europe. This legion of travellers, more or less refined, and rather skilful than learned, formed an artificial nation, a community of intelligent and clever characters, recruited from among all the nations of the world. They did not constitute the Russian people. These are roguish as the slave, who consoles himself by privately ridiculing his master; superstitious, boastful, brave and idle as the soldier; poetical, musical, and contemplative as the shepherd; for the habits of a nomade people for a long time prevailed among the Slavonians. All this is in keeping neither with the style of the architecture nor with the plan of the streets in Petersburg: there has been evidently no connection between the architect and the inhabitant. Peter the Great built the city against the Swedes rather than for the Russians; but the natural character of its population betrays itself, notwithstanding their respect for the caprices of their master; and it is to this involuntary disobedience that Russia owes its stamp of originality. Nothing can efface the primitive character of its people; and this triumph of innate faculties over an ill-directed education is an interesting spectacle to every traveller capable of appreciating it.

Happily for the painter and the poet, the Russians possess an essentially religious sentiment. Their churches, at least, are their own. The unchangeable form of these pious edifices is a part of their religion, and superstition defends her sacred fortresses against the mania for mathematical figures in freestone, oblongs, planes and straight lines; in short, against the military, rather than classic architecture, which imparts to each of the cities of this land the air of a camp destined to remain for a few weeks during the performance of some grand manoeuvres.

The genius of a nomade race is equally recognised in the various vehicles and harness, the carriages and the drowska already described. The latter is so small as quite to disappear under those who occupy it. Its singular appearance, as it passes rapidly between long straight lines of very low houses, over which are seen the steeples of a multitude of churches and other buildings, may be easily imagined.

These gilded or painted spires break the monotonous line of roofs, and rise in the air with shafts so tapered, that the eye can scarcely distinguish the point where their gilding is lost in the mists of a polar sky. They are of Asiatic origin, and appear to be of a height which, for their diameter, is truly extraordinary. It is impossible to conceive how they maintain themselves in air.

Let the reader picture to himself an assemblage of domes, to which are attached the four belfries necessary to constitute a church among the modern Greeks; a multitude of cupolas covered with gold, silver, or azure; palace roofs of emerald green, or ultra-marine; squares ornamented with bronze statues; an immense river bordering and serving as a mirror to the picture—let him add to it the bridge of boats thrown across the river's broadest part—the citadel, where sleep in their unornamented tombs Peter the Great and his family*, and an island covered with edifices built after the model of Grecian temples—let him embrace in one view the whole of these varied parts, and he will understand how Petersburg may be infinitely picturesque, notwithstanding the bad taste of its borrowed architecture, the

* The Greek rite forbids sculpture in churches.

marshes which surround it, the unbroken flatness of its site, and the pale dimness of its finest summer days.

Let me not be reproached for my contradictions; I have myself perceived them without wishing to avoid them, for they lie in the things which I contemplate. I could not give a true idea of objects that I describe, if I did not often seem to contradict myself. If I were less sincere, I should appear more consistent; but in physical as in moral order, truth is only an assemblage of contrasts—contrasts so glaring, that it might be said nature and society have been created only in order to hold together elements which would otherwise oppose and repel each other.

Nothing can be more dull than the sky of Petersburg at midday; but the evenings and mornings, whose twilight occupies three quarters of the whole period of life, are admirable. The summer sun, which is submerged for a moment about midnight, continues for a long time to float along the horizon on a level with the Neva and the lowlands through which it flows. It sheds over the waste, streams of light brilliant enough to beautify nature in her most cheerless aspect. But it is not the enthusiasm produced by the deep colouring of tropic landscapes which this beauty inspires, it is the attraction of a dream, the irresistible influence of a sleep full of memories and of hopes. The promenade of the islands at this hour is the image of a real idyll. No doubt there are many things wanting in these scenes to constitute pictures good as compositions, but nature has more power than art on the imagination of man; her simple aspect suffices under every zone to supply that necessity for admiring which exists in the soul. God has reduced the earth in the vicinity of the pole to the extreme of flatness and nudity; but notwithstanding this poverty, the spectacle of creation will always, in the eye of man, be the most eloquent interpreter of the designs of the Creator. May there not be beauty in the bald head? For my part, I find the environs of Petersburg more than beautiful: they have a sad and sombre dulness about them which is sublime, and which, in the depth of its impression, rivals the richness and variety of the most celebrated landscapes of the earth. They present no pompous, artificial work, nor agreeable invention, but a profound solitude, a solitude terrible and beautiful as death. From one end of her plains, from one shore of her seas to the other, Russia hears that voice of God which nothing can silence, and which says to man, puffed up with the contemptible magnificence of his miserable cities, "Your labour is vain, I am still the greatest!" Often a countenance devoid of beauty has more expression, and engraves itself on our memory in a manner more ineffaceable than those regular traits which display neither passion nor sentiment. Such is the effect of our instinct of immortality, that the things which most highly interest an inhabitant of earth are those which speak to him of something unearthly.

How admirable is the power of the primitive endowment of nations! For more than a hundred years the higher classes of Russians, the nobles, the learned, and the powerful of the land, have been begging ideas and copying models from all the communities of Europe; and yet this absurd phantasy of princes and courtiers has not prevented the people from remaining original.*

The finely endowed Slavonic race has too delicate a touch to mingle indiscriminately with the Teutonic people. The German character has even at this day a less affinity with the Russian than has the Spanish, with its cross of Arab blood. Slowness, heaviness, coarseness, timidity and awkwardness have nothing in common with the genius of the Slavonians. They would rather endure vengeance and tyranny. Even the German virtues are odious to the Russians; thus, in a few years the latter, notwithstanding their religious and political atrocities, have made greater progress in public opinion at Warsaw† than the Prussians, notwithstanding the rare and solid qualities which distinguish the German people. I do not speak of this as desirable, I only note it as an existing fact: it is not all brothers who love, but all understand each other.

As to the analogy which I imagine I can in certain points discover between the Russians and the Spaniards, it is accounted for by the relations which may have originally existed between some of the Arab tribes and some of the hordes which passed

* This reproach, which applies to Peter I. and his immediate successors, completes the eulogy of the Emperor Nicholas, who has begun to stem the torrent of the mania.

† The Poles are of Slavonic race.—Trans.

from Asia into Muscovy. The Moresque architecture bears an affinity to the Byzantine, which is the model of the real Muscovite. The genius of the Asiatic wanderers in Africa could not be contrary to that of other eastern nations but recently established in Europe. History is explained by the progressive influence of races.

But for the difference in religion and the variety of manners among the people, I could fancy myself here on one of the most elevated and barren plains of Castile. In fact we are enduring at present the heat of Africa; for twenty years Petersburg has not known so burning a summer.

Notwithstanding the tropical heats, I see the Russians already preparing their provision of winter fuel. Boats loaded with billets of birch wood, the only fuel used here (for the oak is a tree of luxury), obstruct the large and numerous canals which intersect the city in every direction. It is built on the model of Amsterdam: an arm of the Neva flows through the principal streets, which in winter is filled up by the ice and snow, and in summer by the innumerable boats. The wood is conveyed from the boats in narrow carts of a primitive simplicity of construction, on which it is piled to a height which makes it resemble a moving wall. I have never once seen any of these tottering edifices fall.

The Russian people are singularly adroit: it is against the will of nature that this race of men has been driven by human revolutions towards the pole, and that it is kept there by political circumstances. He who would penetrate further into the designs of Providence, might perhaps recognise a war with the elements as the rough trial to which God has subjected a nation, destined by Him some day to rule over others. A situation demanding a severe struggle is the school of Providence.

Fuel is becoming scarce in Russia. Wood is as dear in Petersburg as in Paris. There are houses here which consume the value of nine or ten thousand francs per winter. In beholding the inroads made upon the forests we may ask, with inquietude, how will the next generation warm themselves.

If the jest be pardonable, I would advise as a measure of prudence on the part of the people who enjoy a genial climate, that they should furnish the Russians wherewith to keep good fires. They might then less covet the southern sun.

The carts used for removing the filth and refuse of the city are small and inconvenient. With such machines a man and horse can do but little work in a day. Generally speaking, the Russians show their skill rather in their manner of using inferior implements than by the pains they take to perfect those which they have. Endowed with little power of invention, they most frequently lack the mechanical appliances suitable to the end they would attain. This people, who possess so much grace and so much facility of character, have no creative genius. Once for all, the Russians are the Romans of the north. Both people have drawn their arts and sciences from strangers. The former have intelligence, but it is an imitative and therefore ironical intelligence; it counterfeits every thing, and imagines nothing. Ridicule is a prevailing trait in the character of tyrants and slaves. All oppressed people are given to slander, satire, and caricature; they revenge themselves for their inaction and degradation by sarcasm. The nature of the relation which exists between nations and their governments has yet to be elucidated. In my opinion, each nation has for a government the only one which it could have. I do not however pretend either to impose or expound this system. It is a labour which I leave to those who are worthier and wiser than I: my present object is the less ambitious one of describing that which has most struck me in the streets and on the quays of Petersburg.

Several parts of the Neva are entirely covered with boats of hay. These rural objects are larger than many houses; they are hung with straw mattings, which give them the picturesque appearance of oriental tents or Chinese junks.

The trade of plasterer is important in a city the interior of whose houses is a prey to swarms of vermin, and the exterior spoilt in appearance every winter. The manner in which the Russian plasterers perform their work is curious. There are only three months in the year during which they can work outside the houses; the number of artificers is therefore considerable, and they are found at the corner of every street. These men, suspended at the peril of their life on little planks attached to a long hanging cord, seem to support themselves like insects against the edifices which they rewhiten.

In the provinces they whitewash the towns through which the emperor may have to pass: is this an honour rendered to the sovereign, or do they seek to deceive him as regards the wretchedness of the land? In general the Russians carry about their persons a disagreeable odour, which is perceptible at a considerable distance. The higher classes smell of musk, the common people of cabbage, mixed with exhalations of onions and old greasy perfumed leather. These scents never vary.

It may be supposed from this, that the thirty thousand subjects of the emperor who enter his palace on the 1st of January, to offer him their felicitations, and the six or seven thousand that we shall see to-morrow pressing into the interior of the palace of Peterhoff, in honour of their empress, must leave on their passage a formidable perfume.

Among all the women of the lower orders whom I have hitherto met in the streets, not a single one has appeared to me to possess beauty, and the greater number among them are ugly and dirty to a degree that is repulsive. Astonishment is excited by the recollection that they are the wives and mothers of men with features so fine and regular, profiles so perfectly Grecian, and forms so elegant and supple as those seen among even the lowest classes of the nation. There are no where old men so handsome, nor old women so hideous, as in Russia. I have seen few of the citizens' wives. One of the singularities of Petersburg is, that the number of women in proportion to that of the men is less than in other capitals. I am assured that the former do not at the utmost form more than a third of the total population of the city. Their scarcity causes them to be only too highly prized. They attract so eager an attention that there are few who risk themselves alone after a certain hour in the streets of the less populous quarters. In the capital of a country altogether military, and among a people addicted to drunkenness, this discreetness appears to me sufficiently well founded. At all times the Russian women show themselves less in public than the French: it is not necessary to go far back to find the time when they passed their lives shut up like the women of Asia. This reserve, the remembrance of which still lingers, recalls, like so many other Russian customs, the origin of the people. It contributes to the dulness of the streets and the fêtes of Petersburg. The finest sights in this city are the parades, which strengthens my former observation, that the Russian capital is a camp, somewhat more stable and pacific than a mere bivouac.

There are few *cafés* in Petersburg, and no authorised public balls in the interior of the city. The promenades are little frequented, and those who are met there exhibit a gravity that conveys but little idea of enjoyment.

But if fear renders the men serious, it also renders them extremely polite. I have never elsewhere seen so many men of all classes treating each other with respect. The driver of the drowska formally salutes his comrade, who never passes him without rendering reverence for reverence; the porters salute the plasterers, and so with all the others. This urbanity is, perhaps, affected; at least, I believe it overstrained: nevertheless, the mere appearance of amenity contributes to the pleasure of life. If a pretended politeness has so much about it that is valuable, what a charm must real politeness possess, the politeness, that is to say, of the heart!

A stay in Petersburg would be agreeable to any traveller who possessed character, and who could believe all that he heard. The greatest difficulty would be the escaping of dinners and soirées, those real plagues of Russia, and it may be added of all societies where strangers are admitted, and consequently where intimacy is excluded.

I have accepted here but few private invitations. I was chiefly curious to view the solemnities of the court, but I have seen enough; one soon wearies of wonders in the contemplation of which the heart has no share.

END OF THE FIRST VOLUME.

❖

CHAPTER XV

❖

It is necessary to view the fête of Peterhoff under two different lights, the material, and the moral; thus viewed, the same spectacle produces very different impressions.

I have never seen any thing more beautiful to contemplate, yet at the same time more saddening to reflect upon, than this pretended national reunion of courtiers and peasants, who mingle together in the same saloons without any interchange of real sympathy. In a social point of view the sight has displeased me, because it seems to me that the emperor, by this false display of popularity, abases the great without exalting the humble. All men are equal before God, and the Russians' God is the emperor. This supreme governor is so raised above earth, that he sees no difference between the serf and the lord. From the height, in which his sublimity dwells, the little distinctions which divide mankind escape his divine inspection, just as the irregularities which appear on the surface of the globe vanish before an inhabitant of the sun.

When the emperor opens his palace to the privileged peasants and the chosen burghers whom he admits twice a year to the honour of paying their court,* he does not say to the labourer or the tradesman, "You are a man like myself," but he says to the great lord, "You are a slave like them, and I, your God, soar

* On the 1st of January, at Petersburg, and at Peterhoff, on the birthday of the Empress.

equally above you all." Such is (all political fiction aside) the moral meaning of the fête: it is this which, in my opinion, spoils it. As a spectator, I remarked that it pleased the sovereign and the serfs, much more than the professed courtiers.

To seek to become a popular idol by reducing all others to a level, is a cruel game, an amusement of despotism, which might dazzle the men of an earlier century, but which cannot deceive any people arrived at the age of experience and reflection.

The Emperor Nicholas did not devise this imposition; and such being the case, it would be the more worthy of him to abolish it. Yet it must be owned, that nothing is abolished in Russia without peril. The people who want the guarantees of law, are protected only by those of custom. An obstinate attachment to usages, which are upheld by insurrection and poison, is one of the bases of the constitution, and the periodical death of sovereigns proves to the Russians that this *constitution* knows how to make itself respected. The equilibrium of such a machine is to me a deep and painful mystery.

In point of magnificent decorations, and of picturesque assemblage of the costumes of all ranks, the fête at Peterhoff cannot be too highly extolled. Nothing that I had read, or that had been related to me concerning it, gave me any adequate idea of this fairy scene; the imagination was surpassed by the reality.

The reader must picture to himself a palace built upon a terrace, the height of which seems that of a mountain in a land of plains extending farther than the eye can reach: a country so flat that, from an elevation of sixty feet, the vision may sweep over an immense horizon. At the foot of this imposing structure lies a vast park, which terminates only with the sea, on whose bosom may be descried a line of vessels of war, which were illuminated on the evening of the fête. This illumination was general; the fire blazed and extended, like a conflagration, from the groves and terraces of the palace to the waves of the Gulf of Finland. In the park, the lamps produced the effect of day-light. The trees were lighted up by suns of every colour. It was not by thousands nor tens of thousands, but by hundreds of thousands, that the lights in these gardens of Armida might be counted; and they could all be seen from the windows of a palace crowded with a people as profoundly respectful as if they had lived all their days at court.

Nevertheless, in this assemblage, the object of which was to efface all distinctions of rank, each class might still be separately traced. Whatever attacks despotism may have made upon the aristocracy, there are yet castes in Russia. Here is presented one more point of resemblance to the East, and not one of the least striking contradictions of social order created by the manners of the people operating in unison with the government of the country. Thus, at this fête of the empress, this true bacchanalian revel of absolute power, I recognised the order which reigns throughout the state, through the apparent disorder of the ball. Those whom I met were always either merchants, soldiers, labourers, or courtiers, and each class was distinguished by its costume. A dress which would not denote the rank of the man, and a man whose only worth should arise from his personal merit, would be considered as anomalies, as European inventions, imported by restless innovators and imprudent travellers. It must never be forgotten that we are here on the confines of Asia: a Russian in a frock coat in his own country appears to me like a foreigner.

True bearded Russians think as I do upon this subject, and they comfort themselves with the idea that a day shall come when they will be able to put to the sword all these coxcombical infidels to ancient usages, who neglect the nation, and betray their country, in order to rival the civilisation of the foreigner.

Russia is placed upon the limits of two continents. It is not in the nature of that which is European to amalgamate perfectly with that which is Asiatic. The Muscovite community has been governed hitherto only by submitting to the violence and incoherence attendant upon the contact of two civilisations, entirely different in character. This presents to the traveller a field of interesting, if not consolatory, speculation.

The ball was a rout: it professed to be a masquerade, for the men wore a small piece of silk called a Venetian mantle, which floated in a ridiculous manner above their uniforms. The saloons of the old palace, filled with people, resembled an ocean of heads of greasy hair, over all of which rose proudly the noble head of the Emperor, whose stature, voice, and will, alike soar above his people. This prince seems worthy and capable of subjugating the minds of men, even as he surpasses their persons. A sort of mysterious influence attaches to his presence; at Peterhoff, on the parade, in war, and in every moment of his life, may be seen in him the power that reigns.

This perpetual reigning, and its perpetual worship, would be a real comedy, if upon such permanent dramatic representation there did not depend the existence of sixty millions of men, who live only because the man whom you see before you playing the part of the emperor, gives them permission to breathe, and dictates to them the mode of using this permission. It is the divine right, applied to the mechanism of social life. Such is the serious side of the representation, wherein are involved incidents of so grave a nature, that fear soon extinguishes the inclination to laughter.

There does not exist on the earth at the present time, not in Turkey, not even in China, a single man who enjoys and exercises such power as the emperor. Let the reader figure to himself all the skilfulness of our governments, perfected as they are by centuries of practice, put into exercise in a still young and uncivilised society; the rubrics of the administrations of the West, aiding by modern experience the despotism of the East: European discipline supporting the tyranny of Asia; the police employed in concealing barbarism, in order, not to destroy, but to perpetuate it; disciplined brute force and the tactics of European armies, serving to strengthen an Eastern policy;—let him conceive the idea of a half-savage people who have been enrolled and drilled, without having been civilised, and he will be able to understand the social and moral state of the Russian nation. To profit by the progressive discoveries in the art of governing made by the European nations, in order to rule sixty millions of Orientals, has been from the time of Peter the First the problem to be studied by those who govern Russia.

The reigns of Catharine the Great and of Alexander did but prolong the systematic infancy* of this nation, which still exists only in name.

* L'enfance systématique.

Catharine had instituted schools to please the French philosophers, whose praises her vanity desired to obtain. The governor of Moscow, one of her old favourites, who was rewarded by a pompous exile in the ancient capital of the empire, wrote to her one day that no one would send their children to the school. The Empress replied pretty nearly in these words:—

"My dear Prince, do not distress yourself because the Russians have no desire for knowledge: if I institute schools it is not for ourselves, but for Europe, in whose estimation we must maintain our standing; but if our peasants should really wish to become enlightened, neither you nor I could continue in our places."

This letter has been read by a person in whose statements I have every confidence. Undoubtedly, in writing it, the Empress forgot herself; and it is precisely because she was subject to such absence of mind that she was considered so amiable, and that she exercised so much power over the minds of men of imagination.

The Russians will, according to their usual tactics, deny the authenticity of the anecdote; but if I cannot be certain of the strict accuracy of the words, I can affirm that they truly express the sentiments of the sovereign. In this trait may be discovered the spirit of vanity which rules over and torments the Russians, and which perverts, even in its source, the power established over them.

Their unfortunate desire for the good opinion of Europe is a phantom which pursues them in the secrecy of thought, and reduces conversation among them to a trick of jugglery, executed more or less adroitly.

The present emperor has, with his sound judgment and his clear apprehension, perceived the shoal, but will he be able to avoid it? More than the strength of Peter the Great is necessary to remedy the evil caused by that first corrupter of the Russians.

At the present time, the difficulty is of a double character; the mind of the peasant remains rude and barbarous, while his habits and his disposition cause him to submit to restraint. At the same time the false refinement of the nobles contravenes the national character, upon which all attempt to ennoble the people can alone be built. What a complication! Who will unloose this modern gordian knot?

❖ 231 ❖

I admire the Emperor Nicholas. A man of genius can alone accomplish the task he has imposed upon himself; he has seen the evil, he has formed an idea of the remedy, and he is endeavouring to apply it.

But can one reign suffice to eradicate evils which were implanted a century and a half ago? The mischief is so deeply rooted, that it strikes even the eye of strangers the least attentive, and that too in a country where every one conspires to deceive the traveller.

In travelling in Russia, a light and superficial mind may feed itself with illusions; but whoever has his eyes open, and adds to some little power of observation an independent humour, will be presented with a continued and painful labour, which consists in discovering and discerning, at every point, the struggle between two nations carried on in one community. These two nations are —Russia as she is, and Russia as they would have her to appear in the eyes of Europe.

The Emperor is less secure than any one against the snares of illusion. The reader will remember the journey of Catherine to Cherson; she traversed deserts, but they built her lines of villages at every half league of the road by which she passed, and as she did not go behind the scenes of this theatre on which the tyrant played the fool, she believed her southern provinces were well-peopled, though they continued cursed with a sterility which was owing to the oppression of her government rather than to the rigour of nature. The finesse of the men charged by the Emperor with the details of Russian administration, still exposes the sovereign to similar deceptions.

The corps diplomatique, and the western people in general, have always been considered by this Byzantine government and by Russia in general, as malignant and jealous spies. There is this similarity between the Russians and the Chinese, that both one and the other always believe that strangers envy them: they judge us by their own sentiments.

The Russian hospitality also, vaunted as it is, has become an art which may be resolved into a refined species of policy. It consists in rendering its guests content at the least possible cost of sincerity. Here, politeness is only the art of reciprocally disguising the double fear that each experiences and inspires. I hear every where spoken the language of philosophy, and every where I see that oppression is the order of the day. They say to me,— "We would gladly dispense with being arbitrary, we should then be more rich and powerful; but we have to do with an Asiatic people:" at the same time they think in their hearts, "we would gladly dispense with talking liberalism and philanthropy, we should then be more happy and more strong, but we have to do with the governments of Europe."

The Russians of all classes conspire with an unanimity which is extraordinary in causing duplicity to triumph among themselves. They have a dexterity in lying, a natural proneness to deceit, which is revolting. Things that I admire elsewhere, I hate here, because I find them too dearly paid for; order, patience, calmness, elegance, respectfulness, the natural and moral relations which ought to exist between those who conceive and those who execute, in short, all that gives a worth and a charm to well-organised societies, all that gives a meaning and an object to political institutions, is lost and confounded here in one single sentiment—that of fear. In Russia, fear replaces, that is, paralyses thought. This sentiment when it reigns alone can never produce more than the appearances of civilisation; whatever short-sighted legislators may say, fear will never be the moving influence of a well organised society; it is not order, it is the veil of chaos; where liberty is wanting, there soul and truth must be wanting also. Russia is a body without life, a colossus which subsists only by its head; and whose members, all equally deprived of force, languish! Thence arises a profound inquietude, an inexpressible uneasiness, an uneasiness which does not, like that of the new French *révolutionnaires*, arise from a vagueness of ideas, from abuses, from the satiety of material prosperity, or the jealousies which a combination of agencies gives birth to, it is the expression of a real state of suffering, the indication of an organic malady.

I believe that in no part of the world do the men enjoy less real happiness than in Russia. We are not happy among ourselves, but we feel that happiness is in our power: among the Russians it is unattainable. Imagine republican passions (for, once again, fictitious equality reigns under a Russian emperor) boiling under the silence of despotism! This is a terrific combination, especially as viewed with regard to its future influence upon the world. Russia is a cauldron of boiling water, well closed, but placed over a fire which is ever becoming more fiercely heated: I dread the explosion, and the Emperor has several times experienced the same dread during the course of his laborious reign; laborious in peace as in war, for, in our days, empires, like machines, are ruined by remaining inactive.

It is, then, this head without a body, this sovereign without a nation, who gives popular fêtes! It appears to me that before creating popularity he should create a people.

In sooth this country lends itself marvellously to every species of fraud: there are slaves elsewhere, but to find a nation of courtly slaves it is necessary to visit Russia. One scarcely knows at which most to wonder, the inconsistency or the hypocrisy. Catharine II. is not dead, for notwithstanding the open character of her grandson, it is still by dissimulation that Russia is governed. Here, to avow the tyranny would be to make a beneficial progress.

On this point, as on many others, the foreigners who have described Russia have combined with the natives to deceive the world. Could any persons be more treacherously complaisant than the greater part of those writers who congregate here from all the corners of Europe, in order to excite a sensibility on the touching familiarity which reigns between the Russian emperor and his people? Are, then, the illusions of despotism so strong as to overpower even the simple spectator? Either this country has not hitherto been described except by men whose position or character does not permit of their being independent, or else minds the most sincere lose their liberty of judgment as soon as they enter Russia.

As regards myself, I oppose to this influence the aversion which I have for disguise.

I hate but one evil, and if I hate it, it is because I believe that it engenders and includes all the others: this evil is falsehood. I therefore endeavour to unmask it wherever I meet with it; it is the horror with which it inspires me that gives me the desire and the courage to write these travels: I undertook them through curiosity, I relate them from a sense of duty. A passion for truth is an inspiration which supplies the place of energy, youth, and enlightened views. This sentiment influences me to such an extent as to cause me to love even the age in which we live: for though it be somewhat coarse, it is, at least, more sincere than that which preceded it. It distinguishes itself by the repugnance, sometimes rude and unmannerly, which it evinces for all affectations. In this repugnance I partake. A hatred for hypocrisy is the torch which serves to guide me through the labyrinth of the world: those who deceive men, whatever means they may use, seem to me as poisoners; and the more elevated and powerful they are, the more are they culpable.

Such are the sentiments which prevented my enjoying, yesterday, a spectacle which, notwithstanding, my eyes admired. It was beautiful, magnificent, singular, novel—but it appeared deceptive: this idea sufficed to deprive it of all real splendour. The passion for truth, which in the present day pervades the hearts of Frenchmen, is still unknown in Russia.

After all, what is this crowd, whose respectful familiarity in presence of its sovereign has been so much extolled in Europe? Do not deceive yourselves: these are the slaves of slaves. The great lords send to the fête of the empress chosen peasants, who, it is pretended, arrive by chance. This *élite* of the serfs is joined by the most respectable and best known tradespeople, for it is necessary to have a few men with beards to satisfy the old-fashioned Russians. Such is, in reality, the people whose excellent disposition has been held up as an example to other people by the sovereigns of Russia from the time of the Empress Elizabeth. It is, I believe, from her reign that this kind of fête dates. At present the Emperor Nicholas, notwithstanding his iron character, his admirable rectitude of intention, and the authority with which his public and private virtues invest him, could not perhaps abolish the usage. It is therefore true that, even under governments the most absolute in appearance, circumstances are stronger than men.

Nothing is so perilous for a man, however elevated his position may be, than to say to a nation "You have been deceived, and I will be no longer accessory to your error." The vulgar cling to falsehood, even to that which injures them, rather than to truth, because human pride prefers that which comes from man to that which comes from God. This is true under all governments, but doubly so under despotism.

An independence like that of the *mugics** of Peterhoff can alarm nobody. It forms the liberty and equality which despots love! It may be boasted of without risk; but advise Russia to a gradual emancipation, and you will soon see what is said of you in the country.

I, yesterday, heard the courtiers as they passed near me boasting of the politeness of their serfs, "I should like to see such a fête in France," they said. I was strongly tempted to answer them: "In order to compare our two people, we must wait until yours exists."

I called to mind at the same time a fête which I once gave to the lower orders at Seville. It was under the despotism of Ferdinand VII., but the true politeness of those Spaniards, free *de facto*, if not *de jure*, furnished me with an object of comparison little favourable to the Russians.†

Russia is a book, the table of whose contents is magnificent, but beware of going further. If you turn over the leaves you will find no performance answering to the promise: all the chapters are headed, but all have to be filled up. How many of the Russian forests are only marshes, where you will never cut a faggot! How many distant regiments are there without men, and cities and roads which exist only in project! The nation itself is as yet nothing more than a puff placarded upon Europe, dupe of a diplomatic fiction. I have found here no real life except that of the emperor's; no constitution except that of the court.

The tradespeople who ought to form a middle class are too few in number to possess any influence in the state; besides, they are almost all foreigners. The authors amount to one or two in each generation: the artists are like the authors, their scarcity causes them to be esteemed; but though this favours their personal pros-

* Russian peasants.
† See "Spain under Ferdinand VII."

pects, it is injurious to their social influence. There are no legal pleaders in a country where there is no justice: where, then, is to be found that middle class which constitutes the strength of other states, and without which the people is only a flock, guided by a few well-trained watch-dogs? I have not mentioned another class of men who are not to be reckoned either among the great or the little. These are the sons of the priests, who almost all become subaltern *employés*—the commissioners and deputies who are the plagues of Russia. They form a species of obscure noblesse, very hostile to the great nobles; a noblesse whose spirit is anti-aristocratic in the true political signification of the word, and who at the same time are very burdensome to the serfs. These are the men (inconvenient to the state, and fruits of the schism which permits the priest to marry) who will commence the approaching revolution of Russia.

The punishment of death does not exist in this land, except for the crime of high treason; but there are certain criminals whom they nevertheless kill. The way in which they reconcile the mildness of the code with the traditional ferocity of manners is this: when a criminal is condemned to more than a hundred strokes of the knout, the executioner, who understands the meaning of such a sentence, kills him through humanity, by striking him at the third blow on a mortal part. And yet the punishment of death is abolished! To making the law thus lie, the proclamation of the most audacious tyranny would be preferable.

If it is thought that I judge Russia too severely, I must plead the involuntary impression that I receive each day from persons and from things, and which every friend of humanity would receive in my place, if like me, he endeavoured to look beyond that which would be shown him.

This empire, immense as it is, is no more than a prison, of which the emperor keeps the key. Nothing can exceed the misery of the subjects unless it be that of the prince. The life of the gaoler has always appeared to me so similar to that of the prisoner, that I am astonished at the mental illusion which makes the one believe himself so much less to be pitied than the other.

Man here knows neither the real social enjoyments of cultivated minds, nor the absolute and animal liberty of the savage, nor yet the independence of action of the half-savage—the barbarian; I can see no compensation for the misery of being born under this system, except the dreams of vanity and the love of command; on these passions I stumble every time I return to the endeavour of analysing the moral life of the inhabitants of Russia. Russia thinks and lives as a soldier! A soldier, to whatever country he may belong, is scarcely a citizen; and here less than any where can he be called one; he is rather a prisoner for life, condemned to look after other prisoners.

It should be observed that the word prison signifies something more here than it does elsewhere. When one thinks on all the subterranean cruelties concealed from our pity by the discipline of silence, in a land where every man performs an apprenticeship to discretion, it makes one tremble. He who would conceive a hatred for reserve should come here. Every little check in conversation, every change of expression, every inflexion of voice, teaches me the danger of confidence and candour.

The very appearance of the houses brings to my mind the unhappy condition of human existence in this land.

If I cross the threshold of the palace of some great nobleman, and see there a disgusting and ill-disguised uncleanliness reigning amidst an ostentatious display of luxury; if I, so to speak, inhale vermin, even under the roof of opulence,—my mind will not stop at that which is presented merely by the senses; it wanders further, and sees all the filth and corruption which must poison the dungeons of a country where even the rich do not shrink from loathsome contact. When I suffer from the dampness of my chamber, I think of the unfortunate beings exposed to that of the sub-marine dungeons of Kronstadt, the fortress of Petersburg, and of many other subterranes of which I forget even the name. The ghastly visages of the soldiers whom I meet in the streets remind me of the plunder of those employed in provisioning the army. The fraud of these traitors, paid by the emperor to feed his guards, is written in lines of lead on the livid faces of the unfortunate wretches, deprived of wholesome and even sufficient nutriment by men who care only to enrich themselves as rapidly as possible, unmindful of the disgrace they are bringing on their government, and of the maledictions of the regiments of slaves whom they kill. Finally, at each step I here take, I see rising before me the phantom of Siberia, and I think of all that is implied in the name of that political desert, that abyss of misery, that tomb of living men,—a land peopled with infamous criminals and sublime heroes, a colony without which this empire would be as incomplete as a palace without cellars.

A traveller who would allow himself to be indoctrinated by the people of the country, might overrun the empire from one end to the other, and return home without having surveyed any thing but a series of façades. This is what he should do in order to please his entertainers. I am aware that such is the case, but so high a price for their hospitality I cannot afford to pay.

Provided a stranger shows himself ridiculously active, rises early after having retired to rest late, never fails to attend every ball and review, in short, provided he keeps too constantly in motion to be able to think, he is well received everywhere, well thought of, and well fêted; a crowd of strangers press his hand every time that the emperor may have spoken to him, smiles are lavishly bestowed, and on leaving, he is pronounced a distinguished traveller. He reminds me of the bourgeois gentleman played upon by the Mufti of Molière. The Russians have coined a French word that admirably designates their political hospitality; in speaking of foreigners whom they blind by means of fêtes— "we must *garland* them,"* they say. But let the stranger be on his guard lest he should for a moment betray any relaxation of zeal; at the least symptom of fatigue, or of penetration, he will see the Russian spirit, the most caustic of all spirits, rising up against him like an enraged serpent.*

Ridicule, that empty consolation of the oppressed, is here the pleasure of the peasant, as sarcasm is the accomplishment of the

---

* Il faut les *enguirlander.*

* A well known means of flattery, and one of which the success is certain, is to exhibit one's self in the streets of Petersburg before the eyes of the Emperor without great coat or cloak: a heroic flattery of the climate which may cost the life of him who practises it. It is not difficult to displease in a land where such modes of pleasing are in use.

noble; irony and imitation are the only natural talents which I have discovered among the Russians. The stranger once exposed to the venom of their criticism would never recover from it; he would be passed from mouth to mouth like a deserter running the gauntlet; and finally be trampled under the feet of a crowd the most hardened and ambitious in the world. The ambitious have always a pleasure in ruining others: "Destroy him as a precaution, there will at any rate be one the less; every man must be viewed as a rival because it is possible that he may become one."

I have no greater belief in the probity of the *magic*. They tell me that he would not conceal a flower in the garden of his emperor; that I do not dispute. I know that fear will produce miracles, but I know also that this model people, these peasant courtiers do not scruple to rob their lordly rivals on a day, when too much affected by their presence at the palace, and too confident in the honourable sentiments of the serf ennobled for the hour, they cease for one moment to watch the movements of the said serf's hands.

Yesterday, at the imperial and popular ball of the palace of Peterhoff, the Sardinian ambassador had his watch very adroitly extracted notwithstanding the chain which formed its guard. Several people lost also their handkerchiefs and other articles in the press. I myself lost a purse lined with a few ducats, and consoled myself for the loss in laughing at the eulogies lavished on the probity of this people by its lords. The latter well know the real value of all their fine phrases, and I am not sorry to know it also. In observing their futile finesses, I seek for the dupes of falsehoods so puerile, and I cry, with Basil, "Who is deceiving here? All the world is in the secret."

In vain do the Russians talk and pretend; every honest observer can only see in them the Greeks of the Lower Empire formed in accordance with the rules of modern strategy by the Prussians of the eighteenth and the French of the nineteenth century.

The popularity of an autocrat appears to me as suspicious in Russia, as does the honesty of the men who in France preach absolute democracy in the name of liberty,—both are murderous sophisms. To destroy liberty in preaching liberality is assassination, for society lives by truth; to make tyranny patriarchal is assassination also.

I have one fixed political principle; it is that men can and ought to be governed without being deceived. If in private life falsehood is degrading, in public life it is criminal; every government that lies, is a conspirator more dangerous than the traitor whom it legally condemns to capital punishment; and—notwithstanding the example of certain great minds spoilt by an age of sophists,—where truth is renounced, genius forsakes its seat, and, by a strange reversion of things, the master humbles himself before the slave; for the man who deceives is below the victim of deception. This is as applicable to politics and to literature as to religion.

My idea of the possibility of making Christian sincerity subservient to politics is not so chimerical as it may appear to men of business; for it is an idea also of the Russian Emperor's, practical and clear-sighted as he undoubtedly is. I do not believe that there is at the present day a prince upon any throne who so detests falsehood and who falsifies so little as this monarch.

He has made himself the champion of monarchical power in Europe, and, it is well known, he boldly and openly maintains this position. He is not seen, as is a certain government, preaching in each different locality a different policy according to varying, and purely commercial local interests; on the contrary, he favours everywhere indiscriminately the principles which accord with his system. Is it thus that England is liberal, constitutional, and philanthropical?

The Emperor reads daily, from one end to the other, one French newspaper, and only one, the *Journal des Débats*. He never looks at the others, unless some interesting article is pointed out to him.

To sustain power in order to preserve social order, is, in France, the object of the best and worthiest minds; it is also the constant aim of the *Journal des Débats,* an aim prosecuted with an intellectual superiority which explains the consideration accorded to this paper in our own country, as well as in the rest of Europe.

France is suffering under the disease common to the age, she is suffering under it more than any other land; this disease is a hatred of authority; the remedy, therefore, consists in fortifying authority: such is the sentiment of the Emperor at Petersburg, and of the *Journal des Débats* at Paris.

But as they agree only in regard to the end to be obtained, they are so much the more opposed as they seem to be united. The choice of means will often cause dissension among those gathered under the same banner; they meet as allies, they separate as enemies.

The legitimacy of hereditary right appears to the Emperor of Russia the only means of attaining his end; and in forcing a little the ordinary sense of the old word "legitimacy," under pretext that there exists another more sure,—that, namely, of election based upon the true interests of the country,—the *Journal des Débats* raises altar against altar, in the name of the salvation of society.

From the contest of these two legitimacies, one of which is blind as fate, the other wavering as passion, results an anger the more lively because the advocates of both systems lack decisive reasons, and use the same terms to arrive at opposite conclusions.

It will be seen ere this that I take pleasure in digressions; this species of irregularity leads me away like everything else that resembles liberty. I could only correct myself by offering excuses, and each time varying their oratorical expression; for then the trouble would exceed the pleasure.

The site of Peterhoff is the most beautiful that I have hitherto seen in Russia. A ridge of small elevation commands the sea, which borders the extremity of the park at about a third of a league from the palace; the latter is built on the edge of this mount, which is almost perpendicular. Magnificent flights of steps have been formed, by which you descend from terrace to terrace into the park, where are found groves of great extent and beauty, jets d'eau, and artificial cascades in the taste of those at Versailles, and structures raised on certain elevated points, from whence may be seen the shores of Finland, the arsenal of the Russian navy, the isle of Kronstadt, and, at about nine leagues towards the right, St. Petersburg, the white city, which at a distance looks bright and lively, and with its palaces with pointed roofs, its temples of plastered columns, its forests of steeples that resemble minarets, has the appearance towards evening of a wood of fir-trees, whose silvered tops are illuminated by the ruddy glare of some great fire.

There is but little variety of vegetation in the scenery of Ingria; that of the gardens is entirely artificial, that of the country consists of a few clumps of birch of a dull green foliage, and of avenues of the same tree planted as limits between marshy meadows, and fields where no wheat grows, for what can grow under the sixtieth degree of latitude?

When I think of all the obstacles which men have conquered here in order to exist as a community, to build a city, and to maintain in it all the magnificence necessary to the vanity of great princes and great folks, I cannot see a lettuce or a rose without being tempted to exclaim—"a miracle!" If Petersburg is a Lapland in stucco, Peterhoff is the palace of Armida under glass. I can scarcely believe in the real existence of so many costly, delicate, and brilliant objects, when I recollect that a few degrees farther north, the year is divided into a day, a night, and two twilights, of three months each.

One may ride a league in the imperial park of Peterhoff without passing twice under the same avenue: imagine, then, such a park all on fire. In this icy and gloomy land the illuminations are perfect conflagrations; it might be said that the night was to make amends for the day. The trees disappear under a decoration of diamonds, in each alley there are as many lamps as leaves; it is Asia, not the real modern Asia, but the fabulous Bagdad of the Arabian Nights, or the more fabulous Babylon of Semiramis.

It is said that on the empress's birth-day, six thousand carriages, thirty thousand pedestrians, and an innumerable quantity of boats leave Petersburg to proceed to, and form encampments around, Peterhoff.

It is the only day on which I have seen a real crowd in Russia. A bivouac of citizens in a country altogether military, is a rarity. Not that the army was wanting at the fête, for a body of guards and the corps of cadets were both cantonned round the residence of the sovereign. All the multitude of officers, soldiers, tradesmen, serfs, lords and masters wandered together among the woods, where night was chased away by two hundred and fifty thousand lamps. Such was the number named to me: and though I do not know whether it was correct or not, I do know that the mass of fire shed an artificial light far exceeding in clearness that of the northern day. In Russia, the emperor casts the sun into the shade. At this period of the summer, the nights recommence and rapidly increase in length; so that, without the illumination, it would have been dark for several hours under the avenues in the park of Peterhoff.

It is said, also, that in thirty-five minutes all the lamps of the illuminations in the park were lighted by eighteen hundred men. Opposite the front of the palace, and proceeding from it in a straight line towards the sea, is a canal, the surface of whose waters was so covered with the reflection of the lights upon its borders, as to produce a perspective that was magical; it might have been taken for a sheet of fire. Ariosto would perhaps have had imagination brilliant enough to describe all the wonders of this illumination: to the various groups of lamps, which were disposed with much taste and fancy, were given numerous original forms; flowers as large as trees, suns, vases, bowers of vine leaves, obelisks, pillars, walls chased with arabesque work; in short, a world of fantastic imagery passed before the eye, and one gorgeous device succeeded another with inexpressible rapidity.

At the extremity of the canal, on an enormous pyramid of fire (it was, I believe, 70 feet high), stood the figure of the Empress, shining in brilliant white above all the red, blue, and green lights which surrounded it. It was like an aigrette of diamonds circled with gems of all hues. Every thing was on so large a scale that the mind doubted the reality which the eye beheld. Such efforts for an annual festival appeared incredible. There was something as extraordinary in the episodes to which it gave rise, as in the fête itself. During two or three nights, all the crowd of which I have spoken encamped around the village. Many women slept in their carriages, and the female peasants in their carts. These conveyances, crowded together by hundreds, formed camps which were very amusing to survey, and which presented scenes worthy of the pencil of an artist.

The Russian has a genius for the picturesque; and the cities of a day which he raises for his festal occasions, are more amusing, and have a much more national character than the real cities built in Russia by foreigners. The painful impression I have received since living among the Russians, is increased as I discover the true value of this oppressed people. The idea of what they could do if they were free, heightens the anger which I feel in seeing them as they now are. The ambassadors with their families and suites, as well as the strangers who have been presented, are boarded and lodged at the expence of the emperor. For this object a large and charming edifice, called the English palace, is reserved. The building is a quarter of a league from the imperial palace, in a beautiful park, laid out in the English taste, and so picturesque that it appears natural. The beauty of the waters, and the irregularities of the surface, an irregularity rarely seen in the environs of Petersburg, render it very pleasant. This year, the number of foreigners being greater than usual, there is not room for them in the English palace. I do not therefore sleep there, but I dine there daily with the diplomatic corps and seven or eight hundred other individuals, at a perfectly well-served table. This is certainly magnificent hospitality. In lodging at the village, it is necessary, after dressing in uniform, to proceed in my carriage, in order to dine at this table, at which presides one of the great officers of the empire.

For the night, the director general of the theatres of the court has placed at my disposal two actor's boxes in the theatre of Peterhoff, and this lodging is the envy of every one.* It lacks nothing except a bed; and fortunately I brought my little iron couch from Petersburg. It is an indispensable necessary for an European travelling in Russia, who does not wish to pass the night on a seat, or on the floor. We carry our beds here as we would our cloaks in Spain. For want of straw, which is a rare thing in a region that grows no wheat, my mattrass is filled with hay.

In any other country, so great an assemblage of people would produce overwhelming noise and disturbance. In Russia every

---

* In the village there are only a small number of dirty houses, in which the rooms are let at the rate of 200 to 500 roubles per night.

thing passes with gravity, every thing takes the character of a ceremony; to see so many young persons united together for their pleasure, or for that of others, not daring either to laugh, to sing, to quarrel, to play, or to dance, one might imagine them a troop of prisoners about to proceed to their destination. That which is wanted in all I see here is not, assuredly, grandeur or magnificence, nor even taste and elegance: it is gaiety. Gaiety cannot be compelled; on the contrary, compulsion makes it fly, just as the line and the level destroy the picturesque in scenery. I see only in Russia that which is symmetrically correct, which carries with it an air of command and regulation; but that which would give a value to this order, variety, from whence springs harmony, is here unknown.

The soldiers at their bivouac are subjected to a more severe discipline than in their barracks. Such rigour, in time of peace, in the open field, and on a day of festival, reminds me of the remark of the Grand Duke Constantine. "I do not like war," he said; "it spoils the soldiers, dirts their uniforms, and destroys discipline."

The prince did not give all his reasons for disliking war, as is proved by his conduct in Poland.

On the day of the ball and the illumination, we repaired to the imperial palace at seven o'clock. The courtiers, the ambassadors, the invited foreigners, and the *soi-disant* populace, entered the state apartments without any prescribed order. All the men, except the mugics, who wore their national costume, and the citizens who were robed in the cafetan, carried the tabarro, or Venetian mantle above their uniform, which was a strictly enforced regulation, this fête being called a masked ball.

We remained a considerable time, much pressed by the crowd, waiting for the appearance of the emperor and his family. As soon as this sun of the palace began to rise, the space opened before him, and, followed by his splendid *cortége*, he proceeded, without being even incommoded by the crowd, through the halls into which the moment before you might have supposed another person could not have penetrated. Wherever his majesty passed, the waves of peasants rolled back, closing instantly behind him like waters in a vessel's track.

The noble aspect of the monarch, whose head rose above all

heads, awed this agitated sea into respect. It reminded me of the Neptune of Virgil;—he could not be more an emperor than he is. He danced, during two or three successive hours, polonaises with the ladies of his family and court. This dance was on former occasions no more than a cadenced and ceremonious march, but on the present, it was a real movement to the sound of music.

The emperor and his cortége wound, in a surprising manner, through the crowd, which, without foreseeing the direction he was about to take, always gave way in time, so as never to incommode the progress of the monarch.

He spoke to several of the men robed and bearded *à la Russe:* at length, towards ten o'clock, at which hour it became dark, the illuminations, of which I have already spoken, commenced.

We had expected, during a great part of the day, that, owing to the weather, they would not have taken place. About three o'clock, while at dinner in the English palace, a squall of wind passed over Peterhoff, violently agitated the trees, and strewed the park with their branches. While coolly watching the storm, we little thought that the sisters, mothers, and friends of crowds seated at the same table with us were perishing on the water, under its terrible agency. Our thoughtless curiosity was approaching to gaiety at the very time that a great number of small vessels, which had left Petersburg for Peterhoff, were foundering in the gulf. It is now admitted that two hundred persons were drowned; others say fifteen hundred or two thousand: no one knows the truth, and the journals will not speak of the occurrence; this would be to distress the empress, and to accuse the emperor.

The disaster was kept a secret during the entire evening, nothing transpired until after the fête; and this morning the court neither appears more nor less sad than usual. There, etiquette forbids to speak of that which occupies the thoughts of all; and even beyond the palace, little is said. The life of man in this country is such as to be deemed of trifling importance even by themselves. Each one feels his existence to hang upon a thread.

Every year accidents, similar, although less extensive, cast a gloom over the fête of Peterhoff, which would change into an act of deep mourning, a solemn funeral, if others, like me, thought upon all that this magnificence costs. But here, I am the only one who reflects. Yesterday, superstitious minds were presented with more than one gloomy prognostic. The weather, which had been fine for three weeks, changed upon the birthday of the empress. The image of that princess would not light up. The man charged with superintending this essential part of the illumination, ascended to the summit of the pyramid, but the wind extinguished his lamps as quickly as he lighted them. He reascended several times; at length his foot slipped, and he fell from a height of seventy feet, and was killed on the spot.

The shocking thinness of the empress, her air of languor, the diminished lustre of her eye, rendered these presages more ominous. Her life, like a disease, may be said to be mortal: fêtes and balls every evening! There is no choice here but that of dying of amusement, or of ennui.

For the empress as well as the zealous courtiers, the spectacle of parades and reviews commences early in the morning. These are always followed by some receptions; the empress then retires for a quarter of an hour, after which she rides out in her carriage for two hours. She next takes a bath before again going out on horseback. Returned a second time, she has some more visitors to receive: this over, she proceeds to inspect certain useful institutions superintended by herself, or by some of those honoured with her intimacy. From thence she follows the emperor to the camp: there being always one somewhere near. They return to dance; and thus her days, her years, and her life are consumed.

Those who have not the courage or the strength necessary to pursue this dreadful life, are not in favour.

The empress said to me the other day, in speaking of a very distinguished but delicate woman, "She is always ill!" The tone and manner in which this was spoken convinced me that the fate of a family was decided. In a sphere where good intentions are not sufficient, an indisposition is equivalent to a disgrace.

The empress does not consider herself more excused than others from paying her personal court. She cannot for a moment bear that the emperor should leave her. Princes are made of iron! This highminded woman wishes, and at moments believes, herself free from human infirmities; but the total privation of physical and mental repose, the want of a continuous occupation, the absence of all solid conversation, the acquired necessity of excitement, all tend to nurse a fever which is sapping life. And this dreadful mode of existence has become as indispensable as it is fatal. She cannot now either abandon it or sustain it. Atrophy is feared, and, above all, the winter of Petersburg is dreaded: but nothing can induce her to pass six months away from the emperor.*

In observing her interesting though emaciated figure wandering like a spectre through a scene of festivity celebrated in her honour, and which she will perhaps never witness again, my heart sunk within me, and, dazzled as I may have been with human pomp and grandeur, I turned to reflect on the miseries to which our nature is exposed. Alas! the loftier the height from which we fall, the severer is the shock. The great expiate in one day, even in this world, all the privations of the poor during a long life.

The inequality of conditions disappears under the levelling pressure of suffering. Time is but an illusion, which passion disperses. The intensity of the feeling, whether of joy or of grief, is the measure of the reality.

Persons, even of the highest elevation, act unwisely when they pretend to amuse themselves on any fixed day. An anniversary regularly celebrated only aids in more deeply impressing the mind with the progress of time, by suggesting comparison between the present and the past. The memories of the past, celebrated with rejoicings, always inspire us with a crowd of melancholy ideas, visions of vanished early youth, and prospects of declining life. At the return of each yearly fête we have ever some fewer joys, some increased sorrows, to contemplate. The change being so sad, were it not better to let the days fly past in silence? Anniversaries are the plaintive voices of the tomb, the solemn echoes of time.

Yesterday, at the close of the ball, we supped; then almost melted, for the heat of the apartments in which the crowd was gathered was insupportable, we entered certain carriages belonging to the court, called *lignes*, and made the tour of the illuminations; beyond the influence of which the night was very dark and

---

* The following year, the waters of Ems restored the health of the empress.

cool. The incredible profusion of lights spread over the enchanted forest produced, however, within its shades an extraordinary heat, and we were warmed as well as dazzled.

The *lignes* are a species of carriage with double seats, on which eight persons can conveniently sit, back to back. Their shape, gilding, and the antique trappings of the horses impart to them an air of grandeur and originality.

Objects of luxury impressed with a really royal character are now rarely seen in Europe.

The number of these equipages is considerable. They form one of the magnificent displays of the fête of Peterhoff. There was room in them for all invited, except the serfs and citizens.

A master of the ceremonies had pointed out to me the *ligne* in which I was to ride, but in the disorder of the departure no one kept his place. I could neither find my servant nor my cloak, and at length was obliged to mount one of the last of the *lignes,* where I seated myself by the side of a Russian lady who had not been to the ball, but who had come from Petersburg to show the illumination to her daughters. The conversation of these ladies, who appeared to know all the families of the court, was frank, in which respect it differed from that of those connected with the palace. The mother immediately commenced conversing with me: her manner had that facility and good taste about it which discovered the woman of rank. I recognised in her conversation, as I had already done elsewhere, that when the Russian women are natural, mildness and indulgence towards others is not a prominent trait in their character. She named to me all the persons we saw passing us; for in this procession the train of *lignes* often divided and filed before each other at the crossings of the alleys.

If I were not afraid of wearying the reader, I should exhaust all the formulae of admiration in repeating that I have never seen any thing so extraordinary as this illuminated park, traversed in solemn silence by the carriages of the court, in the midst of a crowd as dense as was that of the peasants in the saloons of the palace a few minutes before.

We rode for about an hour among enchanted groves, and made the tour of a lake situated at the extremity of the park, and called the lake of Marly. Versailles and all the magical creations of Louis XIV. haunted the imagination of the princes of Europe for more than a hundred years. It was at this lake of Marly that the illuminations appeared to me the most extraordinary. At the extremity of the piece of water,—I was going to say the piece of gold, so luminous and brilliant did it appear,—stands a house which was the residence of Peter the Great, and which was illuminated like the others. The water and the trees added singularly to the effect of the lights. We passed before grottoes, whose radiant interior was seen through a cascade of water falling over the mouth of the brilliant cavern. The imperial palace only was not illuminated, but its white walls became brilliant by the immense masses of light reflected upon them from all parts of the park.

This ride was unquestionably the most interesting feature in the fête of the empress. But I again repeat, scenes of magic splendour do not constitute scenes of gaiety. No one here laughed, sung, or danced; they all spoke low; they amused themselves with precaution; it seemed as though the Russian subjects were so broken into politeness as to be respectful even to their pleasures. In short, liberty was wanting at Peterhoff, as it is every where else in Russia.

I reached my chamber, or rather my box, after midnight. From that time, the retreat of the spectators commenced, and while the torrent swept under my window, I sat down to write, for sleep would have been impossible in the midst of so much uproar. In this country, the horses alone have permission to make a noise. Conveyances of all forms and sizes thundered along amid a crowd of men, women, and children, on foot.

It was natural life recommencing after the constraint of a royal fête. One might have supposed them prisoners delivered from their chains. The people of the road were no longer the disciplined crowd of the park. They rushed along in the direction of Petersburg with a violence and a rapidity that recalled to my mind the descriptions of the retreat from Moscow. Several accidents on the road aided the illusion.

Scarcely had I time to undress and throw myself on my bed, than I found it necessary to be again on foot, to witness the review of the corps of cadets, who were to pass before the emperor.

My surprise was great to find the court already at its post; the women in their morning dresses, the men in their coats of office; everybody awaited the emperor at the place of rendezvous. The desire of proving themselves zealous animated this embroidered crowd, who all showed so much alacrity that it seemed as if the splendour and fatigues of the night had weighed only upon me. I blushed for my indolence, and felt that I was not born to make a good Russian courtier. The chain, though gilded, did not appear to me the less heavy.

I had but just time to make my way through the crowd before the arrival of the empress, and had not yet gained my place, when the emperor commenced inspecting the ranks of his infant officers, while the empress, so overcome with fatigue the previous evening, waited for him in a calèche in the midst of the square. I felt for her, but the extreme exhaustion under which she had seemed to suffer during the ball had disappeared. My pity, therefore, turned upon myself, and I saw with envy the oldest people of the court lightly bearing the burden which I found so heavy. Ambition, here, is the condition of life: without its artificial stimulus the people would be always dull and gloomy. The emperor's own voice directed the manoeuvres of the pupils. After several had been perfectly well executed, his majesty appeared satisfied. He took the hand of one of the youngest of the cadets, led him forth from the ranks to the empress, and then, raising the child in his arms to the height of his head; that is, above the head of every body else, he kissed him publicly. What object had the emperor in showing himself so good-natured on this day before the public? This they either could not or would not tell me.

I asked the people around me who was the happy father of the model cadet, thus loaded with the favour of the sovereign: no one satisfied my curiosity. In Russia everything is turned into mystery. After this sentimental parade, the emperor and empress returned to the palace of Peterhoff, where they received in the state apartments such as wished to pay their court. Afterwards, at about eleven o'clock, they appeared on one of the balconies of the palace, before which the soldiers of the Circassian guard, mounted on their superb Asiatic horses, went through some interesting exercises. The beauty of this gorgeously clad troop adds to the military luxury of a court which, notwithstanding its efforts and pretensions, is, and for a long time will remain, more oriental than European. Towards noon, feeling my curiosity exhausted, and not possessing the all-powerful stimulus of that court ambition which here achieves so many miracles to supply my natural forces, I returned to my bed, from whence I have just risen to finish this recital.

I purpose remaining here the rest of the day, in order to let the crowd pass by; and I am also detained at Peterhoff by the hope of a pleasure to which I attach much value.

To-morrow, if I have time, I will relate the success of my machinations.

❖

CHAPTER XVI*

❖

I had earnestly begged Madame —— to procure for me admission to the English cottage of the emperor and empress. It is a small house which they have built in the midst of the noble park of Peterhoff, in the new Gothic style so much in vogue in England. "Nothing is more difficult than to enter the cottage," replied Madame —— "during the time that their majesties remain here, and nothing would be more easy in their absence. However, I will try."

I therefore prolonged my stay at Peterhoff, waiting, with some impatience, but without much hope, for the answer of Madame ——. Yesterday morning early, I received a little note from her, thus worded, "Let me see you at a quarter before eleven. I am permitted, as a very particular favour, to show you the cottage at the hour when the emperor and empress take their walk; that is at eleven o'clock precisely. You know their punctuality."

I did not fail to keep the appointment. Madame —— resides at a very pretty mansion, built in a corner of the park. She follows the empress everywhere, but she occupies, when possible, some separate house, although in the immediate vicinity of the different imperial residences. I was with her at half past ten. At a quarter before eleven we entered a carriage and four, crossed the park rapidly, and at a few minutes before eleven arrived at the gate of the cottage.

* Written at Petersburg.

❖ 255 ❖

It is, as I have said, quite an English residence, surrounded with flowers, shaded with trees, and built in the style of the prettiest places that may be seen near to London, about Twickenham, on the borders of the Thames. We crossed a rather small vestibule raised a few steps, and had just stopped to examine a room, the furniture of which struck me as a little too *recherché* for the general character of the building, when a *valet de chambre* came to whisper a few words in the ear of Madame ——, who seemed surprised.

"What is the matter?" I asked, when the man had disappeared.

"The empress is returned!"

"How unfair!" I exclaimed, "I shall not have time to see anything."

"Perhaps not; go down into the garden by this terrace, and wait for me at the entrance of the house."

I was scarcely there two minutes before I saw the empress rapidly descending the steps of the house and coming towards me. She was alone. Her tall and slender figure possesses a singular grace; her walk is active, light, and yet noble; she has certain movements of the arms and hands, certain attitudes, a certain turn of the head, that it is impossible to forget. She was dressed in white; her face, surrounded with a white calash appeared calm and composed; her eyes had an expression of gentleness and melancholy; a veil, gracefully thrown back, shaded her features, a transparent scarf fell over her shoulders, and completed the most elegant of morning dresses. Never had I seen her to so much advantage. Before this apparition, the sinister omens of the ball disappeared; the empress seemed resuscitated, and I experienced in beholding her, that sense of security which, after a night of trouble and agitation, returns with the dawn of day. Her majesty must, I thought, be stronger than I, to have thus supported the fête of the day before yesterday, the review and the soirée of yesterday, and to appear to-day so well and beautiful.

"I have shortened my promenade," she said, "because I knew that you were here."

"Ah! Madame, I was far from expecting so much goodness."

"I said nothing of my project to Madame ——, who has been

scolding me for thus coming to surprise you; she pretends that I shall disturb you in your survey. You expect then to discover all our secrets?"

"I should like, Madame; one could not but gain by acquaintance with the ideas of those who know so well how to choose between splendour and elegance."

"The residence at Peterhoff is insupportable to me, and it is to relieve my eyes from the glare of all that massive gold, that I have begged a cottage of the emperor. I have never been so happy as in this house; but now that one of my daughters is married, and that my sons pursue their studies elsewhere, it has become too large for us."

I smiled, without replying: I was under a charm: it seemed to me that this woman, so different from her in whose honour was given the sumptuous fête that had just taken place, could share with me all my impressions; she has felt like me, I thought, the weariness, the emptiness, the false brilliancy of this public magnificence, and she now feels that she is worthy of something better. I compared the flowers of the cottage with the lustres of the palace, the sun of a bright morning to the illuminations of a night of ceremony, the silence of a delicious retreat to the tumult of a palace crowd, the festival of nature to the festival of a court, the woman to the empress; and I was enchanted with the good taste and the sense which this princess had shown in flying the satieties of public display, to surround herself with all that constitutes the charm of private life. It was a new fairy scene, the illusion of which captivated my imagination much more strongly than the magic of splendour and power.

"I would not explain myself to Madame ——," continued the empress. "You shall see all over the cottage, and my son shall show it you. Meanwhile, I will go and visit my flowers, and shall find you again before we allow you to leave."

Such was the reception I met with from this lady, who is represented as haughty, not only in Europe, where she is scarcely known, but in Russia where they see her constantly.

At this moment, the hereditary Grand-duke joined his mother. He was accompanied by Madame ——, and her eldest daughter, a young person about fourteen years of age, fresh as a rose, and pretty as they were in France, in the times of Boucher. This young lady is the living model of one of the most agreeable portraits of that painter.

I expected the empress to give me my *congé*, but she commenced walking backwards and forwards before the house. Her majesty knew the interest I took in all the family of Madame ——, who is a Polish lady. Her majesty knew also that for some years past one of the brothers of Madame —— had lived at Paris. She turned the conversation to this young man's mode of life; and questioned me for a long time, with marked interest, regarding his sentiments, opinions and general character. This gave me every facility for saying of him all that my attachment dictated. She listened to me very attentively. When I had ceased speaking, the Grand-duke addressing his mother, continued the same subject and said, "I met him at Ems, and liked him very well."

"And yet, it is a man thus distinguished whom they forbid to come here, because he retired into Germany after the revolution in Poland," cried Madame ——, moved by her sisterly affection, and using that freedom of expression of which the habit of living at court from her infancy has not deprived her. "But what has he done then?" said the empress, addressing me, with an accent that was inimitable for the mixture of impatience and kindness which it expressed. I was embarrassed to find an answer to a question so direct, for it involved the delicate subject of politics, and to touch upon this subject might spoil everything.

The Grand-duke came to my aid with an affability and a kindness which I should be very ungrateful to forget; no doubt he thought I had too much to say to dare to answer; and anticipating some evasion which might have betrayed my embarrassment, and compromised the cause I desired to plead, "My mother," he said, with vivacity, "who ever asked a child of fifteen years what he had done in politics?"

This answer, full of sense and of good feeling, extricated me from the difficulty, but it put an end to the conversation. If I might dare to interpret the silence of the empress, I should say that this was her thought—"What could now be done, in Russia, with a pardoned Pole? He would always be an object of envy to the old Russians, and he would only inspire his new masters with distrust. His health and life would be lost in the trials to which he would have to be exposed in order to test his fidelity; and if, at length, they came to the conclusion that he might be trusted, they would only despise him. Besides, what could I do for this young man? I have so little influence!"

I do not believe I much deceive myself in saying, that such were the thoughts of the empress; such were also pretty nearly mine. We tacitly agreed in concluding that of two evils, the least for a gentleman who had lost both his fellow citizens and his comrades in arms, was to remain far from the land which had given him birth; the worst of all conditions would be that of a man who should live as a stranger in his own home.

On a sign from the empress, the Grand-duke, Madame ——, her daughter, and myself, re-entered the cottage. I should have wished to have found less luxurious furniture in this house, and a greater number of objects of virtu. The ground-floor resembled that of all the houses of rich and elegant English people, but not one picture of a high order, not one fragment of marble, or of *terra cotta*, announced that the owners of the place had a love for the arts. It is not to be able to draw more or less skilfully, but it is the taste for *chefs-d'oeuvre* that proves a love for and a judgment in the arts. I always regret to see the absence of this passion in those with whom it could be so easily gratified.

It may be said that statues and pictures of great value would be out of place in a cottage; but this house is the chosen and favourite resort of its possessors; and when people form for themselves an abode according to their fancy, if they have much love for the arts, that love will betray itself, at the risk even of some incongruity of style, some fault of harmony: besides, a little anomaly is allowable in an imperial cottage. Over the distribution of the ornaments of this cottage, and the general arrangements of its interior, it could be easily discovered that family affections and habits had chiefly presided; and these are worth even yet more than an appreciation of the beautiful in the works of genius. Only one thing really displeased me in the furniture and the arrangements of this elegant retreat, and that was a too servile adherence to English fashions.

We looked over the ground-floor very hastily, for fear of wearying our guide. The presence of so august a *cicerone* embarrassed me. I know that nothing so annoys princes as our timidity; at least, unless it be affected in order to flatter them. They love to be put at their ease, and we cannot do that without being at ease ourselves. With a grave prince I could have hoped to save myself by conversation, but with a gay and youthful prince, I was left without resource.

A staircase, very narrow, but adorned with an English carpet, conducted us to the upper floor. We there saw the chamber where the Grand-duchess Marie passed a part of her infancy; it is empty: that of the Grand-duchess Olga will not probably remain long occupied. The empress might truly say that the cottage was becoming too large. These two very similar chambers are furnished with a charming simplicity.

The Grand-duke stopped at the top of the stairs, and said with that perfect politeness, of which (notwithstanding his extreme youth) he possesses the secret,—"I am sure that you would rather see everything here without me; and I have seen it all so often, that I would, I confess, as willingly leave you to finish your survey with Madame ———. I will therefore join my mother, and wait for you with her."

Whereupon he saluted us gracefully, and left me, charmed with the flattering ease of his manners. It is a great advantage to a prince to be really well bred. I had not, then, this time, produced the effect that I anticipated; the constraint that I felt had not been communicated. If he had sympathised with my uneasiness, he would have remained, for timidity can do nothing but submit to its torture; it knows not how to free itself; no elevation is safe from its attacks: the victim whom it paralyses, in whatever rank he may be placed, cannot find strength either to confront or to fly from that which produces his discomfort.

This suffering is sometimes the effect of a discontented or overwrought self-love. A man who fears that he stands alone in his opinion of himself, becomes timid through vanity: but more often, timidity is purely physical;—it is a disease.

There are men who cannot, without an inexplicable sense of uneasiness, be conscious that the human eye rests upon them.

That eye paralyses them; fetters their thoughts, their speech, and more especially their movements. This is so true, that I have often suffered from physical timidity, in villages where, as a stranger, I attracted all eyes, much more than in the most stately saloons where nobody paid any attention to me. I could write a treatise on the different kinds of shyness, for I am the accomplished model of them all. No one has suffered more than I have, from my infancy, under the attacks of this incurable disease, scarcely known to the rising generation; which proves that, over and above physical predisposition, timidity is peculiarly the result of education. Familiarity with the world enables us to dissimulate the infirmity, and that is all. The most timid men are often the most eminent in birth. In dignity, and even in merit. I long believed that timidity was modesty combined with an exaggerated respect for social distinctions, or for the gifts of mind; but how then could be explained the timidity of great writers, or of princes? Happily, the princes of the imperial Russian family are by no means timid—they belong to their age; neither in their manners nor language can be perceived any vestiges of that embarrassment, which for a long period tormented the august inmates of Versailles, and their courtiers also; for what can be more embarrassing than a timid prince?

Whatever may have been the cause, I felt relieved when I saw the Grand-duke depart; I thanked him inwardly for having so well guessed my wish, and for having so politely gratified it. A man but half-polished would scarcely have taken it into his head to leave people alone with the view of making himself agreeable to them: nevertheless, it is sometimes the greatest kindness that can be accorded. To know how to leave a guest without wounding his feelings, is the height of urbanity—the *chef-d'oeuvre* of hospitality. This facility is in the fashionable world what liberty without disorder would be in the political—a problem constantly proposed, and never solved.

At the moment when the Grand-duke left us, Mademoiselle —— was standing behind her mother. The prince, as he passed her, stopped, and in a very grave but rather humorous manner, made her a profound reverence, without speaking a word. The young lady, perceiving that this salutation was ironical, remained in a respectful attitude, but without returning the obeisance. I admired this little expression of feeling, which appeared to me to exhibit an exquisite delicacy. I doubt whether at the Russian court, any woman of twenty-five would have distinguished herself by an act of so much courage; it was dictated only by that innocence, which to the regard due to social prerogatives knows how to join a just sentiment of its own dignity. The exhibition of tact did not pass unperceived.

"Always the same!" said the Grand-duke, as he turned away.

They had been children together; a difference of five years in age had not prevented them from often playing at the same games. Such familiarity is not forgotten, even at court. The silent scene which they now enacted together much amused me.

My peep into the interior of the imperial family has interested me extremely. These princes must be nearly approached in order to be appreciated. They are made to be at the head of their country; for they are in every respect superior to their people. The imperial family is the object the most worthy of exciting the admiration and the envy of foreigners that I have seen in Russia.

At the top of the house we found the cabinet of the emperor. It is a tolerably large and very simply ornamented library, opening on a balcony which overlooks the sea. Without leaving this watch-tower, the Emperor can give his orders to his fleet. For this purpose he has a spy-glass, a speaking-trumpet, and a little telegraph which he can work himself.

I should have liked to examine this room and all it contains in detail, and to have asked many questions, but I feared lest my curiosity might seem indiscreet, and I preferred making an imperfect survey, to appearing as if I had come to take an inventory.

Besides, I am more curious about the general appearance of things than about their minute details. I travel to observe, and to form an opinion of objects, but not to measure, catalogue, or sketch them. It is a favour to be admitted into this cottage thus, as it were, in the presence of its occupants;—a favour the more rarely conceded as the house really offers no other interest beyond the curiosity which attaches to their habits and their private life. I therefore felt as though I ought to show myself worthy of the privilege by avoiding too minute an investigation.

After having explained this feeling to Madame ———, who perfectly understood my delicacy, I hastened to take leave of the empress and the grand-duke. We found them in the garden, where, after some further gracious words, they left me, satisfied with everything I had seen; but, above all, grateful for their kindness, and charmed with the singular grace of their accessible manners.

After leaving the cottage, I proceeded to pay a hasty visit to Oranienbaum, the celebrated residence of Catherine II., built by Menzikoff. This unfortunate man was sent to Siberia before he had completed the wonders of a palace deemed too royal for a minister.

It now belongs to the Grand-duchess Helena, sister-in-law of the present emperor. Situated two or three leagues from Peterhoff, in sight of the sea, and on a continuation of the same ridge on which is built the imperial palace, the castle of Oranienbaum, although constructed of wood, is an imposing edifice. Notwithstanding the imprudent luxury of the builder, and the greatness of the personages who have, after him, inhabited it, it is not remarkable for its extent. Terraces, flights of steps, and balconies covered with orange trees and flowering plants, connect the house with the park, and embellish both the one and the other; but the architecture itself is anything but magnificent. The Grand-duchess Helena has shown here the taste which presides throughout all her arrangements, and which has made Oranienbaum a charming residence, notwithstanding the dulness of the landscape, and the besetting memories of the scenes formerly enacted there.

On leaving the palace, I asked permission to see the remains of the small but strong fortress, from whence they obliged Peter III. to come forth, and carried him to Ropscha, where he was assassinated. I was conducted to a retired hamlet, where are to be seen dry ditches, broken mounds, and heaps of stones, a modern ruin, in the production of which policy has had more to do than time. . . .

In looking over the park of Oranienbaum, which is large and beautiful, I visited several of the summerhouses, which were the scenes of the Empress's amorous assignations. Some of them were splendid pavilions, others exhibited bad taste. In general their architecture lacked purity of style, though certainly pure enough for the uses to which the goddess of the place destined them.

I returned to Peterhoff, and slept, for the third night, in the theatre. This morning, in returning to Petersburg, I took the road by Krasnacselo, where a large camp is formed. Forty thousand men of the imperial guard are, it is said, lodged there under tents, or dispersed in the neighbouring villages. Others say the number is seventy thousand. In Russia every one imposes upon me his own estimate, to which I pay little attention, for nothing is more deceptive than these statements. They serve to show, however, the importance that is attached to leading people astray. Nations rise above such childish stratagems when they pass from infancy to a state of manhood.

I was much amused with viewing the variety of uniforms, and with comparing the expressive and savage faces of these soldiers, who are brought from every part of the empire. Long lines of white tents glistened in the sun, on a surface broken into small undulations in a manner that produced a picturesque effect.

I am constantly regretting the insufficiency of words to describe certain scenes in the north, and, above all, certain effects of light. A few strokes of the pencil would give a better idea of the original aspect of this melancholy and singular land, than whole volumes of description.

❖

CHAPTER XVII

❖

According to information that I have obtained this morning respecting the disaster of the fête of Peterhoff, its extent has exceeded my expectations. But we shall never ascertain the exact circumstances of the event. Every accident here, is treated as an affair of state: it is God who has failed in his duty to the emperor.

Political superstition, which is the soul of the Muscovite community, exposes its chieftain to all the complaints that impotence may bring against power, that earth may urge against heaven. If my dog is hurt, it is to me that he comes for the cure of his wound; if God afflicts the Russians, they immediately call upon their czar. This prince, who is responsible for nothing in politics, must answer for every thing in Providence; a natural consequence of man's usurpation of the rights of God. A man who allows himself to be considered as more than a mortal, takes upon himself all the evil that heaven may send upon earth during his reign. There results from this species of political fanaticism, a susceptibility, and jealous delicacy of which no idea can be formed in other lands. Nevertheless, the secrecy which policy believes it necessary to maintain on the subject of misfortunes the least dependent upon human will, fails in its object, inasmuch as it leaves the field open to imagination. Every one relates the same transaction differently, according to his interest, his fears, his ambition, or his humour; according to his situation at court, or his position in the world. Hence it is, that truth, in Petersburg is an imaginary thing, just as it has become in France, although from different causes. An arbitrary censorship and an unlimited liberty may lead to the same results, and render impossible the verification of the most simple fact.

Thus, some say that there were only thirty persons who perished the day before yesterday, while others speak of twelve hundred, others of two thousand, and others again of one hundred and fifty. Imagine the uncertainty in which every thing must be involved, when the circumstances of an event that took place, as it were, under our eyes, will always remain unknown, even to ourselves. I shall never cease to marvel at having seen a people exist, so thoughtless as readily and tranquilly to live and die in the twilight which the policy of its masters accords it. Hitherto I had been accustomed to believe that man could no more dispense with truth for his mind than with sun and air for his body; but my Russian journey has undeceived me. Truth is only needful to elevated minds or to advanced nations; the vulgar accommodate themselves to the falsehoods favourable to their passions and habits; here, to lie, is to protect society, to speak the truth is to overthrow the state. The twilight of politics is less transparent than the polar sky.

For the authenticity of one of the accidents connected with the catastrophe of Peterhoff I can vouch.

Three young Englishmen, the eldest of whom I know, had been some days in Petersburg. Their father is in England, and their mother waits them at Carlsbad. On the day of the fête, the two youngest sailed for Peterhoff without their brother, who constantly refused their solicitations to accompany them, alleging that he felt no curiosity. He saw them embark in their little vessel, and bade them adieu until the morrow. Three hours afterwards both were corpses! They perished together with several women and children and two or three men, who were in the same boat; a sailor, who was a good swimmer, was alone saved. The unhappy surviving brother is plunged in a despair which would be difficult to describe. He is preparing to leave, to join his mother and apprise her of the melancholy tidings. She had written to her sons desiring them not to omit seeing the fête of Peterhoff, nor to hurry their departure, should their curiosity incline them to prolong their stay, intimating that she would wait patiently for them at Carlsbad. A little more urgency on her part would perhaps have saved their lives.

What numberless accounts, discussions, and proposals would not such a catastrophe have given rise to in any other land except this, and more especially in our own! How many newspapers would have said, and how many voices would have repeated, that the police never does its duty, that the boats were not seaworthy, the watermen greedy only of gain, and that the authorities, far from interfering, did but increase the danger by their indifference or their corruption! It would have been added that the marriage of the grand-duchess had been celebrated under very gloomy auspices, like many other royal marriages; and then, dates, allusions, and citations would have followed in great abundance. Nothing of the kind here! A silence more frightful than the evil itself, everywhere reigns. Two lines in the Gazette, without details, is all the information publicly given; and at court, in the city, in the saloons of fashion, not a word is spoken. There are no coffee-houses in Petersburg where people comment upon the journals; there are indeed no journals upon which to comment. The petty employés are more timid than the great lords; what is not dared to be spoken of among the principals, is yet more carefully avoided by subordinates; and as to the merchants and shopkeepers, that wily caution necessary to all who would live and thrive in the land is, by them, especially observed. If they speak on grave, and therefore dangerous subjects, it is only in strict and confidential privacy.*

* I may insert here the extract of a letter received in the present year from a female friend, which, though it does not add to, may serve to illustrate what has been already said, and to give a better idea of the subjection in which minds are held in Russia than anything I can myself say. "An Italian painter who was at Petersburg at the same time that you were, is now in Paris. He related to me, as you had done previously, the circumstances of that catastrophe, in which about four hundred individuals perished. The painter told his story in a very low voice. 'I know all this,' I said to him, 'but why do you whisper it?' 'O! because the Emperor has forbidden that it should be spoken of.' This obedience, in spite of the time that had elapsed, and the distance, excited my astonishment. But you, who cannot conceal one truth, when do you mean to publish your journey?"

I subjoin yet another illustration, taken from an article in the *Journal des Débats* of the 13th October, 1842:—In the month of October, 1840, two trains running in an opposite direction on the railroad of St. Petersburg and Krasnacselo, came into

Russia is instructed to say nothing which could render the empress nervous; and thus is she left to live and die dancing! "She would be distressed, therefore hold your peace." And hereupon, children, friends, relations, all who are loved, die, and no one dares to even weep for them. People here are too unfortunate to complain.

The Russians are all courtiers. Soldiers, spies, gaolers, executioners in this land all do more than their duty; all ply their trade as parasites. Who shall tell me to what lengths a society may not go which is not built on the foundation of human dignity?

I repeat that as much must be undone as done, before there can be here made a people.

This time, the silence of the police is not merely the result of a desire to flatter, it is also the effect of fear. The slave dreads the angry mood of his master, and employs every effort to keep him in a state of benignity and good humour. The chains, the dungeon, the knout and Siberia, are all within reach of an irritated czar; or at the best there is the Caucasus, a Siberia mitigated to the uses of a despotism softened in accordance with the spirit of the century.

It cannot be denied that in this instance the first cause of the evil was the carelessness of the administration. If the authorities had prevented the boatmen of Petersburg from overloading their vessels, or from venturing on the gulf in craft too small or weak to ride the waves, no one would have perished; and yet, who knows? The Russians are generally bad seamen: wherever they are, there is danger. When Asiatics, with their long robes and long beards, are the sailors, there can be little surprise at hearing of shipwrecks.

On the day of the fête, one of the steam-boats that generally

---

collision, owing to their engineers not having seen each other's approach, by reason of a heavy fog. Everything was shattered by the shock. Five hundred persons, it is said, lay around the broken cars, killed, mutilated, or more or less severely wounded. This was scarcely known in Petersburg. Early on the morrow, a few curious persons only ventured to visit the scene of the accident. They found the remains of the carriages cleared away, the dead and the wounded removed, and, as the sole evidence of the accident, a few agents of the police, who after interrogating them as to the motives of their morning visit, reprimanded them for their curiosity, and roughly commanded them all to return home."

run between Petersburg and Kronstadt, started for Peterhoff. Although large and strong, it was in danger of foundering like the smaller vessels, and would have done so had it not been for a foreigner who was among the passengers. This man (who was an Englishman) seeing several vessels capsized around them, knowing the danger they were in, and observing further that the boat was badly served and badly commanded, conceived the happy idea of cutting with his own knife the cords which held the awning raised upon deck for the comfort and convenience of the passengers. The first thing that ought to have been done, upon the least sign of a squall, was to remove this pavilion. The Russians never dreamt of so simple a precaution, and had it not been for the foreigner's presence of mind the boat would have infallibly capsized. It was saved, though too much damaged to continue its voyage, and its crew only too happy in being able to return to Petersburg. If the Englishman who saved it had not been an acquaintance of another Englishman, who is one of my friends, I should not have known the fact. It was confirmed to me by other informed persons, to whom I mentioned it; but they requested that I would keep it secret!

It would not do to talk about the Deluge, if that catastrophe had happened under the reign of a Russian emperor.

Among all the intelligent faculties, the only one that is here valued is that of tact. Imagine a whole nation bending under the yoke of this drawing-room virtue. Picture to your minds an entire people, prudent as a diplomatist who has yet his fortune to make, and you will compass the idea of the substance and worth of conversation in Russia. If the atmosphere of the court oppresses us even when at the court, how unfriendly to life must it not be when it pursues us into the very retirement of the family circle!

Russia is a nation of mutes. Some potent magician has transformed sixty millions of men into automata who must await the wand of another enchanter before they can again enjoy life. Or it reminds me of the palace of Sleeping Beauty in the wood—it is bright and magnificent, but it lacks one thing, which is life, or, in other words, liberty.

The Emperor must suffer from such a state of things. Whoever is born to command, no doubt loves obedience; but the obedience of a man is worth more than that of a machine. A prince surrounded by complaisant flatterers must always remain in ignorance of every thing which it is wished he should not know; he is, therefore, necessarily condemned to doubt every word and to distrust every individual. Such is the lot of an absolute master. In vain would he be amiable, in vain would he live as a man; the force of circumstances makes him unfeeling in spite of himself; he occupies the place of a despot, and is obliged to submit to a despot's destiny—to adopt his sentiments, or, at least, to play his part.

The evils of dissimulation extend here further than may be imagined: the Russian police, so alert to torment people, is slow to aid or enlighten them when they have recourse to its aid in doubtful situations.

The following is an example of this designed inertia. At the last carnival, a lady of my acquaintance had permitted her waiting-woman to go out on the Sunday. Night came, and this person did not return. On the following morning the lady, very uneasy, sent to obtain information from the police.*

They replied that no accident had occurred in Petersburg on the preceding night, and that no doubt the *femme-de-chambre* had lost herself, and would soon return safe and sound.

The day passed in deceitful security. On the day following a relation of the girl's, a young man tolerably versed in the secrets of the police, conceived the idea of going to the Hall of Surgery, to which one of his friends procured him an admission. Scarcely had he entered when he recognised the corpse of his cousin, which the pupils were just about to commence dissecting. Being a good Russian, he preserved self-command sufficient to conceal his emotion, and asked—"Whose body is this?"

"No one knows: it is that of a girl's who was found dead the night before last, in ⸺ street; it is believed that she has been strangled in attempting to defend herself against men who endeavoured to violate her."

* I have been obliged to conceal names, and to change such circumstances as might allow of this account being traced to individuals; but the facts are essentially preserved.

"Who are the men?"

"We do not know: one can only form conjectures on the event; proofs are wanting."

"How did you obtain the body?"

"The police sold it to us secretly; so we will not talk about it."

This last is a common expression in the mouth of a Russ, or an acclimated foreigner. I admit that the above circumstances are not so revolting as those of the crime of Burke in England; but the peculiar characteristic of Russia is the protective silence in which similar atrocities are shrouded.

The cousin was dead. The mistress of the victim dared not complain; and now, after a lapse of six months, I am, perhaps, the only person to whom she has related the death of her *femme-de-chambre*.

It will by this be seen how the subaltern agents of the Russian police perform their duties. These faithless servants gained a double advantage by selling the body of the murdered woman: they obtained a few roubles, and they also concealed the murder, which would have brought upon them severe blame, if the noise of the event had got abroad.

Reprimands addressed to men of this class are, I believe, accompanied with other demonstrations, of a character likely to engrave the words indelibly in the memories of the unfortunate hearers. A Russian of the lower class is as often beaten as saluted. The lifting of the rods (in Russia the rod is a large split cane) and the lifting of the hat are means employed in about equal measure, in the social education of this people. Beating in Russia can only be applied to certain classes and by men of certain other classes. Here ill-treatment is regulated like the tariff of a custom-house; it reminds us of the code of Ivan. The dignity of caste is admitted, but no one dreams of the dignity of man. The reader will recollect what I have already said of the politeness of the Russians of all ranks, and of its real value; I will now confine myself to relating one or two of the illustrative scenes that pass daily before my eyes.

I have seen in the same street two drivers of drowskas ceremoniously lift their hats in passing each other:—this is a common custom: if acquainted, they lift their hand to their mouth with an amicable smile, and kiss it, making at the same time a little expressive and intelligent sign with the eyes: so much for politeness.

A little farther on I have seen a courier, a feld-jäger, or some other government servant, descend from his vehicle, and, running to one of these well-bred coachmen, strike him brutally and unmercifully with whip, stick, or fist, in the breast, the face, or on the head, which punishment the unlucky wight, who had not made way in sufficient haste, received without the least complaint or resistance, out of respect to the uniform and the caste of his tormenter, whose anger, however, is not always in such cases promptly disarmed by the submission of the delinquent.

Have I not seen one of these carriers of dispatches, courier of some minister, or *valet-de-chambre* of some aide-de-camp of the emperor's, drag from his seat a young coachman, and never cease striking him until he had covered his face with blood. The victim submitted to the torture like a real lamb, without the least resistance, and in the same manner as one would yield to some commotion of nature. The passers-by were in no degree moved or excited by the cruelty, and one of the comrades of the sufferer, who was watering his horses a few steps off, obedient to a sign of the enraged feldjäger, approached to hold his horse's bridle during the time that he was pleased to prolong the punishment. In what other country could a man of the lower orders be found who would assist in the infliction of an arbitrary punishment upon one of his companions?

The scene in question took place in the finest part of the city, and at the busiest hour. When the unfortunate man was released, he wiped away the blood, which streamed down his cheeks, remounted his seat, and re-commenced his bows and salutations as usual. It should be recollected that this abomination was enacted in the midst of a silent crowd. A people governed in a Christian manner would protest against a social discipline which destroys all individual liberty. But here the influence of the priest is confined to obtaining from the people and the nobles signs of the cross and genuflexions.

Notwithstanding its worship of the Holy Spirit, this nation has always its god upon earth. Like Tamerlane, the Emperor of Russia receives the idolatrous worship of his subjects; the Russian law has never been baptized.

I hear every day some encomium on the gentleness, politeness, and pacific humour of the people of Saint Petersburg. Elsewhere I should admire this calm; here, I can only view it as the worst symptom of the evil of which I complain. The people are actuated by fear to a degree that urges them to dissimulate, and to assume the appearance of a content and tranquility which conduces to the satisfaction of the oppressor, and the security of the oppressed. Your true tyrant likes to be surrounded with smiles. Under the terror which hovers over all heads, submission becomes the general rule of conduct: victims and executioners, all practise the obedience that perpetuates the evil which they inflict or to which they submit.

The intervention of the police between people who quarrel would expose the combatants to punishment yet more formidable than the blows they bear in silence, and they avoid therefore all noise that might call the executioner to the spot.

Of the following tumultuous scene chance, however, rendered me a witness this morning.

I was passing along a canal covered with boats laden with wood, which the men were carrying on shore. One of these porters got into a quarrel with his comrades, and they all commenced fighting as they might have done among ourselves on a similar occasion. The aggressor, finding himself the weakest, took to flight: he climbed, with the agility of a squirrel, a large mast of the vessel, and perching himself upon a yard, set at defiance his less nimble adversaries. So far I found the scene amusing. The men seeing themselves balked in their hope of vengeance, and forgetting that they were in Russia, manifested their fury by loud cries and savage menaces. There are found at certain distances, in all the streets of the city, agents of the police in uniform: two of these persons, attracted by the vociferations of the combatants, repaired to the scene of action, and commanded the chief offender to descend from his perch. This individual did not obey the summons; one of the policemen sprang on board; the refractory porter clung to the mast; the man of power reiterated his commands, and the rebel persisted in his disobedience. The former, infuriated, tried himself to climb the mast, and succeeded in seizing one of the feet of the fugitive, which, without troubling himself with any consideration as to the manner in which the unfortunate being was to descend, he pulled at with all his force. The other, hopeless of escaping the punishment that awaited him, at length yielded to his fate; he let go his hold, and fell from a height of about twelve feet upon a pile of wood, on which his body lay as motionless as a sack. The severity of the fall may be imagined. The head struck against the wood, and the sound of the concussion reached my ear, though I was about fifty paces off. I supposed the man was dead; his face was bathed in blood; nevertheless, on recovering from the first stunning effect of the fall, this unfortunate savage, thus taken in the snare, rose; his visage, wherever the blood allowed it to be seen, had a frightful paleness, and he began to bellow like an ox. His horrible cries diminished my compassion; he seemed to me as nothing more than a brute, and I could not therefore feel for him as for one of my fellows. The louder the man howled the harder my heart grew; so true it is that the objects of our compassion must exhibit something of their proper dignity, ere we can deeply participate in their trouble. Pity is a sentiment of association, and who would mentally associate with that which he despises? They at length carried him off, although he continued to offer a desperate and protracted resistance. A small boat was brought alongside by other police agents; the prisoner was bound with cords, his hands were fastened behind his back, and he was thrown on his face into the boat. This second rude shock was followed by a shower of blows, nor did the torture here finish; the sergeant who had seized the victim, no sooner saw him thus prostrate, than he jumped upon his body, and began to stamp upon him with all his force, trampling him under his feet as the grapes are trod in the wine press. I had then approached the spot, and am therefore witness of all that I relate. During this horrible torture the frightful yells of the victim were at first redoubled, but when they began to grow fainter and fainter, I felt that I could no longer command myself, and, having no power to interfere, I hastened away.

What most disgusts me is the refined elegance which is exhibited in the same picture with such revolting barbarity. If there were less luxury and delicacy among the higher orders the condition of the lower would inspire me with less indignation. Such occurrences, with all that they involve, would make me hate the most delightful country in the world; how much more, then, a heath of plaster—a painted marsh!

"What exaggeration!" the Russians would say: "what strong expressions for so trifling a matter!!" I know you call it trifling, and it is that for which I reproach you. Your familiarity with these horrors explains your indifference without justifying it: you make no more account of the cords with which you bind a man, than of the collar which you put on your dog.

In broad daylight, in the open street, to beat a man to death before he is tried, appears a very simple matter in the eyes of the public and of the constables of Petersburg. Citizens, lords, and soldiers, the poor and the rich, the great and small, the polite and the vulgar, the clowns and the fops, the Russians of every class consent to let such things quietly go on in their presence, without troubling themselves about their legality. Elsewhere, the citizen is protected by the whole community against the agent of unjust power; here, the public agent is protected against the just accusations of the injured individual. The serf never accuses.

The Emperor Nicholas has made a code! If the facts I have related are in accordance with the laws of this code so much the worse for the legislator; if they are illegal, so much the worse for the administrator of the law. The Emperor is, in both cases, responsible. What a misfortune to be no more than a man in accepting the office of a god, and yet to be forced to accept it! Absolute government should be confided only to angels.

I pledge myself to the accuracy of the facts that are here related. I have neither added nor retrenched one circumstance in the recital, and I recount it while the slightest features of the scene continue present to my mind.*

If such details could be published at Petersburg, with the commentaries indispensable to make them noticed by minds inured to

* It may not be useless to repeat that this chapter, like almost all the others, was preserved and concealed with care during my sojourn in Russia.

all kinds of brutality and injustice, they would not effect the good that might be expected. The Russian administration would so order matters, that the police of Petersburg should henceforth seem to be more mild in its treatment of the people, were it only out of respect for the squeamish sentiments of foreigners; but this would be all.

The manners of a people are gradually formed by the reciprocal action of the laws upon the customs, and of the customs upon the laws; they do not change as by the stroke of a wand. Those of the Russians, in spite of the pretensions of these half-savages, are, and will yet long remain cruel. It is little more than a century since they were true Tartars: it was Peter the Great who first compelled the men to admit females into their social meetings; and under all their modern elegance, several of these parvenus of civilisation still wear the bear skin.

Seeing that they can now no longer avail themselves of the age of chivalry—that age by whose spirit the nations of western Europe were so much benefited in their youth—all that can remain for the Russians is an independent and influential religion. Russia has a faith, but a political faith does not emancipate the human mind; it shuts it up in the narrow circle of its natural interests. With the Catholic faith the Russians would soon acquire general ideas, based on a rational course of instruction, and on a liberty proportioned to their state of enlightenment. Could they but obtain this elevation, I am persuaded that they might rule the world. The evil of their system is deeply seated, and the remedies hitherto employed have only acted upon the surface—they have healed the wound over without curing it. A genuine civilisation spreads from the centre to the circumference, that of Russia tends from the circumference towards the centre; it is a barbarism, plastered over, and nothing more.

Because a savage may have the vanity of a votary of fashion, does it follow that his mind is cultivated? I repeat, and may, perhaps, repeat again, that the Russians care much less for being civilised than for making us believe that they are civilised. So long as this public disease of vanity shall continue to prey upon their hearts and to corrupt their minds, they will have certain great lords who will be able to make a display of refinement both among themselves and us; but they will remain barbarians at heart. Unfortunately, however, savages understand the use of fire-arms.

The endeavours of the Emperor Nicholas justify my views. He has thought, before I did, that the time for the display of appearances is past in Russia, and that the entire edifice of civilisation in that land has to be reconstructed.

Peter the Great would have overthrown it a second time in order to rebuild it. Nicholas is more skilful. I am filled with respect for this man, who, with the whole energy of his mind, struggles in secret against the work of the genius of Peter the Great. While continuing to deify that mighty reformer, he is all the while bringing back to their proper position a nation led astray among the paths of imitation for upwards of a hundred years. The views of the present emperor manifest themselves even in the streets of Petersburg. He does not amuse himself with building, in haste, colonnades of stuccoed bricks; he is everywhere replacing appearance with reality; stone is everywhere superseding plaster, and fabrics of a strong and massive architecture are rising above the showy monuments of a false splendour. It is by first bringing back a people to their primitive character, that they are rendered capable and worthy of true civilisation, without which a nation cannot know how to work for posterity. If a people would rear a monument to their own power and greatness, they must not copy foreigners—they must study to develope the national genius instead of thwarting it. That which in this creation most nearly approaches to Deity, is nature. Nature calls the Russians to great things, while they, under their pretended civilisation, have been occupied with trifles. The Emperor Nicholas has appreciated their capabilities better than his predecessors, and under his reign, by a general return to truth, everything is becoming great. In Petersburg stands a pillar, which is the largest piece of granite that has ever been cut by the hands of man, not excepting the Egyptian monuments. Seventy thousand soldiers, the court, the city, and the surrounding country, gathered together without inconvenience or pressure in the square of the imperial palace, to witness, in a religious silence, the miraculous erection of this monument, conceived, executed, and placed by a

Frenchman, M. de Montferrand; for the French are still necessary to the Russians. The prodigious machines worked successfully, and at the moment when the column, rising from its fetters,
lifted itself up as if animated with a life of its own, the army, the
crowd, the emperor himself, fell on their knees to thank God for
so great a miracle, and to praise him for the stupendous achieve-
ments which he permitted them to accomplish. This I call a real
national fête; not a flattery that might, like the masquerade of
Peterhoff, have been also taken for a satire, but a grand historical
picture. The great, the little, the bad, the sublime, and all other
opposites, enter into the constitution of this singular country,
while silence perpetuates the prodigy and prevents the machine
from breaking.

The Emperor Nicholas extends his reforms even to the language of those who surround him; he requires Russian to be spoken at court. The greater number of the women of the highest
circles, especially those who have been born at Petersburg, are
ignorant of their native language; but they learn a few Russian
phrases, which they utter through obedience to the emperor,
when he passes into the saloons of the palace where their duties
may retain them. One of them acts always as a sentinel, to announce to the others, by some conventional sign, the arrival of
the monarch, on whose appearance French conversation immediately ceases, and Russian phrases, destined to flatter the imperial
ear, are heard on every side. The prince observes, with self-com-
placency, the extent of his power as a reformer; and the fair
rebels begin to laugh as soon as he has passed.

However, like every reformer, the Emperor is endowed with an
obstinacy which must ultimately produce success.

At the extremity of that square, vast as a mighty region, in
which stands the column, is to be seen a mountain of granite—
the church of Saint Isaac, of Petersburg. This edifice, though less
stately, less beautiful in design, and less rich in ornaments than
that of St. Peter's at Rome, is quite as extraordinary. It is not
finished, and one cannot therefore judge of the whole, which will
be a work whose gigantic proportions will far exceed those which
the spirit of the age has produced among other nations. Its mate-

rials are granite, bronze, and iron, and no other. Its colour is imposing, though sombre.

This marvellous temple was commenced under Alexander, and will soon be completed under the reign of Nicholas, by the same Frenchman, (M. de Montferrand), who raised the column.

And such efforts for the benefit of a church crippled by the civil power! Alas! the word of God will never be heard under this roof. The temples of the Greek church no longer serve as roofs for the pulpits of truth. In scorn of the memories of the Athanasiuses and the Chrysostoms, religion is not taught publicly to the Russians. The Greek Muscovites suppress the word of preaching, unlike the Protestants, whose religion consists of nothing but that word.

The Emperor, aided by his armies of soldiers and of artists, exerts himself in vain. He will never invest the Greek church with a power which God has not given it: it may be rendered a persecuting, but it cannot be rendered an apostolical, church,—a church, that is to say which is a *civiliser*, and a conqueror in the moral world. To discipline men is not to convert souls. This political and national church has neither moral nor spiritual life: where independence is wanting, there can be nothing else that is good. Schism, in separating the priest from his independent head, immediately throws him into the hands of his temporal prince; and thus revolt is punished by slavery. In the most bloody periods of history, the Catholic church laboured to emancipate the nations: the adulterous priest sold the God of heaven to the god of the world to enable him to tyrannise over men in the name of Christ; but this impious priest, while even he was killing the body enlightened the mind: for, altogether turned from the right way as he was, he nevertheless formed part of a church which possessed life and light: the Greek priest imparts neither life nor death,—he is himself a dead body.

Signs of the cross, salutations in the streets, bowing of the knees before the chapels, prostrations of old devotees upon the pavements of the churches, kissings of the hands, a wife, children, and universal contempt—such are the fruits of the priest's abdication—such is all that he has been able to obtain from the most superstitious people in the world. What a lesson! and what a punishment! In the midst of the triumph of his schism, the schismatic priest is struck with impotence. A priest, when he wishes to engross temporal power, perishes for the want of views sufficiently elevated to enable him to see the road that God has appointed for him;—a priest who allows himself to be dethroned by the king, for the want of courage to follow that road, equally fails in his high calling.

I cannot apologise for the wandering character of my thoughts and disquisitions, for, in passing freely from object to object, from idea to idea, I describe Russia as a whole, and show the truth as it appears to me, better than if, with a more methodical style, I purposely endeavoured to avoid the reproach of inconsistencies, digressions, or confusion of subjects. The state of the people, the greatness of the Emperor, the aspect of the streets, the beauty of the public buildings, the degraded state of minds consequent upon the degeneration of the religious principle, all struck my eyes at the same moment, and passed so to speak, at once under my pen; and all constitute Russia, the principles of whose life reveal themselves to my thoughts in the contemplation of objects the least significant in appearance.

Yesterday I walked out with a Frenchman, an intelligent person, well acquainted with Petersburg, where he resides as tutor in the family of a great nobleman. He has consequently opportunities for attaining a knowledge of the truth, entirely beyond the reach of passing travellers. He considered my views of Russia too favourable. I laugh at this reproach when I think of those which the Russians will make against me, and I maintain that I am impartial, seeing that I hate only that which appears to me evil, and that I admire all which appears good, in this, as in other lands.

This Frenchman passes his life among Russian aristocrats.

We were walking leisurely along the beautiful promenade of the Perspective Newski, when suddenly a black, or dark green coach passed before us. It was long, low-built, and closed on all sides, and much resembled an enormous coffin raised upon wheels. Four little apertures of about six inches square, crossed with iron bars, gave air and light to this moving tomb; a child of eight, or, at the most, ten years, guided the two horses attached to the machine; and, to my surprise, a considerable number of soldiers escorted it. I had scarcely time to ask my companion the uses of so singular an equipage, when my question was answered by a ghastly face, which appeared at one of the air holes, and at once informed me that this carriage served to transport prisoners to the place of their destination.

"It is the travelling cell of the Russians," said my companion; "elsewhere, no doubt, they have similar odious objects; but then they seek to hide them as much as they can from the public; here they make as much display of them as possible. What a government!"

"Think," I replied, "of the difficulties it has to encounter!"

"Ah! you are still the dupe of their gilded words. I see the Russian authorities impose upon you whatever they please."

"I endeavour to place myself as much as possible in their situation; nothing requires more candid consideration than the position of those who govern, for it is not they who have created the existing state of things; their business is to defend it even while prudently reforming it. If the iron rod which governs this debased people were to be removed but for one moment, society would be overturned."

"They tell you that; but, trust me, they delight in this pretended necessity. Those who most complain of the severities they are obliged, as they say, to put in force, would renounce them with regret. In the bottom of their hearts they love a government without check or counterpoise; such a government works more easily than any other. No man willingly gives up that which makes his task more easy. Could you expect a preacher to dispense with the terrors of hell, in his efforts to convert hardened sinners? Hell is the capital punishment of the theologians*; at first they make use of it with regret, as of a necessary evil, but they soon acquire a taste for dealing out damnation upon the greater part of mankind. It is the same thing with severe measures in politics; they are feared before they are tried, but after

* I would beg the reader to remember that it is not I who thus speak.

❖ 283 ❖

their success is witnessed, they are admired; and such, you may depend upon it, is the feeling too general in this country. I often think that they take pleasure in creating circumstances, under which it is necessary to inflict punishment, for fear they should get out of practice. Are you ignorant of what is now passing on the Wolga?"

"I heard of serious troubles there, but they say that they were promptly repressed."

"No doubt: but at what price? And what should you say, were I to tell you that these frightful disorders were the result of a word of the Emperor's?"

"Never will you induce me to believe that he can have approved such horrors."

"Neither do I say he has. Nevertheless, a word pronounced by him—innocently, I believe, has caused the evil. The fact is as follows: notwithstanding the injustice of the overseers of the crown, the lot of the peasants of the Emperor is still preferable to that of other serfs; and whenever the sovereign becomes proprietor of some new domain, its inhabitants are the envy of all their neighbours. The crown lately purchased a considerable estate in the district that has since revolted. Immediately the peasants sent deputies from every part of the surrounding country to the new superintendants of the imperial lands, to supplicate the emperor to purchase them also. The serfs chosen as ambassadors were sent on to Petersburg. The Emperor received them and treated them with kindness; but, to their great regret, he did not buy them. 'I cannot,' he said to them, 'purchase all Russia, but a time will come, I hope, when each peasant of this empire will be free; if it depended only upon me, the Russians should enjoy from this day forth the independence which I wish for them; and to procure them which, at a future period, I am labouring with all my powers.' "

"Well, this answer seems to me full of reason, candour, and humanity."

"No doubt: but the emperor should have known to whom he addressed such words; and not have murdered his noblemen out of tenderness towards his serfs. These words, interpreted by barbarous and envious men, have set a whole province on fire; and thus has it become necessary to punish a people for crimes which they were instigated to commit. 'Our Father desires our deliverance,' cried the returned deputies on the borders of the Wolga; 'he wishes for nothing but our happiness, he said so to us, himself: it is, then, only the nobles and their agents who are our enemies, and who oppose the good designs of *Our Father!* Let us avenge the Emperor!' After this, the peasants believed they were performing a pious work in rising upon their masters, and thus all the nobles of a canton, and all their agents were massacred together with their families. They spitted one and roasted him alive; they boiled another in a cauldron; they disembowelled and killed in various other ways the stewards and agents of the estates; they murdered all they met, burnt whole towns, and, in short, devastated a province, not in the name of liberty, for they do not know what liberty means, but in the name of deliverance and of the emperor."

"It was perhaps some of these savages whom we saw passing in the prisoner's conveyance. How could such beings be influenced by the gentle means employed by the governments of Western Europe?"

"It would be necessary gradually to change the ideas of the people; instead of which they find it more convenient to change their location. After every scene of this kind, villages and entire cantons are transported. No population is sure of preserving its territory, the result of which is, that men, attached as they become to the soil, are deprived, in their slavery, of the only compensation which could comport with their condition. By an infernal combination they are made moveable, without being made free. A word from the monarch roots them up as though they were trees, tears them from their native soil, and sends them to perish or to languish at the world's end. The peasant, exposed to these storms of supreme power, loves not his cabin, the only thing in this world that he could love; he detests his life, and ill-understands its duties, for it is necessary to impart some happiness to a man in order to make him feel his obligations; misery only instructs him in hypocrisy and revolt. If self interest, when well understood, is not the foundation of morals, it is at least their support."

"Yet it is difficult to change the spirit of a people: it is the work neither of a day, nor of a reign."

"Is it a work at which they sincerely labour?"

"I think so, but with prudence."

"What you call prudence, I call insincerity: you do not know the emperor."

"Reproach him with being inflexible, but not with being false: in a prince, inflexibility is often a virtue."

"Do you believe the character of the emperor to be sincere? Remember his conduct at the death of Pouskine."

"I do not know the circumstances of that event."

Thus talking, we arrived at the Champ de Mars, a vast square which appears a desert, though it occupies the middle of the city. A man may converse there with less danger of being overheard than in his chamber. My cicerone continued:—

"Pouskine was, as you are aware, the greatest poet of Russia."

"We are no judges of that."

"We are, at least, of his reputation. Whether well founded or not, his reputation was great. He was yet young, and of an irascible temper. You know he had Moorish blood on his mother's side. His wife, a very handsome woman, inspired him with more passion than confidence. His poetical temperament and his African blood, made him easily jealous; and it was thus that, exasperated by appearances and by false reports envenomed with a perfidy which calls to mind the conception of Shakespeare, this Russian Othello lost all reason, and sought to force the man by whom he believed himself injured, to fight with him. This person was a Frenchman, and, unfortunately, his brother-in-law; his name was M. de Antés. A duel in Russia is a serious affair, the more so, because, instead of according, as among us, with ideas and customs in opposition to laws, it militates against all preconceived notions: this nation is more oriental than chivalrous. Duelling is illegal here as elsewhere; but, besides this, it is less supported by public opinion than in other lands. M. de Antés did all he could to avoid the difficulty. Urged vehemently by the unhappy husband, he refused him satisfaction, though in a manner that was dignified: but notwithstanding this, he continued his assiduities. Pouskine became almost mad. The constant presence of the man whose death he wished, appeared to him a permanent insult, and in order to rid himself of him, he acted in a way that made a duel inevitable. The two brothers-in-law fought, and M. de Antés killed Pouskine. The man whom public opinion accused, triumphed; and the injured husband, the national poet, the innocent party, fell.

"This death excited public indignation. Pouskine, the Russian poet, *par excellence*, the author of the finest odes in the language, the glory of the country, the restorer of Slavonian poetry, in short, the pride of the age, the hope of the future, to fall by the hand of a Frenchman! this was an event that roused public passion to the highest pitch. Petersburg, Moscow, the whole empire was in excitement. The emperor, who knows the Russians better than any man in Russia, took care to join in the public affliction. He ordered a service to be performed, and I am not sure that he did not carry his pious affectation so far as to assist in person at the ceremony, in order to publish his regret by taking God to witness his admiration of the national genius, removed too soon for his glory.

"However this may be, the sympathy of the sovereign so flattered the Muscovite spirit as to awake a generous patriotism in the breast of a young man, endowed with much talent. This too credulous poet was so enraptured by the august protection accorded to the first of all arts, that he grew bold enough to believe himself inspired! In the ingenuous yearnings of his gratitude, he ventured even to write an ode—a patriotic ode, to thank the emperor for becoming the protector of literature. He concluded his remarkable production by singing the praises of the departed bard. This was all he did; I have read the verses and I can attest the innocent intentions of the author: unless at least it might be a crime to conceal in the depths of his bosom a hope, perhaps, of becoming one day a second Pouskine—a hope very pardonable, it seems to me, in a youthful imagination.

"Audacious youth! to aim at renown, to betray a passion for glory under a despotism! It was the same as if Prometheus had said to Jupiter—'Take care of yourself, I am going to rob you of your thunderbolts.'

"The recompense which this young aspirant received for having thus publicly shown his confidence in his master's love for the fine arts and the belles lettres, was a SECRET order to go and pursue his poetical studies on the Caucasus, a chapel of ease to the ancient Siberia.

"After having remained there two years, he has returned, his health destroyed, his mind cast down, and his imagination radically cured of its chimeras. After this trait will you yet put trust in the official words or the public acts of the Emperor?"

"The Emperor is a man; he shares human weaknesses. Something must have shocked him in the allusions of the young poet. Perhaps they were European rather than national. The emperor proceeds on a principle the very opposite to that of Catherine II., he braves Europe instead of flattering it. This is wrong, I admit; for studied opposition is in itself a species of dependence, since under it a man is only influenced by contradiction; but it is pardonable, especially if you reflect on the evil caused to Russia by princes who were possessed all their life with the mania of imitation."

"You are incorrigible!" exclaimed the advocate of the ancient boyards. "You believe, then, in the possibility of Russian civilisation? It promised well before the time of Peter the Great, but that prince destroyed the fruit in its germ. Go to Moscow, it is the centre of the ancient empire; yet you will see that all minds are turned towards speculations of industry, and that the national character is as much effaced there as at St. Petersburg. The Emperor Nicholas commits to-day, though with different views, a fault analogous to that of Peter the Great. He does not take into account the history of an entire age, the age of the Emperor Peter: history has its fatalities,—the fatalities of *faits accomplis*. Woe to the prince who does not submit to these!"

The day was advanced; we separated, and I continued my walk, musing upon the energetic feeling of opposition which must spring up in minds accustomed to reflect under the silence of despotism. Characters which such a government does not debase, it steels and fortifies.

On my return, I sat down to read again some translations of the poems of Pouskine. They confirmed me in the opinion that a previous reading had imparted. This author has borrowed much of his colouring from the new poetical school of Western Europe. Not that he has adopted the anti-religious opinions of Lord Byron, the social notions of our poets, or the philosophy of those of Germany; but he has adopted their manner of describing. I therefore do not recognise him as a real Muscovite poet. The Pole, Mickiewitch, strikes me as being much more Slavonic, although he, like Pouskine, has bowed to the influence of occidental literature.

The real Russian poet, did one exist, could, in the present day address only the people; he would neither be understood nor read in the *salons*. Where there is no language, there is no poetry; neither indeed are there any thinkers. The Emperor Nicholas has begun to require that Russian be spoken at court; they laugh at present at a novelty which is viewed as merely a caprice of their master's: the next generation will thank him for this victory of good sense over fashion.

How could the national genius develop itself in a society where people speak four languages without knowing one? Originality of thought has a nearer connection than is imagined with purity of idiom. This fact has been forgotten in Russia for a century, and in France for some years. Our children will feel the effects of the rage for English nurses which has, among us, taken possession of all *"fashionable"* mothers.* . . .

❖

DISTURBANCES IN RUSSIA ❖ PARALLEL BETWEEN FRENCH AND RUSSIAN CRIMES AND CRUELTIES ❖ CHARACTERISTICS OF REVOLT IN RUSSIA ❖ ORDER IN DISORDER ❖ DANGER OF INCULCATING LIBERAL IDEAS AMONG IGNORANT POPULATIONS ❖ REASONS FOR RUSSIAN SUPERIORITY IN DIPLOMACY

❖

CHAPTER XVIII

❖

This morning, early, I received a visit from the individual whose conversation is recounted in the last chapter. He brought me a French manuscript, written by the young prince, the son of his patron. It is the relation of an occurrence, only too true, that forms one of the numerous episodes of the yet recent event with which all feeling and thoughtful minds are still silently and secretly occupied. Is it possible to enjoy, without any feelings of uneasiness, the luxury of a magnificent abode, when one thinks that, at a few hundred leagues from the palace, murder is rampant, and society would fall to pieces, were it not for the terrific means employed to uphold it?

The young Prince ——, who has written this story, would be ruined if it could be discovered that he was the author. It is on this account that he has confided his manuscript to me, and entrusted me with its publication. He permits me to insert the account of the death of Thelenef in the text of my travels, where I shall faithfully give it, without, however, compromising the safety of any one. I am assured of the accuracy of the principal facts; the reader can put as much or as little faith in them as he pleases; for my own part, I always believe what people whom I do not know say to me. The suspicion of falsehold never enters my mind until after the proof.

The young Russian, who is the author of the fragment, wishing to justify, by the memory of the horrors of our revolution, the ferocity of his own countrymen, has cited an act of French cruelty, the massacre of M. de Belzunce at Caen. He might have increased his list: Mademoiselle de Sombreuil forced to drink a glass of blood to redeem the life of her father; the heroic death of the archbishop of Arles, and of his glorious companions in martyrdom, within the cloisters of the Carmelite convent at Paris; the massacres of Lyons; the executions, by drowning, at Nantes, surnamed by Carrier, the republican marriages; and many other atrocities which historians have not even recorded, might serve to prove that human ferocity only sleeps among nations even the most civilised. Nevertheless, there is a difference between the cold, methodical, and abiding cruelty of the Mugics, and the passing frenzy of the French. These latter, during the war which they carried on against God and humanity, were not in their natural state; the mood of blood had changed their character; and the extravagances of passion ruled over all their acts; for never were they less free than at the epoch when everything that was done among them was done in the name of liberty. We are, on the contrary, going to see the Russians murder each other without belying their characters; it is still a duty which they are performing.

Among this obedient people, the influence of social institutions is so great in every class—ideas and habits so rule over characters, that the fiercest excesses of vengeance still appear ruled by a certain degree of discipline. Murder is designed and executed in an orderly manner; no rage, no emotion, no words: a calm is preserved more terrible than the delirium of hate. They struggle with, overthrow, trample, and destroy each other, with the steady regularity of machines turning upon their pivots. This physical impassibility in the midst of scenes the most violent, this monstrous audacity in the conception and calmness in the execution, this silent passion and speechless fanaticism seem, if one might so express it, the innocence of crime. A certain order, contrary to nature, presides in this strange country over the most monstrous excesses; tyranny and revolt march in step, and perform their movements in unison.

As everything is in sympathetic accord, the immense extent of the territory does not prevent things being executed from one

end of Russia to the other, with a punctuality, and a simultane-
ous correspondence, which is magical. If ever they should succeed in creating a REAL revolution among the Russian people,
massacre would be performed with the regularity that marks the
evolutions of a regiment. Villages would change into barracks,
and organised murder would stalk forth armed from the cottages,
form in line, and advance in order; in short, the Russians would
prepare for pillage from Smolensk to Irkutsk, as they march to
the parade in Petersburg. From so much uniformity, there results
between the natural dispositions and the social habits of the people, a harmony, the effects of which might become prodigious in
good as in evil.

Everything is obscure in the future prospects of the world;
but, assuredly, it will see strange scenes enacted before the nations by this predestined people.*

It is almost always under the influence of a blind respect for
power, that the Russians disturb public order. Thus, if we are to
believe what is repeated in secret, had it not been for the emper-
or's speech to the deputies of the peasants, the latter would not
have taken up arms.

I trust that this fact, and those that I have elsewhere cited,
will show the danger of inculcating liberal opinions among a population so ill-prepared to receive them. As regards political liberty, the more we love it, the greater care should we take to
avoid pronouncing its name before those who would only compromise a holy cause by their manner of defending it. It is this
which induces me to doubt of the truth of the imprudent reply
attributed to the emperor. That prince knows, better than any
one, the character of his people, and I cannot believe that he
could have provoked the revolt of the peasants, even unwittingly.

The horrors of the insurrection are described by the author of
Thelenef, with an accuracy the more scrupulous, as the principal
incident occurred in the family of the narrator.

---

* There will be some readers who can scarcely read this and similar prophecies in
the present work, without being reminded of the great northern nation of more
inspired prophecy, the chief prince of Meshech (whence the word Muscovite is
generally derived), who, with all his bands, and with numerous Asiatic allies, is to
devastate the Levant and Syria at some period that has yet to come.—*Trans.*

If he have allowed himself to ennoble the character and the passion of his hero and heroine, it is because he has a poetical imagination; but while embellishing the sentiments, he has preserved the picture of national manners: in short, neither in the facts, the sentiments, nor the descriptions, does this little romance appear to me misplaced in the midst of a work, all the merit of which consists in the verisimilitude of its delineations.

I may add that the bloody scenes are yet being daily renewed in various parts of the same country where public order has been disturbed, and reestablished in so terrific a manner. The Russians have no right to reproach France for her political disorders, and to draw from them consequences favourable to despotism. Let but the liberty of the press be accorded to Russia for twenty-four hours, and we should learn things that would make us recoil with horror. Silence is indispensable to oppression. Under an absolute government every indiscretion of speech is equivalent to a crime of high treason.

If there are found among the Russians, better diplomatists than among nations the most advanced in civilisation, it is because our journals inform them of every thing which is done or projected among ourselves, and because, instead of prudently disguising our weaknesses, we display them, with passion, every morning; whilst, on the contrary, the Byzantine policy of the Russians, working in the dark, carefully conceals from us everything that is thought, done, or feared among them. We march exposed on all sides, they advance under cover. The ignorance in which they leave us blinds our view; our sincerity enlightens theirs; we suffer from all the evils of idle talking, they have all the advantages of secrecy; and herein lies all their skill and ability. . . .

❖

PETERSBURG IN THE ABSENCE OF THE EMPEROR ❖ CHARACTER OF THE
COURTIERS ❖ THE TCHINN ❖ ITS NATURE AND ORIGIN ❖ DESTRUCTION OF
THE ARISTOCRACY ❖ CHARACTER OF PETER THE GREAT ❖ THE TCHINN
DIVIDED INTO FOURTEEN CLASSES ❖ AN IMMENSE POWER IN THE HANDS OF
THE EMPEROR ❖ OPPOSITE OPINIONS ON THE FUTURE INFLUENCE OF
RUSSIA ❖ RUSSIAN HOSPITALITY ❖ POLITE FORMALITIES ❖ RESEMBLANCE
TO THE CHINESE ❖ DIFFERENCE BETWEEN THE RUSSIANS AND THE FRENCH
❖ RUSSIAN HONESTY ❖ OPINION OF NAPOLEON ❖ THE ONLY SINCERE
MAN IN THE EMPIRE ❖ SPOILED SAVAGES ❖ ERRORS OF PETER THE GREAT
❖ THE HERMITAGE ❖ PICTURE GALLERY
❖ PRIVATE SOCIAL CODE OF THE
EMPRESS CATHERINE
❖

CHAPTER XIX

❖

I had promised my friends not to return to France without seeing Moscow, the fabulous city—fabulous in spite of history; for the grandeur of the events connected with it, though they recall the most positive and clearly-defined occurrences of our age, renders its name poetical beyond all other names.

This scene of an epic poem has a sublimity which contrasts, in a whimsical manner, with the spirit of an age of mathematicians and stock-jobbers. I am therefore especially impatient to reach Moscow, for which city I set out in two days. My impatience will not, however, prevent my expatiating on all that may strike me before arriving there, for I mean to complete, as far as I am able, the picture of this vast and singular empire.

It is impossible to describe the dulness of St. Petersburg during the absence of the emperor. At no time does the city exhibit what may be called gaiety; but without the court, it is a desert. The reader is aware that it is constantly menaced with destruction by the sea. This morning, while traversing its solitary quays and empty streets, I said to myself, "Surely the city must be about to be inundated; the inhabitants have fled, and the water will soon recover possession of the marsh." Nothing of the kind: Petersburg is lifeless only because the Emperor is at Peterhoff. The water of the Neva, driven back by the sea, rises so high, and the banks are so low, that this large inlet, with its innumerable arms, resembles a stagnant inundation, an overflowing marsh. They call the Neva a river, but it is for want of a more precise signification. At Petersburg the Neva has already become the sea; higher up, it is a channel of a few leagues in length, which serves to convey the superfluous waters of Lake Ladoga into the Gulf of Finland.

At the period when the quays of Petersburg were built, a taste for structures of small elevation prevailed among the Russians. The adoption of this taste was very injudicious in a country where the snow, during eight months in the year, diminishes the height of the walls by six feet; and where the surface of the soil presents no variety that might, in any degree, relieve the monotony of the regular circle which forms the unchangeable line of horizon, serving as a frame for scenes level as the ocean. In my youth, I inhaled enthusiasm at the feet of the mountainous coasts of Calabria, before landscapes all of whose lines, excepting those of the sea, were vertical. Here, on the contrary, I see only one plane surface terminated by a perfectly horizontal line drawn betwixt the sky and the water. The mansions, palaces, and colleges which line the Neva, seem scarcely to rise above the soil, or rather the sea: some have only one story, the loftiest not more than three, and all appear dilapidated. The masts of the vessel overshoot the roofs of the houses. These roofs are of painted iron; they are light and elegant, but very flat, like those of Italy, whereas pointed roofs are alone proper in countries where snow abounds. In Russia, we are shocked at every step by the results of imitation without reflection.

Between the square blocks of an architecture which pretends to be Italian, run wide, straight, and empty vistas, which they call streets, and which, notwithstanding their projecting colonnades, are anything but classical. The scarcity of the women contributes to the dulness of the city. Those who are pretty, seldom appear on foot. Wealthy persons who wish to walk, are invariably followed by a servant. The practice is, here, one of prudence and necessity.

The Emperor alone has the power to people this wearisome abode, abandoned so soon as its master has disappeared. He is the magician who puts thought and motion into the human machines,—a magician in whose presence Russia wakes, and in whose absence she sleeps. After the Court has left, the superb metropolis has the appearance of a theatre when the representation is over. Since my return from Peterhoff I can scarcely recognise the city I left four days ago; but were the Emperor to return this evening, everything to-morrow would assume its former interest. We should have to become Russians to understand the power of the sovereign's eye; it is a very different thing from the lover's eye spoken of by La Fontaine. Do you suppose that a young girl bestows a thought on her love affairs in the presence of the Emperor? Do not deceive yourself; she is occupied with the idea of procuring some promotion for her brother. An old woman, so soon as she breathes the air of the court, feels no longer her infirmities. She may have no family to provide for—no matter, she plays the courtier for the pure love of the game. She is servile without an object, just as others like play for its own sake. Thus, by an endeavour to shake off the burden of years, this wrinkled puppet loses all the dignity of age. We have no pity for busy intriguing decrepitude, because it is ridiculous. At the end of life it is surely time to set about practising the lesson which time is ever teaching, the grand art, namely, of giving up. Happy those who early learn to apply this lesson. To renounce is the great proof of a powerful mind: to abdicate a position before it is lost, —this is the policy of old age.

It is, however, a policy little practised at court, and at that of St. Petersburg less than at any other. Busy, restless old women are the plagues of the court of Russia. The sun of favour dazzles and blinds the ambitious, more especially those of the female sex; it prevents their discerning their true interest, which would be to save their pride by concealing the miseries of their hearts. On the contrary, the Russian courtiers glory in the abject meanness of their souls. The flatterer here shuffles his cards upon the table, and I am only astonished that he can win anything in a game so palpable to all the world. In the presence of the emperor the asthmatic breathes, the paralysed becomes active, the gouty loses his pain, the lovers no longer burn, the young men no longer seek to amuse themselves, the men of mind no longer think. In lieu of all these human states, mental and physical, one combined sentiment of avarice and vanity animates life even to its latest sigh. These two passions are the breath of all courts; but here they impart to their victims a military emulation, a disciplined rivalry, whose agitating influences extend throughout all the stages of society. To rise a step by more carefully dancing attendance—such is the absorbing thought of this etiquette-instructed crowd.

But then, what prostration of strength, when the luminary in whose beam these flattering motes may be seen to move, is no longer above the horizon! It is like the evening dew quenching the dust, or the nuns in Robert le Diable, again repairing to their sepulchres, to wait the signal for another round.

With this continual stretch of all minds towards advancement, conversation is impossible. The eyes of the Russian courtiers are the sunflowers of the palace. They speak without interesting themselves in anything that is said, and their looks remain all the while fascinated by the sun of favour.

The absence of the emperor does not render conversation more free: he is still present to the mind. The thoughts, instead of the eyes, then become the sunflowers. In one word, the emperor is the god, the life, the passion of this unhappy people. Imagine human existence reduced to the hope that an obeisance will procure the acknowledgments of a look! God has implanted too many passions in the human heart for the uses which are here made of it.

If I put myself in the place of the only man who has here the right to live free, I tremble for him. To have to play the part of Providence over sixty millions of souls is a dreadful office. The Divinity has only the choice of two things: either to destroy his own power by showing himself a man, or to lead his votaries to the conquest of the world, in maintaining his character as a god. It is thus that in Russia the whole of life becomes nothing more than a school of ambition.

But by what road have the Russians reached this point of self-abnegation? What human means could produce such a political result? The cause of all is the *tchinn:* the tchinn is the galvanism, the apparent life of souls and bodies here—the passion which survives all other passions. I have shown its effects; it is therefore necessary that I should explain its nature.

The tchinn is a nation formed into a regiment; it is the military system applied to all classes of society, even to those which never go to war. In short, it is the division of the civil population into ranks, which correspond to ranks in the army. Since this institution has been established, a man who has never seen exercise may obtain the title of colonel.

Peter the Great—it is always to him that we must go back in order to understand the actual state of Russia—Peter the Great, troubled by certain national prejudices which had a resemblance to aristocracy, and which incommoded him in the execution of his plans, took it into his head one day to discover that the minds of his people were too independent; and, in order to remedy the evil, this great workman could devise nothing better in his profoundly deep, yet narrow penetration, than to divide the herd, that is to say, the people, into classes, entirely irrelative of name, birth, and family; so that the son of the highest noble in the empire may belong to an inferior class, whilst the son of one of the peasants may rise to the highest classes, if such be the good will of the emperor. Under this division of the people, every man takes his position according to the favour of the prince. Thus it is that Russia has become a regiment of sixty millions strong; and this is the tchinn—the mightiest achievement of Peter the Great.

By its means, that prince freed himself in one day from the fetters of ages. The tyrant, when he undertook to regenerate his people, held sacred neither nature, history, character, nor life. Such sacrifices render great results easy. Peter knew better than any one that, so long as an order of nobility exists in a community, the despotism of one man can be nothing more than a fiction. He therefore said, "To realise my government I must annihilate the remains of the feudal system; and the best way of doing this is to make caricatures of gentlemen—to destroy the nobility by rendering it a creation of my own." It has consequently been, if not destroyed, at least nullified by an institution that occupies its place, though it does not replace it. There are castes in this social system, in which to enter is to acquire hereditary nobility. Peter the Great, whom I should prefer to call Peter the Strong, forestalling our modern revolutions by more than half a century, thus crushed the spirit of feudalism. Less powerful under him than it was among us, it fell beneath the half civil half military institution which constitutes modern Russia. Peter was endowed with a clear and yet a limited understanding. In rearing his system on so great a ruin, he knew not how to profit by the exorbitant powers he had engrossed, except in mimicking more at his case the civilisation of Europe.

With the means of action usurped by this prince, a creative genius would have worked much greater miracles. The Russian nation, ascending after all the others upon the great stage of the world, possessed the gift of imitation in lieu of genius, and had a carpenter's apprentice for its prompter! Under a chief less fond of minutiae, less attached to details, that nation would have distinguished itself, more tardily, it is true, but more gloriously. Its power, corresponding with its own internal requirements, would have been useful to the world: it is now only astonishing.

The successors of this lawgiver in fustian have, during one hundred years, united with the ambition of subjugating their neighbours, the weakness of copying them. In the present day, the Emperor Nicholas believes the time is arrived when Russia has no longer need of looking for models among foreigners in order to conquer and to rule the world. He is the first really Russian sovereign since Ivan IV. Peter I. was a Russian in character, though not in politics; Nicholas is a German by nature, but a Russian by calculation and by necessity.

The tchinn consists of fourteen classes, each of which possesses its own peculiar privileges. The fourteenth is the lowest.

Placed immediately above the serfs, its sole advantage consists in its members having the title of freemen. Their freedom means that no one can strike them without rendering himself liable to prosecution. In return, every member of the class has to inscribe on his door, his registered number, in order that no superior may be led to act under an ignorance that would render him liable to a penalty.

The fourteenth class is composed of persons in the lowest employ under the government, clerks of the post-office, factors, and other subordinates charged with carrying or executing the orders of the heads of departments: it answers to the rank of sub-officer in the imperial army. The men who compose it are servants of the Emperor, and serfs of no one: they possess a sense of their social dignity. But as to human dignity, it is not known in Russia.

All the other classes of the tchinn answer to as many military grades; the order that reigns throughout the entire state is analogous to the order of the army. The first class stands at the summit of the pyramid, and is now composed of one single man—Marshall Paskiewitch, viceroy of Warsaw.

The will of the Emperor is the sole means by which an individual is promoted in the tchinn; so that a man rising step by step, to the highest rank in this artificial nation, may attain the first military dignity without having served in any army. The favour of promotion is never demanded, but always intrigued for.

There is here an immense quantity of fermenting material placed at the disposal of the head of the state. Medical men complain of their inability to communicate fever to certain patients in order to cure them of chronic maladies. The Czar Peter inoculated with the fever of ambition the whole body of his people, in order to render them more pliant, and to govern them according to his humour.

The English aristocracy is equally independent of birth; it depends upon two things which may be acquired, office and estate. If, then, this aristocracy, moderated as it is, still imparts an enormous influence to the crown, how great must be the power of that crown whence all these things—the rank, and also the office and estate—are both *de jure* and *de facto* derived!

There results from such a social organisation a fever of envy so violent, a stretch of mind towards ambition so constant, that the Russian people will needs become incapable of any thing except the conquest of the world. I always return to this expression, because it is the only one that can explain the excessive sacrifices imposed here upon the individual by society. If the extreme of ambition can dry up the heart of a man, it may also stop the fountain of intellect, and so lead astray the judgment of a nation as to induce it to sacrifice its liberty for victory. Without this idea, avowed or disguised, and the influence of which many, perhaps, obey unconsciously, the history of Russia would seem to me an inexplicable enigma.

Here is suggested the grand question: is the idea of conquest that forms the secret aspiration of Russia a lure, suited only to seduce for a period, more or less long, a rude and ignorant population, or is it one day to be realised?

This question besets me unceasingly, and, in spite of all my efforts, I cannot resolve it. All that I can say is, that since I have been in Russia, I take a gloomy view of the future reserved for Europe. At the same time, my conscience obliges me to admit that my opinion is combated by wise and very experienced men. These men say that I exaggerate in my own mind the power of Russia; that every community has its prescribed destiny, and that the destiny of this community is to extend its conquests eastward, and then to become divided. Those minds that refuse to believe in the brilliant future of the Slavonians, agree with me as regards the amiable and happy disposition of that people; they admit that they are endowed with an instinctive sentiment of the picturesque; they allow them a natural talent for music; and they conclude that these dispositions will enable them to cultivate the fine arts to a certain extent, but that they do not suffice to constitute the capacity for conquering and commanding which I attribute to them. They add, that "the Russians lack scientific genius; that they have never shown any inventive power; that they have received from nature an indolent and superficial mind; that if they apply themselves, it is through fear rather than inclination: fear makes them apt to undertake and to draw the rough drafts of things, but also it prevents their proceeding far in any effort: genius is, in its nature, hardy as heroism; it lives on liberty; whilst fear and slavery have a reign and a sphere limited as mediocrity, of which they are the arms. The Russians, though good soldiers, are bad seamen; in general, they are more resigned than reflective, more religious than philosophical; they have more instinct of obedience than will of their own; their thoughts lack a spring as their souls lack liberty. The task which is to them most difficult, and least natural, is seriously to occupy their minds and to fix their imaginations upon useful exercises. Ever children, they might nevertheless for a moment be conquerors in the realm of the sword; but they would never be so in that of thought: and a people who cannot teach any thing to those they conquer, cannot long be the most powerful.

"Even physically, the French and English are more robust

than the Russians; the latter are more agile than muscular, more savage than energetic, more cunning than enterprising; they possess passive courage, but they want daring and perserverance. The army, so remarkable for its discipline and its appearance on days of parade, is composed, with the exception of a few *élites corps*, of men well clad when they show themselves in public, but slovenly and dirty so long as they remain in their barracks. The cadaverous complexions of the soldiers betray hunger and disease: the two campaigns in Turkey have sufficiently demonstrated the weakness of the giant. Finally, a community that has not tasted liberty at its birth, and in which all the great political crises have been brought about by foreign influence, cannot, thus enervated in its germ, have a long existence in prospect."

Such, it seems to me, are the strongest reasons opposed to my fears by the political optimists. From them it is concluded that Russia, powerful at home, and formidable when she struggles with the Asiatic people, would break herself against Europe so soon as she should throw off the mask, and make war in maintenance of her arrogant diplomacy.

I have in no degree weakened the arguments of those who thus think. They accuse me of exaggerating the danger. At any rate my opinions are shared by other minds quite as sober as those of my adversaries, and who do not cease to reproach these optimists with their blindness, in exhorting them to see the evil before it become irremediable.

I stand close by the Colossus, and I find it difficult to persuade myself that the only object of this creation of Providence is to diminish the barbarism of Asia. It appears to me that it is chiefly destined to chastise the corrupt civilisation of Europe by the agency of a new invasion. The eternal tyranny of the East menaces us incessantly; and we shall have to stoop to it, if our extravagances and iniquities render us worthy of the punishment.

The reader must not expect from me a complete account of Russia. I neglect to speak of many celebrated things because they make little impression upon me. I wish only to describe that which strikes or interests me. Nomenclatures and catalogues disgust me with travels, and there are plenty of them without my adding to the list.

Nothing can be seen here without ceremony and preparation. Russian hospitality is so edged round with formalities as to render life unpleasant to the most favoured strangers. It is a civil pretext for restraining the movements of the traveller, and for limiting the freedom of his observations. Owing to the fastidious politeness exercised in doing the honours of the land, the observer can inspect nothing without a guide: never being alone, he has the greater difficulty in forming his judgment upon his own spontaneous impressions; and this is what is desired. To enter Russia you must, with your passport, deposit also your right of opinion on the frontier. Would you see the curiosities of a palace, they give you a chamberlain, with whom you are obliged to view every thing, and, indiscriminately, to admire all that he admires. Would you survey a camp—an officer, sometimes a general officer, accompanies you: if it be an hospital, the head surgeon escorts you; a fortress, the governor, in person, shows it, or rather politely conceals it from you; a school, or any other public institution, the director or the inspector must be previously apprised of your visit, and you find him, under arms, prepared to brave your examination; if an edifice, the architect himself leads you over the whole building, and explains to you all that you do not care to know, in order to avoid informing you on points which you would take interest in knowing.

All this oriental ceremony leads people to renounce seeing many things were it only to avoid the trouble of soliciting admissions: this is the first advantage gained! But if curiosity is hardy enough to persist in importuning official personages, it is at least so carefully watched in its perquisitions, that they end in nothing. You must communicate officially with the heads of the so called public establishments, and you obtain no other permission than that of expressing before the legitimate authorities the admiration which politeness, prudence, and a gratitude of which the Russians are very jealous, demand. They refuse you nothing, but they accompany you every where: politeness becomes a pretext for maintaining a watch over you.

In this manner they tyrannise over us in pretending to do us honour. Such is the fate of privileged travellers. As to those who are not privileged, they see nothing at all. The country is so organised that without the immediate intervention of official persons no stranger can move about agreeably, or even safely. In all this, will be recognised the manners and the policy of the East, disguised under European urbanity. Such alliance of the East and the West, the results of which are discoverable at every step, is the grand characteristic of the Russian empire.

A semi-civilisation is always marked by formalities; refined civilisation dispenses with them, just as perfect good breeding banishes affectation.

The Russians are still persuaded of the efficaciousness of falsehood; and such illusion on the part of a people so well acquainted with it, amazes me. It is not that they lack quick perception, but in a land where the governors do not yet understand the advantages of liberty, even for themselves, the governed naturally shrink from the immediate inconveniences of truth. One is momentarily obliged to repeat that the people here, great and small, resemble the Greeks of the Lower Empire.

I am perhaps not sufficiently grateful for the attentions which these people affect to lavish upon strangers who are at all known; but I cannot help seeing below the surface, and I feel, in spite of myself, that all their eagerness demonstrates less benevolence than it betrays inquietude.

They wish, in accordance with the judicious precept of Monomaque, that the foreigner should leave their country contented.* It is not that the real country cares what is said or thought of it; it is simply that certain influential families are possessed with the puerile desire of reviving the European reputation of Russia.

If I look farther, I perceive under the veil with which they seek to cloke every object, a love of mystery for its own sake. Here reserve is the order of the day, just as imprudence is in Paris. In Russia, secrecy presides over every thing; a silence that is superfluous insures the silence that is necessary; in short, the people are Chinese disguised; they do not like to avow their aversion to foreign observation, but if they dared to brave the re-

* See the motto in the title-page.

❖ 307 ❖

proach of barbarism as the true Chinese do, access to Petersburg would be as difficult for us as is the access to Pekin.

My reasons for wearying of Russian hospitality will be now seen. Of all species of constraint, the most insupportable to me is that of which I have not the right to complain. The gratitude I feel for the attentions of which I am here the object, is like that of a soldier's—made to serve by compulsion. As a traveller who specially piques himself on his independence, I feel that I am passing under the yoke; they trouble themselves unceasingly to discipline my ideas, and every evening on returning to my quarters, I have to examine my thoughts to ascertain what rank they bear, and in what uniform they are clothed.

Having carefully avoided intimacy with many great lords, I have hitherto seen nothing thoroughly except the court. My wish has been to preserve my position as an independent and impartial judge; and I feared to incur accusations of ingratitude or want of good faith; above all, I feared to render subjects of the country responsible for my particular opinions. But at the court I have passed in review all the characteristics of society.

An affectation of French manners, without any of the tone of French conversation, first struck me. It conceals a caustic, sarcastic, Russian spirit of ridicule. If I remained here any time, I would tear away the mask from these puppets, for I am weary of seeing them copy French grimaces. At my age, a man has nothing more to learn from affectation; truth alone can always interest, because it imparts knowledge; truth alone is always new.

I observed from the very first, that the Russians of the lower classes, who are suspicious by nature, detest foreigners through ignorance and national prejudice; I have observed since, that the Russians of the higher classes, who are equally suspicious, fear them because they believe them hostile: "the French and the English are persuaded of their superiority over all other people;" this motive suffices to make a Russian hate foreigners, on the same principle that, in France, the Provincial distrusts the Parisian. A barbarian jealousy, an envy, puerile, but impossible to disarm, influences the greater number of the Russians in their intercourse with the men of other lands.

The Muscovite character is in many respects the very opposite of the German. On this account it is that the Russians say they resemble the French; but the analogy is only apparent: in the inner character there is a great difference. You may, if you choose, admire in Russia pomp and oriental grandeur; you may study there Greek astuteness; but you must not seek for the Gallic naïveté, the sociability and the amiability of the French when they are natural; though I admit that you will find still less of the good faith, the sound intelligence, and the cordial feeling of the German. In Russia you may meet with good temper, because it is to be met with wherever there are men; but good nature is never seen.

Every Russian is born an imitator; he is, by consequence, a great observer.

This talent, which is proper to a people in its infancy, often degenerates into a mean system of espionage. It produces questions often importunate and impolite, and which appear intolerable, coming from people always impenetrable themselves, and whose answers are seldom more than evasions. One would say that friendship itself had here some private understanding with the police. How is it possible to be at ease with people so guarded and circumspect respecting all which concerns themselves, and so inquisitive about others? If they see you assume, in your intercourse with them, manners more natural than those which they show towards you, they fancy you their dupe. Beware then of letting them see you off your guard, beware of giving them your confidence: to men who are without feeling themselves, it is an amusement to observe the emotions of others, an amusement to which I, for one, do not like to administer. To observe our manner of life is the greatest pleasure of the Russians; if we allowed them, they would amuse themselves by striving to read our hearts and analyse our sentiments, just as people study dramatic representations at the theatre.

The extreme mistrust of all classes here with whom you have any business, warns you to be circumspect; the fear that you inspire discloses the danger that you run.

The other day at Peterhoff, a victualler would not permit my servant to provide me with a miserable supper in my actor's box, without being previously paid for it, although the shop of this prudent man is but two steps from the theatre. What you put to your lips with one hand, must be paid for with the other; if you were to give a commission to a merchant without presenting him with money in advance, he would believe you were in jest, and would not undertake your business.

No one can leave Russia until he has forewarned all his creditors of his intentions, that is to say, until he has announced his departure three times in the gazettes at an interval of eight days between each publication.

This is strictly enforced, unless at least you pay the police to shorten the prescribed time, and even then you must make the insertion once or twice. No one can obtain post horses without a document from the authorities certifying that he owes nothing.

So much precaution shows the bad faith that exists in the country; for as, hitherto, the Russians have had little personal intercourse with foreigners, they must have taken lessons in wariness from themselves alone.

Their experience is only such as their position with regard to each other can teach them. These men will not allow us to forget the saying of their favourite sovereign, Peter the Great, "It takes three Jews to cheat a Russian."

At each step you take in the land, you recognise the politics of Constantinople as described by the historians of the crusades, and as discovered by the Emperor Napoleon in the Emperor Alexander, of whom he often said, "He is a Greek of the Lower Empire." Transactions with people whose founders and instructors have always been the sworn foes of chivalry, should be avoided as much as possible. Such people are slaves to their interest, and lords of their word. Hitherto, I have found in the whole empire of Russia but one person who appears to me to be sincere, and that one, I take pleasure in repeating, is the Emperor.

I own it costs less to an autocrat to be candid than it does to his subjects. For the czar to speak without disguise, is the performance of an act of authority. An absolute monarch who flatters and prevaricates must abdicate.

But how many have there not been who, on this point, have forgotten their power and their dignity! Base minds never think themselves above falsehood: we may therefore admire the sincerity even of a powerful ruler. The Emperor Nicholas unites frankness with politeness, and in him these two qualities, which are never seen combined in the vulgar, wonderfully act and re-act upon each other.

Among the nobles, those who do possess good manners, possess them in perfection. The proof of this may be seen daily at Paris and elsewhere; but a drawing-room Russian who has not attained true politeness, that is to say, the facile expression of a real amenity of character, has a coarseness of mind, which is rendered doubly shocking by the false elegance of his language and manners. Such ill-bred and yet well-informed, well-dressed, clever, and self-confident Russians, tread in the steps of European elegance, without knowing that refinement of habits has no value except as it announces the existence of something better in the heart of its possessor. These apprentices of fashion, who confound the appearance with the reality, are trained bears, the sight of which inclines me to regret the wild ones: they have not yet become polished men, although they are spoiled savages.

As there is such a place as Siberia, and as it is appropriated to the uses that are so well known, I could wish it were peopled with fastidious young officers and nervous fair ladies: "You want passports for Paris, you shall have them for Tobolsk!"

In this manner I would recommend the Emperor to check the rage for travelling, which is making fearful progress in Russia, among imaginative sub-lieutenants and fanciful women.

If, at the same time, he were to take back the seat of his empire to Moscow, he would repair the evil caused by Peter the Great, as far as one man may atone for the errors of generations.

Petersburg, a city built rather against Sweden than for Russia, ought to be nothing more than a sea-port, a Russian Dantzic. Instead of this, Peter the First made it a box, from whence his chained boyards might contemplate, with envy, the stage on which is enacted the civilisation of Europe; a civilisation which, in forcing them to copy, he forbade them to emulate!

Peter the Great, in all his works, acted without any regard to humanity, time, or nature. The more we examine Russia, the more strongly shall we be confirmed in the opinion that that prince has been too highly extolled, both at home and abroad.

Had he been as superior a character as is pretended, he would have perceived and shunned the wrong road into which he drove his people; he would have foreseen and detested the frivolity of mind, the superficial acquirements, to which he condemned them for ages.

Great men, in building up the future, do not destroy the past; on the contrary, they avail themselves of it, even in order to modify its consequences. Far from continuing to deify the enemy of their natural genius, the Russians ought to reproach him with being the cause of their possessing no character.*

That crowned missionary forced nature for a moment, because he had the power to do so; but to this his power was circumscribed. Had he been, in reality, what the superstition of his people, and the exaggeration of writers have made him in history, how differently would he have acted! He would have waited, and by that patience have merited his brevet of great man: he preferred obtaining it in advance, and caused himself to be canonised while yet living.

All his ideas, with the faults of character of which they were the consequence, have spread and multiplied under the reigns that followed. The Emperor Nicholas is the first who has endeavoured to stem the torrent, by recalling the Russians to themselves; an enterprise that the world will admire when it shall have recognised the firmness of spirit with which it has been conceived. After such reigns as those of Catherine and Paul, to make the Russia left by the Emperor Alexander a real Russian empire; to speak Russian, to think as a Russian, to avow himself a Russian—and this, while presiding over a court of nobles who are the heirs of the favourites of the *Semiramis of the North*—is an act of true courage. Whatever may be the result of the plan, it does honour to him who devised it.

It is true the courtiers of the Czar have no acknowledged nor assured rights; but they are still strong against their masters, by virtue of the perpetuated, traditional customs of the country. Directly to rebuke the pretensions of these men, to show himself, in the course of a reign already long, as courageous against hypo-

---

* The Russians are superficial in every thing, except the art of feigning.

critical adherents as he was against rebel soldiers, is assuredly the act of a very superior monarch. This double struggle of the sovereign with his infuriated slaves on the one hand, and his imperious courtiers on the other, is a fine spectacle. The Emperor Nicholas fulfils the promise that brightened the day of his elevation to the throne, and this is saying a great deal; for no prince assumed the reins of power under circumstances more critical; none ever faced an imminent danger with more energy and greatness of soul!

After the insurrection of 13th December, M. de la Ferronnays exclaimed, "I see Peter the Great civilised!" an observation that had point because it had truth. In contemplating this prince, in his court, developing his ideas of national regeneration with an indefatigable, yet quiet, unostentatious perseverance, one might exclaim with still greater reason, "I see Peter the Great come to repair the faults of Peter the Blind."

In striving to form a judgment of the present Emperor with all the impartiality of which I am capable, I find in him so many things worthy of praise, that I do not suffer myself to listen to any thing that might disturb my admiration.

Kings are like statues; people examine them with so minute an attention that their smallest faults, magnified by criticism, cause the most rare and genuine merits to be forgotten. But the more I admire the Emperor Nicholas, the more I may be thought unjust towards the Czar Peter. Nevertheless, I appreciate the efforts of determination that were needed to rear a city like Petersburg in a marsh, frozen during eight months of the year; but when my eyes unfortunately encounter one of those miserable caricatures which his passion, and that of his successors, for classic architecture has entailed upon Russia, my shocked senses and taste cause me to lose all that I had gained by reasoning. Antique palaces for barracks of Finns, pillars, cornices, pediments, and Roman peristyles under the pole, and all these things to be renovated every year with fine white stucco,—such parodies of Greece and Italy, *minus* the marble and the sun, are, it must be allowed, calculated to revive all my anger. Besides, I can renounce with the greater resignation the title of impartial traveller, because I am persuaded that I still have a right to it. . . .

I have seen also the paintings of the Hermitage, but I cannot now describe them, as I leave to-morrow for Moscow. The Hermitage! is not this a name strangely applied to the villa of a sovereign, placed in the midst of his capital, close to the palace where he resides! A bridge, thrown across a street, leads from one residence to the other.

All the world knows that there are here some choice pieces, especially of the Dutch school; but I do not like paintings in Russia, any more than music in London, where the manner in which they listen to the most talented performers, and the most sublime compositions, would disgust me with the art.

So near the pole, the light is unfavourable for seeing pictures; no one can enjoy the admirable shading of the colours with eyes, either weakened by snow, or dazzled by an oblique and continuous light. The hall of the Rembrandts is doubtless admirable; nevertheless, I prefer the works of that master, which I have seen at Paris and elsewhere.

The Claude Lorrains, the Poussins, and some works of the Italian masters, especially of Mantegna, Giambellini, and Salvator Rosa, deserve to be mentioned.

The fault of the collection is, the great number of inferior pictures that must be forgotten in order to enjoy the masterpieces. In forming the gallery of the Hermitage, they have gathered together a profusion of names of the great masters; but this does not prevent their genuine productions being rare. These ostentatious baptisms of very ordinary pictures weary the virtuoso, without cheating him. In a collection of objects of art, the contiguity of beauty sets off the beautiful, and that of inferiority detracts from it. A judge who is wearied, is incapable of judging: ennui renders him unjust and severe.

If the Rembrandts and the Claude Lorrains of the Hermitage produce some effect, it is because they are placed in halls where there are no other pictures near them.

This collection is fine; but it appears lost in a city where there are so few that can enjoy it.

An inexpressible sadness reigns throughout the palace, which has been converted into a museum since the death of her who animated it by her presence and her mind. No one ever better understood familiar life and free conversation than did that absolute princess. Not wishing to resign herself to the solitude to which her position condemned her, she discovered the art of conversing familiarly even while reigning arbitrarily.

The finest portrait of the Empress Catherine which exists, is in one of the halls of the Hermitage. I remarked also a portrait of the Empress Mary, wife of Paul I., by Madame Le Brun. There is, by the same artist, a genius writing upon a shield. This latter work is one of her best; its colours, defying alike time and climate, do honour to the French school.

At the entrance of one hall, I found behind a green curtain, the social rules of the Hermitage, for the use of those intimate friends admitted by the Czarina into the asylum of Imperial liberty.

I will translate literally this charter, granted to social intimacy by the caprice of the sovereign of the once enchanted place: it was copied for me in my presence:—

RULES TO BE OBSERVED ON ENTERING.

ARTICLE I.

On entering, the title and rank must be put off, as well as the hat and sword.

ARTICLE II.

Pretensions founded on the prerogatives of birth, pride, or other sentiments of a like nature, must also be left at the door.

ARTICLE III.

Be merry; nevertheless, *break nothing and spoil nothing.*

ARTICLE IV.

Sit, stand, walk, do whatever you please, without caring for any one.

ARTICLE V.

Speak with moderation, and not too often, in order to avoid being troublesome to others.

ARTICLE VI.

Argue without anger, and without warmth.

ARTICLE VII.

Banish sighs and yawns, that you may not communicate ennui, or be a burden to any one.

ARTICLE VIII.

Innocent games proposed by any member of the society, must be accepted by the others.

ARTICLE IX.

Eat slowly and with *appetite:* drink with moderation, that each may walk steadily as he goes out.

ARTICLE X.

Leave all quarrels at the door; that which *enters at one ear must go out at the other* before passing the threshold of the Hermitage. If any member violate the above rules, for each fault witnessed by two persons he must drink *a glass of fresh water (ladies not excepted):* furthermore he must read aloud a page of the Telemachiad (a poem by Frediakofsky). Whoever fails during one evening in three of these articles, must learn by heart six lines of the Telemachiad. He who fails in the tenth article must never more re-enter the Hermitage.

Before reading the above, I believed the Empress Catherine possessed a livelier and more pointed wit. Is this a simple pleasantry? If so it is a bad one, for the shortest jokes are the best. The care which has been taken to preserve the statutes, as though of great value, surprises me not less than the want of good taste which characterises them.

What chiefly provoked my laughter on reading this
social code, was the use that had been made
of the poem of Frediakofsky. Woe to the
poet immortalised by a sovereign!
I leave to-morrow for
Moscow.

❖

THE MINISTER OF WAR ❖ AN EVASION ❖ THE FORTRESS OF SCHLUSSELBURG ❖ FORMALITIES ❖ TROUBLESOME POLITENESS ❖ HALLUCINATIONS ❖ KOTZEBUE IN SIBERIA ❖ THE FELDJÄGER ❖ MANUFACTORIES OF PETERSBURG ❖ HOUSES OF RUSSIAN PEASANTS ❖ A RUSSIAN INN ❖ DIRTINESS OF THE PEOPLE ❖ THE COUNTRY WOMEN ❖ BAD ROADS ❖ THE ENGINEER AND HIS WIFE ❖ THE SLUICES OF SCHLUSSELBURG ❖ UNION OF THE CASPIAN AND BALTIC ❖ THE SOURCE OF THE NEVA ❖ INUNDATIONS OF PETERSBURG ❖ THE INTERIOR OF THE FORTRESS OF SCHLUSSELBURG ❖ THE TOMB OF IVAN ❖ ANGER OF THE COMMANDANT ❖ STATE PRISONERS ❖ A DINNER WITH THE MIDDLE CLASSES IN RUSSIA ❖ NATURAL CAUSTICITY OF THE PEOPLE ❖ POLITE CONVERSATION ❖ MADAME DE GENLIS ❖ FRENCH MODERN LITERATURE PROHIBITED ❖ A NATIONAL DISH ❖ DIFFERENCE IN THE MANNERS OF THE HIGHER AND MIDDLE CLASSES ❖ RETURN TO PETERSBURG

❖

CHAPTER XX

❖

On the day of the fête at Peterhoff, I had asked the minister of war what means I should take in order to obtain permission to see the fortress of Schlusselburg.

This grave person is the Count Tchernicheff. The brilliant aide-de-camp, the elegant envoy of Alexander at the court of Napoleon, is become a sedate man, a man of importance, and one of the most active ministers of the empire. Not a morning passes without his transacting business with the emperor. He replied, "I will communicate your desire to his majesty." This tone of prudence, mingled with an air of surprise, made me feel that the answer was very significative. My request, simple as I had thought it, was evidently an important one in the eyes of the minister. To think of visiting a fortress that had become historical since the imprisonment and death of Ivan VI., which took place in the reign of the Empress Elizabeth, was enormous presumption. I perceived that I had touched a tender chord, and said no more on the subject.

Some days after this, namely, the day before yesterday, at the moment I was preparing to depart for Moscow, I received a letter from the minister of war, announcing permission to see the sluices of Schlusselburg!

The ancient Swedish fortress, called the key of the Baltic by Peter I., is situated precisely at the source of the Neva, on an island in the lake of Ladoga, to which the river serves as a natural canal, that carries its superfluous waters into the Gulf of Finland. This canal, otherwise called the Neva, receives, however, a large accession of water, which is considered as exclusively the source of the river, and which rises up under the waves immediately beneath the wall of the fortress of Schlusselburg, between the river and the lake. The spring is one of the most remarkable natural curiosities in Russia; and the surrounding scenery, though very flat, like all other scenery in the country, is the most interesting in the environs of Petersburg.

By means of a canal, with sluices, the boats avoid the danger caused by the spring: they leave the lake before reaching the source of the Neva, and enter the river about half a league below.

This then was the interesting work which I was permitted to examine.

I had requested to see a state prison; my request was met by a permission to see the floodgates.

The minister of war ended his note by informing me that the aide-de-camp, general director of the roads of the empire, had received orders to give me every facility for making this journey.

Facility! Good heavens! to what trouble had my curiosity exposed me, and what a lesson of discretion had they given me, by the exhibition of so much ceremony, qualified by so much politeness! Not to avail myself of the permission, when orders had been sent respecting me throughout the route, would have been to incur the charge of ingratitude; yet to examine the sluices with Russian minuteness, without even seeing the castle of Schlusselburg, was to fall with my eyes open into the snare and to lose a day; a serious loss, at this already advanced season, if I am to see all that I purpose seeing in Russia, without altogether passing the winter there.

I state facts. The reader can draw the conclusions. They have not here yet ventured to speak freely of the iniquities of the reign of Elizabeth. Any thing that might lead to reflection on the nature of the legitimacy of the present power passes for an impiety. It was therefore necessary to represent my request to the emperor. He would neither grant it nor directly refuse it; he therefore modified it, and granted me permission to admire a wonder of industry which I had no intention of seeing. From the emperor, this permission was forwarded to the minister, from the minister to the director-general, from the director-general to a chief engineer, and, finally, to a sub-officer commissioned to accompany me, to officiate as my guide and to answer for my *safety* during the entire journey: a *favour* which rather reminds one of the janissary with whom they honoured foreigners in Turkey. This protection appears too much like a mark of distrust to flatter me as much as it irks me, and, while crushing in my hands the minister's letter, I think on the justice of the words of the prince, whom I met on the Travemünde steam boat, and with him am ready to exclaim, that "Russia is the land of useless formalities!"

I proceeded to the aide-de-camp general-director. &c. &c. &c. to claim the execution of the supreme command. The director was not at home; I must call to-morrow. Not wishing to lose another day, I persisted, and was told to return in the evening, when I was received with the usual politeness, and after a visit of a quarter of an hour, was dismissed with the necessary orders for the engineer of Schlusselburg, but none for the governor of the castle. In accompanying me to the antechamber, he promised that a sub-officer should be at my door on the morrow, at four o'clock in the morning.

I did not sleep. I became possessed with an idea that will appear sufficiently foolish; the idea that my guard might become my gaoler. If this man, instead of conducting me to Schlusselburg, eighteen leagues from Petersburg, should, when we had left the city, exhibit an order to transport me to Siberia, that I might there expiate my inconvenient curiosity, what should I say or do? It would be necessary, at first, to obey; and afterwards on arriving at Tobolsk, if I ever arrived there, I would claim. . . . The manifestations of politeness by no means re-assured me: on the contrary, I had not forgotten the smiles and kind words of Alexander, addressed to one of his ministers, who was seized by the feldjäger, at the door, even of the emperor's cabinet, and carried direct from the palace to Siberia.

Many other examples of sentences and executions of this character occurred to justify my presentiments and to disturb my imagination.

The being a foreigner is not sufficient guarantee. I called to mind the carrying off of Kotzebue, who, at the commencement of this century, was also seized by a feldjäger, and transported under circumstances similar to mine (for I already felt as if on the road) from Petersburg to Tobolsk. What had been the offence of Kotzebue? He had made himself feared because he had published his opinions, and because they were not thought all equally favourable to the order of things established in Russia. Now, who could assure me that I had not incurred the same reproach? or, which would be sufficient, the same suspicion? If I give the least umbrage here, can I hope that they will have more regard for me than they have had for others? besides, I am watched by spies— every foreigner is. They know, therefore, that I write, and carefully conceal my papers; they are, perhaps, curious to know what these papers are about.

Such were the fancies that possessed me the whole of the night before last; and though I visited yesterday without any accident the fortress of Schlusselburg, they are not so entirely unreasonable as to make me feel quite beyond all danger for the remainder of my journey. I often say to myself, that the Russian police, prudent, enlightened, well-informed, would not have recourse to any *coup d'état*, unless it believed it necessary, and that it would be to attach too much importance to my person and my remarks, to suppose that they could be capable of making uneasy the men who govern this empire. Nevertheless, these reasons for feeling secure, and many others that present themselves, are more specious than solid: experience only too clearly proves the spirit of minutia which actuates those who have too much power: every thing is of importance to him who would conceal the fact that he governs by fear, and whoever depends on opinion, must not despise that of any independent man who writes: a government which lives by mystery, and whose strength lies in dissimulation, is afraid of every thing—every thing appears to it of consequence: in short, my vanity accords with my reflection and my memory of past events, to persuade me that I here run some danger.

If I lay any stress upon these inquietudes, it is simply because they describe the country. As regards my own feelings, they dissipate as soon as it is necessary to act. The phantoms of a sleepless night do not follow me upon the road: I am more adventurous in action than in thought; it is more difficult for me to think than to act with energy. Motion imparts to me as much courage as rest inspires me with doubt.

Yesterday, at five in the morning, I set out in a *calèche* drawn by four horses harnessed abreast. Whenever they journey into the country the Russian coachmen adopt this ancient mode of driving, in which they display much boldness and dexterity. My feldjäger placed himself before me by the side of the coachman, and we quickly traversed St. Petersburg, soon leaving behind us the handsome part of the city, and next passing through that of the manufactories, among which are magnificent glass works and immense mills for the spinning of cotton and other fabrics, for the most part directed by Englishmen. This quarter of the city resembles a colony. As a man is only appreciated here according to his standing with the government, the presence of the feldjäger on my carriage had a great effect. This mark of supreme protection made me a person of consequence in the eyes of my own coachman, who had driven me the whole of the time that I had been in Petersburg. He appeared suddenly to discover and to glory in the too long concealed dignity of his master; his looks testified a respect that they had never done before: it seemed as though he wished to indemnify me for all the honours of which he had, mentally and in ignorance, hitherto deprived me.

The people on foot, the drivers of the carts and drowskas, all bowed to the mystic influence of my sub-officer, who, with a simple sign of his finger, made every obstruction of the road vanish like magic. The crowd was, as it were, annihilated before him, and I could not but think, if he had such power to protect me, what would be his power to destroy me if he had received an order to that effect. The difficulty attending an entrance into this country wearies more than it awes me; the difficulty of flying from it would be more formidable. People say, "To enter Russia the gates are wide, to leave it they become narrow."

Under the guard of my soldier I rapidly followed the banks of the river; frequent views of which, through alleys of birch trees, with the appearance here and there of busy manufactories, and of wooden hamlets, enlivened the landscape, and made the road seem less monotonous than those I had hitherto travelled in Russia; not that the scenery was picturesque in the ordinary acceptation of the word, it was only less desolate than it is on the other side of the city: besides, I have a predilection for melancholy landscapes; there is always a species of grandeur in a scene, the contemplation of which produces reverie. I prefer, as regards poetical effect, the borders of the Neva to the plain between Montmartre and St. Denis, or the rich wheat fields of La Beauce and La Brie.

The appearance of several villages surprised me; they displayed signs of wealth, and even a sort of rustic elegance, which was very pleasing. The neat wooden houses form the line of a single street. They are painted, and their roofs are loaded with ornaments which might be considered rather ostentatious, if a comparison were made between the exterior luxury and the internal lack of conveniences and cleanliness in these architectural toys. One regrets to see a taste for superfluities among a people not yet acquainted with necessaries; besides, on examining them more closely, these habitations are discovered to be ill built.

Always the same taste for that which addresses the eye! Both peasants and lords take more pleasure in ornamenting the road than in beautifying the interior of their dwellings. They feed here upon the admiration, or perhaps the envy, which they excite. But enjoyment, real enjoyment, where is it? The Russians themselves would be puzzled to answer the question.

Wealth in Russia is the food of vanity. The only magnificence that pleases me is that which makes no show, and I therefore find fault with every thing here which they wish me to admire. A nation of decorators will never inspire me with any other feeling than that of fearing lest I should become their dupe. On entering the theatre where their artificial representations are exhibited, I have but one desire; that, namely, of looking behind the curtain, a corner of which I am ever tempted to lift up. I came to see a country, I find only a playhouse.

I had ordered a relay of horses ten leagues from Petersburg. Four, ready harnessed, awaited me in a village, where I found a kind of Russian *Venta*,* which I entered. It was the first time I had seen the peasants in their own houses.

An immense wooden shed, plank walls on three sides, plank flooring and plank ceiling, formed the hall of entrance, and occupied the greater part of the rustic dwelling. Notwithstanding the free currents of air, I found it redolent of that odour of onions, cabbages, and old greasy leather, which Russian villages and Russian villagers invariably exhale.

A superb stallion, tied to a post, occupied the attention of several men who were engaged in the difficult task of shoeing him. The magnificent but untractable animal belonged, I was told, to the stud of a neighbouring lord: the eight persons who were endeavouring to manage him, all displayed a figure, a costume, and a countenance that was striking. The population of the provinces adjoining the capital is not, however, handsome: it is not even Russian, being much mixed with the race of the Finns, who resemble the Laplanders.

They tell me that in the interior of the empire I shall find perfect models of Grecian statues, several of which I have indeed already seen in Petersburg, where the nobles are often attended by the men born on their distant estates.

A low and confined room adjoined this immense shed; it reminded me of the cabin of some river boat; walls, ceiling, floor, seats, and tables, were all of wood rudely hewn. The smell of cabbage and pitch was extremely powerful.

In this retreat, almost deprived of air and light, for the doors were low, and the windows extremely small, I found an old woman busy serving tea to four or five bearded peasants, clothed in pelisses of sheepskin, the wool of which is turned inwards, for it has already, and for some days past, become rather cold.† These men were of short stature. Their leather pelisses were rather tasteful, but they were very ill scented: I know nothing except the perfumes of the nobles that could be more so. On the table stood a bright copper kettle and a teapot. The tea is always of good quality, well made, and, if it is not preferred pure, good

* Venta, a Spanish country inn.—*Trans.*
† This is the 1st of August.

milk is every where to be obtained. This elegant beverage served up in barns, I say barns for politeness-sake, reminds me of the chocolate of the Spaniards. It forms one of the thousand contrasts with which the traveller is struck at every step he takes among these two people, equally singular, though in many of their ways as different as the climates they inhabit.

I have often said that the Russian people have a sentiment of the picturesque: among the groups of men and animals that surrounded me in this interior of a Russian farm house, a painter would have found subjects for several charming pictures.

The red or blue shirt of the peasants is buttoned over the collar bone, and drawn close round the loins by a girdle, above which it lies in antique folds, and below forms an open tunic that falls over the pantaloon. The long Persian robe, often left open, which, when the men do not work, partly covers this blouse, the hair worn long and parted on the forehead, but shaved close behind rather higher than the nape, so as to discover all the strength of the neck—does not this form an original and graceful picture? The wild yet, at the same time, gentle expression of the Russian peasants also possesses grace: their elegant forms, their suppleness, their broad shoulders, the sweet smile of their mouth, the mixture of tenderness and ferocity which is discernible in their wild and melancholy look, render their general appearance as different from that of our labourers as the land they cultivate differs from the rest of Europe. Every thing is new here for a stranger. The natives possess a certain charm which can be felt though not expressed: it is the oriental languor combined with the romantic reverie of a northern people; and all this is exhibited in an uncultured yet noble form, which imparts to it the merit of a primitive endowment. These people inspire much more interest than confidence. The common orders in Russia are amusing knaves: they may be easily led if they are not deceived; but as soon as they see that their masters or their masters' agents lie more than themselves, they plunge into the lowest depths of falsehood and meanness. They who would civilise a people must themselves possess worth of character—the barbarism of the serf accuses the corruptness of the noble.

If the reader be surprised at the ill-nature of my judgments, he will be yet more so when I add that I do but express the general opinion; the only difference is, that I express openly what every one here conceals, with a prudence that none would be surprised at if they saw, as I do, to what extent this virtue, which excludes so many others, is necessary to those who live in Russia.

Dirtiness is very conspicuous in the country, but that of the houses and the clothes strikes me more than that of the individuals. The Russians take much care of their persons. Their vapour baths, it is true, appear to us disgusting; and I should for myself much prefer the contact of pure water; still these boiling fogs cleanse and strengthen the body, though they wrinkle the skin prematurely. By virtue of their use, the peasants may be often seen with clean beards and hair, when as much cannot be said for their garments. Warm clothing costs money, and has to be worn a long time; the rooms also, in which they think only of protecting themselves from the cold, are necessarily less aired than those of southern people. Of the air that purifies, the Russians are deprived for nine months in the year, so that their dirtiness is rather the inevitable effect of their climate than of their negligence.

In some districts the workpeople wear a cap of blue cloth, bulging out in the shape of a balloon. They have several other species of head-dress, all pleasing to the eye, and showing good taste as compared with the saucy affectation of negligence, visible among the lower orders in the environs of Paris.

When they work bare-headed, they remedy the inconvenience of their long hair by binding it with a kind of diadem, or fillet made of a riband, a wreath of rushes, or of some other simple material, always placed with care, and which looks well on the young people; for the men of this race have in general finely formed, oval heads, so that their working head-dress becomes an ornament. But what shall I say of the women? All whom I have hitherto seen have appeared to me repulsive: I had hoped in this excursion to have met some fair villagers; but here, as at Petersburg, they are broad and short in figure, and they gird their forms at the shoulders, a little above the bosom, which spreads freely under the petticoat. It is hideous! Add to this voluntary deformity, large men's boots and a species of riding coat, or jacket of sheep's skin, similar to the pelisses of their husbands, but, doubtless through a laudable economy; much less gracefully cut, and far more worn; falling indeed literally in rags—such is their toilette. Assuredly there is no part of the world where the fair sex so completely dispenses with coquettish finery as in Russia (I speak only of the female peasants and of the corner of the land that I have seen). Nevertheless these women are the mothers of the soldiers of which the Emperor is so proud, and of the handsome coachmen of the streets of Petersburg.

It should be observed that the greater number of the women in the government of Petersburg are of Finnish extraction. I am told that in the interior of the country I shall see very good-looking female peasants.

The road from Petersburg to Schlusselburg is bad in many parts: there are sometimes deep beds of sand, sometimes holes of mud to be passed, over which planks have been very uselessly thrown. What is yet worse, are the small logs of wood rudely laid across each other, on certain marshy portions of the route, which would swallow up any other foundation. This rustic, ill-joined and movable flooring dances under the wheels; and frequent broken bones and broken carriages on Russian *grandes routes*, testify to the wisdom of reducing equipages to their most simple forms, to something about as primitive as the telega. I observed also several dilapidated bridges, one of which seemed dangerous to pass over. Human life is a small matter in Russia. With sixty millions of children how can there be the bowels of a father?

On my arrival at Schlusselburg, where I was expected, the engineer who has the direction of the sluices received me.

The weather was raw and gloomy. My carriage stopped before the comfortable wood-house of the engineer, who introduced me himself into a parlour, where he offered me a light collation, and presented me, with a kind of conjugal pride, to a young and handsome person, his wife. She sat all alone, upon a sofa from which she did not rise on my entering. Not understanding French, she remained silent, and also motionless, I cannot tell why, unless she mistook immovability for good breeding, and starched airs for taste. Her object seemed to be to represent before me the statue of hospitality clothed in white muslin over a pink petticoat. I ate and warmed myself in silence: she watched me without daring to turn away her eyes, for this would be to move them, and immobility was the part she had to perform. If I had suspected there could be timidity at the bottom of this singular reception, I should have experienced sympathy, and felt only surprise; but I could hardly be deceived in such a case, for I am familiar with timidity.

My host suffered me to contemplate at leisure this curious image of rosy wax-work, dressed up in order to dazzle the stranger, though it confirmed him only in his opinion that the women of the North are seldom natural. The worthy engineer seemed flattered with the effect that his wife produced on me. He took my wonder for admiration; nevertheless, desirous of conscientiously acquitting himself of his duty, he at length said, "I regret to disturb you, but we have scarcely sufficient time to visit the works which I have received an order to show to you in detail."

I had foreseen the blow without being able to parry it. I therefore submitted with resignation, and suffered myself to be led from sluice to sluice, my mind still dwelling with useless regret upon the fortress, that tomb of the youthful Ivan, which they would not suffer me to approach. It will be seen shortly how this secret object of my journey was attained.

To enumerate all the structures of granite that I have seen this morning, the floodgates fixed in grooves worked in blocks of that stone, the flags, of the same material, employed as the pavement of a gigantic canal, would fortunately little interest the reader: it will suffice him to know that during the ten years that have elapsed since the first sluices were finished, they have required no repairs. This is an astonishing instance of stability in a climate like that of Lake Ladoga. The object of the magnificent work is to equalise the difference of level that there is between the canal of Ladoga and the course of the Neva near to its source. With this object, sluices have been multiplied, without reference to cost, in order to render as easy and prompt as possible a navigation that the rigour of the seasons leaves open for only three or four months in the year.

Nothing has been spared to perfect the solidity and the precision of the work. The granite of Finland has been used for the bridges, the parapets, and even, I repeat it with admiration, for lining the bed of the canal; in short, all the improvements of modern science have been had recourse to, in order to complete, at Schlusselburg, a work as perfect in its kind as the rigours of the climate will permit.

The interior navigation of Russia deserves the attention of all scientific and commercial men: it constitutes one of the principal sources of the riches of the land. By means of a series of canals, the entire extent of which is, like every other undertaking in this country, colossal, they have, since the reign of Peter the Great, succeeded in joining, so as to form a safe navigation for boats, the Caspian with the Baltic by the Volga, Lake Ladoga, and the Neva. This enterprise, bold in conception, prodigious in execution, is now completed, and forms one of the wonders of the civilised world. Although thus magnificent to contemplate, I found it rather tedious to inspect, especially under the conduct of one of the executors of the *chef-d'oeuvre*. The professional man invests his work with the importance which no doubt it merits; but for a mere general observer, like myself, admiration is extinguished under minute details,—details which, in the present case, I will spare the reader.

When I believed I had strictly accorded the time and the praise that were due to the wonders I was obliged to pass in review in return for the favour which, it was supposed, I had received, I returned to the original motive of my journey, and, disguising my object in order the better to attain it, I asked permission to see the source of the Neva. This wish, the insidious innocence of which could not conceal the indiscretion, was at first eluded by the engineer, who replied, "It rises up under the water at the outlet of Lake Ladoga, at the end of the channel, which separates the lake from the island on which stands the fortress."

I knew this already, but replied: "It is one of the natural curiosities of Russia. Are there no means of reaching this spring?"

"The wind is too high; we could not see the bubbling up of the waters. It is necessary that the weather be calm, in order that the eye may distinguish a fountain which rises from the bottom of

the waves; nevertheless I will do what I can in order to satisfy
your curiosity."

At these words the engineer ordered a very pretty boat to be
manned with six rowers, who were handsomely clad. We immediately proceeded, as was said, to visit the source of the Neva, but,
in reality, to approach the walls of the strong castle, or rather the
enchanted prison to which I had been refused access with so
artful a politeness. But the difficulties only served to excite my
desire: had I had the power to give deliverance to some unhappy
prisoner, my impatience could scarcely have been more lively.

The fortress of Schlusselburg is built on a flat island, a kind of
rock, very little elevated above the level of the water. This rock
divides the river in two parts; it also serves, properly speaking, to
separate the river from the lake, for it indicates the point where
the waters mingle. We rowed round the fortress in order, as we
said, to approach as nearly as possible the source of the Neva.
Our rowers soon brought us immediately over the vortex. They
handled their oars so well that, notwithstanding the rough
weather and the smallness of our boat, we scarcely felt the heave
of the waves, which, nevertheless, rolled at this spot as much as
in the open sea. Being unable to distinguish the source, which was
concealed by the motion of the billows, we took a turn on the
lake; after which, the wind having rather lulled, permitted our
seeing, at a considerable depth, a few waves of foam. This was the
spring of the Neva, above which our boat rode.

When the west wind drives back the waters of the lake, the
channel which serves as its outlet remains almost dry, and then
this beautiful spring is fully exposed. On such occasions, which
are fortunately very rare, the inhabitants of Schlusselburg know
that Petersburg is under water. The news of such catastrophe
never fails to reach them on the morrow; for the same west wind
which causes the reflux of the waters of Lake Ladoga, and leaves
dry the channel of the Neva near its source, drives also, when it is
violent, the waters of the Gulf of Finland into the mouth of the
river. The course of this stream is therefore stopped, and the
water, finding its passage obstructed by the sea, makes a way by
overflowing Petersburg and its environs.

When I had sufficiently admired the site of Schlusselburg, sufficiently surveyed, with a spy glass, the position of the battery
which Peter the Great raised to bombard the strong fort of the
Swedes, and sufficiently praised every thing which scarcely interested me, I said, in the most careless manner imaginable, "Let us
go and see the interior of the fortress:"—"its situation appears
extremely picturesque," I added, a little less adroitly; for in matters of finesse it is, above all, necessary to avoid overdoing any
thing. The Russian cast upon me a scrutinising look, of which I
felt the full force. This diplomatic mathematician answered:

"The fortress, sir, possesses no object of curiosity for a foreigner."

"Never mind: everything is curious in so interesting a land as
yours."

"But if the governor does not expect us, we shall not be suffered to enter."

"You can ask his permission to introduce a traveller into the
fortress; besides, I rather believe he does expect us."

In fact we were admitted at the first application of the engineer; which leads me to surmise that my visit, if not announced
as certain, was indicated as probable.

We were received with military ceremony, conducted under a
vault, through a gate ill defended, and after crossing a court
overgrown with grass, we were introduced into—the prison?
Alas! no: into the apartments of the governor. He did not understand a word of French, but he received me with civility, affecting to take my visit as an act of politeness of which he himself
was the object, and expressing to me his acknowledgments
through the engineer, accordingly. These crafty compliments
were by no means satisfactory. There I was, obliged to talk to the
wife of the commandant, who spoke little more French than her
husband, to sip chocolate, in short, to do every thing except visit
the prison of Ivan—that imaginary prize, for whose sake I had
endured all the toils, the artifices, and the wearisome civilities of
the day.

At length, when the reasonable time for a call had expired, I
asked my companion if it was possible to see the interior of the

fortress. Several words and significant glances were hereupon exchanged between the commandant and the engineer, and we all left the chamber.

I fancied myself at the crowning point of all my labours. The fortress of Schlusselburg is not picturesque: it is a girdle of Swedish walls of small elevation, and the interior of which forms a kind of orchard, wherein are dispersed several very low buildings; including a church, a house for the commandant, a barracks, and the dungeons, masked by windows the height of which does not exceed that of the rampart. Nothing announces violence or mystery. The appearance of this quiet state prison is more terrible to the imagination than to the eye. Gratings, drawbridges, battlements, and all the somewhat theatrical apparatus of the castles of the middle ages, are not here to be seen. The governor commenced by showing me the *superb monuments of the church!* The four copes which were solemnly displayed before me cost, as the governor himself took the trouble to say, thirty thousand roubles. Tired of such sights, I simply asked for the tomb of Ivan VI. They replied by showing me a breach made in the wall by the cannon of the Czar Peter, when he conducted in person the siege of the key of the Baltic.

"The tomb of Ivan," I continued, without suffering myself to be disconcerted, "where is it?" This time they conducted me behind the church, and, pointing near to a rose brier, said, "It is here."

I conclude that victims are allowed no tomb in Russia.

"And the chamber of Ivan," I continued with a pertinacity which must have appeared as singular to my guides, as their scruples, reserve, and tergiversations appeared to me.

The engineer answered in a low voice that they could not show the chamber of Ivan, because it lay in a part of the fortress then occupied by state prisoners.

The excuse was legitimate; I had expected it; but what surprised me was the wrath of the commandant. Whether it was that he understood French better than he spoke it, or that he had only feigned ignorance of our language, he severely reprimanded my guide, whose indiscretion, he added, would some day ruin him.

This, the latter, annoyed with the lecture he had received, found a favourable opportunity of telling me, stating also that the governor had warned him, in a very significant manner, to abstain henceforward from speaking of *public* affairs, and from introducing foreigners into state prisons. This engineer has all the qualities necessary to constitute a good Russian; but he is young, and does not yet understand the mysteries of his trade—it is not of his profession as an engineer that I speak.

I found it was necessary to yield: I was the weakest, and therefore, owning myself vanquished, I renounced the hope of visiting the room where the unhappy heir of the throne of Russia died imbecile, because it was found more convenient to make him an idiot than an emperor. I cannot sufficiently express my astonishment at the manner in which the Russian government is served by its agents. I remember the countenance of the minister of war, the first time that I ventured to testify a wish to visit a castle that had become historical by a crime committed in the times of the Empress Elizabeth; and I compare, with a wonder mixed with fear, the disorder of ideas that reigns among us, with the absence of all private views, of all personal opinion—the blind submission, in short, which forms the rule of conduct among all, whether heads or subordinates, who carry on the administration of affairs in Russia. The unity of action observable in this government astounds me. I admire while I shudder, in noticing the tacit accord with which both superior and inferior *employés* act in making war against ideas and even events. At the time, this sentiment made me as impatient to leave the fortress of Schlusselburg as I had been eager to enter it. I began to fear lest I should become by force one of the inmates of that abode of secret tears and unknown sorrows. In my ever-increasing sense of its oppressive influence, I longed only for the physical pleasure of walking and breathing beyond its limits. I forgot that the country into which I should return was in itself a prison; a prison whose vast size only makes it the more formidable.

A Russian fortress!—this word produces on the imagination an impression very different to that which is felt in visiting the strongholds of people really civilised, sincerely humane. The puerile precautions taken in Russia to hide what are called secrets of state confirms me, more than would open acts of barbarity, in the idea that this government is nothing more than a hypocritical tyranny.

After having myself penetrated into a Russian state prison, and found there the impossibility of speaking of things which every stranger would naturally inquire about in such a place, I argue with myself that such dissimulation must serve as mask to a profound inhumanity: it is not that which is commendable that people conceal with so much care.

I am assured, on good authority, that the submarine dungeons of Kronstadt contain, among other state prisoners, miserable beings who were placed there in the reign of Alexander. These unhappy creatures are reduced to a state below that of the brute, by a punishment the atrocity of which nothing can justify. Could they now come forth out of the earth, they would rise like so many avenging spectres, whose appearance would make the despot himself recoil with horror, and shake the fabric of despotism to its centre. Every thing may be defended by plausible words, and even by good reasons: not any one of the opinions that divide the political, the literary, or the religious world, lacks argument by which to maintain itself: but, let them say what they please, a system, the violence of which requires such means of support, must be radically and intensely vicious.

The victims of this odious policy are no longer men. Those unfortunate beings, denied the commonest rights, cut off from the world, forgotten by every one, abandoned to themselves in the night of their captivity, during which imbecility becomes the fruit, and the only remaining consolation of their never-ending misery, have lost all memory, as well as all that gift of reason, that light of humanity, which no one has a right to extinguish in the breast of his fellow-being. They have even forgotten their own names, which the keepers amuse themselves by asking with a brutal derision, for which there is none to call them to account; for there reigns such confusion in the depths of these abysses of iniquity, the shades are so thick, that all traces of justice are effaced.

Even the crimes of some of the prisoners are not recollected; they are, therefore, retained for ever, because it is not known to whom they should be delivered, and it is deemed less inconvenient to perpetuate the mistake than to publish it. The bad effect of so tardy a justice is feared, and thus the evil is aggravated, that its excess may not require to be justified. Infamous pusillanimity, which is called expediency, respect for *appearances*, prudence, obedience, wisdom, a sacrifice to the public good, a reason of state! Words are never wanted by oppressors; and are there not two names for everything that exists under the sun? We are unceasingly told that there is no punishment of death in Russia. To bury alive is not to kill! In reflecting on so many miseries on one side, and so much injustice and hypocrisy on the other, the guilt of the prisoners is lost sight of, the judge alone seems criminal. My indignation is at its height, when I consider that this iniquitous judge is not cruel by choice. To such extent may a bad government pervert men interested in its duration! But Russia marches in advance of her destiny. This must explain all. If we are to measure the greatness of the end by the extent of the sacrifices, we must, without doubt, prognosticate for this nation the empire of the world.

On returning from my melancholy visit, a new labour awaited me at the engineer's: a ceremonious dinner with persons of the middle classes. The engineer had gathered around him, in order to do me honor, his wife's relations and a few of the neighbouring landholders. This society would have interested me as an observer, had I not at the first moment perceived that it would furnish me with no new ideas. There is no citizen class in Russia, but the petty employés and the small, though ennobled, landed proprietors, represent there the middle orders of other lands. Envying the great, and themselves envied by the little, these men vainly call themselves nobles. They are exactly in the position of the French *bourgeois* before the revolution; the same data produce everywhere the same results.

I felt that there reigned in this society a hostility, ill disguised, against real greatness and true elegance, to whatever land they might belong.

That starchness of manners, that acrimony of sentiment, ill concealed under an air of preciseness and propriety, recalled to my mind only too well, the epoch in which we live, and which I had a little forgotten in Russia, where I had hitherto only seen the society of courtiers. I was now among aspiring subalterns, uneasy as to what might be thought of them, and these people are the same everywhere.

The men did not speak to me, and appeared to take little notice of me; they did not understand French, beyond perhaps being able to read it with difficulty; they therefore formed a circle in a corner of the room, and talked Russian. One or two females of the family bore all the weight of the French conversation. I was surprised to find that they were acquainted with all that portion of our literature that the Russian police suffers to penetrate into their land. The toilette of these ladies, who, with the exception of the mistress of the house, were all elderly, was wanting in taste; the dress of the men was yet more negligent; large brown topcoats, almost trailing upon the ground, had taken the place of the national costume. But what surprised me more than their careless attire, was the caustic and captious tone of their conversation. The Russian feeling, carefully disguised by the tact of the higher orders, exhibited itself here openly. This society was more candid, though less polite, than that of the court; and I clearly saw what I had only felt elsewhere, namely, that the spirit of curiosity, sarcasm, and carping criticism influences the Russians in their intercourse with strangers. They hate us as every imitator hates his model; their scrutinising looks seek faults in us with the desire of finding them. As soon as I recognised this disposition I felt no inclination to be indulgent myself. I had thought it necessary to offer a few words of excuse for my ignorance of the Russian tongue, and I finished my speech by remarking that every traveller ought to know the language of the country he visits, as it is more natural that he should give himself the trouble of learning to speak the language of those whom he seeks, than of imposing upon them the trouble of speaking as he does.

This compliment was answered by the observation, that I must nevertheless resign myself to hearing French murdered by the Russians, unless I would travel as a mute.

"It is of this I complain," I replied; "if I knew how to murder Russian as I ought to do, I would not force you to change your habits in order to speak my language."

"Formerly we spoke only French."

"That was wrong."

"It is not for you to reproach us."

"I invariably speak my real opinions."

"Truth, then, is still thought something of in France?"

"I cannot tell; but I know that it ought to be loved for its own intrinsic merits."

"Such love does not belong to our age."

"In Russia?"

"No where; and especially in no country governed by newspapers."

I was of the same opinion as the lady, which made me desirous of changing the conversation, for I would not speak contrary to my own sentiments, nor yet acquiesce with those of a person who, when she even thought with me, expressed her views with a causticity that was capable of disgusting me with my own.

An incident occurred very *a-propos* to turn the conversation. A sound of voices in the street attracted everybody to the window: it was a quarrel among boatmen, who appeared outrageous in their anger. The conflict was likely to become bloody, when the engineer showed himself upon the balcony, and the sight alone of his uniform produced a miraculous effect. The rage of these rude men calmed, without its being necessary to address them a single word; the courtier, the most perfectly broken in to falsehood, could not have better disguised his resentment.

"What an excellent people!" cried the lady who had undertaken to entertain me.

"What pitiable beings," I thought, as I re-seated myself, for I shall never admire the miracles of fear. However, I deemed it wiser to be silent.

"Order is not so easily re-established in your country," continued my indefatigable enemy, never ceasing to scrutinise me with her inquisitive eyes.

This impoliteness was new to me. In general, I had found the manners of the Russians too obliging for the malignity of mind which I could detect under their fine phrases; here I recognised an accord between the sentiments and their expression, that was yet more disagreeable.

"We have among us the inconveniences of liberty; but we have also the advantages," I replied.

"What are they?"

"They would not be understood in Russia."

"They can be dispensed with."

"As can every thing else that is not known."

My adversary was piqued, and sought to hide her vexation by suddenly changing the subject of discourse.

"Is it of your family that Madame de Genlis speaks so much in the *Souvenirs of Felicia,* and of your person in her Memoirs?"

I answered in the affirmative, and then expressed my surprise that these books were read at Schlusselburg.

"You take us for Laplanders," retorted the lady, with that tone of acrimony which I had not succeeded in softening, and which began to react upon me, until I had nearly reached the same diapason.

"No, madame, but for Russians who have something better to do than to occupy themselves with the gossip of French society."

"Madame de Genlis is no gossip."

"Yet such of her writings as those in which she does no more than gracefully relate the little anecdotes of her times, can only, it appears to me, be interesting to the French."

"You do not wish that we should make much of you and your writers."

"I wish that we should be valued for our real merit."

"If the influence that you have exercised over Europe in matters of social intercourse were taken from you, what would be left you?"

I felt that I had to deal with a powerful adversary. "There would remain to us the glory of our history, and even that of the history of Russia: for this empire owes only its new influence in Europe to the energy with which it avenged itself for the conquest of its capital by the French."

"It is true that you have immensely aided us, without wishing to do so."

"Did you lose any dear friend in that war?"

"No, monsieur."

I had hoped that the aversion against France, which was betrayed by every word in the conversation of this rude lady, would be explained to me by some too legitimate cause of resentment, but my expectation was deceived.

The conversation, which could not become general, was carried on in this manner until dinner. I sought to turn it to our new school of literature, but Balzac alone had been read. He was infinitely admired, and fairly judged. Almost all the works of our modern authors are prohibited in Russia, which proves the influence attributed to them. At last, after a long delay, we seated ourselves at table. The lady of the house, ever faithful to her part as a statue, made that day but one movement: she transported herself, without turning her eyes or opening her lips, from her sofa in the drawing room to her chair in the dining-room. This change of position, performed spontaneously, proved to me that the idol had legs.

The dinner did not pass over without constraint, but it was not long, and appeared to me sufficiently good, with the exception of the soup, the originality of which passed all bounds. This soup was cold, and consisted of pieces of fish, which swam in a broth of strong, highly-seasoned, and highly-sweetened vinegar. With the exception of this infernal ragout, and of the sour quarss, a species of beer which is a national beverage, I ate and drank with good appetite. There was excellent claret and champagne on the table, but I saw clearly that they had put themselves out on my account, which produced mutual formality and constraint. The engineer did not participate in this feeling; though a great man at his sluices, he was nothing at all in his own house, and left his mother-in-law to do its honours, with the grace of which the reader may judge.

At six in the evening my entertainers and myself parted, with a satisfaction that was reciprocal, and, it must be owned, ill-disguised. I left for the castle of ——, where I was expected. The frankness of the fair plebeians had reconciled me to the mincing affectations of certain great ladies. One may hope to triumph over affectation, but natural dispositions are invincible.

It was yet light when I reached ——, which is six or eight leagues from Schlusselburg. I spent there the rest of the evening, walking, in the twilight, in a garden, which, for Russia, is very handsome, sailing in a little boat on the Neva, and enjoying the refined and agreeable conversation of a member of the fashionable circles. What I have seen at Schlusselberg will make me cautious how I place myself again in a position where it is necessary to face such interrogations as I submitted to in that society. Such drawing-rooms resemble fields of battle. The circles of fashion, with all their vices, seem preferable to this petty world, with all its precise virtues.

I was again in Petersburg soon after midnight, having travelled during the day about thirty-six leagues through sandy and miry roads, with two sets of hired horses.

The demands upon the animals are in proportion to those made upon the men. The Russian horses seldom last more than eight or ten years. The pavement of Petersburg is as fatal to them as it is to the carriages, and, it may be said, to the riders, whose heads nearly split as soon as they are off the few wooden roads that can be found. It is true that the Russians have laid their detestable pavement in regularly-figured compartments of large stones,—an ornament which only increases the evil, for it makes riding in the streets yet more jolting. A certain appearance of elegance or magnificence—a boastful display of wealth and grandeur, is all that the Russians care for: they have commenced the work of civilisation by creating its superfluities. If such be the right way of proceeding, let us cry, *"Long live vanity, and down with common sense!*

❖

CHAPTER XXI

❖

. . . I have bid adieu to Petersburg. —Adieu is a magical word! It invests places as well as persons with an attraction previously unknown. Why has Petersburg never appeared to me so beautiful as on this evening? It is because I have seen it for the last time. . . .

Had I been taken to Petersburg by the course of business, should I have seen in so short a time the reverse of things as I now see it? Shut up in the circles of diplomatists, I should have surveyed this land from their point of view, I should have devoted all my thoughts to the affair in hand, I should have been interested in conciliating their good will by the utmost facility of manners; and all this management could not have operated for any length of time without reacting upon the judgment of him who was under its constraint. I should have ended by persuading myself that on many points I thought as they thought, were it only to excuse myself in my own eyes for the weakness of speaking as they spoke. Opinions that you dare not refute, however ill-founded you may find them at first, will finally modify your own; when politeness is carried so far as to become blindly tolerant, it is a treason against self; it perverts the views of the observer, whose business it is to represent persons and things not as he would have them to be, but as he actually sees them. And yet, notwithstanding all the independence on which I plume myself, I am often forced, for the sake of my personal safety, to sooth the rude self-love of this jealous nation, for all semi-barbarous people are suspicious. Let it not be supposed that my opinions on Russia and the Russians will surprise the diplomatic strangers who have had the leisure or the taste to study this empire: their opinions are the same as mine, though they will not confess it openly. Happy is the observer who is so situated that no one may have the right of reproaching him with an abuse of confidence! At the same time, I do not disguise from myself the inconveniences of my liberty: to labour in the cause of truth, it is not sufficient that we perceive it; we must manifest it also to others. The fault of hermit minds is that they are too much influenced by their emotions while changing at each moment their point of view, for the solitude of the mind is favorable to the power of imagination, and this power causes it to be easily moved.

But there are readers who can and ought to extract advantage out of my apparent contradictions, by discerning, through my capricious and movable pictures, the exact shapes of persons and of things. Few writers are courageous enough to leave the reader to perform a part of their task; few dare brave the reproach of inconsistency rather than charge their conscience with an affected merit. When the experience of the day has falsified the conclusions of the previous evening, I do not fear to show it. With the sincerity which I profess, my travels become my confessions. The men whose opinions are formed in advance, are all method, all order, and they consequently escape minute criticism; but those who like me, say what they feel without troubling themselves as regards what they have felt, must expect to pay the penalty of their careless candour. This ingenuous and superstitious respect for truth is no doubt a flattery to the reader, but it is a flattery dangerous in the present day; and I sometimes, therefore, fear that the world in which we live cannot be worthy of the compliment.

I shall, in this case, have risked everything to satisfy the love of truth, a virtue which no one possesses, and by my imprudent zeal in sacrificing to a divinity which has no longer a temple, in taking an allegory for a reality, I shall miss the glory of the martyr and pass only for a simpleton. In a society where false-

hood always obtains its reward, good faith is necessarily punished. The world has its crosses on which to nail every truth.

To meditate on these and many other matters, I stopped for a
long time on the middle of the great bridge of the Neva. I wished
to engrave in my memory the two different pictures which, by
simply turning round, without leaving my place, I could enjoy.

In the east was the dark sky and the bright earth, in the west
the clear sky and the earth involved in shade: in the opposition of
these two faces of Petersburg there was a symbolic meaning, into
which I fancied I could penetrate. In the west I saw the ancient,
in the east, the modern Petersburg; the past, the old city, was
shrouded in night—the new, the future city, was revealed in radiance.

Petersburg appears to me less beautiful than Venice, but more
extraordinary. They are both colossi raised by fear. Venice was
the work of unmixed fear; the last Romans preferred flight to
death, and the fruit of their fear became one of the world's wonders. Petersburg is equally the result of terror, but of a pious
terror, for Russian policy has known how to convert obedience
into a dogma. The Russian people are accounted very religious; it
may be so: but what kind of religion can that be which is forbidden to be taught? They never preach in the Russian churches.
The gospel would proclaim liberty to the Slavonians.

This fear of things being understood, which they desire should
be believed, seems to me suspicious. The more reason and knowledge contract the sphere of faith, and the brighter that divine
light, thus concentrated in its focus, becomes; the less people
believe, the more fervent is their belief. Signs of the cross are no
proofs of devotion; and, notwithstanding their genuflexions and
other external evidences of piety, the Russians, in their prayers,
seem to me to think more of their emperor than their God.
"Awake me when you come to the subject of God," said an ambassador, about to be put to sleep in a Russian church by the
imperial liturgy.

Sometimes I feel ready to participate in the superstition of this
people. Enthusiasm becomes contagious when it is or appears to
be general; but the moment the symptoms lay hold of me, I think

of Siberia, that indispensable auxiliary of Muscovite civilisation, and immediately I recover my calmness and independence.

Political faith is more firm here than religious faith; the unity of the Greek church is only apparent: the sects, reduced to silence, dig their way underground; but nations will only remain mutes for a time; sooner or later the day of discussion must arrive, religion, politics, all will speak and explain themselves at last. Whenever the right of speech shall be restored to this muzzled people, the astonished world will hear so many disputes arise, that it will believe the confusion of Babel again returned. It is by religious dissensions that a social revolution will be one day brought about in Russia.

When I approach the emperor and see his dignity and beauty, I admire the marvel. A man like him is rarely seen any where, but on the throne he is a phoenix. I rejoice in living at a time when such a prodigy exists, for I take as much pleasure in showing respect as others do in offering insult.

Nevertheless, I examine, with scrupulous care, the objects of my respect, from whence it results that when I closely consider this personage, distinguished from all others upon earth, I fancy that his head has two faces like that of Janus, and that the words violence, exile, oppression, or their full equivalent—Siberia, are engraved on the face which is not presented towards me. This idea haunts me unceasingly, even when I speak to him. It is in vain that I strive only to think of what I say to him; my imagination, in spite of myself, travels from Warsaw to Tobolsk, and that single word, Warsaw, revives all my distrust.

Does the world know that, at the present hour, the roads of Asia are once again covered with exiles, torn from their hearths and proceeding on foot to their tomb, as the herds leave their pastures for the slaughter-house? This revival of wrath is attributable to a pretended Polish conspiracy, a conspiracy of *youthful madmen*, who would have been heroes had they succeeded; and who, their attempt being desperate, only appear to me the more generously devoted. My heart bleeds for the exiles, their families, and their country. What will be the result when the oppressors of this corner of the earth, where chivalry once flourished, shall have peopled Tartary with all that was most noble and courageous amongst the sons of ancient Europe? When they have thus crowned their icy policy, let them enjoy their success. Siberia will have become the kingdom and Poland the desert.

Ought not we to blush with shame to pronounce the name of liberalism, when we think that there exists in Europe a people who were independent, and who now know no other liberty but that of apostasy? The Russians, when they turn against the west the arms which they employ successfully against Asia, forget that the same mode of action which aids their progress against the Calmucs, becomes an outrage of humanity when directed against a people that have been long civilised.

The scenes on the Volga continue; and these horrors are attributed to instigations of Polish emissaries; an imputation that reminds one of the justice of the wolf of La Fontaine. These cruelties and reciprocal iniquities are preludes to the convulsions of the coming result, and suffice to apprise us of its character. But in a nation governed like this, passions boil a long time before they explode; the peril may be increasing, yet the crisis is still distant, and the evil meanwhile continues: perhaps our grandchildren will not see the explosion; which, notwithstanding, we can now prognosticate as inevitable, though we cannot predict the time and the season.

We may not cease to repeat that the Russian revolution, when it does come, will be the more terrible, because it will be in the name of religion. The Russian policy has melted the church into the state, and confounded heaven and earth: a man who sees a god in his master, scarcely hopes for paradise, except through the favour of the emperor.

I shall never get away. Fate seems to interfere. Once more a delay—yet, this time, it is a legitimate one. I was just preparing to enter my carriage when a friend insisted upon seeing me. He brought a letter, which he would have me read at the very moment. But what a letter, gracious God! It is from the Princess Troubetzkoi, who addresses it to a member of her family charged to show it to the emperor. I wished to copy it in order to print it without changing a syllable, but this I was not permitted to do. "It would go the round of the whole earth," said my friend, alarmed by the effect which it produced upon me.

"The greater reason to make it known," I replied.

"Impossible. The safety of several individuals would be compromised; besides, it has only been lent me in order to show you on your word of honour, and on condition that it shall be returned in half an hour."

Unhappy land, where every stranger appears as a saviour in the eyes of a herd of oppressed beings, merely because he represents truth, publicity, and liberty among a people deprived of all these blessings.

Before alluding to the contents of this letter, it will be necessary to recount, in a few words, a lamentable history. The principal facts will be known to many, yet vaguely, like every thing else that is known of a distant country, in which people only take a cold interest. Let the public read and blush,—yes, blush; for whoever has not found means to protest, with his utmost power, against the policy of a country where such acts are possible, is to a certain extent an accomplice and a responsible party. I sent back the horses by my feldjäger, under pretext of indisposition, and told him to state at the establishment of the Posts that I should not leave until the morrow. Once rid of this officious spy, I sat down to write.

The Prince Troubetzkoi was condemned as a convict to hard labour, fourteen years ago. He was at that time young, and had taken a very active part in the revolt of the fourteenth December.

The first object of the conspirators on that occasion was to deceive the soldiers as regards the legitimacy of the Emperor Nicholas. They hoped, by the error of the troops, to produce a military revolt, and to profit by this, in order to work a political revolution, of which, fortunately or unfortunately for Russia, they alone at that time felt the necessity. The number of these reformers was too limited to afford any chance that the troubles excited by them could end in the result proposed. The conspiracy was defeated by the presence of mind of the Emperor, or rather by the intrepidity of his countenance. That prince, on the first day of his authority, drew from the energy of his bearing all the future power of his reign.

The revolution thus crushed, it was necessary to proceed to

the punishment of the culpable. The Prince Troubetzkoi, one of the most deeply implicated, unable to exculpate himself, was sentenced to labour in the Uralian mines for fourteen or fifteen years, and for the remainder of his life was exiled to Siberia, among one of those distant colonies that malefactors are destined to people.

The prince had a wife whose family was among the most distinguished in the land. This princess could not be dissuaded from following her husband to his tomb. "It is my duty," she said, "and I will fulfil it; no human power has a right to separate a wife from her husband; I will share the fate of mine."

This noble wife obtained the favour of being buried alive with her unhappy partner. I am astonished, since I have seen Russia and the spirit of its government, that, influenced by a lingering relic of shame, they have thought it right to respect this act of devotion during a period of fourteen years. That they should favour patriotic heroism is very natural, for they profit by it; but to tolerate a sublime virtue that does not accord with the views of the sovereign was an act of remissness for which they must have often reproached themselves. They feared the friends of Troubetzkoi; an aristocracy, however enervated it may be, always preserves a shadow of its independence,—a shadow that serves to cast a cloud over despotism. Contrasts abound in this dreadful society; many men speak among themselves as freely as if they lived in France: this secret liberty consoles them for the public slavery which forms the shame and the curse of their land.

From the fear then of exasperating certain influential families, the government yielded to a kind of prudent compassion. The princess departed with her husband the convict, and, which is more extraordinary, she reached her destination. The journey was alone a frightful trial: hundreds,—thousands of leagues in a telega, a little open cart without springs, over roads that break both carriages and human bodies. The unhappy woman supported these and many other hardships and privations, which I shall not describe for want of the precise details; for I wish to add nothing to the strict truth of this history.

Her conduct will appear the more heroic when it is known that, until the husband's ruin, the married pair had lived somewhat coldly together. But is not a fervent devotion a substitute for love? Or rather, is it not love itself? Love flows from many sources, and of these, self-sacrifice is the most abundant.

They had never had children at Petersburg; they had five in Siberia.

This man, rendered glorious by the generosity of his wife, had become a sacred object in the eyes of all who approached him. Who indeed would not venerate the object of an affection so sacred?

However criminal the Prince Troubetzkoi may have been, his pardon, which the Emperor will perhaps never grant, for he believes that he owes it both to his people and himself to maintain an implacable severity, has been doubtless accorded by the King of Kings. The almost supernatural virtues of a wife could appease the wrath of a God, they could not disarm human justice. The reason is, that Divine Omnipotence is a reality, whilst that of the Emperor of Russia is a fiction.

He would have long since pardoned the criminal had he been as great as he pretends to be; but clemency, independently of its being repugnant to his natural disposition, appears to him a weakness by which a king would degrade the kingly office: habituated as he is to measure his power by the fear which he inspires, he would regard mercy as a violation of his code of political morality.

For my part, I only judge of a man's power over others by that which I see him exercise over himself, and I cannot believe his authority safely established, until he can venture to forgive: the Emperor Nicholas ventures only to punish. Pardon might be a dangerous example to a people who are still so rude in the depths of their hearts. The prince lowers himself to the level of his savage subjects; he hardens himself with them; he does not fear to brutalise them in order to attach them: people and sovereign emulate each other in deceptions, prejudices, and inhumanity. Abominable combination of barbarism and weakness, interchange of ferocity, circulation of falsehood which warms the life of a monster!—a cadaverous body whose blood is poison. Such is despotism in its essence and its action.

The husband and wife have lived for fourteen years by the

side, so to speak, of the Uralian mines; for the arms of a labourer like the prince are little suited to the work of the pick-axe. He is there for the sake of being there, and that is all: but he is a convict, and we shall soon see to what this condition condemns a man—*and his children!*

There is no lack of good Russians in Petersburg, and I have met some, who view the life of the convicts at the mines as very bearable, and who complain of the exaggeration with which the *modern makers of fine speeches* describe the sufferings of the traitors in the Uralian mountains. They own that they are not allowed to receive any money, but their relations are suffered to send them provisions. Provisions! there are few that could be forwarded so great a distance, without being rendered unfit for use. But the courtiers of the executioner always find the punishment too merciful for the crime.

However great may be the luxuries of life in Siberia, the health of the Princess Troubetzkoi is injured by her sojourn at the mines. It is difficult to understand how a woman accustomed to all the delicacies of life in the highest ranks of a luxurious capital, has been able to support so long the privations of every kind to which she has voluntarily submitted. She wished to live, she did live—she even gave life; she reared her offspring under a zone where the length and the rigour of winter seem to us inimical to existence. The thermometer falls there, yearly, to a temperature that might alone suffice to destroy the human race. But this saint-like woman had other cares to think of.

At the conclusion of seven years of exile, as she saw her infants growing around her, she thought it her duty to write to one of her family to beg that they would humbly supplicate the Emperor to suffer them to be sent to Petersburg, or to some other civilised city, in order to receive a suitable education.

The petition was laid at the feet of the Czar, and the worthy successor of the Ivans and of Peter I. answered that the children of a convict,—convicts themselves, would always be sufficiently learned!

After this answer, the family—the mother and the condemned man,—were silent for seven more weary years. Humanity, honour, Christian charity, outraged religion, alone pleaded in their favour; but this was done silently: not a voice was raised to appeal against such *justice*. Nevertheless, a renewal of misery has now called forth a last cry from the depths of this abyss.

The prince has completed his term of labour in the mines, and now the exiles, liberated, as they call it, are condemned to form, they and their young family, a colony in the most remote corner of the desert. The locality of their new residence, *designedly* chosen by the Emperor himself, is so wild that the name of that howling wilderness is not even yet marked on the ordnance maps of Russia, the most exact and minute geographical maps that exist.

It will be easily understood that the condition of the princess (I name her only) is more wretched since she has been permitted to inhabit this solitude. It should be observed that in the language of the oppressed, as interpreted by the oppressor, permissions are obligatory. At the mines, she could find warmth in the bosom of the earth, her family had companions in misfortune, silent consolers, admiring witnesses of her heroism. The human eye contemplated and respectfully deplored her martyrdom, a circumstance which, externally, rendered it the more sublime. Hearts beat in her presence,—in short, without even having to speak, she felt herself in society; for let governments do their worst, pity will still spring to life wherever there are men. But what hope can there be of awakening the sympathy of bears, or of melting eternal ices amid impenetrable woods, or marshes that have no bounds? What means can there be found of excluding the mortal cold from a hovel?—and how is subsistence for five children to be obtained a hundred leagues, perhaps more, from any human abode, unless it be that of the superintendant of the colonies?—for this is called colonising in Siberia!

What I admire as much as the resignation of the princess, is the eloquence, the ingenious tenderness she must have possessed, to overcome the resistance of her husband, and to succeed in persuading him that she was less to be pitied in suffering with him than she would be in Petersburg, surrounded with all the comforts and elegances of life. This triumph of devotion recompensed by success, for her husband finally consented, I view as a miracle of delicacy, of energy, and of sensibility. To know how to sacrifice self is as noble as it is rare,—to know how to accept such a sacrifice, is sublime.

At present this father and mother, abandoned in the desert, without physical powers, stript of every aid, lost to their fellow men, punished in their children, whose innocence only serves to aggravate their anguish, know not how to provide food for themselves and their little ones. These young convicts by birth, these pariahs of the imperial realm, if they have no longer a country, no longer a position in the community, have yet bodies that need food and raiment. A mother, whatever dignity, whatever elevation of soul she may possess, could she see the fruit of her body perish rather than supplicate a pardon? No; she again humbled herself, and this time it was not through Christian virtue: the lofty woman was conquered by the despairing mother. She saw her children ill, and had nothing wherewith to administer to their wants. In this extreme misery, her husband, his heart withered by his misfortune, left her to act according to her impulse, and the princess wrote a second letter from her hut of exile. The letter was addressed to her family, but meant for the Emperor. This was to place herself at the feet of her enemy, to forget what she owed to herself; but who would think the less of her for doing so? God calls his elect to every species of sacrifice, even to the sacrifice of the most legitimate pride. The man who would understand life without recognising eternity, can only have seen the things of this world on their sunny side: he must have lived on illusions, as they would have me do in Russia. The letter of the princess has reached its destination, the Emperor has read it; and it was to communicate to me this letter that I was stopped at the moment of my departure. I cannot regret the delay. I have never read anything more simple and touching. Actions like the writer's can dispense with words; she uses her privileges as a heroine, and is laconic, even in imploring the life of her children. In a few lines, she states her situation, without declamation and without complaint; she concludes by imploring this single favour—the permission to live within reach of an apothecary, in order to be able to get some medicine for her children when they are ill. The environs of Tobolsk, of Irkutsk, or of Orenburg, would appear to her paradise! In the concluding words of her letter, she ceases addressing herself to the Emperor, she forgets every thing except her husband. With a feeling and a dignity which would merit the pardon of the worst crime (and she is innocent of any; the monarch she addresses is all-powerful; God alone judges his acts!) "I am very miserable," she says; "but were it to come over again, I should do as I have done."

There was in the family of this woman an individual bold enough to dare to carry her letter to the Emperor, and even to support with an humble petition the request of a disgraced relative. He spoke only of that relative as a criminal, although, before any other being but the Emperor of Russia, a man would have gloried in avowing his relationship with so noble a victim of conjugal duty. Well! after fourteen years of continued vengeance, continued but not glutted—how can I moderate my indignation? to use gentler terms in recounting such facts would be to betray a sacred cause: let the Russians object against them if they dare; I had rather fail in respect to despotism than to misfortune. They will crush me if they can, but, at least, Europe shall know that a man to whom sixty millions of men never cease saying that he is omnipotent, revenges himself!—Yes, revenge is the proper name for such a justice! After fourteen years, then, of vengeance, this woman, whose misery had been ennobled by so much heroism, obtained from the Emperor Nicholas no other answer than the following:—"I am astonished that any one again dares to speak to me (twice in fifteen years!) of a family, the head of which has conspired against me!" The reader may doubt this answer,—I could yet do so myself, and nevertheless I have clear proof of its truth.

The relations of the exiles, the Troubetzkoï, a powerful family, live at Petersburg, and they attend the court! Such is the spirit, the dignity, the independence of the Russian aristocracy! In this empire of violence, fear justifies every thing,—and yet more, it is the only merit that is sure to receive reward.

I have no more hesitation, no more uncertainty of opinion as regards the character of the Emperor Nicholas; my judgment of that prince is at length formed. He is a man of talent and of resolution; it needs that he should be, to constitute himself the gaoler of the third of the globe; but he wants magnanimity: the use that he makes of his power only too clearly proves this to me. May God pardon him! happily, I shall never see him again.

What heart would not bleed at the idea of the anguish of this unhappy mother? My God! if such be the destiny thou hast ordained upon earth for the sublimest virtue, show to it thy heaven, —open to it the gates thereof before the hour of death! Imagine what must be the feelings of this woman when she casts her eyes on her children; and when, aided by her husband, she labours to supply the education which they need! Education! it will be poison for those who have no names, but are marked and numbered like the beasts of the herd. Can the exiles deny all their recollections, all their habits, in order to hide the misfortune of their position from the innocent victims of their love? Would not the native refinement of their parents inspire these young savages with ideas that they could never realise? What danger, what momentary torment for them, and what insupportable constraint for their mother! This mental torture, added to such a load of physical sufferings, haunts me like a hideous dream from which I cannot awake. Since yesterday morning it has pursued me incessantly, whispering at every moment of the day—What is the Princess Troubetzkoi now doing?—what is she saying to her children?—with what look is she watching over them?—what prayer is she addressing to God for these beings, damned ere they were born by the providence of the Russians? This punishment inflicted upon an innocent generation disgraces an entire people!

I shall finish my journey, but without going to Borodino; without being present at the arrival of the court at the Kremlin; without speaking more of the Emperor. What can I say of this prince that the reader does not now know as well as I? To form an idea of men and things in this land, it is necessary to remember that plenty of occurrences similar to the one I have related take place here, though they remain unknown. It required an extraordinary concurrence of circumstances to reveal to me the facts which my conscience obliges me here to record.

I am about to place in one sealed packet all the papers that I have written since my arrival in Russia, including the present chapter, and to deposit them in safe hands; things which are not easily found in Petersburg. I shall then finish the day by writing an official letter, which will leave by the post to-morrow. In this, every thing will be so carefully praised and admired that I have rational hopes, the letter, seized on the frontier, will assure my tranquillity during the remainder of my journey. If my friends hear no more of me, they must suppose I am sent to Siberia: that journey could alone alter my intention as regards proceeding to Moscow, which intention will be delayed in execution no longer, for my feldjäger has just arrived to inform me that the post-horses will be at my door without fail to-morrow morning.

❖

ROAD FROM PETERSBURG TO MOSCOW ❖ SPEED OF TRAVELLING ❖ A
LIVONIAN ❖ PUNISHMENT OF A POSTILLION ❖ ENGLISH CARRIAGES ON
RUSSIAN ROADS ❖ THE COUNTRY PEOPLE ❖ ASPECT OF THE COUNTRY ❖
THE POST-HOUSE ❖ MOUNTAINS OF VALDAI ❖ COSTUME OF THE PEASANTRY
❖ RUSSIAN LADIES EN DÉSHABILLE ❖ SMALL RUSSIAN TOWNS ❖
TORJECK RUSSIAN LEATHER ❖ CHICKEN
FRICASSEE ❖ A DOUBLE
ROAD
❖

CHAPTER XXII

❖

I am writing at Pomerania, a post town eighteen leagues from Petersburg.

To travel post on the road from Petersburg to Moscow, is to treat one's self for whole days to the sensation experienced in descending the *montagnes Russes* at Paris. It would be well to bring an English carriage to Petersburg, if only for the pleasure of travelling on really elastic springs this famous road, the best chaussée in Europe, according to the Russians, and, I believe, according to strangers also. It must be owned that it is well kept, although hard, by reason of the nature of the materials, which broken as they are in tolerably small pieces, form, in encrusting over the surface, little immovable asperities, which shake the carriages to a degree that causes something to come out of place at every stage. As much time is thus lost as is gained by the speed at which they drive; for we rush along, in a whirlwind of dust, with the rapidity of a hurricane chasing the clouds before it. An English carriage is very pleasant for the few first stages; but in the long run, the necessity of a Russian equipage to withstand the pace of the horses and the hardness of the road, is discovered. The rails of the bridges are formed of handsome iron balustrades, and the granite pillars which support them are carved with the imperial arms. This road is broader than those of England; it is also as even, although less easy; the horses are small, but full of muscle.

My feldjäger has ideas, a bearing, and a person, which prevent my forgetting the spirit which reigns in his country. On arriving at the second stage, one of our four horses fell on the road. Notwithstanding the advanced season, the middle of the day is still excessively hot, and the dust renders the air suffocating. It appeared to me that the horse had fallen under the influence of the heat, and that unless he were instantly bled, he would die. I therefore called the feldjäger, and taking from my pocket a case containing a fleam, I offered it to him, telling him to make prompt use of it if he wished to save the life of the poor brute. He answered, with a malicious phlegm, while declining the instrument I offered, that it was of no consequence, as we were at the end of the stage. Thereupon, without aiding the unfortunate coachman to disengage the animal, he entered the stable hard by, in order to prepare another set of horses.

The Russians are far from having, like the English, a law to protect animals from the ill-treatment of men. On the contrary, it is among them as necessary to plead the cause of the men, as it is in London to plead the cause of the dogs and horses. My feldjäger would not believe in the existence of such a law.

This man, who is a Livonian by birth, fortunately for me, speaks German. Under the exterior of an officious civility and obsequious language, may be discovered much obstinacy and insolence. His figure is slim; his flaxen hair gives to his features an infantile appearance which belies their really dry and harsh expression. That of his eyes, more especially, is crafty and relentless. They are grey edged with almost white lashes; his thick eyebrows are very light, his forehead full but low; his skin would be fair were it not tanned by the constant action of the air; his mouth is finely formed, always closed, and the lips so small that they are not seen until he speaks. His clean and neatly-fitting uniform of Russian green, with a leather belt round his waist, buckled in front, gives him a certain air of elegance. He has a light step, but an extremely slow understanding.

Notwithstanding the discipline under which he has been bred, it can be perceived that he is not of Russian descent. The race, half Swedish, half Teutonic, which peoples the southern side of the Gulf of Finland, is very different from that either of the Finns or the Slavonians. The real Russians are, in their primitive endowments, more to be admired than the mixed populations that defend the frontiers of their land.

This feldjäger inspires me with but little confidence. Officially, he is my guide and protector; nevertheless I see in him only a disguised spy, and feel towards him as towards one who might at any moment receive an order to become my gaoler.

I have already spoken of the mingled interchanges of politeness and brutality, of the bows and blows which the Russians practise among each other; here, among a thousand, is another example. The postillion who brought me to the post-house from whence I write, had incurred at the stage where he set out, by I know not what fault, the wrath of his comrade, the head hostler. The latter trampled him, child as he is, under his feet, and struck him with blows which must have been severe, for I heard them at some distance resounding against the breast of the sufferer. When the executioner was weary of his task, the victim rose, breathless and trembling, and without proffering a word, readjusted his hair, saluted his superior, and, encouraged by the treatment he had received, mounted lightly the box to drive me at a hard gallop four and a half or five leagues in one hour. The Emperor travels at the rate of seven. The trains on the railways would have to do their best to keep up with his carriage. What numbers of men must be beaten and horses killed, in order to render possible so amazing a velocity, and that for one hundred and eighty leagues in succession! Some pretend that the incredible rapidity of these journeys in an open carriage is injurious to the health; and that few lungs can stand the practice of cleaving the air so rapidly. The Emperor is so constituted that he can support every thing; but his son, who is less robust, suffers from the demands made upon his frame, under the pretext of fortifying it. With the character which his manners, expression, and language convey the idea of his possessing, this prince must suffer mentally as well as physically. With reference to him may be applied the words of Champfort,—"In the life of man, an age inevitably arrives at which the heart must either break or harden."

The Russian people give me the idea of being men endowed with gentle dispositions, but who believe themselves born exclusively for violence. With the easy indifference of the Orientals they unite a taste for the arts, which is tantamount to saying that nature has given them the desire of liberty; whilst their masters have made them the machines of oppression. A man, as soon as he rises a grade above the common level, acquires the right, and, furthermore, contracts the obligation to maltreat his inferiors, to whom it is his duty to transmit the blows that he receives from those above him. Thus does the spirit of iniquity descend from stage to stage down to the foundations of this unhappy society, which subsists only by violence—a violence so great, that it forces the slave to falsify himself by thanking his tyrant; and this is what they here call public order; in other words, a gloomy tranquillity, a fearful peace, for it resembles that of the tomb. The Russians, however, are proud of this calm. So long as a man has not made up his mind to go on all-fours, he must necessarily pride himself in something, were it only to preserve his right to the title of a human creature. . . .

Some leagues from this place I met a Russian of my acquaintance, who had been to visit one of his estates, and was returning to Petersburg. We stopped to talk for a short time. The Russian, after casting his eye over my carriage, began to laugh, and, pointing to its various complicated parts, said, "You see all these things, they will not keep together till you reach Moscow: foreigners who persist in using their own carriages when in our country, set out as you did, but return by the diligence."

"In going no farther than Moscow even?"

"No farther even than Moscow."

"The Russians told me that it was the best road in all Europe; I took them at their word."

"There are bridges yet wanting: the road in many parts requires mending; the highway has frequently to be left in order to cross temporary bridges of rude construction, and, owing to the carelessness of our drivers, the carriages of foreigners always break in these awkward places."

"My carriage is an English one, and its goodness has already been well tested by long journeys."

"They drive no where so fast as in Russia; the carriages, under this rapid motion, go through all the movements of a vessel in a storm, the pitching and the rolling combined. To resist such strains on a road like this, even, but whose foundation is hard, it is necessary, I again repeat, that the carriages should be built in the country."

"You have still the old prejudice for heavy and massive equipages; they are not, however, the strongest."

"I wish you a pleasant journey: let me hear if your carriage reaches Moscow."

Scarcely had I left this bird of ill omen when a part of the axle broke. Fortunately, we were near the end of the stage, where I am now detained. I should mention that I have yet only travelled 18 leagues out of the 180. . . . I shall be obliged to deny myself the pleasure of fast driving, and am learning to say in Russian, "gently," which is just the opposite of the usual motto of Russian travellers.

A Russian coachman attired in his cafetan of coarse cloth, or if the weather is warm, as it is to-day, in his coloured shirt or tunic, appears, at first sight, like an oriental. In simply observing the attitude he assumes when placing himself upon his seat, we may recognise the grace of the Asiatic. In travelling post, the Russians drive from the box, dispensing with postillions, unless a very heavy carriage requires a set of six or eight horses, and even in that case one of the men mounts the box. The coachman holds in his hands a whole bundle of cords: these are the eight reins of the team, two for each of the four horses harnessed abreast. The grace, ease, agility, and safety with which he directs this picturesque set-out, the quickness of his slightest movements, the lightness of his step when he reaches the ground, his erect stature, his manner of wearing his dress, in short, his whole person reminds me of the most naturally elegant people on the earth—the Gitanos* of Spain. The Russians are fair-complexioned Gitanos.

I have already noticed some female peasants less ugly than those seen in the streets of Petersburg. Their form invariably wants elegance, but their complexion is fresh and bright. At this season, their head-dress consists of an Indian handkerchief, tied round the head, and the ends of which fall behind with a grace that is natural to the people. They often wear a little pelisse

* Gipsies.—*Trans.*

reaching to the knees, drawn round the waist by a girdle, slit on each side below the hips, and opening in front so as to show the petticoat underneath. The appearance of this dress is tasteful, but it is their boots which disfigure the persons of the women. The leather is greasy, the feet are large and rounded at the toe, and the folds and wrinkles entirely conceal the shape of the legs: so clumsy are they, that it might be supposed the wives had stolen them from their husbands.

The houses resemble those that I described in the excursion to Schlusselburg, but they are not so elegant. The appearance of the villages is monotonous. A village consists always of two lines, more or less extended, of wooden cottages, regularly ranged at a certain distance backwards from the road, for, in general, the street of the village is broader than the embankment of the high-way. Each cabin, constructed of pieces of roughly-hewn wood, presents its gable to the street. All these habitations are of similar construction; but, notwithstanding their wearisome uniformity, an air of comfort, and even prosperity, appears to reign in the villages. They are rural without being picturesque. I breathe in them the calm of pastoral life, which is doubly agreeable after Petersburg. The country people are not gay or smiling, but they have not the miserable appearance of the soldiers and the dependents of the government. Among all the Russians, these are they who suffer least from the want of liberty. The labours of agriculture tend to reconcile man to social life whatever it may cost; they inspire him with patience, and enable him to support every thing, provided he is allowed to give himself up undisturbed to occupations which are so congenial to his nature.

The country that I have hitherto traversed is a poor, marshy forest, covered, as far as the eye can reach over a sterile plain, with miserable, stunted, and thinly-scattered birch and pine; there are neither cultivated lands nor thick flourishing plantations of wood to be seen. The cattle are of a wretched breed. The climate oppresses the animals as much as despotism does the men. It might be said that nature and society vie with each other in their efforts to render life difficult. When we think of the physical obstacles that had here to be encountered in order to organise a society, we have no longer a right to be surprised at any thing, unless it be that material civilisation is so far advanced as we perceive it to be among a people so little favoured by nature.

Can it be true that there are in the unity of ideas, and the fixedness of things, compensations for even the most revolting oppression? I think not; but were it proved to me that this system was the only one under which the Russian empire could have been founded or maintained, I should answer by a simple question: was it essential to the destinies of the human race that the marshes of Finland should be peopled, and that the unfortunate beings brought there should erect a city marvellous to behold, but which is in reality nothing more than a mimicry of Western Europe? The civilised world has only gained from the aggrandisement of the Muscovites, the fear of a new invasion, and the model of a despotism without pity and without precedent, unless it be in ancient history.

The house in which I write exhibits a taste and neatness that contrast strangely with the nakedness of the surrounding country. It is both post-house and tavern, and I find it almost clean. It might be taken for the country-house of some retired, independent person. Stations of this kind, though not so well kept as that of Pomerania, are maintained at certain distances on the road, at the expense of government. The walls and ceilings of the one I am in are painted as in Italy; the ground floor, composed of several spacious rooms, very much resembles a restaurateur in one of the French provinces. The furniture is covered with leather; large sofas are every where to be found, which might serve as a substitute for beds, but I have had too much experience to think of sleeping or even of sitting on them. In Russian inns, not excepting those of the best description, all wooden furniture with stuffed cushions are so many hives where vermin swarm and multiply.

I carry with me my bed, which is a masterpiece of Russian industry. If I break down again before I reach Moscow, I shall have time to make use of this piece of furniture, and shall applaud myself for my precaution.

❖ ❖ ❖

I am now writing at Yedrova, between Great Novgorod and Valdai. There are no distances in Russia—so say the Russians, and all the travellers have agreed to repeat the saying. I had adopted the same notion, but unpleasant experience obliges me to maintain precisely the contrary. There is nothing but distance in Russia; nothing but empty plains extending farther than the eye can reach. Two or three interesting spots are separated from each other by immense spaces. These intervals are deserts, void of all picturesque beauty: the high road destroys the poetry of the steppe; and there remains nothing but extension of space, monotony, and sterility. All is naked and poor; there is nothing to inspire awe as on a soil made illustrious by the glory of its inhabitants,—a soil like Greece or Judea, devastated by history, and become the poetical cemetery of nations; neither is there any of the grandeur of a virgin nature; the scene is merely ugly; it is sometimes a dry plain, sometimes a marshy, and these two species of sterility alone vary the landscape. A few villages, becoming less neat in proportion as the distance from Petersburg increases, sadden the landscape instead of enlivening it. The houses are only piles of the trunks of trees, badly put together, and supporting roofs of plank, to which in winter an extra cover of thatch is sometimes added. These dwellings must be warm, but their appearance is cheerless. The rooms are dark, and tainted for want of air. They have no beds; in summer the inmates sleep on benches which form a divan around the walls of the chamber, and in winter, on the stove, or on the floor around it: in other words, a Russian peasant encamps all his life. The word *reside* implies a comfortable mode of life: domestic habits are unknown to this people.

In passing through Great Novgorod I saw none of the ancient edifices of that city, which was for a long time a republic, and which became the cradle of the Russian empire. I was fast asleep when we drove through it. If I return to Germany by Wilna and Warsaw, I shall neither have seen the Volkof, that river which was the tomb of so many citizens—for the turbulent republic did not spare the life of its children,—nor yet the Church of Saint Sophia, with which is associated the memory of the most glorious events of Russian history, before the devastation and final subjection of Novgorod by Ivan IV., that model of all modern tyrants.

I had heard much of the mountains of Valdai, which the Russians pompously entitle the Muscovite Switzerland. I am approaching this city, and, for the last thirty leagues, have observed that the surface of the soil has become uneven, though not mountainous. It is indented with numerous small ravines, where the road is so formed that we mount and descend the declivities at a gallop. It is only when changing horses that time is lost, for the Russian hostlers are slow in harnessing and putting-to.

The peasants of this canton wear a cap, broad and flat at the top, but fitting very closely round the head; it resembles a mushroom; a peacock's feather is sometimes twisted round the band, and when the men wear a hat, the same ornament is also adopted. Instead of boots they most commonly have plats of reeds, woven by the peasants themselves, and worn as leggings fastened with packthread laces. They look better in sculpture than on the living man. Some ancient statues prove the antiquity of the attire.

The female peasants are rarely to be seen.* We met ten men for one woman. Such as I have noticed wear a dress that indicates a total absence of female vanity. It consists of a species of dressing-gown, very wide and loose, which fastens round the neck and reaches to the ground. A large apron of the same length, fastened across the shoulders by two short straps, completes their rustic and ungainly costume. They nearly all go barefoot; the wealthier wear the clumsy boots I have already described. Indian handkerchiefs or other pieces of stuff are bound closely round the head. The real national female head-dress is only worn on holydays. It is the same as that of the ladies of the court; a species, namely, of shako, open at the top, or rather a very lofty diadem, embroidered with precious stones when worn by the ladies, and with flowers in gold or silver thread when on the heads of the peasants. This crown has an imposing effect, and resembles no other kind of head-dress, unless it be the tower of the goddess Cybele.

The peasant women are not the only Russian females who neglect their persons. I have seen ladies whose dress when travel-

---

* But little more than a hundred years ago the Russian women never went abroad.

ling was of the most slovenly character. This morning, in a post-house where I stopped to breakfast, I encountered an entire family whom I had left in Petersburg, where they inhabit one of those elegant palaces which the Russians are so proud of showing to foreigners. There, these ladies were splendidly attired in the Paris fashions; but at the inn where, thanks to the new accident that had happened to my carriage, I was overtaken by them, they were altogether different persons. So whimsically were they metamorphosed that I could scarcely recognise them: the fairies had become sorceresses. Imagine young ladies whom you had only seen in elegant society, suddenly reappearing before you in a costume worse than that of Cinderella; dressed in old nightcaps that might have once been white, extremely dirty gowns, neck-handkerchiefs that resembled ragged napkins, and old shoes in which they walked slipshod. It was enough to make a man fancy himself bewitched.

The fair travellers were attended by a considerable retinue. The multitude of lacqueys and waiting-women, muffled in old clothes still more loathsome than those of their mistresses, moving about in all directions, and keeping up an infernal noise, completed the illusion that it was the scene of a meeting of witches. They screamed and scampered here and there, drank and stuffed themselves with eatables in a manner that was sufficient to take away the appetite of the most hungry beholder; and yet these ladies could complain before me in an affected manner of the dirtiness of the post-house,—as if they had any right to find fault with slovenliness. I could have imagined myself among a camp of gipsies, except that gipsies are without pretence or affectation. I, who pique myself on not being fastidious when travelling, find the post-houses established on this road by the government, that is, by the Emperor, sufficiently comfortable. I consider that I have fared well in them: a man may even sleep at night, provided he can dispense with a bed; for this nomade people are acquainted only with the Persian carpet or the sheep-skin, or a mat stretched upon a divan under a tent, whether of canvass or of wood, for in either case it is a souvenir of the bivouac. The use of a bed, as an indispensable article of furniture, has not yet been recognised by the people of Slavonian race: beds are rarely seen beyond the Oder.

Sometimes, on the borders of the little lakes which are scattered over the immense marsh called Russia, a distant town is to be seen; a cluster, namely, of small houses built of grey boards, which, reflected in the water, produce a very picturesque effect. I have passed through two or three of these hives of men, but I have only particularly noticed the town of Zimagoy. It consists of a rather steep street of wooden houses, and is a league in length; at some distance, on the other side of one of the creeks of the little lake on which it stands, is seen a romantic convent, whose white towers rise conspicuously above a forest of firs, which appeared to me loftier and more thickly grown than any that I have hitherto observed in Russia. When I think of the consumption of wood in this country, both for the construction and the warming of houses, I am astonished that any forests remain in the land. All that I had hitherto seen were miserable thickets, scattered here and there, which could only serve to interfere with the culture of the soil.

❖   ❖   ❖

I resume my pen at Torjeck. It is impossible to see far on plains, because every object is a barrier to the eye: a bush, a rail, or a building conceals leagues of land between itself and the horizon. It may also be observed that, here, no landscape engraves itself on the memory, no sites attract the eye, not one picturesque line is to be discovered. On a surface void of all objects or variety, there should at least be the hues of the southern sky; but they also are wanting in this part of Russia, where nature must be viewed as an absolute nullity.

What they call the mountains of Valdai are a series of declivities and acclivities as monotonous as the heathy plains of Novgorod.

The town of Torjeck is noted for its manufactures of leather. Here are made those beautifully-wrought boots, those slippers embroidered with gold and silver thread, which are the delight of the *elegants* of Europe, especially of those who love any thing that is singular, provided it comes from a distance. The travellers who pass through Torjeck pay there for its manufactured leathers a much larger price than that at which they are sold at Petersburg or Moscow. The beautiful morocco, or perfumed Russian leather, is made at Kazan; and they say it is at the fair of Nijni that it can be bought most cheaply, and that a selection may be made out of mountains of skins.

Torjeck is also celebrated for its chicken fricassees. The Emperor, stopping one day at a little inn of this town, was served with a hash of fattened chickens, which to his great astonishment he found excellent. Immediately the fricassee of Torjeck became celebrated throughout Russia.* The following is their origin. An unfortunate Frenchman had been well received and treated in this town by a female innkeeper. Before leaving he said to her, "I cannot pay you, but I will make your fortune," whereupon he showed her how to fricasee chickens. As good luck would have it, this precious recipe was, at least so it is said, first prepared for the Emperor. The innkeeper of Torjeck is dead; but her children have inherited her renown, and they maintain it.

Torjeck, when that town first breaks upon the view of the traveller, conveys the idea of a camp in the midst of an immense corn field. Its white houses, its towers and pavilion-shaped domes, remind him of the mosques and minarets of the East. Gilded turrets, round and square steeples, some ornamented with little columns, and all painted green or blue, announce the vicinity of Moscow. The land around is well cultivated. It is a plain covered with rye, which plain, though devoid of all other objects, I greatly prefer to the sickly woods that have wearied my eyes for the last two days. The tilled earth is at any rate fertile, and the richness of a country will lead us to forgive its want of picturesque beauty; but a tract that is sterile, and yet possesses none of the majesty of the wilderness, is of all others the most tedious to travel over.

I had forgotten to mention a singular object which struck me at the commencement of the journey.

---

* There is nothing which an Emperor of Russia could not bring into fashion in his country. At Milan, if the viceroy patronises an actor or singer, the reputation of the artist is at once lost, and he is hissed unmercifully.

Between Petersburg and Novgorod, I remarked, for several successive stages, a second road that ran parallel to the principal highway, though at a considerable distance from it. It was furnished with bridges and every thing else that could render it safe and passable, although it was much less handsome, and less smooth than the grand route. I asked the keeper of a post-house the meaning of this singularity, and was answered, through my feldjäger, that the smaller road was destined for waggons, cattle, and travellers, when the Emperor, or other members of the imperial family, proceeded to Moscow. The dust and obstructions that might incommode or retard the august travellers, if the grand route remained open to the public, were thus avoided. I cannot tell whether the innkeeper was amusing himself at my expense, but he spoke in a very serious manner, and seemed to consider it very natural that the sovereign should engross the road in a land where the sovereign is every thing. The king who said, *"I am France,"* stopped to let a flock of sheep pass; and under his reign, the foot passenger, the waggoner, and the clown who travelled the public road, repeated our old adage to the princes whom they met: "the high road belongs to every body:" what really constitutes a law is the manner in which it is applied.

In France, manners and customs have in every age rectified political institutions; in Russia the harshness of the institutes is increased in their application, so that, there, the consequences are worse than the principles.

❖

CHAPTER XXIII

❖

. . . Once again, a delay on the road, and always from the same cause!—we break down regularly every twenty leagues. Of a truth the Russian officer at Pomerania was a *gettatore!*

There are moments when, notwithstanding my protestations, and the reiterated word *tischné* (gently), the drivers proceed at a rate that obliges me to close my eyes in order to avoid giddiness. Among them, I have not seen one deficient in skill, and some of them possess a dexterity that is extraordinary. The Neapolitans and the Russians are the first coachmen in the world; the best among them are old men and children: the children especially surprise me. The first time that I saw my carriage and my life about to be entrusted to the care of an infant of ten years old, I protested against such imprudence; but my feldjäger assured me it was the custom, and as his person was exposed as much as mine, I believed him. Our four horses, whose fiery eagerness and wild appearance were by no means adapted to re-assure me, set off at a gallop. The experienced child knew better than to endeavour to stop them; on the contrary, he urged them to their utmost speed, and the carriage followed as it best might. This pace, which accorded better with the temperament of the animals than the qualities of the calèche, was kept up throughout the stage, although at the end of the first verst the breathless horses began to tire, and the coachman to become the most impatient. Each time they relaxed their pace he applied the whip until

❖ 373 ❖

they resumed their former speed. The emulation which easily establishes itself between four spirited animals, harnessed abreast, soon brought us to the end of the stage. These horses would rather die than give in. After observing their character, and that of the men who drive them, I soon perceived that the word *tischné,* which I had learned to pronounce with so much care, was utterly useless in this journey, and that I should even expose myself to accident if I persisted in checking the ordinary rate of driving. The Russians have the gift of equilibration; men and horses would lose their perpendicular in a slow trot. Their mode of getting over the ground would greatly divert me if my carriage were of more solid construction, but at each turn of the wheels I expect it to fall to pieces; and we break down so often that my apprehensions are only too well justified. Without my Italian valet, who officiates also as wheelwright and smith, we should already have come to a stand-still. I cannot cease from admiring the air of nonchalance with which the coachmen take their seats; there is a grace about it far preferable to the studied elegance of civilised drivers. In descending the hills, they rise on their feet, and drive standing, the body slightly bent, the arms stretched forward, and the eight reins drawn well up. In this attitude, which may be seen in ancient bas-reliefs, they might be taken for charioteers of the circus. When thus driving, we rush through the air amid clouds of dust, and seem scarcely to touch the earth. The English springs cause the body of the coach to sway like a vessel in a heavy gale, and there appears then to be established between the will of man and the instinct of the animals, a relation which I cannot understand. It is not by a mechanical impulse that the equipage is guided!—there seems to be an interchange of thoughts and sentiments, an animal magic, a real magnetic influence. The coachman is miraculously obeyed; he guides his four steeds abreast as if they were but one horse. Sometimes he draws them together into scarcely more space than is commonly occupied by two wheelers; sometimes he so spreads them out that they cover the half of the high road. In point of civilisation, every thing is incomplete in Russia, because every thing is modern. On the finest road in the world, there are still frequent interruptions; repairs going on, or temporary bridges in place of broken ones, which oblige us to turn off the road; this the driver does without for a moment slackening the pace. The road is also much obstructed by the little carts and waggons of carriers, ten of which are often guided by one man, who cannot possibly keep them all in line. Without great dexterity on the part of the Russian coachmen it would be difficult to find a passage through such moving labyrinths. The bodies of these carriers' carts resemble large casks cut in half lengthways, and open at the top; they are each drawn by one small horse, who, without much capacity as a draught horse, is full of courage and spirit, and will pull until he falls on the road: his life is, therefore, as short as it is devoted: in Russia, a horse twelve years old is a phenomenon.

Nothing can be more original, more different to what is seen elsewhere, than the various vehicles, the men, and the horses that are met on the highways of this country. Every thing that the people touch, wear, or carry, takes, unknown to themselves, a picturesque appearance: condemn a race of men, less naturally elegant, to make use of the houses, dress, and utensils of the Russians, and all these things would appear hideous; but here I find them, though foreign and unusual, striking and deserving of being painted. Oblige the Russians to wear the costume of the Paris workmen, and they would make something out of it agreeable to the eye, though never would a Russian have imagined an attire so devoid of taste. The life of this people is amusing, if not for themselves, at least for a spectator; the ingenious turn of their minds has found means to triumph over the climate, and every other obstacle that nature has opposed to social existence in a desert without poetic imagery. The contrast of the blind political submission of a people attached to the soil, with the energetic and continual struggle of that same people against the tyranny of a climate hostile to life, their conquests over nature showing itself every moment under the yoke of despotism, present an inexhaustible store for lively pictures and serious meditations. To make a journey through Russia with full advantage, it would be necessary to be accompanied by a Montesquieu and a Horace Vernet.

In none of my travels have I so much regretted my little talent for sketching. Russia is less known than India: it has been less often described and pictorially illustrated; it is nevertheless as curious a country as any in Asia, even as relates to the arts, to poetry, and to history.

Every mind seriously occupied with the ideas which ferment in the political world, cannot but profit by examining, on the spot, a community, governed on the principles which directed the most ancient states named in the annals of the world, and yet, already imbued with the ideas that are common among the most modern and revolutionary nations. The patriarchal tyranny of the Asiatic governments, in contact with the theories of modern philanthropy, the character of the people of the East and West, incompatible by nature, yet united together by coercion in a state of society semi-barbarous, but kept in order by fear, present a spectacle that can be only seen in Russia, and, assuredly, one which no man who thinks, would regret the trouble of going to contemplate.

The social, intellectual, and political state of present Russia is the result, and, so to speak, the *résumé* of the reigns of Ivan IV., surnamed, by Russia herself, the Terrible; of Peter the First, called the Great by the men who glory in aping Europe; and of Catharine II., deified by a people that dreams of the conquest of the world. Such is the formidable heritage over which the Emperor Nicholas holds sway—God knows to what purpose, and our posterity will know also!

I continue to meet, here and there, a few female peasants who are tolerably pretty, but I do not cease to exclaim against the ungraceful appearance of their costume. It is not by *their* attire that the taste for the picturesque, which I attribute to the Russians, must be judged. The dress of these women would spoil beauty the most perfect. They are, I think, the only females in the world who have taken it into their heads to make themselves a waist above instead of below the bosom. Their shapeless sacks rather than gowns, are drawn together close under the armpits. At the first sight, their entire person gives me the idea of a bale or large loose parcel, in which all the parts of the body are confounded together without care, and yet without liberty. But this costume has other inconveniences rather difficult to describe. One of the worst is, that a Russian female peasant could suckle her child over her shoulder, as do the Hottentots. Such is the inevitable deformity produced by a fashion which destroys the shape of the body. The Circassian females, who better understand the beauty of woman and the means of preserving it, wear, from their years of childhood, a belt round the waist, which they never cast off.

I observed at Torjeck a variety in the toilette of the women, which perhaps deserves to be mentioned. The females of that town wear a short mantle of velvet, silk, or black cloth, a kind of pelerine which I have not seen elsewhere, it being, unlike any other sort of cape, entirely closed in front, and opening behind between the two shoulders. It is more singular than pretty or convenient; but singularity suffices to amuse a stranger: what we seek in travelling, are proofs that we are not at home; though this is just what the Russians will not comprehend. The talent of imitating is so natural to them, that they are quite shocked when told that their land resembles no other. Originality, which to us appears a merit, is to them the remains of barbarism. They imagine that after we have given ourselves the trouble of coming so far to see them, we ought to esteem ourselves very fortunate to find, a thousand leagues from home, a bad parody of what we have left behind through love of change.

The see-saw is the favourite amusement of the Russian peasants. This exercise developes their natural talent for adjusting the equilibrium of the body; in addition to which, it is a silent pleasure, and quiet diversions best accord with the feelings of a people rendered prudent by fear.

Silence presides over all the festivals of the Russian villagers. They drink plentifully, speak little, and shout less; they either remain silent, or sing in chorus, with a nasal voice, melancholy and prolonged notes, which form a harmonious but by no means noisy accord. I have been surprised, however, to observe that almost all these melodies are deficient in simplicity.

On Sunday, in passing through populous villages, I observed rows of from four to eight young girls balancing themselves, by a scarcely perceptible movement of their bodies, on boards suspended by ropes, while, at a little distance beyond, an equal number of boys were fixed in the same manner, in face of the females. Their mute game lasted a long time; I have never had patience to wait its conclusion. Such gentle balancing is only a kind of interlude, which serves as a relaxation in the intervals of the animated diversion of their real swing or see-saw. This is a very lively game; it even renders the spectator nervous. Four cords hang from a lofty cross-beam, and, at about two feet from the earth, sustain a plank, on whose extremities two persons place themselves. This plank, and the four posts which support it, are placed in such a manner that the balancing may be performed either backwards and forwards or from side to side. The two performers, sometimes of the same, sometimes of the opposite sexes, place themselves, always standing, and with legs firmly planted, on the two extremities of the plank, where they preserve their balance by taking hold of the cords. In this attitude they are impelled through the air to a frightful height, for at every swing the machine reaches the point beyond which it would turn completely over, and its occupiers be dashed to the earth from a height of thirty or forty feet, for I have seen posts at least twenty feet high. The Russians, whose frames are singularly supple, easily maintain a balance that is to us astonishing; they exhibit much grace, boldness, and agility, in this exercise.

I have purposely stopped in several villages to observe the girls and young men thus amuse themselves together; and I have at last seen some female faces perfectly beautiful. Their complexion is of a delicate whiteness; their colour is, so to speak, under the skin, which is transparent and exquisitely smooth. Their teeth are brilliantly white; and—rarely seen beauty!—their mouths are perfectly formed copies of the antique; their eyes, generally blue, have nevertheless the oriental cast of expression, with also that unquiet and furtive glance natural to the Slavonians, who can in general look sideways, and even behind, without turning their heads. Their whole appearance possesses a great charm; but, whether from a caprice of nature, or the effects of costume, these beauties are much less often seen united in the women than in the men. Among a hundred female peasants we perhaps meet with one really beautiful, whilst the great majority of the men are remarkable for the form of their heads, and the gracefulness of their features. Among the old men there are faces with rosy cheeks and silver hair and beard, of which it may be said that time has imparted of dignity more than it has taken of youth. There are heads that would be more beautiful in pictures than any thing that I have seen of Rubens' or Titian's, but I have never observed an elderly female face worthy of being painted.

I sometimes see a regularly Grecian profile united with features of so extreme a delicacy that the expression of the countenance loses nothing by the perfect regularity of the lines. In such cases I am struck with unbounded admiration. The more common mould, however, of the features of both men and women is that of the Calmuc—high cheek-bones and flattened noses.

I have entered into several of the Russian cottages at the hour when the peasants retire to rest. These cabins are almost deprived of vital air, and have no beds: men and women lie stretched pellmell on the wooden benches which form a divan around the chamber; but the dirtiness of these rustic bivouacs has always arrested my progress; I have quickly retreated, though never speedily enough to avoid carrying away in my clothes some living memorial, as a punishment for my indiscreet curiosity.

As a protection against the short but fervent heats of summer, a divan, under a species of veranda, runs round some cottages, and serves as a bed for the family, who even sometimes prefer sleeping on the naked earth. Recollections of the East pursue the traveller everywhere. At all the post-houses into which I have entered at night, I have invariably found, ranged in the street before the door, numerous bundles of black sheep-skins. These fleeces, which I at first took for sacks, were men sleeping under the bright canopy of heaven. We have, this year, heats such as have not been known in the memory of man in Russia.

The sheep-skins, cut out as little over-coats, serve not only for clothes, but likewise for beds, carpets, and tents to the Russian peasants. The workmen, when, during the heat of the day, they take their siesta in the fields, make a picturesque tent of these pelisses to protect themselves from the rays of the sun. With the ingenious address which distinguishes the Russian labourer from those of the west of Europe, they pass the sleeves of their coat over the two handles of their wheelbarrows, and then, turning this moveable roof towards the sun, they sleep tranquilly under the rustic drapery. The sheep-skin coats are graceful in shape, and would be pretty if they were not generally so old and greasy. A poor peasant cannot often renew a vesture which costs so much.

The Russian labourer is industrious, and is ready for every difficulty in which he may be placed. He never goes out without his small hatchet, which is useful for a hundred purposes in the hands of a dexterous man in a country which is not yet in want of woods. With a Russian by your side, were you to lose yourself in a forest, you would in a very few hours have a house to pass the night in, perhaps more commodious, and assuredly more clean, than the houses of the old villages. But if the traveller possessed small articles of leather among his baggage, they would be safe nowhere. The Russians steal, with the address which they exhibit on all occasions, the straps, girths, and leathern aprons of your trunks and carriages, though the same men show every sign of being extremely devout.

I have never travelled a stage without my coachman making at least twenty signs of the cross to salute as many little chapels. Ready to fulfil with the same punctilio his obligations of politeness, he salutes also with his hat every waggoner that he meets, and their number is great. These formalities accomplished, we arrive at the end of the stage, when it is invariably found that either in putting to or detaching the horses, the adroit, pious, polite rogue has abstracted something, perhaps a leather pouch, a strap, or a wrapper; perhaps only a nail, a screw, or a wax candle from the lamps: in short, he never leaves with altogether *clean hands.*

These men are extremely greedy of money; but they dare not complain when ill paid, which has often been the case with those who have driven us the last few days, for my feldjäger retains for himself a portion of the postillion's fees, which, together with the hire of the horses for the entire journey, I paid him in advance at Petersburg. Having once observed this trick, I compensated out of my own pocket the unfortunate postillion, thus deprived of a part of the wages which, according to the ordinary custom of travellers, he had a right to expect from me; but the knavish feldjäger, having perceived my generosity (for this was the name he gave to my justice), had the audacity to complain to me openly,—saying that he could no longer act for me on the journey if I continued to thwart him in the legitimate exercise of his power.

But how can we be surprised at the want of proper feelings among the common people, in a country where the great regard the most simple rules of probity as laws proper for plebeians, but which cannot extend to persons of their rank? Let it not be supposed that I exaggerate, I state what I perceive: an aristocratic pride, degenerated in its character, and at variance with the true sentiment of honour, reigns in Russia among the greater number of influential families. Recently a great lady made to me, little knowing it, an ingenuous confession: it the more surprised me, because such sentiments, sufficiently common here among the men, are less so among the women, who have generally preserved better than their husbands and brothers the traditions of just and noble feelings. "It is impossible for us," she said, "to form any clear idea of a social state like that of yours. They tell me that in France, at present, the highest noble can be put in prison for a debt of two hundred francs; this is revolting: how different from our country! There is not in all Russia a tradesman who would dare to refuse us credit for an unlimited period. With your aristocratic notions," she added, "you must surely find yourself more at home with us. There is greater similarity between the French of the old régime and us, than between any other of the European nations."

I cannot describe the effort of self-command that it required on my part to prevent myself from suddenly and loudly protesting against the affinity of which this lady boasted. Notwithstanding my obligatory prudence, I could not help saying, that a man who would now pass among ourselves for an ultra-aristocrat, might be easily classed at Petersburg with the violent liberals; and I concluded by observing, "When you assure me that, among your families, people do not think it necessary to pay their debts, I must not take you at your word."

"You are wrong: many of us have enormous fortunes, but they would be ruined if they were to pay all they owed."

In order to explain to me the extent to which the fashionable world is imbued with the French genius and spirit, the same lady related to me instances of *impromptu* answers in verse, made in a game at the house of one of her relatives. "You see how completely French we are," she added, with a pride that awoke my inward risibility. "Yes, more so than we ourselves," I replied; and we changed the subject of discourse. I can picture to myself the astonishment of this Franco-Russian lady entering the *salons**** of Madame ———, in Paris, and inquiring of our actual France what has become of the France of Louis XV.?

Under the Empress Catherine, the conversation of the palace, and of some of the nobility, resembled that of the saloons of Paris. In the present day our discourse is more serious, or, at least, more bold than that of any of the other European people; and, in this respect, our modern Frenchmen are far from resembling the Russians, for we talk of every thing, and the Russians speak of nothing.

The reign of Catherine is profoundly impressed on the memories of several Russian ladies. These fair *aspirantes* to the title of female statesmen have a talent for politics; and, as some of them add to that gift manners which altogether remind us of the eighteenth century, they are so many travelling empresses, filling Europe with the sound of their profligacy, but who, under this unfeminine conduct, conceal a commanding and profoundly observing mind. By virtue of the spirit of intrigue that distinguishes these Aspasias of the North, there is scarcely a capital in Europe without two or three Russian ambassadors: the one, public, accredited, recognised, and clothed with all the insignia of office; the others, secret, irresponsible, and playing, in bonnet and petticoat, the double part of independent ambassador, and spy upon the official envoy.

In all ages, women have been employed with success in political negotiations. Many of our modern revolutionists have availed themselves of female aid to conspire more skilfully, more secretly, and more safely. Spain has seen these unfortunate women become heroines in the courage with which they have submitted to

---

* *The salons of a lady*, an expression newly borrowed from the restaurateurs by the people of the fashionable world.

the punishment entailed by their tender devotion—for love always forms a great part of the courage of a Spanish woman.

Among the Russian women love is only the accessory. Russia possesses a completely organised female diplomacy; and Europe is not, perhaps, sufficiently attentive to so singular a means of influence. With its concealed army of amphibious agents, its political Amazons with acute masculine minds and feminine language, the Russian court collects information, obtains reports, and even receives advice, which, if better known, would explain many mysteries, furnish a key to many inconsistencies, and reveal many littlenesses.

The political preoccupation of mind of the greater number of Russian women renders their conversation, interesting as it might be, insipid. This is more especially the case with the most distinguished women, who are naturally the most absent when the conversation does not turn upon important subjects. There is a world between their thoughts and their discourse, from whence there results a want of accord, an absence of natural manner in short, a duplicity, that is disagreeable in the ordinary relations of social life. Politics are, from their nature, but poor amusement; their tediousness is supported by a sense of duty, and sometimes, when statesmen speak, by flashes of mind which animate conversation; but the politics of the amateur are the curses of conversation.

I have been assured that the moral sentiment is scarcely developed among the Russian peasants, and my daily experience confirms the accounts that I have received.

A nobleman has related to me, that a man belonging to him, and skilful in some particular handicraft, had permission to remain in Petersburg, in order to exercise his talent there. After the expiration of two years, he was allowed to return for a few weeks to his native village to visit his wife. He came back to Petersburg on the day appointed.

"Are you satisfied with having seen your family?" asked his master. "Perfectly so," answered the workman, with great simplicity; "my wife has presented me with two more children in my absence, and the sight of them gave me great pleasure."

These poor people have nothing of their own; neither their

cottages, their wives, their children, nor even their own hearts; they have, therefore, no jealousy. Of what could they be jealous? —Of an accident? Love among them is nothing better. Such, however, is the existence of the happiest men in Russia—the serfs! I have often heard the great express envy of their lot, and perhaps with good reason.

They have no cares, they say; we take all the charge of them and their families (God knows how this charge is acquitted when the peasants become old and useless). Assured of the necessaries of life for themselves and their children, they are a hundred times less to be pitied than the free peasants are among you.

I did not reply to this panegyric on servitude; but I thought, if they have no cares, they have also no families, and therefore no affections, no pleasures, no moral sentiment, no compensation for the physical evils of life. They possess nothing; though it is individual property which makes the social man, because it alone constitutes the divisions of family.

Moral truth is the only principle that merits our devotion: to grasp it, all the efforts of the human mind tend, whatever may be their sphere of action. If, in my journeys, I take every pains to describe the world as it is, my object is to excite in the breasts of others, and in my own, regret that it is not as it should be, to arouse in human minds the sentiment of immortality, by recalling, at the sight of every injustice, every abuse inherent in the things of earth, the words of Jesus Christ, "My kingdom is not of this world."

Never have I had so frequent occasion to apply these words as since my sojourn in Russia; they occur to me at every moment. Under a despotism, all the laws are calculated to assist oppression; that is to say, the more the oppressed has reason to complain, the less has he the legal right or the temerity. Surely, before God, the evil actions of a free citizen are more criminal than the evil actions of a serf. He who sees every thing, takes into account the insensibility of conscience in the man debased by the spectacle of iniquity always triumphant.

It will be said that evil is evil, wherever committed; and that the man who steals at Moscow, is just as much a thief as the pickpocket in Paris. It is precisely this which I deny. On the general education that a people receives, depends in a great measure the morality of each individual; from whence it follows that a fearful and mysterious relativeness of merits and of demerits has been established by Providence between governments and subjects, and that moments arrive in the history of communities when the State is judged, condemned, and destroyed, as though it were a single individual.

The virtues, the faults, and the crimes of slaves have not the same signification as those of freemen; therefore, when I examine the character of the Russian people, I can assert as a fact which does not imply the same blame as it would with us, that in general they are deficient in spirit, delicacy, and elevation of sentiment, and that they supply the want of these qualities by patience and artifice.

"The Russian people are gentle," is often said to me. To this I answer, "I cannot give them any credit for being so: it is their habit of submission." Others say, "The Russian people are only gentle because they dare not show what is in their hearts; their fundamental sentiments are superstition and ferocity." To this I reply, "Poor creatures! they are so ill educated!"

From all that I see in this world, and especially in this country, I conclude that happiness is not the real object for which man was placed here upon earth. That object is purely religious in its character: it is moral improvement—the struggle and the victory. . . .

The Russian people are in our days the most believing among all the Christian nations: the chief cause of the little efficacy of their faith is easily seen. When the church abdicates its liberty, it loses its moral virtuality:—a slave, it can only give birth to slavery. It cannot be too often repeated that the only church really independent, is the Catholic church, which has alone preserved the trust of true charity. All the other churches form constituent parts of the state, which uses them as political instruments for maintaining its power. These churches are excellent auxiliaries of the government; complaisant towards the princes or magistrates who are the depositaries of the temporal power, hard upon the subjects, they call in Deity to aid the police. The immediate result is sure; it is good order in society: but the Catholic church, quite as powerful politically, looks higher and reaches farther. The national churches make citizens; the church universal makes men. Among the sectarians, a respect for the church is confounded with a love of country; among the Catholics, the church and regenerated humanity are one and the same thing. In Russia, respect for authority continues still the only spring of the social machine. This respect is necessary, no doubt; but, in order radically to civilise the human heart, it is necessary to teach it something more than blind obedience.

The day when the son of the Emperor Nicholas—I say the son, for this noble task does not belong to the father, obliged as he is to spend his laborious reign in drawing closer the bonds of the old military discipline which constitutes the Muscovite government,—the day when the son of the Emperor shall have taught all the classes of this nation that he who commands owes respect to him who obeys, a moral revolution will be effected in Russia; and the instrument of that revolution will be the gospel.

The longer I stay in this country the more am I impressed with the fact that contempt for the weak is contagious. This sentiment is so natural here, that those who most severely blame it come finally to partake of it. I am myself a proof in question.

In Russia the desire of travelling fast becomes a passion, and this passion serves as a pretext for every species of inhumanity. My courier has communicated it to me, and I often render myself, without at the time perceiving it, an accomplice in his acts of injustice. He is exceedingly angry whenever the coachman leaves his seat to readjust any portion of the harness, or when he stops on the road under any other pretext.

Yesterday evening, at the commencement of a stage, a child who drove us had been several times threatened with blows by the feldjäger for a fault of the kind, and I participated in the impatience and wrath of this man. Suddenly, a foal, not many days old, and well known by the boy, escaped from an inclosure bordering upon the road, and began neighing and galloping after my carriage, for he took one of the mares that drew us for his mother. The young coachman, already guilty of delay, wanted once again to stop and go to the aid of the colt, which he saw every moment in danger of being crushed under the wheels of the carriage. My courier angrily forbade him to leave his seat: the child obeyed like a good Russian, and continued to drive us at a gallop without proffering a complaint. I supported the severity of the feldjäger. I thought to myself, "It is necessary to sustain authority even when it is in fault; this is the spirit of the Russian government: my feldjäger is not over zealous; if I discourage him when he exhibits energy in performing his duty, he will leave every thing to come and go as it pleases, and be of no use to me at all: besides, it is the custom of the country; why should I be less in haste than another? my dignity as a traveller is involved; to have time to spare would be to lose my consequence in this country: here, to be important we must be impatient." While I was thus reasoning, night had come on. I accuse myself with having been more hard-hearted even than the Russians, (for I have not, like them, the habits of early life as an excuse,) thus to leave the poor colt and the unhappy child to mourn in concert; the one by neighing with all his might, the other by crying silently—a difference which gave to the brute a real advantage over the human being. I ought to have interposed my authority to cause this double punishment to cease; but no, I assisted, I contributed to the martyrdom. It was a long one, for the stage was six leagues in length. The boy, obliged to torture the animal that he wished to save, suffered with a resignation that would have touched me, had not my heart been already hardened by my abode in this country. Every time that a peasant appeared on the road, the hope of rescuing his beloved foal again revived in the bosom of the child: he made signs from afar off; he shouted when a hundred paces distant from the foot-passenger, but not daring to slacken the unmerciful gallop of our horses, he never succeeded in making himself understood in time. If ever a peasant, more quick-sighted than the others, endeavoured of himself to turn the foal, the speed of the carriage disconcerted him, and the young animal passed on close to the flank of one of our horses. The case was the same in the villages, and at last the despair of our youthful coachman became so great, that he no longer opened his mouth. The persevering little animal, only eight days old, according to our driver, had the spirit and muscle necessary to perform six leagues at a gallop!*

When this was accomplished, our slave—it is of the boy that I speak—seeing himself at length released from the rigorous yoke of discipline, called the whole village to the rescue of the foal. The energy of this spirited little creature was so great, that, notwithstanding the fatigue of such a course, notwithstanding the stiffness of his limbs, ruined before they were formed, he was still very difficult to catch. They could only take him by driving him into a stable after the mare he had mistaken for his dam. When they had placed a halter round him, they shut him up with another mare, that gave him her milk; but he had not strength left to suck. Some said he would come round by and by, others, that he was foundered and could not live. I begin to understand a little Russian, and heard this sentence pronounced by one of the elders of the village. Our little coachman completely identified himself with the young animal. Foreseeing, no doubt, the treatment that the keeper of the foals would have to suffer, he appeared in as great a consternation as if he was himself to receive the blows with which his comrade would be overwhelmed. Never have I seen the expression of despair more profoundly imprinted on the face of a child; but not one look, not one gesture of reproach against my cruel courier, escaped him. So great an empire over self, so much restraint of feeling at such an age, inspired me with fear and pity.

Meanwhile the courier, without troubling himself for a moment about the foal, or taking the least notice of the disconsolate child, proceeded gravely to make the necessary arrangements for procuring a fresh relay.

On this road, which is the finest and the most frequented in Russia, the villages where relays may be obtained are peopled with peasants purposely established there to attend to the posting. Upon the arrival of a carriage, the imperial director sends from house to house to seek for horses and a disengaged coachman. Sometimes the distances are great enough to cause a considerable delay to the traveller. I should prefer more promptness in

---

* 2⁴/10 miles English is a French *lieue de poste.*—*Trans.*

the changing of horses, and a little less speed in the driving. At the moment of leaving the broken-down foal and the forlorn young postillion, I felt no remorse; it came only upon reflection, and especially upon recording the circumstances in writing: shame then awoke repentance. Thus easily may those who breathe the air of despotism be corrupted. What do I say? In Russia, despotism is only upon the throne, but tyranny pervades the country.

Education and circumstances considered, it must be acknowledged that a Russian lord, the most accustomed to submit to, and to exercise arbitrary power, could not have committed, in the seclusion of his province, an act of cruelty more blamable than that of which I yesterday evening rendered myself guilty by my silence.

I, a Frenchman, who believe myself to possess a naturally kind disposition, who have been educated under a civilisation of ancient date, who travel among a people of whose manners I am a severe observer,—lo! even I, upon the first opportunity for practising a petty act of unnecessary cruelty, yield to the temptation. The Parisian acts like a Tartar! The evil is in the atmosphere.

In France, where they respect life, even that of the brute creation, if my postillion had not thought of rescuing the colt, I should have obliged him to stop. I should myself have appealed to the peasants for aid, and should not have proceeded on my journey until I had seen the animal in safety. Here, I have aided in destroying him by an unmerciful silence. Who would be proud of his virtues, when forced to acknowledge that they depend upon circumstances more than upon self?

A great Russian lord who, in his fits of passion, does not beat to death any of his peasants, merits praise: he is in such case humane; whilst I, a Frenchman, may be cruel for having simply suffered a foal to gallop on the road!

Even Moscow will not recompense me for the trouble I am taking to see it. Shall I give up the idea of Moscow? order the coachman to turn, and depart in all haste for Paris? To this had my reveries brought me when the day dawned. My calèche had remained open, and in my protracted doze I had not perceived the baneful influence of the dews of the north; my clothes were saturated; my hair in a state as if dripping with perspiration; all the leather about my carriage was steeped in noxious moisture; my eyes pained me, a veil seemed to obscure my sight; I remembered the Prince —— who became blind in twenty-four hours after a bivouac in Poland, under the same latitude, in a moist prairie.*

My servant has just entered to announce that my carriage is mended; I am therefore again about to take the road: and unless some new accident detain me, and destine me to make my entrance into Moscow in a cart, or on foot, my next chapter will be written in the holy city of the Russians, where they give me hopes of arriving in a few hours.

I must, however, first set about concealing my papers, for each chapter, even those that will appear the most inoffensive to the friends who receive them in the form of letters, would be sufficient to send me to Siberia. I take care to shut myself up when writing; and if my feldjäger or one of the coachmen knock at the door, I put up my papers before opening it, and appear to be reading. I am going to slip this sheet between the crown and the lining of my hat. These precautions are, I hope, superfluous, but I think it necessary to take them; they at any rate suffice to give an idea of the Russian government.

❖

---

* A similar fate very nearly happened to me; the disorder in my eyes, which commenced when I wrote this sheet, increased during my sojourn in Moscow, and long after; in short, on my return from the fair of Nijni, it degenerated into an ophthalmia, the effects of which I still feel.

CHAPTER XXIV

❖

Does the reader never remember having perceived, when approaching by land some sea-port town in the Bay of Biscay or the British Channel, the masts of a fleet rising behind downs, just elevated enough to conceal the town, the piers, the flat shore, and the sea itself beyond? Above the natural rampart nothing can be discovered but a forest of poles bearing sails of a dazzling white, yards, many-coloured flags, and floating streamers. A fleet, apparently on land—such is the apparition with which my eye has been sometimes surprised in Holland, and once in England, after having penetrated into the interior of the country between Gravesend and the mouth of the Thames. Exactly similar is the effect that has been produced upon me by the first view of Moscow: a multitude of spires gleamed alone above the dust of the road, the undulations of the soil, and the misty line that nearly always clothes the distance, under the summer sun of these parts.

The uneven, thinly-inhabited, and only half-cultivated plain, resembles downs dotted with a few stunted firs. It was out of the midst of this solitude that I saw, as it were suddenly spring up, thousands of pointed steeples, star-spangled belfries, airy turrets, strangely-shaped towers, palaces, and old convents, the bodies of which all remained entirely concealed.

This first view of the capital of the Slavonians, rising brightly in the cold solitudes of the Christian East, produces an impression that cannot easily be forgotten.

Before the eye, spreads a landscape, wild and gloomy, but grand as the ocean; and to animate the dreary void, there rises a poetical city, whose architecture is without either a designating name or a known model.

To understand the peculiarity of the picture, it is necessary to remind the reader of the orthodox plan of every Greek church. The summit of these sacred edifices is always composed of several towers, which vary in form and height, but the number of which is five at the least—a sacramental number, that is often greatly exceeded. The middle steeple is the most lofty; the four others respectfully surround this principal tower. Their form varies: the summits of some resemble pointed caps placed upon a head; the great towers of certain churches, painted and gilded externally, may be severally compared to a bishop's mitre, a tiara adorned with gems, a Chinese pavilion, a minaret, and a clergyman's hat. They often consist of a simple cupola, in the shape of a bowl, and terminating in a point. All these more or less whimsical figures are crowned with large, open-worked copper crosses, gilt, and the complicated designs of which look like work of filagree. The number and disposition of the steeples have always a symbolical religious meaning: they signify the ranks in the ecclesiastical hierarchy. They image the patriarch, surrounded by his priests, his deacons, and subdeacons, lifting between heaven and earth his radiant head. A fanciful variety characterises this more or less richly adorned roof-work; but the primitive intention, the theological idea, is always scrupulously respected.

Bright chains of gilded or plated metal unite the crosses of the inferior steeples to the principal tower; and this metallic net, spread over an entire city, produces an effect that it would be impossible to convey, even in a picture. The holy legion of steeples, without having any precise resemblance to the human form, represents a grotesque assemblage of personages gathered together on the summits of the churches and chapels,—a phalanx of phantoms hovering over the city.

The exteriors of the mystic domes of the Russian churches are worked in a most elaborate manner. They remind the stranger of a cuirass of Damascus steel; and the sight of so many scaly, enamelled, spangled, striped, and chequered roofs, shining in the sun with various but always brilliant colours, strikes him with the most lively astonishment. The desert, with its dull sea-green tint, is, as it were, illuminated by this magical net-work of carbuncles. The play of light, in the aerial city, produces a species of phantasmagoria, in broad day, which reminds one of the reflected brilliance of lamps in the shop of a lapidary. These changing hues impart to Moscow an aspect altogether different from that of the other great European cities. The sky, when viewed from the middle of such a city, is a golden glory, similar to those seen in old paintings. Schnitzler states, that, in 1730, Weber counted at Moscow 1500 churches. Coxe, in 1778, fixes the number at 484. As for myself, I am content with endeavouring to describe the aspect of things, I admire without counting,—I must, therefore, refer the lovers of catalogues to books made up entirely of numerals.

I have said enough, I hope, to impart to the reader a portion of the surprise which the first view of Moscow produced in me. To add to that surprise he must recollect, what he will have often read, that this city is a country within itself, and that fields, lakes, and woods, enclosed within its limits, place a considerable distance between the different edifices that adorn it. The objects being so scattered, greatly increases the effect. The whole plain is covered with a silver guize. Three or four hundred churches, thus spread, present to the eye an immense semi-circle, so that when approaching the city, towards sunset on a stormy evening, it would be easy to fancy you saw a rainbow of fire impending above the churches of Moscow: this is the halo of the holy city. But at about three quarters of a league from the gate, the illusion vanishes. Here, the very real and heavy brick palace of Petrowski arrests the attention. It was built by Catherine after an odd modern design: the ornaments with which it is profusely covered stand in white against the red walls. These decorations, which are formed, I think, of plaster, are in a style of extravagant Gothic. The building is as square as a die, which by no means renders its general effect more imposing. It is here that the sovereign stops, when he means to make a solemn entrance into Moscow. A summer theatre, a ballroom, and a garden have been established, so as to form a kind of public café, which I shall return to see, as it is the rendezvous of the city loungers during the summer season.

After passing Petrowski, the enchantment gradually disperses, so that by the time of entering Moscow, we feel as if waking from a brilliant dream to a very dull and prosaic reality—a vast city without any real monuments of art, that is to say, without a single object worthy of a discriminative and thoughtful approbation. Before so heavy and awkward a copy of Europe, we ask, with wonder, what has become of the Asia whose apparition had struck us with admiration so shortly before? Moscow, viewed from without and as a whole, is a creation of sylphs, a world of chimeras; when inspected close at hand and in detail, it is a vast trading city, without regularity, dusty, ill paved, ill built, thinly peopled; in short, though it unquestionably exhibits the work of a powerful hand, it betrays also the conceptions of a head whose idea of the beautiful has failed to produce one single *chef-d'oeuvre*. The Russian people are strong in arms, that is, in numbers, but in the strength of imagination they are altogether deficient.

Without genius for architecture, without taste for sculpture, they can heap together stones, and create objects enormous in dimension; but they can produce nothing harmonious, nothing great in the perfection of its proportions. Happy privilege of art! masterpieces survive themselves, subsisting in the memory of men ages after they have been devastated by time; they share, by the inspiration which they kindle, even in their latest ruin, the immortality of the minds that created them; whereas, shapeless masses are forgotten while yet untouched by time. Art, when in its perfection, gives a soul to stone; it is a mystic power. This we learn in Greece, where each fragment of sculpture conduces to the general effect of each monument. In architecture, as in the other arts, it is from the superior execution of the smallest details, and from their skilfully interwoven connection with the general plan, that the sentiment of the beautiful springs. Nothing in Russia inspires this sentiment.

Nevertheless, amid the chaos of plaster, brick, and boards, that is called Moscow, two points never cease to attract the eye

—the church of St. Basil, and the Kremlin,—the Kremlin, of which Napoleon himself was only able to disturb a few stones! This prodigious fabric, with its white irregular walls, and its battlements rising above battlements, is in itself large as a city. At the close of day, when I first entered Moscow, the grotesque piles of churches and palaces embraced within the citadel rose in light against a dimly portrayed back-ground, poor in design and cold in colouring, though we are still burning with heat, suffocating with dust, and devoured by mosquitoes. It is the long continuance of the hot season which gives the colour to southern scenery; in the north we feel the effects of the summer, but we do not see it; in vain does the air become heated for a moment, the earth remains always discoloured.

I shall never forget the chilly shudder which came over me at the first sight of the cradle of the modern Russian empire: the Kremlin alone is worth the journey to Moscow.

At the gate of this fortress, but beyond its precincts—at least, according to my feldjäger, for I have not yet been able to visit it —rises the church of St. Basil, *Vassili Blagennoï*; it is also known under the name of the Cathedral of the Protection of the Holy Virgin. In the Greek church they are lavish of the title of cathedral; every ward, every monastery has one of its own; every city possesses several. That of Vassili is certainly the most singular, if it is not the most beautiful edifice in Russia. I have as yet only seen it at a distance. Thus viewed, it appears as an immense cluster of little turrets forming a bush, or rather giving the idea of some kind of tropical fruit all bristled over with excrescences, or a crystallisation of a thousand rays: the scales of a golden fish, the enamelled skin of a serpent, the changeful hues of the lizard, the glossy rose and azure of the pigeon's neck, would all, as regards colour, serve as comparisons: above, rise minarets of a brownish red. The effect of the whole dazzles the eye, and fascinates the imagination. Surely, the land in which such a building is called a house of prayer is not Europe; it must be India, Persia, or China! —and the men who go to worship God in this box of confectionary work, can they be Christians? Such was the exclamation that escaped me at the first view of the church of Vassili. That building must indeed possess an extraordinary style of architecture to have drawn my attention, as it did, from the Kremlin, at the moment when the mighty castle for the first time met my eyes.

Soon, however, my ideas took another turn. Where is the Frenchman who could resist an emotion of respect and of pride (for misfortune has its pride, and it is the most legitimate kind), on entering into the only city where, in our own times, took place a public event, a scene, as imposing as the most striking occurrences of ancient history?

The means that the Asiatic city took to repel its enemy was a sublime deed of despair; and thenceforward the name of Moscow is fatally united with that of the greatest captain of modern times. The sacred bird of the Greeks consumed itself in order to escape the talons of the eagle, and, like the Phoenix, the mystic dove rises again from its ashes.

In this war of giants wherein all was glory, renown does not depend upon success. The fire under the ice, the weapons of the demons of Dante—such were the arms which God placed in the hands of the Russians to repel and to destroy us. An army must be honoured for having advanced so far, though it was only to die there.

But who can excuse the chief whose want of foresight exposed it to such a struggle? At Smolensk, Buonaparte refused the peace which they did not even deign to offer him at Moscow. He hoped for the offer, but he hoped in vain.

It was a modification of that mania for forming collections, for completing catalogues, which narrowed the views of the great politician; he sacrificed his army to the puerile satisfaction of swelling the list of the capitals which he had occupied. Rejecting the wisest councils, he did violence also to his own judgment, in order to have the gratification of installing himself in the fortress of the Czars, and of sleeping there, as he had done in the palaces of nearly all the other potentates of Europe; and this vain triumph of the bold adventurer cost the emperor the sceptre of the world.

A passion for capitals was the cause of the annihilation of the finest army that France and the world ever saw, and two years later, of the fall of the Empire.

The following fact, furnishing one proof more of the unpardonable error committed by Napoleon when he marched upon Moscow, is unknown among us; I can answer for its authenticity.

Smolensk was viewed by the Russians as the bulwark of their land; they hoped that our army would be satisfied with occupying Poland and Lithuania, without venturing farther: but when they learnt the conquest of this city, the key of the empire, a cry of terror rose up from all quarters; both court and country were in consternation, and Russia believed herself in the power of the conqueror. It was at Petersburg that the Emperor Alexander received this disastrous news.

His minister of war partook of the general opinion; and wishing to place beyond the reach of the enemy his chief valuables, he put a considerable quantity of gold, papers, diamonds, and other jewels into a small chest, which he sent to Ladoga by one of his secretaries, the only man to whom he believed he might safely confide such a trust. He directed him to wait at Ladoga for further instructions, announcing that he should probably send him an order to repair with the box to the port of Archangel, and afterwards, from thence to England. Several days elapsed without the further news which was most anxiously expected, being received. At last a courier brought the minister official information of the march of our army upon Moscow. Without hesitating a moment, he sent to Ladoga to order the return of his secretary and valuables, and repaired to the presence of the Emperor, whom he addressed with a triumphant air: "Sire, your majesty is much indebted to Providence: if you persist in following the plan laid down, Russia is saved: it is an expedition *à la* Charles XII.!"

"But Moscow?" responded the Emperor.

"It must be abandoned, Sire: to fight, would be to give away a chance; to retreat, after laying waste the country, will be to destroy the enemy without risking any thing. Famine will begin the work of destruction, the winter and the fire will consummate it: let us burn Moscow, and save the world!"

The Emperor Alexander modified this plan in the execution. He insisted on a last effort being made to save his capital.

The courage with which the Russians fought at Moskowa is well known. That battle, which received from their master the name of Borodino, was glorious not only to them, but to us; for, notwithstanding all their gallant efforts, they could not prevent our entrance into Moscow.

God was willing to furnish the chroniclers of the age—an age the most prosaic that the world has ever seen—with one epic story. Moscow was voluntarily sacrificed, and the flames of that sacred conflagration became the signal for the revolution of Germany and the deliverance of Europe. The nations felt at last that they would have no rest until they had annihilated that indefatigable conqueror who sought peace by means of perpetual war.

Such were the recollections that absorbed my thoughts at the first view of the Kremlin. To have worthily recompensed Moscow, the Emperor of Russia ought to have re-established his residence in that twice holy city.

The Kremlin is not like any other palace, it is a city in itself; a city that forms the root of Moscow, and that serves as the frontier fortress between two quarters of the world. Under the successors of Gengis-Khan, Asia made her last rush upon Europe: in turning to retreat, she struck the earth with her foot, and from thence rose the Kremlin!

The princes who now possess this sacred asylum of oriental despotism, call themselves Europeans, because they have chased the Calmucs, their brethren, their tyrants, and their instructors, out of Muscovy. None resemble the khans of Saraï so much as their antagonists, the czars of Moscow, who have borrowed from them even to their very title. The Russians gave the name of *czars* to the khans of the Tartars. Karamsin says, on this subject, vol. vi. page 438.:—

"This word is not derived from the Latin *Caesar,* as several learned men erroneously suppose. It is an ancient oriental word, as may be seen in the Slavonian translation of the Bible; and it was first given by us to the emperors of the East, and afterwards to the Tartar khans. It signifies, in Persic, a *throne,* or *supreme* authority; and it is to be traced in the termination of the names of the Assyrian and Babylonish kings, as Phalassar, Nabonassar, &c." He adds, in a note, "In our translation of the Holy Scriptures, Kessar is written for Caesar; but tzar, or *czar,* is altogether a different word."

On first entering the city of Moscow, I forgot poetry, and even history; I thought only of what I saw, which was not very striking, for I found myself in streets similar to those in the outskirts of all great cities: I crossed a boulevard which resembled other boulevards, and then, after driving down a gentle descent, found myself among straight and handsome lines of houses built of stone. At last I reached the Dmitriskoï-street, where a handsome and comfortable chamber had been engaged for me in an excellent English hotel. I had, at Petersburg, been commended to Madame Howard, who without this introduction would not have received me into her house. I took care not to reproach her for being so scrupulous, for it is owing to this precaution that one can sleep comfortably in her establishment. The means by which she has succeeded in maintaining in it a cleanliness rarely seen any where, and which is an absolute miracle in Russia, is the having had erected, in her court-yard, a separate building, in which the Russian servants are obliged to sleep. These men never enter the principal edifice except to wait upon their masters. In her judicious precautions, Madame Howard goes yet further. She will scarcely admit any Russian guest: consequently, neither my feldjäger nor coachman knew her house, and we had some difficulty in finding it; although it is, notwithstanding its want of a sign, the best inn in Moscow and in Russia. Immediately on being installed I sat down to write. Night is now approaching, and as there is a bright moon, I lay down my pen in order to take a ramble over the city, which promenade I will describe on my return.

❖   ❖   ❖

I commenced my perambulations at about ten o'clock, without guide or companion, and strolled at hazard from street to street, according to my usual custom. I first traversed several long and wide streets, more hilly than most of those in Russia, but laid out with equal regularity. There can be no complaint of the want of straight lines in the architecture of this country, nevertheless, the line and rule have less spoiled Moscow than Petersburg. There, the imbecile tyrants of modern cities found a level surface ready prepared for them; here, they had to struggle with the inequalities of the soil, and with the ancient national edifices. Thanks to these invincible obstacles presented by nature and history, the aspect of Moscow is still that of an ancient city. It is more picturesque than any other in the empire, which continues to recognise it as its capital, in spite of the almost supernatural efforts of the Czar Peter and his successors: so strong is the law of circumstances against the will of men—men even the most powerful. Despoiled of its religious honours, deprived of its patriarch, abandoned by its sovereign, and by the most courtly of its ancient boyards, without any other attractive association than that of a heroic event, too modern to be as yet duly appreciated, Moscow has been obliged to have recourse to commerce and industry. They boast of its silk manufactories. But the history and the architecture are still here to preserve its imprescriptible rights to political supremacy. The Russian government favours the pursuits of industry: being unable altogether to stem the torrent of the age, it prefers enriching the people to enfranchising them.

This evening, towards ten o'clock, the sun sank, and the moon rose. The turrets of the convents, the spires of the chapels, the towers, the battlements, the palaces, and all the irregular and frowning masses of buildings that form the Kremlin, were here and there swathed with wreaths of light as resplendent as golden fringes, while the body of the city was seen only by the remaining beams of day, which momentarily faded on the painted tiles, the copper cupolas, the gilded chains, and the metallic roofs, that make the firmament of Moscow. These edifices, the general grouping of which gives the idea of some rich tapestry, still however stood in richly coloured relief against the faint blue ground of heaven. It seemed as if the sun had sought to give a parting salute to the ancient capital of Russia. This adieu appeared to me magnificent; although clouds of musquitos buzzed about my ears, whilst my eyes were filled with the dust of the streets, kept in continual motion by the thousands of vehicles moving about, at a gallop, in all directions.

The most numerous were the truly national drowskas, those tiny summer sledges, which being unable conveniently to carry more than one person at a time, are multiplied to infinity in order to meet the wants of an active population, numerous, but lost in the circuit of so immense a city. The dust of Moscow is excessively troublesome, being fine as the lightest ashes. We have still a burning temperature. The Russians are astonished at the intensity and duration of the heat of this summer.

The Slavonian Empire—that rising sun of the political world towards which all the earth is turning its eyes—is it also to be blessed with the sun of heaven? The natives pretend, and often repeat, that the climate is ameliorating. Wonderful power of human civilisation, whose progress is to change even the temperature of the globe! Whatever may be the winters of Moscow and Petersburg, I know few climates more disagreeable than that of these two cities during the summer. It is the fine season which should be called the bad weather of northern lands.

The first thing that struck me in the streets of Moscow was the more lively, free, and careless bearing of the population as compared with that of Petersburg. An air of liberty is here breathed that is unknown to the rest of the empire. It is this which explains to me the secret aversion of the sovereigns to the old city, which they flatter, fear, and fly. The Emperor Nicholas, who is a good Russian, says he is very fond of it; but I cannot see that he resides in it more than did his predecessors, who detested it.

This evening a few streets were partially illuminated. It is difficult to understand the taste of the Russians for illuminations, when we recollect that during the short season, when they can alone enjoy this kind of spectacle, there is scarcely any night in the latitude of Moscow, and still less in that of Petersburg.

On returning to my lodgings, I asked the cause of these moderate demonstrations of joy, and was informed that the illumination was in honour of the anniversaries of the births or baptisms of all the members of the imperial family. There are in Russia so many permanent fêtes of this sort, that they pass almost unnoticed. This indifference proves to me that fear can be sometimes imprudent, that it does not always know how to flatter so well as it would wish to do. Love is the only really skilful flatterer, because its praises, even when most exaggerated, are sincere. This is a truth which conscience vainly preaches in the ear of despots.

The inefficacy of conscience in human affairs, in the greatest as in the least, is, to me, the most wonderful mystery in this world, for it proves to me the existence of another. God creates nothing without an object: since, then, he has given conscience to every individual, and since this internal light is so useless upon earth, it must have its ordained mission to fulfil elsewhere: the evil deeds of this world have for their excusers our passions; the justice of the next world will have for its advocate our conscience.

I slowly followed the promenaders of the streets, and after having ascended and descended several declivities in the wake of a wave of idle loungers, whom I mechanically took for guides, I reached the centre of the city, a shapeless square, adjoining which was a garden, with alleys of trees brilliantly lighted, and under them could be heard the sound of distant music. Several open cafés tended further to remind me of Europe; but I could not interest myself with these amusements: I was under the walls of the Kremlin,—that colossal mountain raised for tyranny by the hands of slaves. For the modern city a public promenade has been made, a species of garden planted in the English taste, round the walls of the ancient fortress of Moscow. How am I to describe the walls of the Kremlin? The word *walls* gives an idea of quite too ordinary an object; it would deceive the reader: the walls of the Kremlin are a chain of mountains. This citadel, reared on the confines of Europe and Asia, is, as compared with ordinary ramparts, what the Alps are to our hills: the Kremlin is the Mont Blanc of fortresses. If the giant that is called the Russia Empire had a heart, I should say that the Kremlin was the heart of the monster; but, as it is, I would call it the head.

I wish I could give an idea of this mighty pile of stones, reared step by step into the heavens; this asylum of despotism, raised in the name of liberty: for the Kremlin was a barrier opposed to the Calmucs by the Russians: its walls have equally aided the independence of the state and the tyranny of the sovereign. They are boldly carried over the deep sinuosities of the soil. When the declivities of the hillocks become too precipitous, the rampart is lowered by steps: these steps, rising between heaven and earth, are enormous; they are the ladder for the giants who make war against the gods.

The line of this first girdle of structures is broken by fantastic towers, so elevated, strong, and grotesque in form, as to remind one of the peaks in Switzerland, with their many-shaped rocks, and their many-coloured glaciers. The obscurity no doubt contributed to increase the size of objects, and to give them unusual forms and tints,—I say tints, for night, like engravings, has its colouring. To behold gentlemen and ladies, dressed *à la parisienne,* promenading at the feet of this fabulous palace, was to fancy myself in a dream. What would Ivan III., the restorer, or, it might be said, the founder of the Kremlin, have thought, could he have beheld at the foot of the sacred fortress, his old Muscovites, shaved, curled, in frock coats, white pantaloons, and yellow gloves, eating ices, seated before a brightly-lighted café? He would have said, as I do, it is impossible! and yet this is now seen every summer evening in Moscow.

I have, then, wandered in the public gardens planted on the glacis of the ancient citadel of the Czars: I have seen the towers, wall above wall, the platforms, terrace upon terrace, and my eyes have swept over an enchanted city. It would need the eloquence of youth, which every thing astonishes and surprises, to find words analogous to these prodigious things. Above a long vault, which I crossed, I perceived a raised viaduct, by which carriages and foot-passengers enter the holy city. The spectacle was bewildering; nothing but towers, gates, and terraces, raised one above the other, steep slopes, and piled arches, all serving to form the road by which the Moscow of the present day, the vulgar Moscow, is left for the Kremlin—the Moscow of miracle and of history. These aqueducts, without water, support other stories of more fantastic edifices. I observed, raised upon one of the hanging passages, a low round tower, all bristling with battlements of spear-heads. The silver brightness of this ornament contrasted singularly with the blood-red of the walls. The tower seemed like a crowned giant standing before the fortress of which he was the guardian. What is there that one could not see, by the light of the moon, wandering at the foot of the Kremlin? There, every thing is supernatural; the mind believes in spectres in spite of itself. Who could approach without a religious terror this sacred bulwark, a stone of which, disturbed by Buonaparte, rebounded even to Saint Helena, to crush the conqueror in the bosom of the ocean! Pardon, reader, I am born in the age of grandiloquence.

The newest of the new schools is endeavouring to banish it,

and to simplify language upon the principle that people the most devoid of imagination that have ever existed, ought most carefully to shun venturing among the tortuous paths of a faculty which they do not possess. I can admire a puritanical style when it is employed by superior talents, talents capable of divesting it of all monotony, but I cannot imitate it.

After having seen all that I have gazed at this evening, it
would be wise to return straight to one's
own country: the excitement
of the journey is
exhausted.

❖

THE KREMLIN BY DAYLIGHT ❖ CHARACTER OF ITS ARCHITECTURE ❖
SYMBOLIC IMAGERY ❖ RELATION BETWEEN THE CHARACTER OF BUILDINGS
AND BUILDERS ❖ IVAN IV ❖ PATIENCE CRIMINAL ❖
INTRODUCTION TO THE HISTORY
OF IVAN IV
❖

CHAPTER XXV

❖

An attack of ophthalmia, which came on between Petersburg and Moscow, gives me much pain and annoyance. Notwithstanding this malady, I resumed to-day my promenade of yesterday evening, in order to compare the Kremlin by daylight with the fantastic Kremlin of the night. The shade increases and distorts every thing: the sun restores to objects their forms and their proportions.

At this second view, the fortress of the Czars still surprises me. The moonlight magnified and threw out in strong relief certain masses of the fabric, but it concealed others; and, while acknowledging that I had imaged to myself too many vaults, and galleries, hanging roads, and lofty portals, I found quite enough of all these objects to justify my enthusiasm. There is something of every thing at the Kremlin: it is a varied landscape of stones. The solidity of its ramparts exceeds that of the rocks on which they stand. The multitude and the multiformity of its parts are a marvel. This labyrinth of palaces, museums, towers, churches and dungeons, is terrific as the architecture of Martin; it is as great and more irregular than the compositions of that English painter. Mysterious sounds rise out of the depth of its subterranes; such abodes must be haunted by spirits, they cannot belong to beings like ourselves. The citadel of Moscow is not merely a palace, a national sanctuary for the historical treasures of the empire; it is the bulwark of Russia, the revered asylum in which sleep the tutelary saints of the country; it is also the prison of spectres.

This morning, still wandering without a guide, I penetrated even to the middle of the fortress, and found my way into the interior of some of the churches which ornament that pious city, as venerated by the Russians for its relics as for the worldly riches and the warlike trophies which it encloses. I am too excited now to describe these objects in detail, but hereafter I shall pay a methodical visit to the Treasury.

The Kremlin, on its hill, gives me the idea of a city of princes, built in the midst of a city of people. This tyrannical castle, this proud heap of stones, looks down scornfully upon the abodes of common men; and, contrary to what is the case in structures of ordinary dimensions, the nearer we approach the indestructible mass the more our wonder increases. Like the bones of certain gigantic animals, the Kremlin proves to us the history of a world of which we might doubt until after seeing the remains. In this prodigious creation strength takes the place of beauty, caprice of elegance: it is like the dream of a tyrant, fearful but full of power; it has something about it that disowns the age; means of defence which are adapted to a system of war that exists no longer; an architecture that has no connection with the wants of modern civilisation: a heritage of the fabulous ages, a gaol, a palace, a sanctuary, a bulwark against the nation's foes, a bastille against the nation, a prop of tyrants, a prison of people,—such is the Kremlin. A kind of northern Acropolis, a Pantheon of barbarism, this national fabric may be called the Alcazar of the Slavonians.

Such, then, was the chosen abode of the old Muscovite princes; and yet these formidable walls were not sufficient shelter for the terror of Ivan IV.

The fear of a man possessing absolute power is the most dreadful thing upon earth; and with all the imagery of this fear visible in the Kremlin, it is still impossible to approach the fabric without a shudder.

Towers of every form, round, square, and with pointed roofs, belfries, donjons, turrets, spires, sentry-boxes upon minarets, steeples of every height, style and colour, palaces, domes, watch-towers, walls, embattlemented and pierced with loopholes, ramparts, fortifications of every species, whimsical inventions, incomprehensible devices, chiosks by the side of cathedrals—every thing announces violation and disorder, every thing betrays the continual *surveillance* necessary to the security of the singular beings who were condemned to live in this supernatural world. Yet these innumerable monuments of pride, caprice, voluptuousness, glory, and piety, notwithstanding their apparent variety, express one single idea which reigns here everywhere—war maintained by fear. The Kremlin is the work of a superhuman being, but that being is malevolent. Glory in slavery—such is the allegory figured by this satanic monument, as extraordinary in architecture as the visions of St. John are in poetry. It is a habitation which would suit some of the personages of the Apocalypse.

In vain is each turret distinguished by its peculiar character and its particular use; all have the same signification,—terror armed.

Some resemble the caps of priests, others the mouth of a dragon, others swords, their points in the air, others the forms and even the colours of various exotic fruits; some again represent a head-dress of the czars, pointed, and adorned with jewels like that of the Doge of Venice; others are simple crowns: and all this multitude of towers of glazed tiles, of metallic cupolas, of enamelled, gilded, azured, and silvered domes, shine in the sun like the colossal stalactites of the salt-mines in the neighbourhood of Cracow. These enormous pillars, these towers and turrets of every shape, pointed, pyramidical, and circular, but always in some manner suggesting the idea of the human form, seem to reign over the city and the land. To see them from afar shining in the sky, one might fancy them an assembly of potentates, richly robed and decorated with the insignia of their dignity, a meeting of ancestral beings, a council of kings, each seated upon his tomb; spectres hovering over the pinnacles of a palace. To inhabit a place like the Kremlin is not to reside, it is to defend one's self. Oppression creates revolt, revolt obliges precautions, precautions increase dangers, and this long series of actions and reactions engenders a monster; that monster is despotism, which has built itself a house at Moscow. The giants of the antediluvian world, were they to return to earth to visit their degenerate successors, might still find a suitable habitation in the Kremlin.

Every thing has a symbolical sense, whether purposely or not, in its architecture; but the real, the abiding, that appears after you have divested yourself of your first emotions in the contemplation of these barbaric splendours, is, after all, only a congregation of dungeons pompously surnamed palaces and cathedrals. The Russians may do their best, but they can never come out of the prison.

The very climate is an accomplice of tyranny. The cold of the country does not permit the construction of vast churches, where the faithful would be frozen at prayer: here the soul is not lifted to heaven by the glories of religious architecture; in this zone man can only build to his God gloomy donjons. The sombre cathedrals of the Kremlin, with their narrow vaults and thick walls, resemble caves; they are painted prisons, just as the palaces are gilded gaols.

As travellers say of the recesses of the Alps, so of the wonders of this architecture—they are horribly beautiful.

❖   ❖   ❖

My eye inflames more and more. I have been obliged to call in a surgeon, who has condemned me to the application of a bandage, and an imprisonment of three days in my chamber. Fortunately, I have one eye left, so that I can still occupy myself with something.

I intend to employ these three days of leisure on a work commenced at Petersburg, but interrupted by the busy gaieties of that city. This work is a brief review of the reign of Ivan IV., the tyrant *par excellence,* and the soul of the Kremlin: not that he built that fortress, but he was born there, he died there, and his spirit still haunts the spot.

Its plan was conceived and executed by his grand-sire Ivan III. I have done my best to give an idea of the place itself, and I will now endeavour to aid the description by painting the colossal figures of the men who were its habitants. If from the arrangements of a house we can form a judgment as to the character of its inhabitants, can we not also, by an analogous operation of mind, picture to ourselves the aspect of edifices by a study of the men for whom they were constructed? Our passions, our habits, our genius, are powerful enough to engrave themselves indelibly on the very stones of our dwellings.

Assuredly, if there be any building to which may be applied such a process of the imagination, it is the Kremlin. Europe and Asia are there seen united, under the influence of the genius of the Lower Empire.

Whether the fortress be viewed under a purely historical, or a poetical and picturesque aspect, it is the most national monument in Russia, and consequently the most interesting both for Russians and for foreigners.

This sanctuary of despotism was re-constructed in stone for Ivan III., in 1485, by two Italian architects, Marco and Pietro Antonio, who were invited to Moscow by the *Great Prince,* * when he wished to again rear the ramparts, formerly wooden, of the fortress more anciently founded under Dmitri Donskoi.

But if this palace was not built by Ivan IV., it was built for him. It was by a spirit of prophecy that the great king, his grandfather, constructed the palace of the tyrant. Italian architects may be found every where, but in no other place have they produced a work similar to that which they raised at Moscow. I may add that there have been elsewhere absolute, unjust, arbitrary, and capricious sovereigns, and yet, that the reign of none of these monsters has resembled that of Ivan IV. The same seed springing under different climates and in different soils, produces plants of the same species, but of many varieties. The earth will never see two masterpieces of despotism similar to the Kremlin, nor two nations as superstitiously patient as was the Muscovite nation under the monstrous reign of its greatest tyrant.

The consequences of that reign are felt even in our days. Had the reader accompanied me in this journey, he would have discovered, as I have done, in the inner depths of the Russian character, the inevitable injuries produced by arbitrary power carried to its last excess; first, namely, a careless indifference to the sanctity of truth in speech, of candour in sentiment, and of justice in

* The title then given to the grand dukes of Moscow.

acts: and afterwards, falsehood rampant in all its forms, fraud triumphant, and the moral sense, in fact, wholly destroyed.

I could fancy I saw a procession of vices pouring forth from all the gates of the Kremlin to inundate Russia.

Other nations have supported oppression, the Russian nation has loved it: it loves it still. Is not such fanaticism of obedience characteristic? It may not, however, be denied that this popular mania has here sometimes become the principle of sublime actions. In this inhuman land, if society has depraved the individual, it has not enervated him: he is not good, but he is also not contemptible. The same may be said of the Kremlin: it is not pleasant to behold, but it inspires awe. It is not beautiful, but it is terrible—terrible as the reign of Ivan IV.

Such a reign blinds to the latest generations the minds of a nation which submitted to it patiently: the crime of treason against humanity attaints the blood of a people even in its most distant posterity. This crime consists not only in exercising injustice, but likewise in tolerating it; a nation which, under the pretext that obedience is the chief virtue, bequeaths tyranny to its children, both mistakes its interests and neglects its duty. Blind endurance, fidelity to insane masters, are contemptible virtues; submission is only praiseworthy, sovereignty is only venerable, when they become the means of insuring the rights of mankind. When kings forget the conditions on which a man is permitted to reign over his fellowmen, the citizens have to look to God, their eternal governor, who absolves them from their oath of fidelity to their temporal master.

Such restrictions the Russians have neither admitted nor understood; yet they are essential to the development of true civilisation: without them circumstances will arise under which the social state becomes more injurious than beneficial to mankind, and when the sophists would be right in sending man back again to the woods. . . .

❖

NOTE TO THE READER

Chapter XXVI
has been omitted in its entirety.

ENGLISH CLUB ❖ REUNION OF NATIONS ❖ PECULIAR CHARACTER OF
ARCHITECTURE IN MOSCOW ❖ OBSERVATION OF MADAME DE STAËL ❖
ADVANTAGE OF OBSCURE TRAVELLERS ❖ KITAIGOROD ❖ MADONNA OF
VIVIELSKI ❖ CHURCH OF VASSILI BLAGENNOÏ ❖ THE HOLY GATE ❖ CHURCH
OF THE ASSUMPTION ❖ FOREIGN ARTISTS ❖ TOWER OF JOHN THE GREAT
❖ CONVENT OF THE ASCENSION ❖ INTERIOR OF
THE TREASURY ❖ NEW WORKS AT
THE KREMLIN
❖

CHAPTER XXVII

❖

The inflammation of my eye being reduced, I left my prison yesterday, in order to dine at the English club. It is a species of restaurateur, to which there is no admission except through the introduction of a member of the society, which is composed of the most distinguished people in Moscow. The institution is newly copied from the English, like our *cercles* of Paris.

In the state which the frequency and facility of communication has produced in modern Europe, one is at a loss where to go to find original manners, and habits which may be taken as the true expression of characters. The customs recently adopted by each people are the results of a crowd of borrowed notions. There arises from this digest of all characters in the crucible of universal civilisation, a monotony that is any thing but conducive to the enjoyment of the traveller, although at no other epoch has the taste for travelling been so universal; owing to the great number of people who travel through ennui instead of for instruction. I am not one of those travellers: curious and indefatigable, I discover each day, to my cost, that differences are the rarest things in the world; and that resemblances are the great annoyances of the traveller, whom they oblige to play the part of dupe, a part the most unpleasant to accept, precisely because it is the most easy to perform.

We travel to escape the world in which we have passed our lives, and we find it is impossible to leave it behind. The civilised world has no longer any limits; it is the whole earth. The human race is reuniting, languages are being lost, nations are disappearing, philosophy is reducing creeds to a matter of private belief—last product of a defaced Catholicism, so ordained until it shall shine forth again with renewed brightness, and serve as the future basis of society. Who shall assign limits to this re-assorting of the human race? It is impossible to avoid seeing in it a design of Providence. The malediction of Babel approaches its prescribed term, and the nations are going to be one, notwithstanding all that has tended to disunite them.

Yesterday I recommenced my travels, by a methodical and minute inspection of the Kremlin, under the conduct of M. ——, to whom I had an introduction. Still the Kremlin! that building is for me all Moscow—all Russia; a world within itself! My footman went in the morning to apprize the keeper, who waited for us. I expected to find an ordinary official, instead of which we were received by a military officer, a polite and intelligent man.

The treasury of the Kremlin is deservedly the pride of Russia. It might serve as a substitute for the chronicles of the country; it is a history in precious stones.

The golden vases, the pieces of armour, the ancient furniture, are not merely to be admired in themselves; every object is associated with some glorious or singular event worthy of commemoration. But before describing, or rather rapidly noticing, the wonders of an arsenal that has not, I believe, its second in Europe, the reader must follow me, step by step, along the way by which I was led to this sanctuary, revered by the Russians, and justly admired by strangers.

After proceeding through several straight but small streets, I arrived in sight of the fortress, when I passed under an archway, before which my footman caused the coach to stop, without deeming it necessary to consult me, so well known is the interest which attaches to the place! The vault forms the under part of a tower, singular in shape, like all the others in the old quarter of Moscow.

I have not seen Constantinople, but I believe that, next to that city, Moscow is the most striking in appearance of all the capitals in Europe. It is the inland Byzantium. Fortunately, the squares of the old capital are not so immense as those of Petersburg, in which even St. Peter's of Rome would be lost. At Moscow the sites are more confined, and therefore the edifices produce greater effect. The despotism of straight lines and symmetrical plans is opposed here both by nature and history: Moscow is everywhere picturesque. The sky, without being clear, has a silvery brightness: the models, of every species of architecture, are heaped together without order or plan; no structures are perfect, nevertheless the whole strikes, not with admiration, but with astonishment. The inequalities of the surface multiply the points of view. The magic glories of multitudes of cupolas sparkle in the air. Innumerable gilded steeples, in form like minarets, Oriental pavilions, and Indian domes, transport you to Delhi; donjon-keeps and turrets bring you back to Europe in the times of the crusades; the sentinel, mounted on the top of his watch-tower, reminds you of the muezzin inviting the faithful to prayer; while, to complete the confusion of ideas, the cross, which glitters in every direction, commanding the people to prostrate themselves before the Word, seems as though fallen from heaven amid an assembly of Asiatic nations, to point out to them all the narrow way of salvation. It was doubtless before this poetical picture that Madame de Staël exclaimed—*Moscow is the Rome of the North!*

The expression wants justice; for, in no respect can a parallel be drawn between these two cities. It is of Nineveh, Palmyra, or Babylon that we think, when we enter Moscow, and not of the *chefs-d'oeuvre* of art in either Pagan or Christian Europe. Nor have the history or religion of this country any nearer connection with Rome. Moscow might have been better compared to Pekin: but Madame de Staël thought of any thing rather than viewing Russia, when she traversed that country to visit Sweden and England, there to carry on the war of genius and of ideas with that enemy of all liberty of thought—Napoleon. She had to deliver herself in a few words of the impressions of a person of superior intellect arrived in a new country. The misfortune of celebrated characters when they travel, is that they are obliged to scatter words behind them; and if they abstain from doing so, other people do it for them.

I place no confidence except in the recitals of unknown travellers. It will be said I am sounding my own trumpet: I do not deny it; for I at least profit by my obscurity, in seeking and endeavouring to discover the truth. The pleasure of rectifying the mistakes and prejudices of some of my friends, and of the few whose minds resemble theirs, will suffice for my glory. My ambition is modest, —for nothing is more easy than to correct the errors of superior characters. It appears to me that if there are any who do not hate despotism as much as I hate it, they will do so, notwithstanding its pomps, after the veracious picture of its works which I offer to their meditation.

The massive tower, at the foot of which my footman made me alight, was picturesquely pierced by two arches; it separates the walls of the Kremlin, properly so called, from their continuation, which serves as a girdle to Kitaigorod, the city of the merchants, another quarter of old Moscow, founded by the mother of the Czar, John Vassilievitch, in 1534. This date appears to us recent, but it is ancient for Russia, the youngest of the European realms.

The Kitaigorod, a species of suburb to the Kremlin, is an immense bazaar, a town intersected with dark and vaulted alleys, which resemble so many subterranes. These catacombs of the merchants form no cemetries, but a permanent fair. They are a labyrinth of galleries, that rather resemble the arcades of Paris, although less elegant, less light, and more solid. This mode of building is essential to the wants of commerce under the climate: in the north, covered streets remedy, as far as it is possible, the inconveniences and severity of the open air. Sellers and buyers are there sheltered from the storm, the snow, and the frost: whereas light colonnades, open to the day, and airy porticoes have an aspect that is ridiculous. Russian architects ought to take the moles and the ants for their models.

At every step that you take in Moscow you find some chapel highly venerated by the people, and saluted by each passenger. These chapels, or niches, generally contain some image of the Virgin kept under glass, and honoured with a lamp that burns unceasingly. Such shrines are guarded by some old soldier. These veterans are to be met with in the antechambers of the rich, and in the churches, which they keep in order. The life of an old Russian soldier, if he could not obtain an asylum among the rich, or among the priests, would be one of extreme wretchedness. A charity void of display is unknown to this government: when it wishes to perform an act of benevolence, it builds palaces for the sick, or for children; and the façades of these pious monuments attract all eyes.

In the pillar which separates the double arcade of the tower, is enshrined the Virgin of Vivielski, an ancient image, painted in the Greek style, and highly venerated at Moscow. I observed that every body who passed this chapel—lords, peasants, trades-people, ladies, and military men,—all bowed and made numerous signs of the cross; many, not satisfied with so humble a homage, stopped, and well-dressed women prostrated themselves to the very earth before the miraculous Virgin, touching even the pavement with their brows; men also, above the rank of peasants, knelt and repeated signs of the cross innumerable. These religious acts in the open street were practised with a careless rapidity which denoted more habit than fervour. My footman is an Italian. Nothing could be more ludicrous than the mixture of conflicting prejudices which are working in the head of this poor foreigner, who has been for a great number of years established in Moscow, his adopted country. His ideas of childhood, brought from Rome, dispose him to believe in the intervention of the saints and the Virgin; and, without losing himself in theological subtilties, he takes for good, in default of better, the miracles of the relics and images of the Greek church. This poor Catholic, converted into a zealous adorer of the Virgin of Vivielski, proves to me the omnipotence of unanimity in creeds. He does not cease repeating to me, with Italian loquacity, "Signor, creda a me, questa madonna fa dei miracoli, ma dei miracoli veri, veri verissimi, non e come da noi altri; in questo paese tutti gli miracoli sono veri."

This Italian, preserving the ingenuous vivacity and the good temper of the people of his country in the empire of silence and reserve, amuses me.

A gossip in Russia is a phenomenon, a rarity delightful to encounter, a thing that is missed every hour by the traveller, wearied with the tact and prudence of the natives of the country. To lead this man to talk, which is not difficult to accomplish, I risked a few doubts as to the authenticity of the miracles of his Virgin of Vivielski: had I denied the spiritual authority of the Pope, my Roman servant could not have been more shocked. In seeing a poor Catholic endeavouring to prove to me the supernatural power of a Greek painting, I thought that it is no longer theology that separates the two churches. The history of all the Christian nations teaches us that princes have known how, in aid of their political schemes, to avail themselves of the obstinacy, the subtilty, and the logic of the priests, to envenom religious controversies.

In the small square to which the vaulted passage leads, stands a group in bronze, executed in a very bad *soi-disant* classic style. I could have fancied myself in a second-rate sculptor's studio at the Louvre during the Empire. The group represents, under the figure of two Romans, Minine and Pojarski, the liberators of Russia, from which country they drove the Poles at the commencement of the seventeenth century,—singular heroes to wear the Roman habit! These two individuals are very much in fashion in the present day. Further on I saw before me the extraordinary church of Vassili Blagennoï. The style of that grotesque edifice contrasts in a whimsical manner with the classic statues of the liberators of Moscow. A quantity of bulbous-shaped cupolas, not one of which resembles the other, a dish of fruits, a vase of Delft ware full of pine-apples, all pointed with golden crosses, a colossal crystallization,—such, on a near approach, were the only things to which I could compare the church that had appeared so imposing on my first approach to the city. This building is small, like most other Russian churches; and, notwithstanding the interminable medley of its colours, it does not long interest the observer. Two fine flights of steps lead to the esplanade on which it stands. The interior is confined, paltry, and without character. Its erection cost the life of the architect. It was built, according to Laveau, by the order of Ivan IV., politely surnamed the Terrible. That prince, as a reward to the architect who had greatly embellished Moscow, caused his eyes to be torn out, under the pretext that he did not wish such a *chef-d'oeuvre* to be built elsewhere.

On leaving the church we passed under the sacred gate of the

Kremlin; and, in accordance with the custom religiously observed by the Russians, I took care to doff my hat before entering the archway, which is not long. The custom is traced back to the time of the last attack of the Calmucs, whom an intervention of the tutelary saints of the empire prevented, they say, from penetrating into the sacred fortress. The saints are sometimes rather inattentive, but on this day they were on the look-out: the Kremlin was saved; and Russia has continued to acknowledge, by a mark of respect renewed every moment, the remembrance of the divine protection in which she glories. . . .

I must not stay to again describe the wonderful aspect of the exterior of the Kremlin—its prodigious walls and towers, carried over hills and ravines, and rising above each other in every variety of style, shape, and design, forming altogether the most original and poetical architecture in the world. But how shall I describe my surprise when, on entering the interior of the enchanted city, I approached the building called the Treasury, and saw before me a little modern palace, with straight lines and sharp angles, ornamented in front by Corinthian pillars. This cold and puny imitation of the antique, for which I ought to have been prepared, appeared to me so ridiculous, that I stepped back some paces and asked my companion permission to delay our visit to the Treasury, under pretext of first admiring some churches. After having been so long in Russia, I ought to be surprised at no incoherence in the inventions of the Imperial architects; but this time, the discordance was so glaring, that it struck me as quite a novelty.

We therefore commenced our survey by a visit to the Cathedral of the Assumption. This church possesses one of those innumerable paintings of the Virgin Mary that good Christians, of all lands, attribute to St. Luke. The edifice reminds me rather of the Saxon and the Norman than of our Gothic churches. It is the work of an Italian architect of the fifteenth century. After the structure had sunk and fallen in several times, while being erected by the bad artificers and worse architects of the land, foreign aid was sought, which succeeded in making the work solid; but, in its ornaments, the taste of the country has been followed.

I am ignorant of the rule prescribed by the Greek church relative to the worship of images: but in seeing this church entirely covered with paintings in fresco, betraying bad taste, and designed in the stiff, monotonous style, called the modern Greek, because its models were brought from Byzantium, I asked myself, what then are the figures, what can be the subjects, the representation of which is forbidden in the Greek church? Apparently they banish nothing from these buildings except good pictures.

In passing before the Virgin of St. Luke, my Italian cicerone assured me that it was genuine: he added, with the faith of a mugic, "Signore, signore, è il paese dei miracoli!" "It is the land of miracles!" I believe him, for fear is a potent thaumaturgist. What a singular journey is this, which in a fortnight conveys you into Europe as it was 400 years ago! Nay, with us, even in the middle ages, man better felt his dignity than he does at the present day in Russia. Princes as false and crafty as the heroes of the Kremlin would never have been surnamed *great* in western Europe.

The ichonostasis of this cathedral is magnificently painted and gilded from the pavement to the roof. The ichonostasis is a partition, or panel, raised in Greek churches between the sanctuary, which is always concealed by doors, and the nave, where the faithful congregate. The church is nearly square, very lofty, and so small that in walking in it you feel as if in a dungeon. The building contains the tombs of numerous patriarchs; it has also very rich shrines and famous relics brought from Asia. Viewed in detail, the cathedral is any thing but beautiful, yet, as a whole, there is something about it which is imposing. If we do not admire, we feel a sense of sadness; and this is something: for sadness disposes the mind to religious sentiments. But in the great structures of the Catholic church there is something more than Christian sadness; there is the song of triumph and victorious faith.

The sacristy contains many curiosities; but I do not pretend to give a list of the wonders of Moscow. I speak of every thing that strikes me, and for more complete accounts refer the reader to Laveau, Schnitzler, and, above all, to my successors. Fresh travellers cannot fail soon to explore Russia; for this country will not long remain so little known as it is at present.

The steeple of John the Great, Ivan Velikoï, is contained within the walls of the Kremlin. It is the loftiest building in the city; its cupola, according to Russian custom, is gilded with the gold of ducats. This singular tower is an object of veneration to the Muscovite peasants. Every thing is holy at Moscow, so strong is the sentiment of respect in the heart of the Russian people.

The church of Spassna Borou (the Saviour in the Garden), the most ancient in Moscow, was also shown to me; and near to it a bell, a piece of which is broken off, the largest bell, I believe, in the world. It is placed on the ground, and is in itself a cupola. It was re-cast after a fire which had caused it to fall, in the reign of the Empress Anne.

We likewise visited two convents within the Kremlin, those of the Miracles and the Ascension, in which latter are the tombs of several Czarinas; among others that of Helena, the mother of Ivan the Terrible. She was worthy of her son: unmerciful like him, talent was her only recommendation. Some of the wives of the same tyrant are also buried here. The churches of the Convent of the Ascension astonish foreigners by their riches.

At last I summoned courage to face the Corinthian columns of the Treasury; so braving with closed eyes those dragons of bad taste, I entered the glorious arsenal, where are ranged, as in a cabinet of curiosities, the most interesting historical relics of Russia. . . .

The group of these varied monuments gives to the Kremlin an aspect of theatrical decoration that is seen nowhere else in the world: but not one of the buildings in that Russian forum will bear a separate examination any better than those dispersed throughout the rest of the city. At the first view, Moscow produces a very powerful impression: to a bearer of despatches, travelling quickly past its walls, it would, with its churches, convents, palaces, and strong castles, any of which might be taken for the abode of unearthly beings, appear the most beautiful of cities.

Unfortunately they are now building at the Kremlin a new palace for the Emperor. Have they considered whether this sacrilegious improvement will not spoil the general aspect, unique as it is in the world, of the ancient edifices of the holy fortress? The present habitation of the sovereign is, I admit, mean in appearance; but, to remedy the inconvenience, they are intrenching upon the most venerable portions of the old national sanctuary. This is profanation. Were I the Emperor, I would rather raise my new palace in the air, than disturb one stone of the old ramparts of the Kremlin.

One day at Petersburg, in speaking to me of these works, the monarch said that they would beautify Moscow. I doubt it, was the answer of my thoughts: you talk as if you could ornament history. I know that the architecture of the old fortress does not conform to any rules of art: but it is the expression of the manners, acts, and ideas of a people and of an age that the world will never see again; it is, therefore, sacred as the irrevocable past. The seal of a power superior to man is there impressed—the power of time. But in Russia, authority spares nothing. The Emperor, who, I believe, saw in my face an expression of regret, left me, assuring me that his new palace would be much larger and better adapted to the wants of his court than the old one. Such a reason would suffice to answer any objection in a country like this in which I travel.

In order that the court may be better lodged, they are going to include within the new palace, the little church of the Saviour in the Garden. That venerable sanctuary, the most ancient, I believe, in the Kremlin and in Moscow, is then to disappear among the fine white walls, with which they will surround it, to the great regret of all lovers of antiquity and of the picturesque.

What more provokes me is the mockery of respect with which the profanation is to be committed. They boast that the old monument will still be preserved; in other words, it will not be destroyed, but only buried alive in a palace. Such is the way in which they here conciliate the official veneration for the past with the passion for "comfort," newly imported from England. This manner of beautifying the national city of the Russians is altogether worthy of Peter the Great. Was it not sufficient that the founder of the new city should abandon the old one? No!— his successors must also demolish it, under the pretext of adorning it.

The Emperor Nicholas might have acquired a glory of his own, instead of crawling along the road laid out by another. He had only to leave the Petersburg winter-palace when it had been burnt for him, and to return and fix the imperial residence in the Kremlin as it stands; building for the wants of his household and for the great fêtes of the court, as many palaces, beyond the sacred walls, as he might think fit. By this return he would have repaired the fault of Peter the Great; who, instead of dragging his boyards into the theatre which he built for them on the Baltic, ought to have been able to civilise them in their own homes, by availing himself of the admirable elements which nature had placed within their reach and at his disposal—elements which he slighted with a contempt and with a superficiality of mind unworthy of a superior man, as, in certain respects, he was. At each step that the stranger takes on the road from Petersburg to Moscow, Russia, with its illimitable territory, its immense agricultural resources, expands and enlarges on the mind in a measure equal to that in which Peter the Great diminished and contracted it. Monomachus, in the eleventh century, was a truly Russian prince; Peter I., in the eighteenth, was, in his false method of improving, nothing more than a tributary of foreigners, an imitator of the Dutch, a mimicker of civilisation, which he copied with the minuteness of a savage.

If I were ever to see the throne of Russia majestically replaced upon its true basis, in the centre of the empire, at Moscow; if St. Petersburg, its stuccoes and gilt work, left to crumble in the marsh whereon it is reared, were to become only what it should have always been, a simple naval port, built of granite, a magnificent entrepôt of commerce between Russia and the West, as, on the other side, Kazan and Nijni serve as steps between Russia and the East; I should say that the Slavonian nation, triumphing by a just pride over the vanity of its leaders, sees at length its proper course, and deserves to attain the object of its ambition. Constantinople waits for it; there arts and riches will naturally flow, in recompense of the efforts of a people, called to be so much the more great and glorious as they have been long obscure and resigned.

Let the mind picture to itself the grandeur of a capital seated in the centre of a plain many thousands of leagues in extent—a plain which stretches from Persia to Lapland, from Astrachan and the Caspian to the Uralian Mountains and the White Sea with its port of Archangel; from thence, bordering the Baltic, where stand Petersburg and Kronstadt, the two arsenals of Moscow, it sweeps to the Vistula in the west, and from thence again to the Bosphorus, where conquest awaits the coming of the Russians, where Constantinople will serve as another portal of communication between Moscow, the holy city of the Muscovites, and the world.

The Emperor Nicholas, notwithstanding his practical sense and his profound sagacity, has not discerned the best means of accomplishing such an end. He comes now and then to promenade in the Kremlin; but this is not sufficient. He ought to have recognised the necessity of permanently fixing himself there: if he has recognised it, he has not had the energy to make such a sacrifice,—this is his error. Under Alexander, the Russians burnt Moscow to save the Empire: under Nicholas, God burnt the palace of Petersburg to advance the destinies of Russia: but Nicholas does not answer to the call of Providence. Russia still waits!— Instead of rooting himself like a cedar in the only fitting soil, he disturbs and upturns that soil to build stables and a palace, in which he may be more conveniently lodged during his journeys; and with this contemptible object in view, he forgets that every stone of the national fortress is, or ought to be, an object of veneration for all true Muscovites. It is not wise in him—a sovereign whose authority depends upon the superstitious sentiments of his people—to shake, by a sacrilege, the respect of the Muscovites for the only truly national monument which they possess. The Kremlin is the work of the Russian genius; but that irregular, picturesque marvel is at length condemned to pass under the yoke of modern art: it is the taste of Catherine II., which still reigns in Russia.

That woman, who, notwithstanding the grasp of her mind, knew nothing of the arts or of poetry, not content with having covered the empire with shapeless monuments copied from the models of antiquity, left behind her a plan for rendering the façade of the Kremlin more regular; and here behold her grandson, in part executing the monstrous project: flat white surfaces, stiff lines, and right angles replace the recesses and projections, the slopes and terraces, where lights and shadows formerly played; where the eye was agreeably bewildered, and the imagination excited by external staircases, walls encrusted with coloured arabesques, and palaces of painted Delft ware. Let them be demolished, let them be concealed;—are they not going to be replaced by smooth white walls, well-squared windows, and ceremonious portals? No! Peter the Great is not dead: the Asiatics whom he enrolled and drilled, travellers and imitators, like him, of the Europe which, while continuing to copy, they affect to disdain, pursue their work of barbarism, miscalled civilisation, deceived by the maxims of a master who adopted uniformity for his motto, and the uniform for his standard.

There are, then, neither artists nor architects in Russia: all who preserve any sentiment of the beautiful ought to throw themselves at the feet of the emperor, and implore him to spare his Kremlin. What the enemy could not do, the emperor is accomplishing. He is destroying the holy ramparts of which the miners of Buonaparte could scarcely disturb a stone.

And I, who am come to the Kremlin to see this historical wonder thus spoiled, dare not raise one cry against the perpetration of the impious work—dare not make one appeal, in the name of history, the arts, and good taste, in favour of these old monuments condemned to make room for the abortive conceptions of modern architecture. I protest, but it is very secretly, against this wrong inflicted upon a nation, upon history and good taste; and if a few of the most intelligent and informed of the men I meet here dare to listen to me, all the answer that they venture to give is, that "the emperor wishes his new residence to be more *suitable* than the old one: of what, then, do you complain?" *(suitable* is the sacramental word of Russian despotism.)* "He has commanded that it should be rebuilt on the very spot, even, where stood the palace of his ancestors: he will have changed nothing."

I am, being a stranger, prudent, and answer nothing to such

* convenable.

reasoning: but were I a Russian, I would defend, stone by stone, the ancient walls and enchanted towers of the fortress of the Ivans; I would almost prefer the dungeon under the Neva, or exile, to the shame of remaining a mute accomplice in this imperial vandalism. The martyr of good taste might yet obtain an honourable place below the martyr of faith: the arts are a religion,—a religion which, in our days, is not the least powerful, nor the least revered. . . .

❖

CHAPTER XXVIII

❖

Moscow is about the only mountainous district in the centre of Russia. Not that this word is to suggest the idea of Switzerland or Italy: the soil is full of inequalities, and that is all. But the contrast presented by these hills, rising in the middle of an expanse, where both the eye and the thoughts lose themselves as on the savannahs of America or the steppes of Asia, produces an effect that is very striking. Moscow is the city of panoramas. With its commanding sites and its grotesque edifices, which might serve as models for the fantastic compositions of Martin, it recalls the idea which we form, without knowing why, of Persepolis, Bagdad, Babylon, or Palmyra,—romantic capitals of fabulous lands, whose history is a poem, and whose architecture is a dream. In a word, at Moscow we forget Europe. This was what I did not know in France, although I had read nearly all the travellers' descriptions of the city. They have then failed in their duty. There is one especially whom I cannot pardon for not having permitted others to enjoy his visit to Russia. No descriptions are equal to the sketches of a painter, exact and, at the same time, picturesque, like Horace Vernet. What man was ever more gifted to perceive, and to make others perceive, the spirit that breathes in things? The truth of painting lies not so much in the form as in the expression of objects: he understood them like a poet, and transferred them like an artist; consequently, every time I feel the insufficiency of my words, I am inclined to be angry with Horace Vernet.

Here, every view is a landscape. If art has done little for Moscow, the caprice of the builders and the force of circumstances have created marvels. The extraordinary forms of the edifices, and the grandeur of the masses, strongly impress the imagination. The enjoyment, it must be owned, is of an inferior order: Moscow is not the product of genius; connoisseurs will there find no monuments of art worthy of a minute examination: those monuments are rather the strange and deserted habitations of some race of giants; they are the works of the cyclops. In a city where no great artist has left the impress of his thoughts we may feel astonishment, but nothing more, and astonishment is soon exhausted. However, there is nothing here, not even the disenchantment that follows the first surprise, from which I cannot draw a lesson: more particularly am I struck with the visible intimate connection between the aspect of the city and the character of the people. The Russians love all that dazzles; they are easily seduced by appearances: to excite envy, no matter at what price, contitutes their happiness. The English are gnawed by pride, the Russians are corroded by vanity.

I feel the necessity of here reminding the reader that generalities always pass for injustices. Once for all, I would state that my observations never exclude exceptions; and I avail myself of the occasion to express the respect and admiration I entertain for the merits and agreeable qualities of individuals to whom my criticisms do not apply.

Other travellers have observed before I did, that the less we know of a Russian the more amiable we find him. The Russians have retorted upon those travellers, that they spoke in their own disparagement, and that the coolness of which they complained only proved their want of merit. "We gave you a good reception," they add, "because we are naturally hospitable; and if we afterwards changed in our manner towards you, it was because we thought more highly of you at first than you deserved." Such an answer was made a considerable time ago to a French traveller, an able writer, but whose position obliged him to be excessively reserved. I do not mean here to cite either his name or his book.

The few truths which, in his prudent recitals, he allowed himself to expose, placed him in a very disagreeable position. This was the penalty for denying himself the exercise of his intellect, in order to submit to expectations which can never be satisfied; not any more by flattering them than by doing them justice. It would cost less to brave them; and on this opinion the reader will perceive I act.

Moscow prides herself on the progress of her manufactures. The Russian silks here contend with those of both East and West. The merchant-quarter, the Kitaigorod, as well as the street called the Bridge of the Marshals, where the most elegant shops are found, are reckoned among the curiosities of the city. If I mention them it is because I think that the efforts of the Russians to free themselves from the tribute which they pay to the industry of other nations, may produce important political consequences in Europe. The liberty that reigns in Moscow is illusive; yet it cannot be denied that in its streets there are men who appear to move spontaneously, who think and act under an impulse of their own. Moscow is in this respect very different from Petersburg. Among the causes of the difference, I place in the first rank the vast extent and the varied surface of the territory in the midst of which it stands. Space and inequality (I here take this word in all its acceptations) are the elements of liberty; for absolute equality is the synonyme of tyranny, though it is the minority who may be placed under the yoke: liberty and equality exclude each other by means of reserves and combinations, more or less abstruse, which neutralise the effect of things while preserving their names.

Moscow remains almost buried in the midst of a country of which it is the capital: hence the seal of originality impressed upon its buildings, the air of liberty which distinguishes its inhabitants, and the little inclination of the Czars for a residence whose aspect is so independent. The Czars, ancient tyrants mitigated by the fashion which has metamorphosed them into emperors, and even into amiable men, fly Moscow. They prefer Petersburg, with all its inconveniences, for they wish to be in continual communication with the West of Europe. Russia, as formed by Peter the Great, does not trust to herself to live and to learn. At Moscow they could not obtain in a week's time the little importations of the current ancedotes and small gossip of Paris, nor the ephemeral literature of Europe. These details, contemptible as they appear to us, furnish the chief excitement of the Russian court, and consequently of Russia.

If the freezing or the melting snow did not render railroads useless in this land during six or eight months of the year, we should see the Russian government surpass all others in the construction of those roads which are, as it were, lessening the size of earth; for that government suffers more than any other from the inconveniences of distance. But, notwithstanding acceleration of the speed of travelling, a vast extent of territory will always be the chief obstacle to the circulation of ideas: for the soil will not allow itself, like the sea, to be crossed in all directions. The water, which, at first sight, appears destined to separate the inhabitants of the world, is the medium which, in reality, unites them. Wonderful problem! Man, the prisoner of God, is yet allowed to be the king of nature. . . .

Moscow is the city for painters of character pieces; but architects, sculptors, and historical painters have nothing to do there. Clusters and masses of edifices, isolated in deserts, present multitudes of striking pictures. This ancient capital is the only large city which, although populous, still retains all the picturesque attributes of the country. It contains as many open roads as streets, as many cultivated fields as hills covered with buildings, as many deserted valleys as public squares. After leaving the crowded centre, we find ourselves among lakes, forests, and villages, rather than in a city. Here, rises a stately monastery, surmounted with its multitudes of church-steeples; there, hills built to the summit; others again bear only crops of corn, between them winds a stream of water; a little further are isolated edifices, as singular as varied in their style; among them are theatres with antique peristyles, and palaces of wood—the only private dwellings that display a national architecture. All these varied structures are half concealed by verdant foliage, whilst the entire poetical decoration is crowned by the old Kremlin, with its indented walls and singular towers. That Parthenon of the Slavonians commands and protects Moscow: it reminds one of the Doge of Venice seated in the midst of his senate.

This evening, the tents where the holiday folks of Devitschie-pol were congregated, emitted various scents, the mixture of which produced an atmosphere that was intolerable. There was perfumed Russian leather, spirituous liquors, sour beer, cabbages, the grease of the boots of Cossacks, and the musk and ambergris of numerous fashionable loiterers, who appeared determined to suffer from ennui, were it only out of aristocratic pride. I found it impossible long to breathe this mephitic air.

The greatest pleasure of the people is drunkenness; in other words, forgetfulness. Unfortunate beings! they must dream if they would be happy. As a proof of the good temper of the Russians, when the mugics get tipsy, these men, brutalised as they are, become softened, instead of infuriated. Unlike the drunkards of our country, who quarrel and fight, they weep and embrace each other. Curious and interesting nation! it would be delightful to make them happy. But the task is hard, if not impossible. Show me how to satisfy the vague desires of a giant,— young, idle, ignorant, ambitious, and so shackled that he can scarcely stir hand or foot. Never do I pity this people without equally pitying the all-powerful man who is their governor.

❖

THE NOBLEMEN'S CLUB ❖ POLITE EDUCATION OF THE RUSSIANS ❖ HABITS OF THE HIGHER CLASSES ❖ A RUSSIAN COFFEE-HOUSE ❖ RELIGIOUS BELIEF OF THE OLD SERFS ❖ SOCIETY IN MOSCOW ❖ A COUNTRY HOUSE IN A CITY ❖ REAL POLITENESS ❖ REVIEW OF RUSSIAN CHARACTER ❖ MURDER IN A NUNNERY ❖ CONVERSATION AT A TABLE-D'HÔTE ❖ THE LOVELACE OF THE KREMLIN ❖ A BURLESQUE PETITION ❖ MODERN PRUDERY ❖ PARTING SCENE WITH PRINCE ——— ❖ AN ELEGANT COACHMAN ❖ MORALS OF THE CITIZENS' WIVES ❖ LIBERTINISM THE FRUIT OF DESPOTISM ❖ MORAL LICENCE IN LIEU OF POLITICAL FREEDOM ❖ CONDITION OF THE SERFS AND OTHER CLASSES ❖ NATURE OF RUSSIAN AMBITION ❖ RESULTS OF THE SYSTEM OF PETER THE GREAT ❖

CHAPTER XXIX

❖

. . . I have also been shown the University, the School of Cadets, the Institutions of St. Catherine and of Saint Alexander, the Hospitals for Widows and for Foundlings, all vast and pompous in appearance. The Russians pride themselves in having so great a number of magnificent public establishments to show to strangers: for my part, I should be content with less of this kind of splendour; for no places are more tedious to wander over than these white and sumptuously-monotonous palaces, where every thing is conducted in military order, and where human life seems reduced to the action of the pendulum of a clock. . . .

The club of the nobles is closed during the present season. I visited it also as a matter of conscience. In the principal hall is a statue of Catherine II. This hall is ornamented with pillars and a semi-rotunda; it will contain about 3000 persons; and, during the winter, magnificent balls are given in it. I can well believe this, for the Russian nobles reserve all their luxury for pleasures of parade. To dazzle is, with them, to display civilisation. It is but little more than one hundred years since Peter the Great dictated to them the first laws of politeness, and instituted assemblies similar to those of old Europe; obliging the men to admit the other sex into these circles, and exhorting them to take off their hats when they entered an apartment. While thus teaching them common civility, he was himself exercising the vilest of all professions—that of the headsman. He has been seen in a single evening to strike off twenty heads with his own hand, and has been heard to boast of his address. Such was the education, and such the example, given to the Russians by this worthy heir of the Ivans, —this prince whom they have made their God, and whom they view as the eternal model of a Russian sovereign!

The new converts to civilisation have not yet lost their taste, as upstarts, for every thing that dazzles—every thing that attracts the eye. Children and savages always love these things. The Russians are children who have the habit, but not the experience of misfortune; hence the mixture of levity and causticity which characterises them. The enjoyments of a calm and equable life, adapted solely to satisfy the affections of intimacy, to administer to the pleasures of conversation and of mind, would never long suffice them: not that these great lords show themselves altogether insensible to refined pleasures; but, to captivate the haughty frivolity of such disguised satraps, to fix their vagrant imaginations, lively excitements are necessary. The love of play, intemperance, libertinism, and the gratifications of vanity, can scarcely fill the void in their satiated hearts: the creation of God does not furnish wherewith these unhappy victims of wealth and indolence can get through their weary days. In their proud misery they summon to their aid the spirit of destruction. All modern Europe is the prey of ennui. It is this which attests the nature of the life led by the youth of the present day: but Russia suffers from the evil worse than the other communities; for here every thing is excessive. To describe the ravages of society in a population like that of Moscow would be difficult: nowhere have the mental maladies engendered in the soul by ennui—that passion of men who have no passions—appeared to me so serious or so frequent as among the higher classes in Russia: it may be said that society has here commenced by its abuses. When vice does not suffice to enable the human heart to shake off the ennui that preys upon it, that heart proceeds to crime.

The interior of a Russian coffee-house is very curious. It consists generally of a large, low apartment, badly lighted, and usually occupying the first floor of the house. The waiters are dressed in white shirts, girded round the middle, and falling like a tunic over loose white pantaloons. Their hair is long and smooth, like that of all the lower orders of Russians; and their whole adjustment reminds one of the theophilanthropes of the French republic, or the priests of the Opera when paganism was the fashion at the theatre. They serve you with excellent tea, superior, indeed, to any found in other lands, with coffee and liqueurs; but this is done with a silence and solemnity very different from the noisy gaiety which reigns in the *cafés* of Paris. In Russia, all popular pleasures are melancholy in their character: mirth is viewed as a privilege; consequently, I always find it assumed, affected, overdone, and worse than the natural sadness. Here, the man who laughs is either an actor, a drunkard, or a flatterer.

This reminds me of the times when the Russian serfs believed, in the simplicity of their abjectness, that heaven was only made for their masters: dreadful humility of misfortune! Such was the manner in which the Greek church taught Christianity to the people.

The society of Moscow is agreeable; the mixture of the patriarchal traditions of the old world with the polished manners of the modern, produces a combination that is, in a manner, original. The hospitable customs of ancient Asia and the elegant language of civilised Europe have met together at this point of the globe, to render life pleasant and easy. Moscow, fixed on the limits of two continents, marks, in the middle of the earth, a spot for rest between London and Pekin.

A small number of letters of introduction suffice to put a stranger in communication with a crowd of persons, distinguished either by fortune, rank, or mind. The *début* of a traveller is here easy.

I was invited a few days ago to dine at a country-house. It is a pavilion situated within the limits of the city, but to reach it, we had to traverse, for more than a league, fields that resemble steppes, to skirt solitary pools of waters; and, at last, on approaching the house, we perceived, beyond the garden, a dark and deep forest of firs, which borders the exterior bounds of Moscow. Who would not have been struck at the sight of these profound shades, these majestic solitudes, in a city where all the luxuries and refinements of modern civilisation are to be found?

Such contrasts are characteristics; nothing similar is to be seen elsewhere.

I entered a wooden house—another singularity. In Moscow both rich and poor are sheltered by planks and boards, as in the primitive cottages. But the interior of these large cabins exhibits the luxury of the finest palaces of Europe. If I lived at Moscow, I would have a wooden house. It is the only kind of habitation the style of which is national, and, what is more important, it is the only kind that is adapted to the climate. Houses of wood are esteemed by the true Muscovites as warmer and healthier than those of stone.

We dined in the garden; and, that nothing should be wanting to the originality of the scene, I found the table laid under a tent. The conversation, although between men only, and very lively, was decent—a thing rarely known among the nations who believe themselves the first in civilisation. The guests were persons who had both seen and read much; and their views appeared to me very clear and just. The Russians are apes in the manners and customs of refined life; but those who think (it is true their number is limited) become themselves again, infamiliar conversation —Greeks, namely, endowed with a quickness and sagacity which is hereditary. . . .

A story of the death of a young man, killed in the convent of——, by the nuns themselves, he told me yesterday at a full table-d'hôte, before several grave and elderly personages, employés and placemen, who listened with an extraordinary patience to this and several other tales of a similar kind, all very contrary to good manners.

I have surnamed this singular young man, Prince ——, the Don Juan of the Old Testament, so greatly does the measure of his madness and audacity exceed the ordinary bounds of an abandoned life among modern nations. Nothing is little or moderate in Russia: if the land is not, as my Italian cicerone calls it, a land of miracles, it is truly a land of giants.

The story in question related to a young man, who, after having passed an entire month concealed within the convent of——, began, at last, to weary of his excess of happiness to a degree that wearied the holy sisters also. He appeared dying: whereupon the nuns, wishing to be rid of him, but fearing the scandal that might ensue should they send him to die in the world, concluded that it would be better to make an end of him themselves. No sooner said than done:—the mangled remains of the wretched being were found a few days after at the bottom of a well. The affair was hushed up.

If we are to believe the same authorities, there are numerous convents in Moscow in which the rules of the cloister are little observed. One of the friends of the prince, yesterday exhibited before me, to the whole legion of libertines, the rosary of a novice, that he said she had forgotten and left that very morning in his chamber. Another made a trophy of a Book of Prayers, which he stated had belonged to one of the sisters who was reputed among the most holy of the community of ——; and the audience warmly applauded.

I shall not go on. Each had his scandalous anecdote to relate, and all excited loud peals of laughter. Gaiety, ever increasing, soon became drunken riot under the influence of the wine of Ai, which overflowed in goblets, whose size was more capable of satisfying Muscovite intemperance than our old-fashioned champagne-glasses. In the midst of the general disorder, the young Prince —— and myself alone preserved our reason,—he, because he can outdrink everybody, I, because I cannot drink at all, and had therefore abstained from attempting.

In the midst of the uproar, the Lovelace of the Kremlin rose with a solemn air, and, with the authority which his fortune, his name, his handsome face, and yet more, his superior mental capacity give him, he commanded silence, and to my great surprise obtained it. I could have fancied I was reading the poetical description of a tempest appeased by the voice of some pagan god. The young god proposed to the friends whom the gravity of his aspect had thus suddenly calmed, to indite a petition, addressed to the proper authorities, humbly remonstrating, in the name of the courtesans of Moscow, that the ancient religious institutions of nunneries so completely interfered with and rivalled their *lay community*, in the exercise of their calling, as to render that calling no longer profitable; and therefore respectfully stating that, as the expenses of these poor cyprians were not diminished in the same proportion as their gains, they ventured to hope an equitable consideration of their case would induce the authorities to see fit to deduct from a part of the revenue of the said convents, a pecuniary aid, which had become absolutely necessary, unless it was wished that the religious orders should entirely take the place of the civil recluses. The motion was put and carried with loud acclamations; ink and paper were called for; and the young madman immediately drew up, in very good French, and with magisterial dignity, a document too scandalously burlesque for me to insert here, though I have a copy. It was thrice read by the author before the meeting, with a loud emphatical voice, and was received with the most flattering marks of approbation.

Such was the scene, of which I have perhaps already recounted too much, that I witnessed yesterday in one of the best frequented taverns of Moscow. It was the day after the agreeable dinner-party in the pretty pavilion of ———. In vain is uniformity the law of the state: nature lives on variety, and knows how, at all costs, to obtain her wants.

I have spared the reader many details, and greatly moderated the expression of those which I have inflicted upon him. If I had been more exact, I should not be read. Montaigne, Rabelais, Shakspeare, and many other great describers, would chasten their style if they wrote in our age; how much more carefully, then, should they who have not the same right to independence watch over their words and allusions. The prudery of the present day, if not respectable, is at least formidable. Virtue blushes; but hypocrisy loudly exclaims.

The captain of the troop of debauchees, whose head-quarters is the tavern before noticed, is endowed with so singular an elegance, his bearing is so distinguished, his person so agreeable, there is so much good taste even in his follies, so much kindly feeling painted on his countenance, so much nobleness in his manner, and even in his wildest language, that we pity more than we blame him. He rules from a high elevation the companions of his excesses; he has no appearance of being born for bad company; and it is impossible to avoid feeling a deep interest in him, although he is, in great part, responsible for the errors of his imitators. Superiority, even in evil, always exerts its influence.

The Imperial Kremlin, Moscow
A familiar view, depicting the Kremlin's many churches and monasteries—
some razed after the Revolution—and spectacular walls and gates.
Lithograph by V. F. Timm.

View from the Kremlin Terrace West
A less familiar perspective of the Kremlin's walls, towers,
and churches, and its surrounding buildings.
Lithograph by A. Durand.

Grand Duchess Elena Pavlovna (1806–75)
Advocate of social reform and sister of Czar Nicholas I, the Grand Duchess
presided over one of St. Petersburg's most influential literary salons.
Engraving by K. P. Briullov.

Grand Duchess Elena Pavlovna's Country Palace
Tinted lithograph by V. F. Timm, 1853.

Panorama of the Ancient Walled City of Kostroma
In Moscow province.
Drawing by L. R. von Klenze.

The Nijni-Novgorod Market
Lithograph by V. F. Timm.

The Market Cathedral and Chinese Stalls in Nijni-Novgorod
An approach to a bridge spanning the Oka River.
Lithograph by V. F. Timm.

Aleksandr Ivanovich Turgenev (1784–1845)
An 1833 portrait of the well-traveled scholar and archaeographer,
elder cousin of the famous novelist. By K. P. Briullov.

Petr Iakovlevich Chaadaev (1794–1856)
Portrait of the controversial "Westernizer" philosopher and social critic.

Rifleman of the Egerski Regiment
A Life Guards regiment.

Prince Petr Borisovich Kozlovsky (1783–1840)
Lithograph by K. I. Pol.

Empress Alexandra Fedorovna (1798–1860), Wife of Czar Nicholas I
Portrait by the miniaturist I. Vinberg.

Provincial Ball
Engraving by A. V. Agin, 1846, an early illustrator
of the Russian realist school.

He had engaged me to-day to accompany him on an excursion into the country, which was to occupy two days. But I have just been to find him in his usual retreat, in order to excuse myself. I pleaded the necessity of hastening my journey to Nijni, and obtained my release. But before leaving him to the course of folly which is dragging him onwards, I must describe the scene that was prepared for me in the court of the tavern, into which they obliged me to descend to view the decampment of this horde of libertines. The farewell was a true bacchanal.

Imagine a dozen young men already more than half drunk, loudly disputing among each other respecting their seats in three calèches, each drawn by four horses. A group of lookers on, the tavern-keeper at their head, followed by all the servants of the house and stables, admired, envied, and ridiculed—although this last was done under the cloak of much outward reverence; meanwhile the leader of the band, standing up in his open carriage, played his part, and ruled, by voice and gesture, with unaffected gravity. There was placed at his feet a bucket, or rather a large tub, full of champagne-bottles in ice. This species of portable cellar was the provision for the journey,—to refresh his throat, as he said, when the dust of the road was troublesome. One of his adjutants, whom he called the general of the corks, had already opened two or three bottles; and the young madman was dispensing huge goblets of the costly wine, the best champagne to be had in Moscow, to the bystanders, as a parting libation. Two cups, quickly emptied and incessantly replenished by his most zealous satellite, the general of the corks, were in his hands. He drank one, and offered the other to the nearest bystander. His servants were all clothed in grand livery, with the exception of the coachman, a young serf whom he had recently brought from his estates. This man was dressed in a most costly manner, far more remarkable in its apparent simplicity than the gold-lace trappings of the other servants. He had on a shirt of precious silken tissue, brought from Persia, and above it a cafetan of the finest cassimere, bordered with beautiful velvet, which, opening at the breast, displayed the shirt, plaited in folds so small as to be scarcely perceptible. The dandies of Petersburg like the youngest and handsomest of their people to be thus dressed on days of ceremony. The rest of the costume corresponded with this luxury. The boots, of fine Torjeck leather, embroidered with flowers in gold and silver thread, glittered at the feet of the rustic, who seemed dazzled with his own splendour, and was so perfumed that I was almost overcome with the essences exhaled from his hair, beard, and clothes, at the distance of several feet from the carriage.

After having drunk with the whole tavern, the young noble leant towards the man thus decked out, and presented him with a foaming cup, saying, "drink." The poor, gilded mugic was, in his inexperience, at a loss how to act. "Drink, I say," continued his master (this was translated to me), "drink, you rascal; it is not to you I give this champagne, but to your horses, who will not have strength to gallop the whole journey if the coachman is not drunk:" upon which the whole assembly laughed and loudly cheered. The coachman was soon persuaded: he was already in the third bumper when his master gave the signal to start, which he did not do till he had renewed to me, with a charming politeness, his regret at having been unable to persuade me to accompany him on this party of pleasure. He appeared so *distingué*, that, while he spoke, I forgot the place and scene, and fancied myself at Versailles in the time of Louis XIV.

At last he departed for the chateau, where he is to spend three days. These gentlemen call such an excursion a summer *hunt*.

We may easily guess how they relieve themselves in the country from the ennui of town life—by continuing the same thing; by pursuing the same career; by reviving the scenes of Moscow, except, at least, that they introduce upon them new *figurantes*. They carry with them, in these journeys, cargoes of engravings of the most celebrated pictures of France and Italy, which furnish them with subjects for *tableaux vivants*, which they cause to be represented with certain modifications of costume.

The villages, and all that they contain, are their own; so that it may easily be supposed the privilege of the nobleman in Russia extends further than at the Opera Comique of Paris.

The ——— tavern, open to all the world, is situated in one of the public squares of the city, a few steps only from a guard-house full of Cossacks, whose stiff bearing and severely gloomy air would impart to foreigners the idea of a country where no one dares to laugh even innocently.

As I have imposed upon myself the duty of communicating the ideas that I have formed of this land, I am obliged to add to the picture already sketched, a few new specimens of the conversation of the parties already brought before the reader.

One boasted of himself and his brothers being the sons of the footmen and the coachmen of their father; and he drank, and made the guests drink, to the health of all his unknown parents. Another claimed the honour of being brother (on the father's side) of all the waiting-maids of his mother.

Many of these vile boasts are no doubt made for the sake of talking: but to invent such infamies in order to glory in them, shows a corruption of mind that proves wickedness to the very core—wickedness worse even than that exhibited in the mad actions of these libertines.

According to them, the citizens' wives in Moscow are no better than the women of rank.

During the months that their husbands go to the fair of Nijni, the officers of the garrison take special care not to leave the city. This is the season of easy assignations. The ladies are generally accompanied to the place of rendezvous by some *respectable* relation, to whose care their absent husbands have confided them. The good-will and silence of these family duennas have also to be paid for. Gallantry of this kind cannot be excused as a love affair: there is no love without bashful modesty,—such is the sentence pronounced from all eternity against women who cheat themselves of happiness, and who degrade instead of purifying themselves by tenderness. The defenders of the Russians pretend that at Moscow the women have no lovers: I agree with them: some other term must be employed to designate the *friends* whose intimacy they seek in the absence of their husbands.

I repeat that I am disposed to doubt many things of this kind that are told to me; but I cannot doubt that they are related pleasantly and complacently to the first newly-arrived foreigner; and the air of triumph of the narrator seems to say—we also, you see, are civilised!

The more I consider these debauchees' manner of life, the

more I wonder at the social position—to use the language of the day—which they here preserve, notwithstanding conduct that in any other land would shut all doors against them. I cannot tell how such notorious offenders are treated in their own families; but I can testify that, in public, every one pays them peculiar deference: their appearance is the signal for general hilarity; their company is the delight even of elderly men, who do not imitate them, but who certainly encourage them.

In observing the general reception which they receive, I ask myself what a person should here do to lose credit and character.

By a procedure altogether contrary to that observable among free people, whose manners become more puritanical, if not more pure, in proportion as democracy gains ground in the constitution, corruptness is here confounded with liberal institutions; and distinguished men of bad character are admired as is with us a talented opposition or minority. The young Prince —— did not commence his career as a libertine until after finishing a three-years' exile at the Caucasus, where the climate ruined his health. It was immediately after leaving college that he incurred this penalty for having broken the window-panes of some shops in Petersburg. The government, having determined to see a political intention in this harmless riot, has, by its excessive severity, converted a hair-brained youth, while yet a child, into a profligate, lost to his country, his family, and himself.* Such are the aberrations into which despotism—that most immoral of governments—can drive the minds of men.

Here all revolt appears legitimate; revolt even against reason and against God! Where order is oppressive, disorder has its martyrs. A Lovelace, a Don Juan, or yet worse if it were possible, would be viewed as a kind of liberator, merely because he had incurred legal punishments. The blame can only fall on the judge. People here, avow their hatred of morals just as others would elsewhere say, "I detest arbitrary government."

I brought with me to Russia a preconceived opinion, which I possess no longer. I believed, with many others, that autocracy

* I have been assured, since my return to France, that he has married, and is living a very orderly life.

derived its chief strength from the equality which it caused to reign beneath it. But this equality is an illusion. I said, and heard it said, that when one man is all-powerful, the others are all equal, that is, all equally nullities; which equality, if not a happiness, is a consolation. The argument was too logical to prove practically true. There is no such thing as absolute power in the world; there are arbitrary and capricious powers; but, however outrageous they may become, they are never heavy enough to establish perfect equality among their subjects.

The Emperor Nicholas can do every thing. But if he often did all that he could do, he would not retain this power very long. So long, therefore, as he forbears, the condition of the nobleman is very different from that of the mugic or the tradesman whom he ruins. I maintain that there is at this day, in Russia, more real inequality in the conditions of men than in any other European land.

The circumstances of human societies are too complicated to be submitted to the rigour of mathematical calculation. I can see reigning under the Emperor, among the castes which constitute his empire, hatreds which have their source solely in the abuses of secondary power.

In general, the men here use a very soft and specious language. They will tell you with the most benign air that the Russian serfs are the happiest peasants upon earth. Do not listen to them, they deceive you: many families of serfs in distant cantons suffer even from hunger; many perish under poverty and ill treatment. In every class in Russia, humanity suffers; and the men who are sold with the land suffer more than the others. It will be pretended that they are protected by a legal right to the necessaries of life; such right is but a mockery for those who have no means of enforcing it.

It will be further said that it is the interest of the nobles to relieve the wants of their peasants. But does every man always understand his interests? Among us, those who act foolishly lose their fortunes, and there is the end of it: but here, as the fortune of man consists in the life of a number of men, he who mismanages his property may cause whole villages to perish of famine. The government, when attracted by too glaring excesses, sometimes puts the unprincipled nobleman under guardianship; but this ever-tardy step does not restore the dead. The mass of sufferings and unknown iniquities that must be produced by such manners, under such a constitution, with so great distances and so dreadful a climate, may be easily imagined. It is difficult to breathe freely in Russia when we think of all these miseries.

The nobleman has, in the government of his estates, the same difficulties to contend with as regards the distances of places, the ignorance of facts, the influence of customs, and the intrigues of subalterns, that the emperor has in his wider sphere of action; but the nobleman has, in addition, temptations that are more difficult to resist; for, being less exposed to public view, he is less controlled by public opinion and by the eye of Europe. From this firmly-established order, or rather disorder of things, there result inequalities, caprices, and injustices, unknown to societies where the law alone can change the relations of society.

It is not correct, then, to say that the force of despotism lies in the equality of its victims; it lies only in the ignorance of liberty and in the fear of tyranny. The power of an absolute master is a monster ever ready to give birth to a yet greater—the tyranny of the people.

It is true that democratic anarchy never lasts; whilst the regularity produced by the abuses of autocracy are perpetuated from generation to generation.

Military discipline, applied to the government of a state, is the powerful means of oppression, which constitutes, far more than the fiction of equality, the absolute power of the Russian sovereign. But this formidable force will sometimes turn against those who employ it. Such are the evils which incessantly menace Russia,—popular anarchy carried to its most frightful excess, if the nation revolt, and the prolongation of tyranny, applied with more or less rigour according to times and circumstances, if she continue in her obedience.

Duly to appreciate the difficulties in the political position of this country, we must not forget that the more ignorant the people are, and the longer they have been patient, the more likely is their vengeance to be dreadful. A government which wields power by maintaining ignorance, is more terrible than stable: a feeling of uneasiness in the nation—a degraded brutality in the army—terror around the administration, a terror shared even by those who govern—servility in the church—hypocrisy in the no- bility—ignorance and misery among the people—and Siberia for them all: such is the land as it has been made by necessity, his- tory, nature, and a Providence ever impenetrable in its designs.

And it is with so decayed a body that this giant, scarcely yet emerged out of Asia, endeavours now to influence by his weight, the balance of European policy, and strives to rule in the councils of the West, without taking into account the progress that Euro- pean diplomacy has made in sincerity during the last thirty years.

At Petersburg, to lie is still to perform the part of a good citizen; to speak the truth, even in apparently unimportant matters, is to conspire. You would lose the favour of the emperor, if you were to observe that he had a cold in his head. . . .

❖

CHAPTER XXX*

❖

I f we are to believe the Russians, all their roads are good during the summer season, even those that are not the great highways. I find them all bad. A road full of inequalities, sometimes as broad as a field, sometimes extremely narrow, passes through beds of sand in which the horses plunge above their knees, lose their wind, break their traces, and refuse to draw at every twenty yards; if these are passed, you soon plunge into pools of mud which conceal large stones and enormous stumps of trees, that are very destructive to the carriages. Such are the roads of this country, except during seasons when they become absolutely impassable, when the extreme of cold renders travelling dangerous, when storms of snow bury the country, or when floods, produced by the thaw, transform, for about three months in the year, the low plains into lakes; namely for about six weeks after summer, and for as many after the winter season; the rest of the year they continue marshes. The landscape remains the same. The villages still present the same double line of small wood houses, more or less ornamented with painted carvings, with their gable always facing the street, and flanked with a kind of enclosed court, or large shed open on one side. The country still continues the same monotonous though undulating plain, sometimes marshy, sometimes sandy; a few fields, wide pasture-ranges bounded by forests of fir, now at a distance, now close upon the

* Written at the convent of Troïtza, twenty leagues from Moscow, 17th of August.

road, sometimes well grown, more frequently scattered and stunted: such is the aspect of all those vast regions. Here and there is to be seen a country-house, or large and mansion-like farm, to which an avenue of birch-trees forms the approach. These are the manor-houses, or residences of the proprietors of the land; and the traveller welcomes them on the road as he would an oasis in the desert.

In some provinces the cottages are built of clay; in which case their appearance is more miserable, though still similar in general character: but from one end of the empire to the other, the greater number of the rustic dwellings are constructed of long and thick beams, carelessly hewn, but carefully caulked with moss and resin. The Crimea, a country altogether southern, is an exception; but, as compared to the whole empire, this country is but a point lost in immensity.

Monotony is the divinity of Russia; yet even this monotony has a certain charm for minds capable of enjoying solitude: the silence is profound in these unvarying scenes; and sometimes it becomes sublime on a desert plain, whose only boundaries are those of our power of vision.

The distant forest, it is true, presents no variety; it is not beautiful: but who can fathom it? When we remember that its only boundary is the wall of China, we feel a kind of reverence. Nature, like music, draws a part of her potent charm from repetitions. Singular mystery!—by means of uniformity she multiplies impressions. In seeking for too much novelty and variety there is danger of finding only the insipid and the clumsy, as may be seen in the case of modern musicians devoid of genius; but on the contrary, when the artist braves the danger of simplicity, art becomes as sublime as nature. The classic style—I use the word in its ancient acceptation—had little variety.

Pastoral life has always a peculiar charm. Its calm and regular occupations accord with the primitive character of men, and for a long time preserve the youth of races. The herdsmen, who never leave their native districts, are unquestionably the least unhappy of the Russians. Their beauty alone, which becomes more striking as I approach the government of Yarowslaw, speaks well of their mode of life.

I have met—which is a novelty to me in Russia—several extremely pretty peasant-girls, with golden hair, excessively delicate and scarcely coloured complexions, and eyes, which though of a light blue, are expressive, owing to their Asiatic form and their languishing glances. If these young virgins, with features similar to those of Greek madonnas, had the *tournure* and the vivacity of movement observable in the Spanish women, they would be the most seductive creatures upon earth. Many of the females in this district are handsomely dressed. They wear over the petticoat a little habit or pelisse bordered with fur, which reaches to the knee, sits well to the shape, and imparts a grace to the whole person.

In no country have I seen so many beautiful bald heads and silver hairs as in this part of Russia. The heads of Jehovah, those chef-d'oeuvres of the first pupil of Leonardo da Vinci, are not such entirely ideal conceptions as I imagined when I admired the frescoes of Luini at Lainate, Lugano, and Milan. These heads may be here recognised, living. Seated in the thresholds of their cabins, I have beheld old men, with fresh complexions, unwrinkled cheeks, blue and sparkling eyes, calm countenances, and silver beards glistening in the sun round mouths the peaceful and benevolent smile of which they heighten, who appear like so many protecting deities placed at the entrance of the villages. The traveller, as he passes, is saluted by these noble figures, majestically seated on the earth which saw them born. Truly antique statues, emblems of hospitality which a Pagan would have worshipped, and which Christians must admire with an involuntary respect: for in old age beauty is no longer physical; it is the depicted triumph of the soul after victory.

We must go among the Russian peasants to find the pure image of patriarchal society; and to thank God for the happy existence he has dispensed, notwithstanding the faults of governments, to these inoffensive beings, whose birth and death are only separated by a long series of years of innocence.

May the angel or demon of industry and of modern enlightened views, pardon me!—but I cannot help finding a great charm in ignorance, when I see its fruits in the celestial countenances of the old Russian peasants.

The modern patriarchs, labourers whose work is no longer a compulsory task, seat themselves, with dignity, towards the close of the day, in the threshold of the cottage which they themselves have, perhaps, rebuilt several times; for under this severe climate the house of man does not last so long as his life. Were I to carry back from my Russian journey no other recollection than that of these old men, with quiet consciences legible on their faces, leaning against doors that want no bolt, I should not regret the trouble I had taken to come and gaze upon beings so different from any other peasants in the world. The majesty of the cottage will always inspire me with profound respect.

Every fixed government, however bad it may be in some respects, has its good results; and every governed people have something wherewith to console themselves for the sacrifices they make to social life.

And yet, at the bottom of this calm which I so much admire, and which I feel so contagious, what disorder! what violence! what false security!

I had written thus much, when an individual of my acquaintance, in whose words I place confidence, having left Moscow a few hours after me, arrived at Troïtza, and, knowing that I was going to pass the night here, asked to see me while his horses were changing: he confirmed to me news that I had already heard, of eighty villages having been just burnt, in the government of Sembirsk, in consequence of the revolt of the peasants. The Russians attribute these troubles to the intrigues of the Poles. "What interest have the Poles in burning Russia?" I asked the person who related to me the fact. "None," he replied, "unless it be that they hope to draw upon themselves the wrath of the Russian government: their only fear is that they should be left in peace."

"You call to my recollection," I observed, "the band of incendiaries who, at the commencement of our first revolution, accused the aristocrats of burning their own chateaux." "You will not believe me," replied the Russian, "but I know, by close observation and by experience, that every time the Poles observe the emperor inclining towards clemency, they form new plots, send among us disguised emissaries, and even feign conspiracies when they cannot excite real ones; all of which they do solely with a view of drawing upon their country the hate of Russia, and of provoking new sentences for themselves and their countrymen: in fact, they dread nothing so much as pardon, because the gentleness of the Russian government would change the feelings of their peasants, who would soon be induced even to love the *enemy.*"

"This appears to me heroical machiavelism," I replied, "but I cannot believe in it. If it be true, why do you not pardon them in order to punish them? You would be then more adroit, as you are already more powerful, than they. But you hate them: and I am much inclined to believe that to justify your rancour, you accuse the victims, and search, in every misfortune that happens to them, some pretext for laying your yoke more heavily upon adversaries whose ancient glory is an unpardonable crime; the more so, as it must be owned that Polish glory was not very modest."

"Not a wit more so than French glory," maliciously responded my friend, whom I had known in Paris: "but you judge unfairly of our policy, because you neither understand the Russians nor the Poles."

"This is always the burden of your countrymen's song whenever any one ventures to tell them unpleasant truths. The Poles are easily known; they are always talking: I can trust in boasters better than in those who say nothing but what we do not care to know."

"You must, however, have a good deal of confidence in me!"

"In you, personally, I have: but when I recollect that you are a Russian, even though I have known you ten years, I reproach myself with my imprudence—I mean my candour."

"I foresee that you will give a bad account of us, on your return home."

"If I write, I perhaps may; but, as you say, I do not know the Russians, and I shall take care not to speak at random of so impenetrable a nation."

"That will be the best course for you to pursue."

"No doubt: but do not forget, that when once known to dissimulate, the most reserved men are appreciated as if already unmasked."

"You are too satirical and discriminating for barbarians such as we."

Whereupon my old friend re-entered his carriage, and went off at full gallop.

I have already spoken of the care I take to conceal my papers, under a sense of the possibility of some secret, if not open means of discovering my thoughts being had recourse to. I place none of these papers in my écritoire or portfolio; hoping that, in the event of any such perquisitions, this might satisfy the inquisitors. I have, also, so arranged that the feldjäger does not enter my room until having asked my permission through Antonio. An Italian may compete in finesse with even a Russian. The Italian in question has been for fifteen years my valet-de-chambre. He has the politic brain of the modern Romans, and the honourable heart of the ancient. Had I ventured in this land with an ordinary servant, I should have abstained from writing my thoughts; but Antonio, countermining the *espionnage* of the feldjäger, assures to me some degree of safety.

❖　❖　❖

If it be necessary that I should offer excuses for repetition and monotony, it is equally necessary that I should apologise for travelling at all in Russia. The frequent recurrence of the same impressions is inevitable in all conscientious books of travels, and more especially of travels in this land. Wishing to give as exact an idea as possible of the country I survey, it is necessary that I should record precisely, and day by day, all that I am impressed with; this is the only means of justifying my after-reflections.

Troïtza is, after Kiew, the most famous and best frequented place of pilgrimage in Russia. This historical monastery, situated twenty leagues from Moscow, was, I thought, of sufficient interest to allow of my losing a day, and passing a night there, in order to visit the sanctuaries revered by the Russian Christians.

To acquit myself of the task required a strong effort of reason: after such a night as the one I have passed, curiosity becomes extinguished, physical disgust overcomes every other feeling.

I had been assured at Moscow that I should find at Troïtza a very tolerable lodging. In fact the building where strangers are accommodated, a kind of inn belonging to the convent, but situated beyond the sacred precinct, is a spacious structure, and contains chambers apparently very habitable. Nevertheless, I had scarcely retired to rest, when I found all my ordinary precautions inefficient. I had kept a candle burning as usual, and by its light I passed the night in making war with an army of vermin, black and brown, of every form, and, I believe, of every species. The death of one of them seemed to draw on me the vengeance of the whole race, who rushed upon the place where the blood had flowed, and drove me almost to desperation. "They only want wings to make this place hell," was the exclamation which escaped me in my rage. These insects are the legacy of the pilgrims who repair to Troïtza from every part of the empire; they multiply under the shelter of the shrine of St. Sergius, the founder of the famous convent. The benediction of heaven seems to attend their increase which proceeds in this sacred asylum at a ratio unknown elsewhere. Seeing the legions with which I had to combat I lost all courage: my skin was burning, my blood boiled; I felt myself devoured by imperceptible enemies, and in my agony I fancied that I should prefer fighting an army of tigers rather than this small pest of beggars, and too often of saints; for extreme austerity sometimes marches hand in hand with filthiness, —impious alliance! against which the real friends of God cannot protest sufficiently loudly.

I rose up, and found calm for a moment at the open window; but the scourge followed me—chairs, tables, ceiling, floor, walls, were teeming with life. My valet entered my room before the usual hour; he had suffered the same agonies, and even greater: for not wishing, nor being able to add to the size of our baggage, he has no bed, and places his paillasse on the floor, in preference to the sofas with all their accessories. If I dwell upon these inconveniences, it is because they form a just accompaniment to the boastings of the Russians, and serve to show the degree of civilisation to which the people of this finest part of the empire have attained. On seeing poor Antonio enter the room, his eyes closed up and his face swollen, I had no need of inquiring the cause. Without uttering a word, he exhibited to me a cloak that had been blue the evening before, but was now become brown:

after he had placed it on a chair, I perceived that it was moveable: at this sight horror seized us both: air, water, fire, and all the elements were put in requisition; though in such a war victory itself is a loss. At length, purified and dressed, I made a shadow of a breakfast, and repaired to the convent, where another army of enemies awaited me: but this time, the light cavalry quartered in the folds of the Greek monks' gowns did not inspire me with the slightest fear; I had sustained the assaults of much more formidable combatants. After the battle of the night, the skirmishes of the day appeared to me a mere child's play: to speak without metaphor, the bites of bugs, and the dread of lice, had so hardened me against the attacks of fleas, that I felt no more annoyance from the light clouds of these creatures that played at our feet in the churches of the convent, than I should have felt from the dust of the road. This past night has awakened all my feelings of pity for the unhappy Frenchmen who remained prisoners in Russia after the retreat from Moscow. Vermin, that inevitable product of poverty, is of all physical evils the one which inspires me with the deepest compassion. When I hear it said of a human being, he is in such wretchedness that he is dirty, my heart bleeds. Personal dirtiness is something viler even than it appears. It betrays, to the eyes of an attentive observer, a moral degradation worse than all bodily evils put together. This leprosy, for being to a certain extent voluntary, is only the more loathsome: it is a phenomenon which springs from our two natures; it embraces both the moral and the physical; it is the result of an infirmity of soul as well as of body; it is at once a vice and a malady.

I have often, in my travels, had reason to remember the sagacious observations of Pestalozzi, that great practical philosopher, the preceptor of the working classes before Fourier and the Saint Simonians. According to his observations on the life of the lower orders, of two men who have the same habits of life, one will be dirty, the other clean. Personal cleanliness has as much to do with the health and the natural habit of body as with the personal habits of the individual. Do we not often see among the better classes people who take great pains with their persons, and who are yet very dirty. Among the Russians there reigns a high degree of sordid negligence: it seems to me they must have trained their vermin to survive the bath.

Notwithstanding my ill-humour, I went carefully over the interior of the patriotic convent of the Trinity. It does not possess the imposing aspect of our old Gothic monasteries. The architecture is not the object that should bring people to a sacred place; but if these famous sanctuaries were worth the trouble of being looked at, they would lose none of their sanctity, nor the pilgrims of their merit.

The convent stands on an eminence, and resembles a town surrounded with strong walls, mounted with battlements. Like those of Moscow, it has gilded spires and cupolas, which, shining in the evening sun, announce to the pilgrims, from afar, the end of their pious journey.

During the fine season, the surrounding roads are crowded with travellers, marching in procession. In the villages, groups of the faithful are to be seen eating and sleeping under the shade of the birch-trees; and at every step a peasant may be met walking in a species of sandal, made of the bark of the lime-tree: a female often accompanies him, who carries his shoes in her hand, whilst with the other she shields herself with an umbrella from the rays of the sun, which the Muscovites dread in summer more than the inhabitants of the south. A kibitka, drawn by one horse, follows, and contains the sleeping appurtenances, and the utensils with which to prepare tea. The kibitka doubtless resembles the chariot of the ancient Sarmatians. This equipage is constructed with primitive simplicity; it consists of the half of a cask severed lengthways, and placed upon axles, resembling the frame of a cannon.

The countrymen and women, who know how to sleep anywhere except in a bed, travel, stretched at their ease, in these light and picturesque vehicles: sometimes one of the pilgrims, watching over the sleepers, sits with his legs hanging over the edge of the kibitka, and lulls with national songs his dreaming comrades. In these dull and plaintive melodies, the sentiments of regret prevail over those of hope; their expression is melancholy but never impassioned: all is repressed, all betrays prudence in this naturally light and cheerful people, rendered taciturn by education. If I did not view the fate of nations as written in heaven, I should say that the Slavonians were born to people a more generous soil than the one on which they established themselves when they came forth from Asia, that great nursery of nations.

The first oppressor of the Russians was the climate. With every respect for Montesquieu, extreme cold appears to me more favourable to despotism than does heat: the men, the freest perhaps on the face of the earth—are they not the Arabs? The rigours of nature inspire man with rudeness and cruelty.

On leaving the hostelry of the convent I crossed an open square, and entered the monastic walls. After passing under an alley of trees, I found myself among several little churches, surnamed cathedrals, with high steeples dividing them from each other; while numerous chapels, and ranges of dwellings, wherein are now lodged the disciples of Saint Sergius, were scattered around without design or order.

This famous hermit founded the convent of Troïtza in 1338: its history, as well as that of its founder, is intimately connected with the general history of Russia. In the war against the Khan Mamaï, the holy man aided Dmitry Ivanowitch with his counsels; and the victory of the grateful prince enriched the politic monks. Afterwards, their monastery was destroyed by fresh hordes of Tartars, but the body of St. Sergius, miraculously discovered under the ruins, imparted a fresh renown to this asylum of prayer, which was rebuilt by means of the pious donations of the Czars. In 1609, the Poles besieged the convent for the space of six months. It had become the retreat of the patriotic defenders of the country; and the enemy, unable to take it, was at length obliged to raise the siege, to the additional glory of St. Sergius, and to the great joy and pecuniary advantage of his successors.

The walls are adorned with turrets, and surmounted with a covered gallery, of which I made the circuit. They are nearly half a league in extent. Of all the historical associations which render this place celebrated, the most interesting is that connected with the flight of Peter the Great, saved by his mother from the fury of the Strelitz, who pursued him into the cathedral of the Trinity, even to the altar of St. Sergius, where the attitude of the hero, ten years of age, disarmed the revolted soldiers.

All the Greek churches resemble each other. The paintings they contain are always Byzantine, that is to say, unnatural, without life and without variety. Sculpture is everywhere wanting: it is replaced by gilded carved work, rich, but not beautiful, and more insipid than magnificent.

All the names of note in Russian history have taken pleasure in enriching the convent, which overflows with gold, pearls, and diamonds. The universe has been placed under contribution to swell the pile of wealth that forms one of the miracles of the place, and which I contemplate with an astonishment more nearly approaching to stupefaction than to admiration. Czars, empresses, nobles, libertines, and true saints, have all vied with each other in enriching the treasury of Troïtza. Amid so many riches, the simple dress and the wooden cup of St. Sergius shine by their very rusticity.

The tomb of the saint in the cathedral of the Trinity blazes with magnificence. The convent would have furnished a rich booty to the French; it has not been taken since the fourteenth century. It contains nine churches. The shrine of the saint is of silver, gilt; it is protected by silver pillars and canopy, the gift of the Empress Anne. The image of Saint Sergius is esteemed miraculous. Peter the Great carried it with him in his wars against Charles XII.

Not far from the shrine, under shelter of the virtues of the hermit, lies the body of the usurping assassin, Boris Godounoff, surrounded by many of his family. The convent contains various other famous but shapeless tombs: they exhibit at once the infancy and the decrepitude of art. The house of the Archimandrite and the palace of the Czars present nothing of interest. The number of monks is now only one hundred; they were formerly thrice as many. Notwithstanding my persevering request, they would not show me the library. "It is forbidden" was always the answer. This modesty of the monks, who conceal the treasures of science, while they parade those of vanity, strikes me as singular. I argue from it that there is more dust on their books than on their jewels.

❖ ❖ ❖

I am now at Dernicki, a village between the small town of Perias-lavle and Yaroslaf, the capital of the province of the same name.

It must be owned that it is a strange notion of enjoyment which can induce a man to travel for his pleasure in a country where there are no high roads,* according to the application of the word in other parts of Europe,—no inns, no beds, no straw even to sleep upon—for I am obliged to fill my mattress and that of my servant with hay,—no white bread, no wine, no drinkable water, not a landscape to gaze upon in the country,—not a work of art to study in the towns; where, in winter, the checks, nose, ears, and feet are in great danger of being frozen; where, in the dog-days, you broil under the sun, and shiver at night. Such are the amusements I am come to seek in the heart of Russia.

The water is unwholesome in nearly every part of the country. You will injure your health if you trust to the protestations of the inhabitants, or do not drink it without correcting it by effervescent powders. To be sure, you may obtain the luxury of Seltzer-water in the large towns: but the necessity of laying in stores of this foreign beverage, as provision for the road, is very inconvenient. The wine of the taverns, generally white, and christened with the name of Sauterne, is scarce, dear, and of bad quality.

As for the scenery, there appears so little variety, that, as regards the habitations which alone enliven it, it may be said that there is but one village in all Russia. The distances are incommensurable, but the Russians diminish them by their rate of travelling: scarcely leaving their carriage until arrived at the place of their destination, they feel as though they had been in bed at home the whole length of the journey; and are astonished to find that we do not share their taste for this mode of travelling while sleeping, inherited by them from their Scythian ancestors. We must not believe, however, that their course is always equally rapid; these northern Gascons do not tell us of all their delays on the route. The coachmen drive fast when they are able, but they are often stopped by insurmountable difficulties.

Even on the road between Petersburg and Moscow I found

---

* With the exception of the road between Petersburg and Moscow, and part of that between Petersburg and Riga.

that we proceeded at very unequal rates, and that at the end of the journey we had scarcely saved more time than is done in other countries. On other routes the inconveniences are multiplied a hundredfold: the horses become scarce, the roads such as would destroy any vehicle; and the traveller asks himself, with a kind of shame, what could have been his motive for imposing upon himself so many discomforts, by coming to a country that has all the wildness, without any of the poetic grandeur of the desert? Such was the question I addressed to myself this evening, when benighted on a road, the difficulty of moving in which was greatly enhanced by a new unfinished chaussée, which crossed it at every fifty yards, and by tottering bridges, which had often lost the pieces of timber the most essential to their security.

My meditations at length determined me to halt, and, to the great annoyance of my coachman and feldjäger, I fixed on a lodging in the little house of some villagers, where I am now writing. This refuge is less disgusting than a real inn: no traveller stops in such a village; and the wood of the cabin serves as a refuge only to the insects brought from the forest. My chamber, a loft reached by a dozen steps, is nine or ten feet square, and six or seven high; it reminds me of the cottage of the imbecile old man in the story of Thelenef. The entire habitation is made of the trunks of fir-trees, caulked with moss and pitch as carefully as if it were a boat. The same eternal smell of tar, cabbage, and perfumed leather, which, combined, pervades every Russian village, annoys me; but I prefer headache to mental distress, and find this bed-chamber far more comfortable than the large plastered hall of the inn at Troïtza. I have fixed in it my iron bedstead: the peasants sleep, wrapped in their sheep-skins, on the seats ranged round the room on the ground-floor. Antonio makes his bed in the coach, which is guarded by him and the feldjäger. Men are pretty safe on Russian highways, but equipages and all their appurtenances are viewed as lawful prizes by the Slavonian serfs; and, without extreme vigilance, I should find my calèche in the morning, stript of cover, braces, curtains, and apron; in short, transformed into a primitive tarandasse, a real telega; and not a soul in the village who would have any idea what had become of the leather: or if, by means of rigid searches, it should be found at the bottom of some shed, the thief, by stating that he had found it and brought it there, would be acquitted. This is the standing defence in Russia: theft is rooted in the habits of the people, and consequently the robber preserves an easy conscience and a serene face that would deceive the very angels. "Our Saviour would have stolen," they say, "if his hands had not been pierced." This is one of their most common adages.

Nor is robbery the vice alone of the peasants: there are as many kinds of theft as there are orders in society. The governor of a province knows that he is constantly in danger of something occurring that may send him to finish his days in Siberia. If, during the time that he continues in office, he has the cleverness to steal enough to defend himself in the legal process which would precede his exile, he may get out of the difficulty; but if he continue poor and honest he must be ruined. This is not my remark, but that of several Russians whom I may not name, but whom I believe to be worthy of faith.

The commissaries of the army rob the soldiers, and enrich themselves by starving them: in short, an honest administration would be here both dangerous and ridiculous.

I hope to-morrow to reach Yaroslaf: it is a central city; and I shall stop there a day or two in order to discover, in the interior of the country, real original Russians. I took care, with this intention, to procure several letters of introduction to that capital of one of the most interesting and important provinces of the empire.

❖

CHAPTER XXXI

❖

The prediction made to me at Moscow is already accomplished, although I have yet scarcely completed a quarter of my journey. I have reached Yaroslaf in a carriage, not one part of which is undamaged. It is to be mended, but I doubt whether it will carry me through.

Summer has now vanished,* not to return until the next year. A cold rain, which they here consider as proper to the season, has driven away the dog-days entirely. I am so accustomed to the inconveniences of the heat, to dust, flies, and musquitos, that I can scarcely realise the idea of my deliverance from these scourges.

The city of Yaroslaf is an important entrepôt for the interior commerce of Russia. By it, Petersburg communicates with Persia, the Caspian, and all Asia. The Volga, that great national and moving road, flows by the city, which is the central point of the interior navigation of the country—a navigation wisely directed, much boasted of by the subjects of the Czar, and one of the principal sources of their prosperity. It is with the Volga that the immense ramifications of canals are connected, that create the wealth of Russia.

The city, like all the other provincial cities in the empire, is vast in extent, and appears empty. The streets are immensely broad, the squares very spacious, and the houses in general stand far apart. The same style of architecture reigns from one end of

* Written 18th of August.

the country to the other. The following dialogue will show the value the Russians place on their pretended classic edifices.

A man of intelligence said to me, at Moscow, that he had seen nothing in Italy which appeared new to him.

"Do you speak seriously?" I asked.

"Quite seriously," he replied.

"It seems to me impossible," I responded, "that any one could descend for the first time the southern side of the Alps, without the aspect of the land producing a revolution in his mind."

"In what manner?" said the Russian, with that disdainful tone and air which here too often pass for a proof of civilisation.

"What!" I replied, "the novelty of those landscapes adorned by art, those hills and slopes, where palaces, convents, and villages stand surrounded with vines, mulberries, and olives, those long ranges of white pillars, which support festoons of vines, and which carry the wonders of architecture into the recesses of the steepest mountains,—all that magnificent scenery, which gives the idea of a park laid out by Lenôtre for the pleasure of princes, rather than of a land cultivated in order to yield the labourer his daily bread; all those creations of man applied to embellish the creations of God,—is it possible that they did not appear to you as something new? Surely, elegantly designed churches, in the steeples of which we recognise a classic taste modified by feudal customs, with so many other stately and extraordinary buildings dispersed in that superb garden, must have caused you some surprise! Roads carried over enormous passes, on arcades as solid as they appear light to the eye,* mountains serving as the base of convents, villages, and palaces,—all announce a land where nature owns art as her sovereign. Woe to him who could tread the soil of Italy, without recognising in the majesty of the sites, as in that of the edifices, the land that is the cradle of civilisation!"

"I congratulate myself," replied my opponent, ironically, "on having seen nothing of all this, as my blindness will serve as an excuse for your eloquence."

"I shall not much care," I answered, coolly, "though my en-

* Witness the town of Bergamo, the lakes Maggiore, Como, &c., and all the southern valleys of the Alps.

thusiasm appears to you ridiculous, if I only succeed in awakening in you a sentiment of the beautiful. The choice of the sites alone of the edifices, villages, and towns of Italy, reveals to me the genius of a people born for the arts. In the localities where commerce has accumulated wealth, as at Genoa, Venice, and the feet of all the great passes of the Alps, what use have the inhabitants made of the treasures they amassed? They have bordered their seas, lakes, rivers, and precipices with enchanted palaces,—ramparts of marble raised by genii. It is not alone on the borders of the Brenta that these miracles are to be seen; every mountain has its prodigy. Towns and villages, churches, castles, convents, bridges, villas, hermitages, the retreats of penitence as well as the abodes of pleasure and luxury, all so strike the imagination of the traveller as to weave a spell over the mind as well as the eye. The grandeur of the masses, the harmony of the lines are new to the men of the north. Add to this the associations of history.—Greece herself, notwithstanding her sublime but too scarce relics, less astonishes the greater number of pilgrims; for the ages of barbarism have left Greece empty, and the land requires to be searched in order to be appreciated. Italy, on the contrary, needs only to be looked at—"

"How," interrupted the impatient Russian,—"how can you expect us inhabitants of Petersburg and Moscow to be astonished, as you are, with Italian architecture? Do you not see models of it at every step you take in even the smallest of our towns and cities?"

This explosion of national vanity silenced me: I was at Moscow; an inclination to laugh was rising within me, but it would have been dangerous to have given way to it. The argument of my adversary was the same as though a person were to refuse to look upon the Apollo Belvidere because he had elsewhere seen plaster-of-Paris casts of it. The influence of the Mongols survives their conquests among the Russians. Was it, then, to imitate them that they drove them out? Detractors make little progress, either in the arts or in general civilisation. The Russians observe with malevolence because they lack the perception of perfection: so long as they envy their models they will never equal them. Their empire is immense, but what of that: who would admire the colossus of an ape?

Such were the angry thoughts that rose in my mind, but of which I suppressed the outward expression, although I believe my disdainful opponent read them on my face, for he did not speak to me any more, unless it was to add, with a nonchalant air, that he had seen olives in the Crimea, and mulberry-trees at Kiew.

For my own part, I congratulate myself that I am only come to Russia for a short time; a long stay in this land might rob me not only of the courage, but of the desire, to say the truth, in answer to things that I hear and see. Despotism discourages and casts a spell of indifference even over minds that are the most determined to struggle against its glaring abuses.

Disdain for things that they do not know, appears to me a dominant trait in the character of the Russians. Instead of endeavouring to comprehend, they endeavour to ridicule. If they ever succeed in bringing to full light their real genius, the world will see, not without some surprise, that it is a genius for caricature. Since I have studied the Russian character, and travelled in this last of the states written in the great book of European history, I have discovered that the talent for ridicule possessed by the *parvenu,* may become the dowry of an entire nation.

The painted and gilded towers, almost as numerous as the houses of Yaroslaf, shine at a distance like those of Moscow, but the city is less picturesque than the old capital of the empire. It is protected on the banks of the Volga by a raised terrace, planted with trees; under it, as under a bridge, the road passes, by which merchandise is carried to and from the river. Notwithstanding its commercial importance, the city is empty, dull, and silent. From the height of the terrace is to be seen the yet more empty, dull, and silent surrounding country, with the immense river, its hue a sombre iron-grey, its banks falling straight upon the water, and forming at their top a level with the leaden tinted plain, here and there dotted with forests of birch and pine. This soil is, however, as well cultivated as it is capable of being; it is boasted of by the Russians as being, with the exception of the Crimea, the richest and most smiling tract in their empire.

Byzantine edifices ought to be the models of the national architecture in Russia. Cities full of structures adapted to their location should animate the banks of the Volga. The interior arrangements of the Russian habitations are rational; their exterior, and the general plan of the towns, are not so. Yaroslaf has its columns and its triumphal arches in imitation of Petersburg, all of which are in the worst taste, and contrast, in the oddest manner, with the style of the churches and steeples. The nearer I approached this city, the more was I struck with the beauty of the population. The villages are rich and well built: I have seen a few stone houses, though too limited a number to vary the monotony of the view.

The Volga is the Loire of Russia; but instead of the gaily-smiling hills of Touraine, crowned with the fairest castles of the middle ages, we here find only flat, unvaried banks, with plains, where the small, gray, mean-looking houses, ranged in lines like tents, sadden rather than animate the landscape: such is the land that the Russians commend to our admiration.

In walking along the borders of the Volga I had to struggle against the wind of the north, omnipotent in this country throughout the year; for three months of which it sweeps the dust before it, and for the remaining nine, the snow. This evening, in the intervals of the blast, the distant songs of the boatmen upon the river caught my ear. The nasal tones, that so much injure the effect of the national songs of the Russians, were lost in the distance, and I heard only a vague, plaintive strain, of which my heart could guess the words. Upon a long float of timber, which they guided skilfully, several men were descending the course of their native Volga. On reaching Yaroslaf they wished to land: when I saw them moor their raft, I stopped. They passed close before me, without taking any notice of my foreign appearance; without even speaking to each other. The Russian peasants are taciturn and devoid of curiosity; I can understand why: what they know disgusts them with all of which they are ignorant.

I admire their noble features and fine expression. With the exception of the Calmuc race, who have broken noses and high cheek bones, I again repeat, the Russians are perfectly beautiful.

Another charm, natural to them, is the gentleness of their

voice, which is always base, and which vibrates without effort. This voice renders euphonious a language, which, spoken by others, would sound harsh and hissing. It is the only one of the European languages which appears to me to lose anything in the mouth of refined and educated persons. My ear prefers the Russian of the streets to the Russian of the drawing-rooms: in the streets, it is a natural tongue; in the *salons,* and at court, it is a newly-imported language, which the policy of the master imposes upon the courtiers.

Melancholy, disguised by irony, is in this land the most ordinary humour of mind; in the saloons especially. There, more than elsewhere, it is necessary to dissimulate sadness; hence the sneering, sarcastic tone of language, and those efforts in conversation, painful both to the speaker and the listener. The common people drown their sadness in silent intoxication; the lords in noisy drunkenness. The same vice assumes a different form in the master and the slave. The former has yet another resource against ennui—ambition, that intoxication of the mind. Among all classes there reigns an innate elegance, a natural refinement, which is neither barbarism nor civilisation; not even their affectation can deprive them of this primitive advantage.

They are, however, deficient in a much more essential quality —the faculty of loving. In ordinary affairs, the Russians want kind heartedness; in great affairs, good faith: a graceful egotism, a polite indifference, are the most conspicuous traits in their intercourse with others. This want of heart prevails among all classes, and betrays itself under various forms, according to the rank of the individuals; but the principal is the same in all. The faculty of being easily affected and tenderly attached, so rare among the Russians, is a ruling characteristic of the Germans, who call it *gemüth.* We should call it expansive sensibility, or cordiality, if we had any need of defining a feeling which is scarcely more common among us than among the Russians. But the refined and ingenuous French *plaisanterie* is here replaced by a malignantly prying, a hostile, closely observing, caustic, satirical, and envious spirit, which appears to me infinitely more objectionable than our jesting frivolity. Here, the rigour of the climate, the severity of the government, and the habit of espionnage, render characters melancholy, and self-love distrustful. Somebody, or something, is always feared; and, what is worse, not without cause. This is not avowed, yet it cannot be concealed from a traveller accustomed to observe and compare different nations.

To a certain point the want of a charitable disposition in the Russians towards strangers appears to me excusable. Before knowing us, they lavish their attentions upon us with apparent eagerness, because they are hospitable like the Orientals; but they are also easily wearied like the Europeans. In welcoming us with a forwardness which has more ostentation than cordiality, they scrutinize our slightest words, they submit our most insignificant actions to a critical examination; and as such work necessarily furnishes them with much subject for blame, they triumph internally, saying, "These, then, are the people who think themselves so superior to us!"

This kind of study suits their quickly discerning, rather than sensitive nature. Such a disposition neither excludes a certain politeness nor a kind of grace, but it is the very opposite of true amability. Perhaps, with care and time, one might succeed in inspiring them with some confidence; nevertheless, I doubt whether all my efforts could achieve this; for the Russians are the most unimpressible, and, at the same time, the most impenetrable people in the world. What have they done to aid the march of human mind? They have not hitherto produced either philosophers, moralists, legislators, or literati whose names belong to history; but, truly, they have never wanted, and never will want good diplomatists, clever, politic heads; and it is the same with their inferior classes, among whom there are no inventive mechanics, but abundance of excellent workmen.

I am leading the reader into the labyrinth of contradictions, that is, I am showing the things of this world as they have appeared to me at the first and at the second view. I must leave to him the task of so reviewing and arranging my remarks as to be able to draw from them a general opinion. My ambition will be satisfied, if a comparing and selecting from this crowded collection of precipitate and carelessly hazarded judgments will allow any solid, impartial, and ripe conclusions to be drawn. I have not attempted to draw them, because I prefer travelling to composing; an author is not independent, a traveller is. I therefore relate my impressions, and leave the reader to complete the book.

The above reflections on the Russian character have been suggested by several visits that I have made in Yaroslaf. I consider this central point as one of the most interesting in my journey.

I will relate to-morrow the result of my visit to the chief personage of the place, the governor, for I have just sent him my letter. I have been told, or rather given to infer, much to his disparagement in the various houses that I have visited this morning.

The primitive drowska is to be seen in this city. It consists of a little board on four wheels, entirely concealed under the occupant, and looks as though the horse were fastened to his person; two of the wheels are covered by his legs, and the other two are so low that they disappear under the rapid motion of the machine.

The female peasants generally go barefoot. The men most frequently wear a species of sandal made of rushes, rudely platted, which resembles those of antiquity. The leg is clothed in a wide pantaloon, the folds of which, drawn together at the ancle by a little fillet, are covered with the shoe. This attire is precisely similar to the Scythian statues of the Roman sculptors.

I am writing in a wretched inn; there are but two good ones in Russia, and they are kept by foreigners: the English boarding-house at Saint Petersburg, and that of Madame Howard, at Moscow, are those to which I refer. In the houses even of independent private people, I cannot seat myself without trembling.

I have seen several public baths, both at Petersburg and Moscow. The people bathe in different ways: some enter chambers heated to a temperature that appears to me insupportable; the penetrating vapour of these stews is absolutely suffocating. In other chambers, naked men, standing upon heated floors, are soaped and washed by others also naked. The people of taste have their own baths, as in other places: but so many individuals resort to these public establishments; the warm humidity there is so favourable to insect life, the clothes laid down in them are nurseries of so many vermin, that the visitor rarely departs without carrying with him some irrefragable proof of the sordid negligence of the lower orders.

Before cleansing their own persons, those who make use of the public baths ought to insist on the cleansing out of these dens where the old Muscovites revel in their dirtiness, and hasten old age by the inordinate use of steam, and by the perspiration it provokes.

It is now ten o'clock in the evening. The governor has sent to inform me that his son and his carriage will presently attend me. I have answered, with many thanks, that having retired for the night, I cannot this evening avail myself of his kindness; but that I shall pass the whole of the morrow at Yaroslaf, and shall then make my acknowledgments in person. I am not sorry to have this opportunity of observing Russian hospitality in the provinces.

❖   ❖   ❖

This morning, about eleven, the governor's son, who is a mere child, arrived in full uniform, to take me in a carriage-and-four, with coachman, and *faleiter* mounted on the off-side horse, an equipage precisely similar to that of the courtiers at Petersburg. This elegant apparition at the door of my inn disappointed me; I saw at once that it was not with old Muscovites, with true boyards, that I had to do. I felt that I should be again among European travellers, courtiers of the Emperor Alexander, and lordly cosmopolites.

"My father knows Paris," said the young man; "he will be delighted to see a Frenchman."

"At what period was he in France?"

The young Russian was silent; my question appeared to disconcert him, although I had thought it a very simple one: at first I was unable to account for his embarrassment; after discovering its cause, I gave him credit for an exquisite delicacy,—a rare sentiment in every country and at every age.

M. ——, governor of Yaroslaf, had visited France, in the suite of the Emperor Alexander, during the campaigns of 1813 and 1814, and this was a reminiscence of which his son was unwilling to remind me. His tact recalled to my memory a very different trait. One day, in a small town of Germany, I dined with the envoy of a petty German government, who, in presenting me to his wife, said that I was a Frenchman.

"He's an enemy, then," interrupted their son, a boy of apparently thirteen or fourteen years old.

That young gentleman had not been sent to school in Russia.

On entering the spacious and brilliant saloon, where the governor, his lady, and their numerous family awaited me, I could have imagined myself in London, or rather in Petersburg, for the lady of the house was ensconced, *à la russe,* in the little cabinet enclosed by gilded trellis, and raised a few steps, which occupied a corner of the saloon, and which is called the *altane.* The governor received me with politeness, and led me across the saloon, past several male and female relatives who had met there, into the verdant cabinet, where I found his wife.

Scarcely had she invited me to sit down in this sanctuary than she thus addressed me: "Monsieur de Custine, does Elzéar still write fables?"

My uncle, Count Elzéar de Sabran, had been from his boyhood celebrated in the society of Versailles for his poetical talent, and he would have been equally so in public society if his friends and relations could have persuaded him to publish his collections of fables—a species of poetical code, enlarged by time and experience; for every circumstance of his life, every public and private event, has inspired him with one of these apologues, always ingenious, and often profound, and to which an elegant and easy versification, an original and piquant turn of expression, impart a peculiar charm. The recollection of this was far from my thoughts when I entered the house of the governor of Yaroslaf, for my mind was occupied with the hope, too rarely satisfied, of finding real Russians in Russia.

I replied to the lady of the governor by a smile of astonishment, which silently said — explain to me this mystery. The explanation was soon given. "I was brought up," continued the lady, "by a friend of your grandmother, Madame de Sabran; that friend often spoke to me of her natural grace and charming wit, as well as of the mind and talents of your uncle and your mother; she often even spoke to me of you, though she had left France before your birth. It is Madame —— to whom I allude; she accompanied into Russia the Polignac family when they became *émigrés*, and since the death of the Duchess de Polignac she has never left me."

In concluding these words Madame —— presented me to her governess, an elderly person, who spoke French better than I, and whose countenance expressed penetration and gentleness.

I saw that I must once again renounce my dream of the boyards, a dream which, notwithstanding its futility, did not leave me without awaking some regret; but I had wherewith to indemnify myself for my mistake. Madame ——, the wife of the governor, belongs to one of the great original families of Lithuania; she was born Princess ——. Over and above the politeness common to nearly all people of this rank, in every land, she has acquired the taste and the tone of French society, as it existed in its most flourishing epoch; and, although yet young, she reminds me, by the noble simplicity of her manners, of the elderly persons whom I knew in my childhood. Those manners are the traditions of the old court, respect for every kind of propriety, good taste in its highest perfection, for it includes even good and kindly dispositions, in short, every thing that was attractive in the higher circles of Paris at the time when our social superiority was denied by none; at the time when Madame de Marsan, limiting herself to an humble pension, retired voluntarily to a small apartment in the Assomption, and for ten years devoted her immense income to paying the debts of her brother, the Prince de Guémenée,—by this noble sacrifice extenuating, as far as was in her power, the disgrace and scandal of a bankrupt nobleman.

All this will teach me nothing about the country I am inspecting, I thought to myself, nevertheless it will afford me a pleasure that I should be loath to deny myself, for it is one that has now become more rare perhaps, than is the satisfaction of the simple curiosity which brought me here.

I fancied myself in the chamber of my grandmother,* though, indeed, on a day when the Chevalier de Boufflers was not there, nor Madame de Coaslin, nor even the lady of the house: for those

---

* The Countess de Sabran, afterwards Marchioness de Boufflers, who died at Paris in 1827, aged 78 years.

brilliant models of the character of intellect which formerly adorned French conversation have gone, never to return, even in Russia; but I found myself in the chosen circle of their friends and disciples, assembled, as it were, in their absence; and I felt as though we were waiting for them, and that they would soon reappear.

I was not in the least prepared for this species of emotion; of all the surprises of my journey it has been for me the most unexpected.

The lady of the house participated in my astonishment; for she told me of the exclamation she had made the previous evening, on perceiving my name at the bottom of the note I had sent to the governor. The singularity of the rencontre, in a region where I supposed myself as little known as a Chinese, immediately gave a familiar and friendly tone to the conversation, which became general, without ceasing to be agreeable and easy. There was nothing concerted or affected in the pleasure they seemed to take in seeing me. The surprise had been reciprocal: no one had expected me at Yaroslaf; I had only decided to take that route the day before leaving Moscow.

The brother of the governor's wife, a Prince ———, writes our language perfectly well. He has published volumes of French verses, and was kind enough to present me with one of his collections. On opening the book, my eyes fell upon this line, full of sentiment; it occurs in a piece entitled *Consolations à une Mère:*

"Les pleurs sont la fontaine ou notre ame s'epure."†

Assuredly, he is fortunate who expresses his idea so well in a foreign language.

All the members of the ——— family vied with each other in doing me the honours of the house and of the city.

My books were loaded with indirect and ingenious praises, and were cited so as to recall to my mind a crowd of details that I had forgotten. The delicate and natural manner in which these quotations were introduced would have pleased me if they had less

† Tears are the fount that purifies the soul.

flattered me. The small number of books which the censorship allows to penetrate so far, remain popular a long time. I may say, not in my own personal praise, but in that of the times in which we live, that in travelling over Europe the only hospitality really worthy of gratitude that I have received has been that which I owe to my writings. They have created for me among strangers a small number of friends, whose kindness, ever new, has in no slight degree contributed to prolong my inborn taste for travelling and for poetry. If a position of so little importance as the one which I occupy in our literature has procured me such advantages, it is easy to conceive the influence which the talents that among us rule the thinking world, must exercise.

This apostleship of our authors constitutes the real power of France: but what responsibility does not such a vocation carry with it! It is, however, viewed as are other offices; the desire of obtaining it causes the danger of exercising it to be forgotten. As regards myself, if, during the course of my life, I have understood and felt one sentiment of ambition, it has been that of sharing, according to my powers, in this government of the human mind, as superior to political power as electricity is to gunpowder.

A great deal was said to me about Jean Sbogar; and when it was known that I had the happiness of being personally acquainted with the author, a thousand questions were asked me regarding him. Would that I had had, in order to answer, the talent for narration which he possesses in so high a degree!

One of the brothers-in-law of the governor has taken me to see the Convent of the Transfiguration, which serves as residence for the archbishop of Yaroslaf. This monastery, like all the Greek religious houses, is a kind of low citadel, enclosing several churches, and numerous small edifices of every style except the good style.

The only thing that appeared to me novel and striking in the visit, was the devotion of my guide, Prince ———. He bent his forehead, and applied his lips, with a fervour that was surprising, to all the objects presented for the veneration of the faithful; and in this convent, which encloses several sanctuaries, he performed the same ceremonies in twenty different places. Meanwhile his drawing-room conversation announced nothing of this devotion of the cloister. He concluded by inviting me also to kiss the relics of a saint whose tomb a monk had opened for us. I saw him make at least fifty signs of the cross; he kissed twenty images and relics: in short, not any one of our nuns in the seclusion of her convent would repeat so many genufluxions, salutations, and inclinations of the head in passing and repassing the high altar of her church, as did this Russian prince, an old officer and aide-de-camp of the Emperor Alexander, in presence of a stranger, in the monastery of the Transfiguration.

The Greeks cover the walls of their churches with fresco paintings in the Byzantine style. A foreigner feels at first some respect for these representations, because he believes them ancient; but when he finds that the churches which appear the most ancient have been recoloured, and often rebuilt but yesterday, his veneration soon changes into profound ennui. The madonnas, even the ones most newly painted, resemble those that were brought into Italy towards the end of the middle ages, to revive there the taste for art. But since then, the Italians—their genius electrized by the conquering spirit of the Roman church—have perceived and pursued the grand and the beautiful, and have produced all that the world has seen of most sublime in every branch of art; during which time the Greeks of the Lower Empire, and the Russians after them, have continued faithfully to chalk their Virgins of the eighth century.

The Eastern Church has never been favourable to the arts. Since schism was declared, she has done nothing but benumb all minds with the subtleties of theology. In the present day, the true believers in Russia dispute seriously among themselves as to whether it is permitted to give the natural flesh-colour to the heads of the Virgin, or if it is necessary to continue to colour them, like the pretended madonnas of St. Luke, with that tint of bistre which is so unnatural. There is also much dispute among them as to the manner of representing the rest of the person: it is uncertain whether the body ought to be painted, or imitated in metal and enclosed in a kind of cuirass, which leaves the face alone visible, or sometimes the eyes only. The reader must explain to himself, as he best can, why a metallic body appears more decent in the eyes of the Greek priests than canvas painted as a woman's robe.

We are not yet at the end of the great points of dispute in the Greek church. Certain doctors, whose number is large enough to form a sect, have conscientiously separated themselves from the mother-church because she now shields within her bosom impious innovators, who permit the priests to give the sacerdotal benediction with three fingers of the hand, whereas the true tradition wills that the fore and middle fingers only shall be charged with the task of dispensing blessings upon the faithful.

Such are the questions now agitated in the Greco-Russian church; and let it not be supposed that they are considered puerile: they inflame passions, provoke heresy, and decide the fate of men in this world and in the next. To return to my entertainers:

The great Russian nobles appear to me more amiable in the provinces than at court.

The wife of the governor of Yaroslaf has, at this moment, all her family united around her; several of her sisters, with their husbands and children, are lodged in her house: she admits also to her table the principal employés of her husband, who are inhabitants of the city; her son also is still attended by a tutor; so that at dinner there were twenty persons to sit down to table.

It is the custom of the north to precede the principal repast by a smaller refection, which is served in the saloon, a quarter of an hour before entering the dining-room. This preliminary, which is destined to sharpen the appetite, is called in Russian, if my ear has not deceived me, zacuska. The servants bring upon trays small plates filled with fresh caviare, such as is only eaten in this country, dried fish, cheese, salt meats, sea biscuits, and pastry; with these, bitter liqueurs, French brandy, London porter, Hungarian wine, &c., are also brought in; and these things are eaten and drunk standing. A stranger, ignorant of the usages of the country, or an appetite easily satisfied, might very soon here make a meal, and remain afterwards a spectator only of the real dinner. The Russians eat plentifully, and keep a liberal table; but they are too fond of hashes, stuffing, little balls of mince-meat, and fish in pâtés.

One of the most delicate fishes in the world is caught in the

Volga, where it abounds. It is called the sterled, and unites the flavour of the sea and fresh water fishes, without, however, resembling any that I have eaten elsewhere. This fish is large, its flesh light and fine; its head, pointed and full of cartilages, is considered delicate; the monster is seasoned very skilfully, but without many spices: the sauce that is served with it unites the flavour of wine, strong meat broth, and lemon-juice. I prefer this national dish to all the other ragouts of the land, and especially to the cold and sour soup, that species of fish-broth, iced, that forms the detestable treat of the Russians. They also make soups of sugared vinegar, of which I have tasted enough to prevent my ever asking for any more.

The governor's dinner was good and well served, without superfluity, and without useless *recherche*. The abundance and excellent quality of the watermelons astonishes me: it is said that they come from the environs of Moscow, but I should rather imagine they send to the Crimea for them. It is the custom in this country to place the dessert upon the table at the commencement of the dinner, and to serve it plate by plate. This method has its advantages and its inconveniences: it seems to me only perfectly proper at great dinners.

The Russian dinners are of a reasonable length; and nearly all the guests disperse upon rising from table. Some practise the Oriental habit of the siesta; others take a promenade or return to their business after drinking coffee. Dinner is not here the repast which finishes the labours of the day; and when I took leave of the lady of the house, she had the kindness to engage me to return and pass the evening with her. I accepted the invitation, for I felt it would be impolite to refuse it: all that is offered to me here, is done with so much good taste, that neither my fatigue nor my wish to retire and write to my friends, are sufficient to preserve my liberty: such hospitality is a pleasant tyranny; it would be indelicate not to accept it; a carriage-and-four and a house are placed at my disposal, a whole family are troubling themselves to amuse me and to show me the country; and this is done without any affected compliments, superfluous protestations, or importunate *empressement:* I do not know how to resist so much rare simplicity, grace, and elegance; I should yield were it only from a patriotic instinct, for there is in these agreeable manners a souvenir of ancient France which affects and attracts me: it seems as though I had come to the frontiers of the civilised world to reap a part of the heritage of the French spirit of the eighteenth century, a spirit that has been long lost among ourselves. This inexpressible charm of good manners, and of simple language, reminds me of a paradox of one of the most intellectual men I have ever known: "There is not," he says, "a bad action nor a bad sentiment that has not its source in a fault of manners; consequently true politeness is virtue; it is all the virtues united." He went yet further; he pretended there was no other vice but that of coarseness.

At nine o'clock this evening I returned to the house of the governor. We had first music, and afterwards a lottery.

One of the brothers of the lady of the house plays the violoncello in a charming manner; he was accompanied on the piano by his wife, a very agreeable woman. This duo, as well as many national airs, sung with taste, made the evening pass rapidly.

The conversation of Madame de ——, the old friend of my grandmother and of Madame de Polignac, contributed in no slight degree to shorten it. This lady has lived in Russia for forty-seven years; she has viewed and judged the country with discernment and justice, and she states the truth without hostility, and yet without oratorical precautions: this is new to me: her frankness strangely contrasts with the universal dissimulation practised by the Russians. An intelligent French woman, who has passed her life among them, ought, I think, to know them better than they know themselves; for they blind themselves in order the better to impose falsehood upon others. Madame de —— said and repeated to me, that in this country the sentiment of honour is without power except in the heart of the women: they have made it a matter of religion to be faithful to their word, to despise falsehood, to observe delicäcy in money affairs, and independence in politics; in short, according to Madame de ——, the greater number of them possess what is wanted in the great majority of the men—probity in all the circumstances of life, whether of greater or less importance. In general, the Russian women think more than the men, because they act less. Leisure, that advantage inherent in a woman's mode of life, is as advantageous to their character as to their understanding; they are better informed, less servile, and possess more energy of sentiment than the other sex. Heroism itself often appears to them natural, and becomes easy. The Princess Troubetzkoï is not the only woman who has followed her husband to Siberia; many exiled men have received from their wives this sublime proof of devotion, which loses none of its value for being less rare than I imagined it: unfortunately I do not know their names. Where will they find a historian and a poet? Were it only on account of unknown virtues, it would be necessary to believe in a last judgment. The glory of the good is a part which would be wanting to the justice of God: we can imagine the pardon of the Omnipotent; we cannot imagine his indifference. Virtue is only so called, because it cannot be recompensed by men. It would lose its perfection and become a matter of mercenary calculation if it were sure of always being appreciated and remunerated upon earth: virtue which did not reach to the supernatural and the sublime would be incomplete. If evil did not exist, where would there be saints? The combat is necessary to the victory, and the victory may even ask from God the crown of conqueror. This beautiful spectacle justifies Providence, which, in order to present it to the attentive Heaven, tolerates the errors of the world.

Towards the close of the evening, before permitting me to leave, my entertainers, with the view of paying me a compliment, expedited, by several days, a ceremony which has been looked forward to for six months in the family: it was the drawing of a lottery, the object of which was charity. All the prizes, consisting of articles made by the lady of the house, her friends and relatives, were tastefully spread upon the tables: the one which fell to me, I cannot say by chance, for my tickets had been carefully selected, was a pretty note-book with a varnished cover. I wrote in it the date, and added a few words by way of remembrance. In the times of our fathers, an impromptu in verse would have been suggested; but, in these days, when public impromptus abound *ad nauseam,* those of the *salon* are out of date. Ephemeral literature, politics, and philosophy have dethroned the quatrain and the sonnet. I had not the ready wit to write a single couplet; but I should, in justice, add, that neither did I feel the ambition.

After bidding farewell to my amiable entertainers, whom I am to meet again at the fair of Nijni, I returned to my inn, very well satisfied with the day. The house of the peasant in which I lodged the day before yesterday, and the saloon of to-day, in other words, Kamtschatka and Versailles within a distance traversed in a few hours, present a contrast which describes Russia.

I sacrifice my nights to relate to my friends the objects that strike me during the day. My chapter is not finished, and dawn already appears.

The contrasts in this empire are abrupt; so much so that the peasant and the lord do not seem to belong to the same land: the grandees are as cultivated as if they lived in another country; the serfs are as ignorant and savage as though they served under lords like themselves.

It is much less with the abuses of aristocracy that I reproach the Russian government, than with the absence of an authorised aristocratic power, whose attributes are clearly and constitution-ally defined. Recognised political aristocracies have always struck me as being beneficent in their influence; whilst the aristocracies that have no other foundation than the chimeras, or the injus-tices of privileges, are pernicious because their attributes remain undefined and ill regulated. It is true the Russian lords are mas-ters, and too absolute masters, in their territories; whence arise those excesses that fear and hypocrisy conceal by humane phrases, softly pronounced, which deceive travellers, and too often the government also. But these men, though monarchs in their far distant domains, have no power in the state; they do what they please on their own estates, defying the power of the emperor, by corrupting or intimidating his secondary agents; but the country is not governed by them; they enjoy no consideration in the general direction of affairs. It is only by becoming court-iers, by labouring for promotion in the tchinn, that they can obtain any public credit or standing. This life of the courtier excludes all elevation of sentiment, independence of spirit, and humane, patriotic views, which are essential elements of aristocratic bodies legally constituted, in states organised to extend their power and to flourish long.

The government, on the other hand, equally excludes the just pride of the man who has made his fortune by his labour. It unites all the disadvantages of democracy with those of despotism, and rejects every thing that is good in both systems.

Russia is governed by a class of subaltern employés, transferred direct from the public schools to the public administration. These individuals, who are very frequently the sons of men born in foreign lands, are noble so soon as they wear a cross at their button-hole; and it is only the Emperor who gives this decoration. Invested with the magical sign, they become proprietors of lands and of men; and thus obtaining power without obtaining also that heritage of magnanimity natural in a chieftain born and habituated to command, the new lords use their authority like upstarts as they are, and render odious to the nation, and the world, the system of servitude established in Russia, at the period when ancient Europe began to destroy her feudal institutions. By virtue of their offices, these despots oppress the country with impunity, and incommode even the Emperor; who perceives, with astonishment, that he is not so powerful as he imagined, though he dares not complain or even confess it to himself. This is the bureaucracy, a power terrible every where, because its abuses are always made in the name of order, but more terrible in Russia than any where else. When we see administrative tyranny substituted for Imperial despotism, we may tremble for a land where is established, without counterbalance, the system of government propagated in Europe under the French Empire.

The emperors of Russia, equally mistaken in their confidence and their suspicion, viewed the nobles as rivals, and sought only to find slaves in the men they needed for ministers. Hence has sprung up the swarms of obscure agents who labour to govern the land in obedience to ideas not their own; from which it follows that they can never satisfy real wants. This class of employés, hostile in their hearts to the order of things which they direct, are recruited in a great measure from among the sons of the popes*

* Greek priests.

—a body of vulgar aspirants, of upstarts without talent, for they need no merit to oblige the state to disembarrass itself of the burden which they are upon it; people who approach to all the ranks without possessing any; minds which participate alike in the popular prejudices and the aristocratic pretensions, without having the energy of the one or the wisdom of the other: to include all in one clause, the sons of the priests are revolutionists charged with maintaining the established order.

Half enlightened, liberal as the ambitious, as fond of oppressing as the slave, imbued with crude philosophical notions utterly inapplicable to the country which they call their own, though all their sentiments and semi-enlightened ideas come from abroad, these men are urging the nation towards a goal of which they are perhaps ignorant themselves, which the Emperor has never imagined, and which is not one that true Russians or true friends of humanity will desire.

This permanent conspiracy dates as far back as the time of Napoleon. The political Italian had foreseen the danger of the Russian power; and wishing to weaken the enemy of revolutionised Europe, he had recourse in the first place to the influence of ideas. He profited by his friendly relations with the Emperor Alexander, and by the innate tendency of that prince towards liberal institutions, to send to Petersburg, under pretext of aiding in the accomplishment of the Emperor's designs, a great number of political workmen,—a kind of masked army, charged with secretly preparing the way for our soldiers. These skilful intriguers were instructed to mix themselves up with the government, and especially with the system of public education, and to instil into the minds of the rising generation doctrines opposed to the political religion of the land. Thus did the great warrior—heir to the French revolution and foe to the liberties of the world—throw from afar the seeds of trouble and of discord, because the unity of despotism appeared to him a dangerous weapon in the military government which constitutes the immense power of Russia.

That empire is now reaping the fruit of the slow and profound policy of the adversary it flattered itself that it had conquered,—an adversary whose posthumous machiavelism survives reverses unheard of in the history of human wars. To the secretly-working influence of these pioneers of our armies, and to that of their children and their disciples, I attribute in a great measure the revolutionary ideas which have taken root in many families, and even in the army; and the explosion of which has produced the conspiracies that we have seen hitherto breaking themselves against the strength of the established government. Perhaps I deceive myself, but I feel persuaded that the present Emperor will triumph over these ideas, by crushing, even to the last man, those who defend them.

I was far from expecting to find in Russia such vestiges of our policy, and to hear from the mouths of Russians reproaches similar to those that the Spaniards have addressed to us for thirty-five years past. If the mischievous intentions which the Russians attribute to Napoleon were real, no interest, no patriotism could justify them. We cannot save one part of the world by deceiving the other. Our religious propagandism appears to me sublime, because the Catholic church accords with every form of government and every degree of civilisation, over which it reigns with all the superiority of mind over body: but political proselytism, that is to say, the narrow spirit of conquest, or to speak yet more justly, the spirit of rapine justified by that skilful sophistry called glory, is odious; for, far from drawing together the human race, this contracted ambition divides them: unity can only give birth to elevated and extended ideas; but the politics of national interference are always little; its liberality is hypocritical or tyrannical; its benefits are ever deceptive: every nation should derive from within itself the means for the improvements it requires.

To resume: the problem proposed, not by men, but by events, by the concatenation of circumstances, to an emperor of Russia, is to favour among the nation the progress of knowledge in order to hasten the emancipation of the serfs; and further to aim at this object by the improving of manners, by the encouraging of humanity and of legal liberty; in short, by ameliorating hearts with the view of alleviating destinies. Such is the condition imperative upon any man who would now reign, even at Moscow: but the peculiarity of the Emperor's position is, that he has to shape his course towards this object, keeping clear on the one side of the mute though well-organised tyranny of a revolutionary administration, and on the other of the arrogance and the conspiracies of an aristocracy so much the more unquiet and formidable as its power is vague and undefined.

It must be owned that no sovereign has yet acquitted himself in this terrible task with so much firmness, talent, and good fortune as have been displayed by the Emperor Nicholas. He is the first of the modern Russian princes who has perceived the necessity of being a Russian in order to confer good upon the Russians. Undoubtedly history will say: This man was a great sovereign.

I have no time left for sleeping: the horses are
already in my carriage, and I shall soon
be on the road
to Nijni.

❖

CHAPTER XXXII*

❖

O ur road follows the course of the Volga. Yesterday I crossed that river at Yaroslaf, and I have re-crossed it to-day at Kunitcha. In many places its two banks differ in physical aspect. On one side stretches an immense plain level with the water, on the other, the bank forms an almost perpendicular wall, sometimes a hundred or a hundred and fifty feet high. This rampart or natural embankment, which extends a considerable way backwards from the river before it again loses itself in gradual slopes upon the plain, is clothed with osiers and birch, and is broken from distance to distance by the river's tributaries. These water-courses form deep furrows in the bank, which they have to pierce in order to reach the mighty stream. The bank is quite a mountain chain, and the furrows are real valleys, across which the road parallel to the Volga is carried.

The Russian coachmen, although so skilful on level ground, are, on mountainous roads, the most dangerous drivers in the world. That on which we are now travelling puts their prudence and my sang-froid to the full proof. The continual ascending and descending would, if the declivities were longer, be, under their mode of driving, extremely perilous. The coachman commences the descent at a foot's pace; when about a third of it is got over, which generally brings you to the steepest part, man and horses

* Written at Yourewetch Powolskoi, a small town between Yaroslaf and Nijni Novgorod.

❖ 493 ❖

begin mutually to weary of their unaccustomed prudence; the latter get into a gallop, the carriage rolls after with constantly increasing velocity until it reaches the middle of a bridge of planks, frail, disjointed, uneven, and movable; for they are placed, but not fixed, upon the beams which support them, and under the poles which serve as rails to the trembling structure. A bridge of this kind is found at the bottom of each ravine. If the horses, in their wild gallop, do not bring the carriage straight on the planks, it will be overturned. The life of the traveller depends entirely upon the address of the driver, and upon the legs of four spirited, but weak and tired animals. If a horse stumbles, or a leather breaks, all is lost.

At the third repetition of this hazardous game I desired that the wheel should be locked, but there was no drag on my Moscow carriage: I had been told that it was never necessary to lock the wheel in Russia. To supply the want, it was necessary to detach one of the horses, and to use its traces. I have ordered the same operation to be repeated, to the great astonishment of the drivers, each time that the length and steepness of the declivity has seemed to threaten the safety of the carriage, the frailness of which I have already only too often experienced. The coachmen, astonished as they appear, do not make the least objection to my strange fancies, nor in any way oppose the orders that I give them through the feldjäger; but I can read their thoughts in their faces. The presence of a government-servant procures me every where marks of deference: such a proof of favour on the part of the authorities renders me an object of respect among the people. I would not advise any stranger, so little experienced as I am, to risk himself without such a guide on Russian roads, especially those of the interior.

When the traveller has been so fortunate as to cross safely the bottom of the ravine, the next difficulty is to climb the opposite bank. The Russian horses know no other pace but the gallop: if the road is not heavy, the hill short, and the carriage light, they bring you to the summit in a moment; but if the ascent is long, or the road, as is frequently the case, sandy, they soon come to a stop; panting and exhausted, in the middle of their task, they turn stupid under the application of the whip, kick, and run back, to the imminent danger of throwing the carriage into the ditches; while at each dilemma of the kind I say to myself, in derision of the pretensions of the Russians, there are no distances in Russia!

The coachmen, however adroit they may be, want experience when they leave their native plains; they do not understand the proper manner of getting horses over mountains. At the first signs of hesitation every body alights; the servants push at the wheels; at every few steps the horses stop to breathe, when the men rub their nostrils with vinegar, and encourage them with voice and hand. In this manner, aided by strokes of the whip, generally applied with admirable judgment, we gain the summit of these formidable ridges, which in other countries would be climbed without difficulty. The road from Yaroslaf to Nijni is one of the most hilly in the interior of Russia; and yet I do not believe that this natural rampart or quay that crowns the banks of the Volga exceeds the height of a house of five or six stories in Paris.

There is one danger when journeying in Russia which could hardly be foreseen—the danger the traveller runs of breaking his head against the cover of his calèche. He who intends visiting the country need not smile, for the peril is actual and imminent. The logs of which the bridges and often the roads themselves are made, render the carriages liable to shocks so violent, that the traveller when not warned would be thrown out if his equipage were open, and would break his neck if the head were up. It is therefore advisable, in Russia, to procure a carriage the top of which is as lofty as possible. A bottle of Seltzer-water, substantial as those bottles are, has, although well packed in hay, been broken under my seat, by the violence of the jolts.

Yesterday I slept in a post-house, where there was a want of every common convenience. My carriage is so uncomfortable, and the roads are so rough, that I cannot journey more than twenty-four hours together without suffering from violent head-ache, and, therefore, as I prefer a bad lodging to brain-fever, I stop wherever we may happen to be. The greatest rarity in these out-of-the-way lodgings, and indeed in all Russia, is clean linen. I carry my bed with me, but I cannot burden myself with much store of bed-clothes; and the table-cloths which they give me at the post-houses have always been in use. Yesterday, at eleven o'clock in the evening, the master of the post-house sent to a village more than a league distant to search for clean sheets on my account. I should have protested against this excess of zeal in my feldjäger, but I did not know of it until the next morning. From the window of my kennel, by the obscured light that is called night in Russia, I could admire at leisure the eternal Roman peristyle, which, with its wooden, whitewashed pediment and its plaster pillars, adorns, on the stable side, the Russian post-houses. This clumsy architecture creates a nightmare that follows me from one end of the empire to the other. The classic column has become the sign of a public building in Russia: false magnificence here displays itself by the side of the most complete penury: but "comfort," and elegance well understood and every where the same, is not to be seen, either in the palaces of the wealthy, where the saloons are superb, but where the bed-chamber is only a screen, or yet in the huts of the peasants. There may, perhaps, be two or three exceptions to this rule in the whole empire. Even Spain appears to me less in want than Russia of objects of convenience and necessity.

Another precaution indispensable to a traveller in this country is a Russian lock. All the Slavonian peasants are thieves, in the houses if not on the highway. When, therefore, you have got your luggage into the room of an inn, full of different classes of people, it is necessary, before going out to walk, either to make your servants mount guard at the door, or to lock it. One of your people will be already engaged in keeping watch over the carriage; and there are no keys, nor even locks, to the doors of apartments in Russian inns. The only expedient, therefore, is to be provided with staples, rings, and padlock. With these you may speedily place your property in safety. The country swarms with the most adroit and audacious of robbers. Their depredations are so frequent, that justice does not dare to be rigorous. Every thing is here done by fits and starts, or with exceptions,—a capricious system, which too well accords with the ill-regulated minds of the people, who are as indifferent to equity in action as to truth in speech.

I yesterday visited the convent of Kostroma, and saw the

apartments of Alexis Romanow and his mother, a retreat which Alexis left to ascend the throne, and to found the actual reigning dynasty. The convent was like all the others. A young monk, who was not fasting, and who smelt of wine at a considerable distance, showed me the house. I prefer old monks with white beards, and popes with bald heads, to these young, well-fed recluses. The Treasury, also, resembled those I had seen elsewhere. Would the reader know in a few words, what is Russia? Russia is a country where the same persons and the same things are every where to be seen. This is so true, that on arriving at any place, we think always that we recognise persons whom we had left elsewhere.

At Kunitcha, the ferry-boat in which we re-crossed the Volga had sides so low, that the smallest thing would have caused it to upset. Nothing has ever appeared to me more dull and gloomy than this little town, which I visited during a cold rain, accompanied with wind, that kept the inhabitants prisoners in their houses. Had the wind increased, we should have run much risk of being drowned in the river. I recollected that at Petersburg no one stirs a step to save those that fall into the Neva; and I thought, that should the same fate happen to me here, not an attempt would be made to save me by any one on these banks—populous though they appear a desert, so gloomy and silent are the soil, the heavens, and the inhabitants. The life of man has little importance in the eyes of the Russians; and, judging by their melancholy air, I should say they are indifferent to their own lives as well as to those of others.

Existence is so fettered and restrained, that every one seems to me secretly to cherish the desire of changing his abode, without possessing the power. The great have no passports, the poor no money, and all remain as they are, patient through despair, that is, as indifferent about death as about life. Resignation, which is every where else a virtue, is in Russia a vice, because it perpetuates the compulsory immobility of things.

The question here, is not one of political liberty, but of personal independence, of freedom of movement, and even of the expression of natural sentiment. The slaves dare only quarrel in a low voice; anger is one of the privileges of power. The greater the appearance of calm under this system, the more do I pity the people: tranquillity or the knout!—this is for them the condition of existence. The knout of the great is Siberia; and Siberia itself is only an exaggeration of Russia.

❖   ❖   ❖

I am writing in the middle of a forest, many leagues from any habitation. We are stopped in a deep bed of sand by an accident that has happened to my carriage; and while my valet is, with the aid of a peasant whom Heaven has sent us, repairing the damage, I, who am humbled by the want of resources which I find within myself for such an occurrence, and who feel that I should only be in the way of the workmen if I attempted to assist them, take up my pen to prove the inutility of mental culture, when man, deprived of all the accessories of civilisation, is obliged to struggle, without any other resource but his own strength, against a wild nature, still armed with all the primitive power that it received from God.

As I have before said, handsome female peasants are scarce in Russia; but, when they are handsome, their beauty is perfect. The oval shape of their eyes imparts a peculiar expression; the eye-lid is finely and delicately chiselled, but the blue of the pupil is often clouded, which reminds one of the ancient Sarmatians, as described by Tacitus: this hue gives to their veiled glances a gentleness and an innocence, the charm of which is irresistible. They possess all the vague and shadowy delicacy of the women of the north, united with all the voluptuousness of the Oriental females. The expression of kindness in these ravishing creatures inspires a singular feeling—a mixture of respect and confidence. He must visit the interior of Russia who would know the real gifts of the primitive man, and all that the refinements of society have lost for him. In this patriarchal land it is civilisation which spoils the inhabitants. The Slavonian was naturally ingenious, musical, and almost tender-hearted; the drilled Russian is false, tyrannical, imitative, and foolishly vain. It would take more than a century to establish an accord between the national manners and the new European ideas; supposing that, all the while, Russia were governed by enlightened princes,—friends of progress, as the expression now is. At present, the complete separation of classes makes social life a violent, immoral thing. It might be supposed that it was from this country Rousseau took the first idea of his system; for it is not even necessary to possess the resources of his magic eloquence to prove that arts and sciences have done more evil than good to the Slavonians. The future will show the world whether military and political glory can compensate the Russian nation for the happiness of which their social organisation deprives them.

Elegance is inborn among the men of pure Slavonian blood. Their characters unite a mixture of simplicity, gentleness, and sensibility, which seduce all hearts: they are often combined with a good deal of irony and some little deceitfulness; but, when the heart is naturally amiable, these faults are transformed into a kind of grace. The people further possess the advantage of a countenance, the delicacy in the expression of which is inimitable; it influences, by an unknown charm, by a tender melancholy, a suffering gentleness, which almost always springs from a secret sense of evil, hid by the sufferer from himself, in order the better to disguise it from others. The Russians are, in short, a resigned nation,—this simple description explains every thing. The man who is deprived of liberty—and here the definition of that word extends to natural rights and real wants,—though he may have all other advantages, is like a plant excluded from the air: in vain do you water its roots, the languishing stem produces a few leaves, but will never send forth flowers.

The true Russians have something peculiar to themselves, both in their character, their countenance, and their whole bearing. Their carriage is light, and all their movements denote a natural superiority. Their eyes are large, of a long oval shape, and the eyelid is but little raised. Their glance combines an expression of sentiment and of mischievousness that is very taking. The Greeks, in their creative language, called the inhabitants of these regions Syromedes, a word which signifies lizard-eyed; the Latin word Sarmatian is derived from it. This expression of the eye then has struck all attentive observers. The forehead of the Russians is neither very lofty nor very broad; but its form is classic and graceful. In the character of the people, both distrust and credulity, roguishness and tenderness, are united,—and these contrasts have a charm. The Slavonians are neither coarse nor apathetic, like most other northern races. Poetical as nature, their imagination mixes with all their affections; with them, love partakes of the nature of superstition; their attachments have more delicacy than vivacity: always refined, even when impassioned, it may be said that their intellect pervades their sentiment. All these fugitive shades of character are expressed in their glance,—that glance which was so well characterised by the Greeks.

The ancient Greeks were endowed with an exquisite talent for appreciating men and things, and for describing them by names; a faculty which renders their language rich among all the European languages, and their poetry divine among all poetic schools.

The passionate fondness of the Russian peasants for tea proves to me the elegance of their nature, and well accords with the description I have given of them. Tea is a refined beverage: it has become in Russia an absolute necessary. When the common people ask for drink-money, they say, for tea, *na tchiai.*

This instinct of good taste has no connection with mental culture; it does not even exclude barbarism and cruelty, but it excludes vulgarity.

The spectacle now before my eyes proves to me the truth of what I have always heard respecting the Russians' singular dexterity and industry.

A Muscovite peasant makes it a principle to recognise no obstacles,—I do not mean to his own desires, unhappy creature! but to the orders he receives. Aided by his inseparable hatchet, he becomes a kind of magician, who creates in a moment all that is wanted in the desert. He repairs your carriage, or, if it is beyond repair, he makes another, a kind of telega, skilfully availing himself of the remains of the old one in the construction of the new. I was advised in Moscow to travel in a tarandasse, and I should have done well to have followed that advice; for, with such an equipage, there is never danger of stopping on the road. It can be repaired, and even re-constructed, by every Russian peasant.

If you wish to encamp, this universal genius will build you a dwelling for the night, and one that will be preferable to the taverns in the towns. After having established you as comfortably as you can expect to be, he wraps himself in his sheep-skin and sleeps at the door of your new house, of which he defends the entrance with the fidelity of a dog; or else he will seat himself at the foot of a tree before the abode that he has erected for you, and, while continuing to gaze at the sky, he will relieve the solitude of your lodging by national songs, the melancholy of which awakes a respond in the gentlest instincts of your heart; for an innate gift of music is still one of the prerogatives of this privileged race. The idea that it would be only just that he should share with you the cabin built by his hands will never enter his head.

Will these *élites* of their race remain much longer concealed in the deserts where Providence, with some design of its own, keeps them in reserve? Providence can only answer! The question as to when the hour of deliverance, and, yet more, of triumph, shall strike for them, is a secret with God.

I am struck with the simplicity of the ideas and sentiments of these men. God, the King of heaven; the Czar, the king of earth —this is all their theory: the orders, and even the caprices, of the master sanctioned by the obedience of the slave; this suffices for their practice. The Russian peasant believes that he owes both body and soul to his lord.

Conforming to this social devotion, he lives without joy, but not without pride; for pride is the moral element essential to the life of the intelligent being. It takes every kind of form, even the form of humility,—that religious modesty discovered by Christians.

A Russian does not know what it is to say *no* to this lord, who represents to him his two other greater masters, God and the Emperor; and he places all his talent, all his glory, in conquering those little difficulties of existence that are magnified, and even valued, by the lower orders of other lands, as auxiliaries in their revenge against the rich, whom they consider as enemies, because they are esteemed the happy of the earth.

The Russians are too completely stripped of all the blessings of life to be envious: the men who are most to be pitied are those who no longer complain. The envious among us are those whose ambitious aims have failed: France, that land of easy living and rapid fortune-making, is a nursery of envious people. I cannot feel sympathy with the regrets, full of malice, that prey on these men, whose souls are enervated by the luxuries of life; but the patience of the peasants here, inspires me with a compassion—I had almost said, with an esteem that is profound. The political self-denial of the Russians is abject and revolting; their domestic resignation is noble and touching. The vice of the nation becomes the virtue of the individual.

The plaintive sadness of the Russian songs strikes every foreigner; but this music is not only melancholy, it is also scientific and complicated: it is composed of inspired melodies; and, at the same time, of harmonious combinations exceedingly abstruse, and that are not elsewhere attained except by study and calculation. Often, in travelling through villages, I stop to listen to pieces executed by several voices with a precision, and a musical instinct, that I am never tired of admiring. The performers, in these rustic quintetti, guess, by intuition, the laws of counterpoint, the rules of composition, the principles of harmony, the effects of the different kinds of voice, and they disdain singing in unison. They execute series of concords, elaborate, unexpected, and interspersed with shakes, and delicate ornaments, which, if not always perfectly correct, are very superior to the national melodies heard in other lands.

The song of the Russian peasants is a nasal lamentation, not very agreeable when executed by one voice; but when sung in chorus, these complaints assume a grave, religious character, and produce effects of harmony that are surprising. I had supposed the Russian music to have been brought from Byzantium, but I am assured that it is indigenous: this will explain the profound melancholy of the airs, especially of those which affect gaiety by their vivacity of movement. If the Russians do not know how to revolt against oppression, they know how to sigh and groan under it.

Were I in the place of the emperor, I should not be content with forbidding my subjects to complain; I should also forbid them to sing, which is a disguised mode of complaining. These accents of lament are avowals, and may become accusations: so

true it is that the arts themselves, under despotism, are not innocent; they are indirect protestations.

Hence, no doubt, the taste of the government and the courtiers for the works, literary or artistical, of foreigners: borrowed
poetry has no roots. Among a people of slaves, when patriotic
sentiments produce profound emotions, they are dreaded: everything that is national, including even music, becomes a means of
opposition.

It is so in Russia, where, from the corners of the farthest
deserts, the voice of man lifts to heaven vengeful complaints;
demanding from God the portion of happiness that is refused him
upon earth. Nothing more strikingly reveals the habitual sufferings of the people than the mournfulness of their pleasures. The
Russians have consolations, but no enjoyments. I am surprised
that no one before me should have warned the government of its
imprudence in allowing the people an amusement which betrays
their misery and their resignation. He who is powerful enough to
oppress men should, for consistency's sake, forbid them to sing.

❖   ❖   ❖

I am now at the last stage on the road to Nijni. We have arrived
on three wheels, and dragging a prop of wood in the place of the
fourth.

A great part of the road from Yaroslaf to Nijni is a long garden
avenue, traced almost always in a straight line, broader than the
great avenue in our Champs-Élysées at Paris, and flanked on
either side by two smaller alleys, carpeted with turf and shaded
by birch-trees. The road is easy, for they drive nearly always
upon the grass, except when crossing marshes by means of elastic
bridges, a kind of floating floors, more curious than safe either for
the carriages or the horses. A road on which grows so much grass
can be little frequented, and is therefore the more easily kept in
repair. Yesterday, before we broke down, I was praising this road,
which we were travelling at full gallop, to my feldjäger. "No
doubt it is beautiful," replied the individual addressed, whose
figure resembles that of a wasp, whose features are sharp and dry,
and whose manners are at once timid and threatening, like hatred

suppressed by fear: "no doubt it is beautiful—it is the great road to Siberia."

These words chilled me through. It is for my pleasure, I said to myself, that I travel this road: but what have been the thoughts and feelings of the many unfortunate beings who have travelled it before me? These thoughts and feelings, evoked by the imagination, took possession of my mind. Siberia!—that Russian hell, is, with all its phantoms, incessantly before me. It has upon me the effect that the eye of the basilisk has upon the fascinated bird.

What a country is this! a plain without limit and without colour; with only here and there some few inequalities in the surface, a few fields of oats and rye, a few scattered birch and pine woods in the distance, villages built of gray boards along the lines of road, on rather more elevated sites, at every twenty, thirty, or fifty leagues, towns the vast size of which swallows up the inhabitants, and immense, colourless rivers, dull as the heavens they reflect! Winter and death are felt to be hovering over these scenes, giving to every object a funereal hue: the terrified traveller, at the end of a few weeks, feels himself buried alive, and, stifling, struggles to burst his coffin-lid, that leaden veil that separates him from the living.

Do not go to the north to amuse yourselves, unless at least you seek your amusement in study; for there is much here to study.

I was, then, travelling upon the great road to Siberia, when I saw in the distance a group of armed men, who had stopped under one of the side alleys of the road.

"What are those soldiers doing there?" I asked my courier.

"They are cossacks," he replied, "conducting exiles to Siberia!"

It is not, then, a dream, it is not the mythology of the gazettes: I see there the real, unhappy beings, the actual exiles, proceeding wearily on foot to seek the land where they must die forgotten by the world, far from all that is dear to them, alone with the God who never created them for such a fate. Perhaps I have met, or shall meet, their wives or mothers: for they are not criminals; on the contrary, they are Poles—the heroes of misfortune and devotion. Tears came into my eyes as I approached these unhappy men, near to whom I dared not even stop lest I should be sus-

pected by my Argus. Alas! before such sufferings the sentiment of
my impotent compassion humiliates me, and anger rises above
commiseration in my heart. I could wish to be far away from a
country where the miserable creature who acts as my courier can
become formidable enough to compel me, in his presence, to dissimulate the most natural feelings of my heart. In vain do I
repeat to myself that, perhaps, our convicts are still worse off
than the colonists of Siberia: there is, in that distant exile, a
vague poetry, which adds to the severity of the sentence all the
influence of the imagination; and this inhuman alliance produces
a frightful result. Besides, our convicts are solemnly convicted;
but a few months' abode in Russia suffices to convince us that
there are no laws there.

There were three exiles, and they were all innocent in my eyes;
for, under a despotism, the only criminal is the man who goes
unpunished. These three convicts were escorted by six cossacks
on horseback. The head of my carriage was closed, and the nearer
we approached the group, the more narrowly did the courier
strive to observe the expression of my countenance. I was greatly
struck with the efforts he made to persuade me that they were
only simple malefactors, and that there was no political convict
among them. I preserved a gloomy silence: the pains that he took
to reply to my thoughts appeared to me very significative.

Frightful sagacity of the subjects of despotism! all are spies,
even as amateurs, and without compensation.

The last stages of the road to Nijni are long and difficult,
owing to the sand-beds, which get deeper and deeper,* until the
carriages become almost buried in them. They conceal immense,
movable blocks of wood and stone, very dangerous to the carriages and horses. This part of the road is bordered by forests, in
which, at every half league, are encampments of cossacks, destined to protect the journeying of the merchants who resort to
the fair. Such a precaution reminds me of the middle ages.

My wheel is repaired, so that I hope to
reach Nijni before
evening.

❖

* A chaussée is being made from Moscow to Nijni, which will be soon completed.

CHAPTER XXXIII

❖

The situation of Nijni is the most beautiful that I have beheld in Russia. I see no longer a little ridge of low banks falling upon a large river, but a real mountain, which looks down on the confluence of the Volga and the Oka, two equally noble rivers; for the Oka, at its mouth, appears as large as the more celebrated stream. The lofty town of Nijni, built on this mountain, commands a plain, vast as the sea. A land without bounds spreads before it, and at its foot is held the largest fair in the world. During six weeks of the year the commerce of the two richest quarters of the globe meet at the confluence of the Oka and the Volga. It is a spot worthy of being painted. Hitherto, the only truly picturesque scenes that I had admired in Russia were the streets of Moscow and the quays of Petersburg. But those scenes were the creations of man: here, the country is naturally beautiful. The ancient city of Nijni, instead, however, of seeking the rivers, and profiting by the riches they offer, hides itself behind the mountain; and there, lost in the country, seems to shrink from its glory and prosperity. This ill-advised situation has struck the Emperor Nicholas, who exclaimed the first time he saw the place—"At Nijni nature has done every thing, but man has spoilt all." To remedy the errors of the founders of Nijni-Novgorod, a suburb, in the form of a quay, has been built under the hill, on that one of the two points of land separating the rivers, which forms the right bank of the Oka. This new town increases every year; it is becoming more populous and important than the ancient city, from which it is separated by the old Kremlin of Nijni; for every Russian city has its Kremlin.

The fair is held on the other side of the Oka, upon a low tract, which forms a triangle between it and the Volga. The Oka is crossed by a bridge of boats, which serves as the road from the city to the fair, and which appears as long as that of the Rhine at Mayence. The two banks of the river thus connected, are very different in character: the one which is the promontory of Nijni, rises majestically in the midst of this immense country; the other, nearly on a level with the water which inundates it during a part of the year, forms a portion of the plain called Russia. The singular beauty of the contrast did not escape the glance of the Emperor Nicholas: that prince, with his characteristic sagacity, has also perceived that Nijni is one of the most important points in his empire. He is very fond of this central spot, thus favoured by nature, and which has become the rendezvous of the most distant populations, who here congregate from all parts, drawn together by a powerful commercial interest. His Majesty has neglected nothing that could tend to beautify, enlarge, and enrich the city. The fair of Makarief, which was held formerly on the estate of a boyard twenty leagues below, following the course of the Volga towards Asia, was forfeited for the benefit of the crown and country; and the Emperor Alexander transferred it to Nijni. I regret the Asiatic fair held on the domains of a Muscovite prince: it must have been more original and picturesque, though less immense and regular, than the one I find here.

I have already said that every Russian city has its Kremlin, just as every Spanish city has its Alcazar. The Kremlin of Nijni, with its many-shaped towers, its pinnacles and embattled ramparts, which circle round a mountain far loftier than the hill of the Kremlin at Moscow, is nearly half a league in circumference.

When the traveller perceives this fortress from the plain he is struck with astonishment. It is the pharos, towards whose shining turrets and white walls, rising above the stunted forest pines, he shapes his course through the sandy deserts which defend the approach to Nijni on the side of Yaroslaf. The effect of this national architecture is always powerful: but here, the grotesque towers and Christian minarets, that constitute the ornament of all the kremlins, are heightened in effect by the striking character of the site, which in certain places opposes real precipices to the creations of the architect. In the thickness of the walls have been worked, as at Moscow, staircases, which serve to ascend, from battlement to battlement, up to the very summit of the crowning ramparts. These commanding stairs, with the towers by which they are flanked, the slopes, the vaults, the arcades which sustain them, form a picture from whichsoever point of approach they are viewed.

The fair of Nijni, now become the most considerable in the world, is the rendezvous of people the least alike in person, costume, language, religion, and manners. Men from Thibet, from Bucharia, from the regions bordering upon China, come to meet Persians, Finns, Greeks, English, and Parisians: it is like the merchants' doomsday. The number of foreigners present at Nijni every day during the fair, exceeds two hundred thousand. The men who compose this yearly gathering come and go daily; but the number always continues pretty nearly the same: nevertheless, on certain days, there are at Nijni as many as three hundred thousand at the same time. The average consumption of bread in the pacific camp amounts to four hundred thousand pounds weight per day. Except at the season of this saturnalia of trade and industry, the city is lifeless. Nijni scarcely numbers twenty thousand stationary inhabitants, who are lost in its vast streets and naked squares during the nine months that the fair-ground remains forsaken.

The fair occasions little disorder. In Russia disorder is unknown: it would be a progressive movement, for it is the child of liberty. The love of gain, and the ever-increasing need of luxuries, felt now by even barbarous nations, cause the semi-barbarous populations who resort here from Persia and Bucharia to recognise the advantages of orderly demeanour and good faith: besides, it must be admitted that in general the Mohammedans are upright in money matters.

Though I have only been a few hours in the city, I have already seen the governor. I had several flattering letters of introduction to him: he appears hospitable, and, for a Russian, open and communicative. His name is illustrious in the ancient history of Russia—it is that of Boutourline. The Boutourlines are a family of old boyards; a class of men that is becoming rare.

I have scarcely encountered any really dense crowd in Russia, except at Nijni, on the bridge over the Oka, the only road which leads from the city to the fair-ground, and the road also by which we approach Nijni from Yaroslaf. At the entrance of the fair you turn to the right to cross the bridge, leaving on the left the booths, and the temporary palace of the governor, a pavilion which forms a species of administrative observatory, whither he repairs every morning, and from whence he surveys all the streets, all the rows of shops, and presides over the general arrangements of the fair. The dust, the din, the carriages, the foot-passengers, the soldiers charged with maintaining order, greatly obstruct the passage of the bridge, whose use and character it is difficult at first to understand; for the surface of the water being covered by a multitude of boats, at the first glance, you suppose the river to be dry. The boats are so crowded together at the confluence of the Volga and the Oka that the latter river may be crossed by striding from junk to junk. I use this Chinese word because a great portion of the vessels which resort to Nijni bring to the fair the merchandise, more especially the tea, of China.

Yesterday, on arriving, I expected that our horses would have run over twenty individuals before reaching the quay of the Oka, which is New Nijni, a suburb that will in a few years more be very extensive.

When I had gained the desired shore, I found that many other difficulties awaited me: before everything else it was necessary to find a lodging, and the inns were full. My feldjäger knocked at every door, and always returned with the same smile, ferocious by its very immobility, to tell me that he could not find a single chamber. He advised me to appeal to the hospitality of the governor; but this I was unwilling to do.

At length, arrived at the extremity of the long street that forms this suburb, at the foot of the steep hill which leads to the old city, and the summit of which is crowned by the Kremlin of Nijni, we perceived a coffee-house, the approach to which was obstructed by a covered public market, from whence exhaled odours that were anything but perfumes. Here I descended, and was politely received by the landlord, who conducted me through a series of apartments, all filled with men in pelisses, drinking tea and other liquors, until, by bringing me to the last room, he demonstrated to me that he had not one single chamber at liberty.

"This room forms the corner of your house," I observed: "has it a private entrance?"

"Yes."

"Very good: lock the door which separates it from the other apartments, and let me have it for a bed-chamber."

The air that I breathed already suffocated me. It was a mixture of the most opposite emanations: the grease of sheep-skins, the musk of dressed leather, the blacking of boots, cabbage, which is the principal food of the peasants, coffee, tea, liqueurs, and brandy, all thickened the atmosphere. The whole was poison: but what could I do? it was my last resource. I hoped, also, that after being cleared of its guests, swept and washed, the bad odours of the apartment would dissipate. I therefore insisted on the feldjäger clearly explaining my proposal to the keeper of the coffee-house.

"I shall lose by it," replied the man.

"I will pay you what you please; provided you also find somewhere a lodging for my valet and my courier."

The bargain was concluded; and here I am, quite proud of having taken by storm, in a dirty public-house, a room for which I have to pay more than the price of the finest apartment in the Hôtel des Princes, at Paris. It is only in Russia, in a country where the whims of men supposed to be powerful, know no obstacle, that one is able to convert, in a moment, the public hall of a coffee-house into a sleeping-apartment.

My feldjäger undertook to make the drinkers retire: they rose without offering the least objection, were crowded into the next room, and the door was fastened upon them by the species of lock I have already mentioned. A score of tables filled up the chamber; but a swarm of priests in their robes, in other words, a troop of waiters in white shirts, precipitated themselves upon the furniture, and left me with bare walls in a few moments. But what a sight then met my eyes! Under each table, under every stool, multitudes of vermin were crawling, of a kind I have never before seen: they were black insects, about half an inch long, thick, soft, viscid, and tolerably nimble in their movements. This loathsome animal is known in a portion of Eastern Europe, in Volhynia, the Ukraine, Russia, and a part of Poland, where it is called, I believe, *persica*, because it was brought from Asia. I cannot make out the name given to it by the coffee-house waiters of Nijni. On seeing the floor of my chamber mottled over with these moving reptiles, crushed under the foot at every step, not by hundreds, but by thousands, and on perceiving the new kind of ill-savour exhaled by this massacre, I was seized with despair, fled from my chamber to the street, and proceeded to present myself to the governor. I did not re-enter my detestable lodging until assured that it had been rendered as clean as practicable. My bed, filled with fresh hay, was placed in the middle of the room, its four feet standing in earthern vessels full of water. Notwithstanding these precautions, I did not fail to find, on awaking from a restless, unrefreshing sleep, two or three persicas on my pillow. The reptiles are not noxious; but I cannot express the disgust with which they inspire me. The filthiness, the apathy, which their presence in the habitations of man betrays, make me regret my journey to this part of the globe. I feel as though there were a moral degradation in being approached by these offal-bred creatures: physical antipathy triumphs over all the efforts of reason.

A merchant of Moscow, who has the most splendid and extensive silk-magazine in the fair, is coming this morning to take me over it, and to show me everything in detail.

❖ ❖ ❖

I again find here the dust and suffocating heat of a southern clime. I was therefore well advised not to go on foot to the fair: but the concourse of strangers is at this time so great at Nijni, that I could not get a vehicle on hire; I was therefore obliged to use the by-no-means elegant one in which I arrived from Moscow, and to attach to it two horses only, which annoyed me as much as though I had been a Russian. It is not through vanity that they drive four horses: the animals have spirit, but they are not robust; they soon fatigue when they have much weight to draw.

On entering the carriage with the merchant who was so good as to act as my cicerone, and with his brother, I told my feldjäger to follow us. He, without hesitating or waiting to ask my permission, deliberately stepped into the calèche, and, with a coolness that amazed me, seated himself by the side of M. ——'s brother, who, notwithstanding my expostulations, was determined to sit with his back to the horses. In this country it is not unusual to see the owner of a carriage seated facing the horses, when even he is not by the side of a lady, whilst his friends place themselves opposite. This impoliteness, which would not be committed among us excepting where there was the strictest intimacy, here astonishes nobody.

Fearing lest the familiarity of the courier should shock my obliging companions, I considered it necessary to make this man remove; and told him, very civilly, to mount the seat by the side of the coachman.

"I shall do nothing of the kind," answered the feldjäger, with imperturbable sang-froid.

"What is the reason that you do not obey me?" I asked, in a yet calmer tone; for I know that among this half-oriental nation, it is necessary to maintain perfect impassibility in order to preserve your authority.

We spoke in German. "It would be a derogation," answered the Russian, in the same quiet tone.

This reminded me of the disputes about precedence among the boyards, which, under the reigns of the Ivans, were often so serious as to fill many pages of the Russian history of that epoch.

"What do you mean by a derogation?" I continued. "Is not that the place which you have occupied since we left Moscow?"

"It is true, sir, that is my place in travelling; but in taking a drive I ought to be in the carriage. I wear a uniform."

This uniform, which I have noticed elsewhere, is that of an agent of the post.

"I wear uniform, sir; I possess a rank in the tchinn; I am not a private servant; I am in the employ of the emperor."

"I care very little what you are; though I never said to you that you were a servant."

"I should have the appearance of being one, were I to sit in that place when you take a ride in the city. I have been many years in service; and, as a recompense for my good conduct, they hold out to me the prospect of nobility: I am endeavouring to obtain it, for I am ambitious."

This confusion of our old aristocratic ideas with the new vanity instilled by despots into a people diseased with envy, took me by surprise. I had before me a specimen of the worst kind of emulation—that of the *parvenant* already giving himself the airs of the *parvenu!*

After a moment's silence, I answered: "I approve your pride, if it is well founded; but being little acquainted with the usages of your country, I shall, before allowing you to enter my coach, submit your claims to the governor. My intention is to require nothing from you beyond what you owe me in accordance with the orders given you when you were sent to me: in my uncertainty as to your pretensions, I dispense with your services for to-day; I shall proceed without you."

I felt inclined to laugh at the tone of importance with which I spoke; but I considered this dramatic dignity necessary to my comfort during the rest of the journey. There is nothing, however ridiculous, which may not be excused by the conditions and the inevitable consequences of despotism.

This aspirant to nobility, and scrupulous observer of the etiquette of the highway, costs me, notwithstanding his pride, three hundred francs, in wages, per month. He reddened when he heard my last words, and, without making any reply, he left the carriage and re-entered the house in silence.

The ground on which the fair is held is very spacious; and I congratulated myself that I did not proceed to that city of a month on foot, for the heat continues to be great during a day in which the sun still darts his rays for fifteen hours.

The men of every land, but especially those of the extreme East, here meet together: these men are however more singular in name than in appearance. All the Asiatics resemble each other, or they may, at least, be divided into two classes: those having the faces of apes, as the Calmucs, Mongols, Baskirs, and Chinese; and those having the Greek profile, as the Circassians, Persians, Georgians, Indians, &c.

The fair of Nijni is held, as I have already said, on an immense triangle of sandy and perfectly level land, which runs to a point between the Oka, at its embouchure into the Volga, and the broad stream of the latter river. It is, therefore, bordered on either side by one of the two rivers. The soil upon which so immense an amount of wealth is heaped scarcely rises above the water. This merchant-city consists of a vast assemblage of long and broad streets: their perfect straightness injures their picturesque effect. A dozen of buildings called Chinese pavilions rise above the shops; but their fantastic style is not sufficient to correct the dulness and monotony of the general aspect of the edifices. The whole forms an oblong bazaar, which appears solitary, so vast is it in extent. The dense crowds that obstruct the approaches disappear as soon as you penetrate the interior lines of stalls. The city of the fair is, like all the other modern Russian cities, too vast for its population, although that population, including the amphibious community scattered in boats on the river, and the flying camps which environ the fair, properly so called, amounts to 200,000 souls. The houses of the merchants stand upon a subterranean city, an immense vaulted sewer; in which labyrinth he would be lost who should attempt to penetrate without an experienced guide. Each street in the fair is doubled by a gallery, which follows its whole length, under earth, and serves as an issue for all refuse. The sewers are constructed of stone, and are cleansed several times daily, by a multitude of pumps, which introduce the water from the neighbouring rivers. They are entered by large and handsome stone staircases.

These catacombs of filth, which are also for the prevention of every thing offensive in the open streets, are placed under the charge of cossacks, who form its police, and who politely invite the individual to descend. They are one of the most imposing works I have seen in Russia, and might suggest models to the constructors of the sewers at Paris. So much vastness and solidity reminds one of the descriptions of Rome. They were built by the Emperor Alexander, who, like his predecessors, pretended to conquer nature by establishing the fair on a soil inundated during one half of the year. He lavished millions in remedying the inconveniences of the injudicious choice made when the fair of Makarief was transported to Nijni.

The Oka, which separates the city of the fair from the permanent city, is here more than four times the breadth of the Seine. Forty thousand men sleep every night upon its bosom, making themselves nests in boats, which form a kind of floating camp. From the surface of the aquatic city rises, at evening, the heavy murmur of voices that might be easily taken for the gurgling of the waves. All these boats have masts, and form a river-forest, peopled by men from every corner of the earth: their faces and their costumes are equally strange. The sight has struck me more than any other in the immense fair. Rivers thus inhabited remind one of the descriptions of China.

Some of the peasants in this part of Russia wear white tunic shirts, ornamented with red borders: the costume is borrowed from the Tartars. At nighttime, the white linen gives them the appearance of spectres moving in the dark. Yet, notwithstanding its many singular and interesting objects, the fair of Nijni is not picturesque: it is a formal plan rather than a graceful sketch. The man devoted to political economy, or arithmetical calculations, has more business here than the poet or the painter: the subjects relate to the commercial balance and progress of the two principal quarters of the world—nothing more and nothing less. From one end of Russia to the other I perceive a minute, Dutch-taught government, hypocritically carrying on war against the primitive faculties of an ingenious, lively, poetical, oriental people, a people born for the arts.

The merchandise of every part of the world is collected in the immense streets of the fair; but it is also lost in them. The scarcest objects are buyers. I have seen nothing yet in this country without exclaiming, "the people are too few for the space!" It is just the contrary in ancient communities, where the land fails the civilisation. The French and English stalls are the most elegant; while viewing them, the beholder might fancy himself at Paris or at London: but this Bond-street of the East, this Palais Royal of the steppes, does not constitute the real wealth of the market of Nijni. To have a just idea of the importance of this fair it is necessary to recollect its origin, and the place where it was first held. Before flourishing at Makarief it was established at Kazan: the two extremes of the ancient world, western Europe and China, met in that ancient capital of Russian Tartary to exchange their various products. This is now done at Nijni. But a very incomplete idea of a market for the commodities of two continents would be formed, if the spectator did not leave the regular stalls and elegant pavilions which adorn the modern bazaar of Alexander, and survey some of the different camps by which it is flanked. The line and rule do not follow the merchant into the suburbs of the fair: these suburbs are like the farm-yard of a château—however stately and orderly the principal habitation, the disorder of nature reigns in its dependencies.

It is no easy task to traverse, even rapidly, these exterior depôts, for they are themselves each as large as cities. A continual and really imposing activity pervades them,—a true mercantile chaos, which it is needful to see in order to believe.

To commence with the city of tea: It is an Asiatic camp, which extends on the banks of the two rivers to the point of land where they meet. The tea comes from China by Kiatka, which is in the back part of Asia. At this first depôt it is exchanged for merchandise, and from thence transported in packages, which resemble small chests, in the shape of dice, about two feet deep every way. These packages are frames, covered with skins; the buyers thrust into them a kind of probe, by withdrawing which they ascertain the quality of the article. From Kiatka the tea travels by land to Tomsk; it is there placed in boats, and sails along several rivers, of which the Irtish and the Tobol are the principal, till it arrives at Tourmine, from whence it is again transported by land to Perm, in Siberia, where it is re-shipped on the Kama, which carries it into the Volga, and up that river it ascends to Nijni. Russia receives yearly 75,000 or 80,000 chests of tea, one half of which remains in Siberia, to be transported to Moscow during the winter, by sledges, and the other half arrives at this fair.

The principal tea-merchant in Russia is the individual who wrote for me the above itinerary. I do not answer for either the orthography or the geography of that opulent man; but a million-naire is generally correct, for he buys the science of others.

It will be seen that this famous tea of the caravans, so delicate, as is said, because it comes over-land, travels nearly always by water: to be sure, it is fresh water; and the mists of rivers do not produce such effects as the ocean fogs.

Forty thousand chests of tea is an amount easily named; but the reader can have no idea of the time it takes to survey them, though it be only by passing before the piles of boxes. This year, thirty-five thousand were sold in three days. A single individual, my geographical merchant, took fourteen thousand, which cost him ten million silver roubles (paper roubles are not current here), a part payable down, the rest in one year.

It is the rate of tea which fixes the price of all the commodities of the fair: before this rate is published, the other bargains are only made conditionally.

There is another city as large, but less elegant, and less per-fumed than the city of tea—that, namely, of rags. Fortunately, before bringing the tatters of all Russia to the fair, those into whose hands they have fallen, cause them to be washed. This commodity, necessary to the manufacture of paper, has become so precious, that the Russian custom-house forbids the exporta-tion with extreme severity.

Another town which attracted my attention among the sub-urbs, was that of barked timber. Like the faubourgs of Vienna, these secondary cities are larger than the principal. The one of which I speak serves as a magazine for the wood, brought from Siberia, destined to form the wheels of the Russian carts, and the collars of the horses—those semicircles formed of a single piece of bended wood, which are seen fixed in so picturesque a manner at the extremities of the shafts, and which rise above the heads of all the shaft-horses in the empire. The store necessary to furnish these wheels and collars to Western Russia forms here, mountains of wood, of which our timber-yards at Paris cannot give even an idea.

Another city, and it is, I believe, the most extensive and curi-ous of all, serves as a depôt for the iron of Siberia. I walked for a quarter of a league under galleries, in which are to be found, artistically arranged, every known species of iron bar, grating, and wrought iron; pyramids built of the utensils of husbandry and house-keeping, magazines full of vessels of cast-iron; in short, a city of the metal which forms one of the principal sources of the wealth of the empire. The sight of such wealth made me shudder. How many criminals must it not have required to dig up those treasures? and if there are not criminals enough in that subterranean world which produces iron, their number is made up by the unfortunate victims of despotism. The system which regulates the miners of the Ural would be a curious subject of inquiry, if it were permitted, to foreigners. But the means of pursuing this study would be as difficult for an European from the West as the journey to Mecca is for a Christian.

All these towns form only chapels-of-ease to the principal fair, round which, as a common centre, they extend without any plan or order. Their outer, or general circumference, would equal that of the larger European capitals. A day would not afford sufficient time to pass through all the temporary suburbs. Amid such an abyss of riches it is impossible to see everything; the spectator is obliged to select.

I must abridge my descriptions. In Russia we resign ourselves to monotony; it is a condition of existence: but in France, where I shall be read, I have no right to expect the reader to submit to it with the same good grace that I do here. He has not the same obligation to be patient as he would have if he had travelled a thousand leagues to learn the practice of that virtue of the vanquished.

I forgot to notice a city of cashmere wool. In seeing this vile, dusty hair, bound in enormous bales, I thought of the beautiful shoulders that it would one day cover; the splendid attires that, when transformed into shawls, it would complete.

I saw also a city of furs, and another of potash. I use this word city purposely; it alone can give an idea of the extent of the various depôts which surround the fair, and which invest it with a character of grandeur that no other fair will ever possess.

Such a commercial phenomenon could only be produced in Russia. To create a fair like Nijni requires that there should be an extreme desire for luxuries among tribes still half barbarous, living in countries separated by incommensurable distances, without prompt or easy means of communication, and where the inclemency of the seasons isolate the population during a great part of the year. The combination of these, and doubtless many other circumstances which I do not discern, could alone induce commercial people to submit to the difficulties, expenses, and personal fatigues of annually resorting, and of bringing all the riches of the soil and of industry to one single point of the country, at a fixed season. The time may be predicted, and I think it is not far distant, when the progress of material civilisation in Russia will greatly diminish the importance of the fair of Nijni, at present, as I have already said, the largest in the world.

In a suburb, separated by an arm of the Oka, is a Persian village, the shops of which are filled exclusively with Persian merchandise. Among these objects I more particularly admired the carpets, which appeared magnificent, the raw silk, and the termolama, a species of silk-cashmere, manufactured, they say, only in Persia.

The forms and dress of the Persians do not greatly strike in this country, where the indigenous population is itself Asiatic, and preserves traces of its origin.

I also traversed a city destined solely as a receptacle for the dried and salted fish which are sent from the Caspian Sea for the Russian Lents.* The Greek devotees are great consumers of these aquatic mummies. Four months of abstinence among the Muscovites enriches the Mohammedans of Persia and Tartary. This city of fishes is situated on the borders of the river: some of the fish are piled upon earth, the remainder lay within the holds of the vessels that brought them. The dead bodies, heaped together in millions, exhale, even in the open air, a disagreeable perfume. Another division forms the city of leather, an article of the first importance at Nijni; as enough is brought there to supply the consumption of all the West of Russia.

Another is the city of furs. The skins of every animal may be seen there, from the sable, the blue fox, and certain bear skins— to obtain a pelisse of which costs twelve thousand francs,—to the

* There are four Lents in the Greek church.—*Trans.*

common foxes and wolves, which cost nothing. The keepers of
the treasures make themselves tents for the night with their merchandise, savage lairs, the aspect of which is picturesque. These
men, although they inhabit cold countries, live on little, clothe
lightly, and sleep in the open air in fine weather. They are the
true lazzaronis of the north, though less gay, witty, or buffoonish,
and more dirty than those of Naples; because, to the uncleanliness of their persons is added that of their garments, which they
never take off.

What I have already written will serve to give an idea of the
exterior of the fair: the interior, I repeat, is much less interesting.
Without, are cars and trucks moving amid a crowd where reign
disorder, cries, songs, and, in short, liberty: within are regularity,
silence, solitude, order, the police, and, in one word, Russia! Immense files of houses, or rather stalls, separate about a dozen long
and broad streets, which terminate in a Russian church and in
twelve Chinese pavilions. The united length of all the streets and
alleys of the fair, properly so called, and without speaking of the
faubourgs, is ten leagues.

The Emperor Alexander, after having selected the new ground
for the fair, ordered the necessary works for its establishment,
but he never saw it. He was ignorant of the immense sums that
had to be added to his budget to make this low land fitted to the
use for which it was destined. By means of amazing efforts and
enormous expenditure the fair is now habitable during summer,
which is all that is required for commerce. But it is not the less
badly situated; being rendered dusty or miry by the first ray of
sun, or smallest rain, and remaining unhealthy at all times; which
is no small evil for the merchants obliged to sleep above their
magazines for the space of six weeks.

Notwithstanding the taste of the Russians for straight lines,
many think with me that it would have been better to have
placed the fair by the side of the old city on the crest of the
mountain, the summit of which might have been rendered accessible by gentle, terraced slopes. At the foot of the hill, on the
borders of the Oka, the objects too heavy and bulky to be carried
up, might have still remained, by the side of their vessels, while
the livelier, retail fair would have been held on a spacious plat-

form at the gate of the lofty city. Imagine a hill crowded with the representatives of all the Asiatic and European nations. Such a peopled mountain would have produced a grand effect: the marsh, where the travelling population now swarms, produces very little.

The modern engineers, so skilful in all lands, would then have had whereon to exercise their talents; the poets, the painters, the admirers of noble sites and picturesque effects, the sight-seers, who are become quite a nation in this century, in which the abuses of activity produce fanatics in idleness,—all these men, useful through the money which they expend, would have enjoyed a magnificent promenade, far more attractive than that afforded them in a bazaar where no point of view can be gained, and where the air breathed is mephitic; while it merits consideration, that such a result would have been obtained at much less expenditure of money than it has cost the emperor to establish his aquatic fair.

The Russian peasants are the principal commercial agents in this prodigious market. Nevertheless, the law forbids the serf to ask, or the freemen to grant him, a credit of more than *five roubles.* And yet they deal with some of these people, on the strength of their word only, for two hundred thousand—five hundred thousand francs; and the dates for payment are very distant. These slavish millionnaires, these Aguados of the globe, do not know how to read. In Russia it is requisite that the men should possess great natural intelligence, to supply the want of acquired. The people are very ignorant of arithmetic. For centuries they have reckoned their accounts by frames, containing series of movable balls. Every line has its colour; each indicates units, tens, hundreds, &c. This mode of calculation is sure and rapid.

It must not be forgotten that the lord of these enormously-wealthy serfs could despoil them in a day of all they possess, provided he did not injure their persons. Such acts of violence, it is true, are rare, but they are possible.

No one remembers that any merchant ever suffered by his confidence in the peasants with whom he dealt: so true it is, that in every society, if only it be stable, the progress of morals corrects the faults of institutions.

I have, however, been told that, on the other hand, the father of a Count Tcheremitcheff, who is now living, once promised liberty to a family of peasants, in consideration of the exorbitant sum of 50,000 roubles. He received the money, and retained among his serfs the despoiled family.

Such is the school of good faith and probity in which the Russian peasants are instructed, under the aristocratic despotism, which crushes them in spite of the autocratic despotism which governs them, and which is often powerless against its rival. Imperial pride contents itself with words, forms, and numbers; aristocratic ambition aims at things, and makes a profit of words. Never did a master receive more adulation and less obedience than the deceived, *soi-disant* absolute sovereign of the Russian empire: disobedience is indeed perilous; but the country is vast, and solitude is dumb.

The governor of Nijni, M. Boutourline, has very politely invited me to dine with him daily during my stay in the city: to-morrow he will explain to me how conduct similar to that of Count Tcheremitcheff, rare everywhere and in every age, cannot be now repeated in Russia. I will give the summary of his conversation, if I can make anything out of it; for hitherto I have gathered little from the lips of the Russians but confused language. Is this owing to the want of logical minds, or is it done purposely, with the view of perplexing foreigners? It is, I believe, attributable to both causes. By continually endeavouring to hide truth from the eyes of others, people become at last unable to perceive it themselves, except through a veil which daily thickens.

Nothing is cheap at the fair of Nijni, except articles that no one cares to buy. The epoch of great differences in price in different localities, is passed: everywhere the value of things is known: the Tartars themselves, who come from the centre of Asia to Nijni to pay very dear for the objects of luxury supplied by Paris and London, bring, in exchange, commodities of which they perfectly well know the value. The merchants may still avail themselves of the situation of the buyers to refuse them articles at a just price; but they cannot deceive them. Yet they do not abate their prices; they coolly ask too much; and their probity consists in never departing from their most exaggerated demands.

In a financial point of view, the importance of the fair continues to increase yearly; but the interest which attaches to the singularity and picturesque appearance of the assemblage diminishes. In general, the fair of Nijni would disappoint the lover of the grotesque and the amusing. Every thing is dull, stiff, and regular in Russia, except, at least, in moments when the long-repressed instinct of liberty bursts forth in an explosion: then the peasants roast their lord, or the lord marries his slave; but these rare outbreaks are little talked of: the distances and the measures taken by the police prevent isolated facts being circulated among the mass.

In my promenades through the central portion of the fair I saw the Bucharians. These people inhabit a corner of Thibet bordering upon China. They come to Nijni to sell precious stones. The turquoises that I bought from them are as dear as those sold in Paris; and all stones of any value are equally high in price. The dealers in these stones pass the year in their journey, for it takes them, they say, more than eight months to go and come only. Neither their persons nor dress struck me as very remarkable. I scarcely believe in the genuineness of the Chinese at Nijni; but the Tartars, Persians, Kirguises, and Calmucs suffice for curiosity.

The two last-named barbarians bring, from the solitudes of their steppes, herds of small wild horses to sell at the fair. These animals have many good qualities, both physical and moral; but their make does not recommend them. They are, nevertheless, excellent for the saddle; and their character causes them to be valued. Poor creatures! they have better hearts than many men: they love each other with a tenderness and a passion that prevents them from ever voluntarily separating. So long as they remain together they forget exile and slavery, and seem to believe themselves in their own country. When one is sold, he has to be cast, and forcibly dragged with cords out of the enclosure where his brethren are confined, who, during this violence, never cease attempting to escape or rebel, and to neigh piteously. Never have I seen the horses of our own country show so many proofs of sensibility. I have seldom been more affected than I was yesterday, by the sight of these unhappy creatures, torn from the freedom of the desert, and violently separated from those they love. I may be answered by the line of Gilbert:

Un papillon souffrant lui fait verser des larmes.

but I shall not care for being laughed at, feeling sure that if the reader had seen the carrying-out of these cruel bargains he would have shared my feeling. Crime, when recognised as such by the laws, has its judges in this world; but permitted cruelty is only punished by the pity of kindly-disposed people for the victims, and, I hope also, by Divine equity. It is this tolerated barbarity which makes me regret the narrow limits of my eloquence: a Rousseau or a Sterne would know how to make the reader weep over the fate of these poor Kirguis horses, destined to carry, in Europe, men as much slaves as themselves, but whose condition does not always deserve as great pity as that of the enslaved brute.

Towards evening the aspect of the plain became imposing. The horizon was lightly veiled in mist, which afterwards fell in dew on the dust of Nijni, a kind of fine brown sand, the reflection of which imparted to the heavens a reddish tint. The depths of the shade were pierced by the fantastic light of a multitude of lamps in the bivouacs by which the fair was surrounded. Everything had a voice;—from the distant forest, from the bosom of the inhabited river, a murmur brought to the attentive ear the sounds of life. What an imposing gathering together of mankind! what different languages and contrasting habits! and yet what uniformity of sentiments and ideas. The object of this great meeting, of each individual it comprised, was simply to gain a little money. Elsewhere the gaiety of the people conceals their cupidity; here commerce stands naked, and the sterile rapacity of the merchant predominates over the frivolity of the lounger: nothing is poetical; everything is mercenary. I am wrong,—the poetry of fear and of sorrow is at the bottom of everything in this country: but where is the voice that dares express it? Nevertheless, there are a few pictures to console the imagination and to refresh the eye.

On the roads which connect the different merchant-encampments, may be seen long files of singular vehicles, being pairs of wheels united by an axle, which, when attached to others, so as to form an equipage of four or six wheels, had served to carry the beams and poles used in the construction of some of the temporary erections of the fair. They return thus detached, drawn by one horse, guided by men who stand upright on the axle, balancing themselves with a savage grace, and managing their half-broken steeds with a dexterity I have seen nowhere but in Russia. They remind me of the charioteers of the Byzantian circus; their shirts form a Greek tunic that is truly antique. As the Russian female peasants are the only women on earth who make themselves a waist above the bosom, so are their male relatives the only men I have ever seen who wear their shirts over their pantaloons.

In wandering at night about the fair, I was struck with the brilliancy of the eating-booths, the little theatres, the taverns, and the coffee-houses. But from the midst of so much light there rose no sound save a dull suppressed murmur; and the contrast formed by the illumination of the place, and the taciturnity of the people, gave the idea of magic. I could have believed the human beings had been touched by the wand of an enchanter. The men of Asia continue grave and serious, even in their diversions: and the Russians are Asiatics, drilled, but not civilised.

I am never tired of hearing their popular songs. The value of music is doubled in a place where a hundred different communities are drawn together by their common interests, though divided by their language and religion. When speech serves only to separate men, they sing to understand each other. Music is the antidote of sophistry; whence the ever-increasing vogue of this art in Europe. There is, in the pieces executed by the mugics of the Volga, an extraordinary complexity, evolving effects of harmony which, notwithstanding, or perhaps owing to their rudeness, we should call scientific in a church or a theatre. These melodies are not sweetly inspired; but, at a distance, the numerous voices counteracting each other in choruses, remarkable for

the mournfulness of the accords, produce a novel and profound impression upon us Western people. The plaintive sadness of the sounds is not diminished by the decoration of the scene. A thick forest of masts bounds the view on two sides; on the other, a solitary plain, lost in a forest of firs: by degrees the lights are seen to diminish; at length they become extinguished; the obscurity heightens the effect of the eternal silence of these pale regions, and spreads in the soul a new surprise: night is the mother of astonishment. All the scenes that a short time before animated the desert are effaced; vague recollections succeed to the movements of life; and the traveller finds himself alone with the Russian police, who render the darkness doubly fearful: he believes himself in a dream, and regains his lodging, his mind full of poetry, that is, of a vague fear, and of mournful presentiments. It is impossible for a moment to forget, while travelling over Russia, that the people are Orientals, who in their former migrations
lost their road, and whose chiefs, by mistake,
led towards the north, a people
born to live in
the sun.

❖

FINANCIAL PHENOMENON ❖ FINANCIAL REFORM OF THE EMPEROR'S ❖
MEANS TAKEN BY THE GOVERNOR OF NIJNI TO INDUCE THE MERCHANTS TO
OBEY ❖ THEIR NOMINAL COMPLIANCE ❖ ENQUIRY INTO THEIR MOTIVES ❖
IMPROVEMENTS AT NIJNI ❖ THE SERF AND THE LORD ❖ THE GOVERNOR OF
NIJNI'S EXPLANATIONS OF DESPOTIC ADMINISTRATION ❖ FORBEARANCE OF
THE AUTHORITIES ❖ A RIDE WITH THE GOVERNOR—VALUE OF THE
COMMODITIES AT THE FAIR OF NIJNI ❖ VISITS WITH THE GOVERNOR ❖ THE
BUREAUCRACY ❖ THE AUTHOR'S FELDJÄGER ❖ FLAG OF MININE ❖ BAD
FAITH OF THE GOVERNMENT ❖ MODERN VANDALISM ❖ PETER THE GREAT ❖
THE GOVERNOR'S CAMP ❖ SONG OF THE SOLDIERS ❖
CHURCH OF THE STROGONOFFS ❖
RUSSIAN VAUDEVILLE
❖

CHAPTER XXXIV

❖

This year, immediately before opening the fair, the governor called around him the ablest commercial heads in Russia, then assembled together at Nijni, and laid before them, in detail, the long-ago-acknowledged and deplored inconveniences of the monetary system of the empire.

The reader is aware that there are in Russia two representative signs of commodities—paper and silver money; but he, perhaps, does not know that the latter, by a singularity that is unique, I believe, in financial history, is constantly varying in value, whilst the worth of the former remains fixed. Nothing but a profound study of the political economy of the country could explain another very extraordinary fact resulting from this singularity, namely, that in Russia, the specie represents the paper, although the latter was only instituted, and only legally exists to represent the former.

Having explained this anomaly to his auditors, and expatiated on all the mischievous consequences arising therefrom, the governor added that the emperor, in his constant solicitude for his people and for the order of his empire, had at length determined to put an end to a disorder, the progress of which threatened seriously to cripple the internal commerce of the land. The only remedy recognised as efficient is the definite and irrevocable fixing of the value of the coined rouble. The edict of the emperor accomplished this revolution in one day, as far at least as words could do it; but in order to realise the reform, the governor con-

cluded his harangue by announcing that it was his majesty's will
that the ukase should be immediately put in execution; and he
added that the superior agents of the administration, and he, the
governor of Nijni, in particular, hoped that no consideration of
personal interest would prevail against the duty of obeying, without delay, the supreme will of the empire's head.

The honest men consulted on this serious question, replied
that the measure, though good in itself, would destroy the most
secure commercial fortunes if it were applied to transactions and
bargains already made, and the terms of which would have to be
fulfilled during the actual fair. While continuing to laud and admire the profound wisdom of the emperor, they humbly represented to the governor that those among the merchants who had
effected sales of goods at a price fixed according to the ancient
rate of money, which they had done, acting in dependence upon
the relations between the paper and the silver rouble being continued as they were at the last fair, would be exposed to the
necessity of submitting to payments that would be not the less
fraudulent because authorised by the law, since they would rob
them of their just profits, and might ruin them if the present
edict were allowed a retro-active effect; the consequences of
which would be a multitude of small bankruptcies, that would
not fail finally to draw in the others.

The governor replied, with the gentleness and calmness which
presides in Russia throughout all administrative, financial, and
political discussions, that he *perfectly* entered into the views of
the chief merchants interested in the business of the fair; but
that, after all, the mischievous results dreaded by these gentlemen only threatened a few individuals, *who would have, as a guarantee, the severity of the existing laws against bankrupts,* whereas,
on the other hand, a delay would always look something like
resistance; and that such example, given by the most important
commercial place in the empire, would involve inconveniences
far more injurious to the country than a few failures, affecting
only a small number of individuals; for disobedience, approved
and justified by men who had hitherto enjoyed the confidence of
the government, would be an attack aimed at the dignity of the
sovereign, at the administrative and financial *unity* of Russia, or,

in other words, at the vital principles of the empire: he added, that, under these peremptory considerations, he did not doubt the gentlemen addressed would, by their compliance, hasten to avoid the *monstrous* reproach of sacrificing the good of the state to their personal interests.

The result of this *pacific* conference was that, on the morrow, the fair opened under the *retro-active* system of the new ukase, the solemn publication of which was made after the assent and the promises of the first merchants in the empire had been thus obtained.

This was related to me by the governor himself, with the intention of proving to me the gentleness with which the machine of despotic government works—that machine so calumniated by people governed under liberal institutions.

I took the liberty of asking my obliging and interesting preceptor in oriental politics, what had been the result of the government measure, and of the cavalier manner in which it was judged right to put it in execution.

"The result has exceeded my hopes," replied the governor, with a satisfied air. "Not one bankrupt! . . . All the new bargains have been concluded under the new monetary system; but what will surprise you is the fact, that no debtor has availed himself, in paying his old engagements, of the power which the law gave him of defrauding his creditors."

I confess that at the first view this result appeared to me astounding; but, on reflection, I recognised the astuteness of the Russians: the law being published, it was obeyed—on paper; and that is enough for the government. It is easily satisfied, I admit; for what it principally requires, at whatever cost, is silence. The political state of Russia may be defined in one sentence: it is a country in which the government says what it pleases, because it alone has the right to speak. Thus, in the case before us, the government says—Such is the law—obey it; but, nevertheless, the mutual accord of interested parties annuls the action of this law in that iniquitous portion of it which could be applied to old debts. In a country where the governing power is patient, it would not have exposed the honest man to the danger of being deprived of his due by thieves: in justice, the law can only regulate the future. And, indeed, theory apart, such is the result here; but to obtain it, it was necessary that the sense and good management of the subjects should be opposed to the blind impetuosity of the authorities, in order to escape the evils which would otherwise be entailed on the country by these freaks of supreme power.

There exists in all governments built on exaggerated theories, a concealed action, a *de-facto* influence, which nearly always opposes the extravagant doctrine adopted. The Russians possess in a high degree the spirit of commerce, which will explain how it was that the merchants of the fair perceived that the real tradesman thrives only by acting, and by being able to act, in confidence,—every sacrifice of credit is a loss to him of cent. per cent. Nor was this all; another influence checked bad faith, and made blind cupidity silent. The temptation that might have been felt by the insolvent would be repressed purely by fear—that real sovereign of Russia. On this occasion, the evil-intentioned will have thought that if they exposed themselves to any process, or even to too notorious animadversion, the judges or the police would turn against them; and that, in such case, what is here called law, would be applied with rigour. They have dreaded incarceration, the blows of the rod in the prison, or, perhaps, something worse! Under these motives, operating with double influence in the universal silence that forms the normal state of Russia, they have given this good example of commercial probity, with which the governor of Nijni took pleasure in dazzling me. If I was dazzled, it was only for an instant; for I was not long in recognising that if the Russian merchants forbore to ruin each other, their reciprocal moderation had precisely the same source as that of the boatmen of Lake Ladoga, and the coachmen and porters of Petersburg, who control their angry passions, not through motives of humanity, but under the dread of the superior authority intervening in their affairs. As I remained silent, I could see that M. Boutourline enjoyed my surprise.

"No one knows the superiority of the emperor," he continued, "unless they have seen this prince engaged in public business, especially at Nijni, where he performs prodigies."

I answered that I greatly admired the sagacity of the emperor.

"When we visit together the works directed by his majesty," replied the governor, "you will yet more admire him. You will see that, owing to the energy of his character and the justness of his views, the monetary revolution, which would elsewhere have required infinite precaution, works among us as if by enchantment."

The courtier-like governor had the modesty to forbear adding a word in favour of his own good management; he equally avoided giving me any occasion to allude to what evil tongues are continually repeating to me in secret, namely, that every financial measure of the kind just taken by the Russian government, gives to the superior authority means of profit, which it well knows how to use, but of which no one dares openly to complain under autocratic rule. I am ignorant of the secret manoeuvres to which recourse has been had on this occasion; but to give myself an idea of them, I imagine the situation of a man who has deposited with another a considerable sum of money. If the receiver has the power to triple the value of each piece of coin of which the sum is composed, it is clear that he can return the deposit, and all the while retain two thirds of the amount deposited. I do not say that such has been the actual result of the measure ordained by the emperor, but I admit the supposition, among many others, to aid me in comprehending the insinuations, or, if you like, the calumnies of the malcontents. They, indeed, add that the profit of this so suddenly executed operation, which consists in depriving, by a decree, the paper-money of a part of its ancient value, to increase in the same proportion that of the silver rouble, is designed to compensate the private treasury of the sovereign for the sums which it was necessary to draw from it, in order to re-build, *at his own cost,* his winter-palace, and to refuse, with a magnanimity which Europe and Russia have admired, the offers of towns and of many private individuals, great merchants, and others, emulous of contributing to the re-construction of a national edifice which serves as habitation for the head of the empire.

The reader may judge, by the detail which I have deemed it my duty to give of this tyrannical charlatanism, of the value here attached to words, and of the real worth of the noblest sentiments and the finest phrases. He may judge also of the constraint imposed upon generous minds and independent spirits, obliged to live under a system in which peace and order are purchased by the sacrifice of truth—that most sacred of all the gifts of heaven to man. In other communities, it is the people who apply the whip, and the government which puts on the drag; here, it is the government which urges onward and the people who hold back: for if the political machine is to keep together at all, it is essential that the spirit of conservatism should exist in some part of it. The displacement of ideas which I here note is a political phenomenon, which I have never seen except in Russia. Under an absolute despotism it is the government which is revolutionary; for the word revolution signifies arbitrary system and violent power.

The governor has kept his promise. He has taken me to see and minutely examine the works ordered by the emperor, with the view of making Nijni all that it is capable of being made, and of repairing the errors of its founders. A superb road rises from the banks of the Oka to the high city, the precipices are filled up, the terraces are laid out, magnificent openings are cut even in the bosom of the mountain, where enormous substructures support squares, streets, and edifices; bridges are constructed; and all these works, worthy of a great commercial city, will soon change Nijni into one of the most beautiful in the empire. As his Majesty has taken it under his special protection, each time that any small difficulty rises as to the mode of carrying on the works commenced, or whenever the face of an old house is to be repaired or a new one to be built, the governor is instructed to cause a special plan to be made, and to submit the question of its adoption to the emperor. What a man! exclaim the Russians. . . . What a country! I should exclaim, if I dared to speak.

While on the road, M. Boutourline, whose obliging civility and hospitality I cannot sufficiently acknowledge, gave me some interesting explanations of the Russian system of administration, and of the improvement which the progress of manners is daily effecting in the condition of the peasants.

A serf may now become the proprietor even of lands, in the name of his lord, without the latter daring to violate the *moral* guarantee by which he is bound to his wealthy slave. To despoil this man of the fruit of his labour and industry would be an abuse of power which the most tyrannical boyard dare not permit himself under the reign of the Emperor Nicholas: but who shall assure me that he dare not do so under another sovereign? Who shall assure me even, that, in spite of the return to equity which forms the glorious characteristic of the present reign, there may yet be no avaricious and needy lords, who, without openly robbing their vassals, know how skilfully, and by turns, to employ threats and kindness, in order gradually to extract from the hands of the slave a portion of the wealth which they dare not carry away at one swoop? It is difficult to believe in the duration of such relations between the master and the serf, and yet the institutions which produce this social singularity are stable.

In Russia nothing is defined by the proper words. In theory, every thing is precisely as is said; but under such a system, if carried out, life would be impossible: in practice there are so many exceptions, that we are ready to say, the confusion caused by customs and usages so contradictory must make all government impossible.

It is necessary to discover the solution of the double problem; the point, that is, where the principle and the application, the theory and the practice, accord, to form a just idea of the state of society in Russia.

If we are to believe the excellent governor of Nijni, nothing can be more simple: the habit of exercising the power renders the forms of command gentle and easy. Angry passions, ill treatment, the abuses of authority, are become extremely rare, precisely because social order is based upon extremely severe laws; every one feels that to preserve for such laws a respect without which the state would be overthrown, they should not be put in force frequently or rashly. It is requisite that the action of despotic government be observed close at hand to understand all its gentleness (it is the governor of Nijni who now speaks): if authority preserves any force in Russia, it is to be attributed to the moderation of the men who exercise it. Constantly placed between an aristocracy which the more easily abuses its power because its prerogatives are ill-defined, and a people who the more willingly misunderstand their duty because the obedience exacted from them is not ennobled by a moral feeling, the men who command can only preserve the *prestige* of sovereignty by using as rarely as possible violent means: these means would expose the measure of the government's strength; and it judges it wiser to conceal than to unveil its resources. If a noble commits any reprehensible act, he would be several times warned in secret by the governor of the province before being admonished officially. If warnings and reprimands were not sufficient, the tribunal of the nobles would threaten to place him under guardianship; and if this had no good effect, the menace would be executed.

All this superabundance of precaution does not appear to me to be very consolatory to the serf, who, if he had as many lives, might die a hundred times under the knout of his master, before the latter, thus prudently warned and duly admonished, should be obliged to give account of his injustices or his atrocities. It is true that the day after, lord, governor, and judges might be all sent to Siberia; but this would be rather a consolation for the imagination of the poor peasants than a real protection from the arbitrary acts of subaltern authorities, who are ever disposed to abuse the power delegated to them.

The common people have very rarely recourse to the legal tribunals in their private disputes. This enlightened instinct appears to me a sure indication of want of equity in the judges. The infrequency of litigation may have two causes—the spirit of justice in the subjects, or the spirit of iniquity in the judges. In Russia, nearly every process is stifled by an administrative decision, which very often *recommends* an arrangement onerous to both parties, who prefer the reciprocal sacrifice of a part of their claims, and even of their best founded rights, to the danger of proceeding against the advice of a man invested with authority by the emperor. This is the reason why the Russians have grounds for boasting that there is very little litigation in their land. Fear produces everywhere the same result—peace without tranquillity.

Will not the reader feel some compassion for a traveller lost in a country where facts are not more conclusive than words? The fictions of the Russians have upon me an effect precisely the contrary to that intended: I see at the very outset the design to blind and dazzle me; I therefore stand upon my guard; and the consequence is, that instead of being the impartial spectator that I should have been but for their vain boasting, I become, in spite of myself, an unfriendly observer.

The governor was also pleased himself to show me the fair; but this time, we made the tour of it rapidly, in a carriage. I admired one point of view that was worthy of forming a panorama. To enjoy the magnificent picture, we ascended the summit of one of the Chinese pavilions, which commands an entire view of the city of a month. I was there more especially struck with the immensity of the piles of wealth annually accumulated on this point of land—a focus of industry the more remarkable, because it is lost, as it were, in the midst of deserts without bounds either to the eye or the imagination.

The governor informs me that the value of the merchandise brought this year to the fair of Nijni exceeds one hundred and fifty millions,* according to the manifestoes of the merchants themselves, who, with the mistrust natural to Orientals, always conceal a part of the value of their stock.

Although all the countries in the world send the tribute of their soil and industry to Nijni, the principal importance of this annual market is owing to its being a depot for the provisions, the precious stones, the stuffs, and the furs of Asia. The wealth of the Tartars, the Persians, and the Bucharians, is the object which most strikes the imagination of the strangers attracted by the reputation of the fair; yet, notwithstanding its commercial importance, I, as merely a curious observer, find it below its reputation. They reply to this, that the Emperor Alexander spoiled its picturesque and amusing aspect. He rendered the streets which separate the stalls more spacious and regular; but such stiffness is dull: besides, everything is gloomy and silent in Russia; everywhere the reciprocal distrust of government and people banishes mirth. Every passion and every pleasure has to answer for its consequences to some rigid confessor, disguised as an agent of police; every Russian is a school-boy liable to the rod; all Russia is a vast college, where discipline is enforced by severe and rigid rule, until

* The author does not state whether these are francs or roubles.—*Trans.*

constraint and ennui, becoming insupportable, occasion here and there an outbreak. When this takes place, it is a regular political saturnalia; but, once again, the acts of violence are isolated, and do not disturb the general quiet. That quiet is the more stable, and appears the more firmly established, because it resembles death: it is only living things that can be exterminated. In Russia, respect for despotism is confounded with the idea of eternity. . . .

This morning early, the governor, whose obliging kindness I can never tire, took me to see the curiosities of the old city. His servants attended him, which enabled me to dispense with putting to a second proof the docility of my feldjäger, whose claims the governor respects.

There is in Russia a class of persons which corresponds to the citizen class among us, though without possessing the firmness of character derived from an independent position, and the experience obtained by means of liberty of thought and cultivation of mind: this is the class of subaltern employés, or secondary nobility. The ideas of these men are generally turned towards innovations, whilst their acts are the most despotic that are committed under despotism: this, indeed, is the class which, in spite of the emperor, governs the empire. They pretend to enlighten the people, and their pretensions incur the dislike and contempt of both great and little. Their impertinences are become proverbial: whoever has any need of making use of these demi-nobles, newly raised by their office and their rank in the tchinn to the honours of territorial proprietors, revenges himself upon their pride by unmerciful ridicule. These men, risen from class to class, and attaining at length, by virtue of some cross or some employ, the class in which a man may possess lands and fellow-men, exercise their seignorial rights with a rigour which renders them objects of execration among their unhappy peasants. What a singular social phenomenon is this liberal or changeable element in a despotic system of government, which system it here renders yet more intolerable! "If we had only the old lords," the peasants say, "we should not complain of our condition." These new men, so hated by the small number who are their serfs, are also masters of the supreme master; and are the preparers likewise of a revolution in

Russia,—first, by the direct influence of their ideas, and, sec-
ondly, by the indirect consequences of the hatred and contempt
which they excite among the people. Republican tyranny under
autocratical!—what a combination of evils!

These are enemies created by the emperors themselves, in their
distrust of the old nobility. An avowed aristocracy, long rooted in
the land, but moderated by the progress of manners and the
amelioration of customs, would have been an instrument of
civilisation preferable to the hypocritical obedience, the destructive influence of a host of commissioners and deputies, the
greater number of foreign origin, and all more or less imbued, in
the secret of their hearts, with revolutionary notions; all as inso-
lent in their thoughts as obsequious in their words and manners.

My courier, unwilling to perform his business because he is
near attaining the prerogatives of this order of nobility, is the
profoundly comic type of its nature and character. I wish I could
describe his slim figure, his carefully-adjusted dress, his sharp,
thin, dry, pitiless, yet humble countenance—humble whilst waiting till it may have the right to become arrogant;—in short, this
type of a puppy, in a country where conceit is not harmless as
with us; for in Russia it is a sure means of rising, if only it unite
itself with servility:—but this person eludes the definition of
words, as an adder glides out of sight. He represents to my eyes
the union of two political forces, the most opposite in appearance although possessing much real affinity, and although detestable when combined—despotism and revolution! I cannot observe his eyes of clouded blue, bordered with nearly white lashes,
his complexion, which would be delicate, but for the bronzing
rays of the sun and the frequent influence of an internal and
always repressed rage, his pale and thin lips, his dry yet civil
words, the intonation of which utters the very opposite of the
phraseology, without viewing him as a protecting spy, a spy respected even by the governor of Nijni; and under the influence of
this idea I am tempted to order post-horses, and never to stop
until beyond the frontiers of Russia.

The powerful governor of Nijni does not dare to command this
ambitious courier to mount the box of my carriage; and, though

the representative of supreme authority, can only advise me to be patient.

Minine, the liberator of Russia—that heroic peasant whose memory has become especially popular since the French invasion —is buried at Nijni. His tomb may be seen in the cathedral, among those of the great dukes.

It was in this city that the cry of deliverance first resounded, at the time when the empire was occupied by the Poles.

Minine, a simple serf, sought the presence of Pojarski, a Russian noble: the language of the peasant breathed enthusiasm and hope. Pojarski, electrified by the sacred though rude eloquence, gathered together a few men. The daring deeds of these heroes attracted others to their standard: they marched upon Moscow, and liberated Russia.

Since the retreat of the Poles, the flag of Pojarski and Minine has always been an object of great veneration among the Russians: the peasants inhabiting a village between Yaroslaf and Nijni preserved it as a national relic. But during the war of 1812 a necessity was felt of exciting the soldiers to enthusiasm; historical associations were revived, especially those connected with Minine; and the keepers of his banner were requested to lend this palladium to the new liberators of their country, that it might be carried at the head of the army. The ancient guardians of the national treasure only consented to part with it through a feeling of devotion to the country, and upon receiving a solemn oath that it should be returned to them after victory, when its new triumphs would render it yet more illustrious. It was thus that the flag of Minine followed our army in its retreat: but, when afterwards carried back to Moscow instead of being returned to its legitimate possessors, it was detained and deposited in the treasury of the Kremlin in contempt of the most solemn promises; while, to satisfy the just appeals of the despoiled peasants, *a copy* of their miraculous ensign was sent to them—a copy which, in the derisive condescension of the robbers, was made exactly similar to the original.

Such are the lessons in good faith which the Russian government gives its people. Nor in this country is historical truth any better respected than the sanctity of oaths: the authenticity of stones is as difficult to establish as that of words or of writings. Under each new reign the edifices are remodelled at the will of the sovereign: none remain where placed by their founders: the very tombs are not shielded from the tempest of imperial caprice: even the dead are exposed to the fantasies of him who rules the living. The Emperor Nicholas, who is now playing the architect in Moscow, and reconstructing the Kremlin, is not at his first attempt of the kind. Nijni has already seen him at work.

This morning, on entering the cathedral, I felt impressed by the ancient appearance of the edifice which contains the tomb of Minine: it, at least, has been respected for more than two hundred years, I thought to myself; and this conclusion caused me to find the aspect of the place the more august.

The governor led me to the sepulchre of the hero; it lies among the monuments of the ancient sovereigns of Nijni: and when the Emperor Nicholas visited it, he descended patriotically into the cave even where the body is deposited.

"This is one of the most beautiful and interesting of the churches that I have seen in your country," I observed to the governor.

"It was I who built it," replied M. Boutourline.

"How? . . . You mean, doubtless, to say that you restored it?"

"No; the ancient church was falling into ruins: the Emperor preferred its being reconstructed rather than repaired: it is only two years ago that it stood *fifty paces further on,* and formed a projection that interfered with the regularity of our Kremlin's interior."

"But the corpse and bones of Minine?" I exclaimed.

"They were disinterred with those of the grand dukes: all are now placed in the new sepulchre, of which you see the stone."

I could not have replied without causing an unpleasant commotion in the mind of a provincial governor as attached to the duties of his office as is the governor of Nijni: I therefore followed him, in silence, to the little obelisk of the square, and towards the immense ramparts of the Kremlin of Nijni.

We here see what is understood by veneration for the dead, and respect for historical monuments in Russia. The emperor, who knows that ancient things are venerable, desires that a church, built yesterday, should be honoured as old; and to produce this, he says that it is old, whereupon it becomes so. The new church of Minine is the ancient one: if you doubt this truth, you are seditious.

Every where is to be seen the same system—that of Peter the Great—perpetuated by his successors. That man believed and proved that the will of a Muscovite czar might serve as a substitute for the laws of nature, for the rules of art, for truth, history, and humanity, for the ties of blood, and of religion. If the Russians still venerate him it is because their vanity outweighs their judgment. "Behold," they say, "what Russia was before the accession of that great prince, and what she has become after: see what a monarch of genius can do!" This is a false mode of appreciating the glory of a nation. I see, among the most civilised states in the world, some whose power extends to none except their own subjects; and these, even, are few in number. Such states have no influence in universal politics. It is not by the pride of conquest, nor by political tyranny exercised over foreign interests, that their governments acquire a right to universal gratitude; it is by good examples, by wise laws, by an enlightened and beneficent administration. With such advantages a small nation may become—not conquerors, not oppressors, but LIGHTS of the world; and this is a hundred times preferable. . . .

We also visited a very pretty convent: the nuns are poor, but their house exhibits edifying marks of cleanliness. Afterwards, the governor took me to see his camp: the rage for manoeuvres, reviews, and bivouacs is universal. The governors of the provinces, like the emperor, pass their life in playing at soldiers; and the more numerous these assemblages are, the more proudly do the governors feel their resemblance to their master. The regiments which form the camp of Nijni are composed of the children of soldiers. It was evening when we reached their tents, reared on a plain which is a continuation of the table of the hill on which stands old Nijni.

Six hundred men were chanting the prayers; and at a distance, in the open air, this religious and military choir produced an astonishing effect; it was like a cloud of perfume rising majestically under a pure and deep sky: prayer ascending from that abyss of passions and sorrows—the heart of man—may be compared to the column of smoke and fire which rises through the torn crater of the volcano, until it reaches the firmament. And who knows if the pillar of the Israelites, so long lost in the desert, did not image the same thing? The voices of these poor Slavonian soldiers, softened by the distance, seemed to come from on high. When the first notes struck our ears, a knoll on the plain hid the tents from our eyes. The weakened echoes of earth responded to these celestial voices; and the music was interrupted by distant discharges of musquetry—a warlike orchestre, which scarcely seemed more loud than the great drums of the Opera, and which appeared much more in place than they do. When the tents, whence issued the harmonious notes, appeared before us, the setting sun, glistening upon their canvas, added the magic of colour to that of sounds.

The governor, who saw the pleasure that I experienced in listening to this music, allowed me to enjoy it, and enjoyed it himself, for a considerable time: nothing gives greater pleasure to this truly hospitable man than to procure enjoyment for his guests. The best way of showing him your gratitude is to let him see your gratification. We finished our ride by twilight; and, returning through the low town, we stopped before a church which has not ceased to attract my eyes since I have been in Nijni. It is a true model of Russian architecture; neither ancient Greek, nor the Greek of the Lower Empire, but a Delft-ware toy, in the style of the Kremlin, or of the church of Vassili Blagennoï, though with less variety in the form and colour. It is so covered with flower-work and carvings of curious form, that one cannot stop before it without thinking of a vessel of Dresden china. This little chef-d'oeuvre of the whimsical is not ancient. It was raised by the munificence of the Strogonoff family; great nobles descended from the merchants, at whose cost was made the conquest of Siberia under Ivan IV. The brothers Strogonoff of that period, themselves raised the adventurous army which conquered a kingdom for Russia. Their soldiers were the buccaneers of *terra firma*.

The interior of the church of the Strogonoffs does not answer to its exterior; but, such as it is, I greatly prefer it to the clumsy copies of Roman temples with which Petersburg and Moscow are encumbered.

To finish the day, we attended the opera of the fair, and listened to a vaudeville in the native language. The Russian vaudevilles are still translations from the French. The people of the country appear to be very proud of this new means of civilisation which they have imported. I was unable to judge of the influence of the spectacle upon the minds of the assembly, owing to the fact of the theatre being empty almost to the letter. Besides the ennui and the compassion one feels in the presence of poor players, when there is no audience, I experienced on this occasion the disagreeable impression which the mixing up of singing and speaking-scenes has always communicated to me in our own theatres. This barbarism, without the salt of French wit, would, but for the governor, have driven me away during the first act. As it was, I remained patient until the conclusion of the performance.

I have been passing the night in writing to dissipate my ennui; but this effort has made me ill, and I am going to bed in a fever.

❖

ASSASSINATION OF A GERMAN LANDHOLDER ❖ RUSSIAN AVERSION TO INNOVATIONS ❖ CONSEQUENCES OF THE ESTABLISHED STATE OF THINGS ❖ SERVILITY OF THE PEASANTS ❖ EXILE OF M. GUIBAL ❖ GYPSIES AT THE FAIR ❖ THE VIRTUES OF OUTCASTS ❖ VICTOR HUGO ❖ PROJECT OF VISITING KAZAN ABANDONED ❖ MEDICAL ADVICE ❖ IDEAS OF THE RUSSIANS RESPECTING FREE GOVERNMENTS ❖ VLADIMIR ❖ THE FORESTS OF RUSSIA ❖ THE USE OF A FELDJÄGER ❖ FALSE DELICACY IMPOSED UPON FOREIGNERS ❖ CENTRALISATION ❖ RENCONTRE WITH AN ELEPHANT ❖ AN ACCIDENT ❖ RETURN TO MOSCOW ❖ A FAREWELL TO THE KREMLIN ❖ EFFECT PRODUCED BY THE VICINITY OF THE EMPEROR ❖ MILITARY FÊTE AT BORODINO ❖ THE AUTHOR'S MOTIVES FOR NOT ATTENDING ❖ PRINCE WITGENSTEIN ❖ HISTORICAL TRAVESTY

❖

CHAPTER XXXV*

❖

A M. Jament related to me, at Nijni, that a German, the new lord of a village, a great agriculturalist and a propagator of modes of husbandry still unused in this country, has just been assassinated on his own domains, contiguous to those of a M. Merline, another foreigner, through whom the fact has come to our knowledge.

Two men presented themselves to this German lord, under the pretext of purchasing horses of him: and in the evening they entered his chamber and murdered him. It was, I am assured, a blow aimed by the peasants of the foreigner in revenge for the innovations which he sought to make in the culture of their lands.

The people of this country have an aversion for every thing that is not Russian. I often hear it repeated, that they will some day rise from one end of the empire to the other upon the men without a beard, and destroy them all. It is by the beard that the Russians know each other. In the eyes of the peasants, a Russian with a shaved chin is a traitor, who has sold himself to foreigners, and who deserves to share their fate. But what will be the punishment inflicted by the survivors upon the authors of these Muscovite Vespers? All Russia cannot be sent to Siberia. Villages may be transported, but it would be difficult to exile provinces. It is worthy of remark, that this kind of punishment strikes the peasants without hurting them. A Russian recognises his country

* Written at Vladimir, between Nijni and Moscow, the 2d of September.

wherever long winters reign: snow has always the same aspect; the winding-sheet of the earth is every where equally white, whether its thickness be six inches or six feet; so that, if they only allow him to re-construct his cabin and his sledge, the Russian finds himself at home to whatever spot he may be exiled. In the deserts of the north it costs little to make a country. To the man who has never seen any thing but icy plains scattered with stunted trees, every cold and desert land represents his native soil. Besides, the inhabitants of these latitudes are always inclined to quit the place of their birth.

Scenes of disorder are multiplying in the country: every day I hear of some new crime: but, by the time it is made public, it has already become ancient, which tends to weaken its impressiveness, especially as from so many isolated atrocities nothing results to disturb the general repose of the country. As I have already said, tranquillity is maintained among this people by the length and difficulties of communication, and by the secrecy of the government, which perpetuates the evil under the fear of disclosing it. To these causes I may add the blind obedience of the troops, and, above all, the complete ignorance of the country people themselves. But, singular conjunction of facts!—the latter remedy is at the same time the first cause of the evil: it is, therefore, difficult to see how the nation will get out of the dangerous circle in which circumstances have placed it. Hitherto the good and the evil, the danger and the safety, have come to it from the same source.

The reader can form no conception of the manner in which a lord, when taking possession of some newly-acquired domain, is received by his peasants. They exhibit a servility which would appear incredible to the people of our country: men, women, and children, all fall on their knees before their new master—all kiss the hands, and sometimes the feet, of the landholder; and, O! miserable profanation of faith!—those who are old enough to err, voluntarily confess to him their sins—he being to them the image and the envoy of God, representing both the King of Heaven and the emperor! Such fanaticism in servitude must end in casting an illusion over the mind of him who is its object, especially if he has not long attained the rank which he possesses: the change of fortune thus marked, must so dazzle him as to persuade him that he is not of the same race as those prostrate at his feet—those whom he suddenly finds himself empowered to command. It is no paradox which I put forward, when I maintain that the aristocracy of birth could alone ameliorate the condition of the serfs, and enable them to profit by emancipation through gentle and gradual transitions. Their slavery becomes insupportable under the new men of wealth. Under the old ones, it is hard enough: but these are at least born above them, and also among them, which is a consolation; besides, the habit of authority is as natural to the one party as that of slavery is to the other; and habit mitigates every thing, mollifying the injustice of the strong, and lightening the yoke of the feeble. But the change of fortunes and conditions produces frightful results in a country subjected to a system of servitude: and yet it is this very change which maintains the duration of the present order of things in Russia, because it conciliates the men who know how to benefit by it—a second example of the remedy being drawn from the source of the evil. Terrible circle, round which revolve all the populations of a vast empire! This lord, this new deity—what title has he to be adored? He is adored because he has had enough money and capacity for intrigue to be able to buy the land to which are attached all the men prostrate before him. An upstart appears to me a monster, in a country where the life of the poor depends upon the rich, and where man is the fortune of man; the onward progress of industrious enterprise, and the immovableness of villenage combined in the same society, produce results that are revolting: but the despot loves the upstart—he is his creature! The position of a new lord is this: yesterday his slave was his equal: his industry more or less honest, his flatteries more or less mean, have put it into his power to purchase a certain number of his comrades. To become the beast of burden of an equal is an intolerable evil. It is, however, a result which an impious alliance of arbitrary customs, and liberal, or, to speak more justly, unstable institutions, can bring upon a people. No where else does the man who makes a fortune have his feet kissed by his vanquished rivals. Anomalies the most shocking have become the basis of the Russian constitution.

I may allude, *en passant,* to a singular confusion of ideas produced in the minds of the people by the system to which they are subjected. Under this system, the individual is intimately connected with the soil, being, indeed, sold with it; but instead of recognising himself as a fixture, and the soil as transferable—in other words, instead of perceiving that he belongs to this soil, by means of which men dispose of him despotically, he fancies that the soil is his own. In truth, his error of perception is reduced to a mere optical illusion; for possessor as he imagines himself of the land, yet he does not understand how it can be sold without the sale also of those who inhabit it. Thus, when he changes masters, he does not say that the soil has been sold to a new proprietor; he considers that it is his own person that has been first sold, and that, over and above the bargain, his land has gone with him— that land which saw him born, and which has supplied him with the means of life. How could liberty be given to men whose acquaintance with social laws is about on a level with that of the trees and plants?

M. Guibal—every time that I am authorised to cite a name, I use the permission—M. Guibal, the son of a schoolmaster, was exiled without cause, or at least without explanation, and without being able to guess his crime, into a Siberian village in the environs of Orenburg. A song, which he composed to beguile his sorrow, was listened to by an inspector, who put it before the eyes of the governor; it attracted the attention of that august personage, who sent his aide-de-camp to the exile to inform himself regarding the circumstances of his situation and his conduct, and to judge if he was good for any thing. The unfortunate man succeeded in interesting the aide-de-camp, who, on his return, made a very favourable report, in consequence of which he was immediately recalled. He has never known the real cause of his misfortune: perhaps it was another song.

Such are the circumstances on which depends the fate of a man in Russia! . . .

I must now give an account of my departure from Nijni, which it will be seen was less brilliant than the nocturnal ride of the captain of hussars.

On the evening that I accompanied the governor to the empty

Russian theatre, I met, after leaving him, an acquaintance who took me to the café of the gypsies, situated in the most lively part of the fair: it was nearly midnight, but this house was still full of people, noise, and light. The women struck me as being very handsome; their costume, although in appearance the same as that of other Russian females, takes a foreign character when worn by them: there is magic in their glances, and their features and attitudes are graceful, and at the same time imposing. In short, they resemble the sibyls of Michael Angelo.

Their singing is about the same as that of the gypsies at Moscow, but if any thing, I thought it yet more expressive, forcible, and varied. I am assured that they have much pride of character, that they have warm passions, yet are neither light nor mercenary, and that they often repel, with disdain, very advantageous offers.

The more I see, the more I am astonished at the remains of virtue in persons who are not virtuous. Individuals whose state is the most decried, are often, like nations degraded by their governments, full of great qualities, ill-understood; whilst, on the contrary, we are disagreeably surprised to discern weakness in people of high character, and a puerile disposition in nations said to be well governed. The conditions of human virtues are nearly always impenetrable mysteries to the mind of man.

The idea of rehabilitation, which I here only vaguely point out, has been laid open and defended, with all the power of talent, by one of the boldest minds of our own or any epoch. It seems as though Victor Hugo had sought to consecrate his theatre to revealing to the world all that remains of human, that is, of divine, in the souls of those creatures of God who are the most reprobated by society: this design is more than moral, it is religious. To extend the sphere of pity is to perform a pious work: the multitude is often cruel by levity, by habit, or by principle, but yet more often by mistake. To cure, if it be possible, the wounds of hearts ill-understood, without yet more deeply injuring other hearts also worthy of compassion, is to associate ourselves in the designs of Providence, and to enlarge the kingdom of heaven.

The night was far advanced when we left the gypsies; stormy

clouds, which swept over the plain, had suddenly changed the temperature. The long, deserted streets of the fair were filled with ponds of water, through which our horses dashed without relaxing their speed; fresh squalls, bringing over black clouds, announced more rain, and drove the water, splashed aside by the horses, in our faces. "Summer is at last gone," said my cicerone. "I feel you are only too right," I answered: "I am as cold as if it were winter." I had no cloak: in the morning we had been suffocated with the heat: on returning to my room, I was freezing. I sat down to write for two hours, and then retired to rest in the icy fit of fever. In the morning, when I wished to get up, a vertigo seized me, and I fell again on my couch, unable to dress myself.

This annoyance was the more disagreeable, as I had intended leaving on that very day for Kazan: I wished at least to set my foot in Asia; and with this view had engaged a boat to descend the Volga, whilst my feldjäger had been directed to bring my carriage empty to Kazan, to convey me back to Nijni by land. However, my zeal had a little cooled after the governor of Nijni had proudly displayed to me plans and drawings of Kazan. It is still the same city from one end of Russia to another: the great square, the broad streets, bordered with diminutive houses, the house of the governor, with ornamented pillars and a pediment; decorations even more out of place in a Tartar than in a Russian town; barracks, cathedrals in the style of temples; nothing, in short, was wanting; and I felt that the whole tiresome architectural repetition was not worth the trouble of prolonging my journey two hundred leagues in order to visit. But the frontiers of Siberia and the recollections of the siege still tempted me. It became necessary, however, to renounce the journey, and to keep quiet for four days.

The governor very politely came to see me in my humble bed. At last, on the fourth day, feeling my indisposition increase, I determined to call in a doctor. This individual said to me,—

"You have no fever, you are not yet ill, but you will be seriously so if you remain three days longer at Nijni. I know the influence of this air upon certain temperaments; leave it; you will not have travelled ten leagues without finding yourself better, and the day after you will be well again."

"But I can neither eat, sleep, nor walk, nor even move without severe pains in my head: what will become of me if I am obliged to stop on the road?"

"Cause yourself to be carried into your coach; the autumn rains have commenced: I repeat, that I cannot answer for you if you remain at Nijni."

This doctor is scientific and experienced: he has passed several years at Paris, after having previously studied in Germany. His look inspired me with confidence; and the day after I received his advice I entered my carriage, in the midst of a beating rain and an icy wind. It was unpleasant enough to discourage the strongest traveller: nevertheless, at the second stage, the prediction of the doctor was fulfilled; I began to breathe more freely, though fatigue so overpowered me that I was obliged to stop and pass the night in a miserable lodging: the next day I was again in health.

During the time spent in my bed at Nijni, my guardian spy grew tired of our prolonged stay at the fair, and of his consequent inaction. One morning he came to my valet-de-chambre, and said to him, in German, "When do we leave?"

"I cannot tell; Monsieur is ill."

"Is he ill?"

"Do you suppose that it is to please himself that he keeps his bed in such a room as you found for him here?"

"What is the matter with him?"

"I do not know at all."

"Why is he ill?"

"Good heavens! you had better go and ask him."

This *why* appears to me worthy of being noted.

The man has never forgiven me the scene in the coach. Since that day his manners and his countenance have changed, which proves to me that there always remains some corner for the natural disposition, and for sincerity in even the most profoundly-dissimulating characters. I therefore think all the better of him for his rancour: I had believed him incapable of any primitive sentiment.

The Russians, like all new comers in the civilised world, are excessively susceptible: they cannot understand generalities; they take every thing for personalities: nowhere is France so ill understood. The liberty of thinking and speaking is more incomprehensible than any thing else to these people. Those who pretend to judge our country, say to me, that they do not really believe our king abstains from punishing the writers who daily abuse him in Paris.

"Nevertheless," I answer them, "the fact is there to convince you."

"Yes, yes, you talk of toleration," they reply, with a knowing air; "it is all very well for the multitude and for foreigners: but your government punishes secretly the too audacious journalists."

When I repeat that every thing is public in France, they laugh sneeringly, politely check themselves; but they do not believe me.

The city of Vladimir is often mentioned in history: its aspect is like all the other Russian cities—that eternal type with which the reader is only too familiar. The country, also, that I have travelled over from Nijni resembles the rest of Russia—a forest without trees, interrupted by towns without life—barracks, raised sometimes upon heaths, sometimes upon marshes, and the spirit of a regiment to animate them. When I tell the Russians that their woods are badly managed, and that their country will in time be without fuel, they laugh me in the face. It has been calculated how many thousands of years it will require to consume the wood which covers the soil of an immense portion of the empire; and this calculation satisfies every body. It is *written* in the estimates sent in by each provincial governor, that each province contains so many acres of forests. Upon these data the statistical department goes to work; but before performing their purely arithmetical labour of adding sums to make a total, the calculators do not think of visiting those forests upon paper. If they did, they would in most cases find only a few thickets of brushwood, amid plains of fern and rushes. But with their written satisfactory reports, the Russians trouble themselves very little about the want of the only riches proper to their soil. Their woods are immense in the bureau of the minister, and this is sufficient for them. The day may be foreseen when, as a consequence of this administrative supineness and security, the people will warm themselves by the fires made of the old dusty papers accumulated in the public offices: these riches increase daily.

My words may appear bold and even revolting; for the sensitive self-love of the Russians imposes upon foreigners duties of delicacy and propriety to which I do not submit. My sincerity will render me culpable in the eyes of the men of this country. What ingratitude! the minister gives me a feldjäger; the presence of his uniform spares me all the difficulties of the journey; and therefore am I bound, in the opinion of the Russians, to approve of every thing with them. That foreigner, they think, would outrage all the laws of hospitality if he permitted himself to criticise a country where so much regard has been shown towards him. Notwithstanding all this, I hold myself free to describe what I see, and to pass my opinion upon it.

To appreciate, as I ought to do, the favour accorded me by the director-general of the posts, in furnishing me with a courier, it will at least be right to state the discomforts which his obliging civility has spared me. Had I set out for Nijni with a common servant only, we should, however well he might have spoken Russian, have been delayed by the tricks and frauds of the postmasters at nearly every stage. They would at first have refused us horses, and then have showed us empty stables, to convince us there were none. After an hour's parley they would have found us a set that they would pretend belonged to some peasant, who would condescend to spare them for twice or thrice the charge established by the imperial post-regulations. We might at first have refused; the horses would have been taken away; till at last, tired of the war, we should have concluded by humbly imploring the return of the animals, and by complying with every demand. The same scene would have been renewed at each out-of-the-way post. This is the manner in which inexperienced and unprotected foreigners here travel.

The Russians are always on their guard against truth, which they dread: but I, who belong to a community where every thing is transacted openly, why should I embarrass myself with the scruples of these men, who say nothing, or merely darkly whisper unmeaning phrases, and beg their neighbours to keep them a secret. Every open and clearly-defined statement causes a stir in a country where not only the expression of opinions, but also the recital of the most undoubted facts, is forbidden. A Frenchman cannot imitate this absurdity; but he ought to note it.

Russia is governed; God knows when she will be civilised.

Putting no faith in persuasion, the monarch draws every thing to himself, under pretext that a rigorous system of centralisation is indispensable to the government of an empire so prodigiously extended as is Russia. This system is perhaps necessary to the principle of blind obedience: but enlightened obedience is opposed to the false idea of simplification, which has for more than a century influenced the successors of the Czar Peter, and their subjects also. Simplification, carried to this excess, is not power, it is death. Absolute authority ceases to be real; it becomes a phantom, when it has only the images of men to exercise itself upon.

Russia will never really become a nation until the day when its prince shall voluntarily repair the evil committed by Peter I. But will there ever be found, in such a country, a sovereign courageous enough to admit that he is only a man?

It is necessary to see Russia, to appreciate all the difficulty of this political reformation, and to understand the energy of character that is necessary to work it.

❖   ❖   ❖

I am now writing at a post-house between Vladimir and Moscow.

Among all the chances and accidents by which a traveller is in danger of losing his life on a Russian high road, the imagination of the reader would be at fault to single out the one by which my life has been just menaced. The danger was so great, that without the address, the strength, and the presence of mind of my Italian servant, I should not be the writer of the following account.

It was necessary that the Schah of Persia should have an object in conciliating the friendship of the Emperor of Russia, and that with this view, building his expectations upon bulky presents, he should send to the Czar one of the most enormous black elephants of Asia; it was also needful that this walking tower should be clothed with superb hangings, serving as a caparison for the colossus, and that he should be escorted by a cortege of horsemen, resembling a cloud of grasshoppers; that the whole should be followed by a file of camels, who appeared no larger than donkeys by the side of this elephant, the most enormous that I have ever beheld; it was yet further necessary, that at the summit of the living monument, should be seen a man with olive complexion and oriental costume, carrying a parasol, and sitting crosslegged upon the back of the monster; and finally, it was necessary, that whilst this potentate of the desert was thus forced to journey on foot towards Petersburg, where the climate will soon transfer him to the collection of the mammoths and the mastodons, I should be travelling post by the same route; and that my departure from Vladimir should so coincide with that of the Persians, that, at a certain point of the deserted road, the gallop of my Russian horses should bring me behind them, and make it necessary to pass by the side of the giant;—it required nothing less, I say, than all these combined circumstances to explain the danger caused by the terror that seized my four horses, on seeing before them an animated pyramid, moving as if by magic in the midst of a crowd of strange-looking men and beasts.

Their astonishment as they approached the colossus was at first shown by a general start aside, by extraordinary neighings and snortings, and by refusing to proceed. But the words and the whip of the coachman at length so far mastered them as to compel them to pass the fantastic object of their terror. They submitted trembling, their manes stood erect, and scarcely were they alongside of the monster than, reproaching themselves as it were for a courage, which was nothing more than fear of another object, they yielded to their panic, and the voice and reins of the driver became useless. The man was conquered at the moment when he thought himself the conqueror: scarcely had the horses felt that the elephant was behind them, than they dashed off at full speed, heedless as to where their blind frenzy might carry them. This furious course had very nearly cost us our lives: the coachman, bewildered and powerless, remained immovable on his seat, and slackened the reins; the feldjäger, placed beside him, partook of his stupefaction and helplessness. Antonio and I, seated within the calèche, which was closed on account of the weather and my ailment, remained pale and mute: our species of tarandasse has no doors; it is a boat, over the sides of which we have to step to get in or out. On a sudden, the maddened horses swerved from the road, and dashed at an almost perpendicular bank, about ten feet high: one of the small fore-wheels was already buried in the bankside; two of the horses had reached the top without breaking their traces; I saw their feet on a level with our heads; one strain more, and the coach would have followed, but certainly not upon its wheels. I thought that it was all over with us. The cossacks who escorted the puissant cause of this peril, seeing our critical situation, had the prudence to avoid following us, for fear of further exciting our horses: I, without even thinking of springing from the carriage, had commended my soul to God, when, suddenly, Antonio disappeared. I thought he was killed: the head and leather curtains of the calèche concealed the scene from me; but at the same moment I felt the horses stop. "We are saved," cried Antonio. This *we* touched me, for he himself was beyond all danger, after having succeeded in getting out of the calèche without accident. His rare presence of mind had indicated to him the moment favourable to springing out with the least risk: afterwards, with that agility which strong emotions impart, but which they cannot explain, he found himself, without knowing how, upon the top of the bank, at the heads of the two horses who had scaled it, and whose desperate efforts threatened to destroy us all. The carriage was just about to overturn when the horses were stopped; but Antonio's activity gave time to the others to follow his example; the coachman was in a moment at the heads of the two other horses, while the courier propped up the coach. At the same moment the cossack-guard of the elephant, who had put their horses to a gallop, arrived to our assistance; they made me alight, and helped my people to hold the still trembling horses. Never was an accident more nearly being disastrous, and never was one repaired at less cost. Not a screw of the coach was disturbed, and scarcely a strap of harness broken.

At the expiration of a quarter of an hour, Antonio was seated quietly by my side in the calèche; in another ten minutes, he was as fast asleep as if he had not been the means of saving all our lives.

While they put the harness in order, I approached the cause of all this mischief. The groom of the elephant had prudently led him into the wood adjoining one of the side-alleys of the road. The formidable beast appeared to me yet larger after the peril to which he had exposed me. His trunk, busy in the top of the birch-trees, reminded me of a boa twisted among the palms. I began to make excuses for my horses, and left him, giving thanks to God for having escaped a death which at one moment appeared to me inevitable.

❖   ❖   ❖

I am now at Moscow. An excessive heat has not ceased to reign there for several months; I find again the same temperature that I left: the summer is indeed quite extraordinary. The drought sends up into the air, above the most populous quarters of the city, a reddish dust, which, towards evening, produces effects as fantastical as the Bengal lights. This evening, at sunset, I contemplated the spectacle from the Kremlin, the survey of which I have made with as much admiration, and almost as much surprise, as I did at first.

The city of men was separated from the palace of giants, by a glory like one of Corregio's: the whole was a sublime union of the marvels of painting and poetry.

The Kremlin, as the loftiest point in the picture, received on its breast the last streaks of day, while the mists of night had already enveloped the rest of the city. The imagination owned no bounds; the universe, the infinite Deity itself, seemed to be grasped by the witness of the majestic spectacle. It was the living model of Martin's most extraordinary paintings. My heart beat with fear and admiration: I saw the whole cohort of the supernatural inmates of the fortress; their forms shone like demons painted on a ground of gold; they moved glittering towards the regions of night, from which they seemed about to tear off the veil; I expected to hear the thunder: it was fearfully beautiful.

The white and irregular masses of the palace reflected unequally the obliquely-borne beams of a flickering twilight. This variety of shades was the effect of the different degrees of inclination of different walls, and of the projections and recesses which constitute the beauty of the barbaric architecture, whose bold caprices, if they do not charm the taste, speak impressively to the imagination. It was so astonishing, so beautiful, that I have not been able to resist once more naming the Kremlin.

But let not the reader be alarmed—this is an adieu.

The plaintive song of some workmen, echoing from vault to vault, from battlement to battlement, from precipice to precipice —precipices built by man—penetrated to my heart, which was absorbed in inexpressible melancholy. Wandering lights appeared in the depths of the royal edifice; and along the deserted galleries, and empty barbicans, came the voice of man, which I was astonished to hear at that hour among these solitary palaces; as was likewise the bird of night, who, disturbed in his mysterious loves, fled from the light of the torches, and, seeking refuge among the highest steeples and towers, there spread the news of the unusual disorder.

That disorder was the consequence of the works commanded by the emperor to welcome his own approaching arrival: he fêtes himself, and illuminates his Kremlin when he comes to Moscow. Meantime, as the darkness increased, the city brightened: its illuminated streets, shops, coffee-houses, and theatres, rose out of the dark like magic. The day was also the anniversary of the emperor's coronation—another motive for illuminating. The Russians have so many joyful days to celebrate that, were I in their place, I should never put out my lamps.

The approach of the magician has already begun to be felt. Three weeks ago Moscow was only inhabited by merchants, who proceeded about their business in drowskas: now, noble coursers, splendid equipages, gilded uniforms, great lords, and numerous valets, enliven the streets and obstruct the porticos. "The emperor is thirty leagues off: who knows if he will not be here to-morrow, or perhaps to-night? It is said he was here yesterday, incognito: who can prove that he is not here now?" And this doubt, this hope, animates all hearts; it changes the faces and languages of all persons, and the aspect of every thing. Moscow, the merchant-city, is now as much troubled and agitated as a citizen's wife expecting the visit of a great nobleman. Deserted palaces and gardens are re-opened; flowers and torches vie with each other in brilliancy; flattering speeches begin to murmur through the crowd: I fear lest I myself should catch the influence of the illusion, if not through selfish motives, at least from a love of the marvellous.

An Emperor of Russia at Moscow, is a king of Assyria in Babylon.

His presence is at this moment, they say, working miracles at Borodino. An entire city is there created—a city just sprung out of the desert, and destined to endure for a week: even gardens have been planted there round a palace; the trees, destined soon to die, have been brought from a distance at great expense, and are so placed as to represent antique shades. The Russians, though they have no past, are, like all enlightened *parvenus,* who well know what is thought of their sudden fortunes, more particularly fond of imitating the effects of time. In this world of fairy work, all that speaks of duration is imitated by things the most ephemeral. Several theatres are also raised on the plain of Borodino; and the drama serves as an interlude between the warlike pantomimes.

The programme of the fête is the exact repetition of the battle, which we called Moskowa, and which the Russians have christened Borodino. Wishing to approach as nearly as possible to the reality, they have convoked from the most distant parts of the empire, all the surviving veterans of 1812 who were in the action. The reader may imagine the astonishment and distress of these brave men, suddenly torn from their repose, and obliged to repair from the extremities of Siberia, Kamtschatka, Lapland, the Caspian, or the Caucasus, to a theatre which they are told was the theatre of their glory—not their fortune, but their renown, a miserable recompence for a superhuman devotion. Why revive these questions and recollections? Why this bold evocation of so many mute and forgotten spectres? It is the last judgment of the conscripts of 1812. If they wished to make a satire upon military life, they could not take a better course: it was thus that Holbein, in his Dance of Death, caricatured human life. Numbers of these men, awakened out of their sleep on the brink of their graves, have not mounted a horse for many years; and here they are obliged, in order to please a master whom they have never seen, again to play over their long-forgotten parts. They have so much dread of not satisfying the expectations of the capricious sovereign who thus troubles their old age, that they say the representation of the battle is more terrible to them than was the reality. This useless ceremony, this fanciful war, will make an end of the soldiers whom the real event spared: it is a cruel pleasure, worthy of one of the successors of the czar who caused living bears to be introduced in the masquerade that he gave on the nuptials of his buffoon: that czar was Peter the Great. All these diversions have their source in the same feeling—contempt for human life.

The emperor had permitted me—which means to say that he commanded me—to be present at Borodino. It is a favour of which I feel myself to have become unworthy. I did not at the time reflect upon the extreme difficulty of the part a Frenchman would have to perform in this historical comedy; and I also had not seen the monstrous work of the Kremlin, which he would expect me to praise; above all, I was then ignorant of the history of the Princess Troubetzkoï, which I have the greater difficulty in banishing from my mind, because I may not speak of it. These reasons united have induced me to decide upon remaining in oblivion. It is an easy resolve; for the contrary would give me trouble, if I may judge by the useless efforts of a crowd of Frenchmen and foreigners of all countries, who in vain solicit permission to be present at Borodino.

All at once the police of the camp has assumed extreme severity: these new precautions are attributed to unpleasant revelations that have been recently made. The sparks of revolt are everywhere feeding under the ashes of liberty. I do not know even whether, under actual circumstances, it would be possible for me to avail myself of the invitation the emperor gave me, both at Petersburg and, afterwards when I took leave of him, at Peterhoff. "I shall be very glad if you will attend the ceremony at Borodino, where we lay the first stone of a monument in honour of General Bagration." These were his last words.*

I see here persons who were invited, yet are not able to ap-

---

* I learnt afterwards, at Petersburg, that orders had been given to permit my reaching Borodino, where I was expected.

proach the camp. Permissions are refused to every body, except a few privileged Englishmen and some members of the diplomatic corps. All the rest, young and old, military men and diplomatists, foreigners and Russians, have returned to Moscow, mortified by their unavailing efforts. I have written to a person connected with the emperor's household, regretting my inability to avail myself of the favour his Majesty had accorded in permitting me to witness the manoeuvres, and pleading as an excuse the state of my eyes, which are not yet cured.

The dust of the camp is, I am told, insupportable to every body; it might cost me the loss of my sight. The Duke of Leuchtenberg must be endowed with an unusual quantum of indifference to be able coolly to witness the spectacle prepared for him. They assure me that in the representation of the battle, the emperor will command the corps of Prince Eugene, father of the young duke.

I should regret not seeing a spectacle so curious in its moral aspect, if I could be present as a disinterested spectator; but, without having the renown of a father to maintain, I am a son of France, and I feel it is not for me to find any pleasure in witnessing a representation of war, made at great cost, solely with the view of exalting the national pride of the Russians, on the occasion of our disasters. As to the sight itself, I can picture it very easily; I have seen plenty of straight lines in Russia. Besides, in reviews and mock fights, the eye never gets beyond a great cloud of dust.

The Russians have reason to pride themselves on the issue of the campaign of 1812; but the general who laid its plan, he who first advised the gradual retreat of the Russian army towards the centre of the empire, with the view of enticing the exhausted French after it,—the man, in fact, to whose genius Russia owed her deliverance—Prince Witgenstein, is not represented in this grand repetition; because, unfortunately for him, he is living, half disgraced; he resides on his estates; his name will not be pronounced at Borodino, though an eternal monument is to be raised to the glory of General Bagration, who fell on the field of battle.

Under despotic governments, dead warriors are great favourites: here, behold one decreed to be the hero of a campaign in which he bravely fell, but which he never directed.

This absence of historical probity, this abuse of the will of one man, who imposes his views upon all, who dictates to the people whatever they are to think on events of national interest, appears to me the most revolting of all the impieties of arbitrary government. Strike, torture bodies, but do not crush minds: let man judge of things according to the intimations of Providence, according to his conscience and his reason. The people must be called impious who devoutly submit to this continual violation of the respect due to all that is most holy in the sight of God and man,—the sanctity of truth.

❖   ❖   ❖

I have received an account of the manoeuvres at Borodino, which is not calculated to calm my wrath.

Every body has read a description of the battle of Moskowa, and history has viewed it as one of those that we have won; for it was hazarded by the Emperor Alexander against the advice of his generals, as a last effort to save his capital, which capital was taken four days later; though a heroic conflagration, combined with a deadly frost, and with the improvidence of our chieftain, blinded on this occasion by an excess of confidence in his lucky star, decided our disaster. Thus favoured by the issue of the campaign, here is the Emperor of Russia flattering himself with treating as a victory, a battle lost by his army within four days' journey of his capital: he has distorted a military scene which he professes to reproduce with scrupulous exactitude. The following is the lie which he has given to history in the eyes of all Europe.

When they came to the moment in which the French, who had been dreadfully galled by the Russian artillery, charged and carried the batteries that decimated them with the daring that is so well known, the Emperor Nicholas, instead of suffering, as both his justice and dignity demanded, that the celebrated manoeuvre should be executed, became the flatterer of the lowest of his people, and caused the corps which represented the division of our army to which we owed the defeat of the Russians and the capture of Moscow, to fall back a distance of three leagues.

Imagine my gratitude to God for having given me grace to refuse being present at this lying pantomime!

The military comedy is followed by an order of the day, which will be considered outrageous in Europe, if it be published there in the shape that it is here. According to this singular exposé of the ideas of an individual—not the events of a campaign—"It was voluntarily that the Russians retired beyond Moscow, which proves that they did not lose the battle of Borodino; (why then did they decline continuing it?) and the bones of their presumptuous enemies," adds the order of the day, "scattered from the holy city to Niemen, attest the triumph of the defenders of the country."

Without waiting for the solemn entry of the emperor into Moscow, I shall leave in two days' time for Petersburg.

❖   ❖   ❖

Here end the chapters that were written by the traveller in the form of letters to his friends: the relation which follows completes his recollections; it was written at various places, commencing at Petersburg, in 1839, afterwards being continued in Germany, and more recently at Paris.

❖

RETURN FROM MOSCOW TO PETERSBURG ❖ HISTORY OF M. PERNET, A FRENCH PRISONER IN RUSSIA ❖ HIS ARREST ❖ CONDUCT OF HIS FELLOW TRAVELLER ❖ THE FRENCH CONSUL AT MOSCOW ❖ EFFECTS OF IMAGINATION ❖ ADVICE OF A RUSSIAN ❖ GREAT NOVGOROD ❖ SOUVENIRS OF IVAN IV ❖ ARRIVAL AT PETERSBURG ❖ M. DE BARANTE ❖ SEQUEL OF THE HISTORY OF M. PERNET ❖ INTERIOR OF A MOSCOW PRISON ❖ A VISIT TO COLPINA ❖ ORIGIN OF THE LAVAL FAMILY IN RUSSIA ❖ THE ACADEMY OF PAINTING ❖ THE ARTS IN RUSSIA ❖ M. BRULOW ❖ INFLUENCE OF THE NORTH UPON THE ARTS ❖ MADEMOISELLE TAGLIONI AT PETERSBURG ❖ ABOLITION OF THE UNIATES ❖ SUPERIORITY OF A REPRESENTATIVE FORM OF GOVERNMENT ❖ DEPARTURE FROM RUSSIA ❖ THE FEELINGS OF THE AUTHOR ❖ A SINCERE LETTER ❖ REASONS FOR

NOT RETURNING THROUGH

POLAND

❖

CHAPTER XXXVI

❖

At the moment I was about to quit Moscow, a singular circumstance attracted all my attention, and obliged me to delay my departure.

I had ordered post-horses at seven o'clock in the morning: to my great surprise my valet-de-chambre awoke me at four, and on my asking the cause of this unnecessary hurry, he answered that he did not like to delay informing me of a fact which he had just learnt, and which appeared to him very serious. The following is the sum of what he related.

A Frenchman, whose name is M. Louis Pernet, and who arrived a few days ago in Moscow, where he lodged at a public hotel, has been arrested in the middle of the night—this very night,—and, after being deprived of his papers, has been taken to the city prison, and there placed in a cell. Such is the account which the waiter at our inn gave to my servant, who, after many questions, further learnt that M. Pernet is a young man about twenty-six years old, and of feeble frame, which redoubles the fears that are entertained for him; that he passed through Moscow last year, when he stayed at the house of a Russian friend, who afterwards took him into the country. This Russian is now absent, and the unfortunate prisoner has no other acquaintance here except another Frenchman, a M. R——, in whose company, it is said, he has been travelling from the north of Russia. This M. R—— lodged in the same hotel with the prisoner. His name struck me the moment I heard it, for it is the same as that of the dark man with whom I dined a few days before at the house of the governor of Nijni. The reader may recollect that his physiognomy had been to me a subject for meditation. Again to stumble upon this personage, in connection with the event of the night, appeared to me quite a circumstance for a novel, and I could scarcely believe what I heard: nevertheless I immediately rose, and sought the waiter myself, to hear from his own lips the version of the story, and to ascertain beyond doubt the correctness of the name of M. R——, whose identity I was particularly desirous of ascertaining. The waiter told me, that having been sent on an errand by a foreigner about to leave Moscow, he was at Kopp's hotel at the moment when the police left it, and he added that M. Kopp had related to him the affair, which he recounted in words that exactly accorded with the statement of Antonio.

As soon as I was dressed, I repaired to M. R——, and found, true enough, that it was the bronze-complexioned man of Nijni. The only difference was, that at Moscow he had an agitated air, very different from his former immobility. I found him out of bed; we recognised each other in a moment; but when I told him the object of my very early morning call, he appeared embarrassed.

"It is true that I have travelled," he said, "with M. Pernet, but it was by mere chance; we met at Archangel, and from thence have proceeded in company: he has a very poor constitution, and his weak health gave me much uneasiness during the journey: I rendered him the services that humanity called for, but nothing more; I am not one of his friends; I know nothing of him."

"I know still less of him," I replied; "but we are all three Frenchmen, and we owe each other mutual aid in a country where our liberty and our life may be menaced any moment by a power which cannot be seen till it strikes."

"Perhaps M. Pernet," replied M. R——, "has got himself into this scrape by some imprudence. A stranger as well as he is, and without credit, what can I do? If he is innocent, the arrest will be followed by no serious consequences; if he is culpable, he will have to submit to the punishment. I can do nothing for him, I owe him nothing; and I advise you, sir, to be yourself very cautious in any steps you may take in his favour, as well as in your language respecting the affair."

"But what will decide his guilt?" I exclaimed. "It will be first of all necessary to see him, to know to what he attributes this arrest, and to ask him what can be said or done for him."

"You forget the country we are in," answered M. R——: "he is in a dungeon; how could we get access to him? the thing is impossible."

"What is also impossible," I replied, rising, "is that Frenchmen —that any men, should leave their countryman in a critical situation, without even inquiring the cause of his misfortune."

On leaving this very prudent travelling companion, I began to think the case more serious than I had at first supposed; and I considered that, to understand the true position of the prisoner, I ought to address myself to the French consul. Being obliged to wait the usual hour for seeing that personage, I ordered back my post-horses, to the great surprise and displeasure of the feldjäger, as they were already at the door when I gave the countermand.

At ten o'clock, I made to the French consul the above relation of facts; and found that official protector of the French full as prudent, and yet more cold, than Doctor R—— had appeared to me. Since he has lived in Moscow, this consul has become almost a Russian. I could not make out whether his answers were dictated by a fear founded on a knowledge of the usages of the country, or by a sentiment of wounded self-love, of ill-understood personal dignity.

"M. Pernet," he said, "passed six months in Moscow and its environs, without having thought fit, during all that time, to make the smallest approach towards the consul of France. M. Pernet must look, therefore, to himself alone to get out of the situation in which his heedlessness has involved him. This answer," added the consul, "is perhaps not sufficiently distinct." He then concluded by repeating that he neither ought, nor could, nor would, mix himself up with the affair.

In vain did I represent to him, that, in his capacity as our consul, he owed to every Frenchman, without distinction of persons, and even if they failed in the laws of etiquette, his aid and protection; that the present question was not one of ceremony, but of the liberty and perhaps the life of a fellow countryman; and that, under such a misfortune, all resentment should be at least suspended till the danger was over. I could not extract one word, not one single expression of interest in favour of the prisoner; nor even, when I reasoned on public grounds, and spoke of the dignity of France, and the safety of all Frenchmen who travelled in Russia, could I make any impression; in short, this second attempt aided the cause no better than the first.

Nevertheless, though I had not even known M. Pernet by name, and though I had no motive to take any personal interest in him, yet, as chance had made me acquainted with his misfortune, it seemed to me that it was no more than my duty to give him all the aid that lay in my power. I was at this moment strongly struck with a truth which is no doubt often present to the thoughts of others, but which had only until then vaguely and fleetingly passed before my mind—the truth that imagination serves to extend the sphere of pity, and to render it more active. I went even so far as to conclude in my own mind, that a man without imagination would be absolutely devoid of feeling. All my imaginative or creative faculties were busy in presenting to me; in spite of myself, this unhappy, unknown man, surrounded by the phantoms of his prison solitude: I suffered with him, I felt his feelings, I shared his fears; I saw him, forsaken by all the world, discovering that his state was hopeless: for who would ever interest themselves in a prisoner in this land, so distant and so different from ours, in a society where friends meet together for enjoyment, and separate in adversity. What a stimulus was this thought to my commiseration! "You believe yourself to be alone in the world; you are unjust towards Providence, which sends you a friend and a brother." These were the words which I mentally addressed to the victim.

Meanwhile, the unhappy man would hope for no succour, and every hour that passed in his dreadful silence and monotony would plunge him deeper in despair: night would come with its train of spectres; and then what terrors, what regrets would seize upon him! How did I pant to tell him that the zeal of a stranger should replace the loss of the faithless protectors on whom he had a right to depend. But all means of communication were impossible: the dismal hallucinations of the dungeon pursued me in the light of the sun, and, notwithstanding the bright arch of heaven above my head, shut me up in dark, dank vaults; for in my distress, forgetting that the Russians apply the classic architecture to the construction even of prisons, I dreamt not of Roman colonnades, but of Gothic subterranes. Had my imagination less deeply impressed me with all these things, I should have been less active and persevering in my efforts in favour of an unknown individual. I was followed by a spectre, and to rid myself of it, no efforts could have been too great.

To have insisted on entering the prison would have been a step no less useless than dangerous. After long and painful doubt, I thought of another plan: I had made the acquaintance of several of the most influential people in Moscow; and though I had two days ago taken leave of every body, I resolved to risk giving my confidence to the man for whom I had, among all the others, conceived the highest opinion.

Not only must I here avoid using his name, I must also take care not to allude to him in any way by which he could be identified.

When he saw me enter his room he at once guessed the business that brought me, and without giving me time to explain myself, he told me that by a singular chance he knew M. Pernet personally, and believed him innocent, which caused his situation to appear inexplicable; but that he was sure political considerations could have alone led to such an imprisonment, because the Russian police never unmasks itself unless compelled; that no doubt the existence of this foreigner had been supposed to have been altogether unknown in Moscow; but that now the blow was struck, his friends could only injure him by showing themselves; for if it were known that parties were interested in him, it would render his position far worse, as he would be removed to avoid all discovery and to stifle all complaints: he added therefore, that, for the victim's sake, extreme circumspection was necessary. "If once he departs for Siberia, God only can say when he will return," exclaimed my counsellor; who afterwards endeavoured to make me understand that he could not openly avow the interest he took in a suspected Frenchman; for, being himself suspected of liberal principles, a word from him, saying merely that he knew the prisoner, would suffice to exile the latter to the farther end of the world. He concluded by saying, "You are neither his relation nor his friend; you only take in him the interest that you believe you ought to take in a countryman, in a man whom you know to be in trouble; you have already acquitted yourself of the duty that this praiseworthy sentiment imposes on you; you have spoken to your consul: you had now, believe me, better abstain from any further steps; it will do no good, and you will compromise yourself for the man whose defence you gratuitously undertake. He does not know you, he expects nothing from you; continue, then, your journey, you will disappoint no hopes that he has conceived; I will keep my eye on him; I cannot appear in the affair, but I have indirect means which may be useful, and I promise to employ them to the utmost of my power. Once again, then, follow my advice, and pursue your journey."

"If I were to set out," I exclaimed, "I should not have a moment's peace; I should be pursued by a feeling that would amount to remorse, when I recollected that the unfortunate man has me only to befriend him, and that I have abandoned him without doing any thing."

"Your presence here," he answered, "will not even serve to console him, as he is and must continue wholly ignorant of the interest you take in him."

"There are, then, no means of gaining access to the dungeon?"

"None," replied the individual addressed, not without some marks of impatience at my thus persisting. "Were you his brother you could do no more for him here than you have done. Your presence at Petersburg may, on the contrary, be useful to M. Pernet. You can inform the French ambassador all that you know about this imprisonment; for I doubt whether he will hear any thing of it from your consul. A representation made to the minister by a personage in the position of your ambassador, and by a man possessing the character of M. de Barante, will do more to hasten the deliverance of your countryman than you, and I, and any twenty others could do in Moscow."

"But the emperor and his ministers are at Borodino or at Moscow," I answered, unwilling to take a refusal.

"All the ministers have not followed his Majesty," he replied, still in a polite tone, but with increasing and scarcely-concealed ill-humour. "Besides, at the worst, their return must be waited. You have, I repeat, no other course to take, unless you would injure the man whom you wish to save, and expose yourself also to many unpleasant surmises, or perhaps to something worse," he added, in a significant manner.

Had the person to whom I addressed myself been a placeman, I should have already fancied I saw the cossacks advancing to seize and convey me to a dungeon like that of M. Pernet's.

I felt that the patience of my adviser was at an end; I had nothing, in fact, to reply to his arguments: I therefore retired, promising to leave, and gratefully thanking him for his counsel.

As it is obvious I can do nothing here I will leave at once, I said to myself: but the slow motions of my feldjäger took up the rest of the morning, and it was past four in the afternoon before I was on the road to Petersburg.

The sulkiness of the courier, the want of horses, felt every where on the road on account of relays being retained for the household of the emperor and for military officers, as well as for couriers proceeding from Borodino to Petersburg, made my journey long and tedious: in my impatience I insisted on travelling all night; but I gained nothing by this haste, being obliged, for want of horses, to pass six whole hours at Great Novgorod, within fifty leagues of Petersburg.

I was scarcely in a fitting mood to visit the cradle of the Slavonian empire, and which became also the tomb of its liberty. The famous church of Saint Sophia encloses the sepulchres of Vladimir Iaroslawitch, who died in 1051, of his mother Anne, and of an emperor of Constantinople. It resembles the other Russian churches, and perhaps is not more authentic than the pretended ancient cathedral that contains the bones of Minine at Nijni Novgorod. I no longer believe in the dates of any old monuments that are shown me in Russia. But I still believe in the names of its rivers: the Volkoff represents to me the frightful scenes connected with the siege of this republican city, taken, retaken, and decimated by Ivan the Terrible. I could fancy I saw the imperial hyena, presiding over carnage and pestilence, couched among the ruins of the city; and the bloody corpses of his subjects seemed to issue out of the river that was choked with their bodies, to prove to me the horrors of intestine wars. It is worthy of remark, that the correspondence of the Archbishop Pinen, and of other principal citizens of Novgorod, with the Poles, was the cause which brought the evil on the city, where thirty thousand innocent persons perished in the combat, and in the executions and massacres invented and presided over by the czar. There were days on which six hundred were at once executed before his eyes; and all these horrors were enacted to punish a crime unpardonable from that epoch—the crime of clandestine communication with the Poles. This took place nearly three hundred years ago, in 1570. Great Novgorod has never recovered the stroke: she could have replaced her dead, but she could not survive the abolition of her democratic institutions: her whitewashed houses are no longer stained with blood; they appear as if they had been built only yesterday; but her streets are deserted, and three parts of her ruins are spread over the plain, beyond the narrow bounds of the actual city, which is but a shadow and a name. This is all that remains of the famous republic of the middle ages. Where are the fruits of the revolutions which never ceased to saturate the now almost desert soil with blood? Here, all is as silent as it was before the history. God has only too often had to teach us, that objects which men, blinded with pride, viewed as a worthy end of their efforts, were really only a means of employing their superfluous powers in the effervescence of youth. Such are the principles of more than one heroic action.

For three centuries the bell of the *vetche** has ceased to summon the people of Novgorod, formerly the most glorious and the most turbulent of the Russian populations, to deliberate upon their affairs. The will of the czars stifles in every heart all sentiments, even regret for the memory of effaced glory. Some years ago, atrocious scenes occurred between the cossacks and the inhabitants of the country in the military colonies established in the vicinity of the decayed city. But the insurrection was stifled,

* Popular assembly.

and every thing has returned to its accustomed order, that is, to the silence and peace of the tomb.

I was very happy to leave this abode, formerly famous for the disorders of liberty, now desolated by what is called *good order,*— a word which is here equivalent to that of death.

Although I made all possible haste, I did not reach Petersburg until the fourth day: immediately after leaving my carriage I repaired to M. de Barante's.

He was quite ignorant of the arrest of M. Pernet, and appeared surprised to hear of it through me, especially when he learnt that I had been nearly four days on the road. His astonishment redoubled when I related to him my unavailing endeavours to influence our consul—that official protector of the French—to take some step in favour of the prisoner.

The attention with which M. de Barante listened to me, the assurance which he gave me that he would neglect nothing to clear up this affair, the importance with which he appeared to invest the smallest facts that could interest the dignity of France and the safety of her citizens, put my conscience at ease, and dissipated the phantoms of my imagination. The fate of M. Pernet was in the hands of his natural protector, whose ability and character became better sureties for the safety of this unfortunate man than my zeal and powerless solicitations. I felt I had done all that I could for him and for the honour of my country. During the twelve or fourteen days that I remained at Petersburg, I purposely abstained from pronouncing the name of Pernet before the ambassador; and I left Russia without knowing the end of a history which had so much absorbed and interested me.

But, while journeying rapidly towards France, my mind was often carried back to the dungeons of Moscow. If I had known all that was passing there, it would have been yet more painfully excited.

❖   ❖   ❖

Not to leave the reader in the ignorance in which I remained for nearly six months respecting the fate of the prisoner at Moscow,

I insert here all that I have learnt since my return to France respecting the imprisonment of M. Pernet, and his deliverance.

One day, near the end of the winter of 1840, I was informed that a stranger was at my door, and wished to speak with me. I desired that he would give his name: he replied that he would give it to me only. I refused to see him; he persisted; I again refused. At last, renewing his entreaties, he sent up a line of writing without any signature, to say that I could not refuse listening to a man who owed to me his life, and who only wished to thank me.

This language appeared extraordinary. I ordered the stranger to be introduced. On entering the room he said—"Sir, it was only yesterday I learnt your address: my name is Pernet; and I come to express to you my gratitude; for I was told at Petersburg that it is to you I owe my liberty, and consequently my life."

After the first surprise which such an address caused me, I began to notice the person of M. Pernet. He is one of that numerous class of young Frenchmen who have the appearance and the temperament of the men of southern lands; his eyes and hair are black, his cheeks hollow, his countenance every where equally pale; he is short and slight in figure; and he appeared to be suffering, though rather morally than physically. He discovered that I knew some members of his family settled in Savoy, who are among the most respectable people of that land of honest men. He told me that he was an advocate; and he related that he had been detained in the prison of Moscow for three weeks, four days of which time he was placed in the cells. We shall see by his recital the way in which a prisoner is treated in this abode. My imagination had not approached the reality.

The two first days he was left *without food!* No one came near him; and he believed for forty-eight hours that it was determined to starve him to death in his prison. The only sound that he heard was that of the strokes of the rod, which, from five o'clock in the morning until night, were inflicted upon the unhappy slaves who were sent by their masters to this place, to receive correction. Add to that frightful sound, the sobs, the tears, the screams of the victims, mingled with the menaces and imprecations of the tormentors, and you will form some faint idea of the moral as well as physical sufferings of our unhappy countryman during four weary days, and while still remaining ignorant of his crime.

After having thus penetrated against his will into the profound mystery of a Russian prison, he believed, not without reason, that he was destined to end his days there; for he said to himself, "If there had been any intention to release me, it is not here that I should be confined by men who fear nothing so much as to have their secret barbarity divulged."

A slight partition alone separated his narrow cell from the inner court, where these executions were perpetrated.

The rod, which, since the amelioration of manners, usually replaces the knout of Mongolic memory, is formed of a cane split into three pieces, an instrument which fetches off the skin at every stroke; at the fifth, the victim loses nearly all power to cry, his weakened voice can then only utter a prolonged, sobbing groan. This horrible rattle in the throat of the tortured creatures pierced the heart of the prisoner, and presaged to him a fate which he dared not look in the face.

M. Pernet understands Russian; he was therefore present, without seeing any thing, at many private tortures; among others, at those of two young girls, who worked under a fashionable milliner in Moscow. These unfortunate creatures were flogged before the eyes even of their mistress, who reproached them with having lovers, and with having so far forgotten themselves as to bring them into her house—the house of a milliner!—what an enormity! Meanwhile this virago exhorted the executioners to strike harder: one of the girls begged for mercy: they said that she was nearly killed, that she was covered with blood. No matter! She had carried her audacity so far as to say that she was less culpable than her mistress; and the latter redoubled her severity. M. Pernet assured me, observing that he thought I might doubt his assertion, that each of the unhappy girls received, at different intervals, a hundred and eighty blows. "I suffered too much in counting them," he added, "to be deceived in the number."

A man feels the approach of insanity when present at such horrors, and yet unable to succour the victims.

Afterwards, serfs and servants were brought by stewards, or

sent by their masters, with the request that they might be punished: there was nothing, in short, but scenes of atrocious vengeance and frightful despair, all hidden from the public eye.* The unhappy prisoner longed for the obscurity of night, because the darkness brought with it silence; and though his thoughts then terrified him, he preferred the evils of imagination to those of reality. This is always the case with real sufferers. It is only the dreamers, who have comfortable beds and good tables, that pretend the evils we fancy exceed those that we feel.

At last, after four times twenty-four hours of a torment which would, I think, surpass all our efforts to picture, M. Pernet was taken from his dungeon, still without any explanation, and transferred to another part of the prison.

From thence he wrote to M. de Barante, by General ———, on whose good offices he thought he could reckon.

The letter did not reach its address; and when afterwards the writer demanded an explanation of this circumstance, the General excused himself by subterfuges, and concluded by swearing to M. Pernet, on the gospel, that the letter had not been put in the hands of the minister of police, and never would be! This was the utmost extent of devotion that the prisoner could obtain from his *friend:* and this is the fate of human affections when they pass under the yoke of despotism.

At the end of three weeks—which had been an eternity to M. Pernet—he was released without any form of process, and without even being able to learn the cause of his imprisonment.

His reiterated questions, addressed to the director of police in Moscow, procured for him no explanations: he was merely told that his ambassador had claimed him; and this was accompanied with an order to leave Russia. He asked, and obtained permission to take the route of Petersburg.

He wished to thank the French ambassador for the liberty which he owed to him; and also to obtain some information as to the cause of the treatment he had undergone. M. de Barante

---

* See, in Dickens's American Journey, extracts from the United States' papers, concerning the treatment of the slaves; presenting a remarkable resemblance between the excesses of despotism and the abuses of democracy.

endeavoured, but in vain, to divert him from the project of addressing M. de Benkendorf, the minister of the Imperial police. The liberated man demanded an audience: it was granted him. He said to the minister that, being ignorant of the cause of the punishment that he had received, he wished to know his crime before leaving Russia.

The statesman briefly answered, that he would do well to carry his inquiries on the subject no further, and dismissed him, repeating the order that he should, without delay, leave the empire.

Such is all the information that I could obtain from M. Pernet. This young man, like every one else who has lived some time in Russia, has acquired a mysterious and reserved tone of language, to which foreigners are as liable as the native inhabitants. One would say that in that empire, a secret weighs upon all minds.

On my continuing my inquiries, M. Pernet further stated, that on his first journey to the country, they had given him, in his passport, the title of merchant, and on the second, that of advocate. He added a more serious circumstance, namely, that before reaching Petersburg, while in a steam-boat on the Baltic, he had freely expressed his opinion of Russian despotism before several individuals whom he did not know.

He assured me, on leaving, that his memory could recall no other circumstance that could account for the treatment he had received at Moscow. I have never seen him since; though, by a singular chance, I met, two years after, a member of his family, who said he knew of the services I had rendered to his young relative, and thanked me for them. This family, I repeat, are respected by all who know them in the kingdom of Sardinia.

❖ ❖ ❖

The last moments of my stay in Petersburg were employed in inspecting various establishments that I had not seen on my visit to that city.

Prince —— showed me, among other curiosities, the immense works of Colpina, the arsenal of the Russian arsenals, which is situated some leagues from the capital. In this manufactory are prepared all the articles required for the Imperial marine. Colpina is reached by a road seven leagues in length, the last half of which is execrable. The establishment is directed by an Englishman, M. Wilson, who is honoured with the rank of General (all Russia is converted into an army). He exhibited to us his machines, like a true Russian engineer, not permitting us to overlook a nail or a screw: under his escort we surveyed about twenty workshops, of enormous size. The extreme complaisance of the director deserved much gratitude, though I expressed but little, and that little was more than I felt: fatigue renders a man almost as ungrateful as ennui.

The object that we most admired in this tedious inspection was a machine of Bramah's, invented to prove the strength of the largest chain-cables: the enormous links that can resist the force of this machine may hold the mightiest vessels of war at anchor in the highest seas. An ingenious application of water-pressure, to measure the strength of iron, is the invention which appeared to me so marvellous.

We also examined sluices destined to serve in extraordinary floods of water. It is especially in springtime that they are useful. Without them, the stream which moves the various machines would cause incalculable damage. The canals of these sluices are lined with thick sheets of copper, because that metal is found to resist the winters better than granite. I was told that I should see nothing like them elsewhere.

When we entered the carriage to return to Petersburg, it was already night, and very cold. The length of the road was lightened by a charming conversation, of which I have retained one anecdote. It will serve to prove to what extent the creative power of an absolute sovereign can be carried. Hitherto I had only seen it exercised upon buildings, upon the dead, upon historic facts, upon prisoners,—in short, upon all things that could not protest against an abuse of power: this time we shall see a Russian emperor imposing upon one of the most illustrious families of France, a relative of whom it knew nothing.

Under the reign of Paul I. a Frenchman of the name of Lovel, young and agreeable in person, gained the affections of a very wealthy and high-born maiden. Her family were hostile to the union, on account of the foreigner's possessing neither name nor fortune. The two lovers, reduced to despair, had recourse to a romantic expedient. They stood in wait for the emperor, in some street by which he was to pass, threw themselves at his feet, and besought his protection. Paul, who was good-natured when he was not mad, promised the consent of the family, which he doubtless procured by more than one means, and among others, by this: "Mademoiselle Kaminska shall marry," said the emperor, "M. *the Count de Laval,* a young French *emigré* of illustrious family, and the possessor of a considerable fortune."

Thus endowed, the young Frenchman was united to the object of his affections.

To prove the words of the sovereign, *M. de Laval* caused his escutcheon to be proudly sculptured over the door of his mansion.

Unfortunately, fifteen years afterwards, a M. de Montmorency Laval journeyed into Russia; and seeing, by chance, his arms above a door, he made inquiries, and learnt the history of M. Lovel.

On his representations, the Emperor Alexander caused the escutcheon of the Lavals to be taken down, and the door of M. Lovel remained stripped of its glory; which has not, however, prevented him up to this day from doing the honours of an excellent house in Petersburg, which will be always called the Hôtel de Laval, out of respect for the memory of the Emperor Paul, to whom an expiatory veneration is indeed owing.

The day after my journey to Colpina, I visited the Academy of Painting, a superb and stately edifice, which up to the present time contains but few good works. How can they be expected in a land where the young artists wear uniform? I found all the pupils of the Academy enrolled, dressed, and commanded like marine cadets. This fact alone denotes a profound contempt for the object pretended to be patronised, or rather a great ignorance of the nature and the mysteries of art; professed indifference would be less indicative of barbarism. There is nothing free in Russia except objects for which the government does not care; it cares only too much for the arts; but it is ignorant that they cannot dispense with liberty, and that this sympathy between the works of genius and the independence of man would alone attest the nobleness of the artist's profession.

I went over numerous studios, and found there distinguished landscape-painters: their compositions display imagination and even colour. I particularly admired a picture representing St. Petersburg on a summer's night, by M. Vorobieff: it is beautiful as nature, poetical as truth. This picture reminded me of my first arrival in Russia, when the summer nights consisted of no more than two twilights: the effect of such perpetual day, which pierces through obscurity like a bright lamp through a gauze veil, could not be better rendered. I saw again the polar light, so different from the colouring of other scenes, which I had first beheld on the Baltic. To be able thus exactly to characterise the special phenomena of nature, proves a high degree of merit.

There is much talk in Russia of the talent of Brulow. His *Last Day of Pompeii* produced, it is said, some sensation even in Italy. This enormous piece of canvass is now the glory of the Russian school: let not the reader ridicule the designation: I saw a saloon, on the door of which these words were inscribed—*"The Russian School!"* The colouring of Brulow's painting appeared to me to be false, though certainly the subject is calculated to conceal this fault: for who knows the shade of the tints that clad the structures of Pompeii on their last day? The painter has a hard, dry touch, but he exhibits power: his conceptions lack neither imagination nor originality. His heads display truth and variety: if he understood the management of the chiaro oscuro, he might some day deserve the reputation that is given to him here: at present he is deficient in natural style, in colouring, in lightness, and in grace: there is no want of a species of wild poetry in his compositions, but their general effect is disagreeable. His style, which is stiff, without being devoid of a certain nobleness, reminds one of the imitators of the school of David. In a painting of the Assumption, which we are obliged to admire at Petersburg, because it is the work of the famous Brulow, I observed clouds so heavy that they might have been sent to represent rocks at the Opera.

There are heads, however, in the Pompeii picture which discover real talent. The painting, notwithstanding its faults as a composition, would gain in celebrity by being engraved; for it is in the colouring that its chief defects lie.

It is said that since his return to Russia, the painter has lost much of his enthusiasm for the art. How I pity him for having seen Italy, since he was obliged to return to the north! He does not work hard; and unfortunately his rapid facility, which is here viewed as a merit, appears but too plainly in his pieces. It is only by assiduous pains and labour that he could succeed in conquering the stiffness of his design, and the crudeness of his colouring. Great painters know the difficulty of learning to design without the pencil, to paint by the intershading and blending of colours, to efface from the canvass, lines which exist nowhere in nature, to show the air, which exists everywhere, to conceal art,—in short, faithfully to depict the real, yet at the same time to ennoble it.

I am told that he passes much more of his time in drinking than in working: I blame him less than I pity him. Here, every thing is good if it only tend to impart a glow: wine is the sun of Russia. If to the misery of being a Russian is added the circumstance of being a painter, the individual ought to expatriate himself. Must not the land, where there is night for three months of the year, and where the snow sheds brighter radiance than the sun, be a land of exile to the painter?

By endeavouring to reproduce the singularities of nature under these latitudes, a few character-painters may win for themselves the honour of a place on the steps of the temple of arts; but an historical painter ought to fly this climate. Peter the Great laboured in vain; nature will always place bounds to the fancies of men, were they justified by the ukases of twenty czars.

I have seen one work of M. Brulow's which is truly admirable: it is unquestionably the best of all the modern paintings in Petersburg; though, indeed, it is a copy of an ancient chef-d'oeuvre, the School of Athens, and is full as large as the original. When an individual knows how thus to reproduce one, perhaps, of Raphael's most inimitable works after his Madonnas, he ought to return to Rome, there to learn to do something better than *"The Last Day of Pompeii"* and *"The Assumption of the Virgin."**

The vicinity of the Pole is unfavourable to the arts, with the exception of poetry, which can sometimes dispense with all mate-

* M. Brulow has copied several of Raphael's works; but I was especially struck with the beauty of the one here mentioned.

❖ 583 ❖

rial except the human soul; it is then the volcano under the ice. But for the inhabitants of these dreadful climates, music, painting, the dance—all those pleasures of sensation which are partially independent of mind—lose their charms in losing their organs. What are Rembrandt, Corregio, Michael Angelo, and Raphael, in a dark room? The north has doubtless its own kind of beauty, but it is still a palace without light: all the attractive train of youth, with their pastimes, their smiles, their graces, and their dances, confine themselves to those blest regions where the rays of the sun, not content with gliding over the surface of the earth, warm and fertilise its bosom by piercing it from on high.

In Russia a double gloom pervades every thing—the fear of power and the want of sun. The national dances resemble rounds led by shadows under the gleam of a twilight which never ends. Mademoiselle Taglioni herself (alas! for Mademoiselle Taglioni!) is not a perfect dancer at St. Petersburg. What a fall for La Sylphide! But when she walks in the streets—for she walks at present—she is followed by footmen in handsome cockades and gold lace; and the newspapers overwhelm her every morning with articles containing the most preposterous praises I have ever seen. This is all the Russians, notwithstanding their cleverness, can do for the arts and for *artistes*. What the latter want is a heaven to give them life, a public which can understand them, a society which can excite and inspire them. These are necessaries: rewards are supererogatory. It is not, however, in a country contiguous to Lapland, and governed under the system of Peter the Great, that such things are to be sought for. I must wait for the Russians' establishment in Constantinople, before I can know of what they are really capable in the fine arts and in civilisation.

The best method of patronising art is to have a sincere desire for the pleasures it procures: a nation that reaches this point of civilisation will not be long compelled to seek for artists among foreigners.

At the time of my leaving St. Petersburg, several persons were secretly deploring the abolition of the Uniates,* and recounting

---

* The Uniates are Greeks reunited to the Catholic church, and therefore regarded as schismatics by the Greek church.

the arbitrary measures by which this irreligious act, celebrated as a triumph by the Greek church, has been accomplished. The unknown persecutions to which many priests among the Uniates have been exposed would be viewed as revolting by even the most indifferent parties; but in a country where distances and secrecy lend their aid to the most tyrannical acts, all these violences remain concealed. This reminds me of the significant words too often repeated by Russians deprived of protectors—"God is so high, and the emperor so far off!"

Here, then, is the Greek church busy making martyrs. What has become of the toleration of which it boasts before men who are ignorant of the East? Glorious confessors of the Catholic faith are now languishing in convent prisons; and their struggle, admirable in the eyes of heaven, remains unknown even to the church for whom they generously fight upon earth,—that church which is mother of all the churches, and the only church universal; for it is the only one untainted by locality, the only one which remains free, and which belongs to no particular country.†

When the sun of publicity shall rise upon Russia, how many injustices will it expose to view!—not only ancient ones, but those which are enacted daily will shock the senses of the world. They will not be sufficiently shocked; for such is the fate of truth upon earth, that, so long as people have a great interest in knowing it, they remain ignorant of it, and when at last they have their eyes opened, it has become to them no longer a matter of importance. The abuses of a destroyed power excite only cold exclamations: those who recount them, pass for ungenerous strikers of the slain; whilst, on the other hand, the excesses of this iniquitous power remain carefully concealed so long as it maintains itself; for its first aim is to stifle the cries of its victim: it exterminates, but avoids lightly wounding; and applauds itself for its mercy in having recourse to none save indispensable cruelties. But its boasting is hypocritical: when the prison is as silent and closely shut as the tomb, there is no mercy in saving from the scaffold.

I left France scared by the abuses of a false liberty; I return to

† Has it not taken three years to carry to Rome the cry of these unfortunate beings?

my country persuaded that, if logically speaking, representative government is not the most moral, it is, practically, the most wise and moderate, preserving the people on one side from democratic licence, and on the other from the most glaring abuses of despotism: I therefore ask myself if we ought not to impose a silence upon our antipathies, and submit without murmur to a necessary policy, and one which, after all, brings to nations prepared for it more good than evil. It is true that hitherto this new and wise form of government has only been able to establish itself by usurpation. Perhaps these final usurpations have been rendered inevitable by preceding errors. This is a religious question, which time, the wisest of God's ministers upon earth, will resolve to our posterity. I am here reminded of the profound idea of one of the most enlightened and cultivated intellects in Germany, M. Varnhagen von der Ense:

"I have often laboured," he wrote to me one day, "to discover who were the prime movers of revolutions; and, after thirty years' meditation, I have come to the conclusion that my earliest opinion was right, and that they are caused by the men against whom they are directed."

Never shall I forget my feelings in travelling from Niemen to Tilsit: it was more especially then that I did justice to the observation of my host at Lübeck. A bird escaped from its cage could not have been more joyous. I can speak, I can write all that I think: I am free! were my exulting exclamations. The first real letter that I despatched to Paris was sent from this frontier: it would cause quite a sensation in the little circle of my friends, who, until they received it, had, no doubt, been the dupes of my official correspondence. The following is the copy of that letter:

"Tilsit, Thursday, 26th September, 1839.

"You will, I hope, have as much pleasure in reading the above date as I have in writing it: here I am beyond the empire of uniformity, minutia, and difficulties. I hear the language of freedom, and I feel as if in a vortex of pleasure, a world carried away by new ideas towards inordinate liberty. And yet I am only in Prussia: but in leaving Russia I have again found houses, the plan of which has not been dictated to a slave by an inflexible master, but which are freely built: I see a lively country freely cultivated (it is of Prussia I am speaking), and the change warms and gladdens my heart.

"In short, I breathe! I can write to you without carefully guarding my words for fear of the police—a precaution almost always insufficient; for there is as much of the susceptibility of self-love as of political prudence in the espionnage of the Russians. Russia is the most gloomy country, and is inhabited by the most handsome men that I have ever beheld: a country in which women are scarcely seen, cannot be gay. Here I am, escaped from it, and without the smallest accident. I have travelled two hundred and fifty leagues in four days, by roads often wretched, often magnificent; for the Russian spirit, friend as it is to uniformity, cannot attain a real state of order: the characteristics of its administration are meddlesomeness, negligence, and corruption. A sincere man in the Empire of the Czar would pass for a fool.

"I have now a journey of two hundred leagues to perform before I reach Berlin; but I look forward to it as a mere excursion of pleasure."

❖ ❖ ❖

Good roads throughout the distance, good inns, beds on which one may lie down, the order of houses managed by women—all seemed delightful and novel. I was particularly struck with the varied architecture of the buildings, the air of freedom in the peasants, and the gaiety of the female sex among them. Their good humour inspired me with a kind of fear: it was an independence, the consequences of which I dreaded for them, for I had myself almost lost the memory of it. I saw towns built spontaneously, before any government had imagined a plan of them. Ducal Prussia does not assuredly pass for a land of licence; and yet, in passing through the streets of Tilsit, and afterwards those of Königsberg, I could have fancied myself at a Venetian carnival. My feelings brought to my memory a German of my acquaintance, who, after having been obliged, by business, to pass whole years in Russia, was at last able to leave that country for ever. He was accompanied by a friend; and had scarcely set foot on the deck of the English vessel, which was about to weigh anchor, when he threw himself into his companion's arms, exclaiming, "God be praised, we may now breathe freely and speak openly!"

Many people have, doubtless, felt the same sensation: but why has no traveller before recorded it? Here, without comprehending, I marvel at the *prestige* which the Russian government exercises over minds. It obtains silence, not only from its own subjects—that were little,—but it makes itself respected, even at a distance, by strangers escaped from its iron discipline. The traveller either praises it or is silent: this is a mystery which I cannot comprehend. If ever the publication of this journey should procure me an explanation of the marvel, I shall have additional reason to applaud myself for my sincerity.

I had purposed returning from Petersburg into Germany, by way of Wilna and Warsaw; but I changed that project.

Miseries like those which Poland suffers cannot be attributed entirely to fatality: in prolonged misfortunes, we may always look to faults as well as to circumstances. To a certain point, nations, like individuals, become accomplices in the fate which pursues them; they appear accountable for the reverses which, blow after blow, they have to suffer: for, to attentive eyes, destinies are only the development of characters. On perceiving the result of the errors of a people punished with so much severity, I might not be able to abstain from reflections of which I should repent. To represent their case to the oppressors would be a task we should impose upon ourselves with a kind of joy, sustained, as we should feel, by the idea of courage and generosity which attaches to the accomplishment of a perilous, or, at least, painful duty: but to wound the heart of the victim, to overwhelm the oppressed, though even with deserved strokes, with just reproaches, is an executioner's office, to which the author who does not despise his own pen will never abase himself.

This was my reason for renouncing my proposed journey through Poland.

❖

RETURN TO EMS ❖ AUTUMN IN THE VICINITY OF THE RHINE ❖ COMPARISON BETWEEN RUSSIAN AND GERMAN SCENERY ❖ THE YOUTH OF THE SOUL ❖ DEFINITION OF MISANTHROPY ❖ MISTAKE OF THE TRAVELLER REGARDING RUSSIA ❖ RÉSUMÉ OF THE JOURNEY ❖ A LAST PORTRAIT OF RUSSIA AND THE RUSSIANS ❖ SECRET OF THEIR POLICY ❖ A GLANCE AT THE CHRISTIAN CHURCHES ❖ THE TASK OF THE AUTHOR ❖ DANGER OF SPEAKING OF THE GREEK RELIGION IN RUSSIA ❖
PARALLEL BETWEEN SPAIN
AND RUSSIA
❖

CHAPTER XXXVII*

❖

I left Ems for Russia five months ago, and return to this elegant village after having made a tour of some thousand leagues. My stay here during the previous spring was disagreeable to me by reason of the crowd of bathers and drinkers: I find it delicious now that I am literally alone, with nothing to do but to enjoy a beautiful autumn sky in the midst of mountains, the solitude of which I admire; and to review my recollections, while I at the same time seek the repose I need after the rapid journey just completed.

With what a contrast am I presented! In Russia, I was deprived of all the scenes of nature; for I cannot give the name of nature to solitudes without one picturesque object,—to seas, lakes, and rivers, whose banks are on a level with the water; to marshes without bounds, and steppes without vegetation, under a sky without light. Those plains are not, indeed, devoid of a kind of beauty; but grandeur without grace soon fatigues. What pleasure can the traveller have in traversing immense spaces, whose surface and whose horizon are always destitute of feature? Such monotony aggravates the fatigue of locomotion, by rendering it fruitless. Surprises must always constitute a great portion of the enjoyment of travelling; and the hope of them must always furnish much of the stimulus that keeps alive the zeal of the traveller.

* Written at Ems, October, 1839.

It is with sensations of real happiness that I find myself at the close of the season in a varied and beautiful country. I cannot express the delight with which I stray, and for a moment lose myself among large woods, where showers of leaves have strewed the earth and obliterated the paths. I am carried back to the descriptions of René; and my heart beats as it beat formerly while reading that sorrowful and sublime conversation between nature and a human soul. That religious and lyrical prose has lost none of its power over me; and I have said to myself, astonished at my own easily-affected feelings, youth will surely never end! Sometimes I perceive through the foliage, brightened by the first hoar-frost, the vapoury distances of the valley of the Lahn, contiguous to the most beautiful river in Europe; and I greatly admire the grace and calm of the landscape.

The points of view formed by the ravines, which serve as channels for the tributaries of the Rhine, are infinitely varied; those of the Volga all resemble each other. The aspect of the elevated plains that are here called mountains, because they separate deep valleys, is in general cold and monotonous; still this cold and monotony is light, life, and motion, after the marshes of Muscovy: the bright rays of the sun spread a southern gladness over the whole face of the northern landscape; in which the dryness of the contour and the stiffness of the broken lines are lost amid the mists of autumn.

The repose of the woods during the autumn season is very striking: it contrasts with the activity of the fields, among which man, warned by the calm forerunner of winter, hastens to complete his labours.

This instructive and solemn spectacle, which is to last as long as the world endures, interests me as much as though I had seen it for the first time, or knew that I was never to see it again: the intellectual life is nothing but a succession of discoveries. The soul, when it has not expended its vigour in the too habitual affectations of people of the world, preserves an inexhaustible faculty of surprise and curiosity; new powers are ever exciting it to new efforts; this world no longer suffices for it; it summons and it apprehends the infinite: its ideas ripen, yet they do not proceed to decay; and this it is which intimates to us that there is something beyond the things which are seen.

It is the intensity of our life which forms its variety; what is strongly felt always appears new: language partakes of this eternal freshness of impressions; each new affection imparts its special harmony to the words destined to express it: and thus it is that the colouring of style is the most certain test of the novelty —I might say, the sincerity of sentiments. When ideas are borrowed, their source is carefully concealed; but the harmony of the language never deceives,—sure proof of the sensibility of the soul. An involuntary revelation—it bursts directly from the heart, and speaks directly to the hearts of others: art can but imperfectly supply it; it is born of emotion: in short, this music of speech reaches beyond the ideas that it conveys; it embodies also the indefinable, involuntary extension of those ideas. Herein lies the reason of Madame Sand's having so quickly obtained among us the reputation which she deserves.

Sacred love of solitude, thou art no less than a real necessary of mental life! The world is so false, that a mind imbued with a passionate love of truth must needs be disposed to shun society. Misanthropy is a calumniated sentiment; it is a hatred of lies. There are no misanthropes; but there are souls which would rather fly than feign.

Alone with God, and man becomes humble under the influence of internal sincerity; in his retreat he expiates, by silence and meditation, all the successful frauds of worldly spirits, their triumphant duplicities, their vanities, their hidden and too often rewarded treacheries: incapable of being duped, unwilling to dupe, he becomes a voluntary victim, and conceals himself with as much care as the courtiers of fashion take to display themselves. Such is undoubtedly the secret of the life of saints,—a secret easily penetrated, but a life difficult to imitate. Were I a saint I should no longer feel curiosity in travelling, nor yet a desire to relate my travels. I am seeking: the saints have found.

While thus seeking, I have surveyed the Russian empire. I wished to see a country where reigns the calm of a power assured of its own strength: but arrived there, I found only the reign of silence maintained by fear; and I have drawn from the spectacle a lesson very different from the one which I came to seek. Russia is a world scarcely known to foreigners: the Russians who travel to escape it, pay, when at a distance, in crafty encomiums, their tribute to their country; and the greater number of travellers who have described it to us have been unwilling to discover in it any thing but that which they went to find. If people will defend their prejudices against evidence, where is the good of travelling? When thus determined to view nations as they wish to view them, there is no longer a necessity for leaving their own country.

❖   ❖   ❖

The following is the *résumé* of my journey, written since my return to Ems.

In Russia, all that strikes the eye, everything that passes around, bears the impress of a regularity that is startling; and the first thought that enters the mind of the traveller, when he contemplates this symmetrical system, is that a uniformity so complete, a regularity so contrary to the natural inclinations of men, cannot have been established, and cannot be maintained except by violence. Imagination vainly implores a little variety, like a bird uselessly beating its wings against a cage. Under such a system, a man may know the first day of his life all that he will see and do until the last. This hard tyranny is called, in official language, respect for unity, love of order; and it is a fruit of despotism so precious to methodical minds, that they think they cannot pay too dear for it.

In France, I had imagined myself in accord with these rigorous disciplinarians; but since I have lived under a despotism which imposes military rule upon the population of an entire empire, I admit that I prefer a little of the disorder which announces vigour to the perfect order which destroys life.

In Russia, the government interferes with every thing and vivifies nothing. In that immense empire, the people, if not tranquil, are mute; death hovers over all heads, and strikes capriciously whom it pleases: man there has two coffins, the cradle and the tomb. The Russian mothers ought to weep the birth more than the death of their children.

I do not believe that suicide is common there: the people suffer too much to kill themselves. Singular disposition of man!—when terror presides over his life, he does not seek death; he knows what it is already.*

But if the number of suicides in Russia were ever so great, no one would know it; the knowledge of numbers is a privilege of the Russian police: I am ignorant whether they arrive correct before the eyes of the Emperor; but I do know that no misfortune is published under his reign until he has consented to the humiliating confession of the superiority of Providence. The pride of despotism is so great that it seeks to rival the power of God. Monstrous jealousy! into what aberrations hast thou not plunged princes and subjects! Who will dare to love truth, who will defend it in a country where idolatry is the principle of the constitution? A man who can do every thing is the crowned impersonification of a lie.

It will be understood that I am not now speaking of the Emperor Nicholas, but of the Emperor of Russia. We often hear mention made of customs which limit his power: I have been struck with its abuse, but have seen no remedy.

In the eyes of real statesmen, and of all practical minds, the laws are, I admit, less important than our precise logicians and political philosophers believe them; for it is the manner in which they are applied that decides the life of the people. True; but the life of the Russian people is more gloomy than that of any other of the European nations; and when I say the people, I speak not only of the peasants attached to the soil, but of the whole empire.

A government that makes profession of being vigorous, and that causes itself to be dreaded on every occasion, must inevitably render men miserable. Wherever the public machine is rigor-

---

* Dickens says—speaking of the solitary prison of Philadelphia—"Suicides are rare among the prisoners; are almost, indeed, unknown. But no argument in favour of the system can reasonably be deduced from this circumstance, although it is very often urged. All men who have made diseases of the mind their study, know perfectly well that such extreme depression and despair, as to change the whole character, and beat down all its powers of elasticity and self-resistance, may be at work within a man, and yet stop short of self-destruction."—*American Notes for General Circulation.*

The great writer, the profound moralist, the Christian philosopher from whom I borrow these lines, has not only the authority of talent, and of a style which engraves his thoughts on brass, but his opinion on this subject is law.

ously exact, there is despotism, whatever be the fiction, monarchical or democratical, which covers it. The best government is that which makes itself the least felt; but such lightness of the yoke is only procured by the labours of genius and superior wisdom, or by a certain relaxation of social discipline. Governments, which were beneficent in the youth of nations, when men, still half savages, honoured every thing that snatched them from a state of disorder, become so again in the old age of communities. At that epoch is seen the birth of mixed institutions. But these institutions, founded on a compact between experience and passion, can suit none but already wearied populations, societies the springs of which are weakened by revolutions. From this it may be concluded, that if they are not the most powerful of political systems, they are the most gentle: the people who have once obtained them cannot too carefully strive to prolong their duration: it is that of a green old age. The old age of states, like that of men, is the most peaceable period of existence when it crowns a glorious life; but the middle age of a nation is always a time of trial and violence: Russia is passing through it.

In this country, which differs from all others, nature itself has become an accomplice in the caprices of the man who has slain liberty to deify unity; it, too, is everywhere the same: two kinds of scattered and stunted trees, the birch and the pine, spread over plains always either sandy or marshy, are the only features on the face of nature throughout that immense expanse of country which constitutes Northern Russia.

What refuge is there against the evils of society in a climate under which men cannot enjoy the country, such as it is, for more than three months of the year? Add to this, that during the six most inclement of the winter months, they dare not breathe the free air more than two hours in the day. Such is the lot that heaven has assigned to man in these regions.

Let us see what man has done for himself: St. Petersburg is unquestionably one of the wonders of the world; Moscow is also a very picturesque city; but what can be said of the aspect of the provinces?

The excess of uniformity engendered by the abuse of unity will be seen described in my chapters. The absence of soul betrays itself in every thing: each step that you take proves to you that you are among a people deprived of independence. At every twenty or thirty leagues the same town greets your eyes.

The passion of both princes and people for classic architecture, for straight lines, buildings of low elevation, and wide streets, is a contradiction of the laws of nature and the wants of life in a cold, misty country, frequently exposed to storms of wind which case the visage in ice. Throughout my journey, I was constantly but vainly endeavouring to account for this mania among the inhabitants of a country so different from those lands whence the architecture has been borrowed: the Russians cannot probably explain it any better than I, for they are no more masters of their tastes than of their actions. The fine arts, as they call them, have been imposed on the people, just as is the military exercise. The regiment, and its spirit of minutia, is the mould of Russian society.

Lofty ramparts, high and crowded edifices, the winding streets of the cities of the middle ages, would have suited better than caricatures of the antique, the climate, and the customs of Muscovy; but the country the wants and genius of which are least consulted by the Russians, is the country they govern.

When Peter the Great published from Tartary to Lapland his edicts of civilisation, the creations of the middle ages had long been out of date in Europe; and the Russians, even those that have been called *great,* have never known how to do more than follow the fashion.

Such disposition to imitate scarcely accords with the ambition which we attribute to them; for man does not rule the things that he copies; but every thing is contradictory in the character of this superficial people: besides, a want of invention is their peculiar characteristic. To invent, there must be independence; with them, mimicry may be seen pervading their very passions: if they wish to take their turn on the scene of the world, it is not to employ faculties which they possess, and the inaction of which torments them; it is simply to act over the history of illustrious communities: they have no creative power; comparison is their talent, imitation is their genius: naturally given to observation, they are not themselves except when aping the creations of others. Such originality as they have, lies in the gift of counterfeit, which they possess more amply than any other people. Their only primitive faculty is an aptitude to re-produce the inventions of foreigners. They would be in history, what they are in literature, able translators. The task of the Russians is to translate European civilisation to the Asiatics.

The talent of imitation may become useful and even admirable in nations, provided it late develops itself; but it destroys all the other talents when it precedes them. Russia is a community of copyists: now, every man who can do nothing else but copy necessarily falls into caricature.

Hesitating for the space of four centuries between Europe and Asia, Russia has not yet succeeded in distinguishing itself by its works in the field of human intellect, because its national characteristics are lost under its borrowed decorations.

Separated from the West by its adherence to the Greek schism, it returns, after many centuries, with the inconsistency of a blind self-love, to demand from nations formed by Catholicism the civilisation of which a religion entirely political has deprived it. This Byzantine religion, which has issued from a palace to maintain order in a camp, does not respond to the most sublime wants of the human soul; it helps the police to deceive the nation, but that is the extent of its power.

It has, in advance, rendered the people unworthy of the culture to which they aspire.

The independence of the church is necessary to the motion of the religious sap; for the development of the noblest faculty of a people, the faculty of believing, depends on the dignity of the man charged with communicating to men the divine revelations. The humiliation of the ministers of religion is the first punishment of heresy; and thus it is that in all schismatic countries the priest is despised by the people, in spite of, or rather because of the protection of the prince. People who understand their liberty will never obey, from the bottom of their hearts, a dependent clergy.

The time is not far distant when it will be acknowledged that, in matters of religion, what is more essential even than obtaining the liberty of the flock, is the assuring that of the pastor.

The multitude always obey the men whom they take for guides: be they priests, doctors, poets, sages, or tyrants, the minds of the people are in their hands; religious liberty for the mass is therefore a chimera; but it is on this account the more important that the man charged with performing the office of priest for them should be free: now, there is not in the world an independent priest except the Catholic.

Slavish pastors can only guide barren minds: a Greek pope will never do more than instruct a people to prostrate themselves before violent power. Let me not be asked, then, whence it comes that the Russians have no imagination, and how it is that they only copy imperfectly.

When, in the West, the descendants of the barbarians studied the ancients with a veneration that partook of idolatry, they modified them in order to appropriate them. Who can recognise Virgil in Dante, or Homer in Tasso, or Justinian and the Roman laws in the codes of feudalism? The passionate respect then professed for the past, far from stifling genius, aroused it: but it is not thus that the Russians have availed themselves of us.

When a people counterfeit the social forms of another community, without penetrating into the spirit which animates it—when they seek lessons in civilisation, not from the ancient founders of human institutions, but from strangers whose riches they envy without respecting their character—when their imitation is hostile, and yet falls into puerile precision—when they borrow from a neighbour whom they affect to disdain, even the very modes of dress and of domestic life, they become a mere echo, a reflection; they exist no longer for themselves.

The society of the middle ages could adore antiquity without being in danger of parodying it; because creative power, when it exists, is never lost, whatever use man may put it to. What a store of imagination is displayed in the erudition of the fifteenth century!

A respect for models is the seal of a creative genius.

Thus it was that the studies of the classics in the West, at the epoch of their revival, scarcely influenced any thing beyond the *belles lettres* and the fine arts: the development of industry, of commerce, of the natural and the exact sciences, is solely the work of modern Europe, which has drawn nearly all the materials of these things out of her own resources. The superstitious admiration which she long professed for pagan literature has not prevented her politics, her religion, her philosophy, her forms of government, her modes of war, her ideas of honour, her manners, her spirit, her social habits from being her own.

Russia alone, more recently civilised, has been deprived by the impatience of her chiefs of an essential fermenting process, and of the benefits of a slow and natural culture.

The internal labour which forms a great people, and renders them fit to rule, has been wanting. The nation will for ever feel the effects of this absence of a proper life that marked the epoch of their political awakening. Adolescence, that laborious age in which the spirit of man assumes all the responsibility of its independence, was lost to them. Their princes, especially Peter the Great, paying no respect to time, suddenly and forcibly made them pass from a state of infancy to a state of virility. Scarcely yet escaped from a foreign yoke, every thing that was not Mongol seemed to them liberty; and it was thus that, in the joy of their inexperience, they accepted servitude itself as a deliverance, because imposed upon them by their legitimate sovereigns. The people, already debased by slavery, were sufficiently happy, sufficiently independent, if only their tyrant bore a Russian instead of a Tartar name.

The effect of such an illusion still remains: originality of thought has shunned this soil, of which the children, broken in to slavery, have only seriously imbibed, even at the present day, two sentiments, terror and ambition. What is fashion for them, except an elegant chain worn only in public? Russian politeness, however well acted it may be, is more ceremonious than natural; for urbanity is a flower that can blossom only on the summit of the social tree: this plant will not graft; it must strike its own roots, and its stalk, like that of the aloe, is centuries in shooting up. Many generations of semi-barbarians have to die in a land before the upper stratum of the social earth gives birth to men really polite. Many ages, teeming with memories and associations, are essential to the education of a civilised people: the mind of a child born of polished parents can alone ripen fast enough to understand all the reality that there is in politeness. It is a secret exchange of voluntary sacrifices. Nothing is more delicate, or, it might be said, more truly moral, than the principles which constitute perfect elegance of manners. Such politeness, to resist the trial of the passions, cannot be altogether distinct from that elevation of sentiment which no man acquires by himself alone, for it is more especially upon the soul that the influences of early education operate; in a word, true urbanity is a heritage. Whatever little value the present age may place on time, nature, in its works, places a great deal. Formerly a certain refinement of taste characterised the Russians of the South; and, owing to the relations kept up during the most barbarous ages with Constantinople by the sovereigns of Kiew, a love of the arts reigned in that part of the Slavonian empire; at the same time that the traditions of the East maintained there a sentiment of the great, and perpetuated a certain dexterity among the artists and workmen; but these advantages, fruits of ancient relations with a people advanced in a civilisation inherited from antiquity, were lost during the invasion of the Mongols.

That crisis forced primitive Russia to forget its history. Slavery debases in a manner that excludes true politeness, which is incompatible with any thing servile, for it is the expression of the most elevated and delicate sentiments. It is only when politeness becomes, so to speak, a current coin among an entire people, that such a people can be said to be civilised; the primitive rudeness, the brutal personality of human nature, are then attacked from the cradle by the lessons which each individual receives in his family: the child of man is not humane; and if he is not at the commencement of life turned from his cruel inclinations, he will never be really polite. Politeness is only the code of pity applied to the every-day affairs of society; this code more especially inculcates pity for the sufferings of self-love: it is also the most universal, the most appropriate, and the most practical remedy that has been hitherto found against egotism.

Whatever pretensions may be made, all these refinements, natural results of the work of time, are unknown to the present Russians, who seem to remember Saraï much better than Constantinople, and who, with a few exceptions, are still nothing better than well-dressed barbarians. They remind me of portraits badly painted, but very finely varnished.

It was Peter the Great, who, with all the imprudence of an untaught genius, all the temerity of a man the more impatient because deemed omnipotent, with all the perseverance of an iron character, sought to snatch from Europe the plants of an already ripened civilisation, instead of resigning himself to the slow progress of sowing the seeds in his own soil. That too highly lauded man produced a merely artificial work: it may be astonishing, but the good done by his barbarous genius was transient, the evil is irreparable.

How does a power to influence the politics of Europe benefit Russia? Factitious interests! vain, foolish passions! Its real interests are to have within itself the principles of life, and to develop them: a nation which possesses nothing within itself but obedience does not live. The nation of which I speak has been posted at the window; it looks out—it listens—it feels like a man witnessing some exhibition. When will this game cease?

Russia ought not only to stop, but to begin anew: is such an effort possible? can so vast an edifice be taken to pieces and reconstructed? The too recent civilisation of the empire, entirely artificial as it is, has already produced real results—results which no human power can annul: it appears to me impossible to controul the future of a people without considering the present. But the present, when it has been violently separated from the past, bodes only evil: to avert that evil from Russia, by obliging it to take into account its ancient history, which was the result only of its primitive character, will be henceforward the ungrateful task, more useful than brilliant, of the men called to govern this land.

The altogether national and highly practical genius of the Emperor Nicholas has perceived the problem: can he resolve it? I do not think so; he does not let enough be done—he trusts too much to himself and too little to others to succeed; for in Russia, the most absolute will is not powerful enough to accomplish good.

It is not against a tyrant, but against tyranny, that the friends of man have here to struggle. There would be injustice in accusing the emperor of the miseries of the empire and the vices of the government: the powers of a man are not equal to the task imposed upon the sovereign who would suddenly seek to reign by humanity over an inhuman people.

He only who has been in Russia, who has seen close at hand how things are there conducted, can understand how little the man can do, who is reputed capable of doing every thing; and how more especially his power is limited, when it is good that he would accomplish.

The unhappy consequences of the work of Peter I. have been still further aggravated under the great, or rather the long reign of a woman who only governed her people to amuse herself and to astonish Europe—Europe, always Europe!—never Russia!

Peter I. and Catherine II. have given to the world a great and useful lesson, for which Russia has had to pay: they have shown to us that despotism is never so much to be dreaded as when it pretends to do good, for then it thinks the most revolting acts may be excused by the intention; and the evil that is applied as a remedy has no longer any bounds. Crime exposed to view can triumph only for a day; but false virtues for ever lead astray the minds of nations. People, dazzled by the brilliant accessories of crime, by the greatness of certain delinquencies justified by the event, believe at last that there are two kinds of villainy, two classes of morals, and that necessity, or reasons of state, as they were formerly called, exculpate criminals of high lineage, provided they have so managed that their excesses should be in accord with the passions of the country.

Avowed, open tyranny would little terrify me after having seen oppression disguised as love of order. The strength of despotism lies in the mask of the despot. When the sovereign can no longer lie, the people are free; thus I see no other evil in this world except that of falsehood. If you dread only violent and avowed arbitrary power, go to Russia; there you will learn to fear above all things the tyranny of hypocrisy. I cannot deny it; I bring back with me from my journey ideas which I did not own when I undertook it. I therefore would not have been spared for any thing in the world the trouble which it has cost me: if I print the relation of it, I do so precisely because it has modified my opinions upon several points. They are known by all who have read me; my disappointment is not: it is a duty to publish it.

❖ 603 ❖

On setting out, I did not intend writing this my last journey: my method is fatiguing, because it consists in reviewing for my friends, during the night, the recollections of the day. Whilst occupied with this labour, which bears the character of confidential communications, the public appeared to my thoughts in only a dim and vapoury distance—so vapoury that I scarcely yet realise its presence; and this will account for the familiar tone of an intimate correspondence being preserved in my printed letters.

I pleased myself with thinking that I should this time be able to travel for myself alone, which would have been a means of observing with tranquillity; but the ideas with which I found the Russians prepossessed with regard to me, from the greatest personages down to the smallest private individuals, gave me to see the measure of my importance, at least of that which I could acquire in Petersburg. "What do you think, or rather, what shall you say of us?" This was at the bottom of every conversation held with me. They drew me from my inaction: I was playing a modest part through apathy, or perhaps cowardice; for Paris renders those humble whom it does not render excessively presumptuous; but the restless self-love of the Russians restored to me my own.

I was sustained in my new resolution by a continual and visible dispersion of illusion. Assuredly the cause of the disappointment must have been strong and active to have allowed disgust to take possession of me in the midst of the most brilliant fêtes that I have ever seen in my life, and in spite of the dazzling hospitality of the Russians. But I recognised at the first glance, that in the demonstrations of interest which they lavish upon us, there is more of the desire to appear engaging, than of true cordiality. Cordiality is unknown to the Russians: it is one of those things which they have not borrowed from their German neighbours. They occupy your every moment; they distract your thoughts; they engross your attention; they tyrannise over you by means of officious politeness; they inquire how you pass your days; they question you with an importunity known only to themselves, and by fête after fête they prevent you seeing their country. They have even coined a French word [*enguirlander* les étrangers] by which to express these falsely polite tactics. Unhappily they have chanced to fall upon a man whom fêtes have always more fatigued than diverted. But when they perceive that their direct attempts upon the mind of a stranger fail, they have recourse to indirect means to discredit his statements among enlightened readers: they can lead him astray with marvellous dexterity. Thus, still to prevent him from seeing things under their true colour, they will falsely depreciate when they can no longer reckon upon his benevolent credulity to permit them falsely to extol. Often have I, in the same conversation, surprised the same person changing his tactics two or three times towards me. I do not always flatter myself with having discerned the truth, but I have discerned that it was concealed from me, and it is always something to know that we are deceived; if not enlightened, we are then at least armed.

All courts are deficient in life and gaiety; but at that of Petersburg one has not even the permission to be weary. The emperor, whose eye is on every thing, takes the affectation of enjoyment as a homage, which reminds me of the observation of M. de Talleyrand upon Napoleon: "L'Empereur ne plaisante pas; il veut qu'on s'amuse."

I shall wound self-love: my incorruptible honesty will draw upon me reproaches; but is it my fault if, in applying to an absolute government for new arguments against the despot that reigns at home, against disorder baptized with the name of liberty, I have been struck only with the abuses of autocracy, in other words, of tyranny designated good order? Russian despotism is a false order, as our republicanism is a false liberty. I make war with falsehood wherever I discover it; but there is more than one kind of lie: I had forgotten those of absolute power; I now recount them in detail, because in relating my travels I describe without reserve all that I see.

I hate pretexts: I have seen that in Russia, order serves as a pretext for oppression, as in France, liberty does for envy. In a word, I love real liberty—all liberty that is possible in a society from whence elegance is not excluded; I am therefore neither demagogue nor despot; I am an aristocrat in the broadest acceptation of the word. The elegance that I wish to preserve in communities is not frivolous, nor yet unfeeling; it is regulated by taste; taste excludes all abuses; it is the surest preservative against them, for it dreads every kind of exaggeration. A certain elegance is essential to the arts, and the arts save the world; for it is through their agency more than any other that people attach themselves to civilisation, of which they are the last and the most precious recompense. By a privilege which belongs to them alone among the various objects that can shed a halo upon a nation, their glory pleases and profits all classes of society equally.

Aristocracy, as I understand it, far from allying itself with tyranny in favour of order, as the demagogues who misunderstand it pretend, cannot exist under an arbitrary government. Its mission is to defend, on one side, the people against the despot, and on the other, civilisation against that most terrible of all tyrants, revolution. Barbarism takes more than one form: crush it in despotism and it springs to life again in anarchy; but true liberty, guarded by a true aristocracy, is neither violent nor inordinate.

Unfortunately, the partisans of a moderating aristocracy in Europe are now blinded, and lend their arms to their adversaries: in their false prudence they seek for aid among the enemies of all political and religious liberty, as though danger could only come from the side of the new revolutionaries; they forget that arbitrary sovereigns were anciently as much usurpers as are the modern jacobins.

Feudal aristocracy has come to an end in all, except in the indelible glory which will for ever shine around great historical names; but in communities which wish to endure, the noblesse of the middle ages will be replaced, as they long have been among the English, by a hereditary magistracy: this new aristocracy, heir of the old, and composed of many different elements, for office, birth and riches all form its bases, will not regain its credit until it supports itself upon a free religion; and I again repeat, the only free religion, the only one that does not depend on a temporal power, is that taught by the Catholic church: for as to the temporal power of the pope himself, it is now only calculated to defend his sacerdotal independence. Aristocracy is the government of independent minds, and it cannot be too often reiterated. Catholicism is the faith of free priests.

Whenever I think I perceive a truth, I utter it without reference to the consequences, for I am persuaded that evil is not caused by published truths, but by truths that are disguised. Under this persuasion, I have always regarded as pernicious that proverb of our fathers, which says that a truth must not be always spoken.

It is because each one picks and chooses in truth only such parts as serve his passions, his fears, or his interest, that it can be rendered more mischievous than error. When I travel, I do not make selections among the facts which I gather, I do not reject those which oppose my favourite opinions. When I relate, I have no other religion than that of a worship of truth; I do not permit myself to be a judge, I am not even a painter, for painters compose; I endeavour to become a mirror; in short, I wish to be, above all things, impartial; and for this object the intention suffices, at least in the eyes of intelligent readers, and I cannot and will not recollect that there are others: such discovery would render the labours of the author too fastidious.

Every time that I have had occasion to communicate with men, the first thought with which their manner has inspired me has been that they possess more ability than I, that they know better how to speak, act, and defend themselves. Such have been, up to this day, the results of my experience in the world; I do not therefore despise any one, and, least of all, my readers. This is the reason that I never flatter them.

If there are men towards whom I find it difficult to be equitable, they are those who weary me; but I scarcely know any such, for I always fly from the indolent.

I have said that there is only one town in Russia: there is also only one drawing-room in Petersburg: every where is to be seen either the court or fractions of the court. You may change the house, but you cannot change the circle; and in that invariable circle all subject of interesting conversation is interdicted; but here I find that there is a compensation, thanks to the sharpened wit of the women, who understand wonderfully well how to inspire thoughts without uttering the words that express them.

Women are in every land the least servile of slaves, because, using so skilfully their weakness as to form for themselves a power out of it, they know better than we do how to evade bad laws; it is they, consequently, who are destined to save individual liberty wherever public liberty is wanting.

What is liberty if it be not the guarantee of the rights of the weakest, whom woman is by nature charged with representing in social life? In France they now pride themselves on every thing being decided by the majority: . . . admirable marvel! When I shall see that some regard is shown to the claims of the minority, I too shall cry *Vive la liberté!* It must be owned that the weakest now, were the strongest formerly, and that then they only too often set the example of the abuse of superior force that I complain of. But one error does not excuse another.

Notwithstanding the secret influence of the women, Russia still remains farther from liberty, not in words, but in things, than most of the countries upon earth. To-morrow, in an insurrection, in the midst of massacre, by the light of a conflagration, the cry of freedom may spread to the frontiers of Siberia; a blind and cruel people may murder their masters, may revolt against obscure tyrants, and dye the waters of the Volga with blood; but they will not be any the more free: barbarism is in itself a yoke.

The best means of emancipating men is not pompously to proclaim their enfranchisement, but to render servitude impossible by developing the sentiment of humanity in the heart of nations: that sentiment is deficient in Russia. To talk liberalism to the Russians, of whatever class they may be, would now be a crime; to preach humanity to all classes without exception is a duty.

The Russian nation has not yet imbibed the sentiment of justice; thus, one day it was mentioned to me in praise of the Emperor Nicholas, that an obscure private individual had gained a cause against some powerful nobleman. In this instance, the encomium on the sovereign appeared to me as a satire upon the community. The too-highly boasted fact proved to me positively that equity is only an exception in Russia.

Every thing duly considered, I would by no means advise obscure men to act in reliance upon the success of the person thus instanced, who was favoured perhaps to assure impunity to the usual course of injustice, and to furnish a specimen of equity which the dispensers of the law were in need of, to serve as a reply to reproaches of servility and corruption.

Another fact, which suggests an inference little favourable to the Russian judiciary, is, that there should be so little litigation in the country. The reason is not obscure; people would more often have recourse to justice if the judges were more equitable. A similar reason accounts for there being no fighting or quarrelling in the streets. A dread of chains and dungeons is the consideration which usually restrains the two parties.

Notwithstanding the melancholy pictures that I draw, two inanimate objects, and one living person, are worth the trouble of the journey. The Neva of Petersburg during the nightless season, the Kremlin of Moscow by moonlight, and the Emperor of Russia: these include picturesque, historical, and political Russia; beyond them, every thing is fatiguing and wearisome to a degree that may be judged of by the preceding chapters.

Many of my friends have already written to advise me not to publish them.

As I was preparing to leave Petersburg, a Russian asked me, as all the Russians do, what I should say of his country. "I have been too well received there to talk about it,"* was my reply.

This avowal, in which I thought I had scarcely politely concealed an epigram, is brought up against me. "Treated as you have been," I am told, "you cannot possibly tell the truth; and as you cannot write except to do so, you had better remain silent." Such is the opinion of a party among those to whom I am accustomed to listen. At any rate, it is not flattering to the Russians.

My opinion is, that without wounding the delicacy, without failing in the gratitude due to individuals, nor yet in the respect due to self, there is always a proper manner of speaking with sincerity of public men and things, and I hope to have discovered this manner. It is pretended that truth only shocks, but in France, at least, no one has the right or the power to close the mouth of him who speaks it. My exclamations of indignation cannot be taken for the disguised expression of wounded vanity. If I had listened only to my self-love it would have told me to be

---

* "J'y ai été trop bien reçu pour en parler."

enchanted with every thing: my heart has been enchanted with nothing.

If every thing related of the Russians and their country turn into personalities, so much the worse for them: this is an inevitable evil, for things do not exist in Russia, since it is the whim of a man who makes and unmakes them; but that is not the fault of travellers.

The emperor appears to me little disposed to lay down a part of his authority. Let him suffer, then, the responsibility of omnipotence: it is the first expiation of the political lie by which a single individual declares himself absolute master of a country and all powerful sovereign of the thoughts of a people.

Forbearance in practice does not excuse the impiety of such a doctrine. I have found among the Russians that the principles of absolute monarchy, applied with inflexible consistency, lead to results that are monstrous; and, this time, my political quietism cannot withhold me from perceiving and proclaiming that there are governments to which people ought never to submit.

The Emperor Alexander, talking confidentially with Madame de Staël about the ameliorations which he projected, said to her, "You praise my philanthropical intentions—I am obliged to you; nevertheless, in the history of Russia, I am only a lucky chance."

That prince spoke the truth: the Russians vainly boast of the prudence and management of the men who direct their affairs; arbitrary power is not the less the fundamental principle of the state; and this principle so works that the emperor makes, or suffers to be made, or allows to exist, laws (excuse the application of this sacred name to impious decrees) which, for example, permit the sovereign to declare that the legitimate children of a man legally married have no father, no name; in short, that they are ciphers and not men.* And am I to be forbidden to accuse at the bar of Europe a prince who, distinguished and superior as he is, consents to reign without abolishing such a law?

His resentment is implacable: with hatred so strong, he may yet be a great sovereign, but he cannot be a great man. The great

---

* See the History of the Princess Troubetzkoï, chap. xxi.

man is merciful, the political character is vindictive: vengeance reigns, pardon converts.

I have now made my last observations upon a prince that one hesitates to judge, after knowing the country where he is condemned to reign; for men are there so dependent upon things, that it is difficult to know how high or how low to look in fixing the responsibility of things done. And the nobles of such a country pretend to resemble the French! The French kings in barbarous times have often cut off the heads of their great vassals; but those princes, when they destroyed their enemies and seized their goods, did not debase by an insulting decree their caste, their family, and their country: such a forgetfulness of all dignity would have rendered the people of France indignant, even in the middle ages. But the people of Russia suffer even worse things than these. I must correct myself—there is no people of Russia: there is an emperor, who has serfs, and there are courtiers who have serfs also; but this does not constitute a people.

The middle class, few in number as compared with the others, is at present almost entirely composed of strangers; a few peasants, enfranchised by their wealth, together with the smallest employés, begin to swell its ranks. The future fate of Russia depends upon this new citizen class, the elements of which are so diverse that it seems scarcely possible they can combine together.

The attempt is now making to create a Russian nation; but the task is difficult for one man. Evil is quickly committed but slowly repaired: the mortifications of despotism must often, I should think, enlighten the despot on the abuses of absolute power. But the embarrassments of the oppressor do not excuse oppression. I can pity them, because evil is always to be pitied; but they inspire me with much less compassion than the sufferings of the oppressed. In Russia, whatever be the appearance of things, violence and arbitrary rule is at the bottom of them all. Tyranny rendered calm by the influence of terror, is the only kind of happiness which this government is able to afford its people.

And when chance has made me a witness of the unspeakable evils endured under a constitution founded on such principles, is the fear of wounding this or that delicate feeling to prevent my describing what I have seen? I should be unworthy of having eyes if I ceded to such pusillanimous partiality, disguised as it has this time been under the name of respect for social propriety, as though my conscience had not the first claim to my respect. What! when I have been allowed to penetrate into a prison, where I have understood the silence of the terrified victims, must I not dare to relate their martyrdom, for fear of being accused of ingratitude, because of the complaisance of the gaolers? Such reserve would be any thing but a virtue. I declare, then, that, after having observed well around me, after endeavouring to see what was attempted to be concealed, to understand what it was not wished I should know, to distinguish between the true and the false in all that was said to me, I do not believe I am exaggerating in affirming, that the empire of Russia is a country whose inhabitants are the most miserable upon earth, because they suffer at one and the same time the evils of barbarism and of civilisation. As regards myself, I should feel that I was a traitor and a coward if, after having already boldly sketched the picture of a great part of Europe, I could hesitate to complete it, for fear either of modifying certain opinions of my own which I once maintained, or of shocking certain parties by a faithful picture of a country which has never been painted as it really is. On what, pray, should I ground a respect for evil things? Am I bound by any other chain than a love of truth?

In general, the Russians have struck me as being men endowed with great tact; extremely quick, but possessing very little sensibility; highly susceptible, but very unfeeling: this I believe to be their real character. As I have already said, a quick-sighted vanity, a sarcastic finesse are dominant traits in their disposition; and I repeat, that it would be pure silliness to spare the self-love of people who are themselves so little merciful: susceptibility is not delicacy. It is time that these men who discern with so much sagacity the vices and the follies of our society, should accustom themselves to bear with our sincerity. The official silence which is maintained among them deceives them: it enervates their intellect: if they wish to be recognised by the European nations, and treated as equals, they must begin by submitting to hear themselves judged. All the nations have had to undergo this kind of process. When did the Germans refuse to receive the English, except on condition that the latter should speak well of Germany? Nations have always good reasons for being what they are, and the best of all is that they cannot be otherwise.

This excuse could not indeed be pleaded by the Russians, at least not by those who read. As they ape every thing, they might be otherwise; and it is just the consciousness of this possibility which renders their government gloomy, even to ferocity! That government knows too well that it can be sure of nothing with characters which are mere reflections.

A more powerful motive might have checked my candour—the fear of being accused of apostasy. "He has long protested," it will be said, "against liberal declamations; here behold him ceding to the torrent, and seeking false popularity after having disdained it."

Perhaps I deceive myself; but the more I reflect, the less I believe that this reproach can reach me, or even that it will be addressed to me.

It is not only in the present day that a fear of being blamed by foreigners has occupied the minds of the Russians. That strange people unite an extremely boasting spirit with an excessive distrust of self; self-sufficiency without, uncomfortable humility within, are traits which I have observed in the greater number of Russians. Their vanity, which never rests, is, like English pride, always suffering. They also lack simplicity. Naïveté, that French word of which no other language can render the exact sense, because the thing it describes is peculiar to ourselves, naïveté, that simplicity which can become pointedly witty, that gift of disposition which can produce laughter without ever wounding the heart, that forgetfulness of oratorical precautions which goes so far as to lend arms against itself to those with whom the individual converses, that fairness of judgment, that altogether involuntary truthfulness of expression, in one word, that Gallic simplicity, is unknown to the Russians. A race of imitators will never be *naïf*; calculation will, with them, always destroy sincerity. . . .

An ambition inordinate and immense, one of those ambitions which could only possibly spring in the bosoms of the oppressed, and could only find nourishment in the miseries of a whole nation, ferments in the heart of the Russian people. That nation, essentially aggressive, greedy under the influence of privation, expiates beforehand, by a debasing submission, the design of exercising a tyranny over other nations: the glory, the riches which it hopes for, consoles it for the disgrace to which it submits. To purify himself from the foul and impious sacrifice of all public and personal liberty, the slave, upon his knees, dreams of the conquest of the world.

It is not the man who is adored in the Emperor Nicholas—it is the ambitious master of a nation more ambitious than himself. The passions of the Russians are shaped in the same mould as those of the people of antiquity: among them every thing reminds us of the Old Testament; their hopes, their tortures, are great like their empire.

There, nothing has any limits,—neither griefs, nor rewards, nor sacrifices, nor hopes: the power of such a people may become enormous, but they will purchase it at the price which the nations of Asia pay for the stability of their governments—the price of happiness.

Russia sees in Europe a prey which our dissensions will sooner or later yield to it: she foments anarchy among us in the hope of profiting by a corruption which she favours because it is favourable to her views: it is the history of Poland recommencing on a larger scale. For many years past Paris has read revolutionary journals paid by Russia. "Europe," they say at Petersburg, "is following the road that Poland took; she is enervating herself by a vain liberalism, whilst we continue powerful precisely because we are not free: let us be patient under the yoke; others shall some day pay for our shame."

The views that I reveal here may appear chimerical to minds engrossed with other matters; their truth will be recognised by every man initiated in the march of European affairs, and in the secrets of cabinets, during the last twenty years. They furnish a key to many a mystery; they explain also, without another word, the extreme importance which thoughtful men, grave both by character and position, attach to the being viewed by strangers only on the favourable side. If the Russians were, as they pretend, the supporters of order and legitimacy, would they make use of men, and, what is worse, of means which are revolutionary? . . .

The distance which separates Russia from the West has wonderfully aided hitherto in veiling all these things from us. If the astute Greek policy so much fears the truth, it is because it so well knows how to profit by falsehood; but what surprises me is that it should succeed in perpetuating the reign of that influence.

Can the reader now understand the importance of an opinion, of a sarcastic word, a letter, a jest, a smile, or, with still greater reason, of a book in the eyes of a government thus favoured by the credulity of its people, and by the complaisance of all foreigners? A word of truth dropped in Russia is a spark that may fall on a barrel of gunpowder.

What do the men who govern the empire care for the want, the pallid visages of the soldiers of the emperor? Those living spectres have the most beautiful uniforms in Europe; what matters, then, the filthy smocks in which the gilded phantoms are concealed in the interior of their barracks? Provided they are only shabby and dirty in secret, and that they shine when they show themselves, nothing is asked from them, nothing is given them. With the Russians, appearance is everything, and among them appearance deceives more than it does among others. It follows, that whoever lifts a corner of the curtain loses his reputation in Petersburg beyond the chance of retrieving it.

Social life in that country is a permanent conspiracy against the truth.

There, whoever is not a dupe, is viewed as a traitor,—there, to laugh at a gasconnade, to refute a falsehood, to contradict a political boast, to find a reason for obedience, is to be guilty of an attempt against the safety of the state and the prince; it is to incur the fate of a revolutionist, a conspirator, an enemy of order, a Pole; and we all know whether this fate is a merciful one. It must be owned the SUSCEPTIBILITY which thus manifests itself is more formidable than laughable; the minute *surveillance* of such a government, in accord with the enlightened vanity of such a people, becomes fearful; it is no longer ludicrous.

People must and ought to employ all manner of precautions under a master who shows mercy to no enemy, who despises no resistance, and who considers vengeance as a duty. This man, or rather this government personified, would view pardon as apostacy, clemency as self-forgetfulness, humanity as a want of respect towards its own majesty, or, I should rather say, its divinity!

Russian civilisation is still so near its source that it resembles barbarism. The Russians are nothing more than a conquering community; their strength does not lie in mind, but in war, that is, in stratagem and ferocity.

Poland, by its last insurrection, has retarded the explosion of the mine; it has forced the batteries to remain masked: Poland will never be pardoned for the dissimulation that she has rendered necessary, not towards herself, for she is immolated with impunity, but towards friends whom it is needful to continue making dupes, while managing their stormy philanthropy. The advance-guard of the new Roman Empire, which will be called the Greek Empire, and the most circumspect at the same time that he is the most blind of the kings of Europe,* to please his neighbour, who is also his master, is commencing a religious war. If he can be thus led astray, it will be easy to seduce others.

If ever the Russians succeed in conquering the West, they will not govern it from their own country, after the manner of the old Mongols; on the contrary, there will be nothing in which they will show such eager haste as to issue from their icy plains: unlike their ancient masters, the Tartars, who tyrannised over the Slavonians from a distance—for the climate of Muscovy frightened even the Mongols—the Muscovites will leave their country the moment the roads of other countries are open to them.

At this moment they talk moderation; they protest against the conquest of Constantinople; they say that they fear every thing that would increase an empire where the distances are already a calamity; they dread—yes! even thus far extends their prudence! —they dread hot climates! . . . Let us wait a little, and we shall see what will become of all these fears.

And am I not to speak of so much falsehood, so many perils, so great an evil? . . . No, no; I would rather have been deceived

* Written of the late King of Prussia, in 1839.

and speak, than have rightly discerned and remain silent. If there is temerity in recounting my observations there would be criminality in concealing them.

The Russians will not answer me; they will say, "A journey of four months!—he cannot have fully seen things."

It is true I have not fully seen, but I have fully devined.

Or, if they do me the honour of refuting me, they will deny facts,—facts which they are accustomed to reckon as nothing in Petersburg, where the past, like the present and the future, is at the mercy of the monarch: for, once again, the Russians have nothing of their own but obedience and imitation; the direction of their mind, their judgment, and their free-will belongs to their master. In Russia, history forms a part of the crown domain: it is the moral estate of the prince, as men and lands are the material; it is placed in cabinets with the other imperial treasures, and only such of it is shown as it is wished should be seen. The emperor modifies at his pleasure the annals of the country, and daily dispenses to his people the historic truths that accord with the fiction of the moment. Thus it was that Minine and Pojarski— heroes forgotten for two centuries—were suddenly exhumed, and became the fashion, during the invasion of Napoleon. At that moment, the government permitted patriotic enthusiasm.

Nevertheless, this exorbitant power injures itself; Russia will not submit to it eternally. A spirit of revolt broods in the army. I say, with the emperor, the Russians have travelled too much; the nation has become greedy of information: the custom-house cannot confiscate ideas, armies cannot exterminate them, ramparts cannot arrest their progress; ideas are in the air, they pervade every region, and they are changing the world.*

From all that has gone before, it follows that the future—that brilliant future dreamt of by the Russians—does not depend upon them; they have no ideas of their own; and the fate of this nation of imitators will be decided by people whose ideas are

* Since this has been written, the emperor has permitted a crowd of Russians to make a stay in Paris. He, perhaps, thinks he may cure the innovators of their dreams, by showing them France, which is represented to him as a volcano of revolutions, as a country, the residence in which must for ever disgust them with political reforms: he deceives himself.

their own. If passions calm in the West, if union be established between the governments and their subjects, the greedy hope of the conquering Slavonians will become a chimera.

Is it proper to repeat, that I write without animosity, that I have described things without traducing persons, and that, in expatiating upon certain facts which have shocked me, I have generally accused less than I have recounted?

I left Paris with the opinion, that the intimate alliance of France and Russia could alone set to rights the affairs of Europe: but since I have seen the Russian nation, and have recognised the true spirit of its government, I have felt that it is isolated from the rest of the civilised world by a powerful political interest, supported by religious fanaticism; and I am of opinion, that France should seek for allies among nations whose interests accord with her own. Alliances are not to be formed on opinions in opposition to wants. Where, in Europe, are wants which accord? I answer, among the French and the Germans, and the people naturally destined to serve as satellites to those two great nations. The destinies of a progressive civilisation, a civilisation sincere and national, will be decided in the heart of Europe: every thing which tends to hasten the perfect agreement of French and German policy is beneficent; every thing which retards that union, however specious be the motive for delay, is pernicious. . . .

The country that I have just surveyed is as sombre and monotonous as that which I described formerly is brilliant and varied. To draw its exact picture is to renounce the hope to please. In Russia, life is as gloomy as in Andalusia it is gay; the Russians are as dull as the Spaniards are full of spirits. In Spain, the absence of political liberty is compensated by a personal independence which perhaps exists nowhere to the same extent, and the effects of which are surprising; whilst in Russia, the one is as little known as the other. A Spaniard lives on love, a Russian lives on calculation; a Spaniard relates every thing, and if he has nothing to relate, he invents; a Russian conceals every thing, or if he has nothing to conceal, he is still silent, that he may appear discreet: Spain is infested with brigands, but they rob only on the road; the Russian roads are safe, but you will be plundered infallibly in the houses: Spain is full of the ruins and the memories of every century; Russia looks back only upon yesterday, her history is rich in nothing but promises: Spain is studded with mountains, whose forms vary at every step taken by the traveller; Russia is but a single unchanging scene, extending from one end of a plain to the other: the sun illumines Seville, and vivifies the whole peninsula; the mists veil the distances in Petersburg, which remain dim during even the finest summer evenings. In short, the two countries are the very opposite of each other; they differ as do day and night, fire and ice, north and south.

He must have sojourned in that solitude without repose, that prison without leisure which is called Russia, to feel all the liberty enjoyed in the other European countries, whatever form of government they may have adopted. It cannot be too emphatically repeated: liberty is wanted in every thing Russian; unless it be in the commerce of Odessa. The emperor, who is endowed with prophetic tact, little loves the spirit of independence that pervades that city, the prosperity of which is due to the intelligence and integrity of a Frenchman*: it is, however, the only point in his vast dominions where men may with sincerity bless his reign.

If ever your sons should be discontented with France, try my recipe; tell them to go to Russia. It is a useful journey for every foreigner: whoever has well examined that country will be content to live anywhere else. It is always well to know that a society exists where no happiness is possible, because, by a law of his nature, man cannot be happy unless he is free.

Such a recollection renders the traveller less fastidious; and, returning to his own hearth, he can say of his country what a man of mind once said of himself: "When I estimate myself, I am modest; but when I compare myself, I am proud."

❖

INDEX

❖

as creatures of the state, 81
deceit of, 233
dinners, 336, 340, 483–84
discourse of, 52, 71
display of, 117
as flatterers, 83, 122, 204–5, 272, 299
and foreigners, 308–9
and formalities, 82–83, 89–91, 306–7, 320–21
heroes of, 108
as imitators, 153–55, 309, 337, 377, 597–98, 599, 617
as individuals, 18
lying of, 233, 234–35, 240, 307
and music, 148–49, 149–50, 502–3, 526–27
national costume of, 99–100
and national glory, 96
as observers, 309
picturesqueness of, 100, 245, 326, 375, 376
as poets, 217–18
politeness of, 90, 177, 225, 232–33, 306–7, 332, 600–1, 604–5
religious intolerance of, 53–54
resignation of, 497, 499, 502
servility of, 21, 131, 191, 548, 549
and strangers' judgments, 70–71
submissiveness of, 21, 121, 191, 216, 375
susceptibility of, 612, 615
vanity of, 231, 434, 542
violence of, 105–6, 272–77, 284–87, 292–94, 361–62
virtue in, 551
as warriors, 51
and world conquest, 303–6
Russian school, 582

S

Sabran, Countess de (later Marchioness de Boufflers) (Custine's grandmother), 478, 479n.
Sabran, Delphine de (Custine's mother), 27–32, 35–41, 151, 478
St. Petersburg, 82, 85, 93, 109, 187, 243, 277, 288, 308, 313, 323, 352, 355, 359, 364, 368, 370, 419, 427, 428, 435, 469, 476, 478, 557, 578, 579, 580, 615, 617
approach to, 77–79
architecture of, 87–89, 105–6, 152–55, 210, 219–20, 279, 280, 298, 401, 473, 544
building of, 69, 218–19, 311–12
as capital, 399
ceremonies and fêtes in, 176, 179–82, 412
contrasts in, 123, 220
court at, 298–99, 605, 607
courtiers in, 115–17, 140, 477
curiosities of, 129
from distance, 242–43
dullness of, 164, 297
environs of, 75–76, 220–21, 244–45
existence in, 118–21
flowers in, 198
fortress of, 110–12, 237–39
fuel in, 222–23
grandeur of, 110, 128, 343
importance of, 160
inhabitants of, 99–100, 101–2, 176, 214, 224–25, 275, 351, 446, 471
insects in, 103–4
liberals at, 381
lower classes of, 99–100
and the Neva, 107, 497
Opera of, 206
overall view of, 218
overflowing, 331
vs. Paris, 177, 179
picturesqueness of, 219–20, 596
population of, 209–10
quays of, 88, 169, 298, 507
races in, 190
representations of, 582
spectacle of, 168–69
statues in, 325
streets of, 87, 107, 204, 209–17, 223–25, 239n., 279, 341
summer in, 90, 103, 155, 222, 403, 619
thaw at, 212
vs. Venice, 345
winter of, 249
Sarmatians, 461, 498

The illustrations that appear at the opening of each chapter are taken from the popular illustrated satirical journal *Nashi, spisannye s natury russkimi (Our Folks, Drawn from Nature by Russians)*, which was published in Russia during the early 1840s. These illustrative figures and vignettes were wood engravings based on drawings by popular artists of the day.

1.   Horse-drawn water carriage.

2.   A woman of gentry birth, drawn by V. Timm.

3.   A gentrywoman reading to her children.

4.   An officer's laundry and billet, drawn by V. Timm.

5.   A one-horse carriage, drawn by V. Timm.

6.   Two soldiers at rest.

7 and 8.   Buffoon and audience, drawn by V. Timm.

9.   The coffin-maker at work.

10.   The undertaker, drawn by V. Timm.

11.   The undertaker serving rum-laced tea.

12 and 13.   The nurse at work and on her way to church, drawn by E. I. Kovrigin.

14.   The nurse gossiping at the samovar, drawn by V. Timm.

15.   Nurse and child.

16.   Lady of the house at her needlepoint, drawn by E. I. Kovrigin.

17.   A healer, drawn by E. I. Kovrigin.

18.   Woman in peasant costume, drawn by E. I. Kovrigin.

19.   Sentry tower.

20.   Peasant woman braiding her hair.

21.   Ural cossack, drawn by V. Timm.

22.   Lancers in battle.

23.   Cattle herder.